GAMBLER'S DIGEST

Edited by Clement McQuaid

DIGEST BOOKS, INC., NORTHFIELD, ILLINOIS

GAMBLER'S DIGEST STAFF

EDITOR—Clement McQuaid

Author, vintner, home gardener and keen student of gambling games, most of which he has played profitably, Mr. McQuaid is an executive in merchandising. He lives with his wife Marion, and children in a suburb of Chicago.

A world traveler, Clem has played all the games from Happy Valley in Hong Kong to Harold's in Reno, from bridge at the Regency Club in New York to gin at the Raffles in Singapore. He's an authority on the correct odds in all sports and an expert at the friendly bar bets which are scattered throughout this book.

ASSOCIATE EDITOR—George B. Anderson

Mr. Anderson is a professional writer who first became interested in the subject of gambling through *Easy Money,* a radio dramatic series on gambling rackets which he sold to NBC. The author of three professional magic books, he wrote more radio mystery dramas during radio's heyday than any other writer in the world.

George's background includes a stint in advertising that ranged from copywriter to agency president. His current books are, *The Dartnell/Anderson 20-Point System for Guaranteed Sales Success,* published by Dartnell, *You, Too, Can Read Minds,* published by Magic, Inc., and *The Sit-In,* a suspense novel published by Ace.

ASSOCIATE EDITOR—Tom James

A native of Southern Ohio where he cut his teeth at the gaming tables of Newport and Covington, Kentucky, Mr. James is a long standing habitué of both standard and thoroughbred race tracks. He is a devoted gambler, be it in Las Vegas, in a friendly poker game or at the local track. Tom is currently an advertising executive in the Chicago area.

ASSISTANT EDITORS

Rosalyn Adler—Research and Permissions
Charles T. Hartigan—Research
John Strauss—Research

DESIGN & PRODUCTION

Allen Carr

PUBLISHER

Sheldon L. Factor

The statements contained in this book represent the judgment of the editors and authors regarding successful means of gambling. None of the publisher, editors, authors or distributors guarantees the result of following the recommendations contained in the book.

ISBN 0-695-80104-X Library of Congress Catalogue Card #73-122378

CONTENTS

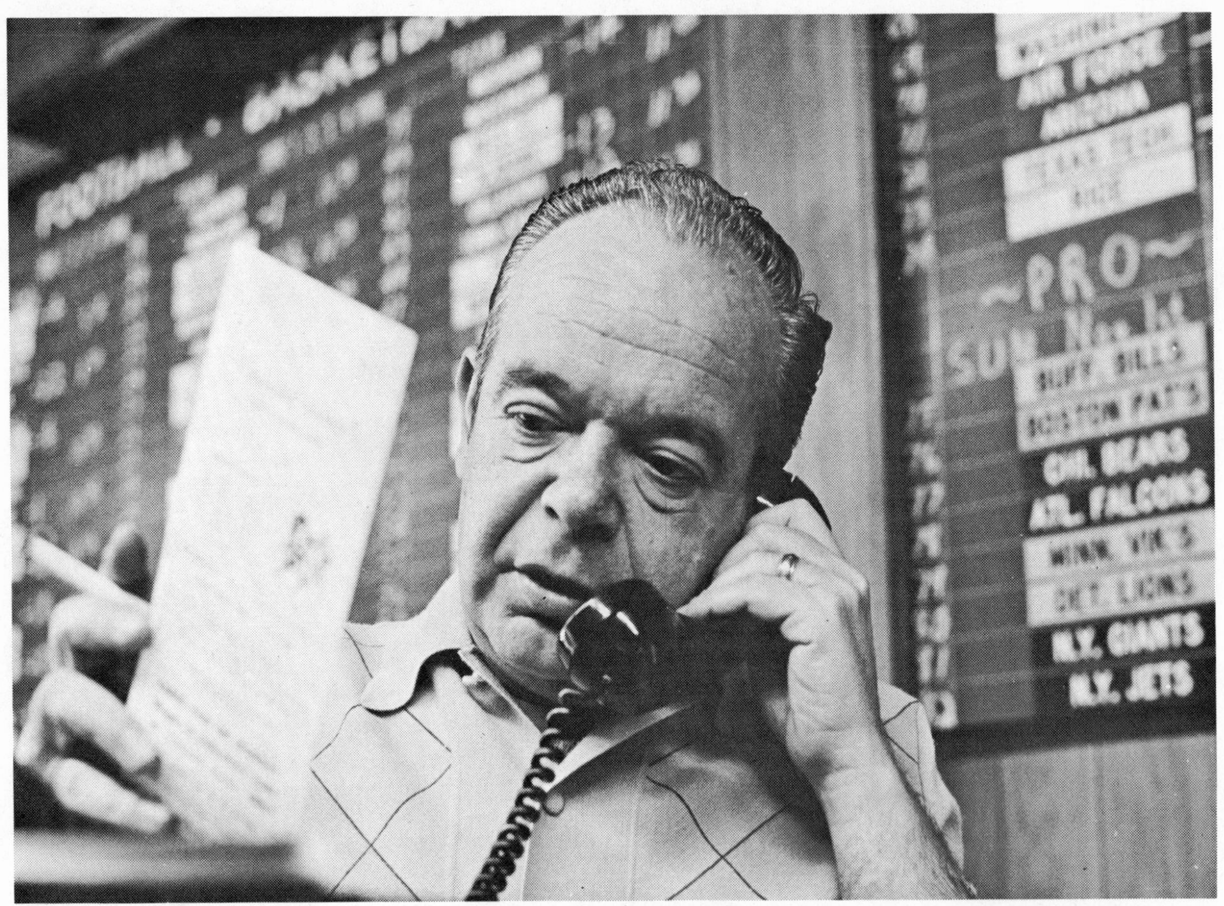

MEET MR. ODDS-MAKER—BOB MARTIN

Charles Einstein, the novelist and free-lance writer, was looking for a reliable estimate on the amount of money illegally bet on sports events every year in the United States, and so he went to an expert.

He not only went to an expert, but chose a man who is generally considered the country's foremost authority on sports wagering, Bob Martin of the Churchill Downs Sports Book on the Las Vegas Strip. Martin told him that a "drastically conservative" estimate would be $12 billion. That tidy sum happens to exceed the combined reported profits last year, Mr. Einstein discovered, of the 20 biggest corporations in the country.

But Einstein got more than the authoritative estimate he was after. He was so impressed with Bob Martin that he wrote a feature story on the man which appeared in a syndicated *Sunday Magazine* widely distributed in metropolitan newspapers.

"Martin," Einstein reported, "is a thick-set, 51-year old native of East New York, and anyone who is from East New York, which is a fail-safe section of Brooklyn, has by definition been setting a price all his life. For the past seven years, he has been doing it legally, having migrated to Las Vegas, where he is in charge of the sports-betting operation at the Churchill Downs race book on the strip. He is a patient man: In the eyes of his not-unhandsome face there is the look of somebody who was already waited on. But, though he is by no means the only man who will quote you a price on a sporting event, the preliminary odds he sets for, say, a football game are used, with slight variation, if any, by bookmakers from coast to coast, including most of the 11 other licensed sports-betting parlors in Nevada. Other names may be more familiar, such as that of Jimmie the Greek, Snyder, the Las Vegas newspaper columnist. But long-time Chicago sports editor Joe Rein has observed that 'Snyder, Las Vegas' most famous handicapper, uses Martin's figures'.

"So it tends to come back to Martin, and it is an interesting business. Unlike Snyder, he has no newspaper salary to fall back on. Unlike Lockheed, if the price he quotes is wrong, he can't go back to the government for more."

Martin's attitude toward sports-betting is objective, factual and unemotional. Einstein observes, "Martin does not say if he thinks there are fixes going on today, but he has an educated way of checking up. If an uncommonly big bet comes in, he will probably accept it, but he will watch the outcome of the game, and if the bettor wins, then bets again and wins again, it will take Martin a remarkably short time to figure out why. Once he has come to that, he 'plays' the bettor, and regulates his odds accordingly."

"I'm not ashamed that a bettor knows more than I do," Martin says. "In fact, I depend on it. The big money thinks I don't know what's going on, and the big money may be right. But the big money also thinks I won't know what's going on next week, and the week after, and there the big money's wrong. I had a guy come in and bet big on three games three weeks in a row. He was using me the first week. The second and third weeks, I was using him.

"I caught what he was doing, and I changed the point spread." It happened to be a football bet, and the big bettor was betting in terms of not who was playing but who was officiating. With a certain team a five-point favorite, he explains, it can go for a field goal or a touchdown in the closing minutes of a tie game. Should a lineman be called for offside, it has to settle for a field goal. So, as a five-point favorite, it wins by three points instead of seven.

What hurts the bookmaker most, Martin explained to Einstein, is not the crooked bettor but the informed bettor. He pointed out that many heavy plungers are close to athletes, coaches, and sports writers, any of whom may be aware of something that can help or hurt a team's chances in a given game. It is when their big bets come in that Martin must make a judgment—usually on whether to change his "line"—something he dislikes to do—for the remaining bets made before the game.

In these days of instant communication and fast travel, there is what Martin calls a "visible grapevine."

"Though he can discount a certain amount of loyalty betting," Einstein says, "such as Southern Methodist getting a big play in Dallas, if the play on Southern Methodist is heavy in Boston, it will be heavy in Las Vegas, too, and Martin will see it instantly. It is in the big bettor's favor to make his bets in Las Vegas. In Vegas, he's not violating the law.

"You get to the point," Martin says, "where if one guy comes in and bets $10,000, you don't bat an eyelash. If another comes in and bets $500, you have to be careful."

He likes to encourage informed bettors to make their football bets early in the week. "Nothing so interferes with a bookmaker's digestion," Einstein says, "as a $25,000 bet that comes in 10 minutes before game time. But since the odds are guaranteed to pay off at whatever they were at the moment the bet was made, bettors don't mind placing their bets early. Indeed, they prefer it. If they make bets at the last minute, Martin is as likely to know why as they do, and will shift his odds accordingly."

In football, for example, weather is a definite last-minute regulator of the odds. Bad weather holds down the score, at least, most of the time.

Much of Martin's acknowledged skill as an odds-maker lies in his knowledge of what he doesn't know, Einstein points out. In years gone by, he knew just about everybody in boxing circles in New York and could act from personal assurance, but now that he functions nationwide, such intimacy isn't possible.

Martin admits to advantages in his being at a certain arm's length. "There is a water's edge," Einstein says, "at which his information stops, and his skill lies in knowing this for the fact it is. Hockey, for instance, represents a very small part of his action, but he knows nothing about hockey and has the intelligence to confess so. So, each hockey season, he imports Billy Clarke from Boston to set the hockey odds for him."

Martin will work till 4 a.m. of a Sunday to set up his line for the college football games of the next Saturday. Some things that can effect a change in the odds during the week, like injuries, may be public knowledge or privately known only to a few. "Thirty-five years in the business is a long time," he says—and those years have created rare sensitivity.

He subscribes to eight or 10 newspapers from around the country and studies their sports pages, as much for little grace notes as anything else. Past performances mean something, but so does the certain good hitter who says in an interview that he has trouble with a certain good pitcher.

"This will click into the Martin brain," Einstein says, "and the next time those two teams meet, the odds may be shaded accordingly. If a top athlete has had a divorce, or illness in his family, the papers will say so, and Martin will note it as a possible distraction to the man's concentration next time out."

Martin projects his thinking beyond the pale, particularly in his college football line. "It isn't just who's playing whom this Saturday," he says. "I want to know about the Saturday after that."

Einstein cites an example. If UCLA should be a 14-point favorite over Washington, he asks himself if UCLA is looking ahead to Southern Cal the next week, with a Rose Bowl bid at stake. If so, the 14 points will shrink. He checks what happened last year. If UCLA won, 52-0, Washington is going to want revenge. He speculates as to whether the rival coaches are friends, or once worked together. If they're buddies, the coach who's a long favorite may try to hold down the score. Martin asks other questions, too. With a bowl bid at stake, a team has an extra reason to pour it on. With a conference championship possible, a team with a non-conference game this week may be resting its star players.

The greatest number of games handicapped by Martin are professional baseball games. They are put up as a matter of odds, not runs, and depend totally on the starting pitchers. Some major league pitchers are known as "action" pitchers, meaning the betting is heavy when they work.

Martin regards football as the big betting sport, and Martin loves its challenge. "I want the odds on a football game to be good," he says. "By good, I mean I want as many people betting on one side as on the other. In addition to being good, I like them to be right, at least most of the time. If I pick 35 college games every week in football season, I want to be right on 27 of them. I'll give up the other eight."

"He is Mr. Odds-Maker," Einstein says, "and what that comes down to is this—if he tells you that when you go outside it is going to be raining nickels, then you'd better wear a hard hat."

Bob Martin is a class by himself as an odds-maker, which is the reason he was chosen to reveal the "Best Bets" in the field of sports for GAMBLER'S DIGEST. His knowledge of the whole wagering operation carries over into other phases of gambling, and his methods and techniques have been applied to Mr. Odds-Maker's "Best Bets" far afield from sports.

A high percentage of these other best bets have the approval of hard-core professional gamblers who make their living by being right. Some of the experts, not operating in the legality of Las Vegas as Martin does, are understandably reticent about the use of their names.

Some of the "Best Bets" are actually composites of smart opinion, culled from as many as a dozen sources. All of them have the benefit of Bob Martin's incomparable experience with gambling and his intimate acquaintance with the people who know every phase of it best.

A few of the "Best Bets" in some areas of gambling may be questioned by GAMBLER'S DIGEST readers. They are open to discussion, certainly, but you can't argue with success.

The success of Bob Martin as an authority on gambling can't be questioned. The editors of GAMBLER'S DIGEST feel that he and his consultants in their respective fields are pre-eminent. GAMBLER'S DIGEST doubts that ever before has anyone in Mr. Odds-Maker's class ever given readers so much inside information—practical information—about so many areas of gambling.

A professional gambler designated as Smart Sam observes, "Anybody who sticks with the GAMBLER'S DIGEST "Best Bets" should do considerably better than he'd do without 'em. They take everything into consideration except luck—and that's something nobody can control. If you want the odds in your favor or as close to it as you can get, GAMBLER'S DIGEST is your book and Mr. Odds-Maker is your man."

It started a long time ago

"I'm fed up with nothing but berries, berries, berries for meals," Eve pouted. "Come on, Adam, don't be a panty-waist. These apples look absolutely super-delicious. Don't you want a little variety in your diet?"

"I've got strict orders from The Boss to leave those apples alone," Adam replied.

"They're not doing Him any good, just hanging there. And it's a cinch he's not going to sell them to anyone else. Be a sport, Adam."

Adam was adamant. "Orders are orders, Eve. And this is too nice a piece of property to lose."

The serpent, who'd been listening, slithered forward. "He won't even know you've eaten one of His old apples, Adam. And I'll bet you two to one that even if He finds out, He won't care."

Adam considered. "Make it six to one," he said, "and you've got a bet."

Reconstruction of the dialogue is fictitious, but we know that Adam gambled on not getting caught. And man has been gambling ever since!

The New Century Dictionary traces the word, "gambling," back to the Anglo-Saxon word, gamenian — to sport or play, and defines gambling as "the staking or risking of money or anything of value on a matter of chance or uncertainty."

Since almost everything was uncertain when man distinguished himself from all other forms of life by standing on his hind legs and smiling, back in the Lower Pleistocene era, he had to risk his existence on many matters of chance or uncertainty — and has been taking risks ever since!

A tablet in the Egyptian Cheops pyramid, built around 3,000 B.C., tells the story of how the Goddess of the Sky angered the God of Creation by marrying her twin brother. The God of Creation declared that, as punishment, the Goddess of the Sky should bear no children on any day of the year. The God of Night came to her rescue and gambled with the moon for part of the moon's light, enough to add five new days to the 360-day Egyptian calendar. Since the five new days were not the property of the God of Creation, the Sky Goddess used them to give birth to her children. The "gaming" between the God of Night and the Moon was probably with dice, since crude forms of dice date back that far. Copper bowls from an early Egyptian gambling game are displayed in the Cairo museum.

In India, according to ancient Vedic hymns, great herds of cattle were wagered on the outcome of chariot races, and dice games were popular as far back at 1500 B.C.

The casting of lots, or lottery, was a part of almost every tribe's life. Nobody knows for sure how far the Chinese enthusiasm for gambling goes back into history, but it has been intense for many centuries.

Greek legend tells the story of a daughter of Tyche, the goddess of fortune, who devoted most of her time to inventing games of chance and who founded the ancient Grecian gambling houses. The Romans had cubic dice, lotteries, a kind of Backgammon, and the fore-runner of coin-tossing, played with a shell colored black on one side and white on the other. Gambling was legal only during the Feast of the Saturnalia, but was an important part of Roman life, nevertheless, throughout the year.

Chess, probably an outgrowth of a game called shah-mat which was played in Persia in 500 B.C., has little opportunity for chance in its makeup, but has been played for huge sums.

The Bettmann Archive

Most historians are agreed that long before the birth of Christ, all the basic forms of gambling had been created. King Henry III found it necessary to warn his clergy to "leave diceing and chesseing undone on pain of durance vile." By the fifteenth century, the lottery had become a popular method of raising funds for both the church and the government.

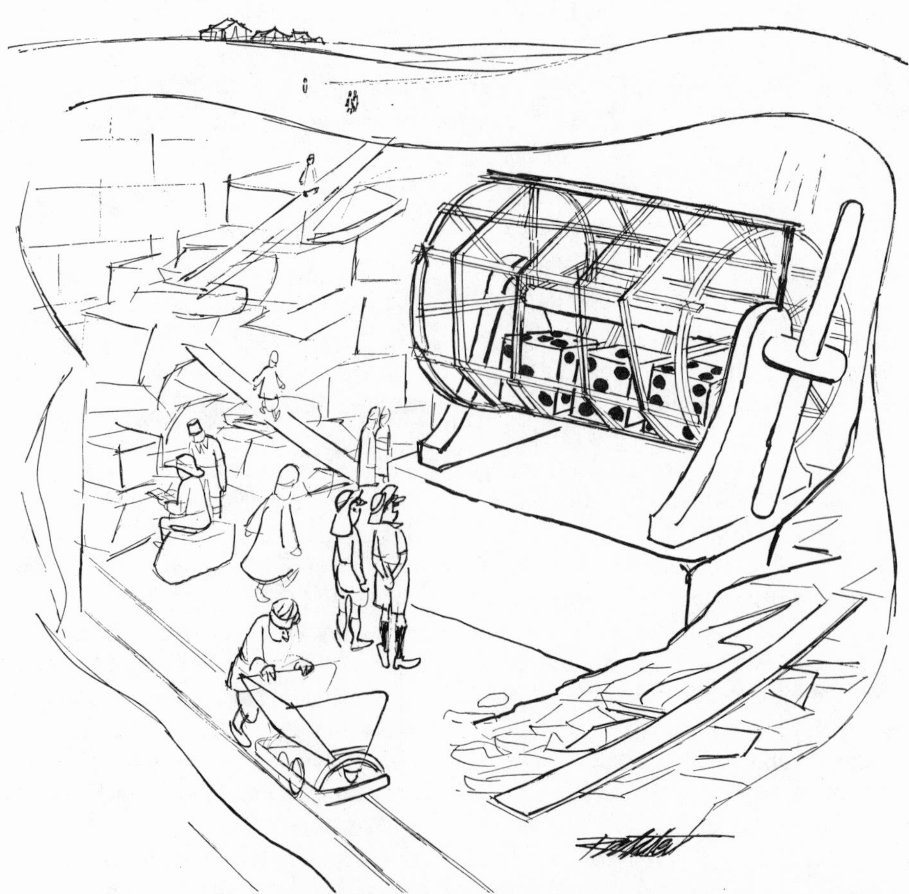

"Well, I think we might not go too far wrong in drawing at least two conclusions about them. They were gigantic in size and addicted to gambling."

Form **11–C**
(Rev. Feb. 1970)
Department of the Treasury
Internal Revenue Service

Special Tax Return and Application For Registry—Wagering

Return for period from ...., 19........... to June 30, 19...........
(Month, day, and year)

See Instructions on back for time and place for filing return.

Check one: ☐ First return and application ☐ Renewal return and application ☐ Supplemental return and application

1. Name: True name...

Alias, style, or trade name, if any.......................................

For Internal Revenue Use Only

The American Indians had been enthusiastic gamblers for centuries before the discovery of America, but the colonists introduced them to playing cards, dice, horse racing, bear-baiting and cockfights.

There is a federal tax on gambling and while the Internal Revenue Service tries diligently to collect income tax on earnings from gambling, Alan Wykes is authority for the statement that no federal law regulates gambling; it is in the hands of the states. Nearly every country, including Russia, permits some form of gambling, and no country of any substantial size permits all forms.

Everywhere, of course, speculation in the stock and grain markets is permitted. Some people, mostly those who are active and winning in the market, refuse to regard such speculation as gambling, but the loser often refers to Wall Street, with validity, as Las Vegas East.

The owner of a Nevada Casino who doesn't want his name used says, "They talk about us being gamblers! If we manipulated payoffs the way stock prices are manipulated, we'd land in jail."

Richard Ney, in his great expose of the stock market, *The Wall Street Jungle,* published by Grove Press, tells how "investors lose and the house wins in the greatest gambling casino in the world—Wall Street."

Las Vegas East maintains that its operation is necessary to the national economy — which is probably so. But the great bulk of the money that's speculated every day is not invested to help the national economy; it is gambled by speculators who hope to win. And gambling in commodities, particularly in grain, is a part of life.

Wherever you go, at every economic level, you find gambling. Even little children become involved in guessing games at an early age. The small boy who acquires some degree of skill at marbles and doesn't play "for keeps" is a rarity. Penny-pitching and the matching of coins are simple forms of gambling that youngsters are quick to embrace. "I'll bet my dad can beat your dad" is a standard ploy in juvenile confrontation.

Card games have always been in the upper social strata of gambling. First played by royalty, they have continued for centuries to rank high in the scale of social cachet. The professional contract bridge player is probably the elite leader of present-day gamblers.

The Chinese dictionary, *Ching-tze-tung,* published in 1678, sets the invention of playing cards at 1120 A.D. They almost certainly originated in the East, and one popular theory is that Arabs and Saracens who had learned their use from traveling bands of gypsies brought the fascinating pasteboards to Europe. A fact that seems to strengthen this theory is that playing cards first appeared in Europe in the southern and eastern countries.

The first known European cards appeared in Italy in 1299 and were hand-painted, far too costly for any except the extremely wealthy. The only name we have for the man who first manufactured engraved cards is The Master of the Playing Cards. Some authorities say he lived in Basle, Switzerland. He was an engraver of armor who realized that common people would be eager to own cards that had been available up to that time only to kings or princes, so he began to engrave and print them.

There were no printed books at the time, because movable type was not to be invented until 1455. With nothing to read, people bought pictures, and the engraving process put them within reach of the mass market.

The first engraved pictures on the market were playing cards and Biblical illustrations. The Boston

SPECIAL OPTIONS

CALLS ★ PUTS

PER 100 SHARES (PLUS TAX) PER 100 SHARES

Subject to Prior Sale or Price Change

CLOSE					CLOSE				
52⅛	Amer So African	.50⅜	June 22	$587.50	26½	Action Indus	..27	Apr. 22	$225.00
9½	Atlantic Rich wt	.10	11 mos.	275.00	48⅞	Amer Tel & Tel	.50.85	10 mos	425.00
35¼	Amer Mach & Fdy	31¼	May 24	550.00	33	Apco Oil	.....34¾	Aug. 11	425.00
121¼	Burroughs	...109.85	May 6	1387.50	67½	Atlantic Rich	..68½	1 year	987.50
15⅛	Buttes Gas Oil	..14⅝	Sept.22	350.00	19	Asamera	......19¾	June 21	287.50
239	Corning Glass	.231½	May 17	1987.50	32¼	Babcock Wilcox	.34	Sept.22	450.00
29¾	Calif Computer	..29⅝	Apr. 20	287.50	121¼	Burroghs	.....110.85	Apr. 15	225.00
39¾	Computer Softw	.36	Apr. 22	525.00	239	Corning Glass	.210⅞	May 10	275.00
88½	Dome Pete	....88¼	Apr. 15	550.00	97½	Disney, Walt	..96½	6 mos.	1187.50
65⅝	Fed Natl Mtge	.61¼	Apr. 15	587.50	61¼	Digital Equip	.63½	May 17	662.50
38	Fairchild Cam	.37	May 7	387.50	78¾	Eastman Kodak	.73½	8 mos.	450.00
27½	Gulf & Western	.26¼	May 19	287.50	41½	Flying Tiger	..38.80	6 mos.	450.00
358½	Intl Bus Mach	.360	Aug. 19	2225.00	65⅝	Fed Natl Mgte	.62	Apr. 19	187.50
75¾	Kresge	70	June 14	825.00	28⅛	Flying Tiger wts	.24½	Apr. 26	137.50
46⅝	Loews Theatre	.38½	Apr. 19	950.00	44¼	Farah Mfg	....44½	June 25	387.50
73¾	Memorex	67	May 14	1050.00	85	Getty	.........85½	May 21	525.00
18¾	Milgo	22	June 25	137.50	56½	Georgia Pac	..58¼	May 19	487.50
43⅛	Natl Cash Reg	.39⅞	Apr. 30	525.00	26⅜	Home Oil A	...27	May 25	275.00
121	New Process Old	.83½	June 21	4050.00	358½	Intl Bus Mach	.340	Aug. 19	1375.00
33	Pennzoil	......30⅛	Apr. 28	425.00	100⅛	Merck	........95.45	May 3	387.50
[illegible]	Saxon Indus	...22⅞	Apr. 28	450.00	57¾	[illegible]	57	Apr. 19	387[illegible]

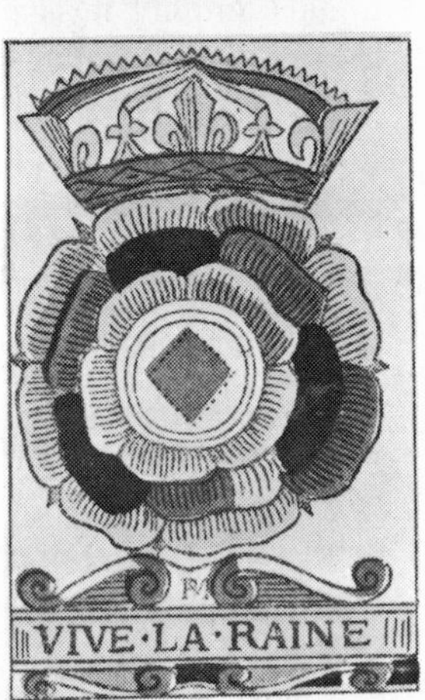

The Bettmann Archive

EARLY EDGE

First serious study of the mathematical percentages in gambling was written in 1520 by Gerolamo Cardano, while he was, of all things, student rector at the University of Padua. It outdates the commonly accepted beginning of the mathematical theory of probability by about 130 years. A man of varied scientific and scholarly interests, he was also a chronic gambler.

Today's bookmakers can thank Cardano for being the first person to determine and set mathematical odds on the probabilities of various occurrences in gambling. He even worked out the probabilities of a few simple draws in a card game called *primero,* a forerunner of poker.

The theory of probability has modern-day applications in almost every area of science, but it began in and with gambling.

A translation of the Cardano book was published by the Princeton University Press in 1953 and was later reprinted by Holt, Rinehart and Winston, translated by Sydney Henry Gould.

Museum of Art has the only original "Master" playing card in the United States, the Queen of Cyclamen. It is estimated that a pack of 52 of these original cards would, today, be worth well over $1 million.

If bringing playing cards within reach of the common man stimulated gambling, it also spurred the invention of the printing press and the consequent increase in literacy which changed the world.

The pasteboards arrived in France in 1360, and the French contributed the design that became standard with card players everywhere. The figures of the four suits originally represented the four divisions of society. Hearts symbolized the *gens de coeur,* the choir-men or ecclesiastics. The *Espads* (sword) of Spain stood for the nobility and military, and the English word for it soom became Spade. Trefoil leaves acknowledged the peasantry, and were called Clubs. Diamonds represented merchants.

From their invention, cards were associated with chance and fate. Gypsies devised a system of foretelling the future with cards, and the Tarot cards are even today consulted by the superstitious.

While not all card games involve wagering and some that usually do could be played without it, the pasteboards were used for gambling as well as recreation from the date of their creation. The King of Castile, John I, prohibited card playing in 1387 because of heavy gambling losses by members of his court.

Cards and gambling have always been linked in the public mind. Strangely, the first definitive book linking cards and gambling to be published in the United States did not appear until 1890. By an author named Van Rensselaer, it bore the title, *The Devil's Picture Books.* So much had been written on the subject that a bibliography, *Works in English on Playing Cards and Gambling,* was published in London in 1905.

Gambling had been a popular activity long before the introduction of playing cards, but cards quickly achieved and have maintained high status as a vehicle for gambling, probably because card games can be a combination of skill and chance. In almost every card game, the play of the cards calls for exercise of judgment, but the outcome hinges in some part on what cards have been dealt to a hand.

The variations of hands to be dealt from a shuffled deck are almost infinite, and the variety of winning combinations in various games is staggering. A man who idly suggested that it might be a good idea to take a computer into a card game was told by a computer programming expert to forget it.

"A computer is no better than its programming," he said, "and programming a computer for the game of bridge, for example, would be virtually impossible. Nobody could live long enough to feed all the possible combinations into the machine. On top of that, there'd still be no way of knowing the distribution of your

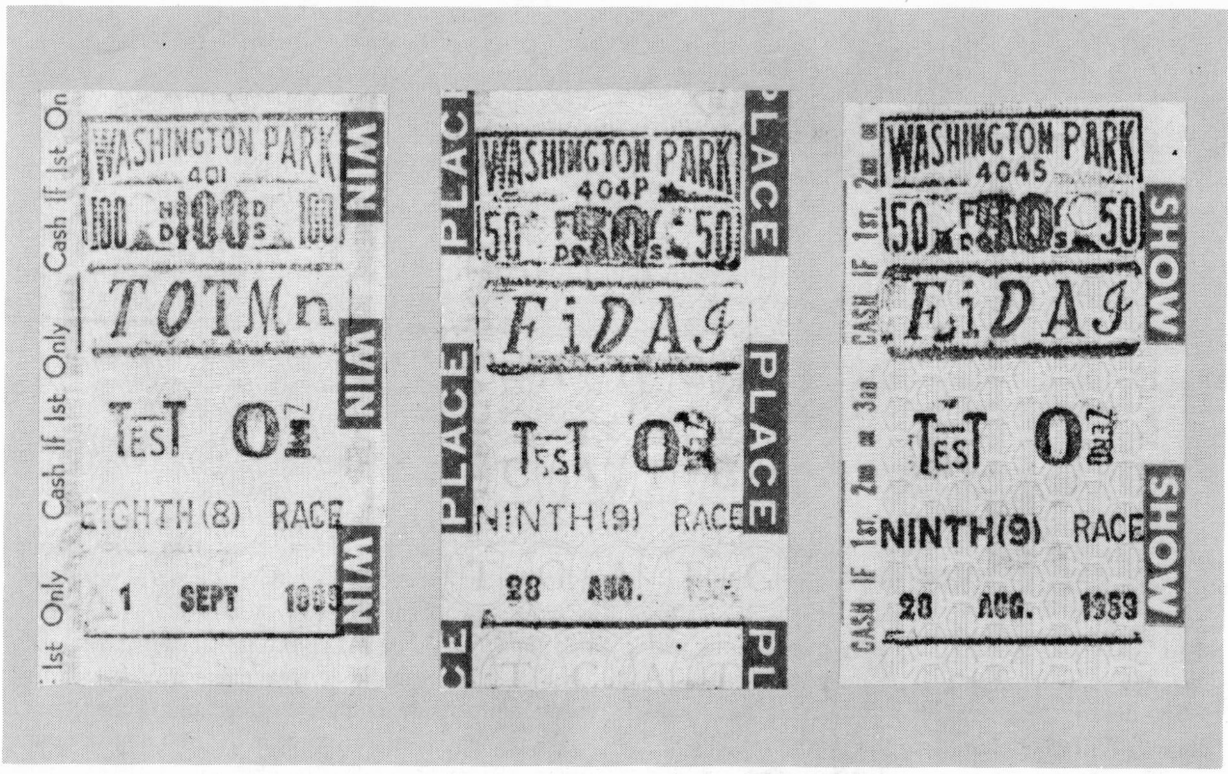

Courtesy Chicago Thoroughbred Enterprises, Inc.

opponents' hands, variations of which could be almost endless and all of which could affect the outcome of the game. Furthermore, as you well know, one smart play or one error by an opponent can change the entire course of the game, and that play may be anywhere from the first trick to the last."

Some parts of society have always expressed active opposition to gambling. Often, it has been a case of, "Do as I say, don't do as I do." Many churches and civic organizations which frown on gambling in general have been eager to accept the profits from their own lotteries and Bingo. Management of private clubs whose members publicly frown on gambling is quick to admit that substantial club revenue comes from slot machines. Posted rules of some clubs forbid playing cards for money on the premises — and it would be difficult to find a table in the crowded card rooms where no money is changing hands.

Economic pressure has often brought increased tolerance toward gambling. Following the Civil War, some Southern states which were in bad financial condition instituted state lotteries to refill their depleted coffers. Nevada had repealed open gambling laws following unfortunate experiences with gangsters and other undesirables, but legalized gambling again during the depression that followed the 1929 financial crash.

Public gaming houses had been prevalent in the United States until 1881, when the state of New York began to crack down on them. By 1885, many other states had started similar action, and open gambling "shut down" in most major cities.

Anti-gambling legislation has always been difficult to enforce, a major reason being that it is so easy to gamble in private. In some countries where certain forms of state-controlled gambling are permitted but private gambling is forbidden, the unapproved gambling continues to thrive, probably more vigorously than it would if it were legal.

In the United States, confusion results from state control of gambling legislation. With 50 states, there are 50 different sets of laws, regulations and penalties. At the time of this writing, Nevada is the only state in the union to permit open, legal gambling on games usually played in Casinos, such as Roulette, Baccarat, Blackjack and dice — although debate on casino gambling for New Jersey, Florida and New York is attracting much interest.

In about half the 50 states, pari-mutuel betting on thoroughbred and harness races is legal, but similar betting on dog races is legal in only one state out of seven. Only in Nevada is betting your horse selections with a public bookmaker legal, although New York has set up a state-sponsored and owned bookmaking operation. While there are no accurate figures on the number of illegal bookmakers in the country, general opinion is that, strangely, more illegal bookies operate in states having pari-mutuel betting than in those that do not. Ask where to make a bet in any major city and the answer is prompt and accurate.

New York State Lottery Ticket.

The New Hampshire and New York State lotteries are legal, but lotteries conducted by charitable organizations for the benefit of charity are not. While so-called "sweepstakes" conducted by publications and substantial manufacturers to promote sales are technically illegal, they are seldom questioned. Many "drawings" in which purchase of a product is, in common practice, a requirement for participation, get around the "consideration" angle by requiring either a product label or "reasonable facsimile thereof." In a strict interpretation, even that reasonable facsimile which must accompany the entry could be considered illegal. The "lucky number" promotions which appear in magazines and contain a number that must be checked at some point of purchase to determine whether or not it is a winner require the purchase of the magazine to get a number and require expenditure of time and effort to learn whether or not it is a winner.

Postal regulations clearly stipulate against the dissemination of news that might encourage participation in lotteries, and yet, stories about big winners in lotteries are commonplace. In several large cities, several pages of Irish Sweepstakes winning numbers are published by local newspapers.

It is legal in some states to manufacture and sell gaming devices, even such obvious ones as slot machines, but it is illegal to gamble with them. Prestigious department stores and sporting goods shops commonly display and sell Roulette wheels and layouts, chuck-a-luck games, Bingo games and similar devices. It is perfectly legal for a customer to buy any of these items but illegal to use them for gambling purposes after purchase.

Manufacturers of such equipment run mail-order advertisements offering their wares, with the small-print stipulation that purchases are to be used "for amusement purposes only."

In communities where gambling is illegal, many law enforcement officers complain that it is virtually impossible to get anything other than token convictions in their local courts. Jury convictions are almost non-existent. Illegal gambling is, naturally, conducted in an atmosphere of privacy, and many judges who follow the strict rules of law take a dim view of any invasion of any citizen's privacy, under any conditions.

To compound the enforcement problem, national and local investigations of gambling in localities where it is illegal have shown that there have been and are numerous unhealthy alliances between gambling and "on the take" law enforcement officers.

Gambling today is Big Business. How big? Nobody can say with certainty, but consensus of most authorities on the subject puts the total at a $400 billion exchange.

Some gambling revenues and losses are not recorded anywhere. The money that changes hands in friendly Friday night poker games the length and breadth of the land is impossible to estimate. How much do comfortably well-to-do housewives win or lose in friendly bridge games every year? Even their husbands can't tell you.

A professional gambler who operates a poker room in back of a pool hall in a city of 150,000 says, "My gross take runs about three thousand bucks a week, and it averages to about five percent of every pot. That means there's sixty thousand bucks changing hands at my tables. My setup is small potatoes compared to one other game in town, the big one where the heavy money shows, and there's a couple dozen little dollar-limit tables running, that I know of. What's the total? Does Macy tell Gimble? Well, one poker table operator sure doesn't tell another."

Who could possibly estimate the total amount wagered on golf courses every day? We often read of Calcuttas, betting pools on golf tournaments, that run to a quarter of a million dollars. A few years ago, a retired sports celebrity polished up his golf game, turned golf hustler, and was said to be making about $3,000 a week in private play. He never entered any tournaments and his golfing skill was never publicized. He boasted to a confidante, "All over the country, there's rich guys who wanta brag to their buddies that they lost five thousand bucks to me in a golf game, and I'm tryin' to oblige all of 'em." This sports star's substantial wagers never attracted public attention. He was just another minor golf hustler.

If wagering on golf is substantial—$500 million a year, by one conservative estimate—the betting on baseball, football and basketball games is astronomical. One estimate is that $2 billion a year is bet through bookmakers on big-league baseball games. College and pro football games are said to account for another two billion dollars. As a result of "fixing" scandals, the betting on basketball is considerably lower. Baseball and football "pools" undoubtedly account for much more than individual team bets.

The bulk of the betting on sports, however, is done by individuals, with each other on private "Betchas." Who could possibly estimate how many millions of dollars are wagered on sports, friend to friend, one self-styled sports fan and expert against another? These bets pass through no business organization, and nobody has a shingle out to announce that he's open to all bets against his favorite team.

The pools, on which some estimates run five times the amount of individual bets, are regarded by professional gamblers as pure lotteries. These pools are by no means confined to the United States. In other countries, where soccer is the big spectator sport, pools thrive. In Great Britain, for example, where bookmaking activity is a matter of record, soccer pools account for betting up to $350 million a year. Australia adds another quarter of a billion dollars. In France, Germany, Italy, Spain, Norway, Denmark, Sweden and the South American countries, soccer or association football pools do a booming business.

Despite its size, activity in football pool betting on soccer probably falls far short of football pool betting on the American brand of football. The popularity of football pools has grown by leaps and bounds in recent years.

Even the game of Jai-Alai, comparatively little-known in the United States, is an appealing game to gamblers. Florida has had legal pari-mutuel betting on the sport since 1933, and the Miami fronton attracts capacity crowds of bettors during a season of about 100 nights.

Bingo is considered by many to be a minor, innocuous form of gambling. From the money wagered on Bingo in the 11 states where it is legal, it is estimated that in excess of two billion dollars a year is spent on the little game. In Great Britain, where Bingo is legal, the annual take is over $70 million.

A typical parlay card.

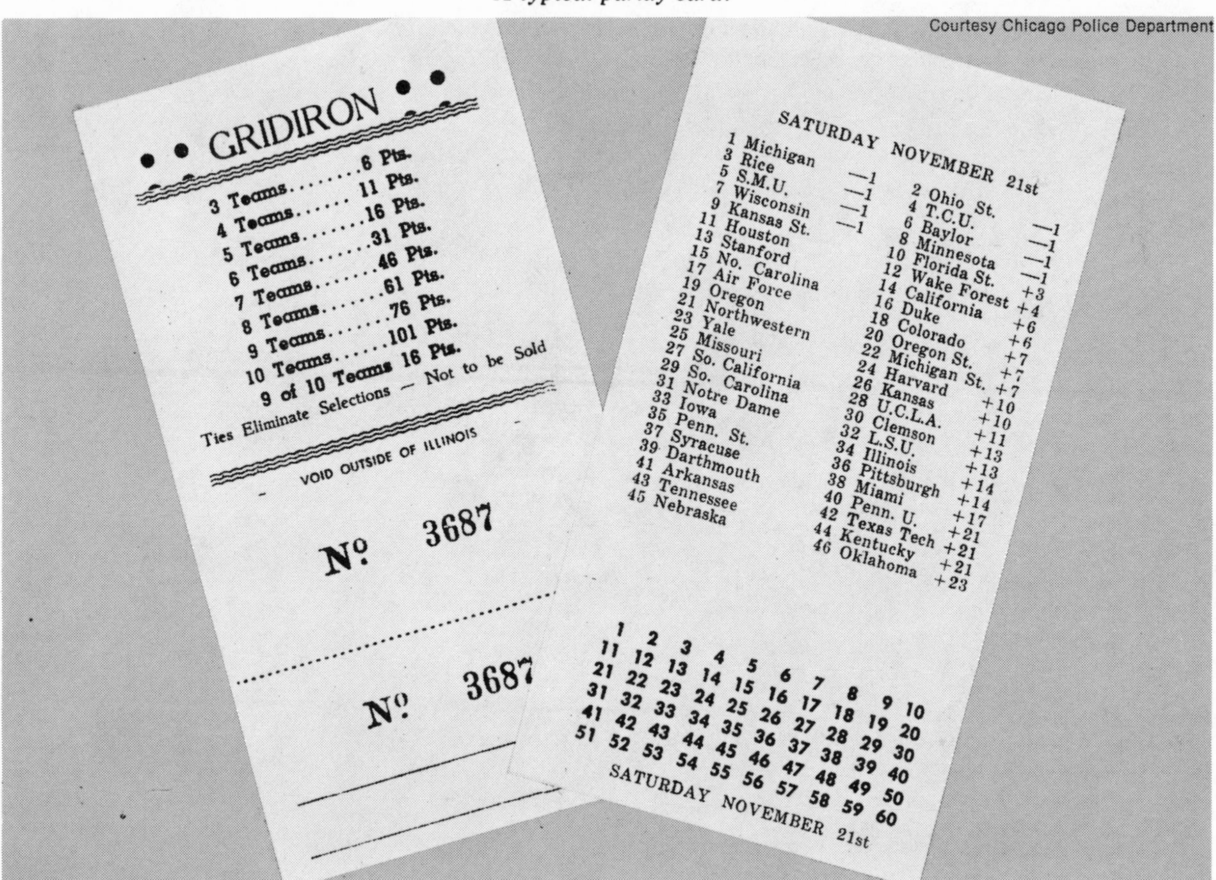

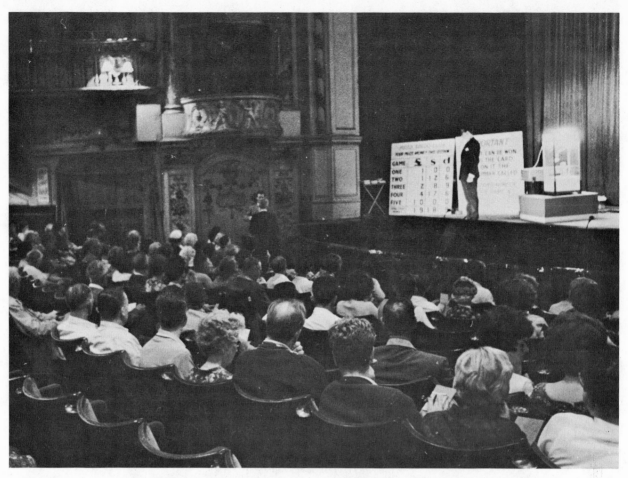

Above—A typical "Bingo Parlor" in London. Below—The British government's "Premium Bond," a type of lottery.

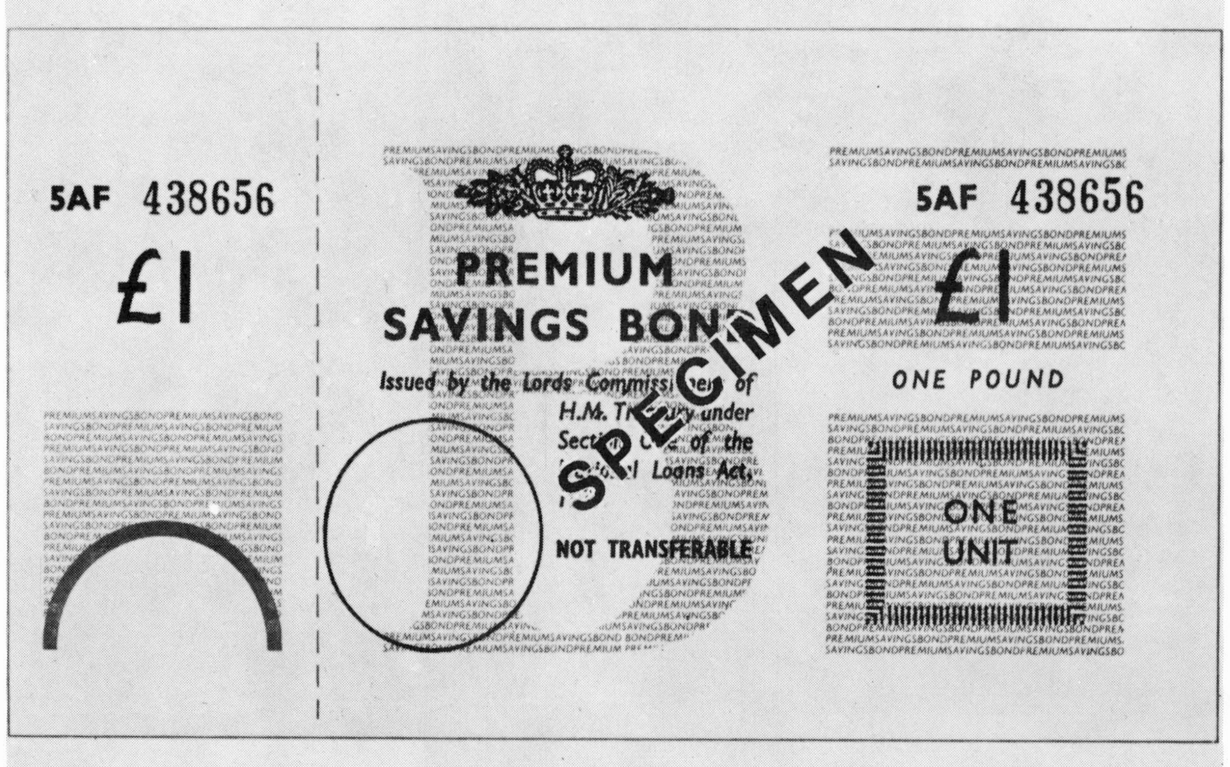

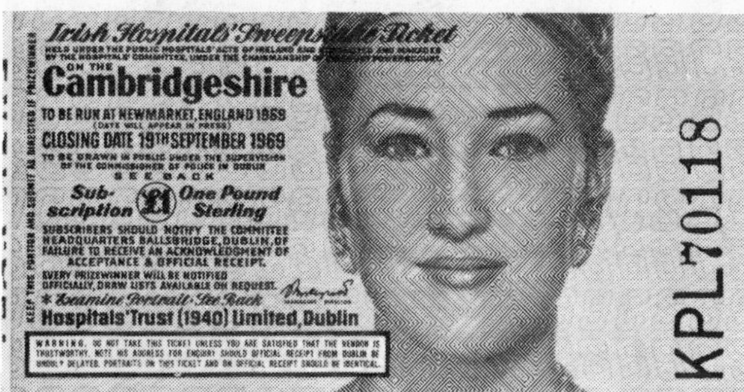

Irish Sweepstakes Ticket

The game, which stemmed from an old children's game, is, indeed, minor when compared to the Numbers Game, also called "Policy" and "Bolita." This form of lottery which began in Harlem in the early part of the twentieth century was probably about the same size operation as Bingo until racketeers took it over in 1932, with the repeal of prohibition. A simple game, it involves picking the final three digits of some number that can't be pre-determined. The superstitious rely on astrology, numerology and "dream books" to arrive at their three-digit selections, and wager anything from 10¢ a day up on their ability to predict the unpredictable.

Despite gang warfare, murders and police harrassment, the Numbers Game continues to flourish — and to draw in excess of $5 billion a year. It is to be found in virtually every American city. Unlike legal lotteries and pools where the size of winnings is determined by the amount bet, the prizes are arbitrarily set by the promoters, and the "vigorish" or house percentage is probably higher than in any other American form of gambling.

The lottery is comparatively small in the gambling picture in the United States, although it rivals horse betting in other countries. One of the main reasons for the success of lotteries is that participation in them requires nothing more than the purchase of a ticket. Another reason is that while the odds against winning are staggeringly high, the return on a modest investment can be stupendous when the gambler hits.

Lotteries and pools will be delt with in detail in a later chapter, but their history is interesting. They have almost invariably come into existence as a result of economic pressure, and they thrive best in depressed countries or localities.

With a financial pinch, Italy approved the first state-owned lottery, Lotto, in 1863. France and Germany, both in need of money, soon saw the dependable profitability of the Italian venture and entered the field. Italy's current income from Lotto, half of whatever is taken in through the sale of tickets, amounts to over $75 million a year. Every Italian town has a government lottery office, with 2200 such places holding weekly drawings.

Most European countries and many in other parts of the world have lotteries, and the "take," everywhere, is impressive. When a government suffers from serious economic ills, a lottery seems to be a popular prescription.

Great Britain's government lottery, called "Premium Bonds," is unique. It is in actuality a sale of government bonds at a price of one pound each, with interest of 4½ percent drawn by the bonds going into a lottery pool instead of to the bonds' owners. The only game involved is with the interest money.

State lotteries flourish in most of the Communist countries. In Hungary, for example, 125 government-operated lottery shops sell about 5 million tickets a week.

Most widely known of all the lotteries is the Irish Hospital Sweepstakes, whose tickets are in demand almost everywhere, despite their illegality outside of Ireland. Take away the illegal sale of tickets, and the size of the Irish Sweepstakes would be about four percent of what it now is.

Roughly two-thirds of the tickets are sold in the United States, where any kind of lottery is illegal in three-fourths of the states. In countries that have their own government-controlled lotteries and forbid all competition, such as Brazil, Peru, Italy, Hungary, Finland and Israel, Irish Sweeps tickets still find a ready sale.

The first state lottery in the United States since the Louisiana state lottery in 1895 was authorized in New Hampshire in 1963. When the state of New York later instituted a state lottery, many gamblers considered it indicative of a trend. The *Wall Street Journal* of Monday, Jan. 11, 1971, broke the news of a powerful move to introduce gambling casinos on the Boardwalk at Altantic City, New Jersey, and *Variety* magazine reported that the campaign was causing Atlantic City property values to soar.

Two New York state senators promptly prepared a bill to bring back casino gambling to the Empire State. Two city councilmen with an eye to answering criticism immediately suggested that a $5 admission fee be charged to the New York Casino to keep out the city's poor. A fee is normally charged at most European spas, for the same reason.

Profit possibilities of casino operations are apparent from the quarterly reports of the Nevada gaming commission. These reports list the gross taxable revenues of casinos in the state. This gross taxable revenue is the total of all sums received by the casinos as winnings, less the total of all sums paid out as losses, and does not take operating expenses into account.

The gross taxable revenue of Nevada casinos in a good year runs close to half a billion dollars. The revenue for 1969, for example, was roughly $460 million.

Despite this awesome gross revenue, the *Wall Street Journal* of December 8, 1970, carried the headline,

Courtesy Chicago Thoroughbred Enterprises, Inc.

"Tarnished Las Vegas . . . Hughes Will Return, But He, Others, Learn Gambling Isn't Golden . . . Corporations Find Casinos Aren't Gold Mines . . . Big Losers on Wall Street." A long story reported, "But there is one rumor Mr. (Howard) Hughes did not deny . . . owning Las Vegas, or a large part of it, hasn't turned out to be nearly as profitable as Mr. Hughes had planned it to be. In that, he's not alone. For Las Vegas casinos have turned out to be something less than the automatic money makers the Hughes organization, as well as a whole flock of major corporations, assumed them to be. In fact, compared to the good old days — like last year — this town is in the doldrums. Mr. Hughes' own experience illustrates how the bloom is off the gross."

Half a billion dollars still seems like a lot of taxable gross revenue, until you consider pari-mutuel betting on the horse races.

Harland B. Adams, author of *The Guide to Legal Gambling,* published by Citadel Press, is responsible for the statement that the California state revenue from one race track, Hollywood Park, is more than the Nevada state revenue from all its casinos. A bullring track at the Los Angeles county fair grounds has a daily handle of over $1 million for its 20-day meet. DelMar, a little seaside track near Oceanside, California, puts $1 million through its pari-mutuel windows on weekdays, with substantially higher weekend business. Add the Santa Anita handle, and it's easy to see why California likes pari-mutuel racing.

With over 100 race tracks operating in the United States, annual attendance as far back as 1960 hit close to the 47 million mark, with a pari-mutuel handle of 3⅓ billion dollars.

Of all forms of gambling that are legal, pari-mutuel betting on horses is the largest. Add illegal off-track betting and by the most conservative estimates, you have at least double the mutuel gross wagered on the horses.

While bookies have long been legally licensed in England, New York City is the first place outside of Nevada to grant legal sanction to off-track betting. Howard Samuels, a former U. S. Under-Secretary of Commerce and self-made millionaire, is board chairman of the Off-Track Betting Corporation. He hopes within five years to yield the city a profit of $100 million a year on a betting handle of $1 billion annually, according to the *Wall Street Journal.* If the business Samuels hopes to lure away from illegal bookies in New York City can approximate $1 billion a year, a figure of $10 billion a year would seem most conservative for off-track betting on horses throughout the country.

New York's increasing tolerance toward gambling is not unique. In recent years, a dozen states have legalized some form of lottery and/or Bingo.

Reading the news stories about gambling in the *Wall Street Journal,* some people have wondered why the eminently respectable publication, the newspaper of business, devotes so much space to gambling.

Gambling is a business. It is a big business. On the figures that are available — and nobody knows how much money is gambled privately and illegally — gambling must be rated as the world's largest industry.

In the United States, despite all the restrictions against it, gambling retains its position as the Number One industry. It surpasses the combined total volume of the 75 largest industrial organizations in the country, including General Motors, U.S. Steel, the oil companies and any other giants you care to name.

Gambling is a growing business, increasing its clientele every year, except for occasional economically "tight" years. The Nevada gaming commission states that some 13 million people patronize its casinos during every 12-month period, and attendance at race tracks is estimated at well over 70 million.

Gambling is Big Business, the biggest there is. To ignore such a gigantic part of our activity and economy goes beyond hypocrisy to the point of sheer stupidity.

Big Business, and popular business. Gambling is as accepted as apple pie, and as entrenched as sex. Like life, gambling is here to stay. ♠

PROFILE OF A GAMBLER

Who gambles?

Everybody!

Some people don't want to gamble but are forced into it by circumstances. Every person finds himself in a situation where he has two or more possible courses of action and must elect to take one of them. He must gamble on his judgement. To some people, making a chance decision is sheer agony. Such people gravitate toward routine jobs in large organizations where the rules of the game are rigidly set. They want security, above everything else. When they can, they become Organization Men, avoiding all possible risk and staying comfortable under Big Daddy's protective wing. Even with the Employer-Protector, there are times when they must "take a chance," and these are moments of pure hell.

They disapprove of gambling and do it only when and because they must. Forced into taking a gamble in either their business or private lives, they will usually "hedge" their decisions as much as possible, cutting the chance for personal gain but also reducing the chance of loss.

They resent "lucky" people, and regard the man who takes chances as a fool. When a risk pays off, they are outraged at the triumph of foolhardiness.

They try to sell the world on their attitude. Afraid to gamble, they don't want anyone to regard any gambler with favor. Over the years, such people have built up a picture of the gambler that shows a completely unreliable, untrustworthy, selfish, greedy, erratic, mentally-ill wastrel. They've sold their belief so hard that they sometimes get some people to accept it.

They take chances only when there's no alternative.

Other people, and they are in the majority, gamble by choice. They love to bet on their judgement. The "safe" course, to them, is the dull course. They are eager to take risks whenever the reward for betting right justifies it. They may not enjoy taking a loss, but the chance of losing is part of what makes gambling exciting to them.

Nearly every successful man the world has ever known has been a gambler. At least once in his career, he has staked everything on his judgement. In the biographies of most great men, there is a critical turning point where the right gamble paid off. Most successful men say that had they listened to the cautions and warnings of well-meaning friends, they would never have attained their eminence.

They not only gamble on business and personal decisions, but they find zestful recreation in gambling in casinos or in private games of chance. Stories of highly successful men winning or losing huge sums of money at the gaming tables are common.

If the non-gambler resents the gambler, the gambler looks down on the play-it-safe type of person. He regards the non-gambler as stodgy, timid, unambitious and cowardly.

The word "gambler" is too broad a designation for precise definition or discussion. Just as there are many degrees of gambling interest and enthusiasm, there are numerous types of gamblers, motivated by widely different causes. The gambler at one economic level may be and often is an entirely different kind of person from gamblers of different economic status. Psychologists say that feminine gambling instincts usually spring from much different sources than do masculine gambling urges.

There are as many different kinds of gamblers as there are kinds of people. There are mentally ill gamblers, just as there are mentally ill drinkers. To condemn all gamblers because of a few neurotic, compulsive gamblers is no more logical than to condemn religion because of a few religious fanatics.

Mr. Odds-Maker defines a professional gambler as one who makes a living from gambling. He is either a "house" man or an independent bettor, but usually prefers being the latter. He likes to be independent and dislikes the confining restrictions of a job.

Mr. Odds-Maker is, himself, a professional gambler who seldom gambles. He employs experts to analyze betting situations and, if necessary, pays for computerization of odds in certain peculiar betting situations. He makes money by accurate analyses of betting odds, and so is somewhat unique among professional gamblers. He is an actuarial advisor.

The professional gambler is at the top of the heap. Gambling is his business and he's in business for profit. Gambling is a major industry, such a large and profitable one that it has attracted Big Business. Major corporations and holding companies, looking for lucrative expansion, have moved into legal gambling. And Big Business has discovered, to its sorrow, that the gambling business requires just as much know-how as any other kind of business, a know-how of a specialized kind and one that its management has not yet acquired. Professional gamblers knew how to make casinos lucrative; Big Business is having a rough time trying to hit the break-even point.

Smart Sam, a professional gambler who bucks the house in Las Vegas, says he never depends on luck. "Sure, every player has ups and downs, but the law of averages will give you a down for every up, sooner or later," he says. "I've made a study of every gambling game there is, and I stay away from the ones I can't beat. Also, I only bet the others when I think I can win."

Like Smart Sam, most professional gamblers are solid business men. They may have warm personalities, but they don't get emotional when they're doing business. All of them admit to enjoying the competition with other gamblers, but they don't gamble for kicks. They gamble for money.

Smart Sam is constantly on the alert for "edges," advantages which will operate to his profit. Like another professional gambler, the casino operator,

DRAWING LOTS

The "casting of lots" in Biblical times was done in the belief that God would control the results to show His will. (Proverbs 16:33) In national crises, it was a common occurence. It happened in the plans for the conquest of Canaan, in the campaign against the Benjamites, in David's indecision after the death of Saul, and in wars. The Phoenicians cast lots to discover the cause of the tempest.

It was employed to discover wrongdoers, as in the case of Achon. (Jos. 7:14).

Lots were used in dividing the land of Canaan, in the election of Saul (Isaiah 10:20), the choice of men to attack Gibeah, and to settle the division of duties among the priests.

One method of casting lots was by Urim and Thummin, which were probably two variant stones carried in a pouch under a priest's breastplate and drawn out as indicative of choices. "Kasam" was the drawing of lots with headless arrows, and rhabdomoney was with sticks of varying length.

The Book of Jonah, 1:7, says, "And they said everyone to his fellow, Come, and let us cast lots, and the lot fell upon Jonah. Then they said unto him, Tell us, we pray thee, for whose cause this evil is upon us."

he knows that a percentage in his favor will eventually pay off.

He explains how his theory operates. "Now, you might argue that every player in a poker game has an even chance. That's hog-wash. Most of the players in a poker game are going to make mistakes — and when they do, I'm going to clobber 'em.

"The house has a very slight advantage in a casino Blackjack game — but the dealer's not allowed to use any judgment. The rules make him a machine. That means that there are times in every Blackjack game when the advantage is on my side, and I use it.

"In casino craps, you've got close to an even gamble if you know what you're doing. And if you're hep in the average private crap game, you can walk out with all the money that was in the place. An expert in any business does better than a dub."

Mr. Odds-Maker says that, surprisingly, the true professional gambler is seldom greedy. He neither expects to break the bank nor tries to do it. He only goes for the big kill when he thinks the percentage is so heavy on his side that it would take a repeal of the law of averages to beat him. But if he doesn't make many big hauls, he almost never loses his shirt, either.

Two young accountants in Aurora, Illinois, became professional horse players during the Depression years. They rented an office and put in an eight-hour day, six days a week, handicapping the horses and playing their system. They refused to explain it to anyone, but they made about $12,000 a year apiece with it. When the national economy picked up, they refused to take lucrative auditing jobs with nice fringe benefits. They preferred being professional gamblers.

Charlie Tillek, a quiet, intelligent man about 40 years old, was a racing writer and handicapper. He sold enough copy to various tout sheets and racing publications to make a modest living. When anyone asked his occupation, he replied, "Waiting for the big one." Several times, he had spotted maneuvers where a horse was being built up for a big killing, and he had decided that whenever another such deal came along, he'd gamble on it.

Charlie lived modestly and put his money in the bank. He was a mousey, colorless fellow who never said much but had many casual friends. One Tuesday afternoon in a coffee shop, he announced to them, "Well, boys, by late Saturday afternoon, I'll either be broke or ready to retire. I've nosed out a big one."

The following Monday morning, he went around to the coffee shop to say goodbye. "I'm buying a beautiful log house and acreage up in northern Wisconsin," he told his friends. "I'm getting it for 20,000 bucks and it's a steal. A lot of wild life, good hunting and fishing, a nice lake at the front door, everything I've ever wanted. From now on, it's all downhill and shady."

His big one had hit. He had passed up dozens of little bets while he waited for it. He said he'd never bet on another horse. "That was my business," he explained, "and I've retired."

Mr. Odds-Maker points out that not all professional gamblers devote all their time to gambling. "In one way," he says, "being a pro is an attitude. There's a Texas oil millionaire who bets heavily on sports events—and nearly always wins. He certainly doesn't need the money, but he has a professional attitude toward gambling. His personal friends, who are in the same income bracket as his, have no business gambling with him. They are gambling for fun and he's gambling for profit. They don't know what they're doing, and he does."

Psychologists have discovered that true professional gamblers never indulge in crooked trickery. Smart Sam explains why. "To start with," he says, "we don't have to cheat. We're better gamblers than the amateurs, and we've always got some percentages going for us. But on top of that, we don't dare take the risk of getting caught. If an amateur's caught doing something crooked, he's kicked out of the game; if a pro gets caught cheating, he's out of business."

The professional gambler constitutes a small segment of the gambling fraternity. Another small group ranks right down at the bottom, the compulsive, neurotic or psychopathic gamblers. While they're not numerous, they're the gamblers who get the publicity —unfavorable publicity. Dostoevski wrote what has been accepted as the master picture of the compulsive gambler in his novel, *The Gambler*. Since the novelist was, himself, a pathalogic gambler, the character may be a self-portrait.

The most pronounced characteristics of the mentally ill gambler are that gambling is an obsession with him, he risks more than he can afford to lose, he will

---

I'll Betcha!

Bets on little-known facts or commonly accepted inaccuracies have gone on for years, with the bettor usually having a sure thing and leading his victims into a trap that has only one avenue of escape — a pay-off.

An erudite bettor in Pittsburgh has won free drinks for years by betting that genuine ivory doesn't have to come from elephant tusks. He wagers that he can name at least three other sources of real ivory.

When challenged, he names the other three — the boar, the hippopotamus and the walrus. A check-up shows that he's right. The losers pay — but who says gambling isn't educational?

WHO'S AFRAID?

The late Nick Zographos of the Greek Syndicate once said, "Keep close track of how much money every opponent you face has lost, and make it your business to know how much he can afford to lose. The information is vital and should influence your style of play. When a player is under heavy financial pressure, and you know it, his betting can almost tell you what cards he's holding."

"Of course," he smiled, "nobody can use that technique against me because I have always taken the attitude that when I consider the odds to be in my favor, I can afford to lose any given amount. I've never in my life let the possibility of losing a large wager frighten me."

Over the years, he had an occasional loss of astronomical size—but he never "bet scared."

never stop while he's winning, and consistent losses never teach him anything. Some psychologists say that the compulsive gambler doesn't *want* to win, that a big loss is a "cleansing punishment" for him.

The professional gambler wants no part of the compulsive, psychopathic gambler, easy as it is to get his money. "He's the worst publicity the house can have," a casino operator explains. "He cries long and loud about the money he dropped in your game, and gives folks the idea that you took him. In a good many cases, the house gets so fed up with the compulsive gambler who's been wiped out that we give him some money on condition that he stay away."

The great bulk of gamblers can best be classified as "Casual" gamblers. Gambling isn't a compulsion, and while they sometimes gamble for more than they can afford to lose, they don't make a practice of it. If a gambling loss hurts them financially, they learn a lesson from it.

The casual gambler believes in luck. He knows it exists. Doesn't somebody win the top money in the Irish Sweepstakes Lottery every year? When he makes a wager, he hopes that this is his lucky day. If he doesn't win, he hopes that luck will favor him some other time.

He gambles primarily for entertainment and "kicks," although the hope of a lucky streak is always there. One of the pleasures he gets is exercise of the competitive urge in its most basic form. He pits himself against an adversary and there is a reward for the victor. Penny-ante poker games and bridge for a tenth of a cent a point give players enough enjoyment to keep them coming back, and nobody can say that greed is the motivation.

Every man likes to think he's daring, and gambling gives him the opportunity to prove it, without undue risk. The casual crap-shooter who "lets it ride" after three consecutive passes regards himself as a dashing, devil-may-care fellow who isn't afraid to take a chance—although the money that's "riding" wasn't his at the start of the game.

The casual gambler is part of a society that restricts him, and gambling is a mild defiance of The Establishment, which he thoroughly enjoys.

Gambling is often his hobby, and he makes a study of a certain game or games to increase his efficiency, just as a golfer takes lessons from a pro. Sometimes he's good enough at a game to be a pro, but it remains a hobby, not a career.

The casual gambler is an optimist, but not a crazy optimist. He knows that lightning doesn't strike often but figures that, some time, it may hit him. Whether he knows the percentages or not, he's not stupid.

The casual gambler is the healthiest of all. He gambles for fun, where the pro puts in long hours in a business that calls for tremendous concentration and is, at best, hazardous.

The casual gambler is the backbone of the gambling industry. Without him, the casinos and sports pools would fold. Lotteries would be small-time operations. Racing wouldn't amount to much.

Psychologists and psychiatrists are fairly well agreed that every member of our current culture is a potential gambler. The urge to gamble is always there, and considerable disagreement exists as to how strongly that urge should be disciplined.

The casual gambler's enthusiasm for wagers varies. In the few instances where it becomes a pathologic concentration that's more important than his business or profession, his family or his economic status, he becomes a compulsive and neurotic gambler!

Does the professional gambler respect the non-gambler?

Smart Sam says, "Show me a person who won't ever take a chance on anything and I'll show you the dullest guy in town. What's more, the odds are that he's no great success. You never get far without taking some chances, and a routine life, without kicks, dulls your imagination. I wouldn't trade one minute of my life for the narrow, play-it-safe, unexciting routine of the non-gambler. What I have beats Social Security."

GAMBLING FOR FUN AND PROFIT

Nobody except a sick compulsive gambler deliberately gambles to lose, yet many gamblers take approaches that almost inevitably lead to a loss of money.

Stacey Horn, an avid gambler who has fun, winning or losing, says, "Don't let anybody kid you; it's more fun to win than to lose, but you *can* enjoy a losing session if you adopt the right mental attitude. Take the stand that you're gambling for recreation and possible profit. If you don't get the profit, you've spent a certain amount of money on recreation. You've had an evening in congenial company. You've had the fun of matching wits and testing skills against other gamblers. At times when larger-than-usual sums were at stake, you've had some 'kicks,' some thrills. For an evening, you've forgotten all your problems. You've been practically unconscious of time. In short, you've gotten a large amount of recreation in return for your expenditure. If the evening's fun wasn't worth what it cost, you were gambling for too much money and should change your gambling habits.

"When gambling ceases to be fun, even if you're winning, it's time to lay off. You wouldn't keep spending money on another form of recreation if you quit enjoying it, and gambling shouldn't differ from other pastimes in that respect.

"A good many casual gamblers handicap themselves so severely that their chances of winning are greatly diminished—and so are their chances of having fun. I always stick by Clement McQuaid's 11 basic rules for winning."

McQuaid's rules are simple, and they're easy to follow.

1. Don't gamble unless you have a positive mental attitude.

What this boils down to is, don't get into a game or make a bet unless you expect to win. Maybe you'll lose, even with a positive mental attitude, but going in with the expectation of defeat almost guarantees failure. When you're in a mood where you're convinced that everything is going wrong and the world's against you, don't even consider gambling. Always have the intention of winning.

2. Never gamble when you're tired or ill.

Good gambling requires alertness. No form of recreation is much fun when you're mentally and physically fatigued or when you're ill, and you seldom handle yourself well under such circumstances. If you go into a long session feeling fine and later find yourself fagged out or with a headache, it's time to quit. Maybe all you need is a little fresh air and a bit of exercise. Try it, and if you still feel below par, call it a day.

3. Dress comfortably.

Tight, uncomfortable shoes, a collar that scratches your neck, a jacket or sweater that binds your shoulders, tight socks, binding underwear, or even a necktie that's too tightly tied can be distracting. A shower and a splash of cologne or after-shave lotion on your face can add to your feeling of comfort. Almost every form of gambling puts you in close proximity with other people and fresh, clean clothes, regardless of what they do for your personal comfort, are a consideration that those around you have a right to expect.

4. Set a losing limit before you gamble, and stick with it.

Nearly everyone *does* set a limit on losses before starting to gamble, but a great many people don't adhere to their self-made limit. "Easy Credit" is available in many gambling operations. Personal checks aren't hard to cash if you have proper identification. If you're with personal friends, somebody will almost inevitably accommodate you with a loan. More people get into trouble by exceeding their loss limit than any other single reason.

When you hit your pre-determined limit, resign yourself to the fact that this isn't your night, and quit. There's always a strong temptation to try for a comeback, but resist it. If you succumb to it, you're not a good gambler.

5. Never gamble with "tough" money.

"Tough" money is money you can't afford to lose, money that's needed for essentials. If you have obligations to meet, you have no right to gamble the money that will meet them.

Nobody can gamble right with tough money. The tough-money gambler is under tension. He presses. Almost always, he is frightened and worried. He can't possibly wager with the calculated coolness that's a part of good gambling. The tough-money gambler is a miserable gambler who isn't having any fun. He doesn't follow the procedures of money management because he's desperate.

6. Have a plan for money management.

In casino games, there is usually a percentage of from roughly one and a half to five percent in favor of the house. In private games, you have no better than an even chance, aside from your superior skill. On horse bets, under the pari-mutuel system, up to 17 percent is taken off the top! In bets with bookmakers, the bookie, theoretically, at least, gets his profit percentage out of every dollar you bet.

This means that if you bet an identical sum on every bet and the law of mathematical probability operates, which it always does, over the long haul, the best you can do in a private game is break even and the best you can do betting against a "house" is lose a little money.

If you're going to have a like number of wins and losses, there is only one way to show a profit. Bet

MONEY MANAGEMENT SYSTEMS

Best known of all gambling money-management systems and one of the oldest, is the Martingale, in which the stakes are doubled every time you lose. It has never worked consistently for anyone, since a few losses brings the bettor up against the house maximum bet—if he hasn't already run out of money. Starting with a $1 bet, 21 straight losses would bring you to a bet of $1,048,576—to get your original dollar back!

The Great Martingale has you double your stakes and add a dollar after each loss, breaking you a little quicker.

The Alembert has you add one betting unit after each loss and subtract one after each win, thus taking a little longer to lose your money. The Contre-Alembert adds a unit after a win and subtracts one after a loss.

With the Ascot, you have a formula: 3, 6, 9, 12, 20, 25, 35, 50, 75, 125, 200. You start betting from the middle, with $25, moving one up if you win and one down if you lose. Once, somewhere, at some time, it must have worked—but not lately.

The Labouchere starts with the digits, 1, 2, 3, 4. You add the two outside numbers, one and four, for your first wager. If you lose, you add 5 to your list of numbers and bet 6. When you win, you cross off the last outside numbers on both ends. If you won with 1 and 6, for example, your next bet would be 2 and 5, so you bet 7.

The Contre-Labouchere adds numbers when you win, crosses off the last number when you lose. It doesn't work, either—unless luck is with you.

light on your losses and heavy on your wins.

Many good gamblers follow a specific procedure.

a. *Bet minimums when you're losing.* Never "double up" after a loss. The Martingale system of doubling and redoubling after losses, until you win, has bankrupted more gamblers than any other system known to man. Even if you have enough money to do it—which almost nobody in a real losing streak has—you soon hit the house maximum limit and have taken a whopping loss.

b. *Bet heavy when you're winning.* Following a win with your minimum bet, bet the original minimum plus the amount you won. If you win a second time, "drag" the amount of the minimum bet and bet the rest. On a third win, drag the minimum and bet the rest. You now have a one-minimum-bet profit on the round, regardless of what happens. If you win a fourth time, you have an eleven-minimum-bet profit. At this point, either hold at a five-minimum-bet level or continue to increase your bets, dragging a profit from each win. As soon as you lose, go back to the minimum bet.

c. *Always make your heavy bets with the other fellow's money, not your own.* The worst you can do betting house money against the house on a bet is break even on that particular wager. Actually, you've lost money on the round—but it was money that you got from the other fellow, not part of your original venture-money.

d. *Quit on a losing streak, not a winning streak.* While the law of mathematic probability averages out, it doesn't operate in a set pattern. Wins and losses go in streaks more often than they alternate. If you've had a good winning streak and a loss follows it, bet minimums long enough to see whether or not another winning streak is coming up. If it isn't, quit while you're still ahead.

e. *Don't limit your winnings.*

It's surprising how many people do. Gamblers who limit their winnings to covering expenses on a trip to casino-land save the house a lot of money. Always ride out a winning streak, pushing your luck to the hilt.

f. *Gamble for a winning streak.*

You never make much money continuing to bet minimums after a win. To beat the house or an opponent substantially, you need streaks of at least four consecutive wins. Play for them. If you alternate streaks of four consecutive wins and four consecutive losses, you can wind up a heavy winner by the use of money management.

7. Never drink while you're gambling.

Liquor is one of a gambler's worst enemies. A big winner who starts celebrating while he's still gambling almost always winds up in the red. Alcohol creates a false optimism and a disregard for money. It blunts the judgment and the perception.

Good gamblers may drink, but not while they're gambling. They want their mental faculties to be acute and sensitive. If you're thirsty, have a cup of coffee or a glass of ice water.

8. Concentrate on your gambling.

A good gambler doesn't think of anything else while he's gambling. In a casino, he'll be polite and pleasant to other players, but he won't become involved with them. In a private game, he won't let the conversation take his mind off the game, no matter how entertaining the chatter is. If he has personal problems that won't let him concentrate on his gambling, he gets out. While chance is involved in most gambles, there is also an element of skill. He considers the odds and the probabilities on every move he makes, and he keeps money management constantly in mind. He has things to think about, things that can make him a winner or a loser, and he refuses to be distracted.

9. Don't let a winning streak give you a disregard for money.

Many novice gamblers who get a big win develop a disregard for money that is almost incredible. They bet with a recklessness that seems unbelievable. They let their winnings ride on win after win, without taking out a profit, reasoning that they're far enough ahead so they can afford it. After a couple of losses, they make a big bet on a "hunch." They literally throw a large part of their profits away.

Tomorrow, they will haggle over a $10 charge for services, but tonight, $10 means absolutely nothing.

Money is always money, and you should be gambling to win. Regardless of how much you're ahead of the game, each new bet is a new venture and you should be making it with the intention of maximizing profits and minimizing losses. When money ceases to mean anything to you, it's time to get out of the game.

10. Don't try to recoup losses.

Don't fight a losing streak by increasing the size of your bets. Each new bet is the same gamble as the last one was. The fact that you've lost ten times in a row doesn't mean that the odds are nine to one in favor of your winning the next bet. They're roughly even—slightly against you — just as they were on your previous bets.

You recoup losses by betting house money against the house, not your own. When you win with a minimum bet, let the winnings ride and manage to come up with a few more wins, you're back in business. Trying to force or "bull" your way back doesn't work.

11. Don't try to "break" the opposition.

Breaking the house may be a pleasant dream, but that's what it is—a dream. It almost never happens.

The house has more funds than you have and the odds are slightly in its favor. Letting everything ride, time after time after time, has to result in an eventual loss. Don't be greedy. Never refuse to take a sure profit in the hope of breaking the bank. One reason why compulsive gamblers always lose is that they won't let themselves win. They have a delusion that they're suddenly invincible, and they let their winnings ride until they lose.

When you gamble, nothing in the world can guarantee that you'll win. These 11 rules can't do it. But they can increase your chances of winning and they can keep you from getting badly hurt by losses.

They can also make gambling more fun. They can guarantee that even when you lose, you'll get your money's worth.

Most novices gamble without rhyme or reason.

One Nevada casino operator who has read McQuaid's 11 rules says, "Anybody who follows them will be a better-than-average gambler. One thing I'd add, and I guess it would come under Rule Six, a plan for money management, is—don't count on a 'system' to make you rich. We welcome system gamblers with open arms. They're so convinced that their system is infallible that they spend a bundle before they change their minds. Some gamblers beat us every day, but not with systems. The big secret of winning is money management, knowing how to bet a hot hand, and McQuaid's advice in Rule Six hits the nail on the head. Most amateur gamblers don't know how to make a hot streak pay off. We get amateurs every day who are lucky as the devil, have fantastic runs of luck, and leave with a few dollars profit when they should be $20,000 ahead of us. And Clem is so right about betting minimums when you're losing. The losers who keep going up and up on the size of their bets, thinking it will somehow change their luck, represent a good-sized chunk of our casino profit.

"A good example of what Clem says about money management is a fellow, a regular patron, a resident of this town, who is just plain unlucky. He comes around every night to the crap table and always makes more losing bets than winning ones. But on his worst nights, he walks out of here with 15 or 20 bucks profit. His losing bets are peanuts and his winning ones are substantial. He knows how to win and how to lose. One of the pit bosses remarked the other day, 'Give that guy average luck and he'd own half the town.'

"I like McQuaid's Rule One on mental attitude, too. There's a type of amateur gambler who comes in expecting to lose. He has an air of resignation as if he's about to say, 'Let's hurry up and get this over with.'

"It's a funny thing, but he's almost never surprised. He loses, just as he expects to do.

"Then there's another type who has all the confidence in the world. He expects to win. He came here for that purpose and is matter-of-fact about the whole thing. If he happens to lose, he's astounded.

"Talk about positive mental attitude, every summer, we get a visit from a prim, proper, middle-aged woman who's an algebra teacher in a little Iowa town. She heads straight for a blackjack table with all the assurance in the world and makes small bets. When she's won $1,000, which usually takes her three or four nights, she quits and leaves. She's never failed to get her $1,000; she seems to *know* she's going to get it. She told me once that the trip out here is the high spot of her year, and she added that there are a few things we could learn about blackjack."

He emphasizes the importance of Clem's rule on setting a loss limit. "We don't want anybody to leave our place barefoot," he says. "The people who don't limit their losses are responsible for most of the criticism against gambling.

"An attractive young couple from Los Angeles show up here every three or four months with exactly $200 in gambling money. Sometimes they win and sometimes they lose, but they always have a ball. We get a kick out of watching them. The dealers love 'em. She told one of our dealers that her husband got into bad trouble with gambling losses when they were first married. Instead of trying to stop his gambling, she decided to regulate it—and succeeded. They're good gamblers and they have a great time.

"I wish there were some way we could enforce Clem's Rule Four, set a loss limit and stick with it, and Rule Five, never gamble with tough money. It's good business from our standpoint to have everyone follow these rules. Our profit depends on traffic and

". . . but of course I'm cheating, aren't you . . .?!"

repeat business. It's no fun to lose money you can't afford to lose, and people who lose too much won't come back.

"McQuaid's Rule Seven is another that should be emphasized. We serve liquor because our clientele demands it and because it's a profitable part of our business. But I have to admit that drinking and winning don't go together.

"I'd say that the best gamblers already follow most of the 11 rules. Every gambler would profit from observing them."

Gambling Etiquette

Gambling etiquette is no problem when you're visiting the bookmaker or going to the Friday night poker game or betting a few dollars with a friend on a round of golf. It's established, and everyone knows it.

People who are visiting a gambling casino for the first time are uneasy about the clothes problem. An uncomfortable gambler is a bad gambler, and the person who senses that his clothes are wrong is bound to be uncomfortable.

Anyone doing casino gambling within the continental limits of the United States does it in Nevada, where informality and sports clothes are typical. The casinos on The Strip, however, have spent millions to create an atmosphere of elegance, and management likes to maintain it.

Wives or girl-friends who go to Nevada on vacations have read about the glamorous night spots and excellent dining rooms, and look forward to "dressing up." The management loves them for it, and encourages them to look their lovely best.

The husband or boy-friend who accompanies a beautifully-dressed woman into a Las Vegas Strip spot, wearing an old pair of golf slacks, a wrinkled cotton sports jacket, short-sleeved sport shirt open at the neck and a pair of scuffed loafers is likely to feel foolish.

Business men who attend Las Vegas conventions with nothing in their luggage except the kind of clothes they wear to the office feel equally uncomfortable, and stand out as "squares."

A general rule of thumb is that the better the casino, the more fastidiously its customers dress.

Most Las Vegas dining rooms enforce the rules that any man entering must be wearing a jacket and necktie. They don't go much farther than that. Even a Western "bolo" tie will suffice in most places, although the management won't cheer about it.

Many places have posted regulations that women will not be admitted to a dining room in shorts or swim suit — and have arguments every day with guests who think the rule is silly. Maitre d's are unhappy when a woman diner isn't wearing a skirt or slacks. Anyone who wants to eat while wearing shorts or swimming togs should do it at pool-side, where it's quite acceptable.

Nevada casinos operate around the clock, and the time of day or night influences dress. From the dinner hour to midnight, when the night clubs are presenting their spectacular shows, is the "dressiest" time. And formal and semi-formal evening wear are the same in Las Vegas as anywhere else.

Most of the time, sports attire is in order. The person who plans to buy such clothes especially for a trip to Nevada might do well to wait and purchase them after arrival.

The hotels have excellent shops, and downtown Las Vegas and Reno offer sports wear in the widest possible price range. The important thing is that Nevada shops stock what is being worn in the locality. Nevada sports wear has a Western flavor. Most of it isn't "Gung Ho" western, the cowboy and cowgirl type, but it is easily identifiable as distinctive to Nevada. Also, the clothes are the right weight —and Nevada temperatures may be quite different from those in other parts of the country.

Because the Nevada casinos cater to everyone from the extremely wealthy to the great mass market, prices range from stiff to modest. Clothes displayed in the better hotel shops are generally much more expensive than those shown in downtown stores. The safest "bargains" are probably to be found in a downtown department store.

A word of caution — don't buy "far out" Western clothes if you want maximum value. Novelty apparel, extreme in style, looks fine in its intended setting but all wrong back home.

Take along at least two comfortable, well broken-in pairs of shoes. Nevada vacationers are on their feet much of the time and do considerable walking. Laboring over a hot crap table for two or three hours can tire anyone, and the feet are normally the first part of the anatomy to cry for help.

Take along plenty of undergarments and hose. Both men and women have a tendency to change their underclothes more often than usual, probably because of the climate and increased activity.

And while the climate is wonderful, nights can be either chilly or warm. The visitor should be prepared for both.

For some reason, the best-dressed people in the casinos are usually to be found at the roulette and baccarat tables.

There is no "standard" casino atmosphere. That in Lucaya/Freeport, for example, is quite different from that in Pleasure Island in Nassau. Dress is different, and the character of the patronage is different.

The average American gambler regards the atmosphere of Monte Carlo as the "stuffiest" of any casino in the world, perhaps because he is unprepared for its dignity. Formal attire is almost obligatory in certain of Monte Carlo's gaming rooms.

At the other extreme is Casino Center in downtown Las Vegas, where customers can wear almost anything — and do. Some are garishly over-dressed and some look like panhandlers. Clothing is neither questioned nor noticed. Anything is all right, just so the wearer stays with the action.

On a Nevada vacation, don't plan on spending all your time in the casinos. You'll need to get out and about. And you should eat regularly and well. Superb food is available in beautiful dining spots. You'd be doing yourself a disservice to miss the night-club floor shows, which are the best to be found anywhere in the country.

A Maitre d' in a hotel supper room confided, "While we don't demand semi-formal wear, we at least encourage it. But a good many of the wealthy who come here come to relax and let their hair down. The men don't want to dress for dinner, and the competition is too stiff for us to insist on it.

"There's no question, though, men's semi-formal wear does something for a dining room or supper club. And there's really no reason any more why men should grumble about dressing for dinner. Dinner jackets today are almost sports jackets. The old, stiff-starched tux shirts were uncomfortable, but today's are just as comfortable as any other shirt a man wears."

What will a Nevada vacation cost you, aside from gambling money?

As luxury hotels go, those in Nevada probably give you better value than you'll find anywhere else in the country. Aside from the transportation, a Nevada vacation should cost you less than one in any other popular resort area.

There's the matter of tipping to be considered. Whether you approve of it or not, it's done, and since you're stuck with it, you might as well do it graciously.

People without previous casino experience wonder if they are expected to tip the dealers at the gaming tables. Some customers do, usually with chips rather than money, and some don't. One way of tipping that meets with their approval is to make a separate bet for "the boys." The dealers don't demand tips and aren't disgruntled if they don't get them. Certainly, you don't tip an impatient or surly dealer. If he's helpful, tip him because you want to rather than because you think it's necessary.

As to tipping for hotel services, remember that you're in a luxury spot. The atmosphere of the Strip hotels in Las Vegas tends to promote a little larger tips than are customary in most localities. Big winners in the casinos sometimes get carried away by their good fortune and tip with lavish recklessness. If a bellhop isn't impressed with a fifty-cent tip, consider that a crap game winner may just have tossed him a twenty-dollar bill.

Don't tip lavishly to impress anyone, because you won't succeed. Tip because you're getting good service and want to show your appreciation.

If you have any doubts about proper procedure or custom, ask. Everybody wants to be helpful, and nobody expects a newcomer to know the ropes.

If you feel like a tenderfoot, look around. Most of the people who rub elbows with you are greenhorns, too. There's no stigma about being a newcomer, and everyone wants you to get comfortable as quickly as you can. Visitor revenue has been a bonanza, and Nevada wants to keep it coming.

Hotel and casino competition is stiff, and management wants your patronage. If there's anything wrong with the way you're treated in a Strip hotel, complain. The management would far rather make amends than have you go elsewhere.

Everything's available for a varied, action-crammed, fun-packed vacation, and the natives are friendly. With all this and a chance to win some money, too, all you have to do is get with it. ♠

BOOK ONE

"IT'S JUST A FRIENDLY GAME"

Gambling and winning ways in all the card and board games.
The rules.
How to play and win.
Best Bets by Mr. Odds-Maker, himself.

"It's just a friendly game"

More than thirteen million people who visit the legal gambling casinos in the United States every year are, for the most part, not habitués of gambling salons. Neither are they constant, day-in-and-day-out gamblers. They spend a few days in Nevada or the Bahamas, or on a world-wide trip, visit the famous gambling casinos they've read or heard about, concentrate on the form of gambling they enjoy most, have a wonderful time and go home.

If they're not professional gamblers, neither do they represent the bulk of the population. They're a small part of it. It would be interesting to know if the "typical" American has ever been inside a gambling casino.

While we don't know if the "Typical" American has ever been to Nevada or to the site of a foreign casino, we do know that he gambles. Available records on pari-mutuel horse-race wagering indicate that just the legal betting on the part of just those Americans who are intrigued by racing makes casino gambling insignificant by comparison.

And for every horse player, there are at least a dozen casual gamblers who never go near the tracks or bookies. Horses aren't their "thing."

"Friendly games" probably account for more gambling than any other form of wagering. There is hardly a participant-game existent that doesn't have money bet on it, from marbles on up. Get into the spectator sports of baseball, football and basketball and the amount of money wagered on their outcomes staggers the imagination.

Most of the "friendly game" gambling is gambling at its pleasant best, done with friends in a congenial atmosphere. An evening of cards with "the boys" would be a pleasant experience under any circumstances, but competing for the other fellow's money and risking one's own adds the real spice to the event.

Since most forms of gambling are illegal—although common—in most parts of the United States, so-called "public" gambling is, in most communities, in the hands of people who can, at best, only be called "undesirable." To participate in it, the player must visit shabby backrooms of pool halls, shady night spots and questionable secret meeting places where he feels uncomfortable and apprehensive. These games that are run by undesirables are, we might as well face it, frequented and patronized by many who belong in the same category. Joe Average would have a miserable time gambling in such a spot and if he won would be scared to death about getting home without being slugged over the head.

Joe Average enjoys gambling, but he disapproves of the conditions surrounding "public" gambling and is frightened of it.

And so, gambling for the great rank and file of American citizenry has become a private thing, done privately in company with others who are members of the same social class. Some of it is done at the office, but most of it is done in private clubs or in private homes.

All things considered, it is gambling in which every participant gets the most even break possible. There are no "house" percentages and no massing of house know-how and skill against the individual player. The players compete against each other, not against a "house." The only advantage one player has over another is a superior ability at a certain game.

The other players are almost never willing to acknowledge such a superiority, and the competition is not only intense but healthy.

Since the players are usually of a class, the wagering is ordinarily in keeping with income. A player may occasionally get hurt by a larger-than-usual bet, but he seldom gets mortally wounded. There's no place for a compulsive gambler in such a group, and he's quick to sense it. He moves on to some area where he can gamble more desperately and grimly.

Most popular of all the "friendly games" from the start of the United States down to the present has been Poker. The game has been eulogized and cursed, depending on the speaker's current point of view. As a gambling card game, it has stood the test of time and goes merrily on its way. Bridge and Gin Rummy are the other two "friendly games" rating highest in popularity. All three are classified as "friendly games" because they are most often played in the congenial atmosphere of the home or private club, but the competitive spirit in any of them sometimes reaches a level where "friendly" seems a misnomer.

Backgammon, a board game that was once regarded as innocuous entertainment for children, has had a tremendous rise in popularity as a gambling game for adults, particularly with well-to-do sophisticates. People who have held it in low regard and have been inveigled into playing it for money with backgammon experts have learned to their sorrow that there is nothing childish about it as a gambling game.

The checker-board that belonged to Queen Hatasu, who reigned over the ancient Egyptians in 1600 B.C. is on display in the British Museum. Chess probably

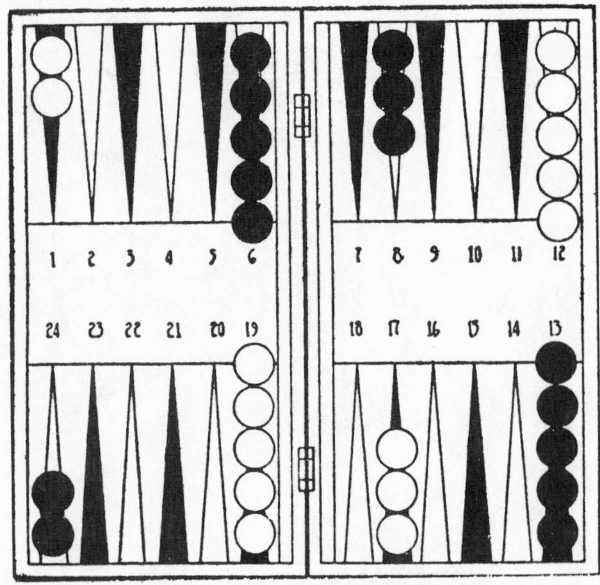

A Backgammon Board

stemmed from a game known as shah-mat that was popular in Persia around 500 B.C. Scholars have gambled on both games from their inception, the appeal being that the games are contests of wits. It was King Henry III who ordered his clergy to abstain from "diceing and chesseing under pain of durance vile."

"Heads or tails" type gambling was done before coins existed, with flat stones or pieces of wood marked to distinguish one side from the other. Australia today has a slightly more complicated version of coin-tossing in which two coins are flipped into the air from a stick. The gambler wagers on whether the two coins will light heads up or tails up. If they light without matching sides up, the toss is a "no-throw," and is done over. The game—illegal, of course—is called "Two-Up," and is too popular to be successfully policed.

Matching coins has always been one of the most prevalent forms of gambling in the United States. "I'll match you for it" may well be one of the most frequently used sentences in the English language. Even in football, the team that first goes on the offensive is determined by the toss of a coin.

Serious students of gambling have matched or flipped coins for hours, days and weeks at a stretch, trying to determine some law of probability hitherto undiscovered. Invariably, they have reached the conclusion that, if heads comes up six or seven times in a row, the chance of "tails" being thrown on the next flip remains 1 to 1, no better and no worse than the "norm."

Many parlor games which involve both luck and skill, such as Mah-Jongg, are played for money. Considered strictly a recreational game, Monopoly has been played and is still being played by some of its devotees for substantial sums. Even Dominoes is played for money, particularly in Ireland and China where the game draws large wagers. The public was surprised to learn, a few years ago, that respectable sums of money change hands in, of all things, Tiddly Winks tournaments.

Word games have won and lost considerable sums in the intellectual set, and the "Match Game" is often played by those with a mathematical bent, often for high stakes. "Yotsey," "Chice" or "Yahtze," a game with five dice and a score pad, has developed quite a following in recent years.

Guessing games have always been popular. Oddly, Oriental Fan-Tan, which falls into this category and is one of the most popular gambling games in the East, is seldom played in the United States except by Orientals. Four players participate, drawing beans or other markers from a pile containing an unknown number. Each withdrawal consists of four markers, and the players bet on whether there will be none, one, two or three markers left at the conclusion of the game. Even Charades is a betting game, a popular one in some sets on the West and East coasts.

Cheating has always been a potential factor in "friendly games." Wherever a large amount of money is at stake, temptation rears its ugly head, and weak gamblers sometimes succumb to it. Cheating in a "friendly game" is much easier to get away with than in a professional game, not only because of the friendly, trustful atmosphere but because most of the participants lack any knowledge of what to look for.

Casino games are run by experts and are well policed. Illegal "house" games are usually run by rough, tough professional gamblers who may not be above doing some cheating, themselves, but who know what to look for whenever they suspect a player's luck is too good to be true. An amateur who tries to cheat one of these hardened professionals is almost literally taking his life in his hands.

"Oops, Sorry" Technique

Cheating at Gin requires sure knowledge of two important points: which cards are near the top of the pack, and which cards have already been played. No guesswork is permitted, it must be a dead certainty. Al Zilch really perfected this gambit, partly because Al has always been known as old "fumble fingers," and also because he doesn't like to lose at gin.

When drawing from the pack, Al picks up *three* cards "by accident." He promptly expresses horror and shame at his clumsiness and replaces the cards in the middle of the stack, but not before he has had a good look at them. Figure this out mathematically: Suppose ten cards have been dealt each player, plus one turned up. That's 21 cards. Suppose further that 5 cards are already discarded. Half the pack is now gone, so that when Al gets a look at 3 cards (and then puts them back) he knows the position of roughly 12 per cent of the remaining cards. You think that's not a helping hand?

While on the subject, we are often asked what to do to PREVENT being cheated. Usually, cheating calls for stacking the deck, dealing off the bottom, dealing "second cards," etc. The cheat always KNOWS FOR SURE the position of the cards, otherwise he's as much in the dark as his victim. To that end we have designed the CLEMFELDT CUT (also known in some areas as the "Chuck Shuffle"), and it is illustrated on this page. Note that we use 6 different stacks. Any amount can be used, from at least 6 through 17. Make sure the cuts are put back in mishmash order. If a character can stack the deck (without reshuffling, of course) after the Clemfeldt Cut, he deserves whatever he can get. Genius should not be interfered with.

HOLDING HANDS—CHEATER'S STYLE

"If you're in a poker game with strangers, perish the thought," the old gambler said, "watch how every player holds the deck when he deals the cards.

"When a dealer holds the cards with a wide space between his first and second fingers, he may not be cheating, but he's holding the deck in such a way that he can, whenever he has a mind to. He always holds the deck that way, so that nobody will notice anything different about his deal if he decides to cheat.

"It's known as a 'Mechanic's Grip,' and a good card mechanic can deal cards off the bottom of the deck without anybody in the game knowin' what's happening. He can't do it if he's holding that left-hand first and second finger close together.

"Whenever I spot a mechanic's grip in a card game, I get out. The guy may not be cheating me, but I know he can do it and get away with it if he wants to. Somehow, I can't play my usual game under such conditions."

Aside from moral scruples, few "friendly game" participants are willing to risk getting caught. Not many social stigmas equal that faced by the known gambling cheat, and the ostracism carries over into other parts of his life.

A player who "welches" on his gambling losses faces social ostracism, too. Gambling debts are uncollectable in a court of law, and so a strict Code of Honor has been built up to assure payment of them. A man may be excused for non-payment of his grocery bill or the interest on his mortgage, but let him ignore a gambling loss and he is in deep trouble with his area of society.

For the most part, the player has a right to assume that most friendly games are honest and that those involved will pay their losses. He knows there is no built-in house "edge." He is matching his luck and ability against those of other players and if he is properly informed has an "even money" chance of winning.

Let's consider some of the more popular "friendly games." Let's say you're invited to sit in on a game of Poker.

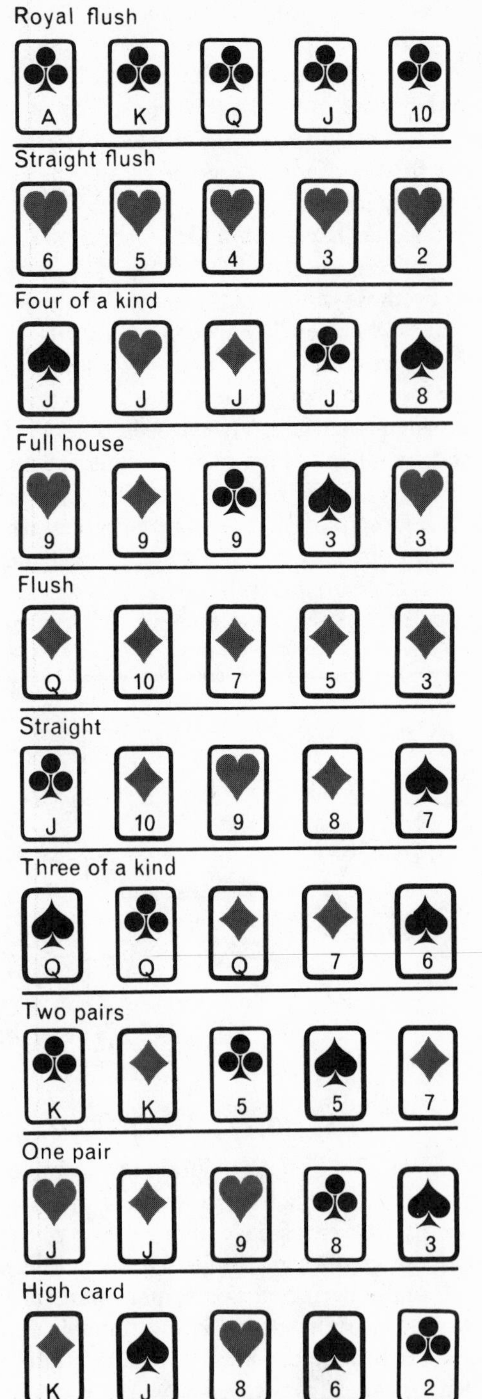

From "The Complete Illustrated Guide To Gambling" by Alan Wykes, copyright ©1964 by Aldus Books Limited, London. Reprinted by permission of Aldus Books Ltd. and Doubleday & Company, Inc.

POKER

Poker is, in the final analysis, a kind of rummy game, a game in which you try to acquire certain combinations of cards. The two main types of poker are Draw and Stud, but there are as many variations as there are cards in a deck. Even a long-experienced poker player in a "Dealer's Choice" game occasionally comes up against a variation he's never seen before.

A Bold Bluff

The variations are usually a combination of wild cards and wild rule changes. The expert player may not like some of these off-beat games, but he isn't bothered by them because he knows that the most skillful player has the advantage in "wild" games.

The object of all poker games except "Low" games is to wind up with the best hand in the game. The chart of Hand Values on this page comes from Alan Wykes' excellent and beautifully-printed book, *The Complete Illustrated Guide to Gambling,* published by Doubleday and Company. The hands are shown in order of their value, from top to bottom.

Draw Poker

In draw poker, each player is dealt five face-down cards. The players are, in turn starting at the dealer's left, given an opportunity to "open," or make a bet. A common variation is the requirement of a pair of Jacks or better to open.

Those who want to "stay" in the game either match the opener's bet or raise it, in accordance with rules for betting which have been established before the cards are dealt. The three general classifications of betting start with table stakes, and any player may bet all his chips at any time. The second is pot-limit table stakes, in which a raise may be made up to the current amount of the pot until the table stake is reached, and

HAND	NUMBER OF WAYS	ODDS
Royal Flush	4	1 in 649,740
Straight Flush	36	1 in 72,193
Four of a kind	624	1 in 4,165
Full house	3,744	1 in 694
Flush	5,108	1 in 509
Straight	10,200	1 in 255
Three of a kind	54,912	1 in 47
Two pairs	123,552	1 in 21
One pair	1,098,240	1 in 2

the third and commonest is the fixed limit game. This is often linked with a fixed number of raises.

Each player who "stays" has the privilege of discarding part of his hand and drawing new cards, with the dealer dealing around the table, starting at his left. A player may discard up to three cards, and in some rule variations may discard four cards or draw an entire new hand. With the hands completed, betting resumes.

The original opener either bets or "checks." Each player in rotation has the opportunity to "stay" by meeting whatever bet has been made or "raise" by meeting the previous bet and betting an additional amount. If he elects not to meet the bet or raise, he drops out. When all players meet a bet without raising, a bettor is said to be "called," and exposes his hand, along with the hands of the "callers." The best hand wins the pot.

From a deck of 52 cards, it is possible to deal 2,598,960 different five-card hands—poker hands. Of those hands, 1,098,240 will contain a pair. Other possibilities out of 2,598,960 possible hands will result in:

4 Royal Flushes
36 Straight Flushes
624 Four-of-a-Kind Hands
3,744 Full Houses
5,108 Flushes
10,200 Straights
54,912 Three-of-a-Kind Hands
123,552 Two Pair Hands

This means you have one chance out of 21 of being dealt two pairs, 1 chance in 47 of getting three of a kind, 1 in 255 of getting a straight, 1 in 509 of getting a flush, 1 in 694 of a full house, and 1 in 4,165 of getting four of a kind in a pat hand.

From the multi-million possibilities, any player quickly realizes that the odds in draw poker are fairly complex. In drawing three cards to a pair, the odds against making any improvement are roughly 2½ to 1. Other percentages are:

Arriving at:	*Odds Against:*
Two Pairs	5.25 to 1
Three of a Kind	7.74 to 1
Full House	97.3 to 1
Four of a Kind	359 to 1

Knowing the rules of the game is elementary in poker. Knowing the mathematical possibilities of filling out a hand is tremendously important. There's much more to the game, however, than knowing the data. You can get the necessary information from books, but it won't make you a superior poker player.

For one thing, you have to know the Poker Attitude of the other players in the game. Knowing them away from the poker table isn't enough; you must know how they bet and how they play. You need to be a good psychologist.

While poker is one of the greatest of all gambling games, never forget that it is also a game of skill. In his book, *Oswald Jacoby on Gambling,* published by Hart Publishing Company, Inc., the card expert says, "If you play poker and lose more often than you win, don't place the blame upon your luck—you are being outplayed."

Remember that the best hand doesn't always win in poker; the best hand still in at the finish of the game is the winner, and many winning hands are frozen out or bluffed out before the showdown.

A good poker player needs something you can't buy —daring. Call it "guts," courage or what you will, every superior poker player has it. When he thinks he holds the winning hand, he backs his judgment to the limit.

Shaggy Dog Poker

Jay Marshall, the magician-comedian, tells the story about the circus performer who trained one of his dogs to play poker.

Envisioning a fortune, he took the dog to a booking agent, who was dubious. "Let's see him do it," the agent demanded.

The circus performer dealt three hands of draw poker, The dog picked his hand up in his teeth turned his back on the other two players, and then turned around, putting the cards face down on the table. With his nose, he shoved aside two of the cards and made two sharp barks. The circus performer dealt him two cards.

After five hands, the booking agent made his decision. "You got nothin' there, mister, he said. "Sure, the dog can play poker—but he wags his tail every time he gets a good hand."

People who make money at poker are generally agreed that the best hand going *into* a draw poker game is usually the best hand at the finish. In a six or seven-handed game, a pair of Kings will stand up more often than it will lose.

Tom James says, "I've spent a lifetime learning to play winning poker, and the big thing I've learned is how to figure what the other players have in their hands. I don't often miss, but when I do, I get hurt bad, because I back my judgment to the limit. Teaching anybody else how to read draw poker hands is out of the question. It's something you've gotta learn for yourself.

"One important thing I've learned is to run for the

woods when I think I'm beat. There's players who think it's a sign of weakness to drop out of a round. They're real proud of saying that they can't be bluffed. Man, I'd like to play against those dudes seven days a week.

"A poor player sticks in the game because he's already got a big investment in the pot. That's absolutely crazy. The minute you think you're gonna lose a hand, toss in your cards. What you already have in the pot has nothin' to do with it. Throwin' good money after bad is no way to get ahead.

"Bluffing's an important part of the game, but you gotta know when to bluff. One thing I can tell you, don't try to bluff a big winner or a big loser and get away with it.

"Like in any gambling game, try to lose small and win big. If you think you've got the winning tickets, bet 'em for all they're worth. Don't lose the old moxie. If you're afraid with what you think is the best hand in the game, you shouldn't be playing poker.

"Another thing, gamble when the odds are right. Let's say you're holding a medium high pair and you think the guy who just raised has a pair of Aces. If the pot's small, toss in your hand. But count the pot. Let's say there's fifteen bucks in it and the guy with the Aces has just raised a buck. Call.

"The chances against improving your hand to two pair are five to one against you, and the chances against winding up with three of a kind are eight to one against you. But the payoff is 15 to 1. Don't pass up good odds in your favor."

MR. ODDS-MAKER'S BEST BET

Mr. Odds-Maker says, "The game doesn't call for as much skill as Stud. Mix up your play; don't set a pattern. If you stay with a weak hand that doesn't get better with the draw, toss it in. There's no point in throwing good money after bad. One of the great old-time poker players once told me, 'The hardest poker player in the world to bluff is a lousey player.' He also said, 'Know what's saved me more money than anything else in poker? Knowing when I'm over-matched and having the sense to get out of the game.' Of course, he was seldom over-matched."

"RUNNING UP" POKER HANDS

When the dealer in a "friendly" game of poker overhand shuffles, he's either incompetent or a card mechanic getting ready to take someone to the cleaners. The overhand or "slop" shuffle in which the deck is held in the right hand and cards are pulled into the left hand singly or in groups by the left thumb and fingers is an easy way to run up a good hand for a victim and a better hand for the dealer.

To do it, he must get the two hands together, face up, in the process of assembling the cards for shuffling, with the cards for the two hands alternating, one of the victim's cards face up, a dealer's card on top of it, victim's card, dealer's card, etc., ten cards in all, with a card for the dealer on top. These cards are assembled at the bottom of the deck, face down. The deck may be riffle-shuffled a few times, not disturbing the bottom stock of ten cards, if the dealer so desires.

Then he goes to an overhand shuffle. Let's say it's a five-handed game and the victim is third player to the left of the dealer. The dealer pulls the top card from the deck with his left thumb and the bottom card with his left fingers, simultaneously, letting them drop into his left palm perfectly aligned. He repeats the process, and then runs a single card from the top. He does this routine rapidly, five times. Then he pulls the next top card off sloppily so that it extends inward about half an inch toward his body, and runs off the balance of the deck in equally sloppy fashion. He then picks up the deck with his right hand, and his right thumb holds the break below the in-jogged card. It and the cards above it are shuffled off sloppily and the balance of the deck, 25 cards which form the setup, are dropped on top. The bottom card is crimped and cut to roughly the middle. The dealer offers the deck for a cut. If the cutter doesn't cut to the crimp, the card mechanic makes "the pass," one of the commonest sleights in card manipulation, a move which invisibly cuts the deck again as he draws his hands back in front of himself to deal. Every third card he deals off is one of the five pre-arranged for the victim and every fifth card is part of his own pre-set hand.

Five-Card Stud Poker

In five-card Stud Poker, a first card is dealt face down to each player in rotation, and a second card face up. High card showing opens the betting. Three more cards are dealt face up, with betting after each round.

A rule of thumb in a conservative game is not to stay unless you can beat what's showing. If one player has an Ace up and you have nothing as good, get out. Only if you have another Ace up or a pair do you stay. A pair of deuces on the first two cards, incidentally, will win more pots than it will lose, depending in some measure, of course, on how many people are in the game. On the first two cards, however, any pair is considered worth staying on. A high pair is always a betting hand.

As the hands progress, you must observe all the up-cards. If one player has an Ace up, and so do two others, the chance of any one of them having an Ace in the hole is lessened.

When an up-pair shows in an opponent's hand and has you beaten, you are playing a losing game to stay for another card or cards in the hope of beating his hand.

How to bet your hands in five-card Stud depends in large part on the characteristics of the game. If all the players are playing cautiously, it behooves you to play the same way. If everybody is staying, let 'em, but you get out if you don't have the cards.

Tom James says, "There's times in Stud when you know for sure that you've got the best hand. There's no guesswork. You've got a high pair, with one of 'em face down—let's say, a pair of Aces. Nobody else has anything higher than a King up, and there's no possible flushes or straights.

"You've got a sure winner, but your object oughta be to win as much as you can. If you start bettin' big, you'll scare everybody out. Wait 'til the last round to raise, and then kick the pot as high as it'll go.

"Here's another tip that's made me a bundle over the years. Once in a blue moon, you'll find a really smart poker player who'll fool you on this, but not often. When a player keeps lookin' at his hole card, the chances are 99 to 1 that it's a big, fat nothing. If it's any good, he'll remember it after one glance.

"Another thing, you gotta bet a face-up pair to the limit. If the other players know what they're doin', they'll drop out unless they got you beaten, but you gotta do it to win the maximum when your hole card makes what's showin' three of a kind.

"Only a lame-brain draws to two or three-card flushes or straights in five-card stud. Another thing, don't bet into a hand that must either raise or drop, like a possible flush or straight. If he has it, he'll raise you right back, and if he doesn't, he won't even call."

MR. ODDS-MAKER'S BEST BET

Mr. Odds-Maker says, "Stud Poker (Table Stakes) requires great perception and heart. It's a game where you must feel the pulse of your opponent, where one deuce can beat three Aces. About eight years ago, I witnessed a no-limit game at the Dunes Hotel. Seated around the table were seven or eight of the best players in the world and at no time was there less than half a million dollars on the table. Sid Wyman, owner of the Dunes and one of the three top players in the world had just bet $6,500 and was caught bluffing. A few minutes later, he was nailed bluffing again, this time for $8,000.

"During the course of the game, he was later involved in a big pot with two other players, one a famous oil man and the other an old-time gambler, now deceased. On the last card, he bet $51,000. After studying the situation for more than ten minutes, both called. Wyman turned over the best hand and raked in the pot. I learned two things—1. It sometimes pays to get caught bluffing. 2. When you move in for the big bet, be there."

Five Aces

The stranger bought into the bar-room poker game in the little Western town, and the dealer smiled at him.

"It's draw poker, deuces wild, jacks or better to open, mister," he said. "The rules are the same as anywhere else, I guess, except in this game there ain't no such thing as five of a kind."

"Why is that?" the stranger asked.

"Mostly, a matter of keepin' the peace," the dealer answered. "Of course, if the Good Lord had intended for there to be five of a kind in poker, there'd be five suits, but that ain't the reason for the house rule. Over the years, there's been more arguments and disputes and accusations of cheatin' over a hand that was five of a kind than any other reason.

"We got a little cemetery up on the mesa with a lot of deceased gamblers in it. And the commonest cause of death to be found in that final restin' place is five Aces."

Seven-Card Stud

While the object of the game is the same, seven-card Stud is as different from the five-card variety as day is from night. The big difference is that each player makes a five-card hand from seven cards. Given this extra choice, the hands are invariably better than in draw or five-card stud.

The game is much more deceptive than five-card stud in another respect. With three cards face down and four face-up, a powerful winning hand can be well concealed.

Many good players won't stay in a seven-card stud game unless they get a concealed pair, a 7-spot or better split pair (one up and one in the hole) or three cards of the same suit on the first three cards.

Other good players contend that it takes a second up-card to let you know whether your hand is going anywhere or not. They stay for a second up-card, but drop fast if it doesn't improve the original holding.

Betting is much the same in seven-card as in five-card, but the player must bear in mind that the winning hand will almost invariably be better.

There is usually more money in the pot than in the five-card game, not only because there's an extra round of betting, but because the potentialities for good betting hands are better.

Tom James says, "I love the game. To me, it combines the best features of both Stud and Draw. And it's the game where the experts come off best.

"There's a tendency in seven-card to stick around, even when you have a rotten hand. Most players do it. Actually, you don't have to stay as often to make a lot of money as you do in five-card, because the pots are bigger. It costs money to stay, and there's no point unless you think you're gonna win.

"Whenever anybody in the game has two cards face up that have me beaten, I get out. I'll take the second face-up card to see what happens, but when it's on the table and I'm beaten, I won't stick around to make anybody prove it to me.

'Studying the face-up cards is even more important in Seven-Card than in Five-Card. Like in Draw, you gotta try to figure what everybody has, and the face-up cards can tell you a lot."

Lowball

This is a weird variation of draw poker in which the low hand wins. The official rules say that straights and flushes don't count and Ace is low, so the perfect hand is Ace,2,3,4 and 5. A pair of Aces, incidently, is considered lower than a pair of deuces. In some variations, straights count, in which case Ace,2,3,4 and 6 is a perfect hand.

Most hands that stay draw one card or are pat. The lowest hand after the draw is usually an eight-high bust.

CONTACT!

The marked deck of cards whose markings could be read only when the card-sharp was wearing tinted glasses was the easiest marked deck to read that was ever put into play. Unfortunately for the card mechanic, so many people read about the ruse or heard about it that a pair of tinted glasses on a player almost branded him as a cheat. No card hustler dared to use it, and it became extinct.

The tint-marked deck is back again, alive and well and flourishing in crooked card games throughout the country, with victims blissfully unaware of what is happening to them.

The cheater no longer wears tinted glasses. He wears contact lenses! The sharper's eyes may have a slight pink cast, but nobody thinks anything about it. The other players have all had red eyes, themselves, at times.

High-Low Draw

This is draw poker in which high hand and low hand split the pot. The Ace is not customarily ranked as low card, and straights and flushes count as in regular draw poker.

For some reason, more players go for "low" in this game than for "high," although it is usually sounder to draw to a good high hand than to a good low one, because a low hand may be "improved" right out of contention.

Political Poker

The late Ed Wynn insisted that Congress is like a poker game. "It takes more than a pair of Jacks to open a congressional session; it takes a lot of Jack," he explained. "When it looks like there's money in the pot, a Congressional session opens with a Full House. Half are in favor of a new deal, and half want to cut. Sometimes, everything's wild. Some of the Congressmen don't want to show their hands when a vote is called for. Regardless of what the opposition proves, some of 'em will always stand pat. A few trouble-makers are always ready to raise the deuce and a few have a Queen or two hidden. No matter how good a thing they have going, they want your Jack, and there's nearly always a Joker in the deck.

Holding Hands

Mr. Milquetoast dragged in at four o'clock in the morning, despondent and much the worse for wear. His wife was waiting for him.

"All right," she said, "let's hear your excuse. I suppose you were sitting up with a sick friend, holding his hand."

"If I'd been holding his hands," Mr. Milquetoast replied sadly, "you could buy yourself a mink coat."

High-Low Seven-Card Stud

This variation is popular because it is often possible for one hand to win both "high" and "low." The player is entitled to use his seven cards in any way he likes to put together both a high and low hand.

Tom James advises the player to try for low. Sometimes, he points out, low cards can be put together so that they will not only win "low" but will make a flush or straight that will win "high."

One variation of this game stipulates that you must win both high and low or you lose, if you try for both high and low.

Wild Card Poker

All forms of poker are sometimes played with "wild" cards, the commonest being deuces, one-eyed Jacks and Joker. With any wild cards, the hands are naturally better. Two pairs will often induce an optimistic player to bet, although anything less than three Aces seldom wins. Since the wild cards increase every player's chance for a good hand, heavier betting results.

Wild-card varieties of poker such as Baseball, Spit in the Ocean, Whiskey Poker, Wild Widow and others enjoy regional popularity. In most wild-card games, five-of-a-kind beats a straight flush. Any player in a wild-card game should get comparative values of various holdings stipulated before play starts.

MR. ODDS-MAKER'S BEST BET

Mr. Odds-Maker says, "Poker experts don't like Wild Card games, but they win at them. The wilder the game is, the better the expert does. You see, he's trained to figure odds quickly, and he knows instantly whether they're in his favor or not. The average player is impressed by the holding the wild cards give him and doesn't figure that everyone else in the game is faring proportionately better."

WINNING HANDS

The best hand still in the game at the show-down is the winner, and it may vary from a Royal Flush to a face-card high "bust."

To say that any hand other than a Royal Flush or four-of-a-kind is a "sure-winner" has to be imprecise—and in the case of four-of-a-kind, four Aces beat four Kings.

Any flat statement as to what hand will win an "average" game is open to argument. What constitutes an "average" game? How many hands contain an "average" run of cards?

Tom James approaches the problem from a slightly different angle. He says, "You've gotta have certain minimums to stand any *chance* of winning in an average game. For example, any player who expects to win a hand of draw poker with less than Jacks Up is too optimistic for me. I've lost more three-of-a-kind hands to Full Houses than I like to remember, but I'd bet 'em again.

"I'd say you've got a fair chance of winning a hand of Draw with Queens Up. In five-card stud, I'd be happy with Aces or Kings. In seven-card stud, I'd want three-of-a-kind, preferably tens or face cards. In Deuces Wild Draw, it takes three Aces to make me feel I've got a chance.

"Even though these hands will win an 'average' round, I wouldn't bet a dime on 'em without knowing the circumstances. How many cards the other players draw and how they bet may make me think I've got a lead-pipe cinch or may convince me that my hand is borderline, a 'maybe' winner.

"Don't ever forget that your chances of winning depend on who you're playing with, almost as much as on the cards you draw. A Big-League poker player wins more often than he loses, but he doesn't always win on the best hand in the game. He may win with a 'bust,' and he may win with what's really the second or third-high hand. But one thing for sure, he *never, never* loses on the best hand in the game. He plays it right down to his bottom dollar."

Left At The Switch

Pat Buttram remembers Zeb Fink as the best poker player who ever hit Winston County, Alabama. Zeb got rich playing poker, but finally had to retire.

According to Pat, it happened like this. A traveling buggy whip salesman got into the game and did well—too well to suit Zeb, who finally accused him of cheating.

"That's crazy talk," the buggy whip salesman argued. "What in the world ever gave you the idea?"

"I know danged well you're cheatin', "Zeb declared. "You ain't playin' the hand I dealt you."

THE "SHINER" OR "READER"

A Denver card mechanic has done well for years with a broad-band ring he wears on the third finger of his right hand. The side of the band opposite the star saphire setting is polished to a mirror surface. When he deals, taking off each card between his right thumb and forefinger, he reads the value of every card in the ring's mirror-like surface.

A chrome-plated cigaret lighter serves as a "reader" for a card cheat in Toledo. Tossed carelessly (?) on the table with a pack of cigarettes, it never seems to arouse suspicion.

It is harder to use a "shiner" or "reader" well than one would guess. The average novice, trying to use one, would make it painfully obvious what he was doing as he stared intently at the shiner. The expert never seems to be looking at the device, and his movement and conversation as he deals are natural and normal — which is quite a trick.

GIN RUMMY

Gin Rummy probably accounts for the exchange of as much money as poker or Bridge, largely because it has achieved such popularity as a two-handed gambling game. Whenever two people who want "a friendly game" get together, they can play Gin, which isn't true of Poker or Bridge.

The "Oklahoma" and "Hollywood" variations of Gin, aimed at making it a better gambling game, have been highly successful.

The "Hollywood" feature of playing three games simultaneously has unquestionably added interest and action. The score of the first hand a player wins is entered only in the first of three columns. His second winning hand is entered in both the first and second columns, and with the winning of a third hand, he is scoring on all three games. It frequently happens that a player who gets off to a bad start will lose two of the games but salvage the third.

One Gin devotee who is highly enthusiastic about the Hollywood feature of playing three games at once explains his liking by explaining, "You can win three times as much money in the same length of time that one game used to take."

Learning the rudiments of Gin is simple, and luck involved in the game convinces every new player that he's good at it. Actually, considerable skill is involved, and the pat hands, called "No Brainers" by Gin experts, don't occur with any great frequency. Much less complicated than Bridge, it still demands know-how. The good player is a psychologist, knows the mathematical percentages, has a good memory for cards, and has the knack of adapting his style of play to different types of opponents.

A business man who makes about $100 a week playing Gin at lunch says, "It's a game of small edges. Give me one little edge over my competition and I'll clobber him. For example, I play against one fellow who always makes a break in his hand between his melds and miscellaneous cards. Another player usually exposes the new bottom card when he cuts the deck for me to deal, and he holds the deck so carelessly on his deal that I can't help but see the bottom card. I never cheat, but I'd have to close my eyes not to see those things."

As in all rummy games, the object is to draw cards which will form or add to sequences and three or four of a kind holdings. When a hand is matched so that the remaining cards count less than ten, the player may "call," "knock," or "go down." The dealer deals ten cards to his opponent and to himself, one at a time and alternately. The twenty-first card is placed face-up beside the remainder of the deck, which is face down on the table between the two players. After the first hand each succeeding one is dealt by the winner of the previous one.

The dealer's opponent has the option of taking the exposed card. If he does not want it, the dealer may take it. If the dealer doesn't want it, either, the opponent takes a card from the stock (top of deck) and discards a card upon the exposed one. Play continues with the players alternately taking either the exposed card in the discard pile or the top card from the unexposed stock, until either the dealer or opponent elects to "knock" or Gin, which he may do when all ten of his cards are in melds or runs of at least three.

All face cards count ten and all others count their pip value. When a player with a count of less than ten calls, he discards and then exposes his hand on the table. The opponent lays his hand down face up, too, and plays any of his unmatched cards upon sequences or three-of-a-kind melds wherever they fit into the other hand. If the caller's unmatched card count is still less than his opponent's, he scores the difference and gets credit for a "box." If, on the other hand, the player who did not call has an equal or lower count of unmatched cards after playing on his opponent's hand, he scores the difference in count plus an overcall penalty of either ten or 25, whichever has been agreed upon.

A bonus, usually 25 points, is given to a player who melds all ten of his cards before calling. This is a "Gin," and his opponent may not play off on it.

Game is usually 100 points, except in the "Oklahoma" version where a call card in Spades doubles all scoring. Scoring varies. Some players add a game bonus. Most players add points for each call or box. If one side fails to score during a game, it is called a "Blitz" or "Schneider," and calls for a heavy penalty, either 100 points added to the winner's score or doubling it. The latter is more popular.

Hollywood

This, as mentioned previously, is scoring three games simultaneously. The first hand won by either player is scored on the first game. The second hand won by a player who is already on Game One is scored twice, as the second score on Game One and the first score on Game Two. A third win by the same player is scored three times—on the first, second and third games. After a player is "on" all three games, all subsequent scores are scored on all games.

Oklahoma

This is an exciting variation for gambling in which the twenty-first card, dealt face up beside the stock, determines the amount of the call. A face-card or ten-spot retains the normal call of ten, but all other cards establish the call for the round at their pip value. If the card happens to be a spade, the score for that hand is doubled, including any bonuses. Because the spade doubling causes some large scores, Game in the Oklahoma version is usually 150 or 200, rather than 100.

Partnership Gin

In partnership Gin, two players against two, two games are going simultaneously, with partners alternating opponents. Each of the two games is played as two-handed Gin, which it is, in fact. There is a glaring difference, however. The two partners' scores are added together for each hand and scored as one hand. This means that if one partner wins and the other loses, as often happens, the difference between the two winning scores determines the winner of the round. Consequently, it behooves partners to watch each other's scores and govern themselves accordingly. For example, if one player suffers a substantial loss, it usually behooves his partner to go for "Gin" to try to offset the loss. If a partner "knocks" quickly and makes a few points, his partner should usually try to "knock" as quickly as possible. The object of each hand, from a partnership standpoint, is to wind up with a plus rather than a minus for the two hands.

One of the interesting things about Partnership Gin

A Typical Hollywood Score Pad

USE INNER BOXES TO RECORD PARTNER'S HALF OF SCORE

PLAYER	PLAYER	PLAYER	PLAYER	PLAYER	PLAYER	PLAYER	PLAYER	PLAYER	PLAYER	PLAYER	PLAYER

PLAYERS NET SCORES

is the variation that will show in a good player's technique from hand to hand, depending on what his partner is doing.

Scoring is identical with that of other Gin games, except that "Game" is usually slightly higher. With each round's score a composite of the scores made by two partners. "Game" might otherwise be made too quickly.

PLAYING GIN TO WIN

Whether your hand is good, bad or indifferent, you play to better it for the first few rounds, holding combinations and discarding useless cards. Until your opponent has made a few discards, you have no way of knowing what he can use, so you get rid of what you can't use.

As play continues, you may have to go from offense to defense. Your continuing strategy is determined by your opponent's discards and pickups, but even with a bad hand, you play the first few rounds to improve it. With a poor hand, if the up-card on first draw is an Ace, most experts agree that you should take it, if only to get rid of a useless high card. Even with a good hand, it is often advisable to take the Ace, unless you have all the low cards you want.

Normally, you take the up-card only when it will complete a meld. Proper discarding is probably the most important part of the game. "Advertising," or discarding a card to lure your opponent into discarding another card of the same rank which you want, is normally done only in the early rounds. After that, throw another "safe" card in preference to an "advertiser." Your opponent will advertise, too, in the early rounds. With another safe discard, don't answer his "bait" discard.

A major problem for most Gin players is whether to knock or play for Gin. If there's any question about it, you have your answer—knock. A good player usually plays for Gin only when he feels reasonably sure of making it, when he feels he'll be undercut if he knocks, or when he has a sure play into an opponent's hand if the opponent calls.

And when does a good Gin player feel reasonably sure of making Gin? The first requirement is nine cards melded. Once he has that, he asks, how many different cards will give me Gin? If he has four chances of going Gin, he regards it as a good bet. With three chances, he asks himself how much his opponent knows about his hand. To that information, he adds what he knows about his opponent's hand and makes his decision. More often than not, in the three-chance situation, he elects to knock. When

Reproduced from "Bridge and Gin Gambitry" by Clem Stein, Jr. © 1963 Home Library Press.

Fast-Draw Partner Tactic

The CCC Club, a commuting gang of gin Gambiteers, has developed dozens of effective ploys, and the authors have left their names on some chosen victims too. For example, double gin can be fun, but it's more fun when we win. To that end one of our favorites is picking the right partner, the one we know to be the best of the available three. To be effective this gambit must be worked fast and loudly. Charlie, a life master of this ploy, says for all to hear, "Cut the cards, let's go!" And, no matter how they turn out, Charlie quickly tosses his pick back into the pack and announces, "Clem and I against you two." He's never questioned, either!

READING THE BOTTOM CARD OF A DECK

It's the card mechanic's deal. The cards are cut, and he'd like to know what the bottom card is.

He holds the deck on his left hand, face down, getting ready to deal. He squares up the cards. In doing it, his right hand moves the deck slightly forward, the fingers covering the front end of the deck, the thumb holding the back end and pushing forward. The deck slides forward over the left forefinger — all except the bottom card, which arcs downward between the left forefinger and right thumb. The face of the card is bowed sufficiently so that it is readable to the dealer — and visible to nobody else. The deck is now moved backward again, in a squaring motion, releasing the pressure on the bottom card. The cards are dealt.

A New York gin rummy player declares that knowing the bottom card on his deal is enough of an advantage to make him a consistent winner.

CUTTING HIGH CARD

An Omaha gin rummy player uses a cheat that professional card sharps have used for years. Win or lose, he suggests cutting high card, double or nothing. If his suggestion is accepted and he was a loser, he winds up even. If he was a winner, he doubles his winnings.

Whenever he buys a deck of cards, he removes the Ace of Spades and coats the face of it lightly with carnauba wax, letting it dry and then polishing it with a flannel cloth. Lacking carnauba wax, he has found that any good commercial floor wax will work almost as well. Once polished on its face, the Ace is put back into the deck and the deck carefully resealed in its pack.

When he cuts high card, he holds the deck in his left hand and quickly pushes a block of cards to the right. He picks these up in his right hand as his cut. As he pushed cards to the right with his left thumb, he applies a little pressure — and the deck invariably breaks at the Ace of Spades.

Throughout the gin game, when he's asked to cut the cards for the other fellow's deal, he cuts in the same way — and knows that the bottom card is the Ace of Spades.

---

you're playing for Gin, it is usually unwise to hold a five-card run, and runs are preferable to matching cards. You normally have two chances of adding a fourth card to a sequence, where you never have more than one chance to get a fourth matching card.

Clement McQuaid says, "Those Blitzes kill you when you're playing for money. Get on all three games before you go for any big scores. And just like in Poker and Blackjack, make the move that gives you the odds. Play the percentages. Another thing, late in the game you've got two possible discards. One is a card you're sure is 'live.' It'll give the other guy either an extra card in a sequence or will give him four of a kind. Your other possible discard is 'fresh,' a new face. Give him the card you know will add to a sequence or group, always. The 'fresh' card may complete a meld to give him Gin.

"Analyze the other guy's Gin habits. If he likes to go for Gin, don't be too quick to knock, late in the game. He may be laying for you, with a possible Gin and a low count. If he's a quick knocker and you've got a lousy hand, get rid of high cards fast, even if they're 'blind.' On the other hand, if he's a quick knocker and doesn't knock, call as fast as you can.

"And here's a rule of thumb that's money in the bank. Most of the time, your safest early discard is a card next in sequence above or below a card your opponent throws, but in another suit. Your safest 'blind' discard is a King and the next safest is a Queen.

"There's a couple of players who've taken me at Gin that I wouldn't play against again if my life depended on it. Their card memory is better than mine. At the end of a long Gin hand, they can tell you every card in the discard pile, in order. I could play them from now 'til Doomsday and the only way I'd ever beat 'em is with No-Brainers. When you find a player who beats you consistently, over a number of games, don't let your competitive spirit overcome your judgement. Quit trying to beat that player. You're not gonna do it, and trying is gonna cost you money. If you think you're gonna get good enough to beat him, get your practice against other players.

"Whatever you do, don't be a card sorter. I've played against pretty fair Gin players who kept rearranging their cards every time they drew, *if* the draw did 'em any good. I play against one fellow who always keeps his high cards on the right-hand side and his low cards on the left. Don't be that kind of a pigeon. And don't be sloppy with the cards. Every time you expose a card, you give your opponent a big advantage. I don't feel a bit guilty about taking advantage of sloppy card handling. If you're gonna play cards for money, the first thing you should learn is how to shuffle, cut and deal professionally. Use two decks, and shuffle at least four times while your opponent is dealing a new hand.

"Some people never disturb the order of the bottom few cards when they shuffle. In Gin, those bottom cards are often one of the laydowns from the previous hand. Against a player like that, I cut the deck as close to the middle as I can. He deals off 21 cards,

---

Divorce—Gambler's Style

Jack E. Leonard tells the story about a fellow who caught another man with his wife. "I admit everything," the offender said. "I'm in love with your wife, madly in love with her, and she's in love with me. I'll make you a sporting proposition. I'll play you a game of Gin for her. If I win, you divorce her. If you beat me, I walk out of here and promise never to see her again."

The husband thought about it. "Okay," he finally said, "but how about a penny a point on the side to make it interesting?"

right? And when the first of those bottom laydown cards appears, I know what the next cards are gonna be! Some dealers toss out cards so carelessly that they give you a flash of some of the cards in their own hand. I remember 'em, with no apologies. It's a part of Gin to figure out what the opposition is holding. If he lets me see any part of his hand, he deserves to lose."

Stephen Potter of One Upsmanship fame invented ploys, and Clem Stein, Jr., added gambits to the game of Gin to help you win all the time. Stein gives a great psychological treatise on Gin in his highly entertaining book, *Bridge and Gin Gambitry,* published by Home Library Press. Since playing a good game of Gin requires intense concentration, Stein has developed gambits that will irritate an opponent to utter distraction and ultimate loss of money.

MR. ODDS-MAKER'S BEST BET

Mr. Odds-Maker says, "Every hand poses a new problem. Always set your hand up in a way that offers the most available chances of completing runs or making melds. Remember that only one card in the deck will give you four-of-a-kind, where either of two cards will complete a four-card run unless it has an Ace or King at one end."

CONTRACT BRIDGE

Bridge is the most "social" of all card games, the one that enjoys the most prestige at every level, even having the respect of those who don't play it. A man who would be known as a "card hustler" in any other game is a Bridge Expert, and the expert is not only accepted in the best society but lionized.

The game stems from Whist, which has been played for nearly 200 years, and is a refinement of Auction Bridge.

Harold S. Vanderbilt, wealthy American sportsman, originated the "Contract" feature of Bridge in 1925, as a result of playing the Continental game of Plafond while on a cruise. A feature of Plafond was that tricks must be contracted for in order to be scored toward game.

When he returned to New York, he added the contract feature to Auction Bridge, adding such features as vulnerability, bonuses for slams, penalties for sets and a new scoring setup. The game was introduced at the Knickerbocker Whist Club in New York as Contract Bridge. It soon supplanted Auction Bridge and is generally regarded as the most advanced card game ever devised.

Contract Bridge is a team game, with two players on each side. Among amateurs, there's a tendency to blame all mistakes on one's partner, a ploy which saves face but hardly makes for harmonious team play.

Two decks of cards are used, although only one is in play at any time. While one player deals, his partner shuffles the other deck—at least four riffle shuffles—and places it at the corner of the table nearest his right hand, in readiness for the next dealer who, at the proper time, offers the deck to the player at his right for a cut, and then deals while his partner shuffles the deck not in use.

Cards rank in order from high Ace to low Deuce, and the suit ranking is Spades, Hearts, Diamonds and Clubs, Spades being the highest suit and Clubs the lowest. A No-Trump bid ranks above Spades.

The dealer deals out the entire pack in a clockwise direction, each player receiving 13 cards. As soon as the players have sorted their hands according to suits, the dealer makes the first bid, and bidding goes around the table clockwise. Bidding establishes the trump suit or, in the case of a winning No-Trump bid, that the hand is to be played without a trump suit.

The bidder states the number of tricks over six that he agrees to win, and in the suit he wants to play. A bid of One Club, for example, is a contract to take seven tricks with Clubs as trumps. A Three No-Trump bid is a contract to take nine tricks without there being a trump suit. Each bid must name a greater number of tricks than the previous bid, or a similar number of tricks in a higher suit. No-Trump is higher than any suit.

A player who doesn't want to bid may pass, and if all four players pass, the hand is thrown in without being played and the deal passes.

Any player may, in his turn, double an opponent's bid. The double increases the score, whether the contract is made or not. A player whose bid is doubled may, in his turn, redouble, increasing the score still more. The doubling and redoubling affect only the scoring and not the size of the contract. The contract is determined when the last and highest bid has been followed by three passes, and the player who first mentioned the final Trump suit is the declarer.

The player to the left of the declarer leads a card and the declarer's partner lays his cards face-up on the table as dummy. He takes no part in the play of the hand.

Play travels clockwise. A player must follow suit to the led card, if he has any cards in that suit. If he hasn't, he may either discard from any other suit or play a trump. The player who plays the highest card of that led suit or the highest trump takes the trick. The player who takes a trick then leads a card for the next trick, and this process continues until all 13 tricks have been played.

Scoring is done "above and below the line." A team that makes its contract puts its score for tricks bid below a horizontal line. Scores for additional tricks above the contract, for honors and penalties for sets go above the horizontal line.

A game is completed when a side scores at least 100 points below the line, either in one hand or more. Less than 100 points below the line is called a "part-score" or "leg." If the opponents score game, the part-score is not applicable to the next game. Whenever game is won, both sides begin the next game with nothing credited below the line.

A team that wins a game becomes vulnerable, which means that it faces higher penalties if it fails to make its contract and increased bonuses if it does. Vulnerability does not affect the number of tricks contracted for.

Main object of each team is to win a "rubber," the best out of three games.

Scoring for bids made is as follows:

No-Trump—40 points for the first trick and 30 for each subsequent trick. A Three No-Trump bid achieves Game.

Spades and Hearts—30 points for each trick. A four bid is Game.

Diamonds and Clubs—20 points for each trick. A Five Bid is Game.

Scores are doubled if the contract is doubled, and quadrupled if the contract is redoubled.

Tricks made in excess of the contract score as follows:

Undoubled—trick value, above the line.

Doubled—100 points for each trick if not vulnerable; 200 points if vulnerable, above the line.

Redoubled—200 points per trick if not vulnerable, 400 if vulnerable, above the line.

Penalties for failure to make contract are:

Undoubled—50 points for each trick, scored for the opponent, above the line, if not vulnerable; 100 points if vulnerable.

Doubled—100 points for the first trick and 200 for each subsequent trick, if not vulnerable, credited to the opponents, above the line. If vulnerable, 200 points for the first trick and 300 for each additional trick.

Redoubled—200 points for the first trick and 400 for each subsequent trick, if not vulnerable. If vulnerable, 400 for the first trick and 600 for each additional one.

Winning a rubber scores as follows:

If won in two games. 700

If won in three games. 500

Bonus scores are as follows:

50 points above the line for making a contract when doubled.

Grand Slam (13 tricks) bid and made: 1,000 points above the line if not vulnerable; 1,500 points if vulnerable.

Small Slam (12 tricks) bid and made: 500 points if not vulnerable; 750 points if vulnerable.

In a No-Trump contract, all four Aces in one hand —150 points.

All five honors in the bid suit in one hand (A,K,Q,J,10)—150 points.

Any four honors of Trump suit in one hand—100 points.

Since making game and winning a 500 or 700 rubber is the object of the play, and since a side scores below the line toward game only the number of tricks it bids, estimating the maximum trick-taking capacity of every hand becomes of the utmost importance. A team's bids and responses should convey to its mem-

---

New Cards

Kibitzers are inclined to regard a gambler who asks for a new deck every hour or so in a high-stakes card game as being overly fussy.

Not so, according to a professional.

"Without anybody doing a thing to mark the backs of the cards, a few of them become identifiable in the course of an evening's play," he explains. "A speck of cigar or cigarette ash may cling to the backs of certain cards, in certain spots. Sweat from a drink glass may mark another card. A dealer who 'breaks' the cards hard in shuffling will unwittingly leave some of them more bent than others, once they're well broken in. A card may get a nick in its edge where a chip or coin hits it.

"I've seen gamblers who could study a worn, dirty deck and read ten or twelve high cards from their backs.

"Another thing, one card in a worn deck will be 'slicker' than the others or will have an almost unnoticeable bend in it that will cause it to be cut to more often than any other card in the deck. Take a worn deck in your left hand and push off about half of it by pressing the top stock firmly to the right with your left thumb. Notice the card you cut to. Now, put the cards back together and make the same kind of cut again. The deck will break at that same card, more often than not.

"When a 'hep' player asks for a new deck, it isn't that he thinks anyone in the game is dishonest. He simply wants to play with clean cards that aren't identifiable from use.

bers the most information about each other's hands that can possibly be shown.

There are numerous bidding "systems" to accomplish this. The late Ely Culbertson's original bidding system has been followed by the Jacoby, Italian, Stayman, Goren, Fry and other systems, all of which have their adherents and most of which are quite similar except for bidding "conventions" peculiar to a specific system.

Most bidding systems rate an Ace as 4 points, King as 3, Queen as 2 and Jack as 1. With four suits, this means there are 40 such points. There are additional points either for long suits or for doubletons, singletons and voids. A void in a suit usually counts 3 points, a singleton, 2 points, and a doubleton, 1 point. Some systems deduct a point for the absence of an Ace in a hand. Any five-card suit is biddable, but a four-card suit should contain at least four high-card points (K-J or A). No four-card suit should be rebid. To rebid a five-card suit, it should be topped by Q-J or better. Any holding in a six-card suit is rebiddable. Any hand that opens should contain two quick tricks (A-K, A-Q and K-x [any card 2 thru 9], or K-Q, K-Q). Meeting the minimum requirements for biddable suit and quick tricks, a 14-point hand must be opened. A 13-point hand may be opened if a good re-bid is available, and an 11-point hand may be opened in third position if it contains a good suit.

A two opening bid, which is forcing to game requires 25 points with a good five-card suit, 24 points with two good five-card suits, 23 points with a good six-card suit, and 21 points with a good seven-card suit. An opening suit bid of three indicates less than ten high-card points but the strength to take within two tricks of the contract, vulnerable, or within three tricks of the contract, not vulnerable. The opening three bid is usually made with a good biddable suit that is seven cards or longer. A one No-Trump opening bid requires 16 to 18 high-card points with no points for short suits, and even distribution, with at least Q-x in any doubleton.

The first requirement the partner must have to respond with a raise in the bid suit is adequate trump support: three with a face card, four trump without a face card. With seven to ten points and adequate trump support, the response is to raise the partner's bid by one. With 13 to 16 points and a minimum of four trumps, responder "jumps" or raises by two.

With a count of six or more, the responder may change the suit if the new bid can stay at the one level. To bid two of a new suit requires a count of ten or more. A jump-bid to a new suit requires 19 points minimum. A one-No-Trump response may be made to a one bid with six to nine points and such a bid is often made when the responder's biddable suit is lower than the original bidder's.

An opening bid of two is a forcing bid that demands the responder keep the bidding open to game. With a "bust" hand, six points or less, the responder bids two no-trump. With seven points and a quick trick, he may bid a new suit or, if his hand so indicates, raise the opening bid. With nine points and unbid suits protected, he may bid three No-Trump.

Usually, 25 points in the partners' two hands are required to make game; 33 will often make a Small Slam, and 37 points will usually make a Grand Slam.

Regardless of the system played, most players want a minimum count of 12 points in their hand to make an opening bid, except in third position and barring unusually long runs in a trump suit. Some players won't open on 14 points with poor distribution. Regardless of poor distribution, a 15-point hand should open.

It is recommended that a player learn at least one of the bidding systems thoroughly—Jacoby, Goren, Stayman, Fry or the Italian. He should try to know the bidding "conventions" that distinguish each system.

The story of the out-of-towner who was trying to find Carnegie Hall in New York is particularly pertinent to Contract Bridge.

The visitor approached a far-out Love Cultist and asked, "Pardon me, sir, but could you tell me how to get to Carnegie Hall?"

The long-haired, bead-bedecked cultist smiled at the stranger and answered, "Practice, man! Practice!"

It takes a lot of practice to become a good bridge

BRIDGETTE

Promise of a good two-handed bridge game has been held out for years without ever materializing. A new entry in the field in the Summer of 1970 was *Bridgette,* the invention of Joel D. Gaines, one-time assistant to the late Albert Morehead, bridge editor of the *New York Times.* The new game has the endorsement of such bridge experts as Sheinwold, Root, Schenken, Crawford, Jacoby, Truscott, Kaplan and von Zedtwitz. Oswald Jacoby has prepared a booklet on Bridgette winning strategy.

In addition to the usual 52 cards, the game employs three additional ones called "Colons." Unlike "Honeymoon" and other two-handed attempts, the game retains the bidding features of Contract. Among the unique features are a bid of "Zero No-Trump," no passed hands, and "cue" bids that extract information from an opponent. The Colon cards add a special strategy.

Bridge World gave the new game an excellent review.

THE EASY BRIDGE CHEAT

A team of crooked bridge players in New York has used a dodge for years that makes them practically unbeatable. Both players have learned how to do a convincing false riffle-shuffle and that's all they need.

The cheat depends on the fact that one partner shuffles and the other partner cuts on the opponents' deal.

Whenever a game bid is made by either side, the high card falls either first or third on the majority of the tricks. It is a simple matter to bring the high card to first or third position on the others is taking them up from the table. At the conclusion of the round, the crooked player picks up the two stacks of tricks and assembles them. Then he false-shuffles, vigorously and loudly. At the conclusion of his false-shuffling, he crimps the bottom card of the deck and cuts slightly less than half the cards from top to bottom. Then he puts the deck on the table at his right hand, ready for the opponent's deal.

The opponent picks up the deck when it's time to deal and offers it to the crook's partner for a cut. The partner cuts to the crimp.

The opponent deals, dealing high card first and third until all cards are dealt.

The crooked team has a sure game. Since it comes on their opponent's deal, nobody even considers that there might be skullduggery involved.

---

player. Many bridge enthusiasts, like golfers, take lessons from Pros. YMCA's, adult education courses and clubs often have both beginners' and advanced courses in Contract, with qualified teachers who are dedicated to improving their students' play. Every system has its body of literature, with the definitive book usually written by the inventor or sponsor of the system. "Auto-Bridge" sets are available in the adult games depar'ments of many stores, and enable a player to play, in effect, with experts, analyzing the bids, responses and play of the hands.

Thousands and thousands of "pretty fair" bridge players play what is commonly called "Party Bridge" and have a thoroughly enjoyable time doing it. They play for prizes or low stakes, and the play is casual. The question, "What's trump?" is not unheard-of in such games. Mistakes in bidding and play are passed off lightly—well, *fairly* lightly. If the "average" player wants to play for money, he should be in such games. It is a fact of life that good "party bridge" players usually get massacred in a cut-throat, high stake bridge game.

Like golf, bridge has various levels of competition. The PGA pros who make tournament play their business win the big tournaments, and the professional bridge teams do likewise. Bridge at the top level demands concentration and skill. It calls for daring bids and daring play. Mistakes are not tolerated.

Bridge authorities estimate that at least a billion dollars a year changes hands in bridge games in the United States. The legendary John "Bet a Million" Gates is said to have played bridge on occasion for $1,000 a point.

Contract bridge, with its bonus of 700 for a rubber in which the opponents don't get a game below the line, can and often does put a team 1,000 points behind after two hands in which their opponents bid and make game.

Whether at the professional level, the local tournament level or the "Party Bridge" level, bridge teams are usually matched closely enough to make the game interesting.

Unfortunately, a few casual bridge players in nearly every group secretly think of themselves as experts. Haven't they won prizes at numerous local gatherings? These people are potential victims for any skillful team of bridge hustlers that happens along.

Whatever your level of competition, bridge is a challenging game. Bidding and play have become scientific, but judgement must always play a part, thanks to the dissimilarity of one round to another. In bridge as in no other card game, the player's "Card Sense" is given opportunity to prove itself. Bridge appeals to both the intellect and the imagination, and every new hand offers a new challenge. The game also offers a sociability found in few other card games.

Chicago Bridge

This is four-deal bridge, and is commonly credited to the Standard Club, in Chicago. Four deals make a round, each player dealing in turn. On the first hand, neither team is vulnerable. On the second and third hands, the dealer's team is vulnerable and the other team is not. On the fourth hand, both teams are vulnerable. A passed hand is dealt over by the same dealer. Bonus for making game when not vulnerable is 300; 500 when vulnerable. A part-score applies to the next hand but is canceled if opponents make game. On fourth hand, a team that makes part-score gets a 100 point bonus. Scores are totaled at the end of the fourth hand, just as they are at the end of a game in rubber bridge.

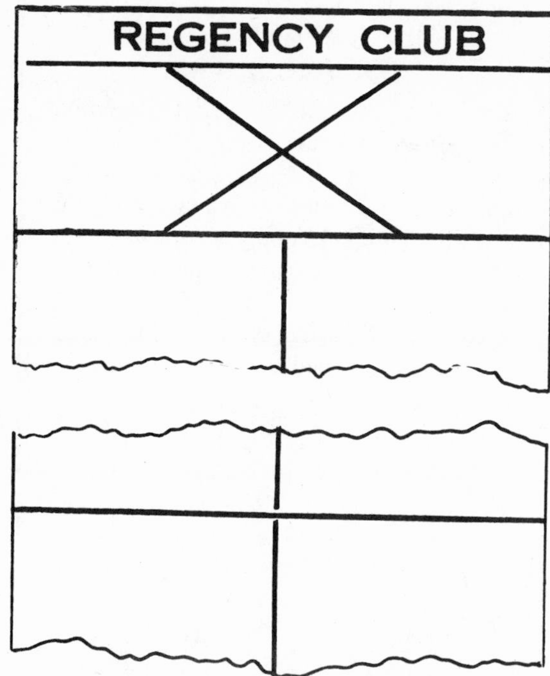

Chicago Bridge is scored on a modified score pad as used here by the Regency Club.

GAMBLING AT BRIDGE

Gamble on bridge with players whose ability is comparable to your own.

The greatest fault of the average money-bridge player is a distaste for taking deliberate "sets" when it would be to his financial advantage to do so.

Mathematics prove that it is profitable to go down 400 or 500 points, depending on the vulnerability situation, to *prevent* your opponents from making game. Experts agree that a 200 set is preferable to letting your opponents make a part-score. Any player who lets his opponents make game because he knows he would go down one trick if he increased the contract is playing losing bridge.

While most bridge systems allow it, opening major-suit bids with only four cards in the suit often leads to trouble, and some successful money-bridge players won't make such a bid unless they have 100 honors in the suit.

Sometimes, two hands can add up to a good count without fitting. Continue bidding with the utmost caution whenever you think the two hands may not fit.

You can bid a small slam with the *possibility* of losing two tricks. You should never bid a grand slam with the *probability* of losing one trick.

Most players bid more cautiously when vulnerable. The expert will stick his neck out a little further, will take more chance to reach game, when he's vulnerable than when he isn't. And aside from deliberate protective losses, he won't bid game when he isn't vulnerable unless he thinks he has an even chance of making it.

Remember that an opponent whose bidding has indicated a long, strong suit must also inevitably have at least one short suit. This knowledge may often profitably influence your decision on possible finesses.

CODE BIDDING

Two bridge cheats in the Chicago area have used a simple code similar to those used by so-called "mind-readers" to convey information.

"A heart" or whatever the suit happens to be means that it's a four-card suit. "One heart" means that it's a five-card suit. "I'll bid a heart" indicates a six-card suit, and "I'll bid one heart" indicates a seven-card suit.

When an "mmm" or "uh" immediately preceeds the bid, it means, "I don't have the ace." If the "mmm" or "uh" is followed by a slight break before the bidder continues with his bid, it means, "I don't have the king."

On the partner's response, an "mmm" or "uh" preceeding the bid, whatever it is, means that the partner has the Ace or King the original bidder asked for. "Two hearts" means the barest minimum. "I'll bid two hearts" means better than the barest minimum but not enough points to change suits.

A flat bid by the responder in another suit means from nine to 12 points. "I'll bid" means more than twelve points. "Pass" means insufficient count without adequate trump support. "I'll pass" means insufficient count but adequate trump support.

When either partner bids "Four no-trump" as a slam invitation, asking for aces, a response of "Five diamonds" would indicate one ace and no kings. "I'll bid five diamonds" would indicate an ace and a king. An "mmm" or "uh" preceeding the bid indicates two or more kings.

"CHaSeD" is their key word for suits. One card slightly up from the others or spread slightly at either end means, "Lead me a club." Two cards means "Lead me a Heart," three means "A spade, please" and four means "A diamond."

MR. ODDS-MAKER'S BEST BET

Mr. Odds-Maker says, "Lose hands to win rubbers. Going set is nearly always preferable to letting your opponents score below the line. If your opponents aren't vulnerable, take a deliberate two set any time to keep them from getting that way. If they are vulnerable, take a three set. When you're playing for money, know your partner like a book."

THE MISSISSIPPI HEART HAND

The classic of all the "cold deck" switches is the famous Mississippi Heart hand in Bridge. With the victim sitting to the dealer's right, he switches in the set-up deck after the victim has cut the cards, just before he starts dealing. Only the third and fourth hands are stacked. The victim thinks he has a Grand Slam laydown in Hearts. Actually, he can take only six tricks, while the dealer takes seven.

Here is the "cold deck" setup of the two hands:

NORTH
S—5 4 3 2
H—Void
D—8 7 6 5
C—6 5 4 3 2

DEALER
S—A K Q J 10 9
H—8 7 6 5 4 3 2
D—Void
C—Void

EAST
S—8 7 6
H—Void
D—10 9 4 3 2
C—J 10 9 8 7

VICTIM
S—Void
H—A K Q J 10 9
D—A K Q J
C—A K Q

The hand gets its name from the dealer's suggestion, made earlier, that they play "Mississippi style," meaning that if a bid is doubled and redoubled, the redoubling may continue on both sides. Three redoubles causes the hand to be played for 16 times the original stakes. The set penalties, of course, take it even higher.

Kevin Kimkennel, a noted cold-deck artist, not only takes his victims to the cleaners but coaxes an additional side-bet that they won't make even one Heart, let alone the tempting Seven Hearts that seem to be a sure thing.

THE "SNEAKY SPADE" SMALL SLAM

Probably one of the most deceptive Bridge hands is the "Sneaky Spade," in which the original bidder has a count of only 13 points and only one face card, the Ace, in Spades. His only other face cards are the Ace of Diamonds and the Queen and Jack of Hearts. The bidder makes a small slam in Spades against any defense. West's opening lead is the King of Hearts.

NORTH
S—K Q 9
H—Void
D—Q x x
C—A Kxxxxx

WEST
S—J 8 5
H—A K x x x
D—K x x
C—J x

EAST
S—Void
H—10 9 x x x
D—J x x x
C—Q x x

SOUTH
S—A 10 x x x x
H—Q J x
D—A x x
C—x

"Pressing" is fatal. When you're behind, reckless, desperate bidding won't put you ahead. One reason why bridge experts can afford to play for high stakes is that when two teams are evenly matched, their scores over a long period of play will usually be close.

Gamesmanship, as illustrated in Stein's *Bridge and Gin Gambitry,* plays a great part in winning at bridge. For example, Stein and his partner sometimes explain their "Up Trick, Down Suit" convention before play starts. It involves keeping the bidding open by raising the bid a trick in a suit immediately lower in rank than the suit the partners hope to play the hand in. The explanation of the convention's uses and variations becomes so complicated that the other team is completely befuddled before play starts. And the situation never seems to arise for Stein and his partner to use the convention — but the opponents spend the evening looking for it, wondering on every opponent bid whether it's operative or not.

Another player invariably tells "the classic story" about the time he won $6,000 in less than an hour of play against two famous experts, as if the mythical story were a part of bridge history. The two experts, he reveals, would never play against him again. He smiles, and says, "I assure you, it was sheer luck that I made what won the trophy as the play of the year, *regardless* of what those two big-shots thought."

One player has memorized the rules of etiquette for tournament play and the penalties for violation of them — and gets his opponents so self-conscious that their game falls apart.

Another player has actually mimeographed copies of his "Minimax" system, "a system for minimizing losses and maximizing winning hands." He offers copies of it for sale at $100 each and says it is strictly a system for money-bridge. Nobody buys the system, but everyone is impressed.

ONE-WAY DECKS

A one-way deck of cards is one in which the back of the card has a top and a bottom. Most bridge decks, with illustrations on the back, are one-way cards. Some popular poker decks whose backs seem to have neither top nor bottom are one-way cards if you know what to look for — a slight difference in the design at either end.

The bridge cheat using a one-way deck will set the backs all facing the same way. Then he will reverse the four aces or whatever cards he wishes to keep track of, so that the bottom of the illustration on those cards is in line with the top of the illustration on the other cards in the deck.

He legitimately shuffles the deck, and his opponent is given an opportunity to make a fair cut. But the cheat knows where every ace in the deck is.

Quite often, an innocent victim will riffle or overhand shuffle without disturbing the one-way arrangement of the backs of the cards. There is no easier way to spot a face-down card than to have its back facing the wrong way in a one-way deck.

MORE FRIENDLY GAMES

Oh, Hell!

This popular party gambling game may be played by from four to ten people and is played for predetermined stakes. The amount of money involved may be substantial or small.

As many cards are dealt out on the first round as may be dealt so that every player receives the same number. For example, with six players, eight cards are dealt to each hand; with seven players, seven cards, etc.

The top card left on the remainder of the pack is turned face up and determines the trump suit. Players must follow suit whenever possible, but may trump when void in the led suit.

The scorekeeper asks each player to declare the number of tricks he will take, and notes the declaration under the player's name. Players declare in turn, starting to the left of the dealer and going clockwise back to him. If a player believes he will take no tricks, he so declares.

The first lead is made by the player to the left of the dealer and the other players play in rotation. The person who takes each trick makes the following lead until all cards are gone.

If a player makes his declaration, he gets three points, even if his declaration was Zero. For each trick he declares and takes, he gets an extra point, if the number taken matches his declaration. For example, a player who declares one trick and takes it scores four points; a player who declares three tricks and takes them scores six points. However, the number of tricks taken must exactly match the declaration. Any player who fails to take the number declared loses the three points for making his bid and loses one point for each trick over or under his declaration.

For example, a player who declares one trick and takes three would get a −2 score on the round; a player who declares one trick and takes none would get a −1, as would a player who declares no tricks and takes one.

At the end of the round, a new hand is dealt by the next dealer, the player immediately to the left of the first dealer, but one less card is dealt to each player than was dealt in the previous hand. For example, if eight cards were dealt to each player on the first round, seven cards constitute each hand in the second round. Again, the top card turned up on the remainder of the pack determines trump and again, the players declare how many tricks they will take.

This continues down to one card, at which time every player must declare whether he will take one trick or none. After this round, the deal goes up to two cards and runs progressively back up to the number of cards dealt in the first round. When the players have played their hands with the same number of cards they held on the first round, the game is over.

The person with the highest score is paid the maximum amount agreed upon by the person with the lowest score. Second lowest score pays second highest and third lowest pays third highest. With an odd number of players, the middle scorer is "free," neither winning nor losing any money. With six or seven players, the amount may be $1.00, 75¢ and 50¢, or whatever the group agrees upon.

An interesting variation of the game is a stipulation that the dealer, who is the last to declare, may not let the total of declarations match the number of cards dealt. For example, if five cards are dealt and five tricks have been declared up to the dealer's declaration, he must declare one or more tricks. If four have been declared, he cannot declare one trick and must declare either none or two or more.

Bidding strategy varies from hand to hand, depending on the number of cards in the "blind." While much depends on chance, it is interesting to note that the best card players in the game usually get the best scores.

Boo-Ray

A gambling game for from four to ten players, Boo-Ray is often played for much higher stakes than the players anticipated.

It is a simple game. Three cards are dealt face down to each player and a few "blind" hands are also dealt out. The dealer antes 15¢ on every round and on this round and any subsequent rounds where only 15¢ is in the pot, all players must stay.

A card is turned face up from the remaining stock, and this card determines trump. There are three tricks, and the three tricks split the pot three ways. The player to the left of the dealer leads and all players must follow suit if possible. Any player who fails to take a trick must put the amount of the pot into it for the next round. On the first round, all players must stay, as is the case whenever the pot gets down to 15¢. On all other rounds, a player with a poor hand may either drop out or take one of the extra "blind" hands, which he then must play.

If the second pot is 30¢ and two players fail to take a trick, the next pot is 75¢: the two 30¢ antes and the dealer's 15¢. Should two players fail to take a trick on this round, the pot for the next hand becomes $1.65.

With six or seven players, including a few optimists, the pots can soon become substantial. The bigger the pot, of course, the greater the temptation to stay in—and the more a player can lose if he fails to take a trick.

Most experienced Boo-Ray players insist on a "limit," 90¢ and $3 being popular ones, for failure to take a trick. Without such a limit, $60 or $90 in a pot is not uncommon.

The game is fast, and easy to understand. Chance plays a large part, but weighing the value of the pot against the odds of taking a trick is important.

Canasta

Canasta, a great favorite of the gals, which may be played by any number of players from two to six, is most commonly played by two or four. When there are four or more players, play is by partnership. Otherwise, each player plays for himself. With five players, a pair of partners are opposed by three players, one of the three sitting out each hand in rotation. With six players, one member of each team sits out, in rotation.

Two full decks plus four Jokers are used, being shuffled together. Jokers and deuces are wild, and a wild card may be melded with natural cards. Depending on the number of players, the deal alternates or rotates. Eleven cards are dealt, one at a time, to each player, clockwise. The remainder of the deck, the "stock," goes face down on the table, with its top card being turned face up, beside the stock. Whenever the upcard is a Joker, two, black or red three, additional cards are put face up on top of it until a natural card from Ace down to four shows up.

A player who has a red three in his hand must, at his turn, put it face up on the table in front of him and draw a replacement from the stock. When a player draws a red three from the stock, it is immediately put face up on the table and a replacement is drawn. A player who picks up the discard pile and finds a red three places it face up on the table, without drawing any replacement. Red threes have a bonus score of 100 points each, with an extra bonus of 400 points if all four are assembled by one side. Value of the red threes is credited to a side that has made a meld or debited against a side that has no melds by the time the hand ends. Play goes clockwise, with each player's turn consisting of a draw, an optional meld and a discard. The player always has the option of drawing the top card from the stock. In two-hand Canasta, the stock draw is two cards. He may, instead, take the top card of the discard pile to use in a meld, but must then take the rest of the discard pile. The discard is one card from the hand, onto the pile beside the stock.

Main object of the game is to form melds, three or more cards of the same rank, with or without wild cards. Sequences are not played in Canasta. A meld must contain two natural cards of the same rank and not more than three wild cards. Jokers and deuces may never be melded by themselves, and three or four black threes without wild cards may be melded only in going out.

To count for a player, a meld must be laid face up on the table in the player's proper turn. Cards left in the hand at the end of a hand count minus, even when they form melds. A player may meld as many cards as he wishes in his turn, of one rank or various ones, forming new melds and adding to previous ones.

In partnership play, all melds of the partnership are

placed in front of one of the two active players. A partnership may meld a rank already melded by the opposition but may never make two different melds of the same rank. A player may add additional cards to any meld of his side, providing the meld remains legitimate, but he may not add any cards to the opposition's melds.

A meld of seven or more cards is a Canasta. In addition to the point value of the cards, a Canasta gets a bonus: 500 if it contains no wild cards and 300 if it contains one to three wild cards. A completed canasta is squared up with a red card on top to show a natural, a black card to show a mixed. Additional cards may be added to Canasta to score their point values but do not affect their bonus except that the addition of a wild card to a natural canasta reduces the bonus from 500 to 300.

Point values of cards are as follows:

Joker	50
Deuce	20
Ace	20
King, Queen, Jack, 10, 9 and 8	10
7, 6, 5 and 4	5
Black 3	5

The first meld a side makes has a minimum count requirement, depending on the player's accumulated score:

Minus	15
0 to 1495	50
1500 to 2995	90
3,000 or more	120

EVERY DECK A MARKED DECK

During the course of an evening's play, a good card mechanic can mark every key card in the deck with finger-nail nicks or crimps. The markings are made at different positions on the back of the cards to indicate different card values. The nail-nick marking is more practical when the card-sharp is dealing, because it is easier to feel than to see—although sharp eyes can detect it.

The "crimp" or "bump" can be spotted across the table, in every hand—*if* you know what to look for—and only the crook who did the marking has that information.

Spotting it won't do the victim much good. He doesn't know which player is responsible, and he doesn't know the marking system employed.

A Denver card mechanic confides, "It's unbelievable what glaring crimps and nicks will go through an evening's play without anyone getting wise. It's one of the safest cheats going. By the time it can be detected, the dirty work is done—and nobody can say who did it."

A meld's "count" is the point value of the cards within it. To meet the minimum requirement, a player may meld two or more different sets of cards. Bonuses for red threes and Canastas do not count toward the minimum. After its initial meld, a side may make any further melds without any minimum count.

DISCARD PILE — The discard pile is frozen against a side until that side has made its first meld, which unfreezes it unless it contains a red three or wild card. In the latter event, a player may take the discard pile only to meld its top card with a natural pair of the same rank held in his hand. He should show the meld cards before picking up the discard pile. If the discard pile is not frozen, a player may pick it up to meld one matching card and one wild card from his hand or to add the top card to a previous meld made by his side. When he has melded the top card of the discard pile, the player may then meld any additional cards he wishes. The discard pile may never be picked up when its top card is a wild card or black three.

A player goes out when he gets rid of the last card in his hand, either by discarding it or by melding it. When any player goes out, play stops and the deal is scored. A player is permitted to go out only when his side has melded at least one Canasta, except in a two-handed game, where two Canastas must be melded. Unless he meets this stipulation, he must keep at least one card in his hand. A player with only one card in his hand may not take a discard pile of only one card. If he can go out, a player may ask his partner's permission, before or after drawing from the stock, and must obey the partner's decision. A player may not ask his partner's permission to go out after having melded any card or after having indicated he is taking the discard pile, but he may go out without asking permission. A player goes out "concealed" when he melds his whole hand in one turn, including at least one Canasta. If his partner has not made a meld, he must make the minimum count, without the Canasta bonus, if he has taken the discard pile but not if he has drawn from the stock.

If the last card of the stock is a red three, the player who draws it faces it without melding or discard, and play ends. If the last card of the stock is not a red three, play continues so long as each player in turn takes the discard. At this time, a player must take the discard if it matches a meld made by his side but need not take it to make a new meld. Play ends when a player cannot take or legally refuses the discard.

SCORING—

Going out 100
Going out concealed . . . . 100 (bonus)
Each red three 100
Each natural Canasta 500
Each mixed Canasta 300

A side scores the total point values of all cards melded, less the point value of the cards left in the hand or hands. The side that first scores 5,000 points is the winner of the game. The difference between winner's and loser's total points determines the gambling loss.

SAMBA is a faster variation of Canasta, played with three decks instead of two.

Roz Adler says, "It's not my game, and I always thought it was a panty-waist game 'til I saw two old ladies play cut-throat Canasta for high stakes. A good Canasta player holds back for a big, big score on each deal. Going out fast is just a defensive thing. She lays back and doesn't meld until the pack is taken. Experts tell me that they never worry about bonuses for natural Canastas or a concealed hand.

"Just because I don't care for the game, I can't knock it. Any game that involves such big point scores is a good gambling game. Maybe the reason I don't like it is because I have to play Canasta one night a week with my old aunt for a twentieth of a cent a point when I could otherwise be in a poker game."

Last Hand

Damon Runyan gets credit for the story about a Broadway character who died of a heart attack during a high-stakes poker game. After the body had been removed from the premises, one of the other players saw the dead man's hand, face down, in front of the vacant spot at the table. He reached out and picked up the hand.

He shook his head sadly. "He never woulda made it, anyway," he declared.

Between The Sheets

No game could be simpler. Every player antes. Each player in rotation is dealt two cards, face up. Ace is low and King is high. In his turn, each player may either fold or bet any part of the pot that a "hit" or third card dealt him will have a face value *between* his two original cards. If the "hit" card has a value above, below or matching either of his two dealt cards, he loses. A player may call for an ante whenever the pot falls below its original starting level. Being dealt an Ace and a King, the player usually bets the pot. The only way he can lose is to draw another Ace or King. The dealer "burns" one card before starting the deal and continues dealing until there are insufficient cards for another round, at which time the deal passes.

John Strauss says, "A good card 'counter' will murder you in this game. Pots build up because the average player takes chances he shouldn't. Every bet is at even money, so always fold unless there are at least as many cards left in the deck that will win for you as cards that will lose for you. On the first round, let's say you're dealt a four and a ten. Only 20 cards in the deck will win for you. A good rule of thumb is to subtract the value of the low card from the value of the high card, counting Jacks as 11, Queens as 12 and Kings as 13. If you get a remainder of eight or more, the betting odds are in your favor. If you're a 'counter' and remember what cards have been played that fall between your high and low ones, you're in like Flynn."

Concentration

Originally a children's game, John Strauss says, "I've seen professional gamblers play Concentration by the hour. They regard it as an exercise and conditioner, and they don't play for small stakes. Watch real pros play this simple game and you'll get some idea of why they win at poker and gin."

The deck is shuffled and the cards laid face down on the table haphazardly, but not overlapping. On the first round of play, each player in turn turns up any two cards. If they match, he takes the pair, and turns up two more. If the cards do not form a pair, they are immediately turned face down again and left in the position they occupied. A player's turn passes when he fails to match a pair. Play continues until all cards are paired.

Spite And Malice

Two packs of playing cards are used, one without Jokers and one with four Jokers. The packs are not matching and are not shuffled together. Pack One, without Jokers, is shuffled and dealt into two face-down piles of 26 cards each, one for each of the two players. These are called the "pay-off piles," and the top card of each is turned face up. Higher card turned is the first player. The other player deals hands of five cards to his opponent and himself from Pack Two and puts the stock on the table.

The winner is the player who first gets rid of his pay-off pile.

Card ranking is King, high, down to Ace, low.

The first player immediately plays any Ace or Aces to the center of the board to start a center stack. Four center stacks are permitted at any one time. Center stacks are built in order from Ace up to King, regard-

RUB-A-DAUB-DAUB

"Daub" is a greaseless, quick-drying colored paste that comes in a tiny pill box, in red, blue or gold metallic. The red and blue are exact matches of the colors in poker-deck backs. The gold is almost impossible to detect on the back of any dark card, unless you know what you're trying to find.

"Daub" is almost never used to mark a whole deck. It is primarily used to mark Aces or key cards.

The card mechanic has the daub box in his pocket, minus the lid. He gets a tiny speck of daub under a finger-nail and smears it onto the back of a card he wants to be able to identify at a later time. He can then identify that card face-down from six feet away —but nobody else sees anything wrong with it.

In a "friendly" gin or Blackjack game, it can give the mechanic all the edge he needs. It gives him only one problem. He has to put his hand back into his pocket to wipe off a trace of daub that may possibly remain on his finger-tip.

---

less of suit. Any deuce may go on any Ace, any trey on any deuce, etc. Both players play to any center stacks.

Both players are permitted four side stacks or discard piles. These piles are built in descending order. A player plays only upon his own side stacks.

The top face-up card of the pay-off pile may be played only to a center stack. When it is played, the next card is turned face up. Only one card from the hand may be played to a side stack in one turn, and the turn ends with play to such a side stack. Cards cannot be moved from one side stack to another. In addition to ending play by playing to a side stack a player ends his turn if he cannot or doesn't want to make a further play. At the beginning of each turn, a player draws enough cards from the stock to restore his hand to five cards. Jokers are wild and may be used instead of any card except an Ace. A Joker at the top of a side stack may be played to the center. Whenever a center stack is completed, running from Ace up to King, it is shuffled into the stock. The player who first depletes his pay-off pile is the winner, and the score is determined by the number of cards remaining in his opponent's pay-off pile at that time. The game is usually played for a stipulated number of cents per point.

Eights

Eights may be played by any number from two to eight, and makes a good four-handed game with partners. With two players, seven cards are dealt to each hand. With more players, five cards constitute a hand. With the hands dealt, the stock is placed in the center of the table and a card turned face up. If an eight is turned, it is buried face down in the center of the pack and another card turned. The face up card starts a "play" pile. Players play in rotation, from left to right. Each player must play one card — a card that matches the "up" card in face value or is of the same suit. If he cannot make a play from his hand, the player must draw from the stock until he gets a card which will play, or until the stock is exhausted, when he passes his turn. Eights are wild. Any eight may be played upon any card and the player who plays it names the suit of his choice. The following player must then play a card of the specified suit or another eight, in which case he may change the suit to one of his choice.

The player who gets rid of all his cards first is the winner, and the other players' losses depend on what they are holding at the time when the winner goes out. An eight in the hand counts 50; face cards and tens count ten, and all other cards count their face value. Thus, a hand with an eight, three and Jack left in it would cost its holder 63 points. In the four-handed partnership game, both partners must go out. After the first hand goes out, the three remaining continue to play.

One two-handed version of the game is called Hollywood Eights and is scored like Gin, with the score pad marked off to score three games simultaneously. A player must be "on" Game 1 before he scores on Game 2, and "on" Game 2 before he scores anything on Game 3. After he is on all three games, further points are scored on all three. When this game is played for 100 points, eights count 20; Aces, 15; face cards, 10; and lower cards, their face value.

Cassino

Cassino is undoubtedly of Italian origin, and a widely held theory is that it was first played in Cassino, Italy. It is quite different from most other card games. Playable by either two, three or four players, the four-handed game is usually played by pairs of partners, facing each other at the card table.

Unlike most card games, face cards have no numerical value. Aces count one, and all other pip cards have their face value.

Four cards are dealt to each player, along with four cards face-up on the table. The balance of the deck is held for continuation of play.

Each player tries to take in cards, particularly those that score. Big Cassino, the ten of Diamonds, scores two points, Little Cassino, the two of Spades, scores one point, and each Ace scores a point. A "sweep," not usually counted in the two-handed game, counts a point. The player or team taking in the greatest number of cards scores three points for it, and the greatest number of Spades taken in scores one point.

A "sweep" is taking in all the cards on the table. In partnership play, everything taken by a team is counted on one score. In case of a tie on number of cards or Spades, no points are counted for those items.

After the first round of four cards is played, the deal passes to the left and four more are dealt to each player, without any addition to the face-up cards on the table. Play continues until the deck is exhausted.

Players, starting with the one to the dealer's left, have the following choice of plays:

Taking in a combination — A card in a player's hand, of the same denomination as one on the board, may be played on it, and the player takes in both of them. He may also take in any other cards, the total of which is identical with the one he plays. For example, an eight will take all the eights on the table and will also take a six and deuce, a five and trey, etc.

Building a combination — A player may add a card from his hand to one or more cards on the board, in the event that the total will match another card in his hand. He can then take in the "build" on his next play, unless another player has taken it with another card of the same denomination or built higher on it. For example, if a six is on the board and he holds a deuce and eight, he can build his deuce on the six and take it with his eight on his next turn — unless another player has built it higher or taken it with another eight.

Calling a combination — For example, if he holds two sixes and a third six, or a pair of threes or a four and deuce are on the board, he has the option of playing one of his sixes, calling it "sixes," and taking the combinations on his next turn, unless a previous player takes it with another six. While a "build" may be built higher, a "call" may not.

Making a Sweep — This is taking every card on the table in one play. A sweep is marked by reversing one card of the combination in which it's made.

If a player cannot make any combination, he plays a single card onto the board. On the last deal of the pack, the player taking the last combination takes in all the remaining cards on the board, but this does not constitute a sweep.

No player may increase his own build unless he has the cards to take in either the first or second build. A player who can make a second build or call or take in a combination or capture another player's build may do so before taking in his original build. Otherwise, he must take his original build on his next play. Builds may be raised with cards from the hand, but not with cards from the board. A builder or caller must name the build or call when he makes it.

Spades are desirable in making pairs and combinations, because of their scoring count. Given a choice, take up a card put on the board by an opponent. Holding a pair, put one of them on the board unless there's already one there and the fourth hasn't been played.

Until Big and Little Cassino have been played, don't lay down a ten or a deuce. Play of Aces depends on how many are still out. Try for combinations before you try for matching pairs, but don't hesitate to take either.

In two-handed, a deal through the deck usually constitutes a game, and sweeps don't count. One popular scoring method is that in which 11 points constitutes a game and if a side scores 11 points in one deal, its score is redoubled. Scoring 11 points in two hands doubles the score. In still another method of scoring, 21 points constitutes a game.

Variations of the game include:

Royal Casino, in which Jacks are 11-spots, Queens, 12 and Kings, 13.

Royal Draw Casino, in which each player, after playing a card from his hand, draws another from the face-down pack, keeping the number of cards in his hand at four until all cards are drawn from the stock, when the hands are played to a finish.

Spade Casino, in which each Spade counts one

The Old Gambler

"Son," the old gambler said, "the best advice I can give you is not to get into any friendly card game with strangers.

"I got into a pool-hall poker game one time out in Montana, and one of the players was filthy dirty. His fingernails were almost black. But after I'd lost about $200 to him, I realized that it wasn't dirt under his nails. It was grease, and in five or six hands, he'd marked every face card in the deck, from the back. Aces had a little dot of grease right in the center of the card. On Kings, it was in the upper right or lower left-hand corner. Queens had a dab of grease along one side, about halfway, and Jacks, the same thing only at the top or bottom.

"I wasn't in any position to accuse him of cheating. Anyway, there was no way I could prove he was responsible. So I just stayed in the game, using the marks the same way he was using 'em, until I got back my $200.

"When I left the game, he followed me and thanked me for not exposing him. 'I've got a nice thing goin' here,' he said, 'and I'd sure hate to lose it.'"

THE BOTTOM-DEAL

The card mechanic gets a good hand together at the bottom of the deck in the course of assembling the cards to shuffle. He either riffle-shuffles or overhand shuffles, being careful not to disturb the position of the bottom four cards. In the course of shuffling, he crimps the lower right-hand corner of the bottom card downward with his left little finger, brings the bottom stock to approximately the center of the deck or slightly above, and offers the deck for a cut. Nine times out of ten, the victim will cut to the crimped card. If the dealer has a confederate sitting at his right, he doesn't even take that one chance in ten of failing to get the good hand to the bottom of the deck.

He deals top cards fairly to every player except himself. He deals "bottoms" for his own hand.

To deal "bottoms" properly, he must hold the deck in the "mechanic's grip," with a space between the first and second fingers of the left hand. The deck is actually held by the thumb and first finger. When he wants to deal a "bottom," he moves a top card off to the right in dealing position. His right thumb goes on top of it and his first finger beneath. His second finger, however, goes down into the gap between his left forefinger and the others and pivots off the bottom card while the left thumb moves the top card back into position. A good bottom dealer can tell you what he's doing and you still can't seem him do it. More important, there is no way in the world to prove he's cheating.

---

point toward game. The Ace, Jack and deuce actually count two points each, one point as Ace and Jack and Little Casino and one point as a Spade. The game is 61 points.

Hearts

Hearts is a home gambling game whose popularity has waxed and waned, over the years, but always comes back, probably because of its well-balanced mixture of skill and chance. Said to be an offshoot of Whist, it resembles that game except that the object is to avoid taking any Hearts or the Queen of Spades.

As a gambling game in college fraternities, it is usually played with chips, each player putting a chip into the pot for each Heart he takes, along with 13 chips for the Queen of Spades, and the player who takes the least number of Hearts takes the pot—or splits it, in the event of a tie.

As a home game, it is usually played with scores tallied on a pad, and settlement made at the conclusion of a pre-determined period of play. Low score is the winner, and highest score is the heaviest loser.

While it may be played by any number from three to seven, four players constitute the ideal game. It is not a partnership game.

Players are dealt the largest possible equal number of cards, with the remainder going into a "blind," which is taken by the taker of the first trick and must not be looked at until the end of the game.

After sorting his hand, each player passes three of his cards, face down, to the player to his right. No player may look at the cards passed to him until he has selected the three cards to be given face down to his neighbor. In six and seven-handed Hearts, only two cards are passed. The passed cards become a part of each hand.

The player to the dealer's left makes the first lead. Tricks are taken by high card in a suit, Ace being high and deuce, low. A player must follow suit if possible. If he cannot follow suit, he discards—usually Hearts. A player holding the Queen of Spades must discard it at his first opportunity. The object of the game is not to take tricks but to avoid taking any Hearts or the Queen of Spades.

An interesting variation is that in which a player tries to take all 13 hearts and the Queen of Spades. If he is successful, every other player in the game has 26 points marked against him. If unsuccessful, he scores the number of Heart and Q S points he has taken.

DEAD MAN'S HAND

The true story of Wild Bill Hickok's untimely demise in a Deadwood, South Dakota, saloon, has became gambling history.

Doing well in a game of draw poker, seated with his back to the door, he was shot in the back just after drawing his cards. His murderer was one Jack McCall, acting on behalf of some crooked gamblers who felt Wild Bill's imminent appointment as town marshall would be detrimental to their interests.

As Hickok collapsed over the table, his poker hand was exposed—a pair of Aces and a pair of eights.

From that moment on, Aces and eights have been known as "Dead Man's Hand."

Numerous variations known as Domino Hearts, Cancellation Hearts, Auction Hearts, etc., are popular in various localities.

Marion Gillet says, "Most players pass cards to hurt the opponents. Pass cards to protect your own hand! If you have less than four spades, pass the A S, K S or Q S. With four Spades, hold onto 'em. It's usually easier to keep from taking the Q S when it's in your hand than when it's somewhere else. Never pass Spades below the Queen.

"Keep track of how many cards are played in each suit, just as if you were playing Bridge. It'll make you a winner.

"Going for a slam is fun, but you'll miss more often than you'll succeed. It's a long shot that you take only when you have no other choice."

Auction Pitch

Pitch evolved from an old English game called "All Fours" or "High-Low-Jack," which was extremely popular in the United States in the nineteenth century. It may be played by from two to seven players, but is usually played by four. It is not a partnership game.

Each player is dealt six cards. Ace is high and deuce is low. The first player to score seven points is the winner.

Highest trump in play counts one point; holding the lowest trump in play counts one point, although some variations in scoring give this point to the player taking the low trump in play; taking the Jack of trumps counts one point, and Game counts one point. Game consists of taking scoring cards to the greatest total value. Each Jack counts one point, each Queen counts two points, each King counts three points and each Ace counts four points. Each ten counts ten points. If the Jack of Trumps is not played, no one counts it. If two players count identically for game, no one counts it.

Players examine their hands and bid or pass in rotation. The lowest bid is two, and successive bidders must top the previous bids, except for the dealer, who may make trump without bidding over the previous bid. Any player may "pitch" or "smudge" (bid for all four scores, high, low, Jack and game) and nobody can take the bid away from him.

The pitcher (high bidder) leads for the first trick, and the card he leads becomes trump suit. All players must follow suit if they can on a trump lead. A player may either follow suit or trump on any other suit led. Unable to follow suit, a player may play an indifferent card if he chooses not to trump. Player of the highest trump or the highest card of the led suit, if no trump is played, takes the trick and leads to the next one.

If a player fails to make his bid, he is set back by the amount of his bid. The first player to get seven points is the winner. The pitcher's score is counted first, and if both he and another player reach seven points on the same hand, the pitcher wins, by virtue of going out first. A player who "smudges" wins the game then and there, unless he was in the hole, in which case he counts four.

Variations of Auction Pitch, popular in different localities, are Smudge, Auction Pitch with a Joker, Sell-Out and Cinch. More complicated versions are Seven-Up, California Jack and Shasta Sam. In recent years, most devotees of these more complicated versions have switched to Contract Bridge.

Tom James says, "Never bid a smudge without the Jack in your hand. Don't worry about going set. You can't bid cautiously in Pitch and win. And remember that while luck determines the high, low and Jack, the way the hands are played decides who gets game. Deliberately throw points to somebody else to keep a high player from going out. If the bidder pitches his high trump and then switches suit, try to get the lead and then lead *your* high trump. Unlike Bridge, a three-card suit is as good as anybody'll have, barring freak hands. I never play it for much money because the hands can be so inconsistent."

Tunk

Tunk probably came to the United States from France, and was popular on the levees in New Orleans in the nineteenth century. The idea of the game is similar to Gin, except that it is much wilder.

Any number of players from two to seven may participate, but when more than two people are playing, two packs of cards constitute the deck. Deuces are wild. This means that in games with three or more players, there are eight wild cards.

The dealer deals seven cards to each player. A "tunk" or call comes when a hand is matched except for five or less points. The caller must be able to "tunk" or call without drawing or discarding. After his call, the other players in the game each have one draw and one discard. All hands are then laid down face up, and the players who didn't call may, in rotation, play upon the hand of the caller, wherever possible. When this has been done, each player's unmatched remaining cards are counted and put on the score pad against him. When a player reaches 100, he is out of the game. All players ante on every round, and play continues until only one player is left with a score of under 100. He wins the pot, which may be substantial, depending on the size of the ante.

Euchre

Euchre is a trick-taking game, as distinguished from the "meld" games such as Rummy, and was probably a forerunner to Whist. It is the original "nickel on the corner" game, and is usually played with antes by the player, anywhere from a nickel to a dollar a game. "Euchres" cost additional antes, and winners take the pot.

While the official rules designate five points as a game, most present-day players make ten points the game, by agreement.

All cards below the sevens are thrown out of the deck, making a Euchre pack of 32 cards. Score is kept by two cards, a four and a six, called the "counters."

One side uses black cards as counters, the other side, red. Card values are as in Bridge, except for the Jack of Trump, which is highest and is called the "Right Bower." The other Jack of the same color is second-highest trump and is designated as "Left Bower." The remaining two Jacks have no special value.

Players cut for deal, and it is considered an advantage to be dealer. The dealer deals two cards on the first round and three on the second, to each player. With five cards dealt to each hand, the dealer turns up the top card from the pack which designates the trump suit. The basic object of the game is to take three tricks, which count one point. If all the tricks are taken by one side, it is called a "Marche" and counts 2 points. If a player in a partnership game elects to play it "alone," his partner throws in his hand and the declarer then tries to take all five tricks. If successful, he makes four points. He still makes one point if he takes only three tricks.

Whenever the player who determines the trump takes less than three tricks, he is "euchred," and the opponents score two points.

If the player to the left of the dealer feels he has sufficient strength to take three tricks, he "orders it up." The suit of the exposed card becomes trump and the dealer puts the card into his hand, discarding a card of his choice, face down. Ordinarily, he doesn't pick up the exposed card until he is ready to play it, but can do so whenever he chooses.

If the player to the left of the dealer passes, and the dealer's partner either passes or "assists." He elects to assist when he has enough, with the help of the card the dealer has turned up, to take three tricks. If he passes, the third hand may either order up or pass. If all players pass, the dealer may either "take it up," in which case the turned-up card is trump, or "turn it down," in which case he places the upturned card face down on the pack. The player to dealer's left then is entitled to make trump in whatever suit he prefers, except the suit just turned down. If the bidder's hand isn't strong enough in any suit, he can pass again, and the next bidder may declare trump. If all players refuse to name trump, the deal passes and a new hand is dealt. Once trump is declared and the dealer has discarded, the player to his left leads. High card takes the trick, and leads. Play continues until all five cards in the hands have been played. Players must follow suit whenever possible and when they cannot, may either trump or discard.

Helen Stein, a champion at Euchre claims that three trumps and a side Ace are enough to attempt a point. The score affects the player's action. With both sides a point away from going out, a player normally makes trump with a weak hand. With both sides two points away from going out, he is more cautious.

With a three-point lead over his opponents, a player often orders up the trump to keep the opposition from going alone.

DEALING SECONDS

Dealing off the second card from the top of the deck instead of the top one is a standard manipulative move that is indetectable in the hands of a good card mechanic. It is most commonly used with a marked deck. If the top card that should be dealt to a player would improve his holding, the mechanic simply deals the second card instead of the good one.

The top two cards of the deck are moved off for dealing in perfect alignment. As the right hand reaches for the card(s), the left thumb pulls the top card back and the lower of the two is dealt. There is no change of pace or movement from the dealer's procedure when he is dealing legitimately. The hands are in motion as the card is dealt, and the broader motion covers the quarter-of-an-inch movement of the top card back to the squared deck. Even an expert who knows what the dealer is doing can't detect it.

Two-Hand And Three-Hand

The only scoring difference from four-hand Euchre is that in three-hand, a "Marche" tallies three points rather than two. In both of these games, each player plays for himself. In three-hand, the declarer is opposed by two players. In two-hand, he may stand on a much poorer hand than in the three-contestant game, where two people play against him.

VARIATIONS

Bidding Euchre is popular in the Midwest. "Call-Ace" Euchre, in which the bidder says, "I call on the best" and names a trump, is big in some localities.

The player who holds the Ace in the bid suit becomes his partner, but the partnership is not revealed until the Ace is played.

Set-back Euchre is an amusing gambling variation. Each of four players puts a dollar or a previously determined amount into the pot. At the offset, each player has five points, and the object of the game is to get your score down to zero. A player who doesn't take a trick gets a point added to his score. Anyone who is euchred adds a dollar to the pot and gets two points added. Any player who thinks he cannot take a trick has the right to toss in his hand. First player to reduce his score to zero is the pot winner.

Pinochle

Pinochle, combining melding and trick-taking, stems from the old French game of *Piquet*. It originated in Switzerland, where it is still highly popular and probably gets its name from the French word, *binocle* (binocular).

In the United States, the old Pinochle game, played by two, three or four players, has been succeeded by Auction Pinochle with a Widow, played by three or four players. Variations of the game call for adding eights and sevens, but the standard Pinochle deck holds two each of Ace, K,Q,J, ten and nine of each suit, 48 cards in all.

Let's consider the old standard game first. Twelve cards are dealt to each player, four at a time, with the 25th card turned up to indicate trump. If the trump card is a nine, lowest of its suit, the dealer scores ten points for it. The trump card or "Dix" (pronounced deese) is beside the face-down stock.

The object of the game is to score melds and to take tricks containing cards that count. Here are the melds:

CLASS A—Marriage (K and Q of any suit), 20; Royal Marriage (K and Q of trump suit), 40; Royal Sequence (A, K,Q,J and 10 of trumps), 150.

CLASS B—Pinochle (Q of Spades and J of Diamonds), 40; Double Pinochle, (Two Q S and two J D), 80. Some players count Double Pinochle as 500, by agreement.

CLASS C—Four Jacks, one each of the four suits, 40; Four Queens, one each of the four suits, 60; Four Kings, one each of the four suits, 80; Four Aces, one each of the four suits, 100. Eight of each card counts double the value.

Cards taken on tricks have these values: Aces and 10's, 10 points; Kings and Queens, 5 points. The last trick counts an additional ten points for the player who takes it.

"Dix," the lowest trump, counts ten points to a dealer who turns it up or to its holder if he takes a trick and exchanges the Dix for the trump card originally turned up. If he makes any other meld on the same trick, he does not get the ten points for Dix.

A SHAVE AND A TRIM

One card sharp who would never dream of using marked cards always carefully trims one end of the Ace of Diamonds, never more than 1/16th of an inch. The short card is replaced and the deck resealed in its pack.

After such a deck is shuffled, riffling the deck either up or down will produce a noticeable "click" when he reaches the trimmed card.

If he riffles from the bottom up and cuts at the break, the Ace of Diamonds will be the top card when the cut is completed. If he riffles from the top down, the Ace of Diamonds will be the bottom card upon completion of the cut.

Throughout an evening's play, he uses the short card as a "locater." On his deal, he will place a known group of cards just beneath it, at the bottom of the deck, and shuffle without disturbing their order. He lets another player make a legitimate cut before he deals. When he comes to the short card, he then knows what the next few cards are.

Melds are valueless unless the player wins at least one trick in play.

After the dealer has turned the trump, the player to his left, or in two-handed, the other player leads any card, and the dealer plays any card he chooses on it. It is not required to follow suit until the stock is exhausted. The high card of suit led wins, unless trumped. The cards rank A (high), 10, K,Q,J and 9 The winner of a trick may meld (or announce) any one combination he holds, but must do it before he draws a card from the stock, laying the combination face up on the table. The meld is immediately scored.

Cards used in one combination cannot be used in another of less or equal value if both melds are in the same class. A lower combination must always be laid down first and any higher added to it. At least one new card from the hand must be added to cards already on the table for each additional meld.

After he has melded, the winner of a trick draws the top card from the stock, his opponent taking the next, and leads for the next trick. Play continues until the stock is used up. After all cards are gone from the stock, the second player on each trick must follow suit and must take the trick if he can; if he cannot follow suit, he must trump if his hand contains any trump.

Only one combination can be melded for each trick taken. Cards used for melds may afterwards be led or played on tricks.

Calling Out—First player to correctly announce he has 1,000 points wins the game, regardless of the opponent's score. A player may call out any time before the last trick is taken, but not after he has picked up his hand to count his points. If he calls when he is not out, he loses the game. If both players are 1,000 and neither has called out, the game continues to 1,250 points.

When a meld is enough to put a player out, he does not have to take another trick to make the meld good. If the ten points for the last trick complete a player's score, he must call out before he takes the trick.

When the hands have been played, points taken in tricks by each player are counted and added to the meld scores.

Three-handed Pinochle is played with 48 cards, and four-hand is played with either 48 or 64, eights and sevens being added. Four-hand is a team game. In both games, players rotate to play or score Dix card. The holder of a second Dix card may also score it, in turn. Dix is a meld in three-hand and is scored with other melds after a trick is won.

Each player in turn exposes his melds and their values are scored. In the four-hand game, partners may not combine hands to form combinations. At least one new card must be added from player's hand for each extra meld. The trump run scores 190 if the K,Q marriage is laid down first, the A,J and 10 being added later.

Once the melds are scored, they are taken back into the hand and a card is led. Players must follow suit and must take the trick if they can. A player holding no card of suit must trump, and in the event the trick has already been trumped, must play a higher trump if he has it, even if he is over-trumping his partner's trick. Player with neither suit nor trump discards card of his choice. Winner of each trick makes the next lead. A player may score all of his melds after taking a trick. In partnership game, both partners may score their melds if either takes a trick.

Game is 1,000 points. In a four-hand game, player "calling out" obligates his partner.

Auction Pinochle With Widow

This is the currently popular Pinochle game, played with 48 cards by three or four persons. If four play, the dealer takes no cards and scores with the two opposed to high bidder.

Three hands of 15 cards each are dealt, three at a time, and three laid aside, face down, after the first round, for a Widow.

Player to the left of dealer bids first and bidding continues until two players in succession pass. Every bid must be at least ten points higher than the last one. A player who passes is permitted to bid in the next round.

At the conclusion of bidding, Widow is turned face up and the high bidder takes them into his hand and calls the trump. He then lays out three cards in place of the widow, with their points counting for him at the end of play. The bidder must discard before melding and no part of his melds may be laid away.

Melds and scoring points are identical to those in two-hand Pinochle. The bidder makes his melds, and since he makes them all at once, the trump sequence counts 150 and there is no count for the royal marriage. Opponents are not allowed to make any melds or to score anything for cards in the tricks they take.

Play then begins, with the successful bidder leading. The rules of Three-hand Pinochle apply to the play.

If the bidder's melds equal his bid, the hand is not played, as only the amount bid can be scored. If the melds do not score enough, he may play the hand and try to win by cards enough to equal his bid. If he succeeds, he scores the amount of his bid. If he turns up the Widow and decides he cannot meet his bid, he may acknowledge and accept a loss equal to his bid, but if he plays the hand and still misses his bid, his loss is doubled in the scoring.

An optional rule makes one suit better than the others. When that suit is trump, the bidder scores double. Another variation is to give substantially higher scores for double melds.

On The Table

Cactus Pete is the legendary gambler who took the poker players of Deadwood, South Dakota, to the cleaners.

He dressed like a prospector. "He sure was a prospector," Belle Starr said. "He found the gold in the pokes of everybody at the poker table. He looked like an ignorant old coot who was ripe for the plucking, and the pros welcomed him into the game.

"He glared around the table and said, 'Boys, I don't mind gittin' beat fair and square, but I won't stand for no cheating.' He pulled a big, shiny, toad-stabber knife from its sheath, a knife with a gleaming six-inch blade, and laid it on the table in front of him. 'The first varmint I catch cheating gets this right through his gizzard,' he threatened.

"The knife stayed on the table in front of him throughout the game. And every time he got the deal, he read the value of every card he dealt to every player. That knife blade was a 'shiner,' and every card was reflected in it. He was the only cheat in the game."

COLD-DECKING

The "Cold Deck Switch" is one of the commonest, simplest, least detectable and most vicious forms of cheating in a private card game. Usually, it is employed only once in the course of an evening's play—for the Big Kill.

A deck of cards that matches the deck in use is set up in advance, so that the "mark" or "chump" will have an excellent hand. It is also stacked so that the dealer or his confederate will have a better one. The stacked deck is concealed in a hold-out up the dealer's sleeve or in a spring clip under the edge of his suit coat.

When the time arrives for the Big Haul, the dealer shuffles the legitimate deck and offers it for a cut. He picks up the cut deck, gets ready to deal—and sneezes violently. He reaches quickly for his handkerchief—and during that second while his hand is beneath the top of the table, the legitimate deck is switched for the cold one. The cards are dealt, and the pigeon is taken to the cleaners.

The cards are not marked, there have been no tricky shuffles, and no unusual moves during the course of the deal. The dealer knows what cards are in every hand and knows that he has the winner. A favorite stack is one that gives the "mark" four Tens and the dealer four Queens.

Some card mechanics are so adept with the hold-out that they can switch decks above the table top, in the course of pulling the cut deck toward themselves, without detection.

As a gambling game, chips may be used at the end of each deal or a running score may be kept of points won and lost by each player, with settlement at the end of the game. The "kitty" is a separate score or pile of chips, which belongs to all the participants in the game. At conclusion of play, the players divide the kitty equally or, if it is in the red, make up its loss equally.

Pinochle is a complex game, requiring considerable skill, and good pinochle players almost invariably clobber poor ones. It is a scientific game in which knowledge of the principles is vital. Many good tips may be found in John R. Crawford's book, *How to Be a Consistent Winner in the Most Popular Card Games,* published in paperback by Dolphin Books. *The Key to Winning Pinochle,* available from Gamblers' Book Club, Las Vegas, is also recommended.

Herman Schneider says, "The people who gamble on Pinochle take the game seriously, and most of 'em play well. Don't expect to beat 'em unless you're good, too. Become familiar with the game through play.

"Pinochle isn't as easy as it looks. If you're playing with opponents who are better 'leaders' than you are, don't bid unless you're pretty sure you can make it. Play of the hand is real important, and there's a lot to learn about it. For example, the Queen's a better lead from a flush than the King is. And Ace of Trumps is a sucker lead, most of the time, unless you've got enough trump to keep leading 'em.

"Play a hand when making it isn't more than two to one against you—except if it's Spades. Don't play a Spade hand unless you've got an even chance. When you're playing against a bidder, try to lead through him. And if he's about to go out, lead trump."

Thirty-One

The player's stake in "Thirty-One" may be three nickels, three dimes, three quarters, or three dollars, with one-third of it payable for each of three losses.

The game is for any number from two to seven players. Four cards are dealt to each player, with values as indicated by the pips, except that face cards count 10. The Ace counts one.

Object of the game is to knock the others out of the game by elimination. Three losses puts a player out, and the last player takes the entire pot.

The game is played in hands. The player to the left of the dealer can either "knock" or improve his hand by drawing a card and discarding one. If he elects to knock, he announces his count. All players then turn their cards face-up and announce their totals. The player with the lowest count pays his first one-third stipend to the pot and a new hand is dealt. If a player reaches 31 before a "knock" is made, all players except the one making 31 put a third of their stake into the pot. As soon as players lose 3/3rds of their stake, they are eliminated.

Last player in the game collects the entire pot. Danny Foxstein, the Ohio Wizard of 31, says "Knock fast, particularly if you have a count of 20 or more, before any player has an opportunity to improve his hand."

The game is fast, easy, and lots of fun.

Snip, Snap, Snore 'Em

Bob Cromie relays this game from his 1845 first American edition of Hoyle's Games, published by Henry Anners of Philadelphia.

"Snip, Snap, Snore 'Em—This is a very laughable game, and is extremely simple. It may be played by any number of persons, and with a complete deck of cards. Each places before him 5¢ or counters as his stock, and all the cards are dealt out in the usual order. The game consists in playing a card of equal value with the person immediately before you, which *snips* him; if the player next to you has a third card of the same value, you are *snapped;* and the fourth produces a *snore*.

"For example, if the elder hand A plays a six and B likewise plays a six, A is snipped and puts one counter into the pool. If C also has a six, B is snapped and pays two into the pool. If D has the other six, C is snored and pays in three. The fourth, of course, is safe, because all four sixes are now played. No person can play out of his turn, but everyone must snip or snap when it is in his power. When anyone has paid into the pool his 5¢, he retires from the game; and the pool becomes the property of the person whose stock holds out longest. The cards are sometimes dealt three or four times before the game is decided; but if the players are reduced to two or three, they only get 13 cards each."

Seven-Twenty-Seven

Seven-Twenty-Seven is a high-low gambling game for from two to ten players.

Object of the game is to come as close to seven or 27 as possible, seven being "low" and 27 "high."

Each player is dealt two cards at the outset, one face up and one face down, and the betting commences. A player with a total of seven points in his first two cards has an unbeatable hand for "low," and will bet as heavily as possible. After all players have either bet or dropped out on the first round, each player is given a choice of taking a third card or standing pat. Betting is permitted on every round until nobody wants to draw any more cards.

At that point, holder of the cards whose total comes closest to seven, either over or under, and the holder of the cards whose total come closest to 27, either under or over, split the pot.

It is a fast-action gambling game, with stakes often running high. Bluffing is prevalent.

Waterloo Sulentic, a rabid Seven-Twenty-Seven fan and heavy winner attributes his winnings to early round passing and courageous bluffing at low—if his opponents stick it out with him—he always has another chance at 27.

Red Dog

Every player, usually not more than seven, antes, and three cards are dealt face down to everyone in the game.

The first player to the dealer's left makes the first bet, and may bet any part of the pot. The dealer then turns up the top card of the deck. If the bettor has a higher card of the same suit in his hand, he collects the amount of the bet. Without a higher card in the same suit, his bet goes into the pot. Each player in rotation bets that he will have a higher card of the same suit as the one the dealer turns up for him.

When the pot becomes empty, everybody antes again. The deal passes from left to right in order. Aces are high and deuces are low.

Carolina Jim is quite an expert at this game—his advice is, "Count the cards—watch for the best opportunity with your three cards to beat the deck turnover—a good counter can increase his odds to win appreciably."

The game is sometimes called High Card Pool.

MARKED CARDS

Gambling supply houses that make a specialty of marked decks continue in business year after year, apparently selling enough of them to remain prosperous. The marking is usually done by hand, and the craftsmanship is excellent.

"Shading" is one of the best methods of card marking, with various white areas of the card backs delicately shaded with ink that matches the deck's printed back. "Blocking out" employs white ink to block out various parts of the back design. Little curlicues on the backs of some decks are made heavier or additionally embellished with matching ink.

All you have to do to detect the usual marked deck is riffle the deck slowly, backs facing you. You'll be treated to a moving picture, similar to the movement in a riffle-through animated cartoon booklet. The markings of the cards are in different places, and they dance around as you riffle.

Big Game

Milton Berle was bored stiff with the conversation about big-game hunting and decided to call a halt to it.

"Last winter when I was in Canada," he announced, "I shot five bucks in one day."

"But you're not allowed to shoot five bucks in one day," a sportsman protested.

"You were in this game?" Berle inquired.

BOARD GAMES

Dominoes

Some time around 1600 A.D., Dominoes first appeared in the Western world, probably deriving from earlier Oriental games. The last strongholds of dominoes as a form of heavy gambling are China and Ireland, although the game vies with darts and skittles as a bar competition in some English pubs.

The only element of chance in Dominoes is the dealing of the pieces. The pieces, small, flat blocks, are bare on the back and have dots similar to those on dice on the other side. Each piece's face is divided into two halves, in each of which there is either a blank or dots, varying in number from one to six. There are double-blank, blank-ace, blank-deuce, etc., up to blank-six, and double-ace, double-deuce, etc., up through double-six—28 dominoes in the set.

The simple Block and Draw games are augmented by Matador, Bergen, Rounce, Muggins, Poker, Euchre, and others. In all games, the pieces are mixed around, face down, on the center of the table, before the game starts.

In the Block game, each player draws seven pieces from the pool. After the first piece is played, every subsequent piece played must match the end of a piece that does not join another. When a player cannot play, he loses his turn. If nobody can play, the set is blocked and the players count the number of spots on the pieces they still hold. If a player is able to play his last piece, he shouts "Dominoes" and wins the hand, scoring the number of spots the rest still have in their possession. Game is usually 100 points.

The Draw game is similar to Block, except that a player who cannot make a play is forced to draw dominoes from the pool until he can or until the pool is depleted.

Bar Bet

The old grifter announced to the men at the bar, "Any one of you, give me any half-dollar you happen to have in your pocket. Put it into my hands behind my back, and I'll bet you a dime I can tell you the date on it without looking at it."

He rarely won the bet. And when he lost, he cheerfully handed the bettor a dime. When the victim asked for his half-dollar back, the old man smiled. "But a part of the bet was that you would give me a half-dollar. You see, even when I lose, I come out all right."

None of his victims ever complained. They were thinking too hard about which of their friends would become their victims on the same bet.

In Muggins, each player draws five dominoes, and the highest double starts play, with play then alternating. The count is by fives. If the player can put down any domino with total spots amounting to five or ten, he adds that number to his score. If a matching piece can be placed so it makes five, ten, 15 or 20 by adding the spots on both ends of the row, that amount is credited to the player's score. With a three at one end and a five at the other, a player putting down a five-deuce would score five. With a double trey at one end, a player who could get a double deuce at the other end would score ten. With a double five at one end and a double deuce at the other, a deuce-four would count 20. If a player fails to state his count when he plays and an opponent calls out "Muggins," he cannot score the points. A player who cannot match draws, as in the draw game. The first player to play his last piece adds to his score the count of the spots still held by his opponents. The game is usually 200 points.

In the Bergen game, each player draws six. The lowest double, called the "double-header," starts play, which then alternates. If there is no double, the player with the lowest piece starts. When a player puts down a piece which makes the ends of the line the same, it is a "double-header." If either end is a double and the next player can make the other end of the same value, it becomes a triple-header. A player who cannot match, draws from the pool. A player who makes domino wins the hand. A hand won by either domino or counting scores one point. A double-header scores two and a triple-header three.

In the Matador game, the player must make up a total of seven, rather than match the pieces. A four requires a three to be played on it, and a six requires a one. Since no piece will score seven with a blank, there are four matadors—the double blank, and three seven-spots: six, ace; five, two; and four, three. The matadors can be played anywhere, at any time. Each player draws three pieces at the start, and the highest double begins play. If a double-four is the lead, the next player must play a three. Without a three in his hand, he must draw until he gets one. The player to domino first counts the spots in the other hand or hands and scores them for himself. Game is usually 100.

Best Bets depend on what particular domino game you are playing. Since the object of the game is to domino, you try to make plays that will force your opponent to draw from the pool, and you also try to play your largest counters before your opponent is ready to domino. Since it is a "numbers" game—either matching or adding to make certain totals, the good player figures out the mathematical possibilities. The pieces already played cut the possibilities of an opponent being able to play on certain numbers.

Shel Factor says, "There's more skill to it than

meets the eye. An old Irishman who's played the game for money for years will beat you blind without half trying. The answer is that he knows his percentages. He'll also lay back and then play a piece he knows will block you. He plays to domino, but he tries to do it when he can catch you with the most points unplayed."

MR. ODDS-MAKER'S BEST BET

Mr. Odds-Maker says, "I recognize the little white spots on the black dominoes, ranging from one to six, but I somehow associate them with a game played with cubes. From what I've heard about the gambling on Dominoes in Ireland, my best bet would be, never play against an old-country Irishman."

Monopoly

During the grim depression years of the 1930's when thousands of people were losing their shirts, Charles B. Darrow became a wealthy man through his invention of the board game, Monopoly, a game in which players speculated mythical fortunes. Copyright on the game is held by Parker Bros., Inc., and detailed rules accompany the board and equipment. In addition to the board, there are a pair of dice, tokens to be used as playing pieces, 32 houses and 12 hotels, two sets of cards for "Chance" and "Community Chest," title deed cards for every property, and "pretend" money in large quantities.

While it is a board game played with dice and tokens, do not be mislead into thinking of it as primarily a children's game. Following a tremendous Monopoly craze, Monopoly has become a standard adult game combining chance and judgement. Among business and professional men, particularly, it has become a popular gambling game.

Players buy, rent and sell properties with the idea of accumulating the most wealth and thus becoming the winner. Each player starts with $1,500 in scrip, with the balance of the money and properties held by the bank—a bank, incidentally, which never goes broke and which may create additional money when necessary. During the course of the game, players bid for various pieces of property. Undeveloped lots, railroads and utilities may be sold in private transactions, and mortgages may be secured from the bank in order to raise cash.

When players enter enthusiastically into the spirit of the game, it can take a long time to play. Consequently, two versions of a "short" game have been approved by Parker Bros. One is the "time limit" game, in which play stops at a stipulated time, when the wealthiest player is declared the winner. The other version has the banker deal two title deed cards to each player at the start, with players immediately paying the bank the printed price on both properties. Only three houses are required on a piece of property before a player may buy a hotel, instead of four houses as in the long game. The first player to go bankrupt leaves the game. When a second player goes bankrupt, the game is over, and the wealthiest player wins. In the standard game, play continues until all but one of the players have gone bankrupt.

Two forms of betting on the game are fairly common. In one, each player puts a stipulated amount, say a dollar, into a pot and the winner takes the pot. In the other, the players play for a stipulated amount per point—say, a penny. At the conclusion, in the regular game, the bankrupt players pay the stipulated sum per point. In the short version where the game ends after two bankruptcies, players remaining in the game pay on the difference between their holdings and the winner's.

MR. ODDS-MAKER'S BEST BET

Mr. Odds-Maker says, "Unless you're already a winning Monopoly player when money's wagered on the game, avoid it like you'd avoid a quarantine sign. I've seen good gamblers become expert at various little-played board games and clean up whenever they could get competition. You see, they invariably know things about the game that their opponents don't. I used to think Backgammon was a simple child's game until I saw two professional gamblers play it."

Chess

Nobody seems to know the origin of chess, which probably stemmed from a Persian game, Shah-mat, but everyone seems agreed that playing the game well requires more skill than is needed in any other table game.

Chess is a game of strategy. There are nearly 170, 000,000,000,000,000,000,000,000 different ways to play the ten opening moves. The only time chance enters the picture is when the player who gets the white pieces is decided by lot. White, which makes the opening move, is always one move ahead of Black.

Contrary to general opinion, chess is easy to learn. It is not too difficult to learn to play a passable game, but becoming an expert is anything but easy. A basic requirement for a good chess player is knowledge of some of the opening "gambits" used by the great Chess masters.

Gambling on chess is matching your skill at the game against that of another player. Most chess games

A chess player who plays for money and wins has a ploy against a new opponent of unknown strength which he says invariably wins.

After the opponent's fifth or sixth move, early in the game, this player smiles and remarks, "I see you've made a study of Capablanca's deliberate sacrifice of his queen in his famous match with Laskar in Paris in 1922."

He says, "The last thing the player does is admit that he never heard of Capablanca's sacrifice of his queen in the game you mentioned — which, of course, never happened. He looks wildly at the board. His queen doesn't seem to be in any danger, but he has apparently made a move inadvertently that will lead to its sacrifice. And he reasons that since you know the move, you also know how to counteract it.

"The more he studies the board, the more befuddled he becomes. If you can't beat a player with this ploy, you have no business competing against him. I've only had it backfire once, when my opponent laughed and replied, 'Oh, no, this isn't the Capablanca gambit at all, although I'll admit it starts from a similar series of moves. I'm trying to set up my men for the attack Alekhine used to win the British championship in 1931. Believe me, it doesn't involve the sacrifice of even a pawn.'

"He beat me. He was not only a better chess player but a better gamesman."

are decided, not by luck but by a player's error. Opportunities for error are almost constant, which creates uncertainty—and uncertainty lends itself to gambling. What intrigues chess devotees about gambling on the game is the minor role played by chance. Players have gambled on chess from the game's creation. There's the classic story of Ivan, The Terrible, on his deathbed, playing Boris Godunov for Ivan's entire treasury.

A Chess board is identical with a checkerboard, and is so placed that each player has a white right-hand corner. Each player has 16 men: eight pawns, two bishops, two knights, two rooks, a king and a queen. Each player's men are lined up at his end of the board, two rows across. White's first row is, in order from left to right, a rook, a knight, a bishop, queen, king, bishop, knight and rook. Black's lineup is the same except that the king and queen are directly opposite the white king and queen. Both queens start on a square of their own color and both kings on squares of opposite color. The second row for each player consists of eight pawns.

Object of the game is to capture or "checkmate" an opponent's king. The king moves only one square at a time, in any direction and can take a piece on any adjacent square not defended by the opponent.

The queen is the most powerful piece on the board and may move any number of unblocked squares in any direction, forward, backward, sideways and diagonally.

The rook is next in strength, and may move forward, backward, sideways, but not diagonally, on unblocked squares.

The bishop may move diagonally in any direction, always on squares of its own color.

The knight moves one square forward, backward or sideways and then one square diagonally. He can move over blocking men and is the only piece that can move prior to movement by the pawns.

A pawn moves one square forward, except on the first move when it may move either one or two squares. The pawn does not move straight ahead to capture an enemy piece, however. It may move right or left diagonally to capture an enemy piece on the diagonally adjacent square.

A king and rook may "castle." In this move, the two pieces are moved simultaneously, the king moving two squares toward the rook and the rook moving to the adjacent square on the opposite side of the king from that which he previously occupied.

A player may not move his king into check nor move one of his intervening pieces that will put his king into check. When a player makes a move that puts the enemy king into check, he must so announce, and the opponent must move his king out of check before he makes any other play, either by moving his king, moving one of his pieces to an intervening square that voids the check, or by taking the piece that is

MR. ODDS-MAKER'S BEST BET

Mr. Odds-Maker says, "Don't play over your head. The better of two players will win consistently. If you lose a real close game with the black pieces, make the same bet on the next game. Remember the White always has the advantage. I've watched chess games where it was apparent to everyone on the sidelines that one player had no business at the same board with his opponent. He was simply outclassed. Play against players whose ability is a known quantity. And learn one opening gambit so thoroughly that you're an expert at it."

checking his king. If he cannot get his king out of check, he is checkmated, and the game is over.

When a pawn reaches the eighth row, his opponent's king row, it may be designated as any piece and assumes that piece's moves. Usually, a player elects to have the pawn become a queen.

Your Guide to Winning Chess, by Fred Reinfeld, published by Follett, is recommended to any chess player who is ambitious to progress from his own class of competition to a higher one.

The only "best bet" advice is elementary. Don't bet on yourself against a player who is more skillful. Play for money only against players of comparable ability.

Checkers

As in chess, the only chance element is determining which player gets the opening move. Also as in chess, the only wager is on the outcome of the game. The rules are simple enough so that checkers has been played by children in all parts of the United States for many years.

As played by experts, checkers is a game of science and strategy, but people who fail to qualify as experts have always played checkers against players of their own caliber with small wagers on the outcome. Every hamlet has its Checker Champ who will take on all comers for small bets. Old patriarchs in city parks who will play anybody for 50c a game win much more often than they lose.

The playing board is identical with a chess board and is placed with a white square in each player's lower right-hand corner. Each player has 12 men, which are placed on his first three rows of colored squares. Two rows of colored squares between the men are vacant.

Players move alternately, the men progressing diagonally forward, a square at a move. The farthest row away from each player is his "King Row," and he tries to move his men across the board to that row. When one of his men reaches "King Row," the man is crowned by having a second man put on top of it, and becomes a king. A king may move either backward or forward, always diagonally and always on the dark squares.

Enemy men are captured by "jumping" them, moving over the occupied space to a vacant diagonal square on the other side. Whenever a jump is possible, the player must take it if the opponent so orders.

The object of the game is to "jump" or capture all of an opponent's men. In the event that a player's men are blocked so that he cannot move, he loses the game.

Checkers, like chess, has many opening gambits, which few casual players know.

Hoyle's Standard Games gives only this advice about playing to win: "It is better to keep the men as near the center of the board as possible . . . Giving away . . . certain men . . . often aids by exposing a greater number of the opponent's men."

Nobody knows whether checkers preceded or followed chess, and there is no record of the present version of the game before the 12th century.

Played by opponents of similar ability, it is a "fun" game and a good gambling game. N. Marks' *Winning Checkers* and W. Ryan's *It's Your Move* are among the oldest standard works on the game, and both aim at improving the reader's skill. *America's Best Checkers,* written by Thomas Wiswell and published by McKay is a more recent book containing much good information.

MR. ODDS-MAKER'S BEST BET

Mr. Odds-Maker says, "The game requires a great deal of concentration. Depending on your opponent, never go into the next room to answer the phone while a game's in progress. Good players head for the King Row as quickly as possible, with 'back-up' men to protect them against heavy losses."

Shaggy Bird Gambling

Myron Cohen tells the story in his book, Laughing Out Loud, *published by Citadel Press, about the bookmaker who acquired a particularly bright mynah bird. The bird became so proficient at English that the bookie taught it some French. Once the bird could say a few sentences in French, he got a Spanish dancer to teach it some Spanish, and the bird became proficient at that language. Then he had one of his runners, Otto Schultz, teach the bird some German.*

He carefully kept the bird's linguistic ability under wraps until one evening when he needed money. He walked into his favorite bar with the mynah bird on his shoulder. The bird attracted attention, naturally, and the bookie bragged that it could speak three languages besides English. The bartender was skeptical, just as the bookie had expected, and wound up making a $50 bet.

The bookie talked to the bird in French without getting the slightest response. Then he barked out some German phrases. Still no response. Spanish did no better.

The bartender took the $50 wager from the bar and stuck it in his pocket as the bookie stalked out, the mynah bird still on his shoulder. Once outside, the bookie screamed, "I oughta wring your blasted neck. Do you realize, you just cost me $50?"

"Don't be a jerk," the mynah bird protested. "Just think of the odds you'll be able to get in that joint tomorrow!"

A NEW SHELL GAME

The ancient shell game in which the gullible gambler bets he can pick the one of three English Walnut shells that has a little rubber pea beneath it has been successfully revived by a crook who stages "Carnival Nights" for charity benefits.

The pea he uses is a little ball of steel wool covered with liquid latex that has been tinted to match the coloring of plastic wood. Actually, he uses three such peas.

A tiny Alnico magnet is imbedded in plastic wood at the top of each walnut shell, covered with the plastic so it can't be seen. A pea clings to the magnet in the top of each shell.

The operator has the three shells on his table and lifts all three to show there is nothing (?) inside any of them. He puts the pea he is showing under the shell it originally came from, rolling it to the top and the magnet as he does so.

He moves the three shells around until he gets a bet. He lifts the shell the victim points to and shows there is nothing beneath it. He puts it down and lifts another, showing that it, too, is empty. Then with his left hand, he gives the third shell a sharp rap on the table top, saying "*This* was the right one." The rap dislodges the pea, and he lifts the shell to show that the "mark" has guessed wrong. He puts the pea back under the shell it came from and starts over again.

The old-time grifter did it by sleight-of-hand, with only one pea.

Mah-Jongg

The ancient Chinese game of ma-tsiang or sparrows was trademarked by a manufacturer as "Mah-Jongg" when introduced to the Western world. Basically, it is a form of rummy played with tiles rather than cards. Long a popular gambling game in China, Japan, Korea and other Oriental countries where gambling has always thrived, it became a fad in the United States during the 1920's and waned in popularity during the depression years that followed.

The first thing you need, if you intend to play Mah-Jongg , is a Mah-Jongg set, an important part of which is an attractive and colorful set of 144 tiles. The complex rules for playing and scoring are included with the set.

There are three suits—bamboos, circles and characters—and each suit has nine ranks. There are also the Four Winds, the Four Seasons, Four Flowers and red, green and white Dragons. To start with, the tiles are face down, as in dominoes. Three of four players take 13 tiles and the fourth takes 14. Winning hands are achieved by drawing and discarding tiles.

The winner is the first player to assemble four sets of three and a pair, or seven pairs, or a run of 13 with a pair of any number in the run. Payment of bets is similar to that in dominoes, except for a complex system of cumulative doubling which may take total scores to astronomical heights. This cumulative doubling makes it difficult to set stakes that will not prove excessive.

Because there are 144 tiles, rather than 52 cards, and the suits and combinations are different from those in rummy, it is extremely difficult to apply the law of mathematical chance that governs rummy games. But the mathematical probabilities are always present, whether a player is able to determine them or not.

As in rummy games, the outcome depends on the luck of the draw and the skill of the play. A *Mah-Jongg Handbook,* by Eleanor Ross Whitney, published by the Charles E. Tuttle Company, is an authoritative work on the game.

MR. ODDS-MAKER'S BEST BET

Mr. Odds-Maker says, "Your best bet in Mah-Jongg is to get an Oriental to sit in for you. He'll at least know what the game is all about. Frankly, I don't."

Yotsy

In recent years, a game played with five dice has become popular. Known by various names, including "Chice" (your choice with dice) and Yotsy, slightly different rules are in effect in various communities. The E. S. Lowe Company, Inc., version has the registered name of Yahtzee, the rules for which are copyrighted.

A score pad is necessary to play the game. It is divided into eleven or more boxes for each player, depending on the version being played, and each player tries to score in all boxes.

The players in turn roll five dice from a dicecup. A player has the option of three rolls on each round. For example, if he rolls three fours on the first shake, he would leave the three fours on the table and shake two dice on his second shake. Should he roll a fourth four on the second shake, he would put it with the other three and roll one die on the third shake, trying for five of a kind.

After his play, which may consist of one, two or three rolls at his option, the player enters his score for that round in the box where it will be most beneficial.

The score card looks something like this, depending on the version that is being played:

PLAYER	Geo	Clem	Mary	Edna	Milt	Roz
ACES	2	3	3	3	2	3
DEUCES	6	6	4	6	6	2
TRAYS	6	9	9	9	9	9
FOURS	12	12	12	12	12	16
FIVES	15	15	10	15	20	15
SIXES	18	18	18	24	18	18
3 of a Kind	18	18	18	15	15	18
4 of a Kind	16	20	12	16	16	20
Full House	28	28	28	28	28	28
Straight	0	0	35	0	35	0
5 of a Kind	0	0	0	50	0	0
High	21	23	20	0	27	23
Low	20	18	0	24	21	22
TOTAL	162	170	169	202	207	174

A typical Yotsy score pad.

On the first round, the player has a choice of trying to score in any of the boxes. Once a score is entered in a box, it stands and cannot be moved to another box where it might also fit, so that on the last round, he has only one box open and must try to score in it.

The scoring is simple. In the upper six boxes, a player scores whatever total he rolls for the elected die face. For example, if he rolls four fives, he would score 20; if he rolls three deuces, he would score six. Two Aces would score two in the ace box.

The 3 of a kind box may score from 3 to 18, depending on which die face comes up three times. The same is true of the 4 of a kind box. The Full House box is one of the bonus boxes and scores a flat 28, whether the full house is sixes and fives or deuces and aces. A straight, another bonus box, scores 35. Five of a Kind scores 50. The High and Low boxes are open to fill with throws that cannot be fit into any other boxes. The total of the faces up on the five dice is added together and constitutes the score for the box. If either box is already filled, the total for the other box must fit. For example, if a throw of 23 were entered in high, a throw of 23 or more could not be entered in low and low would be scored a 0. If 23 were already entered in the Low box, a score of 23 or lower could not be entered in High, and High would be scored as a 0. Five of a Kind is the most desirable box to fill, since it scores highest, but it is also the most difficult.

With the scoring as illustrated, a game ends at the conclusion of the 13th round. Scores are totaled, and the player with the highest score is the winner.

The player does not have to decide on the box he wishes to fill until he has completed his three shakes on a round. For example, he may have three deuces and be trying for the Deuce box. If on his last shake, he throws two other deuces, he would naturally elect to use the 5 of a kind box. Should he roll, for example, two fours on his third shake, he would probably elect to fill the Full House box.

When playing for money, scoring may be done in various ways. In some localities, each player antes at the start of a game and high score takes the pot. Some players pay off with low paying high a stipulated amount, second low paying second high, etc. One popular scoring method has each loser paying the holder of high score a penny for each point difference.

Stakes may be as high or as low as you care to make them. Side bets as to whether or not a player will fill a specific box are common. Another popular side bet is which of two players' "High" will be higher, or "Low," lower.

Friendly Craps

Any adult male who doesn't know the rules of the home crap game has led a sheltered life. The main differences from Bank Craps, the casino game, are that players bet with each other rather than against the house, there is no layout to keep bets straight, and the odds on any number are whatever some player in the game will offer.

Because so few home crap-shooters know the correct odds, an informed player can bet even money on situations where he should be offering 6 to 5, 3 to 2 or even 2 to 1 odds. Correct odds are explained in the Casino Games section.

The value of the "house" men and the layout in Casino Craps are apparent in private crap games where both bets and points are often confused. Since the shooter is covered by other players in the game, there is sometimes confusion as to what part of a bet a player is covering.

Despite these problems, the home crap game is always able to find eager players. Particularly at conventions and meetings, adjournment is often followed by "a friendly game."

Tom James says, "Whenever you can, try to 'bank'

the game as much as possible. Some of the players are rank amateurs and most of the players who know the odds aren't expert Money Managers. Whenever a shooter says, 'Five bucks I make my point,' cover it fast. You've got an edge on such bets that's almost sure-fire. On some points, you've got a percentage advantage of 100 percent.

"It's interesting to me that the guy who goes into a home crap game with the most ready cash on him, the guy who 'bulls' the game, who banks it, is nearly always the big winner.

"If you're not in a position to bank the game, lay back and make good bets—even-money bets—against a point being made, for example. And follow the same Money Management plans when you're shooting that you'd follow in a casino game.

"There's nearly always at least one dude in a home game who has a hot streak. His trouble is that he doesn't know how to handle it. Either he drags his winnings after every pass or he lets everything ride, time after time, trying to see how much he can build up before he craps out.

"Cover him, either way. Figure it out for yourself. The bank does fine in a casino crap game, covering all bets. If you can do the same thing in a home game and not offer correct odds, you should walk out with plenty of loot."

CROOKED DICE

If variety is the spice of life, it is also the key word in the world of crooked dice.

Most basic of all are the mis-spotted dice, commonest among them being dice with which it is impossible to roll a seven. Another set has double the usual number of combinations that will make seven or eleven. Mis-spotted dice are never left in a game for any appreciable length of time, because they are too easy for an alert player to spot.

The crudest "loaded" dice won't pass the Water Test, in which a pair of dice are dropped several times into a tumbler of water. But the water test won't reveal "Suction" dice, "roughing," or razor-edge work. Neither is it a sure-fire indication of beveling or mis-shapen dice.

Today's dice mechanic seldom has the nerve to try "switching" in a casino game, where he is usually detected in short order. He operates mostly in illegal floating crap games and in "friendly" games—particularly, big games that develop at trade shows and conventions.

Private games are almost never properly watched for cheating, and the "switch" can be as simple as rolling the dice off the table and making the switch in the process of retrieving them. The dice mechanic may switch a pair of six-ace flats, mildly loaded, into a game and leave them for the duration of play, always betting against the shooter and betting light on his own roll. These dice will come up craps and seven more often than anything else and will make it extremely difficult for a shooter to make a point.

Opaque dice can be more heavily loaded than transparent ones, but today's dice hustler doesn't want sure-shot loads, anyway. They're either so hot or so cold that they attract undue attention. The smart hustler is happy with a lightly loaded pair of dice that will give him a 20 or 25 percent edge over normal probability.

THE BLANKET ROLL

Would you believe that some dice experts can roll a pair of dice out across a blanket, a bedspread or a soft rug and control the numbers?

You better believe it, and don't bet that they can't do it with your dice.

They put the dice into their cupped palm with the two sixes facing each other and the two aces on the outside, which means that with a precision roll, the possibility of "craps" has been eliminated. Other possibilities for a seven are lined up so that if the pair are rolled in perfect unison, a seven has a better than good chance of coming up.

If the shooter doesn't seven on his first role, the dice are then stacked in the palm to try to make the point. As the palm is closed, the dice are vigorously clicked against each other to simulate shaking, but their position isn't disturbed. The roll onto the soft surface is a symphony of rhythm and timing that is sheer art.

The dice are perfectly honest. How do you prove that the blanket roll expert is cheating? You don't. You simply refrain from betting against him when he has the dice — or bet with him. Of course, if you bet with him, knowing what he's doing, you're cheating, too.

Backgammon

Basically, a defensive game, Backgammon is a race to a finish line between two players. Each player's goal is to get all his pieces off the board before his opponent accomplishes that end. The throw of dice determines how quickly or how slowly the men will reach their destination.

The game is played with 30 checkers, 15 white and 15 black, placed on the board as illustrated. The left-hand half of the board is called the "Inner Table" and contains numbers 1 to 6 and 19 to 24. The right-hand half is called the "Outer Table", and the division between the two halves is referred to as the "Bar."

Here is a Backgammon board:

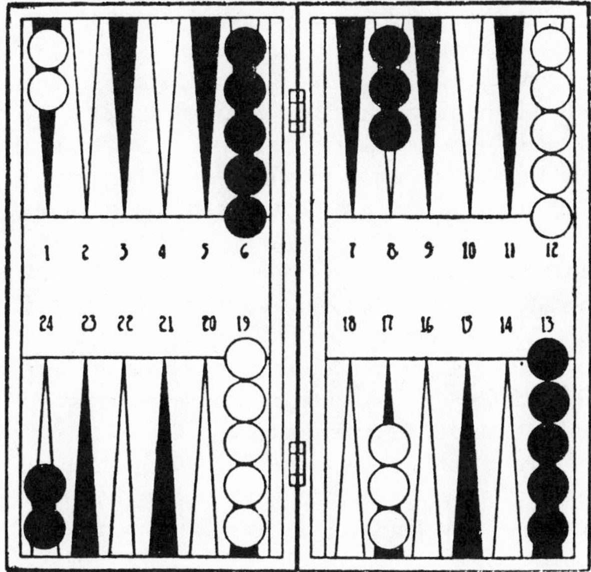

From "Look It Up in Hoyle." Edited by Thomas M. Smith. Copyright © Arco Publishing Company, Inc., 1969. Published by Arco Publishing Company, Inc., New York.

The game opens with the men placed as illustrated. The lower half of the Inner Table is the Home Table for White and the upper half is the Home Table for Black. Men are moved from the opponent's home table around to the player's home table to the finish. The player who first throws off all his men wins. Two dice decide the move of the men, each player getting a throw in turn and moving any of his men as far as the dice number indicates. Once a player has all his men in his Home Table, he throws them off according to the throw of the dice, points in the home table being numbered from one to six. If a player should throw, say a five-four, he has the option of moving one piece five points and another four or moving one man five points and then four more. The point to which the dice bring a man must be vacant or have only the player's men on it or not more than one of the opponent's men. If two of the opponent's men are on it, the point is closed and the move can't be made. Only one man on a point is called a Blot, and if the opponent can reach this point by a move, he can capture a man and place him on the Bar. The man's owner must, in his turn, enter that man in his opponent's home table on a point corresponding to his number on the dice. He must do this before he moves any other man. If the two points he throws on the dice are closed on the board, the player can't play and loses his turn.

If a player throws "Doublets," he plays the throw twice. This means that with double sixes, a player may move one man 24 points or two men 12 points or four men six points, but each sixth point must be available. A player can pass over any number of men on intervening points between a man played and the point reached by the dice number, and a single man belonging to the opponent is not captured in this case.

Once a player's men are all in his home table, he begins to throw off, according to the numbers coming up on the dice. Throwing a six-two, he may throw off one man from the six point and one from the two point. If he hasn't a man on the two points, he may move up any man two points. If he hasn't a man on the six point, he may throw off any man from the highest point occupied. If a player begins to throw off, the opponent captures a man in a Blot and puts him on the Bar, the piece must be entered in the opponent's home table and brought home again before any more men can be thrown off. If an opponent has taken off some of his men when the other player finishes, a single game is won by the latter. If the opponent hasn't thrown off any man, the game counts double and is called a "Gammon." If the opponent not only has all his men on the table but still has one or more men in the inner table of the winner, the game is called a "Backgammon" and counts triple.

Hoyle's Standard Games mentions "a number of innovations which create additional interest when the game is played for stakes." Chief among these are the automatic and optional doubles and the Chouette (pronounced shoe-et) or team play.

"Automatic doubles" establishes the fact that a tie when throwing the dice for the first play doubles the stakes. "Optional doubling" may be done at any time a player's turn comes and he thinks he is ahead. The opponent may either accept the double or forfeit the game at the original stakes. The option of redoubling belongs to the player who was doubled, so that neither player may double twice in succession.

The Chouette makes Backgammon a game for any number of players up to six. All the players throw two dice and the highest becomes the "Man in the Box" who plays alone against all the other players. Second highest becomes Captain of the Team, and the others rank in order of the numbers they cast, with third highest second in command. Team members may consult as to plays and doubles, but the captain's decision stands. If the Man in the Box issues a double and the Captain accepts, a member of the team who disagrees may withdraw by paying

A SMOOTH DICE-SWITCH

A Cicero, Ill., dice hustler is a regular attendant at many Chicago conventions, usually as a guest of a registered conventioneer who gets a part of the Cicero Flash's crap game take. The attache case this fellow carries is loaded—and loaded is the right word—with dice of every known size, color and composition, loaded for every contingency.

He spends hours in a Cicero pool hall practicing his "switch," and it is beautiful to see. Instead of picking up the dice from the table with his left hand, he scoops them toward his right hand, which has been below the table top and comes up to take them as he gives them a flip into the hand.

Only, he doesn't flip them into the right hand. He flips them up his right sleeve, much as a magician "sleeves" coins and other small objects. His right hand, in a continuous move, comes out over the table top with the dice plainly visible—only these are the "loaded" dice that were already in his palm while his hand was below table-top level.

Rarely does a die miss his cuff. When it does, it clatters to the floor and he bends over to pick it up. To others in the game, it looks as if he simply failed to catch the die in his hand—and while he's retrieving it, he can make a crude switch and get away with it.

---

his losses up to that time to the team. Remaining members of the team assume the withdrawer's interest and win or lose more, pro rata. Should the Man in the Box win, he is paid the accumulated stakes by each member of the Team. The Captain of the team moves down to the lowest position on the team and each members moves up one place. If the Man in the Box loses, he pays each member of the team and goes to the foot of the team, while the Captain of the winning team moves over to become Man in the Box.

Hindering the opponent's progress is an important strategy in Backgammon. Leaving as few Blots as possible cuts down the opponent's chance of capturing men and forcing them to start over. The point next to the Bar on both sides is called the Bar Point and should be closed on both sides as quickly as possible. When a player is forced to leave a Blot, he should cover it as quickly as possible.

A beautiful new book, *The Backgammon Book,* by Oswald Jacoby and John R. Crawford, published by The Viking Press, is the equivalent of a college course in the game, revealing complexities and subtleties that convince the reader Backgammon is definitely not a children's game. The consistent Backgammon winner is an expert.

Errit Smithe says, "It would do most Martengale System gamblers good to play a little high-pressure Backgammon and see how the Double-Up can mount. With optional doubles and redoubles, what looks at the start like a possible one-buck loss can soon have you screaming for help."

A Backgammon expert recommends, "Make your five point as quickly as possible, then your Bar point and then your four.

"In a running game, get your men into your inner board as fast as you can.

"Never agree to unlimited automatic doubles unless you're willing to play for extremely high stakes. Know the odds before you double or redouble. Don't accept doubles that are stacked against you. Whenever the odds are more than two to one against you, turn a double down. It's always to your advantage to have the doubling cube on your side of the table. Regardless of how great an advantage your opponent has, he can't double you—but if the complexion of the game changes, you can double him. Against an expert whose doubles are sound, you will lose less money in the long run refusing his doubles.

"A good gambler who knows Backgammon doubles with a 20 percent edge and does whatever he can to keep increasing the stakes as long as he continues to hold the edge.

"A good gambler who learns to play good Backgammon has the added advantage of knowing more about a pair of dice than his opposition. He knows, for example, that a total of seven is going to come up more often than any other. He knows that the odds against throwing a 12 are 35 to 1. He knows which numbers have the best chance of being thrown by both himself and his opponent. That's a substantial edge at certain stages of the game.

"Know who you're playing against. Is he a quick doubler or a slow doubler? Does he accept doubles, even when they're bad? How much of an expert is he? The number of Backgammon experts increases each day. Unless you qualify, going up against a brilliant player gives you a lot in common with a lamb being led to slaughter."

Acey-Deucy

This is a variant of Backgammon in which a roll of 2-1 with the dice gives the player certain privileges, as choice of any doublet and a second roll. Unlike standard Backgammon, the game starts with all the men off the board and entering by throws of the dice.

Rules for Acey-Deucy are quite flexible, differing in various sections of the country

MR. ODDS-MAKER'S BEST BET

Mr. Odds-Maker says, "There are good Backgammon players who don't know the probabilities with a pair of dice and lose games because of it. Out of 36 throws, the chances are that a double of each number will come up only once. A 6 and a 5 will come up only twice, as will most other combinations. Six, seven and eight are the easiest combinations to throw, so you can count on their turning up more often. Don't be too quick to double in Backgammon unless you have your opponent over a barrel."

Cribbage

Along with Bezique, Cribbage is one of the oldest card games involving a scoring board. A deck of 52 cards, a Cribbage board and four pegs are the physical equipment for this two-handed game. While other numbers of cards are sometimes used, six-card is the commonest game.

Sixty-one points constitutes a game, and the scoring is done with pegs, inserted into holes on the board. The player marks his first score with one of his pegs. His second score is marked with his second peg, counting from the first. When he moves again, the back peg is used to count ahead from the front one, throughout the play. Face cards and tens count ten and pip cards count their numerical value.

Players cut for deal, with high card dealing. Each player gets a hand of six cards, of which they place two on the table, face down. These four cards are called "the crib" and are the property of the dealer. The remainder of the deck is cut by the non-dealer and the dealer turns up the top card. If it is a Jack, he immediately scores two points.

The other player leads a card, calling it. If it is a seven, he calls "Seven." The dealer, playing an eight, calls "Fifteen," scoring two points. The other player plays again and calls the increased score until the total reaches 31 or as near to it as possible without going over. At each 15 count the player scores 2 points—pairs also score 2 points, triples 6, and quadruples 12 points. If the count reaches 29 or 30 and a player's opponent has only cards of a value above two, he calls "Go," and the opponent scores one point. The remaining cards in the hand, if any, are again counted until all are used.

The game is divided into two phases, counting and scoring. When the points in play have been marked on the board and the counting is over, each player then scores his hand and tallies the amount of scoring points he has. The dealer counts both the points in his hand and in the "crib." Another deal is made and the hands played, until one of the players reaches 61 on the board.

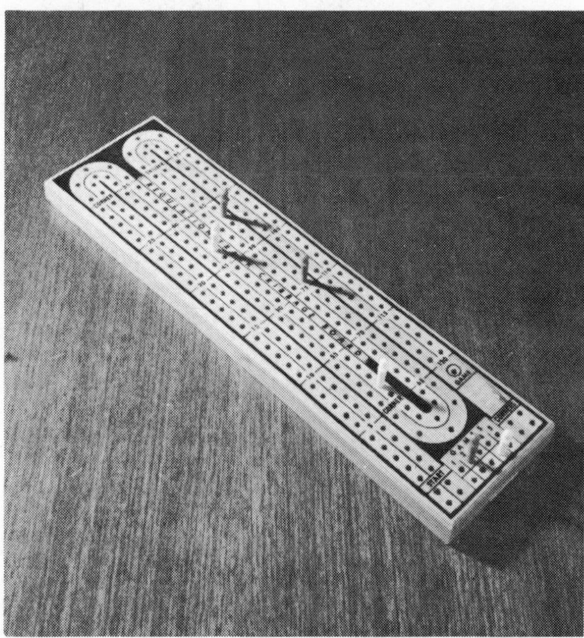

Each Cribbage player keeps his own score by moving two pegs on the special Cribbage board.

COUNTING AND SCORING

Fifteens—Whenever a player calls the number 15 in play, he counts two. At the conclusion of play, each player scores his hand for 15's, getting two points for every combination of 15 he can get by adding his cards together. With a King and two tens along with a five-spot, for example, a player has three two-count 15's, or six points. The dealer totals the "crib" for 15's in the same way as his hand, but cannot combine his hand with the crib to make combinations. The only card added to either hand in combinations is the turn-up card, which is counted in both.

Pairs—Every pair made in the play of a hand counts two. To "pair," the player plays a card of the same denomination played by his opponent. If the dealer plays a nine and his opponent plays a nine next, without exceeding 31, the opponent counts two points. In pairing, face cards must match, King for King, Queen for Queen and Jack for Jack. At the end of the deal, the turn-up card may be used by both sides in pairing.

Pair-Royal—This is three cards of a kind, either in the hand or crib, or occurring in play, as three Aces, three tens, etc. In play, the player who plays the second matching card scores two for a pair and the other player, if he plays the third of a kind, scores six for a pair-royal. In scoring at the end of a hand, a pair-royal in the hand or the crib also counts six. Holding a pair which the turn-up card matches also counts six.

Double Pair-Royal—Four of a kind makes this combination, and the score for it is 12, whether in play, in the hand or in the crib. The turn-up card can be used to make it. If one player makes a pair-royal by playing the third of a kind, the other player who plays the fourth of a kind gets a double pair-royal and 12 points.

Sequences—Three or more sequences, regardless of suit, score a point per card, in counting or in scoring. In scoring sequences at the end of a hand, the turn-up card may be used. Since a minimum sequence is three cards, the minimum sequence score is 3. With two tens, two nines and an eight, the player may score 12 sequence points, since he can make four sequences.

Jack—A Jack of the same suit as the turn-up card gives the player a point, which he scores when he tallies his hand. If such a Jack is in the crib, it scores a point for the dealer. If the turn-up card is a Jack, the dealer immediately counts two points.

Flush—A flush is tallied only in scoring the hand or crib and consists of four or more cards of the same suit. The player having it scores one point for each card in the flush. A flush in the crib does not score unless it is of the same suit as the turn-up card.

At the end of the hand, the non-dealer counts first. If he has enough points to "show out," (score game!) he wins the game, although the dealer may have enough points to put him more than out.

In single-game play, there is a cut for deal on each game.

A "Lurch" is when one player scores 61 before his opponent reaches 31, and counts as a double game when agreed on by the players before play starts.

Clement McQuaid's dad—an authority on winning at Cribbage—says, "Fives are the most valuable cards in the deck, since they make 'Fifteen' with any of 16 ten-count cards in the pack.

"Best cards to spoil the dealer's crib are a King, with a ten, nine, eight, seven, six or Ace, or a Queen, with nine, eight, seven, six or Ace. Never put a Jack in your opponent's crib.

"Best cards for your own crib are a pair of fives, five and six, five and a ten-counter, three and two, seven and eight, four and one, nine and six and similar pairs.

"Whenever you can hold a pair-royal in your hand, you should usually lay out the other two cards for the crib, unless they are extremely hazardous.

"The first dealer has an advantage.

"With a bad hand, save low cards to score with a 'Go.' The safest lead is a Four."

MR. ODDS-MAKER'S BEST BET

Mr. Odds-Maker says, "If you have a four in your hand, lead it. There's no other lead as safe. With a poor hand, hold on to your low cards on the chance that you may be able to score a go with them. And whatever you do, keep one eye on the score, every minute."

Liar's Poker

All you need to play Liar's Poker is one or more other players and a big supply of dollar bills. The bills are the equipment for play and also the stakes.

Here's how the game is played. Each player takes one dollar bill out of his stake and places it face (serial number) side down in the center of the table. The bills are shuffled together then each player extracts a bill from the shuffled pile. Care should be taken not to flash or expose the serial number of your bill to your opponents. U. S. and Canadian dollar bills have eight numbers in their serial number, the idea of the game is to use the serial numbers of *all* players' bills to make up the best "hand." Now, how do you figure the numbers on your opponents' bills when you haven't seen them? That's what makes Liar's Poker the fascinating game that it is!

One player opens the game by bidding, say a pair of nines (Aces are ones, tens are zeros and either may be ranked high or low before the game starts), the player to the opener's left then must either overbid the opener with, say three threes or challenge the opener. Then the next player must either over-call the prior bid, or the opener, if challenged, or challenge. This continues until all players have had an opportunity to either over-call the previous bid or challenge the last bid. Passing or checking is not permitted.

When all opposition has challenged the last bidder, serial numbers are exposed and the bidder counts the numbers that appear on the bills. If the numbers fall short of the bid he must pay off all

---

A Marksman

The young army sergeant in the audience was wearing the most impressive array of medals Johnny Carson had ever seen. His curiosity aroused, he buttonholed the young man after the show.

"I've never seen so many medals on one man in my life," he said. "You must be a real sharpshooter."

The sergeant grinned. "You're half right, Johnny," he answered.

"What do you mean, half right?"

"I won most of these medals from the other guys in my outfit," he explained. "I'm not much of a sharpshooter, but I'm a real crapshooter."

players. On the other hand, if the numbers equal or exceed his bid, all players must pay him. Liar's Poker gets its name from the fact that when a player bids he doesn't necessarily have to have those numbers on his bill. The Poker half of the name is rather misleading because there are no flushes and a straight or full house looks real puny against six tens or eight deuces.

This table will give you a fast grasp of the game:

PLAYER NUMBER	BIDS				PLAYER'S SERIAL NUMBERS
	#1	#2	#3	#4	
1	2-2's	4-9's	6-6's	C	13464608
2	3-3's	C	C	C	01133485
3	4-2's	C	C	C	22273546
4	C	5-5's	7-5's	9-5's	30556590
5	4-6's	6-4's	C	C	87544129
6	4-8's	6-5's	8-5's	C	32667545

C=Challenge

Player No. 4 loses on his bid of 9-5's, the total number of fives on his opponents bill is one short of his bid of nine. He pays everyone and those bills just used are retired, fresh ones brought out, put in the middle and shuffled for the next game. After the first game, the winner or loser always opens bidding.

Noting the table, you'll see that player number 1 lied on his first and second bids and players number 5 and 6 lied on their first bids. Player number 1 was misled by number 5's first bid of 4-6's and went to 6-6's on his third bid and caught two challenges for his trouble.

Anyone who challenges out of turn is fined. This fine is usually a pay-off to all players. State this rule at the beginning of the game. An out-of-turn challenge is extremely unfair to the last bidder and takes the pressure off the person who should be challeng-lied on his first and second bids and players numbers ing or increasing a bid.

Moe James says, "This is definitely one of my favorite games. Skill and strategy payoff big and when the stakes are 5, 10, or 20 dollar bills instead of ones a good player can make a real nice bundle in a few hours time.

"Strategy can be defined as offensive and defensive. The offensive player goes for the big win, the payoff from everybody. The defensive is satisfied with the smaller income of good challenges and an occasional big win. There are times when you're in a tough spot, the last bid was a good one, maybe even a great one, and you're holding a couple of his numbers. You know your opposition and you figure the bid was right on. The smart player will always prefer losing one instead of five if there are six in the game, so challenge, put the heat on the next guy in line. He may overbid and you know he's got a loser or he, too, may challenge and reinforce your position. An offensive strategy works well against conservative players and conversely, a defensive strategy is good against several agressively offensive players.

"Also, spot habitual liars early. Remember their bids and check their bills. I've seen habitual liars consistently draw challenges on their opening bids and lose heavy. They can't bear telling the truth early in the game and some never wise up. You can really hurt 'em in two or three man games. When you've got a good bill, three or four of a kind, don't give it away by bidding it up right away, lay back and ambush 'em when it'll count. Vary your play as far as lying and telling the truth. Don't get in either rut. Everybody has always got the equipment for this game on him. Play it smart and you'll be one of the best equipped guys around!"

Marbles

One of the first forms of gambling indulged in by most males is playing marbles "for keeps."

The game has many variations, but is normally played with a circle scratched into the ground. The "object" marbles are lined up in a row, a specified distance apart, within the ring.

The shooter must shoot his "shooter" marble from outside the ring, holding it between his thumb and forefinger, aiming it at the "object" marbles and shooting with sufficient force to knock one or more of the "commies" or common clay marbles within the ring to the area outside the ring boundary. His "shooter" marble must not go outside the ring.

In the most skillful versions of the game, the "shooter" must touch the forefinger large knuckle to the ground while shooting. A form of shooting permitted in some areas is called "drop-eyes," in which the shooter picks up his marble and holds it approximately the same distance above the object marbles as it was away from them on the ground. He then drops the "shooter" marble, attempting to hit and dislodge a "commie."

Expert players sometimes gamble for "aggies," or agate marbles, and other superior marbles that are much more expensive than the baked-clay "commies." Some early-day glass marbles with intricate color patterns are now quite valuable as collector's items, and some are formed from what are now designated as semi-precious stone.

The game retains its popularity from generation to generation, and local rules, which vary from locality to locality, remain constant. In recent years, national marble tournaments with valuable prizes have become popular sales promotions for manufacturers appealing to the youth market.

Little girls seldom play the game. "Jacks" is their substitute.

A STICKY SITUATION

A Southern California dice hustler uses a switch for bringing loaded dice into the game that requires more timing than dexterity. The optical illusion it creates is most convincing.

The fellow has the palm of his left hand coated with "Adhero," a colorless, invisible liquid which magicians use to make light objects cling to their finger-tips, apparently held in place by personal magnetism. He gathers up the straight dice in his left hand. His right cupped palm, hanging naturally at his side, contains the pair of loaded dice.

He makes a tossing motion with his left hand toward the right, turning the left hand face down in the process. The right palm clicks the dice together as it opens. The left hand drops to his side and he begins shaking the dice with his right, meanwhile putting his left hand into his left pants pocket, where he scrapes the clinging dice from the palm.

The tossing motion is natural and the left hand is opened, palm down, following it, so other players in the game never question but what the dice they see in the hustler's right palm are the original ones.

Frisco

The late Joe Frisco, talented cigar-chewing, stuttering comedian, loved to gamble, and particularly enjoyed playing the horses, win or lose. When he worked, he made big money. If he lost it, another engagement would bring more. Unfortunately, his salary demands were so high that jobs were infrequent, and during periods when he wasn't "holding," he borrowed money from other comedians and performers, all of whom loved him.

One day, he hit Bing Crosby for $10 to bet on the first race at DelMar, and his horse ran out. Before the second race, he was back for a second ten-spot. Crosby gave him $10 after every race, up through the seventh.

Joe failed to show up for money to bet on the eighth race, and it was almost post time. Crosby found him and asked, "Joe, do you want a ten for the eighth race?"

Frisco looked at him coldly. "G-get l-lost, Crosby," he said. "You're b-b-bad luck."

Frisco liked to tell about the time he went to Las Vegas in an $8,000 Cadillac and returned to Hollywood in a $70,000 Greyhound bus.

When he found out he had terminal cancer, he announced blithely to his friends, "I got Big Casino." The Masquers Club held a banquet in his honor, and Joe sat on the dais, attended by a nurse. He got more laughs than any of the stellar performers and celebrities who spoke, which was par for the course. Most of the stories that were told dealt with his horse-betting.

When a group of his cronies went to the hospital to visit him, Joe immediately organized a betting pool based on the time it would take an intravenous feeding to go from the suspended bottle through the tube and into his body. An intern passing by put $1 into the pool. A few minutes later, a nurse came in, saw how slowly the fluid was draining from the bottle and gave it a sharp shake.

"The fix is on, boys," Joe shouted. "I shoulda realized that intern knew something."

A doctor came in and asked him how he felt. "Th-that d-depends on what h-happens in the f-fourth at Hollywood P-park," Joe replied.

When the doctor left, one of his friends asked Joe if he'd like them to send a clergyman to see him. Joe shook his head. "D-don't worry, boys," he said. "Old c-crapshooters never die; they just f-fade away."

A few days before his death, a $10 bet on a 20-to-1 shot paid off. The nurse said, "How wonderful!"

Joe grinned at her. "T-two b-bills is about as much use to m-me right now as a t-television set in a bridal suite."

Two days before the end, a doctor hinted tactfully to him that he wasn't making any progress and, in fact, wasn't holding his own.

"D-don't talk like a bookie, doc," Frisco said. "G-gimme the correct odds."

Some of his relatives came from Dubuque, Iowa, his home town, for the funeral. "I know they say Joe gambled and drank," one of them said, "but he was a God-fearing, religious man at heart."

Cully Richards, a West Coast comedian and one of Joe's closest friends, nodded hearty agreement. "That's for sure," he agreed. "I remember one time when he had 100 bucks on a 40 to one shot, and he prayed for that nag like crazy." ♠

BOOK TWO

GAMBLING AT THE CASINOS

Mr. Odds-Maker tells you how to manage your money, how to make the best bets at every game in the casinos from slots to casino poker.

The Casino Games

The word "casino" connotes glamour and excitement, even to the person who's never patronized one. Monte Carlo, to the average gambler, is the Magic Mecca, the grand-daddy of casinos, the legendary spot where gambling reaches its romantic peak.

Monte Carlo has the tradition, but Las Vegas has the play. The gross "handle" of Las Vegas casinos makes Monte Carlo look like Amateur Night at the Bijou.

Other Nevada localities have casinos, too. Certainly, Harold's Club in Reno is one of the most widely advertised ones. Lake Tahoe has beautiful casinos in a beautiful setting. Both Reno and Tahoe offer attractive entertainment to lure customers. Puerto Rico has attractive and busy casinos, and they do a good volume of business.

Las Vegas, though, is Casino Town to the average American. And if Las Vegas casinos lack the old-world elegance of Monte Carlo, they certainly try to make up for it in sheer luxury. Nowhere else in the world has so much money been invested to make a gambling atmosphere create the feeling that the player has finally arrived. If the decor in some of the casinos is garish, it's meant to be—for the benefit of a market that regards the rococo as a symbol of plush living. Other casinos are decorated in excellent good taste and cater to a market that knows the difference. Most of the casinos on the Las Vegas Strip are a part of hotels, and the hotels are, for the most part, good examples of what an innkeeper can do if he has enough money.

The Las Vegas hostelries pamper and nurture their guests. History has shown that the longer they stay, the more money they'll spend. Time was when life in a Las Vegas hotel cost ridiculously little, a gift from the management to encourage casino patronage. As the ratio of sight-seeing tourists to gamblers increased hotel-casino owners found themselves being taken by hordes of "Lookers," who took the hospitality but didn't reciprocate by gambling. The system had to change, and today, most departments of most hotels are expected to be self-sustaining.

Las Vegas, Reno and Tahoe, however, are still among the world's greatest recreational buys. If night club and dining room tariffs have increased, what hasn't? And the service, food, drink and entertainment

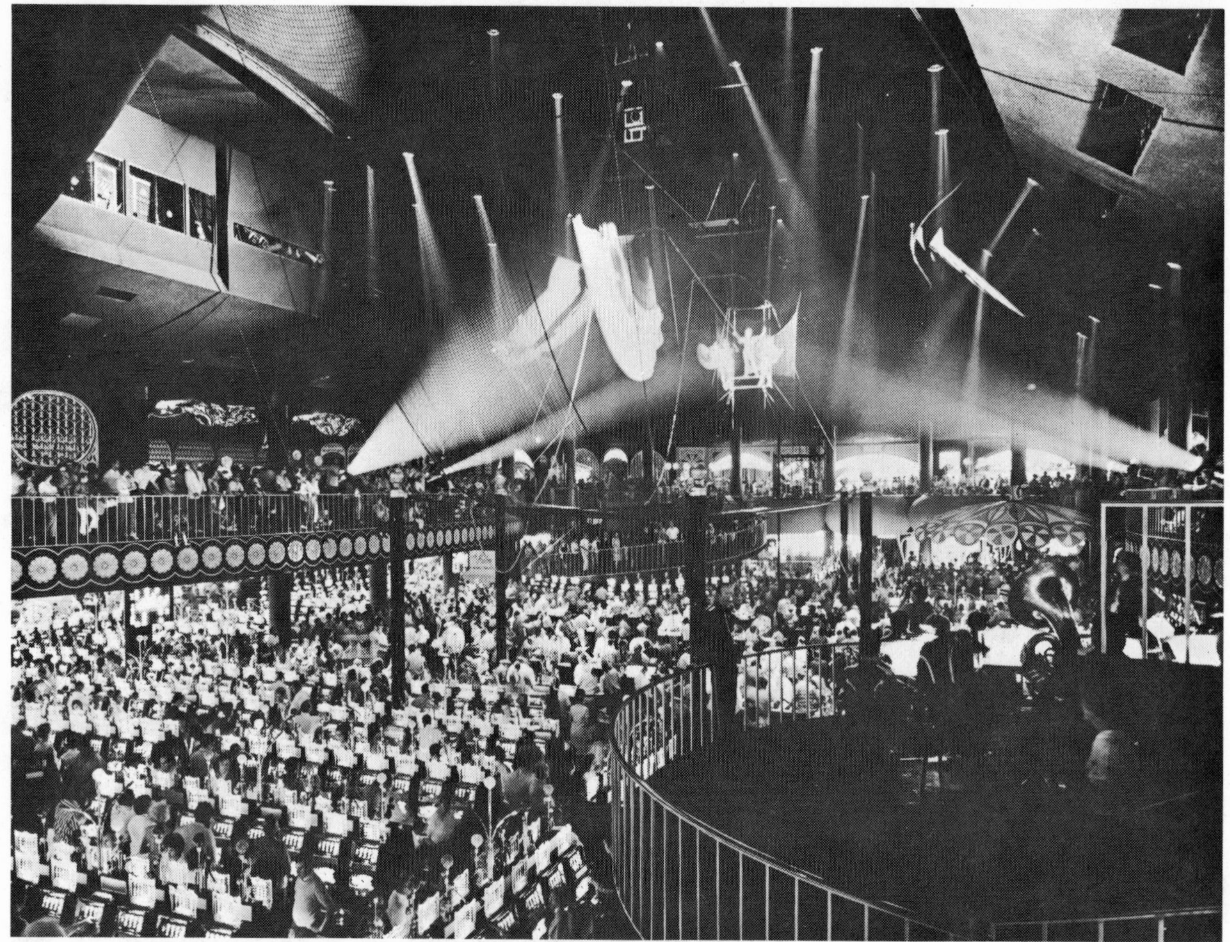

One of the great trapeze acts appearing at CIRCUS CIRCUS, Las Vegas, performs high above the casino floor where gaming tables and slot machines are set in a plush casino atmosphere.

are so good that they would inevitably cost more, if you could get them at all, in another locality.

The night club entertainment is the finest there is. Stars who won't make personal appearances anywhere else consistently play Nevada because nowhere else can they make so much money in such a short time.

Every casino is after traffic. The big gamblers who used to drop upwards of $100,000 a night are few and far between, ghosts of another era that shows no sign of ever returning. It takes a lot of "Hundred Buck" gamblers to replace one of the big spenders, and Las Vegas has done a remarkable merchandising job in going after them. Stellar entertainment, it has learned, is a sure-fire magnet. The costliest entertainment, from management's viewpoint, is the low-priced act that won't pack the place.

In the lounges, popular bands, vocalists and comedians whose presence elsewhere would command a $5 per head cover charge are offered the public without any charge at all.

Opulence is in the air, and it has a psychological effect on all except the old-school, hard-core gamblers. When you're entertained like a millionaire, you soon begin to feel like one.

But the entertainment, lavish as it is, plays second fiddle to the gambling. Legal gambling is what Las Vegas casinos are all about, and the most profitable customers wouldn't come to town for the greatest floor show ever presented if it weren't for the gambling. "The Strip" is Endsville, the greatest concentration of high-quality gambling facilities in the world.

The Strip is by no means the only casino location in Las Vegas. Downtown Vegas, which likes to be known as Casino Center, is big, busy and brassy, but it's a different world. This is gambling for the masses, the area where the working stiff blows a ten-spot on Lady Luck, the home of the penny slot machines, the bingo halls and two-bit crap games. Here is gambling without social polish, with sawdust on the floor. It's a gambler's Hamburger Heaven as contrasted to Le Pavillon. More than anything else, it's living proof that the wealthy and the elite have no corner on gambling enthusiasm.

You pay your money and you take your choice, but whether you patronize downtown Casino Center or more than a dozen luxurious casinos on the Strip, you can gamble with the assurance that you're getting as fair a shake and as good a run for your money as you'll get anywhere in the world.

Nevada realizes what the gambling industry has

done for it, and recognizes an obligation to the customers. The faintest hint of scandal brings instant investigation, and, if anything's wrong, which it seldom is, prompt action.

Everybody in the industry and in the state offices that control it is determined to keep Nevada gambling scrupulously honest. Much money is spent in policing the business. Gamblers with unsavory backgrounds are quickly discouraged, and, if they refuse to take the hint, treated harshly. Casino ownership, which in the early days of Las Vegas gambling was open to suspicion, has undergone close scrutiny in recent years. When an undesirable element is detected, it is soon sifted out.

The casino games are under careful watch, almost fanatical supervision. Attempts at cheating are rare, and when they do occur, they are the efforts of optimistic if misguided customers, not Casino management.

Since gambling is a big, legitimate business in Nevada, the men who run the casinos are business men —and realists. They have a house percentage in their favor that insures a profit if they do sufficient business, and they know that if they're ever caught cheating, they're out of business.

Las Vegas is every bit as conscious of "Public Image" as Madison Avenue—and does considerably more to police itself. It recognizes that the big, free spending which is characteristic of the business will always draw an undesirable element that's hopeful of getting some of the money—and it discourages that shabby fringe as determinedly as it's humanly possible to do. Where states which have pari-mutuel betting on horse races levy a tax on the "handle" that gives the bettor a big handicap to overcome, Nevada casinos have learned that the better the break they give the customer, the more he will gamble. In Blackjack or Twenty-One, for example, the "house" has a percentage advantage of less than one percent at certain times in the game.

While a player in an illegal clip joint may wonder, and often with good reason, whether or not he's getting a fair break, the gambler can dispense with that worry in a legal casino almost anywhere in the world. There was an instance of a casino in Freeport, the Bahamas, being shut down a few years ago for a six month period for reasons not clearly defined, but such occurrences are almost on a par with hen's teeth in the matter of frequency. And the assuring thing, to the gambler, was that the casino was promptly closed.

It is always possible for any player to win in a casino. Since there is a percentage in favor of the house in every game, however slight, it is almost impossible for a player to come out ahead over a long period of play. The gambler with an allegedly infallible "system" is up against the hard fact that with a house percentage of five percent, he will get back only 95¢ for every $1 he wagers, over the long haul. Only when the odds favor the player is it possible for him to beat the house over an extended period of play. The "counter" player in Blackjack sometimes finds such a situation and shows a handsome profit, but even with the "counter," the favorable odds are not consistently present. The rare player who wins more money than he loses, playing day in and day out, does his real gambling with "house money," money he's already won, minimizing his losses and maximizing his winnings. He also has the ability to quit while he's ahead. And even with all his gambling know-how, he needs some luck.

If the average player cannot hope to make a career of beating the house, however, neither does he have to be a heavy loser—if he knows what he's doing. Playing in a game where the house percentage is five percent, he can experience all the thrills and pleasure a gambler gets from gambling—at a low cost, less than he would pay for many other forms of amusement that offer far less excitement.

Let's assume that you are an out-lander, visiting Las Vegas for the first time. You will realize almost immediately that you're in a world foreign to your own. Aside from the bright, clear sky and clean desert air, probably the first points of difference to strike you will be slot machines and marriage chapels. Las Vegas abounds with both.

A person flying into Vegas for an initial visit is inevitably startled at the banks of slot machines in the airport. Life at home was never like this! Flying in at night, he will see the neon glow of the town lighting up the sky from 50 miles away. And when he reaches his destination, he quickly realizes that the bright lights of Broadway in their brightest days never equaled this. He sees a fairyland of colorful and spectacular signs, and most of them hold out a promise of entertainment.

The sense of excitement is contagious, and when

Complaints

Part of the Nevada Gaming Control Board's job is to see that all licensed Nevada gaming is honest.

A member of the board assures Gambler's Digest *that any reader of this book who believes he has been cheated in any way in a Nevada casino or who feels that any game is not being properly run will receive courteous attention and prompt action.*

Immediately upon receipt of such a complaint, the board will investigate the matter.

Complaints may be filed at either of two Gaming Control Board offices, one in Suite 120 at 302 East Carson street in Las Vegas and the other at 515 Musser street, Carson City.

Just tell 'em G.D. sent you.

he visits his first casino, whether downtown or on the Strip, he realizes the cause of the excitement. It's action! The action is always there, 24 hours a day, and nearly always fast and furious. On the Strip, it's not only fast and frenzied, but big-time. The games are big, the stakes are big, and the entertainment is colossal. The accommodations are luxurious and the service is sometimes informal but always excellent.

Whether he's ever been an enthusiastic gambler or not, he realizes that this can be Funtown and that if he doesn't have a good time, it will be his own fault.

Inevitably, he drifts to the fountainhead of all the action, the Casino. The first thing that hits him is the unceasing whir of the slot machines. It's unlike any sound he's ever heard before, a constant, high, metallic hum. And while he's accustoming himself to the background sound, he discovers something else that's different. There are no clocks! He searches the place for one, without any success. There simply aren't any.

He's bewildered by all the games, all busy. And he sees more slot machines than he knew existed. They line the walls, and additional banks of them are strategically placed throughout the room.

If he's a swinger, he disdains the nickel machines. He hesitates in front of a dollar machine and ends up by putting 25¢ in one of the quarter machines. He is now a part of the action.

Since the slot machine is the first thing to attract the novice's money, let's look into it.

SLOT MACHINES

You've heard all your life "you can't beat the slot machines," and it's quite true. Then why do so many people play them with so much enthusiasm?

Do they? For the first three-quarters of 1969, which was a typical "good" year for Nevada casinos, the Nevada Gaming Commission reports show a gross game-and-table revenue of $260,477,248. That's the total of all winnings by the casinos less the total of all sums paid out, before operating expenses. It's the revenue from all the games and tables—everything except the slot machines. For the same period, the Gaming Commission report shows a gross slot machine revenue of $132,793,716.

In other words, slot machines grossed over half as much money as everything else combined. Slightly over a third of the casinos' revenue came from the slots.

Why? Of all the games in the casino, the slot machine is the one where the house percentage is always operative, never varying. In states where the so-called "one-arm bandits" are illegal, they often operate with pay-outs as low as 50 percent. In other words, over a long period of play, if you feed a dollar into a machine, you will consistently get 50¢ back. Even in the face of such unbeatable odds, these illegal machines prosper, perhaps because they're "the only game in town."

Charles Fey, a young mechanic who emigrated from Bavaria to San Francisco in 1887, invented the slot machine and put it into operation in the Bay area in 1895. The first one was called "The Liberty Bell," accepted and paid out nickels, and sat on the bar in a saloon. It operated with a house percentage of 25 percent and was an immediate success. There was no jackpot. Demand for the machines was almost instantaneous and Fey not only refused to sell manufacturing rights but refused to sell the machines outright. He put them into locations on a lease basis, with 50 percent of the revenue going to Fey and the other 50 percent to the location owner.

Herbert Mills of Chicago, a carnival game manufacturer up to that time, put the slots on a nationwide basis. Fey's small output had stayed mostly in the San Francisco area.

Gambling devices are not patentable, and Fey's only protection had been his ownership of all the machines and his exclusive knowledge of how to manufacture them. Mills sold his first output in 1906 and had slot machines throughout the United States by 1910. He made various improvements, the most notable of which was the jackpot feature, first available in 1920.

The slot machine is a rugged, sturdy, complex device with over 600 parts and many springs. Changing the payout percentage, imagined by most people to be extremely simple, actually is highly complicated, requiring that the machine be dismantled and the reels changed, as well as the discs inside the reels. The job is so difficult that the casinos have their own workshops to handle it.

In the late 30's, when an undesirable element that had lost its bootlegging revenue had begun operating the machines in many localities, public opinion against the slots began to crystallize. In the 40's, they were outlawed in most states, and a Federal law passed in 1950 made it illegal to ship them across state lines except into states where they were still legal. Aside from a few local-option places of minor importance, they are now illegal everywhere in the United States except in Nevada, where more than 30,000 of them keep their wheels busily spinning, day and night.

Since the slot machine is mechanically constructed in such a way that the customer can never win consistently, what accounts for its persistent popularity?

It's the easiest gambling game known to man. The little old lady from Dubuque can play the slots just as adeptly as the person who's been playing them for 50 years. You drop a coin into the slot, pull the handle, watch the wheels spin and hear them hum, and wait for them to come to a stop. You not only

Photo courtesy Las Vegas News Bureau

The Big Bertha slot machine at the Dunes Hotel & Country Club, Las Vegas, accepts half-dollars or dollar bills.

REEL 1 REEL 2 REEL 3

WINNING COMBINATIONS			PAYOFF IN COINS	CHANCE OF APPEARING IN 8,000 PLAYS	TOTAL COINS PAID OUT
			JACKPOT 85	1 x 3 x 1 - 3	255
			18	1 x 3 x 3 - 9	162
			18	1 x 3 x 1 - 3	54
			14	5 x 1 x 5 - 25	350
			14	5 x 1 x 1 - 5	70
			10	3 x 6 x 7 - 126	1260
			10	3 x 6 x 1 - 18	180
			5	7 x 7 x 4 - 196	980
			5	7 x 7 x 3 - 147	735
		ANY	3	7 x 7 x 13 - 637	1911

From "The Facts of Slots" ©Gambler's Book Club, Las Vegas, Nev.

see immediately whether you've won or lost, but the payoff is automatic. There's nothing to learn and no variation in the percentage of the machine you happen to be playing. Your chance of winning is no better and no worse on every play than it was on the previous one.

The naive belief that chances for hitting a jackpot improve with every play is completely erroneous. There's no control and no mathematical formula to make a jackpot any more imminent on one pull of the wheel than on another. With a three-reel machine, there are 8,000 possible combinations—and with a four-reeler, 160,000. You can see 27 possible combinations that are "close" on a three-reel machine. Seeing three jackpot bars or three oranges or three of anything in the window doesn't mean that such a combination is about to come up. Nothing could be farther from the truth.

Despite the indisputability of a slot machine's mechanical construction, some people persist in the belief that the way you pull the handle in some way controls the progression of stopping the reels. There are slow pullers, fast pullers, those who pull it with a sharp jerk, those who pull it hard and those who pull it gently. Regardless of how you pull it, the handle releases certain springs when it reaches a certain point. Any way in which the machines might possibly be beaten was circumvented long ago.

The machines are honest and inexorable. The State of Nevada regularly checks the reliability of posted pay-offs. If a sign on a machine says, "Thirty-Six Jackpot Combinations," you may be sure that there are 36 possible jackpot pay-out combinations. Every casino receives regular visits from state inspectors, and if the payout possibilities of a machine have been misrepresented, management is in deep trouble.

Then how do you get the best run for your money in playing the slots?

The house percentage varies greatly from one machine to another. The poorest bets are usually machines to be found in drug stores, restaurants, grocery stores and other places where they are almost incidental sidelines. The loosest machines are invariably located in the casinos where competition is the greatest. Slots can be programmed to pay out any percentage the operator or owner wants. When new machines are bought, the manufacturer sets the percentage to match the customer's request. Tests have shown that the payouts won't vary from this percentage as much as one percent. Occasionally, some part of a machine may suffer from metal fatigue or a breakdown of some part which will result in a change in payoff percentage, but accurate records are kept on every machine and such a situation is never allowed to continue for long.

Since the house percentage is different on different machines, it's obvious that you get the best run for your money by playing the "loosest" ones, the slots that return the highest percentage of what they take in.

There is no way that anyone in the world can look

Some casinos issue "Boodle Bags" to their patrons. The bag is used to conveniently carry chips and coins.

at a slot without disassembling it and determine its percentage of payout.

Your only method of determining the best machine to play is to watch the slots in action and pick one that is giving its players a run for their money.

The slot machines in the Nevada casinos are probably the "loosest" machines in the world. Where "tight" machines in minor locations that get only a casual play may be set as low as 50 percent and many non-casino machines are set for a 75 percent payout, the casino slots average somewhere around a 90 percent payout—90¢ back for every $1 put into them.

This is not due to any great, public-spirited, benefactory impulse on the part of management. Completition for the gambling dollar is intense in Nevada, and "loose" slot machines attract customers. Not only do they draw patronage but they often show a bigger profit than "tight machines."

Slot machine operators learned long ago that machines which pay out 75 percent will make more money than those that pay out 50 percent, for the simple reason that they encourage play. "A 75 percent payout machine will always do at least four times the business that a 50 percent payout machine will do," one of them said.

Casino management has determined that when you have a large number of potential players, you will make more money with a 90 percent payout than with a 75 percent payout, and so they have set their machines for an average payout of roughly 90 percent.

But "average" is the key word. They want to draw business away from their competition and one way of accomplishing it is to get a reputation for "loose" machines. And so, in most casinos, some machines are set for as high as a 95 percent payout!

Some of them. A 95 percent payout machine usually sits beside a machine that pays out somewhere in the neighborhood of 80 to 85 percent, for the simple but sound reason that management knows the tendency of dedicated slot players to play the machines in tandem.

So you look for a machine that's "loose." Don't be frightened by the fact that the person who leaves it has done well. It won't get "cold" for any appreciable length of time. Mathematically programmed machinery doesn't get psychic or emotional streaks, and a machine that pays out well today will pay out equally well tomorrow.

If you spot several machines that seem equally loose, play the one with the greatest jackpot potential. Sometimes, a casino offers a particularly attractive jackpot to attract business. On a machine that has two jackpot bars on the first reel, three on the second and two on the third, the jackpot should hit 12 times in 8,000 plays. On the other hand, a machine with one jackpot bar on the first reel, three on the second and one on the third will pay out three times in 8,000 plays. Neither one is what you'd call a sure thing, but your chances on the jackpot with the first machine are four times as good as with the second.

There is nothing you can do to increase your chance

ROMANTIC GAMBLERS

Because of his notorious amatory exploits, it is not commonly known that Casanova was one of the famous gamblers of his time. From the age of 20, gambling was his occupation. While he sometimes suffered reverses and had to call on women under his spell for gambling funds, he was such a successful gambler that he was often suspected of being a cheat at the gaming tables as well as in the boudoir.

Beau Brummel, whose interest in clothes probably exceeded his predilection for women, was also a persistant gambler. The son of wealthy parents, he was far less successful at the gaming tables than Casanova. His supply of funds, unfortunately, was not inexhaustible, and gambling losses broke him. After a term in gaol for nonpayment of debts, the British dandy died in confinement as a lunatic.

of winning. On a single slot machine, there's no way you can "double up" on your bets. Neither can you bet light when you're losing and heavy when you're winning. Every play is for the same amount of money, with the same odds.

Obviously, the only way to win is to get lucky. And some people manage to do that, all the time. And even if you don't have a lucky streak, you have the consolation that it's taking you longer to lose your money than it would take at any other slot machine location you ever visited.

Richard Bueschel says, "There's no best bet on the slots because every bet is just like every other one, and you're betting against a piece of machinery that wasn't built to lose. Outside of the Nevada casinos, there ain't even a *good* bet on the slots.

"There's a way to beat the slots, though, in Nevada. Anywhere else, forget it, because the house odds kill you too fast.

"To do it, you gotta get lucky. First, you've gotta win some money on a nickel machine. Now, there's an old saying that you never go broke betting the house's money. So you take that money you've won and you stick it into a quarter machine. If you get a payoff there, you move on to a 50¢ machine, and if your luck holds, go to a dollar machine. If you lose your house money in the $1 machine, don't stick with it. Go back to the nickel machine and start over again. You can win more and lose less with that routine than any way I know. Myself, I get no kicks from the slots, even when I'm winning. I like to compete against people, not machines."

He has one other bit of advice. "If you feed seven or eight coins into the slot without getting any return, either quit or move to another machine."

Finally, he warns, "Start with a stake of a certain size. If you're playing a nickel machine, let's say it's five bucks. Get that five bucks changed into nickels, and if you lose it, quit. It ain't your night. And the chance of that hundred and first nickel starting a payoff to you is no better than it was on the first nickel."

A typical Casino Crap table scene. The table pictured here is in the Dunes Hotel & Country Club, Las Vegas.

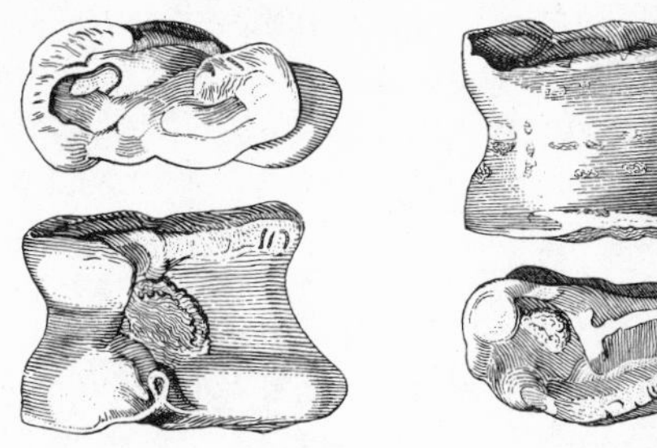

Each of the four faces of an astragalus had a specific value in ancient games. Top left is six, right is four, bottom, left is three, right is one.

CRAPS

When or where "Craps" began is a mystery, but gambling with dice is almost as old as the human race. Prehistoric man gambled with a six-sided sheep ankle bone, called astragalus, that qualifies as the first die. So dice were, literally, "bones" at their beginning. And they have been rattling out with money wagered on them from the beginning of money's existence.

The ancient ruins of Pompeii, the royal tombs of ancient Egypt and other archeological excavations, including some in Great Britain, have yielded dice. Some have been wooden, some made of clay and some of more precious ivory. Interestingly, a few have been crudely "loaded," weighted to make certain numbers come up more often than mathematical probability would cause. The probable forerunner of craps as we know the game was Hazard, probably invented by the Arabs, which was brought to Corsica by Saracen invaders in the eighth century. It swept through Europe and became a high-stakes game in which fortunes were won and lost.

"Ten" was the simple name of the reigning dice game in the Roman Empire and was probably the game played for Christ's clothing by soldiers at the foot of the cross, certainly the most notable game recorded in Christian history. The game, called passe-dix in France and ten-spot or dicey in Great Britain and the United States, still exists.

Stevedores along the levees in the New Orleans area developed craps from Hazard, and the game spread. In Hazard, the game from which it stemmed, the losing numbers two, three and 12, were known as "Crabs." Whether the new game was called "Crabs" or the mispronunciation that stuck, "Craps," it quickly replaced Faro as the major gambling game in casinos.

Although Craps is illegal almost everywhere except Nevada, nobody has been able to stop it. When the police raided known crap games in New York City, the "floating" crap game came into existence and thrived. The game was popular in millionaires' mansions and working-men's tenements, but Nicholas Dandolos, the legendary "Nick, the Greek," is generally credited with giving it social acceptance.

Craps devotees call it the fastest gambling game ever invented. The action is fast and exciting. Tom James says, "I've seen crap games start with nickels and dimes, but I've never seen one go very far without big folding money on the line. It's a friendly, noisy, informal game where there's action every second, and it's a game where every player has a chance to win — and not just an outside chance, either. You can be hitting rock bottom, too, and five or six passes can make you well again. What's more, you don't have to be a college professor to play a good game. Craps is almost as simple as it is exciting, but you've still gotta know what it's all about. In private crap games, I've seen guys make even-money bets that shoulda been against the law, the odds were so heavy against them. And wnen they lost, they complained about bein' unlucky. In Bank Craps, even the beginner who doesn't know gets decent odds on most of his bets."

"Bank Craps" is the casino crap game, and it's the most popular game in the house.

Even if it didn't offer the player the most attractive odds of any game available, it would probably maintain its Number One position because of the fun and excitement it offers.

To the player who's done all his crap-shooting with friends on a living room or home game-room floor, the first sight of a Bank Craps table is often awesome and intimidating. Craps has always been a simple, informal game, and this looks complicated and different.

It isn't. There may be a good many players in this game, and the layout is necessary to keep an accurate record of every bet that's down. It has nothing to do with the mechanics of the game and is necessary only because neither the players nor the dealers could possibly keep every bet straight if it weren't there.

The layout looks like this, although the odds may vary slightly from one casino to another:

Players put down their own bets on the Pass Line, Don't Pass Line, Odds on these bets, "Field" and "Come", and Big 6 and 8. Other bets are handed to the dealer to be properly placed by him. Actually, the layout is as much of a help to the player as to the dealers, since it enables him to keep track of several wagers he may have going at one time.

The Stickman runs the game. He calls the result of each roll, and the dealers collect all losing bets and pay all winners. The Boxman supervises the game and drops all the money the dealers collect into a drop-box.

The mechanics of Craps is simple. When a die is rolled, each of its six sides has an equal chance of being on top when the die stops rolling. Since the sides of the die bear numbers from one through six, each of those numbers should, over an extended period, come up once in six rolls.

When you add a second die, any number from two through 12 may be rolled. There are 36 ways of arriving at these 11 totals — 6 x 6. Some numbers have more mathematical potential than others. Basically, that's what Craps is all about — the appearance at certain times of certain numbers from 2 through 12.

Here is a chart showing the 36 possible combinations, how many of them will produce each number from 2 through 12, and what the mathematical probability is for any number's appearance:

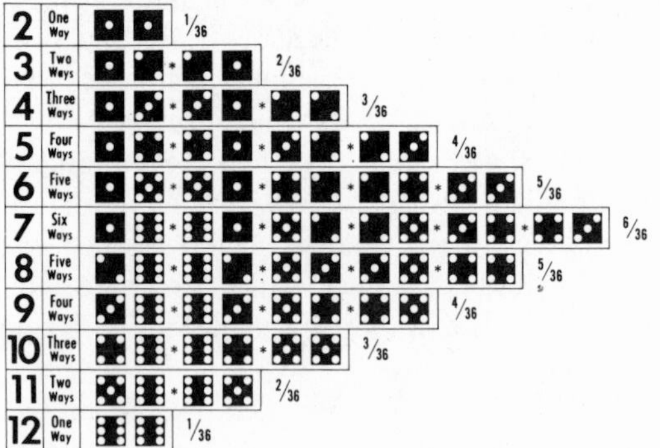

From "The Facts of Craps" ©Gambler's Book Club, Las Vegas, Nev.

Since both 2 and 12 can only be rolled one way and 3 can only be rolled two ways, four rolls out of 36 should produce "craps." In other words, if the dice follow the mathematical pattern, you should throw "craps" once in every nine rolls.

The 11 is a two-way number, so it should appear once in 18 rolls.

The 4 and 10 are three-way numbers, so each should appear once in 12 rolls. Four-way numbers are 5 and 9, and percentages indicate that each should turn up in one roll out of nine. Since 8 and 6 are five-way numbers, they should show once in approximately seven throws.

Seven is the Magic Number. Six of the 36 possible combinations arrive at 7, so mathematical probability indicates that once out of every six times you roll the dice, they should come up with a 7. It's what you want on your first throw and what you don't want when you've rolled another point. There's no other game where any one number is as important as the 7 in Craps. It can make you and it can break you. It has caused many a system player to wire home for money, but it has been almost equally unkind to the Don't Pass bettor who counts on it.

Betting Procedure

Since more bets are made on the Pass Line than anywhere else, as a rule, let's consider Pass Line bets first.

PASS LINE — Betting even money that the shooter will win is a Pass. The bet must be made before his first throw, or after he's won or lost. When the shooter rolls the dice, he is "coming out." You win a Pass Line bet, at even money, when the shooter's come-out roll of the dice is 7 or 11. When the come-out roll is a 4, 5, 6, 8, 9 or 10, that number is the shooter's point, and you win if he repeats it before he rolls a 7.

You lose a Pass Line bet when the shooter's come-out roll is craps — 2, 3 or 12. You also lose when the shooter's point number is not repeated before he rolls a 7.

PASS LINE — Taking Odds. When a Point number is determined by the shooter's come-out, anyone who has a bet on the Pass Line may make an additional bet that the number will be rolled before a 7. Usually, the amount of this Odds bet can't be any larger than the Line bet, except that the player is permitted to bet even units. Odds bets are paid at the correct odds:

Points 4 or 10—Odds paid, 2 to 1.
Points 5 or 9—Odds paid, 3 to 2.
Points 6 or 8—Odds paid, 6 to 5.

With a Pass Line bet of only $1, the bettor is usually permitted to make a $2 bet on five or 9. With 6 or 8, the player cannot take odds unless he has $3 on the line, in which case he can make an Odds bet of $5.

DON'T PASS LINE—This is the opposite of a Pass Line bet, an even-money bet that the shooter loses, and must be made before the come-out roll. You win a Don't Pass Line bet when the come-out roll is a 2 or 3 Craps (but not 12). A throw of 12 is a stand-off or "push." You also win when the shooter fails to repeat his point before rolling a 7.

You lose Don't Pass Line bets when the shooter comes out with a 7 or 11, or when he makes his point before throwing a 7.

Comparatively few players bet the Don't Pass Line, although the disadvantge to bettors is practically the same. The Pass Line disadvantage is 1.414 percent and the Don't Pass Line disadvantage is 1.402 percent.

DON'T PASS LINE—Laying Odds. Similar to Pass Line odds bets, except that the player lays the odds, within the limits of the original Don't Pass bet. The Odds bets are paid at the correct odds:

Point 4 or 10—Paid 1 to 2.
Points 5 or 9—Paid 2 to 3.
Points 6 or 8—Paid 5 to 6.

Odds bets on both the Pass Line and Don't Pass line should be made whenever possible, since the casino has no percentage in its favor.

COME BETS—Another area of the layout is designated simply, "Come." It is the same as a Pass Line bet, except that it is made after the first roll, when the shooter has a point. When you place a "Come" bet, the next roll of the dice is the come-out roll as far as your bet is concerned. You win if the roll turns up a

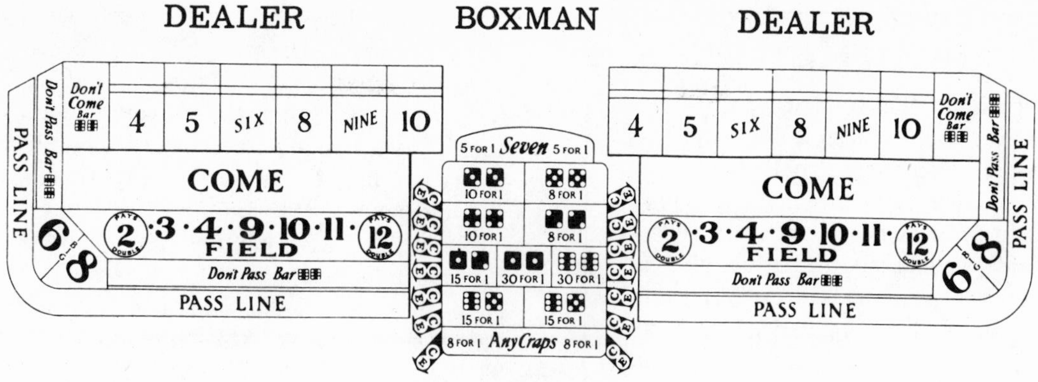

STICKMAN

Typical Las Vegas style Crap layout — the standard for the industry except for very minor changes in each casino. The arrows around the center portion contain the letters C-E. They stand for Crap-Eleven and each arrow represents a position at the table.

From "The Facts of Craps" ©Gambler's Book Club, Las Vegas, Nev.

7 or 11, and you lose if 2,3 or 12 come up. Rolls of 4,5,6,8,9 or 10 become the Point number for your come bet, and the dealer moves your chips or money to the correspondingly numbered box on the layout.

Odds bets can be made with Come bets, and should be, if possible.

DON'T COME BETS—These are the same as Don't Pass Line bets, except that they're made after the shooter has a point. Here again, odds bets are permissable and should be placed, if you want to take advantage of the most favorable odds.

PLACE BETS—A Place bet is a wager that a Point number of your choice will come up before a 7. It doesn't require playing the Pass Line or Come and can be made with the dealer at any time. Place bets on 6 and 8 are the fifth and sixth best bets at casino crap tables. Place bets on these two numbers pay off 7 to 6, so it is necessary to bet a minimum of $6. At a $5 table, the minimum place bet on 6 or 8 would be $30. The house percentage of these two numbers is 1.5 percent.

Pass Line and Come bets, with full odds taken on Point Numbers in both instances, are the best bets in Bank Craps, along with Don't Pass and Don't Come bets with full odds against the Point numbers. The only other bets that the experts consider good are Place bets on the 6 and 8.

A beginning player should probably confine himself to Pass Line and Come bets, taking the odds on Point numbers, until he acquires familiarity with the game and methods of play. Many experienced players will tell you never to have more than three bets in action simultaneously. Most of them will tell you to stay away from "Field" and Big 6 and Big 8 bets, which they regard as poor risks. Taking the Point Odds on Line and Come bets, however, they regard as sound, since this action reduces the house percentage to less than one percent.

Tom James says, "If you stick to Pass Line bets and then make the Odds bets, you're bucking the house on nearly even terms. Let's say the casino has a one percent edge. Barring freak luck on either side, you should only be out a buck on a hundred dollars play.

"But you've got some advantages over the house. You can quit when you want to, decide how much to bet, within the house limits, skip bets, go heavy, go light and pick your spots. The house has to cover you. By always taking odds on your point, you force

---

Oops!

A dice-switch story that's been a favorite with crap shooters for years is the one about the brash young dice hustler who accidentally let both of the loaded dice and one of the original straight dice roll out onto the table, three dice in all.

As the other players glared at him, he shrugged his shoulders and said, "Okay, fourteen's my point."

In one unlikely version of the story, the pit boss, ready to throw the fellow out of the casino, sees that he's betting $100 on the line. The pit boss picks up one of the three dice and hands the other two to the hustler. "Okay," he says, "fourteen's your point."

Another story which probably never happened deals with the hustler who always held the dice up to his lips and blew on them before he rolled. One evening, he sneezed violently as he tossed the dice against the backboard—and a third die spurted onto the table from between his lips. He had been switching dice in his mouth.

THE DICE MAKER

Craps is a game of chance, and casino operators want to keep it that way. Their dice are custom-made to their specifications, milled to a ten-thousandth of an inch to form as nearly perfect a cube as possible. While cheap plastic dice are polished in a mechanical tumbler similar to those used by lapidarists, such mechanical polishing also gives them rounded edges, and casinos want their dice to have sharp, true edges on all sides.

Most casino dice are made of celluloid. The raw celluloic is "cured" over a period of time to dry it out and give it stability. Then it goes through a series of milling operations to form it into a perfect cube. Following that, shallow indentations to form the spots are made on all six sides. These indentations are filled with a white polyester resin, and the dice are then subjected to a final grinding which leaves them with smooth, even surfaces.

Some casinos order their dice made in "off" sizes, as a safeguard against "switching" by dishonest players.

Even the heat of a shooter's hands may slightly alter the size of a pair of dice. Bud Jones of Las Vegas, whose factory furnishes casinos with about 12,000 pairs of dice a month, says that dice should never be held for more than 30 days if precise sizing is desired.

Dice in most casinos are changed frequently, and many pairs of "used" dice are given to customers as souvenirs. The price of custom-made dice in quantity runs about $1.50 a pair.

the casino to make one bet where it has nothing in its favor.

"Now, whatever you do, don't press if you're losing. The loser who doubles up to try to get even is almost a lead-pipe cinch to go home a loser. What you want to do is gamble with the casino's money, not your own. So when you get a winning bet, let it ride. Put whatever you won on the Pass Line plus your winning on the Point odds all on the Pass Line. If you roll a natural, fine. If you get a Point, make the maximum odds bet allowed by the house. You're betting with some of the Casino's money and you have a larger odds bet than before, which is an even-money bet.

"Now, there's one school of thought that plays it close to the chest, and it tells you to go right back to your minimum bet after this one, whether you win or lose. What this advice amounts to is, let a winner ride. If you win again, pull out your winnings and go back to your minimum bet. Here's how it works. Say you've bet three bucks, with your odds bet. You win, and the house pays you four. You put the seven bucks on the Pass Line, and get a Point of 6 or 8. You make an odds bet of $5. If you win, the house pays six bucks on the Odds bet and seven on the Pass Line. You've got $17 in house money plus your $8 investment. Go back to your original minimum bet and you've got a $17 profit.

"That's fine, but it's not my way. You've made 17 bucks on two passes, sure, but I take a flyer on tryin' to make three passes. I drag out my $8 investment and bet $17 on the line, only I'm betting casino money, not mine. If I lose, I'm out nothing. But if I win, I'm ahead $34 without risking a penny in doubling the 17. Then I go back to my original minimum bet. Mathematically, my chances of making that third pass are just the same as they were for the first one—but on that third come-out, the house is betting against its own money.

"I guess my rule of thumb is, make a pass and let it ride. If I win, again, I drag my own money and let the house money ride. And I go back to my minimum bet after the third bet, win or lose."

"Another thing, don't quit while you're winning. Say you're 100 bucks ahead of the game and still doing all right. Keep betting. Then, with minimum bets that you keep losing, pull outta' the game when your original profit is down to 75 or 80 bucks."

He admits that his advice to always ride a winner and always walk away from a losing streak sent him to a hospital one time. "I'd been at the table for 37 hours," he says, "and was still hotter than a depot stove. When I caved in, I was $22,000 ahead and who knows how much it mighta been if I'da managed to stay on my feet?"

The recollection made him think of something else. "Let's say you're losing—not much, because you're sticking to minimum bets. But you keep playing, waiting for your luck to change. That's no fun. It wears you out. So leave the game. You're not like the dealers; you don't have to stay there. Get something to eat or drink. Maybe even catch a floor show. Take a walk. Do anything that relieves the tension and makes you feel fresher. Then go back to the game. If the same consistent losing streak is still with you, don't fight it. Give up and wait for tomorrow."

Nick, the Greek, once observed that any sport involving a ball was much too strenuous and that craps offered the perfect exercise. Walking from game to game, he added, promoted meditation and contemplation.

Tom James puts his finger on one danger faced by every crap-shooter. "It's a fast, exciting game," he says, "and it can get to you. Matter of fact, it grabs most players. They start out cool and collected —good gamblers. They've got a plan mapped out with their money and they stick with it until they hit a winning streak. And at that point, money ceases to mean what it should. They're out to break the bank. Judgement flies out the window and they lose a bundle. Try to remember that each chip in that big pile in front of you represents a dollar. Don't let it become just a plastic chip, because tomorrow morning, sure as anything, a buck is gonna be worth a buck again."

MR. ODDS-MAKER'S BEST BET

Mr. Odds-Maker says, "By all means, lay or take the odds. By doing so, you reduce the percentage against you. Don't place bets on points and avoid all "propositions." These are top percentage bets for the casino and worst bets you can make. Bear in mind that there is a slight percentage against the shooter when he picks up the dice, and you have the right to bet against him."

BLACKJACK OR TWENTY-ONE

Number Two game to Craps in the casinos is Blackjack. Although it is the one casino game requiring judgment and skill to play it well, anyone can get the basic idea and play passably in a few minutes.

Up until a few years ago, not even many casino dealers really knew much about the game or its strategy, and a house percentage that was too high discouraged play. While Blackjack is a descendant of European counting games played in the fifteenth and sixteenth centuries, it achieved its big popularity in the United States from the thousands of men who had played it in military service. It first became a strong contender for casino popularity in the late 1950's and early 1960's when players discovered that it was possible to maneuver much shorter house odds if you played with skill.

The big break-through came when Edward O. Thorp, a mathematics professor, developed a unique system, based on the fact that the odds change after certain cards have been played. Playing his system in a Las Vegas casino, Thorp won $2,000 in about four hours. He was soon barred from several blackjack games he patronized, because his winnings were too consistent. Thorp had used a computer to work out all the odds changes as certain cards were removed from the deck, and got from the computer the percentages for or against the player in each situation.

Casino management is well aware of what's going on, and doesn't like it. A person who counts the cards is known to the casino as "a counter," and is soon eased out if his winnings are consistent. With a "counter," or somebody suspected of being one, at a blackjack table, the speed of the game picks up, the deck is loudly riffled, and chatter from both the pit boss and the dealer increase. The idea is to keep the "counter" from counting the values of the cards that are played, and any "counter" who can do it in the face of so much distraction is a good man.

WHO'S BARRED?

Several gamblers have stated that they are barred from Nevada casinos because of their winning techniques, and they are quoted in GAMBLER'S DIGEST. Confirmation of such statements has been elusive.

One Las Vegas casino operator says, "We have never barred any gambler from our place because he has a winning system. The only people we bar are proven cheats.

"Allegedly successful 'counters' in Blackjack are welcome in my casino. Some casino may have stopped their play at one time or another; I have no way of knowing about that. I do know that we never bar anyone for being a consistent winner. We watch any player closely whose luck exceeds the law of probability over a long period, but we watch for cheating, not for use of a system.

"Stories that they are barred from Nevada casinos help to sell their systems — and the only sure way to make money on any system I've ever seen is to sell it to other gamblers. In Blackjack, a skillful 'counter' is a student of the game and would probably be an above-average player whether he 'counted' or not. My personal belief is that the 'counting' advantage was dissipated when the casinos went to two and four decks, 'burning' additional cards.

"If I had a sure-fire system for beating any casino game, I wouldn't sell it to anyone at any price. I'd keep it for my own exclusive use."

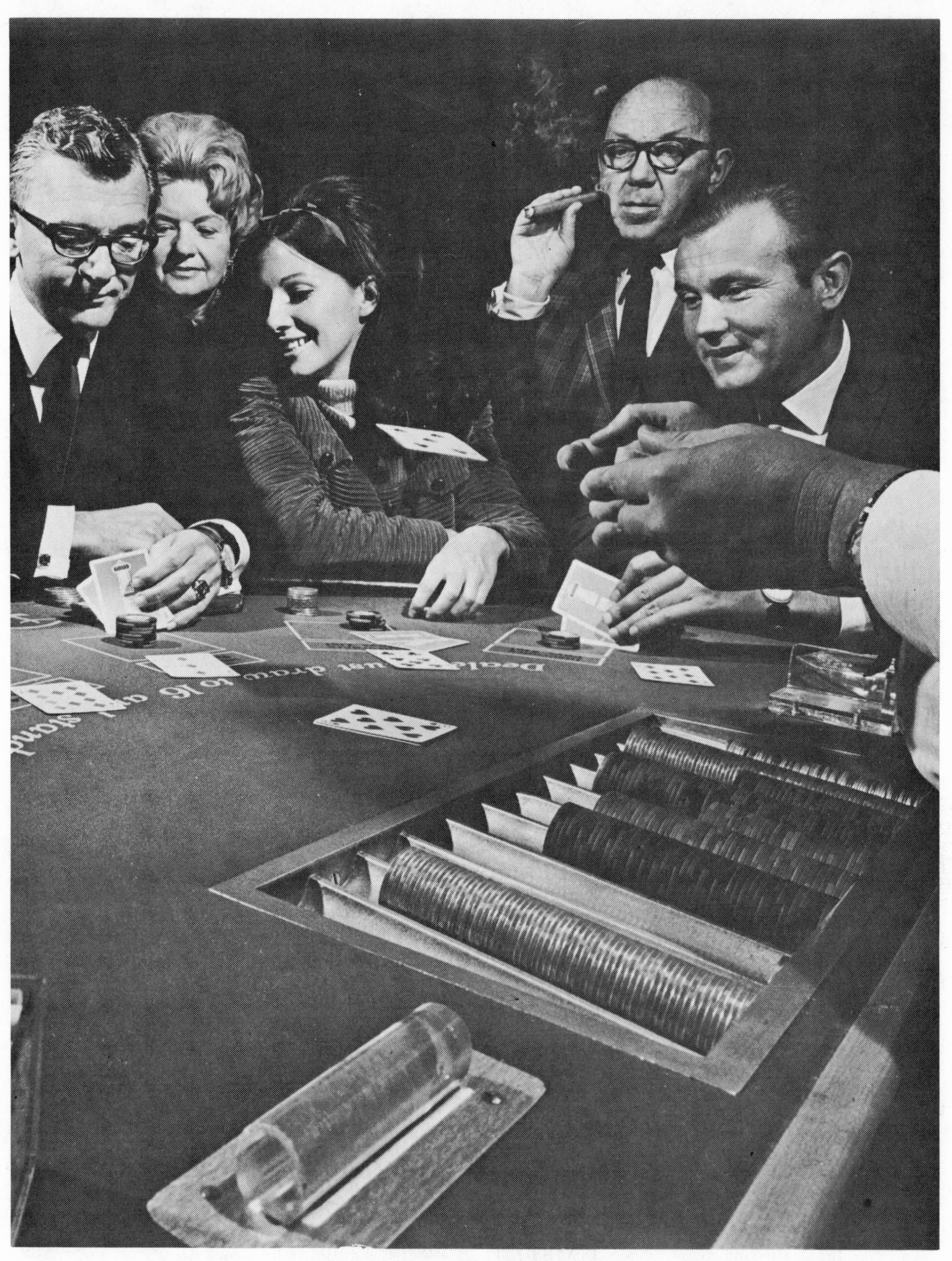

Although Blackjack is a game that requires skill and judgment, anyone can get the basic idea and play passably well in a few minutes.

CARD VALUES-ONE DECK

4 each - 16 cards counting 10

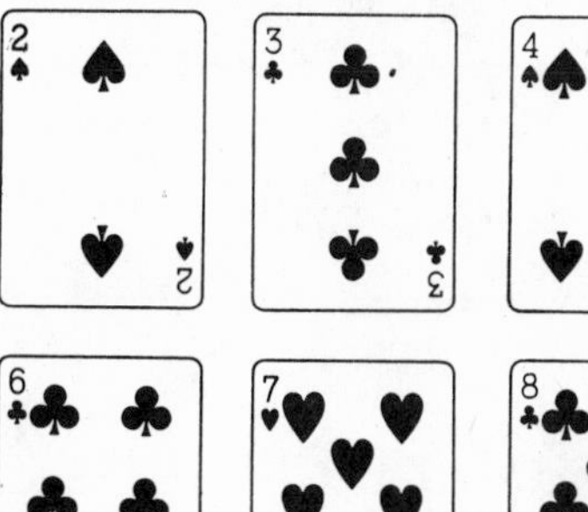  

4 each - 32 cards counting face value

  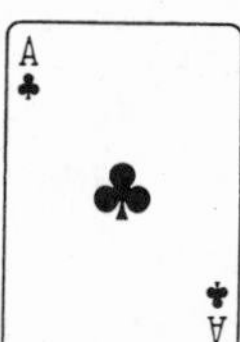 

4 aces - 4 cards counting 1 or 11

2 CARDS	COMBINATIONS		TOTAL	PERCENT	CHANCE
21	ACE-10	64	64	4.827	1 in 20.7187
20	10-10 ACE-9	120 16	136	10.256	1 in 9.7500
19	10-9 ACE-8	64 16	80	6.033	1 in 16.5750
18	10-8 9-9 ACE-7	64 6 16	86	6.486	1 in 15.4186
17	10-7 9-8 ACE-6	64 16 16	96	7.240	1 in 13.8125
16	10-6 9-7 8-8	64 16 6	86	6.486	1 in 15.4186
15	10-5 9-6 8-7	64 16 16	96	7.240	1 in 13.8125
14	10-4 9-5 8-6 7-7	64 16 16 6	102	7.692	1 in 13.0000
13	10-3 9-4 8-5 7-6	64 16 16 16	112	8.446	1 in 11.8392
12	10-2 9-3 8-4 7-5 6-6	64 16 16 16 6	118	8.900	1 in 11.2372
11	9-2 8-3 7-4 6-5	16 16 16 16	64	4.827	1 in 20.7187
10	8-2 7-3 6-4 5-5	16 16 16 6	54	4.072	1 in 24.5555
9	7-2 6-3 5-4	16 16 16	48	3.620	1 in 27.6250
8	6-2 5-3 4-4	16 16 6	38	2.866	1 in 34.8947
7	5-2 4-3	16 16	32	2.413	1 in 41.4375
6	ACE-5 4-2 3-3	16 16 6	38	2.866	1 in 34.8947
5	ACE-4 3-2	16 16	32	2.413	1 in 41.4375
4	ACE-3 2-2	16 6	22	1.660	1 in 60.2727
3	ACE-2	16	16	1.207	1 in 82.8750
2	ACE-ACE	6	6	.452	1 in 221.0000

From "The Facts of Blackjack" ©Gambler's Book Club, Las Vegas, Nev.

The rules of the game are simple. The object of the game is to beat the dealer, and the goal is to accumulate cards adding up to 21 or as close to 21 as you can get without going over the 21 figure. If you go over, you "bust" and the dealer wins. Ties "push," and you neither win nor lose.

Some games are played with one deck and some with two or four decks of cards. After the cards are shuffled by the dealer, a player cuts and the dealer completes the cut. He then removes the top card of the deck, turns it face up and places it on the bottom.

Before any cards are dealt, the players make their bets. Some tables have a $1 minimum bet and some have a $5 minimum. Once the bets are down in front of the players, the dealer, starting at his left, deals one card face-down to each player and one face-up to himself. Another face-down card is dealt to each player, and the dealer's second card, too, is dealt face down.

If the dealer has an Ace and a ten-count card (Blackjack), the round is over and he wins from everyone except a player who has another Blackjack. This player "pushes."

In the event that the dealer doesn't have Blackjack, the players look at their hands. If a player has Blackjack, he shows it immediately and is paid off 1½ to 1. Otherwise, the player has two choices. He can "stand" on the two cards he has, putting them under his bet, or he can draw. One variation of the draw is the "double down." The player has the option to double the size of his bet, turning both of his cards face up and drawing only one additional card, face down. Another variation of the draw is pair splitting. Any time the player is dealt two of a kind, he has the option to separate the pair and make two Blackjack hands, betting the same amount on the second hand as he had already bet on the deal. In some casinos, there is a "surrender" option which gives the player the right to call off his bet by paying half of it to the dealer.

Another option is called "insurance." The dealer offers it when his up-card is an Ace. He gives two to one odds that his down card is not a ten-counter. The player may bet not more than half his original bet. It should never be made by the average player unless he has Blackjack, himself, in which case he is guaranteed a profit.

THE BASIC BLACKJACK STRATEGY

	2	3	4	5	6	7	8	9	X	A
12	H	H	S	S	S	H	H	H	H	H
13	S	S	S	S	S	H	H	H	H	H
14	S	S	S	S	S	H	H	H	H	H
15	S	S	S	S	S	H	H	H	H	H
16	S	S	S	S	S	H	H	H	H	H

WHEN DEALER HAS A SMALL CARD

2 3 4 5 6

YOU NEVER HIT 13-14-15-16

HIT 12 IF DEALER HAS 2 OR 3

WHEN DEALER HAS A LARGE CARD

7 8 9 10 ACE

HIT UNTIL YOU GET 17

DOUBLE DOWN

DOUBLE ON 10	EXCEPT 10 OR ACE
DOUBLE ON 9	2 THRU 6
DOUBLE ON 8	5 OR 6 (NO 6-2)
DOUBLE A2-A5	4-5-6
DOUBLE ON A6	2 THRU 6
DOUBLE ON A7	3 THRU 6
DOUBLE ON A8	6 ONLY

SPLIT PAIRS

22		3 THRU 7
33		4 THRU 7
66		2 THRU 6
77		2 THRU 7
99	EXCEPT	A-7-10

A2 TO A6

IF YOU CANT DOUBLE DOWN ALWAYS HIT

YOU HAVE A-7

A-2-7-8	STAND
3-4-5-6	DOUBLE
9 OR 10	HIT

A8 OR A9

IF YOU CANT DOUBLE DOWN ALWAYS STAND

WHEN DO YOU DOUBLE ON A-9
WHEN DO YOU STAND ON 9-9
WHEN DO YOU DOUBLE ON A-2
WHEN DO YOU HIT 14
WHEN DO YOU SPLIT 2-2
WHEN DO YOU HIT A-7
WHEN DO YOU DOUBLE ON 8
WHEN DO YOU STAND ON 15
WHEN DO YOU SPLIT 4-4
WHEN DO YOU STAND ON A-5
WHEN DO YOU DOUBLE ON A-7
WHEN DO YOU HIT 16
WHEN DO YOU SPLIT 6-6
WHEN DO YOU HIT A-8
WHEN DO YOU DOUBLE ON A-4
WHEN DO YOU STAND ON 13
WHEN DO YOU SPLIT 8-8
WHEN DO YOU STAND ON A-6
WHEN DO YOU DOUBLE ON 11
WHEN DO YOU HIT 12
WHEN DO YOU SPLIT 3-3
WHEN DO YOU HIT A-5
WHEN DO YOU STAND ON 14
WHEN DO YOU DOUBLE ON A-5
WHEN DO YOU SPLIT 5-5
WHEN DO YOU STAND ON A-7
WHEN DO YOU DOUBLE ON 9
WHEN DO YOU HIT 15
WHEN DO YOU SPLIT 7-7
WHEN DO YOU HIT A-6
WHEN DO YOU DOUBLE ON A-8
WHEN DO YOU STAND ON 12
WHEN DO YOU DOUBLE ON A-3
WHEN DO YOU HIT 13
WHEN DO YOU SPLIT 9-9
WHEN DO YOU STAND ON A-8
WHEN DO YOU DOUBLE ON 10
WHEN DO YOU STAND ON 16
WHEN DO YOU DOUBLE ON A-6
WHEN DO YOU SPLIT A-A
WHEN DO YOU STAND ON 7-7

ASK YOURSELF THE QUESTIONS ABOVE THEN CHECK THE ANSWERS TO THE LEFT. GO OVER AND OVER THESE QUESTIONS. THIS IS THE EASIEST WAY TO LEARN HOW TO PLAY.

EVERYTHING YOU SEE HERE IS ABSOLUTELY CORRECT. YOU MUST BELIEVE THIS.

DO NOT ATTEMPT TO LEARN ANYTHING ELSE UNTIL YOU CAN GO OVER THESE QUESTIONS AND ANSWER THEM INSTANTLY.

From "Playing Blackjack as a Business" by Lawrence Revere, published by Mann Publishing Company, Las Vegas, Nev.

A Good Gamble

For the player who follows a good, sound playing strategy, Blackjack becomes an excellent gamble with a house percentage of little more than half of one percent, thanks to things that have been learned about the game from computer research.

Computer findings also revealed that the odds fluctuate as hand after hand is played from the deck, depending on the frequency with which certain cards appear. Obviously, at a time when most of the ten-count cards have been played and the remaining cards in the deck are low denominations, the probabilities are much different from what they are at the start of a game when 16 of the cards are ten-counters.

This discovery led immediately to the development of a system known as "counting."

Now, casino management loves systems, because

system players do notoriously badly in nearly all gambling games. One of the surest ways to lose money, most gamblers agree, is to play a system.

Yes, casino management loves system players—but it doesn't love "counters," players who use the "counting" system in Blackjack. From the time Edward Thorp first demonstrated "counting," the "counter" has been anathema to the blackjack dealer.

Lawrence Revere, a "counter" of considerable skill and author of an excellent book, *Playing Blackjack as a Business,* is responsible for the statement that seven known "counters" are barred from Nevada casinos.

In an attempt to thwart "counters," some casinos went from single-deck Blackjack games to two-deck and four-deck deals, but the "counters" still beat the house. In the Dealer's Instructions in a downtown Las Vegas casino, quoted by Walter Nolan in his informative booklet, *The Facts of Blackjack,* a point is made that "a player playing more than one hand must play each hand in turn, although he may look at all of them, unless the floorman knows the player is a counter, then he cannot look at all of them."

Revere's advice to a "counter" is never to play for more than an hour in any casino, to keep the management from becoming aware that you are counting.

In Blackjack the player's chips must be placed in the square in front of his seat—otherwise there's no bet.

Photo courtesy of Dunes Hotel & Country Club

He says that it takes hours of patient practice to become a good counter, along with a thorough knowledge of what you're doing. Interestingly, he did not publish any information concerning his system until after he said he had been barred from Nevada casinos.

If you want to become a "counter," you will find a number of books available on the subject, and some "counters" are said to be available for personal instruction.

For the person who wants to give the house a good, stiff battle in blackjack and do it without becoming involved in the complex intricacies of a counting system, our revised basic strategy of Blackjack can do the job without making you persona non grata to the casinos.

Even a beginner should know certain things. For example, his bet is put into a square in front of his seat. If the money isn't in that square, there's no bet. Shoving chips out in the general direction of the square may mean to the player that he's betting that much, but it doesn't hold the same meaning for anyone else.

When you've been dealt your two cards, look at them immediately and decide what you want to do. If you don't want to be hit, slide your two cards under your bet, in the square. If you want a card, brush the two cards toward yourself on the table's surface. If you want another card, repeat the process. If you go "bust," turn your down cards up immediately and throw in the hand. If you're dealt a blackjack, an ace and ten-count card, turn your hand up immediately at the conclusion of the two-card deal, before any "hit" cards are dealt.

The poorest seat at the table for a beginning player is the "third base" seat, the one that draws immediately before the dealer does. If you sit there and your strategy doesn't agree with that of other players at the table, you may be loudly criticized. For example, if you draw a "bust" card that would have "busted" the dealer had you stood pat, the other players will blame you in the event they lose.

The first seat isn't the right place for a beginner,

Handicap 21

Peter Lind Hayes sat at a table in a Las Vegas club where everyone was bemoaning his luck. Each man at the table topped the hard luck story of those who had wailed out their woes before him. One grim-faced man remained silent.

"I take it that you had a good night, Joe," Peter observed.

The fellow sighed. "I'll tell you how unlucky I was. I was playing Blackjack and my cards ran so bad that they let me play '22' instead of '21' to keep me in the game."

either. Dealers are impatient and like to work fast. If you hold up the play, trying to make a decision, you won't be popular. Preferably, take a seat somewhere around the middle.

Try to be pleasant to those around you, but avoid any lengthy conversation. You want to concentrate on your cards, and so, if they know the game, do the other players.

While experts differ slightly on some points of the play, they are in surprisingly close agreement on the player's basic strategy.

Gambler's Digest Basic Strategy For Blackjack

SPLITS—Always split a pair of Aces or Eights. Never split a pair of fives or ten-count cards. Split threes if dealer has 4 through 7 face up; with any other face-up card, hit. Double down on Fours if dealer shows 5 or 6. Any other card, hit. Double down on a pair of Fives if dealer shows 2 through 9. If dealer shows Ace or ten-count card, hit. Split a pair of Sixes with dealer showing 2 through 6. With any other card showing, hit. Split a pair of Sevens if dealer shows 2 through 7. Hit if he shows 8,9 or Ace. You may split a pair of Nines unless dealer shows Ace, ten or seven, in which case you stand.

DOUBLE DOWNS—With Ace-Seven, double down if dealer shows three through six; stand if he shows 2, 7, 8 or Ace. Draw if his up card is 9 or 10.

With Ace-6, double down if dealer's up card is 2 through 6. Draw if it is any other card.

Double down with Ace-5,Ace-4,Ace-3 or Ace-2 if dealer's up card is a 4,5 or 6. Otherwise, draw.

With a count of 11, always double down.

With a count of 10, double down unless dealer's up card is an Ace or ten-counter.

With a count of 9, double down if dealer's up card is 2 through 6. Otherwise, draw.

STANDING—Stand on a count of 17 through 21, always.

Stand on a count of 13 through 16 if dealer's up card is 2 through 6. Otherwise, draw.

Stand on a count of 12 if dealer's up card is a 4,5 or 6. Otherwise, draw.

Here is a chart of this basic strategy, from *The Facts of Blackjack,* by Walter I. Nolan, published by Gambler's Book Club of Las Vegas.

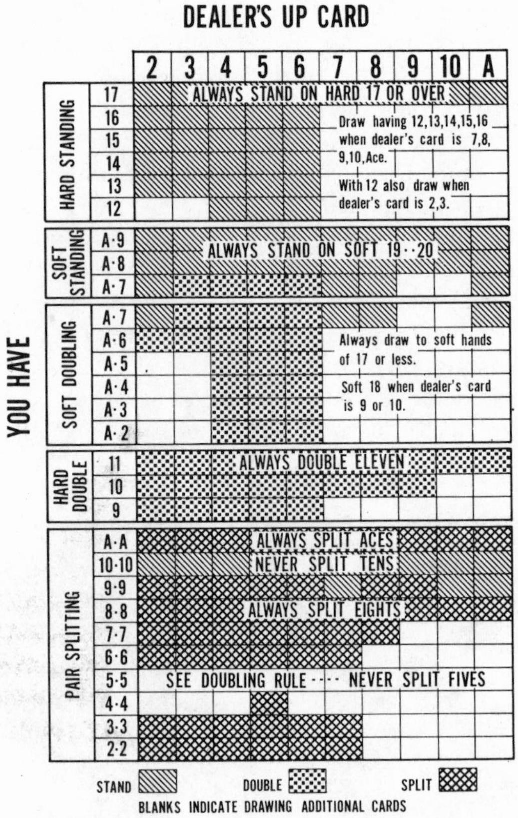

DEALER'S UP CARD

2 3 4 5 6 7 8 9 10 A

YOU HAVE

HARD STANDING: 17, 16, 15, 14, 13, 12

ALWAYS STAND ON HARD 17 OR OVER

Draw having 12,13,14,15,16 when dealer's card is 7,8, 9,10,Ace.

With 12 also draw when dealer's card is 2,3.

SOFT STANDING: A·9, A·8, A·7

ALWAYS STAND ON SOFT 19··20

SOFT DOUBLING: A·7, A·6, A·5, A·4, A·3, A·2

Always draw to soft hands of 17 or less.

Soft 18 when dealer's card is 9 or 10.

HARD DOUBLE: 11, 10, 9

ALWAYS DOUBLE ELEVEN

PAIR SPLITTING: A·A, 10·10, 9·9, 8·8, 7·7, 6·6, 5·5, 4·4, 3·3, 2·2

ALWAYS SPLIT ACES

NEVER SPLIT TENS

ALWAYS SPLIT EIGHTS

SEE DOUBLING RULE···· NEVER SPLIT FIVES

STAND DOUBLE SPLIT

BLANKS INDICATE DRAWING ADDITIONAL CARDS

If you learn the basic strategy and stick with it, you will play a good game of Blackjack and the house percentage against you will be so small that, given a little luck, you can win. Never play hunches if you want to depend on the laws of Mathematical Probability. Nolan says, "It is now known that the player who draws with knowledge of the basic strategy gives the casino a lesser amount of percentage than in any other game."

Clement McQuaid says, "If the dealer had any chance to exercise judgement, he'd probably beat your brains out, but he's held to set rules. He has to stay on 17, even when he's pretty sure he's beaten, and he has to draw on 16. He has no control over his play in an honest game. The cards could be dealt by a machine and the results would be the same. That's your big edge. You can go along with the laws of probability; he can't.

"Now, I'm not a counter, but I watch the play, and

One For The Road

Myron Cohen tells the story of a couple who went to Las Vegas on their second honeymoon. Every night, the husband went directly to the Blackjack table after dinner and his wife was left alone in their room until three o'clock in the morning.

One night he was doing exceptionally well when a bellhop ran up to him and whispered, "Mr. Bindle, your wife is upstairs making love to your best friend."

Furious, Bindle shouted to the dealer, "Hurry up and deal! This is positively my last hand!"

if not many face cards or nines or tens are coming up, I know it. And I also know that the higher the percentage of ten-count cards is left in the deck, the greater my edge over the dealer is, so I bet accordingly.

"As a rule of thumb during the play of one, two or four decks, the house will have a percentage advantage about a third of the time, it'll be about even a third of the time, and the advantage will be with the player the other third of the time. The trick is to know when that percentage edge is with you.

"I'll always make one parlay when I've won a hand, but if I know the deck is light on face cards and tens, I may go back to a one-unit bet after I've won my second bet. On the other hand, if I know the remainder of the deck is loaded with high cards, I may continue to double up, after dragging my original one unit because I know the edge is with me.

"I never double my bet unless I've won the last hand. And when I've won four straight hands, I always go back to my original one-unit bet, *unless* I think the rest of the deck is loaded with face cards and tens, in which case, I let five units ride. A good gambler takes his big gambles with the house's money, not his own. He bets big when he's winning and light when he's losing.

"The main thing is to remember the basic betting strategy. Most of the players in the average Blackjack game deserve to lose because they don't know what they're doing. A player who knows when to stand on 12 will do all right. And a player who draws to 17 because the dealer has an eight up will get clobbered. Always remember that a dealer must draw on 16, and 32 of the 52 cards in the deck will make him go bust.

"Playing Blackjack requires more concentration than most casino games, and it calls for knowledge. A smart gambler doesn't play the game when he's too tired to think quickly or when he's been drinking too much. I never play the game for more than two hours without taking a break and relaxing. Another thing, if I'm at a table where the dealer gets under my skin by his attitude toward the players, I don't put up with it. I move to another table. Whether you're a beginner or an expert, you've got a right to enjoy yourself while you're playing Blackjack. Besides, a dealer who annoys you can color your judgement."

MR. ODDS-MAKER'S BEST BET

Mr. Odds-Maker says, "When properly played, Blackjack produces the least amount of percentage for the house of any casino game now being played. Always double-down when you have 11, no matter what the dealer shows. Always split Aces. For the novice who doesn't know the new drawing procedures, follow the same rules as the dealer."

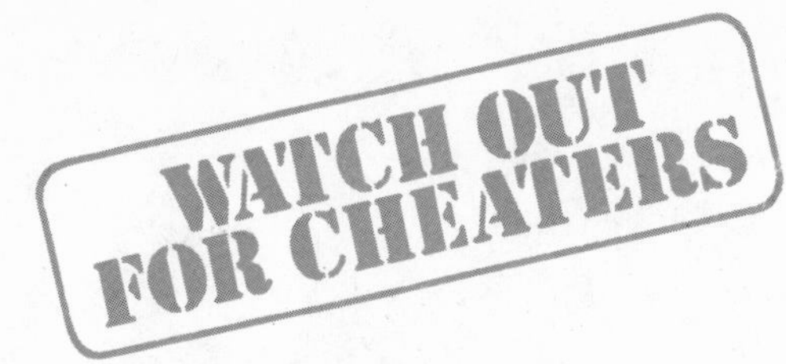

THE CHIP COPPER

Probably tops of all the petty annoyances in private poker games and in casinos is the professional chip copper.

He—or often in casinos, she—maneuvers a position next to a substantial winner whose chips have gotten out of hand. The chip copper's small supply of chips is placed in close proximity—and somehow or another, some of the big winner's chips end up in the pile.

A magician's product called Adhero is sometimes applied to the chip copper's palm. A brush of the palm against a neighbor's pile of chips makes the top chip of the stack adhere to the palm, usually without anyone realizing what has happened.

A Las Vegas pit boss who suspected an attractive young woman of habitual chip-copping once put a new shill into the game with a haphazardly stacked pile of chips that were glued together into a solid mass. When the beautiful larcenist made a deft move to steal a chip, her hand came away from the table with the solid pile. She very calmly replaced it and walked away, out of the casino, where she was never seen again.

BACCARAT

When Faro, the big casino gambling game of the Old West, gasped its last breath a few years ago in the casinos of the United States, it had already been replaced, for all practical purposes by Baccarat. When the latter game was introduced in Las Vegas in 1958, it got off to an inauspicious start as far as casino owners were concerned. The Strip dropped close to a quarter of a million dollars to players in the course of the first night's play.

The game probably started during the reign of Charles VIII, in the latter quarter of the 1400's. Two versions developed, one a banking game called Baccarat Banque, and the other, a non-banking game called Chemin de Fer. The biggest difference between Chemin de Fer and Nevada-style Baccarat is that in Chemin de Fer, players compete against each other without the participation of the "house." The game's first bid for popularity in this country was short-lived, in the early 1900's, but the current version is thriving.

One of the reasons for the current popularity of Baccarat may be the "snob appeal" with which it has

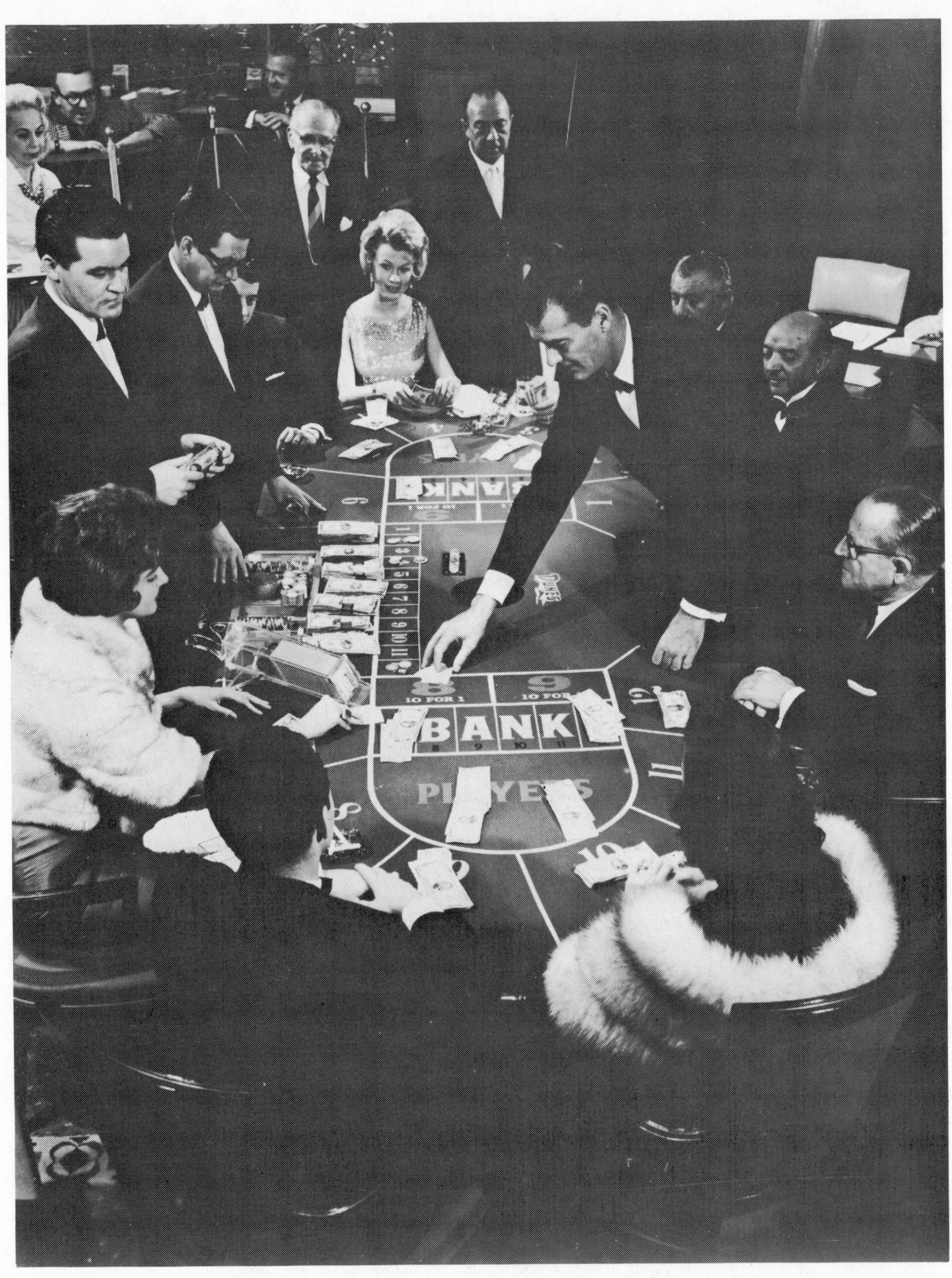

Baccarat has traditionally been a big money game and the casino Baccarat tables are surrounded with an aura of elegance.

Photo courtesy Dunes Hotel & Country Club

been surrounded. The beginning player may be awed and intimidated by the terminology and the physical setup—without reason.

The atmosphere is there, certainly. Casinos try to surround their Baccarat tables with an aura of elegance. The tables and chairs are of a substantially higher quality than those at a Blackjack table, for example. The area surrounding the table is roped off as a safeguard against too close contact with the hoi polloi. The dealers are formally attired and so, for that matter, are a majority of the female customers.

The "tone" of the game is set more by the stakes than by anything else, however. The minimum bet may vary from \$5 to \$20, depending on the casino, and the maximum is usually \$2,000—with a higher lid for heavy gamblers.

Baccarat has traditionally been a big-money game. Continental stories about \$400,000 and \$500,000 being risked on one hand are common and seem to be authentic. The French automobile manufacturer, Andre Citroen, lost approximately \$500,000 in one night's Baccarat play. Gordon Selfridge, the British department store magnate, not only gambled heavily himself but financed the famous Dolly Sisters of Ziegfield Follies fame, who are said to have gambled away nearly \$8 million of his money, mostly at Baccarat. They often lost \$10,000 or \$15,000 at the game. Nicholas Zagrophos of the group known as the Greek Syndicate, won astronomical sums at Baccarat, once winning three straight hands for a total profit of over half a million dollars. At another time, he lost \$100,000 more than that in a week's play. At one time when he was down to his last million francs, he bet it all on a hand of Baccarat, won, and continued to win.

The Nevada game actually came, not from the Continent, but from Cuba. It was a feature of the Havana casinos before Castro's rise to power and not only won popularity with American players but with Europeans, who found it much faster than Baccarat Banque or Chemin de Fer.

Because the American version of the game is still undergoing changes, a player may find minor differences in rules from one casino to another.

Edward Thorp, the man who originated the "counting system" for beating Blackjack, caused one of the original Cuban rules to be changed. At the time Thorp went to Las Vegas, a side bet was available at odds of 9 to 1 that the Bank hand would have a natural 9. The same bet could be made on a Natural 8 in the Bank hand, at the same odds. Thorp, using the "counting" system he pioneered in Blackjack, bet on natural 8's and 9's when the percentage was in his favor, and the game owners, when they discovered what was hitting them so hard, removed the betting option from the Baccarat layout.

Many gambling experts agree that Baccarat is the fairest, most even bet of any game to be found in the casinos, even not excluding craps and Blackjack where advantageous odds may be secured by using true odds and card-counting systems.

Because of the rules which are posted at every table, and the terminology, Baccarat seems at first glance to be a complicated game. Nothing could be further from the truth. The game is completely mechanical, and the only control or option a player has is which hand to bet and how much to wager on it. There is no possible way for a player to exercise skill, and the money management comes in betting, not in play.

You do not even need to know the slightest thing about the rules to play Baccarat. The dealer will see that you follow them, since they're inflexible. You take your seat at the Baccarat table and make a bet, either on the "Bank" hand or the "Player" hand. From then on, what happens to you depends on the fall of the cards.

Here is an illustration of a Baccarat table, with

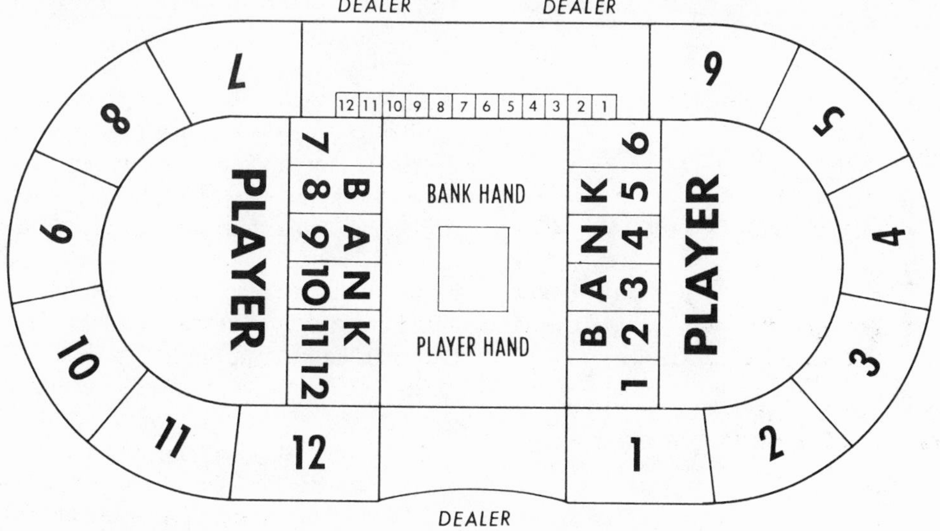

From "The Facts of Baccarat" ©Gambler's Book Club, Las Vegas, Nev.

Hand Values

tens and pictures do not count

hands counting zero

hands counting 5

naturals 8 and 9

Card Values—Six Decks

96 pictures and tens
have no value—they count zero

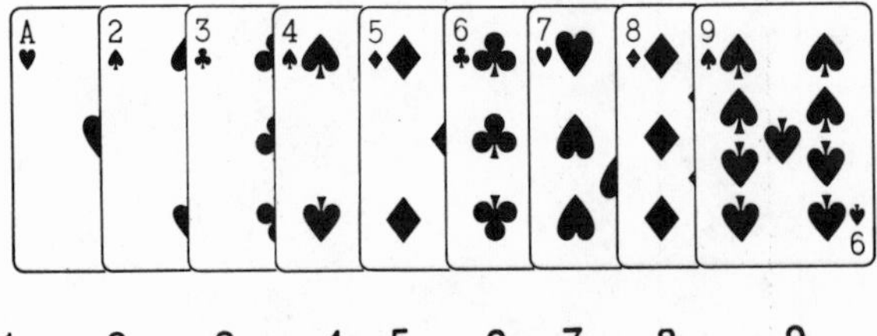

1 2 3 4 5 6 7 8 9

24 each—216 cards of index value

space for 12 players and three dealers. The dealer between seats 1 and 12 supervises the play and announces the winners. The two dealers between seats 6 and 7 collect losing bets and pay off winners. The boxes numbered from 1 through 12 and labeled "Bank" refer to seat numbers and are used by the dealer for bookkeeping purposes. Winning Player hands are paid 1 to 1. The five percent commission on winnings on Bank hands is noted in the center squares and the player settles with the dealer when he quits the game.

Object Of The Game

Nine is the highest possible count in Baccarat, and the higher hand wins. Face cards and tens have no value, with counts of over 9 acquiring the value of the second digit. A hand of 17 has a 7 value and a hand of 14 a 4 value, for example.

Two hands are dealt from a dealing box or "shoe." The one farthest from the shoe is the player hand and the one immediately in front of it is the Bank hand. The names, "Bank" and "Player" mean absolutely nothing except that they distinguish one hand from the other. The "Bank" hand is not the casino hand and the "Player" hand is not the sole choice of the players. Any player may wager on either hand, and no balance between amounts bet on the two hands is required. Theoretically, every bet can be on either hand.

All cards except face cards and tens have the value indicated on their faces, with the picture cards and tens counting zero. Suit means nothing. At the start, each hand contains two cards, the value of which is added together. When the total is more than 10, the first digit is dropped. A 7-8 hand, for example, becomes 5, and a 9-4 hand becomes 3.

A third card is drawn to a hand when the rules specify it, and if they total more than 20, the first digit is dropped. Six or eight decks are sometimes used, and this has no effect on the mathematical probabilities.

After all wagers are down, the dealer asks the person holding the shoe to deal. The player dealing has the Bank hand and the hand in front of the dealer is the Player hand. The Bank hand is shoved under the front edge of the shoe and the dealer puts the Player hand in front of whoever at the table has the largest wager on it. This player is asked to turn the hand up, and the dealer announces its value. Then he asks for the Bank hand to be turned face up and announces its value. If either hand has a natural 8 or 9, it is declared the winner.

If the rules demand the drawing of a third card to the Player hand, the dealer so indicates and the card is dealt, face up. If a third card is indicated by the rules for the Bank Hand, it, too, is dealt face up.

When the dealing is concluded, the dealer announces the winner.

If the winning hand is the Player hand, the shoe moves counterclockwise to the next customer at the table, who does the dealing but can bet on either the Bank hand or Player hand. As long as the Bank hand wins, the person with the shoe keeps dealing. Having the deal means absolutely nothing to the player.

The rules, which are precise, indicate when a third card is to be dealt. The Player hand must draw a third card if its two-card total is 0,1,2,3,4 or 5, and cannot draw with a 6,7,8 or 9.

The Bank hand, too stays on a 7,8 or 9 and cannot draw. If the Player hand's third card was either a 6 or 7, the Bank hand is compelled to take a third card if it holds a 6 total. If the Player hand third card was 1,2,3,4,5, 8, 9 or 10, the Bank must stand with a 6.

If the Bank hand totals 5 and the Player hand has drawn a third card which was a 4,5,6 or 7, the Bank hand must take a third card. If the Player hand third card was a 1,2,3,8, 9 or 10, the Bank hand must stand.

With a total of 4 the Bank hand must draw a third card if the Player hand has drawn a 2,3,4,5,6 or 7. The Bank hand must stand on its 4 total if the Player hand third card was 1,8,9 or 10.

With a three total, the Bank hand must draw a third card if the third card drawn by the player hand was a 1,2,3,4,5,6,7,0 or 10. The Bank hand cannot draw a third card if the Player hand third card was an 8.

With a total of 0,1 or 2, the Bank hand always draws a third card.

The only choice the bettor has is which hand to bet. Player hand winners are paid even money. Banker hand winners pay a five percent commission to the house. This is not a five percent commission in the strict sense, since the bettor playing the bank hand pays only when he wins.

The beginning player invariably asks why the Bank hand pays a commission on winnings and the Player hand doesn't. The rules permit the Bank hand to win more often than the Player hand. Then, the beginner ponders, wouldn't it be a good idea to always play the Bank hand. The answer is that, because of the five percent commission on winning Bank hands, the choice of sides is a "push." Over a long period of play, the casino should win 1.25 percent of money bet on Player hands. If the advantage is with the Bank hand, it is minute.

If any game is a toss-up for the person playing, it's Baccarat. You can't do anything to improve your chance of winning or anything to lessen it. It is a pure gamble, with all playing options controlled.

Because the two choices open to the player are so even, Baccarat is an execellent spot for the "hot" gam-

Baccarat Rules

PLAYER

HAVING	
0,1,2,3,4,5	DRAWS A CARD
6,7	STANDS
8,9	NATURAL-BANK CANNOT DRAW

BANKER

HAVING	DRAWS WHEN PLAYER DRAWS	STANDS WHEN PLAYER DRAWS
3	1,2,3,4,5,6,7,9,10	8
4	2,3,4,5,6,7	1,8,9,10
5	4,5,6,7	1,2,3,8,9,10
6	6,7	
7	STANDS	
8,9	NATURAL-PLAYER CANNOT DRAW	
BANK HAND STANDS WITH 6 WHEN PLAYER HAND STANDS WITH 6 OR 7		

Pictures and tens have no value

If Player takes no card, Banker stands on 6

Frequency of starting hands—6 Decks
Total two-card combination—48516

HAND TOTAL	HOW MANY IN 48516	PERCENT OF TOTAL	CHANCE IN ONE HAND
0	7140	14.71	6.80
1	4608	9.50	10.52
2	4584	9.44	10.58
3	4608	9.50	10.52
4	4584	9.44	10.58
5	4608	9.50	10.52
6	4584	9.44	10.58
7	4608	9.50	10.52
8	4584	9.44	10.58
9	4608	9.50	10.52
	48516	100.00	

From "The Facts of Baccarat" ©Gambler's Book Club, Las Vegas, Nev.

bler to parlay his winnings. Major A. Riddle, in his interesting book, *The Weekend Gambler's Handbook,* published in hard-cover by Random House, Inc., and then in paperback by Signet Books, tells the story of a friend who asked him how to bet $100 at Baccarat. Riddle recommended alternating bets, Bank, Player, starting with a $20 bet and parlaying after "dragging" $20 from the second win. His friend, Riddle relates, won 14 consecutive hands, holding at a $1,000 maximum bet, before losing on the 15th—and walked away from the table with $8,060 of the casino's money.

If it is possible to win a large sum at Baccarat by lucky parlays, don't mislead yourself into any "double up" or Martingale system of doubling wagers after each loss. Starting with a $20 bet, eight straight losses will find you past the double-up limit at the $2,000 maximum bet, with no hope of recouping a heavy loss without a long, miraculous streak of luck.

Clement McQuaid says, "One bet's as good as another in Baccarat. There's no way you can louse up a hand, like there is in Blackjack, and no way you can improve it, which you can do in Blackjack.

"Because it's such an even bet, it's a great spot for parlays if you're riding a lucky streak. Everything's chance, either hand you bet.

"If you're in a game with a $20 minimum, stick to the minimum while you're losing. If you win one, don't drag. Bet the 40 bucks. I have many friends who immediately double bets in Baccarat after one win and redouble after two! If you win the second bet, who knows, this may be your lucky night. Drag the 20 you started with, if you win, and bet 60. With a fourth win, you've got $120 out there. Your chance of winning the next hand is just the same as it was on the first hand, no better and no worse. Only there's one big difference. That's right, you're betting the house's money now.

"I almost never let a parlay ride in craps after four or, at the most, five passes—but I'd string along heavier on Baccarat. There aren't all the variables there are in craps. You've got as close to an even money bet as you'll get that you'll win again. It's a toss-up that you'll lose, but if you do, you've still got that $20 you dragged after your second win. If you win your sixth straight bet, you've got $960 out there. Put $460 into your pocket and bet $500. Keep betting $500 as long as you win, which probably won't be long. When you lose $500, go right back to your $20 minimum bet.

"The best way to gamble to win is to gamble with house money, not your own. Regardless of whose money it is, you've gotta hit three or more consecutive times to do yourself any real good. Alternating winners and losers won't ever line your pockets. Maybe the reason I'm advising you to try for five or six straight wins at Baccarat is that you can't make any misplays. If you're lucky, you'll win a bundle—and if you aren't, what's new?"

MR. ODDS-MAKER'S BEST BET

Mr. Odds-Maker says, "Baccarat is a great game for the casino player because you can't make a bad bet at bad odds or make a mistake in playing judgment that will be to your disadvantage. Take advantage of your luck. When you're winning, play for higher stakes."

Odds Against Romance

Numerous observers have reached the conclusion that gambling and romance don't seem to go together.

The widely known Palace of Pleasure operated by the Everleigh Sisters in the early days of Chicago contained a beautiful, tastefully decorated, comfortable gaming room, where gambling was permitted for a half-hour immediately following dinner every evening.

Patrons of the place protested the short period of gaming, but Ada Everleigh was adamant. "The most beautiful, charming girls in the world can't arouse any interest in men who are gambling," she explained.

The story of how Nick, the Greek, Dandolos' romance was broken up by a long gambling session is told in his biography, "Nick the Greek, King of the Gamblers, *by Cy Rice, published by Funk and Wagnalls.*

CHEMIN DE FER

Chemin de Fer, one of the most popular gambling games in Europe, is seldom played in American casinos. The major difference between it and Baccarat is that where in Baccarat the "house" is banker, in Chemin de Fer, the bank passes from player to player, with the players playing against each other.

The player designated as banker puts up a stake and the other players in the game play against it. A single player may bet the entire amount of the player's bank by calling out, "Banco!"

The "house" takes no part in the actual game, but extracts a percentage from every winning bank. Most players in the United States are reluctant to assume the bank's responsibilities and feel that the house "cut" into bank winnings makes banking the game a bad bet.

Big Max, an American stationed in Italy disagrees —the odds are with the banker and thus he'll always take his shoe.

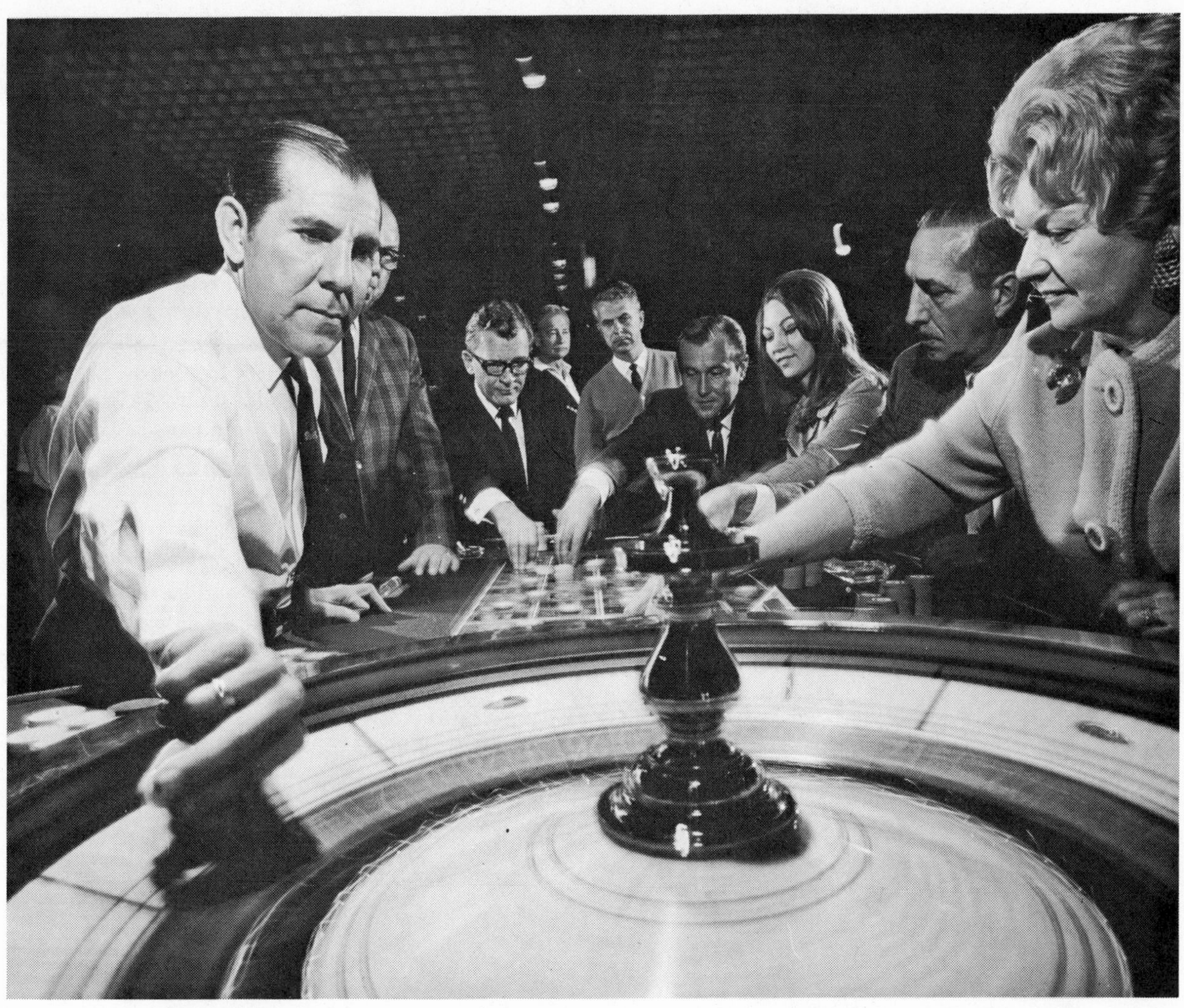

ROULETTE

If Baccarat has built-in snob appeal, so does Roulette, along with a tradition of being socially "in." For some reason, the Roulette wheel has always been mentally associated with the aristocracy. Pascal, a French mathematics scholar, is supposed to have invented the game in the 17th century, as an offshoot of experimentation with perpetual motion devices.

Gambling with wheels started almost with the invention of the wheel. The Romans are said to have gambled with spinning chariot wheels, and various "wheel of fortune" devices have existed in nearly every age of man. A *Modern Hoyle* edition dated 1814 shows that the English were playing a game called E.O. (Even-Odd) that used a wheel almost identical to the Roulette wheel but with even-odd designations on the slots instead of numbers.

French Roulette reached England some time around 1820 and soon replaced E.O. Descriptions of the game show that it was identical with the Roulette game now played in the Nevada casinos. It probably reached the United States via New Orleans. Wherever it was introduced, it was a top game in American casinos until after World War II. Men who became familiar with Craps and Blackjack in the armed forces stuck with those games in civilian life. Currently, two and a half times as many crap tables as Roulette tables operate in the Nevada casinos.

The game is simple, easy to play, and exciting, with a wide variety of possible bets and combinations of bets, some at long odds and some practically even.

The Roulette wheel is a beautifully-made piece of equipment, built with precision and delicately balanced. Shaped like a bowl, the wheel is spun counterclockwise by the dealer, who then spins the ball clockwise around the outer rim of the bowl. When the ball slows down, it drops into one of 38 pockets in the wheel. The pockets are identical in size and shape, each bearing a number (1 through 36, 0 and

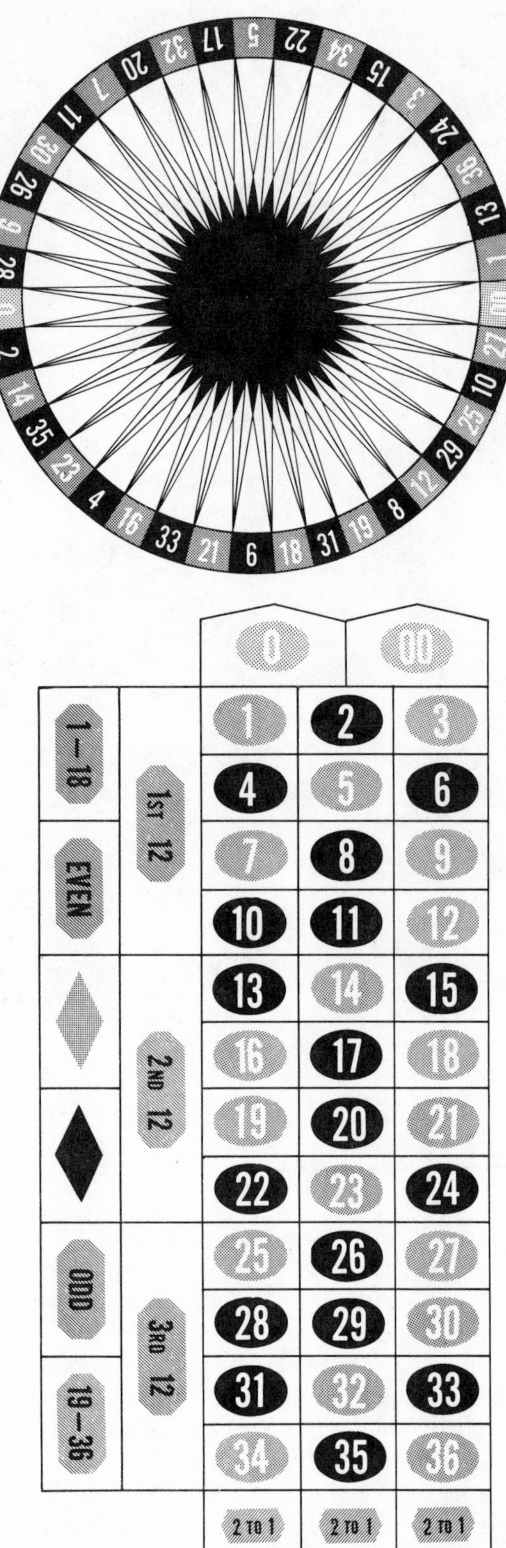

From the "Facts of Roulette"
@ Gambler's Book Club, Las Vegas, Nev.

Wheel and Layout

The zero, double-zero Roulette wheel used in Nevada today is the same as those used over 200 years ago. The layout is American design and the standard model used today.

Las Vegas Honeymoon

Frank Sinatra has a favorite gambling story about a young couple who decided to go to Las Vegas on their honeymoon. The bridegroom was fascinated by the casinos, and bet so heavily and unwisely that the newlyweds were soon down to their last two dollars.

They were all ready to check out, but the husband wasn't quite ready to give up. "Let me take the two bucks down to the casino," he pleaded. "I can't explain it, but I have a feeling that my luck has turned."

The bride reluctantly agreed, and the young man headed straight for a roulette table, where he bought two dollars' worth of chips and put them on Number 13. Thirteen won, and he let his winnings ride. When 13 came up a second time, he moved his winnings to Number 14, and 14 won.

Within an hour, he won $50,000. So he picked up his winnings and headed for the cashier's cage. A sudden wild impulse seized him and he spun around, went back to the table and put his entire winnings on Number 33. The wheel spun, and stopped on Number 10. The bridegroom shrugged, and walked slowly back to his room.

"How'd you come out?" his wife asked hopefully.

He shook his head. "I lost the two dollars."

---

00). Alternate red and black colors are applied to the numbers, except for 0 and 00, which are green.

Here, at left, is an illustration of the Roulette table layout.

It looks complicated but is actually simple, and is the basis for identifying all bets. In addition to Odd, Even, Red and Black, it offers the basis for betting on individual numbers and many combinations of them.

To avoid confusion and disputes, each player has chips of one color, different from the color used by other players in the game. These chips have a value from 10¢ upwards in casinos. Oddly, the most famous Roulette game—at Monte Carlo—does not use different color chips; confusion and arguments often result—pity the poor American, without the gift of the French tongue, trying to claim his bets and wins!

The numbers 0 and 00 are important to casino management, representing an important part of the house percentage. When either 0 or 00 comes up, the house wins all 1 to 1 bets except those that may have been placed on 0 and 00.

A straight-up bet on a single number pays 35 to 1. A "split" bet, made by placing a chip on the line between any two numbers on the Roulette layout, pays 17 to 1. Sixty-two possible two-number bets are available to the player. A three-number bet is made by

30	26	9	28	0	2	14	35	23
29	25	10	27	00	1	13	36	24
25	10	27	00	1	13	36	24	3
26	9	28	0	2	14	35	23	4
1	13	36	24	3	15	34	22	5
2	14	35	23	4	16	33	21	6
3	15	34	22	5	17	32	20	7
4	16	33	21	6	18	31	19	8
5	17	32	20	7	11	30	26	9
6	18	31	19	8	12	29	25	10
7	11	30	26	9	28	0	2	14
8	12	29	25	10	27	00	1	13
17	32	20	7	11	30	26	9	28
18	31	19	8	12	29	25	10	27
10	27	00	1	13	36	24	3	15
9	28	0	2	14	35	23	4	16
13	36	24	3	15	34	22	5	17
14	35	23	4	16	33	21	6	18
15	34	22	5	17	32	20	7	11
16	33	21	6	18	31	19	8	12
21	6	18	31	19	8	12	29	25
22	5	17	32	20	7	11	30	26
23	4	16	33	21	6	18	31	19
24	3	15	34	22	5	17	32	20
0	2	14	35	23	4	16	33	21
00	1	13	36	24	3	15	34	22
19	8	12	29	25	10	27	00	1
20	7	11	30	26	9	28	0	2
12	29	25	10	27	00	1	13	36
11	30	26	9	28	0	2	14	35
31	19	8	12	29	25	10	27	00
32	20	7	11	30	26	9	28	0
33	21	6	18	31	19	8	12	29
34	22	5	17	32	20	7	11	30
35	23	4	16	33	21	6	18	31
36	24	3	15	34	22	5	17	32
28	0	2	14	35	23	4	16	33
27	00	1	13	36	24	3	15	34

Sequence of Numbers

From the "Facts of Roulette"
@ Gambler's Book Club, Las Vegas, Nev.

KNOWLEDGE IN PRINT

John Luckman, once a dealer in Nevada casinos, got a bright idea when he started the Gambler's Book Club, a Las Vegas company which now stocks close to 500 books on gambling. The books are classified, with Cards and a sub-classification, Card Magic, and Racing being the largest categories. Some of the books are published by Gambler's Book Club and some have been authored by Luckman, using the pen name of Walter I. Nolan. There is a ten-day return privilege on any book ordered from the club, and a list of titles and prices is available upon request from Gambler's Book Club, Box 4115, Las Vegas, Nev. 89106.

Magic, Inc., a Chicago firm, has a large and interesting catalogue of magic books, and some of the listed volumes include everything there is to know about trickery with cards and dice. The catalogue even lists books on the Shell Game and Three-Card Monte, two classic gambling swindles.

placing a chip on the line at the end of a row of three numbers. It pays 11 to 1 and there are 15 such bets possible.

If the player wants to bet four numbers, he may bet them individually with separate chips or make a "corner" bet, placing his chip at the juncture of four numbers so that it actually touches a part of all four. This bet pays 8 to 1, and there are 22 possible combinations. There is only one 5-number bet, a wager on 0, 00, 1,2 and 3. Since it pays 6 to 1 and should pay 6 and 1/5 to 1 to be on a par with other number bets, gamblers consider it a poor risk.

A six-number bet is made by putting a chip on the end of the line between two rows of three numbers. This bet pays 5 to 1 and has 11 possible combinations.

Bets on the first 12 numbers, the second 12 or the third 12 are placed on spaces marked "1st 12" "2nd 12" and "3rd 12." Another way of betting on 12 numbers is to place your wager in the space marked "2 to 1" at the end of each of the three long columns of numbers. There are six possible 12-number combinations, and they pay 2 to 1.

Red or Black, Even or Odd and 1-18 and 19-36 are paid 1 to 1. A substantial part of the wagering usually falls on the six possible 1 to 1 bets.

If there were no house percentage, a straight-up bet on a number would pay 37 to 1 instead of 35 to 1. At 35 to 1, the house advantage is slightly over five percent. Every bet in the Nevada Roulette game gives the house an exact 5.26 percent advantage, except for the five-number bet, which has a built-in house advantage of 7.89 percent.

Roulette is the oldest casino game still in operation, and the house loves it because of its steady 5.26 percent house advantage. Over the years, more systems have been developed for beating Roulette than for any other game—and none of them works consistently. Most of the systems are based on increasing bets after losses, a practice which experienced gamblers shun. The way to beat the Roulette game is to win quickly and get out! To win any appreciable amount of money, winnings must be successfully parlayed. Most casual Roulette players are in the game for fun and don't want to leave after a short period of play.

Roulette offers fun and excitement of an entirely

different kind from that offered by craps. The atmosphere is entirely different and the pace is much slower and seats are available. Where craps is one of the noisiest gambling games known to man, Roulette is one of the quietest. And where a 2 to 1 payoff on some bets is about the longest odds in craps, the 35 to 1 payoff on a single number in Roulette is a thrilling possibility to the optimistic gambler.

Clement McQuaid says, "The best bet in Roulette is to play for fun. Buy in with a few dollars' worth of chips and see how long you can keep going without having to buy more.

"There've been more systems in Roulette than there are beans in chili, and some of 'em work—for a little while. Keep playin' any Roulette system, though, and you're gonna go for broke.

"I've seen players with charts of Roulette number sequences, and they studied the numbers comin' up on the wheel like they were crammin' for a history exam. They'd get the idea that the numbers were following a pattern. But somehow, when they started betting, the pattern seemed to change. Actually, every drop of the ball into a slot depends on chance. Chance will come up with a few odd number sequences, a few strange arrangements, but there's no way of knowing when it's going to happen or what it'll be.

"I knew one fellow who had a numerology system. It was very deep and he worked hard at it. That is, he worked hard at it until he ran out of scratch. The Martingale players take the worst beating of all, doubling up after each loss. I saw one fellow wait for red to come up five times in a row, and then he bet on black on the next spin of the wheel. It happened six times during the evening, and every time, he bet a bundle. And luck was with him. He almost broke even. Black came up twice, a double 0 once, and red three times.

"If I wanted to win at Roulette, I'd play like I was hitting the slot machines. I'd put in a few bucks, and if I won, try to parlay an even-money bet, dragging after the second win. And if I got ahead on the parlay, I'd quit the game.

"Most Roulette players don't go into the game expecting to break the house. They play for fun, and they enjoy seeing how well they can do. The average player who goes in determined to win plays too long and tries to win too much. In any game that's pure chance and has a house percentage of better than five percent, you're gonna lose if you play very long. You've gotta get lucky fast and quit fast, while you're still ahead.

"If you ever see me at a roulette table, you'll know that I'm playing for kicks, not because I expect to break the bank."

MR. ODDS-MAKER'S BEST BET

Mr. Odds-Maker says, "The house percentage is 5.26 against you. If you're the conservative type, play the colors or odd 'n' even. Only the more daring player should bet individual numbers."

MARK PRICE HERE

KENO
$25,000.00
LIMIT TO AGGREGATE PLAYERS EACH GAME

CAESARS PALACE

WINNING TICKETS MUST BE COLLECTED IMMEDIATELY AFTER EACH KENO GAME IS CALLED.

1	2	3	4	5	6	7	8	9	10
11	12	13	14	15	16	17	18	19	20
21	22	23	24	25	26	27	28	29	30
31	32	33	34	35	36	37	38	39	40

WE PAY ON TICKET PLAYED BY PLAYER EACH GAME

41	42	43	44	45	46	47	48	49	50
51	52	53	54	55	56	57	58	59	60
61	62	63	64	65	66	67	68	69	70
71	72	73	74	75	76	77	78	79	80

KENO RUNNERS ARE AVAILABLE FOR YOUR CONVENIENCE
WE ARE NOT RESPONSIBLE IF TICKETS ARE TOO LATE FOR CURRENT GAME

A typical Keno ticket

KENO

The Keno Lounge is usually one of the most comfortable places in the casino—and management hopes you'll find it so comfortable that you'll stay right there and play.

Casino owners say, "Love that Keno!" If everyone who visits the casinos were to become a rabid Keno fan, casino owners would soon have more money than the United States mint.

Keno is for the gambler who believes in miracles and not only believes in them but thinks he's due for one. There's a strong house percentage of 25 percent upwards. On top of this, on a 10-Spot ticket, only six out of a hundred ever win anything, with five of the six returning even money. You get even money on a 5-Spot win and your chance of getting it is 1 in 20. Your chance of scoring a 6-spot win is 1 in 88; a 7-Spot, 1 in 620; an 8-spot, 1 in 74,000; a 9-spot, 1 in 163,000, and a 10-spot, 1 in 9,000,000!

Keno offers the largest prizes of any game in the casino—a remotely possible $25,000 payoff. In return for the long odds, it gives you the least chance of winning. It's a little like buying a ticket in a big lottery. The bettor has many possibilities, all at long odds. There are 80 numbers on the ticket. To play an 8-

The relaxing atmosphere of a Las Vegas Keno Lounge makes it one of the most comfortable places in the casino.

Spot card, the player marks through eight numbers on his card with a crayon. He gives the card to a Keno writer, pays 60¢ and gets back a copy of his ticket with the number of the game printed on it. Shortly thereafter, a Keno "goose" selects 20 numbers at random and these are posted on a Keno board. If five or more of the numbers coincide with those marked on the player's ticket, he wins. On a 60¢ ticket, he gets $5 back. Six numbers gets $50, seven pays $1,100, and eight pays $12,500. There are 15 basic Keno tickets, 1-spot through 15-spot, with millions of possible combinations. With the High-Low tickets and "Way" tickets added to the basic combinations, the possible combinations run into the zillions, and it's a safe bet that millions of them will never be written.

Play Keno because you enjoy the relaxing atmosphere of the Lounge, because you like the free cocktails, because you're intrigued by the almost infinite combinations of the game, because you're interested in numerology, or because you want a break from serious gambling. Play for any of these reasons, but don't play to win.

That is, don't play to win unless you're convinced that Fate has singled you out to play the fantastic long-shot against overwhelming odds and win.

Chinese laborers brought to the United States to build the railroads in the 1800's brought a game with them that had been played in China for more than 2,000 years. The game was Kino, or what is now called Keno. Occidentals who ran into it during America's pioneer years referred to it as "The Chinese Lottery," and most western towns had at least one Keno game going.

Casino owners defend the high percentage against the player. The cost of operating the game, they maintain, is the highest of any game in the house. Operation of the Lounge, maintenance of equipment, constant use of tickets that can't be re-used, and the large number of people required to keep the game going smoothly unquestionably make Keno an expensive

Business Expense

A tourist who won $50,000 at Keno in Las Vegas was visited immediately by an Internal Revenue agent.

"It's not clear profit," the tourist said quickly. "I had to invest $2.40 in Keno tickets."

---

game to operate — but the game's overhead in no way alters the fact that Keno has a high percentage working against the player.

Chuck Hartigan says, "You gotta be joking! How do you pick a Best Bet in buying an Irish Sweepstakes ticket? But I'm making a point there. People *do* buy Irish Sweepstakes tickets, year after year—and a few of them make the Big Killing every year.

"I'd buy a Keno ticket the same way I'd buy a Sweepstakes ticket—hoping to be the guy lightning strikes but not expecting it.

"You want a Best Bet for Keno? I'll give you one. Wait until a Friday, the thirteenth, when you have a dream in which 80 beautiful girls are competing in a beauty contest. The 15 winners step out in front, with their numbers hanging around their necks. Remember those numbers and bet them on a Keno card the next day, Saturday, the Fourteenth.

"So what if you never have a dream like that? You're better off. You've saved yourself 60¢."

MR. ODDS-MAKER'S BEST BET

Mr. Odds-Maker says, "Keno is an exciting game, with an extremely high percentage against you. What makes it interesting to the average player is that you win a lot for a small amount. The best bet for the player is the Eight Spot ticket, where you can win $25,000 for an investment of $1.20."

WHEEL OF FORTUNE, CHUCK-A-LUCK AND OTHER COME-ONS

Some games that are found in some casinos should be dismissed as "bait," games that no informed gambler would dream of playing.

Don't blame the casino owner for having them. A good part of the wear-and-tear on his thick carpeting comes from the shoes of "lookers," tourists who are out to see the sights and get anything for nothing that's available.

There are a lot of them in the Nevada casinos, watching the shows, eating the appetizers, maneuvering an occasional free drink, crowding up around the players for further free entertainment, and having themselves a great time without any expenditure.

When they decide to gamble a couple of dollars, to have something to talk about when they go home, they almost invariably gravitate to the Wheel of Fortune or Chuck-a-Luck or some other come-on.

The Wheel of Fortune appeals to them because they understand it. They've seen variations of it at carnivals in their home towns, they've been assured that the games here are all honest, and the odds look pretty good.

Of course, the odds on almost any of the many variations of the Wheel of Fortune are terrible, as any experienced gambler knows. They aren't meant to be good, and neither are they meant to attract any real gambler. If the "lookers" want to play them, welcome aboard!

THE WIZARD OF ID

FARO-WELL!

Nevada casino owners breathed a collective sigh of relief when Faro gasped its last breath as a casino game—not because they had lost great sums of money to Faro players but because the game simply didn't pay its way.

The game employs a layout of 13 cards, from Ace down to deuce. Players put their bets on individual cards. A shuffled deck is put into a shoe and the dealer deals one card at a time from it. The first card means nothing, but after it, the second card is a loser and the third is a winner. The cards alternate, loser and winner, until only three are left. If the dealer turns two consecutive cards of matching value, he gets half of whatever is bet on that card.

"The game got to be an exercise," one casino owner says. "Nobody won or lost enough to stick in your eye—including the house. Faro was the champion time-killer of casino gambling."

The "lookers" have seen Chuck-a-Luck games, too, and the shrewdest of them leave the Wheel of Fortune after a few unfortunate spins and look for a Chuck-a-Luck layout. They see a revolving cage containing three dice, along with a layout with numbers from 1 through 6. The payoff for winners is at even money. If the three dice come up 4,5 and 6, the dealer picks up the money from the 1,2 and 3 squares and deposits it in the winning 4,5 and 6 squares. The house has no percentage at all. What could be fairer?

Almost any game in the casino, with the exception of Keno, that's what could be fairer. On the next spin of the cage, suppose two aces and a 6 come up. Two dollars are deposited in front of the $1 bet on Number 1, along with $1 in the square occupied by 6. The house has taken in $4 and paid out three. Not a bad percentage for the casino. Now, on the next roll, let's say that three 4's come up. The house pays out $3 to No. 4 and makes $2 profit. That's even better for the house, isn't it? A 40 percent advantage. Of the 216 combinations to be made with three dice, 90 make pairs and six make three of a kind. In other words, the players can break even only 120 times out of 216. In other words, betting $6 a round, a dollar per number, for 216 times, the house will win $108. And if every bet is a $1 bet, never at any time does the casino risk a dollar of its own money. Every cent in the game belongs to the players—or belonged to them at the outset.

Faro went the way of all flesh in Nevada not so much because it had lost its appeal to players but because the house percentage was too low and casinos got hurt by expert Faro players.

Games cease to exist for only two reasons, because people quit playing them or because they don't show a profit for their owners. As long as there are uninformed "lookers" to patronize Wheels of Fortune, those wheels will continue to spin.

If you can invent a game that's fun to play, looks like a good gamble and has a built-in house percentage of ten percent or more, you can write your own ticket. You have the kind of game that casino operators dream about.

Roz Adler says, "I have no sympathy for people who lose a bundle at Keno or the slots or Roulette and then cry about it. There's no law compelling anybody to play games that have long house odds. And Blackjack, Craps and Baccarat offer the player a good run for his money, with a nearly even chance. Look at the good casinos and the way they're operated. It's remarkable to me that a first-class casino can give you so much and still show a fair profit.

"That brings up another point. The percentage is usually the same in the best casino in town and the worst. In the best, you get treated great, you're comfortable, the air's kept clean, the tables are neat and you enjoy yourself. On top of that, the policing's usually better. The grifters and hustlers who flock wherever there's money, hoping to take advantage of the players, are watched so closely that they give up and leave. In a second-rate casino, nothing's as nice and you're usually getting prodded to part with more of your money. It's one of the few cases I know where going first-class doesn't cost any more than going steerage."

MR. ODDS-MAKER'S BEST BET

Mr. Odds-Maker says, "Regardless of what the game is called or what color the layout is, wheels of fortune give management a top percentage—anywhere from five to 20 percent. Your best bet is to watch, or move on."

CASINO POKER

Confirmed poker devotees accept no substitute for poker, and feel that they're discriminated against in the more elegant casinos of Nevada. Poker is not considered a casino game on The Strip in Las Vegas, and the would-be player has to go downtown to get a game.

If he's determined to play Casino Poker, his best bet is to go to Gardena, California. That's right—Gardena, California, about ten miles south of the Hollywood Park race track. For many years, poker

Downtown Las Vegas.

Nevada's Casinos— Housed in Splendor

Above—The Sands Hotel, Las Vegas.
Below—Dunes Hotel & Country Club, Las Vegas.

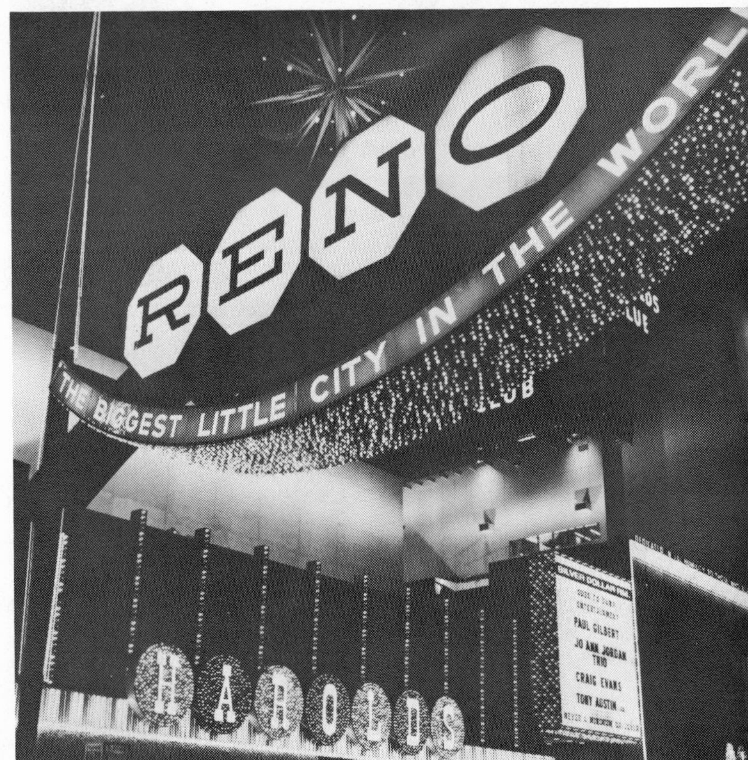

Harold's Club, Reno.

Above and below right—Tropicana Hotel and Country Club.

Binion's Horseshoe Hotel and Casino, Las Vegas.

Circus Circus, Las Vegas.

THE FIRST "COUNTER"?

Nick Zographos, legendary member of the Greek Syndicate who died in 1953, made his first big gambling money at Baccarat. The "shoe" contained 312 cards at the outset of the game, but Zographos, with an incredible memory, kept mental note of every card that was played, and had worked out in advance the mathematical effect on the game of every card that was no longer in the "shoe."

Once when he had lost nearly $700,000 in a week's play at Cannes, he came back to the Baccarat table with his last million francs and bet the whole amount. His first two cards were face cards, which don't count in Baccarat, but his third card was the nine of Diamonds, a sure winner. It was the turning point, and he recouped his heavy loss in a few evenings' play.

The nine of Diamonds became his trademark, engraved on his jewelry and embroidered on his linen. With it as his good luck charm, he never again found himself near financial disaster.

casinos have thrived in the little community, with the approval of city and state officials. At last count, there were about six licensed and legal poker casinos. The city government gets no argument from poker players in its contention that it is licensing a game of skill.

While operations may vary slightly from place to place, the two clubs operated by the Bow Herbert Organization, the Gardena Club and the Horseshoe Club, serve as good examples. They are open from 9 a.m. to 5 a.m., except on Wednesdays, when they are closed, and on Sundays, when they don't open until noon. Approximately 350 Herbert employees are unionized, and many of them have been with the clubs for over 20 years. TV lounges and restaurants are available in both clubs. Liquor is taboo.

House rules are detailed and specific, covering every imaginable contingency. One of the most interesting house rules is that "husband and wife and immediate relatives are not allowed to play at the same table."

Classic draw poker, with five cards, is the usual game. Stakes vary from table to table, but are clearly stipulated as to maximum bets and raises.

When a player has tested his luck and skill in all of the Gardena casinos, he can go to San Diego's Mission Valley Strip and open the yellow pages of the phone book to "Card Rooms." He may find as many as a dozen listed.

Tom James, who has a passion for poker, plays Casino Poker only when it's "the only game in town." His reasoning is, "I like to know the people I'm playing against. Psychology is an important part of the game. When I know the players, I get a big kick out of figuring what they're going to do. On top of that, my father told me never to play cards with strangers.

"On the other hand, most of the players in a casino game love poker. That's why they're there. And you get the fun of playing against good, stiff competition, people who know what the game is all about. A casino game is a good place to test your skill."

Casino Poker differs from most casino games in that the players are playing against each other, not against the house. The casino furnishes facilities, management and supervision, for a fee. Many good poker players feel that the expert management and supervision make Casino Poker more desirable than private games.

Obviously, the successful Gardena clubs are proof that there's a good market for well-conducted casino poker.

MR. ODDS-MAKER'S BEST BET

Mr. Odds-Maker says, "Casino management does not consider Casino Poker as a profit potential. It's simply an accomodation for the guest who wants it—and a highly relaxing game. If you're the best poker player at the table, you should win. Just remember that most of the people who play Casino Poker are good at the game or they wouldn't be there." ♠

Easy Credit

Nick, the Greek, Dandelos, the gambler who became a legend during his lifetime, died broke—but he could get a thousand dollars in gambling stake money from at least one Las Vegas casino whenever he wanted to gamble.

Either he had become a compulsive gambler in his declining years or his luck had run out. Whatever the cause, he invariably lost the stake money—and nobody ever tried to collect from him. He was welcome to another thousand on another night, without argument.

An intimate of Nick's explains. "It was a sure thing for the casino. The house was reasonably sure he was going to lose, because it always happened. If he happened to win, the thousand would be paid back immediately from his winnings. The house wasn't out any commodity or product. They had given Nick the use of some chips for an hour or so. They not only got the money back; they even got the chips back.

"What it amounted to was that the house had a celebrity shill, without cost. Even when he was through as a gambler, the public was interested in him and he had a certain value as window dressing."

BOOK THREE:

YA WANNA BET?

Gambling without a rule book—how to make bets on any sport and when. Bob Martin, Mr. Odds-Maker from Las Vegas, gives you the low-down on the best ways to make sure you're a winner in spectator and participating sports.

Ya wanna bet?

It started with man betting on himself against other creatures and the elements. If he lost, what he lost was his life. If he won, he had the privilege of continuing to exist. Sometimes the odds were heavily against him, but the bet wasn't one he could take or leave.

As man rose above his competition, he began to have choices and the opportunity to exercise judgement. That's when he first said to his associates, "I'll betcha!" And he's been making bets ever since.

From the time one child says to another, "I'll bet you can't do this," he is making bets. Even the simplest children's games are, basically, bets.

Run, Sheep, Run is "I'll bet you can't catch me."

Blind Man's Buff is "I'll bet you can't find me."

Musical Chairs is "I'll bet I'm quicker than you are."

Simple children's games like "Old Maid" are picture versions of games with playing cards.

An infant learning to walk is encouraged with, "I'll bet you can't walk from that chair to me."

From the moment of comprehension, a child is taught to bet on himself. And since children are natural hero worshippers, they soon start to bet on others, both children and adults. As their reasoning powers grow, they try to figure the outcome of situations in which they find themselves and they make a stand or take a course of action based on their decisions. In other words, they bet on their judgement.

Without man's willingness to bet on himself and his ideas, progress would stop. Business would cease to exist.

A great and thriving business, the insurance business, is a form of betting that touches nearly everyone. The insurance company's odds-makers (actuaries) determine the odds against catastrophe striking an individual and make a bet, based on those odds. If the odds have been correctly determined, with a fair margin of profit allowed, the insurance company prospers.

The major difference between the insurance operation and bookmaking is that the insurance company does an aggressive selling job because it is legally allowed to promote. The bookmaker doesn't have to,

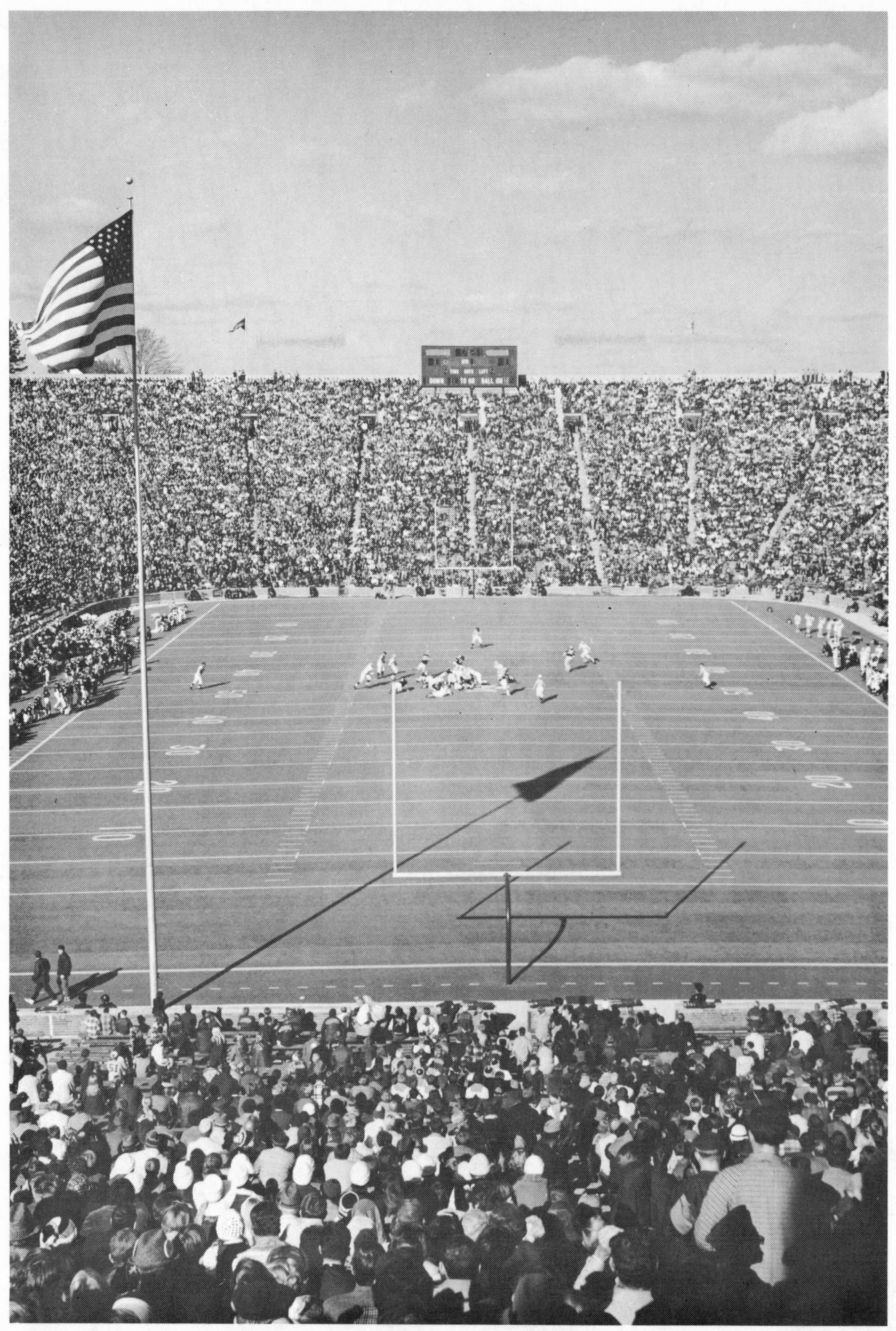

and even if he were so inclined, couldn't safely advertise and market his wares in most parts of the United States where his business is illegal.

Insurance companies will bet that a person will live to a certain age. They will bet that rain won't fall on certain specified days. They will bet against damage by fire, tornado, flood and earthquake. They will bet against the theft of personal property. A company like Lloyd's of London will bet against almost any conceivable calamity.

Most of the people who buy insurance buy it as a form of protection. Without insurance, disaster could conceivably wipe them out. Insurance is almost universally regarded as a wise precaution.

Aside from his insurance bets, the average man bets not for protection but for personal gain. Required to gamble in his business or professional career, man sharpens his betting instinct and ability by betting on propositions not related to his working hours, for fun and possible profit.

If he has any ability at any sport, and sometimes even if he hasn't, he bets on himself to defeat his opponent. In golf, bowling, skeet and trap shooting, handball, badminton, horseshoes, croquet, Indian wrestling, coin tossing, darts, and other games of skill, a bet adds to the excitement and pleasure. Even when he knows he is outclassed, he works out a satisfactory handicap that makes the match more even, and still bets on himself.

The average American male is sports-minded, and from betting on himself, it is a short and logical step to bet on others. He bets on the sports teams of his favorite school, as well as on his favorite professional teams. He follows sports closely, either attends events or watches them on television, and forms strong opinions as to the merits of competing teams, backing his choice with money.

He not only bets on teams but on individuals. He bets on boxers, automobile racing drivers, professional golfers and bowlers, pool and billiards champions, tennis stars and others.

He not only bets on sports but on almost anything that happens where an element of doubt exists. He bets substantially on candidates for public office. He bets on the stock and grain markets. He bets on the outcome of well-publicized court cases. He bets on the passage of certain bills in Congress. He bets on the weather. He bets on the attendance at public events. He bets not only on the outcome of wars but on the length of their duration. He bets that a new play will be a hit or a flop. In the absence of anything else, he bets heads or tails, odd or even.

He makes freak bets. He bets which of two frogs will jump farther. He puts two peanuts on the ground and bets on which one a squirrel will pick up first. On a fishing trip, he bets that he will catch a fish before the person who's fishing with him does, and bets that his fish will be larger. He bets on which of two toboggans will coast farther.

He bets on his accuracy at tossing cards into a hat. In many rural communities, he bets his expectoration ability for both distance and accuracy.

He bets on how deep a well digger will drill before he strikes water. He bets the size of his garden produce against a neighbor's. He bets on whether an expected baby will be a boy or a girl, and, with the proper odds, he'll even bet that the baby will turn out to be twins. He bets that his car will travel more miles on a gallon of gas than a friend's.

He works out elaborate "catch" bets, wagers which he seems almost certain to lose but which are so contrived that he's almost sure to win. There's the classic example of the bettor who proposed to a heavy-drinking friend, "I'll bet you ten bucks that you can't drink three of the Galway Pub's martinis before lunch today and then get out of the restaurant without help." The friend took the bet, before he realized it was election day and all bars were closed until after sundown.

He often bets the lunch check. He bets a new hat, a new necktie, theater tickets, a bottle of liquor or whatever seems like a good wager at the moment. After almost every election, some losing bettor attracts crowds as he pays off a bet by rolling a peanut a certain distance on the sidewalk with his nose, or something equally outlandish.

One rabid group of golfers often makes a side bet for "Announcements." For one week after his loss, the loser is obligated to rise and state in a loud, clear voice, regardless of where he is, whenever the winner asks him, "Joe Blank (the winner's name) is the greatest golfer in the whole world." It was probably the ultimate in announcement bets when this two column by three inch advertisement appeared in a Detroit newspaper, "Vincent Vernon is the world's greatest putter. (Signed) George Gaines."

The betting isn't entirely masculine. Although women sometimes bet on their favorite teams in sports and on themselves in golf and bowling, their wagering generally goes into different fields. They're big on "romance" bets. Whether or not a certain couple will become engaged calls for wagering, as does a rivalry between two suitors. Let a marriage show indications of going on the rocks and there will be betting on whether or not it ends in divorce. Let an attractive grass-widow set her sights on an attractive and eligible male, and the betting begins. Will she get him or won't she?

A mother who scarcely knows one sport from another will bet on her son's team to win, not because she thinks it's a good bet but because it seems like the right thing to do.

Day in and day out, the heavy betting is on sports. Betting on sports events and personal sports partici-

THE MATCH GAME

"One of the most expensive games in the world to learn to play is a form of the Match Game," the head of the Confidence detail in a mid-western police department says. "Every year, we get a few protests from a few would-be gamblers who have finally learned the secret.

"The rules are simple. You start with 15 matches in a heap, and two players alternate, removing one, two or three at their option. The object of the game is *not* to take the last match. The person who takes it loses. If the insider draws first, he takes two matches and then continues to draw so that the victim will have an odd number to draw from each time. If he can force the victim to draw from 5 matches, he has him. Only when the victim can draw from four, three or two matches can he win.

"By the time a beginner catches on, he is so far in the hole that he either complains of being swindled or works the same swindle on others to try to recoup his loss.

"Believe it or not, we still get occasional complaints from the victim of the old 'Odd Man Wins' coin-matching game in which a team of confederates slap down a Heads and a Tails every time, so that the third man is bound to lose to one or the other."

---

pation is exceeded only by betting on the horses.

Over 2,000 bookmakers in the United States specialize in handling sports wagers, and there's little gamble involved in their operation. Their handling of a sports event is such that backers of one team are actually betting against backers of another, with the bookmaker getting from 4.6 to 8.3 percent on every bet, as long as the betting on both teams is even.

There's the six-to-five, pick-your-team betting line for small bettors and the $11 to $10 line for larger ones. In both cases, the extra dollar goes to the bookmaker.

A "sports line" is determined by skillful sports event handicappers who sell their information to bookmakers throughout the United States. From the moment the opening line is set, bookmakers and handicappers keep track of the betting action, and the odds are maneuvered to keep an even flow of betting money coming from both sides. By game time, the amount of money bet on one team against another has had more to do with the odds than the comparative abilities of the two teams.

Odds-making is a big business. For example, one sports service that employs 18 people collects around $8 million a year in service fees from bookmakers.

The bookmakers usually set a $20,000 top limit on sports bets, although the lid is removed for baseball's World Series every year. Baseball accounts for slightly less than half of the money bet, football is about 40 percent and hockey, boxing and basketball account for most of the remainder. Hockey and football betting are on the increase. Basketball gets little action, and betting on boxing has sharply declined in recent years.

Newsweek Magazine estimated as long ago as 1960 that $10 billion a year was being bet illegally on American sports events. It credited $10 million a week to New York City, $8 million to Los Angeles, $5 million to San Francisco, $4 million to Chicago, and about the same amount to Pittsburgh, Detroit, Cleveland and Baltimore.

If you want to bet, you're not alone. And even if a friend won't bet with you, there's no problem. Your neighborhood bookmaker is eager to serve you.

BASEBALL

Following the infamous Black Sox scandal of 1919, major league baseball instituted a police action that has continued through the years. The faintest hint of misconduct on a player's part results in thorough investigation and prompt discipline.

With major league salaries as high as they currently are and with the side benefits that go with star status, it is hard to think of a lure that would tempt any successful ball player — unless he happened to be stupid.

With the purity of baseball certified and practically insured, bookmakers have found the sport something of a bonanza. When both the National and American leagues expanded their membership a few years ago and increased the number of games on their schedules, the vein became even richer. Day-to-day wagers through bookmakers on individual teams jumped from roughly $2 billion a season to close to $3 billion. To that you can add at least $10 billion on personal bets.

This is money bet on single games through bookies. All a potential gambler needs to do to risk a few dollars on his favorite team is pick up the phone and contact his friendly neighborhood bookmaker. Strangely, most of the handicapping on which these bets are based is done in a city and state where major league baseball doesn't exist, Las Vegas, Nevada.

The expert handicappers know just about everything that any close follower of a team is likely to know, and the handicapping is done with a fine eye

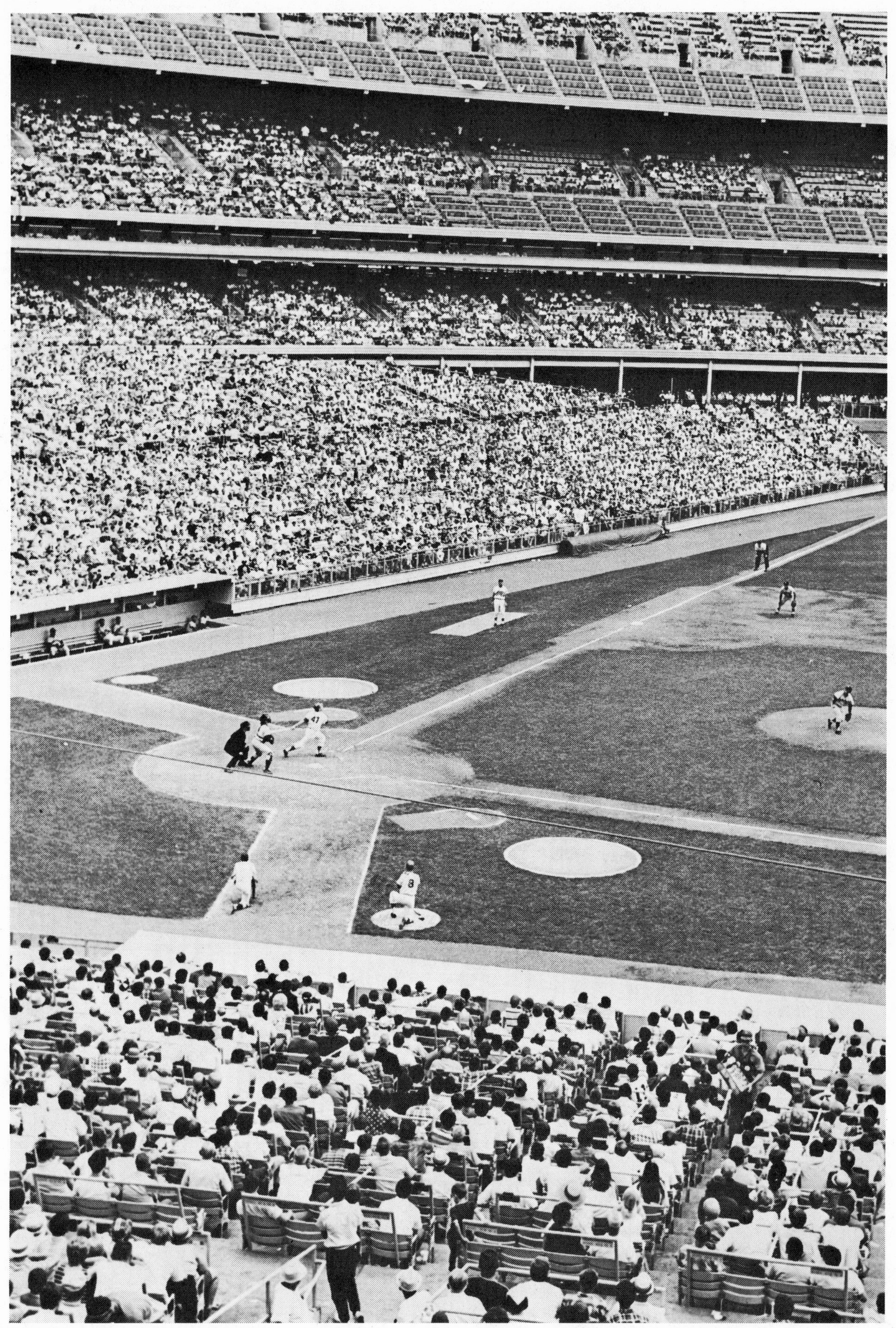

to encouraging backers of both teams in a game to bet on their favorite. The bookmakers don't care which team wins, just so both teams have substantial backing. The odds are usually so set that, whichever team wins, so does the bookie, if—and it's an important if—the amount bet on the two teams is somewhere near even.

If announcement that an almost invincible Sandy Koufax is pitching scares off bets on the opposition, it behooves the handicappers to give the opposition team enough of an edge to bring out money.

An early addition to baseball betting was the private "office" pool, in which employees of a business organization put up a dollar to draw a number. These pools were usually based on total number of runs scored, runs by the winning team, or the inning in which the winning run was scored.

They were a natural forerunner to the professional baseball pool. Always alert to the law of supply and demand, professional gamblers came up with various types of parlay cards, usually available for a dollar, usually based on the number of runs scored by five or six different teams. The handy little parlay cards immediately proved immensely popular, although illegal in most states.

As in lotteries and the numbers game, the payoff is fabulously high in baseball pools—and almost impossible to attain. The arbitrary amounts that are paid to winners probably represent a small part of the money collected. In other words, the odds are heavily stacked in favor of the pool operators. Although astute gamblers who examine the odds closely won't touch the pools with a 20-foot pole, this seems to have no deterrent effect on the vast rank and file of baseball fans who cheerfully contribute, week after week.

Nobody seems willing to hazard a guess on the total "take" of baseball pools in the United States. There are, of course, no official records, and the pools operate at various levels. A hole-in-the-wall cigar store proprietor in Chicago's Loop confided that his ten percent cut on pool tickets sold in his little shop averages around $500 a week. One small pool that operates solely in a mid-western industrial plant, is said by its operator to show a net profit, after all expenses, of roughly $2,000 a week.

The plant manager of a prosperous supplier to the automotive industry, located in Michigan, says, "I get a salary of $25,000 a year for running this whole operation. And the guy who runs baseball and football pools in the plant probably makes four times what I do. It makes a guy think—and burn."

While the pool bets are smaller than the wagers on individual games, placed with bookmakers, there are many more of them and they are usually made on a regular, steady basis. It would not seem out of line to guess that the parlay pool volume at least equals the game bets, which would mean another $3 billion.

By far the most exciting betting that's done on baseball, and the most fun to watch, takes place in the bleachers at nearly every major league ball park.

The hard core of bleacher bettors is usually to be found in a permanent bleacher location, where the daily action is. They will bet on anything that might possibly happen in a baseball game, even to strikes and balls on single pitches.

At least one of the bettors in these bleacher wagers is far from whimsical. He knows what he's doing. In the Bleacher Bet section, anywhere in the United States, there are baseball statistical experts who are walking encyclopedias of the sport. They can not only come up with the current batting averages of every major league player but, with a little thought, can recall Hank Greenberg's average in 1944.

The Bleacher Bettors are loaded with "trick" bets to entice casual spectators who aren't a regular part

I'll Betcha!

With the proper buildup, bettors have collected wagers on these little-known facts.

What living creatures predominate in the world? Ants.

Which has a faster current, a crooked river or a straight one? A straight one.

Where is the quotation, "Cleanliness is next to Godliness" to be found in the Bible? Nowhere. It was used in a sermon by John Wesley.

Washington, D.C., is the third capitol of the United States. It was preceeded by both New York and Philadelphia.

And here's another little-known fact to bear in mind. When a smart gambler makes what seems to be a preposterous statement and offers to back it with money, he's hoping to get a bet on a sure thing.

MR. ODDS-MAKER'S BEST BET

Mr. Odds-Maker says, "Baseball offers the best opportunity for profitable betting of any sport. The bookmaker's (if you can find one) percentage is minute, often less than two percent. If you're located in an area where you can shop for the best price, many times there is no percentage at all.

"Moreover, as opposed to casino gambling where the odds are mathematically fixed, baseball odds are man-made and subject to error.

"A sure-fire way to beat baseball is to follow certain pitchers who seem to have a hex on certain clubs. If a Juan Marichal is 19 and 1 at home against the Dodgers, he has to be a good bet every time he faces them in his own ball park."

of their group. When they offer to bet that the three current top hitters in the league won't get two hits apiece on that particular day, they know that it almost never happens. When they offer to bet that the top hitter on a team won't get more than two hits, they know he will probably have four official trips to the plate and one walk—and that he's batting .329.

They not only know batting averages but which players hit best in the clutches and which ones choke up under pressure. They know which pitchers have trouble with which teams. They've even been known to bet that a pitcher who is pitching great ball will be taken out before the end of the seventh inning, because they know that's when he folds.

Mr. Odds-Maker says, "Over the years, we've simplified the handicapping of baseball games to the point where almost our sole consideration is pitching. We give the nod to the pitcher with the better record."

The late Rogers Hornsby said, after his retirement from baseball, "Bet on pitching. Managers who say that pitching is 90 percent of the game aren't just whistling Dixie. When a pitcher's record shows more wins than losses, you can't go far wrong betting on him.

"Hitting is always iffier than pitching. When a good pitcher's got it, he'll handcuff good hitters most of the time. To win with hitting, you need big innings when everybody gets on base—like the old Yankees did. But don't forget that the Yankees had great pitching, too. To win with hitting, you need a group of good hitters bunching hits. One good pitcher is all you need."

Mr. Odds-Maker adds, "In betting on pitching, don't just look at the won and lost column. See what the pitcher's record is against the other team. Sometimes a pitcher who can tie the top teams in the league into knots is a patsy for one particular second-division team.

"Bookmakers take pre-season bets on the final standings of the teams in both leagues. In the pre-season line, a team may be a 100 to 1 shot against winning the pennant.

"The previous year's champions and runners-up are the teams to beat, at least, early in the season. At Spring Training time, we try to estimate the improvement or decline for each team from the preceding year. For example, if a team folded last year because of poor relief pitching and has acquired greatly increased strength in the bull pen during the off-season, it becomes a potential winner. If a team that was plagued with dissension has rid itself of the trouble-makers without weakening its lineup, you rate it better than last year.

"Conversely, a strong team made up of older ball players has no way to go but down unless it starts a youth movement. It seldom dares to drop popular, established but aging players because of home-town public opinion. It has to have a bad season before it can start rebuilding.

"In rating teams at the start of the season, study the trades. A deal for ballplayers is seldom an even swap, and the team that gets money as well as players in an exchange has usually weakened its lineup. If a team fills a hole without weakening itself somewhere else, you have to rate that team as improved.

"Any baseball fan should be able to look over the lineups for a new season and have a good idea of a team's chances in the coming year.

"One last word of advice. Most bets on single plays in a game are bad bets. Betting that any player will get a hit is always a sucker bet. So, for that matter, is betting that he'll strike out. He may walk, get hit by a wild pitch, ground out, fly out, get to base on an error, or get a solid hit. With a three and two count on the batter, betting that the next pitch will be either a strike or a ball is another sucker bet. There are the additional possibilities that it will be a hit, an infield out or fly, or a hit batter, or safe on an error—long odds against you, either way you bet. Betting that a batter will strike out is a sucker bet, too, when you consider how seldom a pitcher strikes out half the players who face him. Betting that a team will score in its next turn at bat is another loser. At least, the odds are stacked against it. When the top hitters on both teams have comparable batting averages, a bet that the leading hitter on the home team will out-hit the visitor shouldn't be even money. If the home team is ahead

---

Does Japan have a potential Black Sox baseball scandal?

Newsweek Magazine for March 30, 1970, reported rumors that a Japanese pitcher allegedly rigged games by tossing up "nothing" pitches to batters. Following the charges, the pitcher disappeared and Japan debated the possibility that he had been kidnapped by gangsters.

Professor Suzuki of Meiji University, a popular baseball commentator, insisted that gangsters are seldom interested in fixing games. They bet on who will strike out, who will make a hit or commit an error, or what the margin of victory will be, he maintained.

Baseball gambling started in Osaka in 1955 and has grown to the point where it is the largest source of revenue for the gangster combine, somewhere in the neighborhood of $5 million a day.

A parallel with the Black Sox is that Japanese players are poorly paid and look like easy prey for the gamblers.

---

after eight and a half innings, it gets one less turn at bat. Betting on the leading base-stealer in the league to steal two bases in a game is one of the worst sucker bets of all time. Bet that he won't do it and you'll win a lot more than you'll lose. On the other hand, when a pitcher is behind at the end of six innings, betting that he won't go all the way isn't too bad a bet. If he stays behind, the manager is almost obligated to lift him for a pinch-hitter.

"Baseball probably has the most complete, detailed records of past performance of any sport extant, and the facts are available to anyone."

FOOTBALL

Residents of the United States are prone to think of football as an American sport, and it is—but this country is not alone in its enthusiasm. Soccer, or, to use its official name, association football, is a top spectator sport practically everywhere except in the United States—throughout Europe, South America, Africa, Australia and even the USSR.

Attendance at soccer games far exceeds attendance at American-type football. It is the top sport in most countries where it is played, although in Great Britain it must share top billing with cricket.

Since 1924, most of the wagering on association football has been done through postal pools. Pool tickets are mailed every week to anyone who wants them, and marked tickets are returned by mail, along with payment. There are several kinds of pools, so that the bettor has a choice as to what predictions he wants to make. Operating on a basis similar to the pari-mutuel, all money wagered is pooled, and then allotted to winners on a carefully worked out system, minus a profit for the promoters and, in quite a few countries, a government tax. Scandinavian pool ticket buyers spend over $150 million a season, the Australians go over the $250 million mark, and Great Britain hits $350 million.

The return on a pool ticket depends on the number of people who have correctly determined the outcome of games. When winners are easily predictable, winnings are low. In the event of upsets, they may conceivably hit from half a million to a $1 million.

College football in the United States was popular long before the start of the professional game. Up until the appearance of "Red" Grange of the University of Illinois, the immortal "77", in the ranks of the pros, the game as played for money by former college players could best be described as semi-professional. Grange and his manager, C. C. "Cash and Carry" Pyle, drew the first substantial gates that made pro football a business.

A national professional football league was formed, and ownership of most of the teams in the league turned out to be a source of income beyond the wildest dreams of the pioneers who got in on the ground floor.

There had been betting on college football, mostly friendly wagers between supporters of rival teams, and collegiate athletic associations had tried, with little luck, to discourage it.

As the pro game's popularity grew, so did gambling on the sport. Bookmakers found a new and substantial source of revenue, and the point-handicapping of games became an important business.

Professional gamblers were aware of the enormous "take" of soccer pools, and football pools were activated in the United States, first only in the cities where professional teams operated. The parlay tickets were so popular that they soon spread across the country and could be purchased almost everywhere—in most cases, illegally.

Several attempts to challenge the monopoly of the National League proved unsuccessful, largely because owners of teams in the "upstart" leagues lacked the money to weather a break-in and shake-down period or, if they had it, were afraid to risk it.

The American football league was a different story. A population explosion in the United States had created new and prosperous markets. Television rights in some of them virtually insured a profit. Owners had been carefully picked for their ability and inclination to compete with the National League, and they refused to be frightened. With one league, the football draft had put players in a poor bargaining position. Once the American League showed an inclination to compete for top players, the National League became annoyed and, finally, conciliatory.

Perhaps the American League would have remained a secondary league had it not been for Joe Namath, New York Jets quarterback, and the Super-Bowl game of 1969. Namath, like "Dizzy" Dean and Cassius Clay before him, a pop-off who delivered, seemed to be about the only person in the country

---

I'll Betcha!

"I'll bet you can't tell me what country the cigar store wooden Indian originated in," the bettor challenged.

"Why, of course I can," his friend replied. "In the United States."

"Want to bet?" the bettor asked. His friend was so inclined, and lost what seemed to him like a sure-thing bet.

The cigar store wooden Indian originated in England and was prevalent there long before it made its first appearance in the United States. The idea for it came from the American colonies, but the wooden Indian, itself, was of English origin. As a matter of fact, there were cigar store wooden Indians in England before there were cigar stores in the United States.

who thought the Jets had a chance against the Baltimore Colts. The football handicappers gave Baltimore a 17-point edge over the Jets—and Namath, with the confidence and poise of a champion, passed and maneuvered the underdog team to victory by a nine-point margin. The American League had arrived, and pro football was on its way to becoming the greatest sports attraction in the history of the country.

Had the odds-makers made a terrific boo-boo? Not at all. A bettor had to put up $11 on either team to win $10, and betting on the two teams had been about equal. Without the 17-point handicap, it is doubtful that much Jet money would have appeared. As things worked out, the 1969 Super-Bowl game was the largest single betting event in sports history. The bookmakers couldn't have been happier.

Despite the greatest number of baseball games played, bookmakers now handle about as much each year in football bets, both pro and amateur, as in baseball. Even before the American football league had become important, from $50 to $60 million was bet on a typical fall weekend on from 30 to 35 college and and pro games on the bookmakers' slates.

While there's no way of knowing the total take of the football pools because of their illegality, it seems obvious that they have grown at least as much as bookmaker-placed individual bets.

A retired college football coach says, "Point handicaps are always a risky bet in college football. While a few college coaches pour it on whenever they can, most college coaches don't like to humiliate a fellow-coach. Also, they're inclined to put sophomore third-stringers into the game as soon as they have a comfortable lead, to give them expeirence.

"Then, too, a college team with a big game against a bitter rival coming up next week may 'coast' this week. It's almost impossible to keep a college team 'up' for every game. The players are apt to dog it when they're playing an inferior team. The size of the score may depend on last week's game, too. Whether it was won or lost, a rough, tough, hard-nose game may leave the squad weary and dragging.

"For those reasons, it's always better to give odds on college games rather than points. If you're convinced a team is going to win, give odds rather than points, every time.

"I look closely at the first two games of the college season and then try to pick the teams that I think are going to win championships. Then I bet 'em all the way.

"For example, if you knew anything about football, it wasn't hard to pick Ohio State as the Big Ten winner, right from the start of the 1970 season. Michigan was the only tough competition, and Michigan had been to the Rose Bowl the year before. You knew Ohio State was going to have extra incentive and Michigan wasn't.

"If you want a sure thing, certain college coaches come up with a lot more winners than losers, year after year. They coach winning football. For example, Woody Hayes and Ara Parseghian will have a loser now and then, but not for long."

Mr. Odds-Maker says, "Points are easier to figure in pro ball than college ball. The pro teams are more consistent. The players are playing for money, and they want all the touchdowns they can get, every game. Scoring is worth money when they're negotiating next year's contracts. There's seldom any gentlemanly 'coasting' when a pro team is ahead.

"When you're giving points, study both offense and defense. Pro defensive lineups are generally tougher than college ones. On the other hand, they have to be better because the pros play a more open offensive game and take more chances to try to score. The passing and pass reception are superior.

"Consider how the teams do on first down. A team that makes one yard or two yards on first down, time after time, isn't going to do well. It needs a few four and five-yard first downs to sustain a drive.

"Now, consider third down and short yardage. A team with a power back who can grind out that two or three yards has a potent weapon. A team that doesn't have one is in trouble.

"A pro team needs a lot more than a quarterback, but it can't go anywhere without him. Superior quarterbacking is vital. Bettors who bet on Bart Starr and Johnny Unitas over the years did fine. Gayle Sayers in his prime was the best ball carrier in pro ball, but without that superior quarterback, the Bears didn't have it.

"Rate the coaches, if your estimate of the two teams puts them close. Some pro coaches consistently do a better job than others. The late Vince Lombardi was starting a rebuilding process at Washington when he died, but had he lived, he'd soon have been fielding winning teams.

"Don't look for betting information in the sports section of a team's home newspaper. Some local sports writers get carried away by civic pride and would have you believe their team's a winner when it doesn't have an outside chance.

MR. ODDS-MAKER'S BEST BET

"In college football, I look for a psychological or emotional edge and wait until I think a team is sky-high or due for a let-down. A case in point was the Ohio State vs. Michigan game in 1970, a game for which Ohio State had pointed for a whole year to avenge a 24-12 1969 loss. Michigan had been to the Rose Bowl in 1969 and didn't have the Rose Bowl incentive. Ohio state covered the six-point spread by winning 20 to 9."

"That leads to an important point. Don't let emotion influence your betting on pro ball. In 1970, for example, it was much easier to tell which teams weren't going anywhere than to pick the final winners. Smart bettors didn't bet on their favorites; they bet against teams that looked like natural losers.

"Remember, too, that the handicapping line sent out at the start of the week to bookmakers doesn't necessarily mean that one team is a certain number of points better than another. The handicapper's primary concern is bringing out money on the underdog team. He may feel that two teams are an even bet, but if public opinion strongly favors one, a point handicap is necessary.

"Regardless of how you bet, weather is always a factor. When there's a chance that bad weather will affect your team adversely, don't take the good odds at the beginning of the week. Wait until you're reasonably sure of the weather before you place your bet.

"As for the parlay cards and pool tickets, bet them for fun if you can afford it. You're playing long-shots and, lets face it—you're really tossing away your money. Parlay cards, like the jar tickets in the old saloons, are really poor bets. The best football handicapper in the world can't beat them consistently. For one thing, you don't get anywhere near the true odds. You'll be money ahead to bet with friends on individual games."

First of the charges of "fixing" by gamblers in professional football was the persistent one of "point shaving" by quarterbacks. The charge was never made that any quarterback "threw" a game, but unhappy bettors grumbled that certain quarterbacks whose teams were ahead by more than the handicap given by the odds-makers to the opposition deliberately threw pass interceptions to narrow the margin. And if their teams were getting close to the point of beating the handicap, these bettors alleged, their hitherto-perfect passes began to be slightly off the mark. Nothing was ever proved.

The first serious punitive action to discourage gambling came in 1963. It was charged that during a party in Miami in December of 1962, five Detroit Lions bet $50 apiece on the Green Bay Packers to win the NFL championship. Pete Rozelle, the football league commissioner, fined the five players $2,000 apiece and fined the Detroit club $4,000. Then he issued "indefinite" suspensions to two of the players involved. Both players were later reinstated.

I'll Betcha!

"I was a great reader when I was a kid," the bettor says, "and my favorite book was Joe Kipling's Jungle Book."

"You mean Rudyard Kipling's," somebody corrects him. "Rudyard Kipling wrote the Jungle Book."

"I must have read it half a dozen times," the indignant bettor protests, "and I guess I ought to know. I'll bet you anything you want to bet that the first name of the Kipling who wrote the Jungle Book *was Joseph. My memory may not be so hot, but that's one thing I* do *remember. Want to bet I'm wrong?"*

Everybody does—and everybody loses. Kipling's full name was Joseph Rudyard Kipling.

MR. ODDS-MAKER'S BEST BET

"In pro football, always try to bet on a team that has momentum. If you have patience, wait until the end of the season and bet on a team looking for a play-off berth to beat a team that's out of the running."

BASKETBALL

Following the basketball betting scandals some years back, bookmakers for a time took bets on the total score in a basketball game, rather than the winner or loser. You had the unusual situation where bettors who had picked a high total score were exhorting the players with the frenzied shout, "Come on, anybody!"

Even today, with the game vigorously policed, bookmakers approach it with reluctance, and more betting is done by fans with each other than through the usual gambling channels. While the players are scrupulously honest, professional odds-makers admit that it is the most difficult of all games to handicap.

The whole tenor of the game has changed since the 1930's, when the rulemakers decided to speed it up. Present rules have put the emphasis on offense, with the two competing teams taking turns at shooting baskets—or trying to. The advent of the giant player, often over 6′5″, has changed the game, too.

In the amateur game, one or two teams every year seem to dominate each athletic conference. In the Big Ten, there's an axiom that when you've lost two games, you can't expect to win a conference championship if you lose another.

Betting consistently on any team that has over a .500 average makes you at least a small winner, if you're betting even money. Betting on a team that loses two games out of a 15-game schedule puts you in clover. Basketball fans pick teams they think have a good chance at their conference championship and bet on all their games.

With two evenly matched teams, the team that has the home floor will win more often than not. But there is an even more important factor. Teams all have "hot" nights and "cold" nights. Even an all-American sharpshooter will occasionally hit a night when he can't buy a basket, when even easy layup shots go wrong. In a strong collegiate conference, a team's shooting accuracy percentage may vary from as low as 32 percent to as high as 68 percent. If it runs into a "hot" team on a night when its shooting percentage is down to 32, it faces defeat.

MR. ODDS-MAKER'S BEST BET

Mr. Odds-Maker says, "If you're a student of basketball, you'll know which college teams are tremendous 'homers.' On the road, away from the friendly confines which help them, bet against these teams."

The professional teams, made up of super-stars, play grueling schedules, and the pace wears the men down. A tired team that plays a fresh professional team is going to have a bad night, even if its shooting percentage is normal. The problem will be that it won't get as many shots, possibly because it won't be as aggressive on rebounds.

Smart Sam's complaint about basketball as a gamble has nothing to do with the players. He says, "It's the only athletic contest I know about where the officials can control the outcome of a close game—and I mean, control. A couple of weeks ago, I watched a game between two college teams. The score was tied, 115 to 115, with 32 seconds left. The Golds got the ball in the back court, and the player who had it tripped over the leg of a Blue guard. The ref called him for traveling and gave the ball to the Blues, out of bounds. Was it tripping or traveling? Your guess is as good as mine—and as good as the ref's. So Blue holds on to the ball for a last shot. With six seconds left, the Blue forward charged in and hit a Gold player like it was football, taking a shot at the same time. The shot missed, and Gold got the ball, with four seconds left. But the ref called a foul on the Gold player who hadn't gotten out of the shooter's way in time. All right, was it offensive charging or defensive blocking? Anyway, the Blue player got two free throws, and Blue won, 117 to 115. As far as I was concerned, the ref determined the outcome of the game.

"Sure, most of the officials try to do a good job. But don't tell me there aren't 'homer' officials, because I see 'em at work. They call all the close ones in favor of the home team. On a close match, with one of those homers on the floor, I'll bet on the home team, every time. Really, I'll be bettin' on the referee.

"Some officials call fouls close, and some call 'em loose. A rough, tough, aggressive team is in like Flynn with one of the loose boys, and it's in bad trouble with one of the sticklers.

"Before basketball becomes a good game to gamble on, something's gotta be done to take the decision outta the hands of the officials."

As things stand, the bulk of the betting on basketball is done by fans backing their favorite team, against fans who support rival teams.

One bookmaker says, "We try to take a vacation during the basketball season, but if I were betting on the game, I'd bear certain things in mind.

"A good tall team beats a good small team.

"The home floor is worth six points.

"A player who dominates on rebounds is worth ten points.

"A team that makes eight out of ten of its free throws will usually beat a team that only makes five out of ten.

"Know the shooting percentages of both teams. In a tight game, the team that's the most accurate usually wins."

"Don't give points if you can avoid it. If you have to give more than eight points, walk away from the bet. Basketball is a free-scoring game, and scores can be close even when one team is definitely superior. Give odds rather than points, always.

"Write off a top star who isn't in good physical condition. An injured or 'dragging' star can be more of a hindrance than a help.

"Balanced scoring is always better than one scoring ace. A dead-eye shooter can be bottled up; a scoring team can't be.

"A good team that has played together for three seasons should beat a good team in its first season. Basketball is a team game, and when a team jells—becomes a unit—it has a tremendous advantage over competition.

"A player who can hit 50 percent of his outside shots can break a game wide open, if his coach will let him.

"The won and lost records of competing teams always give you a good indication of how to bet."

MR. ODDS-MAKER'S BEST BET

"In pro basketball, study match-ups—position vs. position, and you'll find that certain teams beat other teams consistently because they match up well. Other things being equal, bet on the teams that handle certain opponents consistently well."

JAI-ALAI

Jai-Alai, often billed as "the fastest game in the world," is a Basque game that came to the United States by way of Cuba. It has always been a gambling game, and is particularly popular in Latin-America. It is played with baskets or *cestas* and ball, the ball being heavier and less resilient than a golf ball, but not much larger.

Florida has this country's only legal Jai-Alai frontons, where pari-mutuel betting is sanctioned, and draws capacity crowds during a three-month season. Betting is heavy.

The game is somewhat similar to handball, played in a court with three walls. The ball is thrown from the cesta and must be caught either on the fly or on the first bounce and returned by an opposing player. Both singles and doubles games are played.

An evening's play usually consists of nine games, and bettors bet players to win and place, as in horse races. A $2 ticket may pay off as much as 100 to 1, although such odds are unusual.

The players are importations, and must be extremely durable. Because of the high speed of the game and the energy and stamina required, the playing life of a Jai-Alai star is usually short.

A Jai-Alai fan points out that few people in this country understand the fine points of the game and are incapable of picking winners on form. For that reason, he recommends that anyone who intends to bet on Jai-Alai try to pick up a form chart or dope sheet, available at the frontons.

"Your best bet is to bet on Jai-Alai for fun," he says. "Pick a couple of players you like, and bet them to win and place. Your chance of winning is as good as anybody else's, and you get pari-mutuel odds."

I'll Betcha!

"We certainly owe a lot to Nathan Stubblefield," the sure-thing bettor says solemnly.

Others in the group frown. "What for?" one asks.

"Why, for his invention of radio," the bettor says.

"Marconi invented radio," somebody corrected him.

"Nate Stubblefield invented radio when Marconi was only 18 years old," the bettor says, "back in 1892. I thought everybody knew that."

Everybody challenges him, and he takes all bets.

Nathan Stubblefield demonstrated his wireless telegraph invention time after time, to the complete satisfaction of scientists and press. In 1902, he even demonstrated with ship-to-shore conversation. Everyone was impressed—and nothing happened. He died a bitter old man, in his little home on his farm near Murray, Kentucky. The documented source is Frank Edwards' intriguing book, Stranger Than Science.

Win or lose, Jai-Alai is an exciting game to watch, with fast action and skillful execution. People who attend a Jai-Alai game for the first time soon become enthusiastic—and their interest is heightened by a small wager.

MR. ODDS-MAKER'S BEST BET

Mr. Odds-Maker says, "The only successful way to win at Jai-Alai is to follow one of the players' wives or girl-friends to the window. Bet exactly as she does."

HOCKEY

Hockey has attracted gamblers in Canada, particularly in Montreal, for years, to the tune of about twenty million dollars annually. Up until recent years when the major hockey league increased its size, its games were no substantial gambling lure in the United States. The betting action ran to around $1 million a weekend.

With more teams and more public interest in the sport, gambling has increased. "It was always a good bet," according to one bookie, "but people wouldn't buy it. Now, it's drawing some action—not much, but more than it did." Because of increased interest, one of the foremost odds-makers in the country, Mr. Odds-Maker, has brought in a hockey expert to set the odds on every game.

Much of the wagering on the sport has always been done in the stands, by spectators who are true fans and who get carried away by their enthusiasm. The hockey fan is among the most violent sports enthusiasts in the world, and he doesn't hesitate to back his judgement with money.

A hockey handicapper says, "Americans don't dig the fine points of hockey like Canadians do. They like the fast action and the violent body contact, but they don't see the difference between an average major league player and a great one. The novice bettor doesn't have much to rely on except over-all past team performance."

Mr. Odds-Maker says, "The home team starts with a slight edge. If you know as little about the game as most fans do, check the records of the goalies. A team has to get that puck past the goalie to win. The goalie who consistently makes the highest percentage of 'saves' is pretty good insurance for your bet.

"At home or on the road, hockey's one game where the better team is going to win more often than it loses. Half-way through the season, when a performance record has been established, you'll win money betting

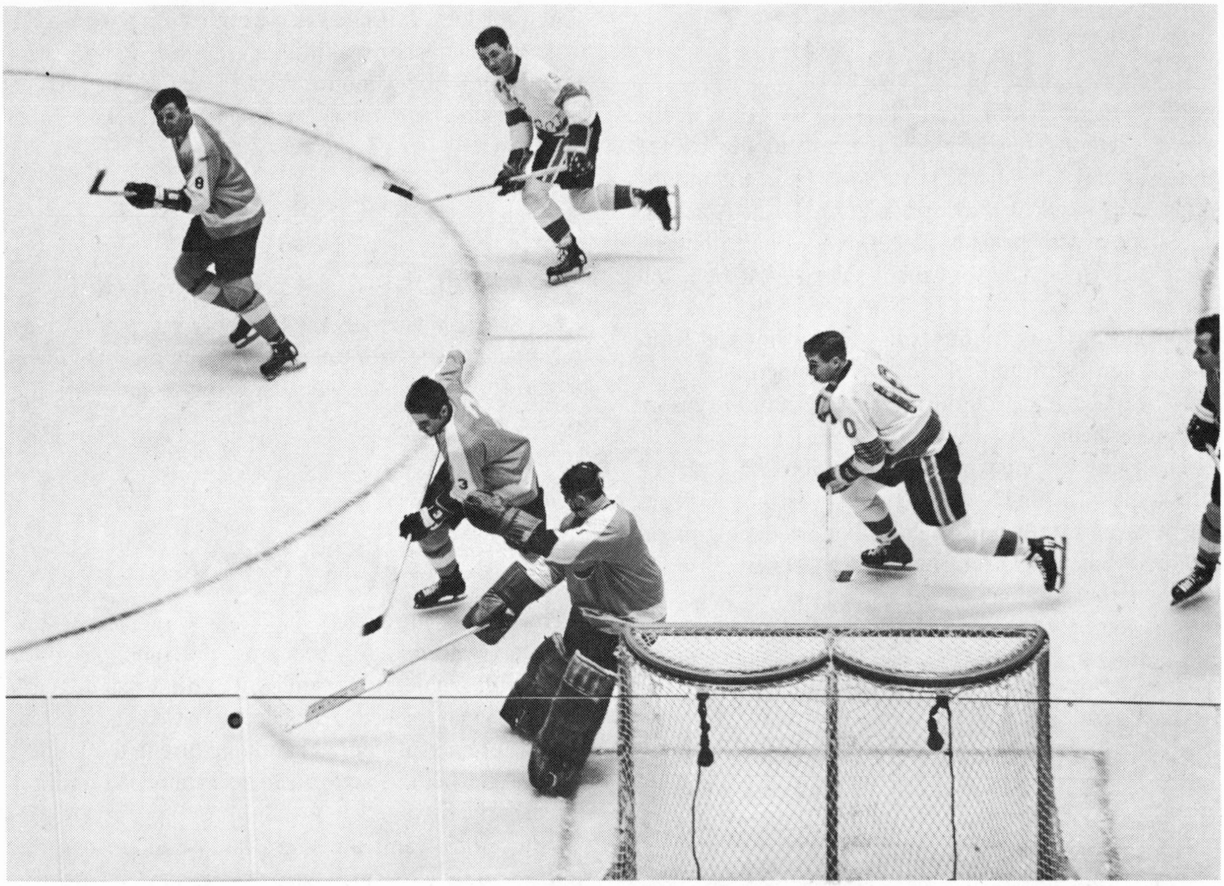

on the top teams unless the handicappers over-handicap the underdogs. When a team gets too good and attracts too much money, your best bet is to lay off.

"In a few years, the league will be better-balanced, but as of right now, a few first-rate teams stand out and the others aren't of the same quality. The standings as published in the newspapers should show you the teams that have winning ways."

MR. ODDS-MAKER'S BEST BET

Mr. Odds-Maker says, "In hockey, beware of the spread line. If Montreal is playing Boston and the line reads, 'Boston 1½-2 goals,' pass. Translated, this means you take Montreal plus a goal and a half, but in order to bet on Boston, you must give two goals. Never bet into a spread line. You are taking more than 40 percent the worst of it."

BOXING

Ancient Greeks were the first people to bring any semblance of science and rules to the sport of fighting. The "anything goes" atmosphere of a rough-and-tumble brawl was not for them. Their fighters wore gloves on their fists and also wore belts. A blow below the belt was a foul. The Romans made a gory spectacle of boxing by "improving" the gloves, adding weight and metal spikes to them. The savage display proved too violent for subsequent generations, and fighting as a sport virtually died.

Bare-knuckle fighting became popular in England in the 1700's and was still a bloody mess until the Marquis of Queensbury prepared a set of rules, late in the 1860's. The rules, which have been revised several times since then, brought the birth of modern boxing.

In the first half of the twentieth century, boxing reached a peak as a spectator sport, due to colorful champions and, even more, the promotional efforts of Tex Rickard, who was the father of the "million dollar gate." As the rewards grew richer, competition increased and boxing thrived. Particularly in the heavyweight division, it became big business. Such champions as Jack Dempsey, Gene Tunney, Max Baer and Joe Louis had the color that paid off at the box-office.

Even before the 1929 depression, the underworld, attracted by the enormous money in boxing, began to move in, and the names of unsavory gangsters began to be linked with the sport. Rumors of "fixed" fights were heard with increasing frequency. Secret contracts between champions and challengers came to light. Even so, the turnstiles clicked merrily and the money rolled in.

There were tragic stories of champions who never received more than a fraction of the money their fists had earned.

Joe Louis, one of the greatest and most active champions of all time, was one of the fighters who wound up broke, but it was his honesty and sheer capability that kept boxing prosperous. In 1946, when he defended his championship against Billy Conn and Tami Mauriello, wagering on boxing was estimated at over $500 million.

The Madison Square Garden corporation achieved what was close to a monopoly on championship fights, and fight managers who resisted the Garden promoters hurled bitter charges that their fighters couldn't get matches unless they agreed to fight under Garden auspices.

Strangely, it was not the hoodlum element or attempts at commercial control of boxing that contributed most to its decline. It was television. At one time, three fight cards a week were nationally televised. The first effect of this was to deal a death blow to small fight clubs. Boxers had up to that time received their training in club fights. Fight clubs were the minor leagues of the boxing game and they were unable to stand the competition of free major fights.

The decline of the fight clubs in turn created a shortage of capable fighters. It became impossible for the promoters of televised fights to come up with a quality product, week after week. As the quality of fights hit the skids, so did audience ratings. The TV promoters finally had to give up.

Outside of Madison Square Garden, boxing was virtually dead. Sporadic attempts by optimistic promoters in other cities met with failure.

Probably all that saved boxing from complete oblivion was the appearance of a heavyweight, Cassius Clay, a superb boxer with a punch, who was that rare and precious commodity, a pop-off who delivers. It looked like he had everything necessary to revitalize boxing.

Unfortunately, in addition to his glib facility to pop off and his boxing prowess, he had convictions, and the convictions were highly unpopular. A follower of the Muslim religious sect, he adopted the Muslim name of Muhammad Ali and refused to be drafted into the U.S. armed forces, basing his refusal on religious convictions. He was one of the first of many to refuse participation in the Viet Nam conflict.

What his stand on military service had to do with his ability as a boxer was never made clear, but the heavyweight championship was taken away from him, and the heavyweight division became a shambles. By 1971, boxing had hit its low point in the twentieth century.

As his stand on Viet Nam drew more followers and, consequently, more respectability, a situation in which a heavyweight champion had lost his championship outside the ring became more ludicrous. Boxing made its first real effort on the comeback trail when a fight between Joe Frazier and Muhammad Ali for the heavyweight championship was approved.

At the time, wagering on boxing had declined from half a billion dollars a year to somewhere in the neighborhood of $11 or $12 million.

In spite of this, gamblers still love to bet on boxing—when there is something that constitutes a bet. The only sport in which victory is achieved by rendering an opponent helpless, boxing has a basic appeal. It is one man pitted against another in a contest of skill and strength. Once a match begins, the two participants are on their own.

When boxing was in its prime, fans became serious students of the manly art and rated fighters with surprising accuracy.

What made boxing a good bet was the fact that, even when overmatched with a boxer of superior skill, a boxer with a knockout punch had a chance of winning a fight, as long as he remained on his feet. Long odds against an underdog with a punch attracted backing—and the backers of the long-shot won often enough to maintain high interest.

The Frazier-Ali fight was unique in the history of boxing. Frazier had been designated the heavyweight champion of the world. Muhammad Ali had won the championship and had never willingly relinquished it. The title had been stripped from him outside the ring.

Frazier was rated as a good boxer with a good punch. Ali, in spite of his unpopularity in certain areas, was considered by many boxing afficionados to be one of the most capable boxers of all time. Had he been a working, active champion at the time of the confrontation with Frazier, it is doubtful if much Frazier money would have appeared.

As it was, after several years of ring inactivity, broken only by a "warm-up," the so-called "smart" money favored Frazier. Students of fistiana felt that Ali's layoff had been too long, and Frazier became a 7-5 favorite. Ali had always predicted victory for himself in every fight of his career, however, and had always delivered.

The late Tex Rickard had been hailed as the father of the "Million Dollar Gate," and boxing writers in recent years had wondered if a box office return of such magnitude was fading into oblivion.

Thanks to closed-circuit television in theaters throughout the country and even in Europe, the Frazier-Ali fight became the $20 million gate event. Each fighter received the incredible guarantee of $2½ million.

Boxing, which had been in the doldrums, suddenly attracted world-wide interest and created the greatest excitement in the sport's history. In one of the closed-circuit showings, in Chicago's ancient Coliseum, an

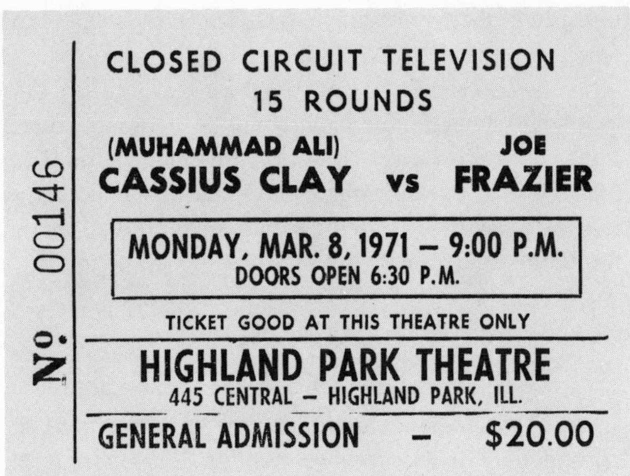
CLOSED CIRCUIT TELEVISION
15 ROUNDS
(MUHAMMAD ALI) JOE
CASSIUS CLAY vs FRAZIER
MONDAY, MAR. 8, 1971 – 9:00 P.M.
DOORS OPEN 6:30 P.M.
TICKET GOOD AT THIS THEATRE ONLY
HIGHLAND PARK THEATRE
445 CENTRAL – HIGHLAND PARK, ILL.
GENERAL ADMISSION – $20.00
Nº 00146

equipment failure during the fight created a riot that brought out 40 squad cars and resulted, in spite of police action, in considerable damage.

Usually, the fight that has the biggest buildup turns out to be a dud, as in the case of the Dempsey-Carpentier fiasco. Fortunately, the Frazier-Ali fight was, the sports writers agreed, a bang-up affair, one well worth the advance excitement it had caused.

The fight was close until the 15th round, when Ali was decked by a hard right to the head, a punch that boxing experts agreed would have been a knockout if taken by most boxers. There was some disagreement as to which fighter was ahead at the time, but everyone agreed that Frazier had been coming on strong in the latter rounds, and nobody found much fault with the decision, which gave the nod to Frazier.

Ali, who had always been a boastful, flamboyant winner, turned out to be a surprisingly gracious loser, giving full credit to Frazier, who, he admitted, turned out to be considerably smarter than Ali had thought he would be.

Almost before the fighters were out of the ring, the buildup had started for a return match.

Here, again, the betting situation gave promise of being almost perfect from the bookmaker's standpoint. Ali's backers now admitted that he had been out of the ring too long and that he had needed a good, hard fight under his belt. They were also of the opinion that he hadn't taken Frazier seriously enough and that he had clowned too much at times when he should have been building up points. Another time around, they were convinced, would find Ali victorious.

Some of this may have been wishful thinking on their part. Both fighters were black, and yet Ali was the overwhelming favorite with the majority of the many black spectators who helped swell the gate. Perhaps this was due in part to Ali's affiliation with the Muslim religion and his adamant stand against military service. Certainly, Frazier had never done anything to indicate the slightest disloyalty to his race.

Frazier emerged from the fight with new stature

and respect, now the owner of a boxing title that was no longer tarnished. Ali lost little except his hitherto perfect ring record. Frazier went into a hospital with abnormally high blood pressure and Ali started a tour of universities. Whatever the fight cost either man physically or mentally, he was indemnified with a comforting $2½ million.

It was generally agreed that a return match would shatter every record ever even dreamed of by the wildest optimist in boxing.

A boxing ref. says, "There's never been but one best bet in boxing and it's been said often enough to become an adage, 'Always bet on the champion.' The only time it doesn't apply is in a case like the Willard-Dempsey fight where the champion had been inactive too long and was obviously through. In most cases, you have to bet on the champ as long as he continues to hold the crown. The records show few champions who have ever lost their titles in their first defense.

"For one thing, a champion can pick his opponents most of the time. The championship is worth a lot of money to him and is a source of pride. When public opinion forces a champion into a fight he regards as risky, he tries to dictate terms that will be advantageous to him.

"Sugar Ray Robinson was a perfect example. When he was in his prime, taking the short end of the odds in order to bet on him meant nothing. He was going to win. He could not only outbox any fighter who ever entered the ring, but it was almost impossible for a stiff puncher to hurt him enough to slow him up. Joe Louis at his peak was the same kind of a bet.

"Aside from championship fights, you never have a sure thing when the fighter you're betting against has a knockout punch. He can always get lucky and land it, no matter how good a boxer his opponent is.

"Don't bet on a bleeder. Some officials are quick to stop a match when blood is drawn.

"If a fighter hasn't become a top contender in 40 professional fights, the odds are against him.

"A good fighter's legs are his weakest spot. When his legs go, so does he. Any fighter who fights flat-footed after four or five rounds is a risky bet.

"Betting on a fighter just because he can take a solid punch is unwise. Preferably, bet on a fighter who stays out of the way of solid punches.

"A home-town favorite who is a big drawing-card is a good bet to win at home. Promoters won't overmatch him if they can avoid it.

"When a good manager comes up with a promising young fighter, that fighter is a good bet. The manager will nurse him along until he's ready for a championship fight and won't put him into the ring against anybody who can beat him.

"A retired champion told me, 'Present boxing regulations on fouls give a good dirty fighter the edge over a good clean fighter. He won't care if he loses a round on fouls if in doing it he sets up his opponent for the kill.'

"A fighter who is slated to go a longer distance than he's ever done before is seldom a good bet.

"Experience is a big advantage, but age is a big disadvantage. The bettor has to decide at what point experience is offset by slower reflexes."

MR. ODDS-MAKER'S BEST BET

"In boxing, always bet against the fighter who has had a long layoff. No better example can be cited than the recent Clay-Frazier fight. Clay's long absence from the ring deprived him of his main asset; the speed in his legs was gone. Had they fought three years ago, he would have been an easy winner."

ANIMAL FIGHTS

Spain and Mexico are the last strongholds of bullfighting, but it was not always thus. Frescoes painted in approximately 1500 B.C., show that bullfighting was a tremendously popular sport. The ancient Greeks and, later, the Romans, were avid gamblers on their favorite bulls and matadors.

Today, bullfighting is Spain's national sport. Even sleepy little Spanish hamlets have their arenas. A *corrida* of six or more fights draws capacity crowds, and the sport is surrounded by colorful pageantry. And wagering. If you're a stranger in a *plaza de toros* and want to place a bet, just give your money to a program hawker or beverage vendor. Ten to one, he's an agent for a bookmaker. Betting is wide open, usually on which of the six or so matadors will be rated highest in technique.

Cockfighting, which began in Greece several hun-

I'll Betcha!

"Publicity can make people believe anything," the bettor says. "For example, the camel's had so much publicity about being able to go for days without water that people think it's the champion. Why, I'll bet a common rat can go longer without water than a camel."

Everyone immediately thinks of the little rat's water-storage capacity in comparison to the camel's, and the bettor gets plenty of takers.

The rat can go longer without water than any other mammal. The bettor's source is the Haskins Information Service, and the truth of his statement is attested by all zoologists.

Challengers don't even have an outside chance of winning.

dred years before Christ, has persisted through the centuries despite persistent efforts to stop it. While it has all but disappeared in Europe, it continues to thrive in the United States, the Philippine Islands, the West Indies, Mexico, Latin America, Spain and, to a lesser degree, elsewhere. It is illegal nearly everywhere, but that doesn't discourage it.

Surprisingly to most people, cockfighting has enjoyed legal approval in recent years in Florida, Kansas and New Mexico. A single tournament at the Orlando Game Club in Florida is said to have prompted a betting "handle" of well over $1 million.

Most of the cockfighting in the world draws rabid cockfighting enthusiasts, who are thoroughly conversant with all facets of the competition. Casual spectators contribute little, in either attendance or wagering. Most of the betting is illegal, but bets are made not only between spectators but by bookmakers who specialize in this one particular gamble. In the United States, where most cockfighting is hush-hush, afficionados travel from all over the country to major meets and bring their money with them.

Where cockfights were at one time usually to the death, most fights today are stopped when one of the birds is sufficiently hurt to be an obvious loser. A bird that dies in the ring today is a rarity.

MR. ODDS-MAKER'S BEST BET

Mr. Odds-Maker admits to a lack of knowledge about handicapping cockfights. He passes along a "best bet" from Smart Sam, who will gamble on anything.

"I know from nothing about cockfighting," Smart Sam acknowledges, "so the only times I've ever gone to the fights, I've tried to pick the most prosperous-looking owner. He bets not only on his own cocks but others when his aren't in the ring. I bet right along with him, and I did fine."

The gambler who wants something more bizarre than cockfighting can go to Thailand. There, he can bet on fighting fish or fighting crickets. And, whichever combatant he chooses, he'll find plenty of takers.

Mr. Odds-Maker throws up his hands and grins. "The best bet here," he says, "would obviously be to bet on the toughest, meanest-looking fish or cricket."

WRESTLING

Wrestling, a noble sport that dates back 2,000 years before Christ, was once a contest of classic beauty and champion wrestlers were highly respected.

In the first 20 years of the twentieth century, championship wrestling matches drew substantial gates, and betting was heavy. Then, as boxing's popularity grew, attendance at wrestling matches declined. Wrestling was "too slow" for the on-the-move audience of the Roaring Twenties. When the chips were down, two expert wrestlers moved warily around each other, looking for a possible opening and not finding one. This sometimes went on for hours, and spectators voiced their displeasure and boredom.

After the sport had languished for about ten years, promoters came up with what insiders called "hippodrome" wrestling. If the public wanted action, the new-style wrestling was designed to give it to them.

What resulted was more an acrobatic extravaganza than a contest. It was a show, often carefully rehearsed in advance, full of furious action, body slams, eye-gouging, hair-pulling, fisticuffs, loud taunts, vehement complaints to the referee, and tumbling. It was as phoney as a three-dollar bill, and a certain segment of society loved it—not as a legitimate contest but as entertainment.

Main-event matches usually pitted a handsome hero type against an ugly villain, a "dirty" wrestler who gave the crowd plenty of opportunity to exercise their vocal chords with lusty boos.

The villains, surprisingly, commanded better pay than the heroes. Promoters had discovered that more people would come out and plank down their money at the boxoffice to see a despised villain defeated than their favorite hero win.

Freaks thrived. Masked marvels, pseudo Counts, ridiculously effeminate giants, men with Neanderthal faces, drew admissions. Every wrestler had some kind of a "gimmick" to distinguish him from others.

What had once been a sport became a burlesque. Strangely, even the people who attended the shows seemed to know that the matches weren't legitimate contests. The *Chicago Daily News* moved its reports of such matches from the sports section to the drama page.

Wrestling had become a joke, and not a particularly funny one. A sport that once had prompted substantial betting action no longer presented anything on which to wager.

MR. ODDS-MAKER'S BEST BET

Mr. Odds-Maker's best bet on wrestling is terse. "Stay home."

GOLF

It's a far cry from the ancient Roman game played with a feather ball and a crude stick to modern golf. For that matter, it's more than a loud shout from the sparsely-attended club tournaments in the early part of the twentieth century to the multitude of televised tournaments with rich purses that are sponsored almost everywhere today.

Just as the crowds have grown, so has the interest

in gambling. Despite PGA protests, parlay betting cards have made an appearance at many professional tournaments. In England, bookmakers have put in an appearance at tourneys from time to time, despite the vigorous protest of the golf association.

Calcuttas, pools in which players are auctioned off to the highest bidders, are common, and disciplinary action by the PGA seems to have driven them outside the clubhouse rather than stopped them. Instances of a Calcutta winner collecting $100,000 on his player are not common, but are not unknown. Some Calcutta pools at major tournaments run well over a quarter of a million dollars.

Executives of golf associations are fearful that the parlay cards and Calcuttas may lead to betting scandals similar to those that have sometimes plagued other sports. With so much money involved, unscrupulous manipulators are attracted, and the lure of the "big money fix" is ominous.

Counting all forms of betting, the amount wagered on golf every year in the United States approaches $1 billion.

The part of this money—and it is a substantial part —which is put up in friendly wagers between players is of little concern to guardians of the game's purity, although as Milton Klein, publisher of *Golfer's Digest* says, in the present era of affluence, private golf bets have a tendency to reach unhealthy importance.

Mr. Klein points out that the publinx golfer is particularly vulnerable to being a patsy when high stakes are involved, thanks to inadequate handicapping of publinx players. In most private golf clubs, the handicapping is excellent, and the average players goes around the course with friends who are fairly well matched in skill.

There are almost as many different ways of wagering on golf as there are courses. There's the "Contract" or "Bridge" bet common at some clubs, in which each member of the foursome predicts his score. He receives $1 for making his contract and $1 for every stroke below it. He pays $1 a stroke for every stroke above his contract.

There's also the "Hedge" bet, in which a player who loses the hole and outdrives any member of the foursome on the next hole collects $1.

There's the "Backgammon," in which any player making a putt of 15 feet or more has the privilege of doubling the stakes on the next hole. If any player sinks a putt of 15 feet or more on the following hole, he may redouble. Unless a long putt is made, stakes revert to the original amount.

There is also the "Blitz" bet. A member of the foursome must make the longest drive, get on the green first, make the longest putt or be closest to the pin on his approach shot. Failing to do at least one of those things, he pays double on the hole.

The "Bingle-Bangle-Bungo" is a more expensive variation. The first player to reach the green is the "Bingle," the player whose ball is closest to the pin is the "Bangle," and the player sinking the longest putt is the "Bungo." Each wins from the other members of the foursome.

The Nassau, with $1 on the first nine holes, $1 on the second nine and a third dollar on over-all score, is the commonest bet. A variation of it is the "Press" bet. Playing in a foursome, a player and his partner who get two strokes behind may "press." This means that they start playing a new bet, identical to the original one, beginning with the next hole. It is not unusual for both teams to "press" before the end of the game, sometimes as late as the seventeenth hole.

A weird variation or addition to the press bet is the "Heckle." It is almost identical with the press, except that when a team is two down, the player shouts "Heckle!" as an opponent is driving off the tee. A golfer who knows that his opponents are in a position to "heckle" is often unnerved as he gets ready to drive, waiting for the shout. And the players who are two down often wait to "Heckle" until the opponents think they aren't going to do it.

"Skin" Edge of Georgia reports a new fun game, "The Rabbit." The game is bet by the first nine and the second nine holes. The rabbit is "loose" when neither team has scored any points or the score is tied. The rabbit is "owned" by the team that scores

---

Dice isn't the only form of shooting that men gamble on. Trap-shooting and skeet-shooting prompt substantial wagers between contestants.

One expert has a secret for winning his bets that he never has much trouble getting his friends to try. Gambler's Digest, however, does not recommend the practice.

"Have a good, stiff shot of liquor before you start shooting," he says. "A drink of bourbon, Scotch or brandy, whichever you prefer, will relax nervous tension and steady your nerves. At least, it works for me. Most trap and skeet champions, whether they admit it or not, follow the practice.

"Of course, you can overdo it. If you see two or three clay pigeons in the air simultaneously, you know you've overshot the mark. You're *too* relaxed. Nevertheless, a nervous, taut trap or skeet shooter doesn't do well. Add a little gamesmanship to my secret weapon, to get your opponent irritated and nervous, and in addition to the pigeon in the air, you've got one as competition."

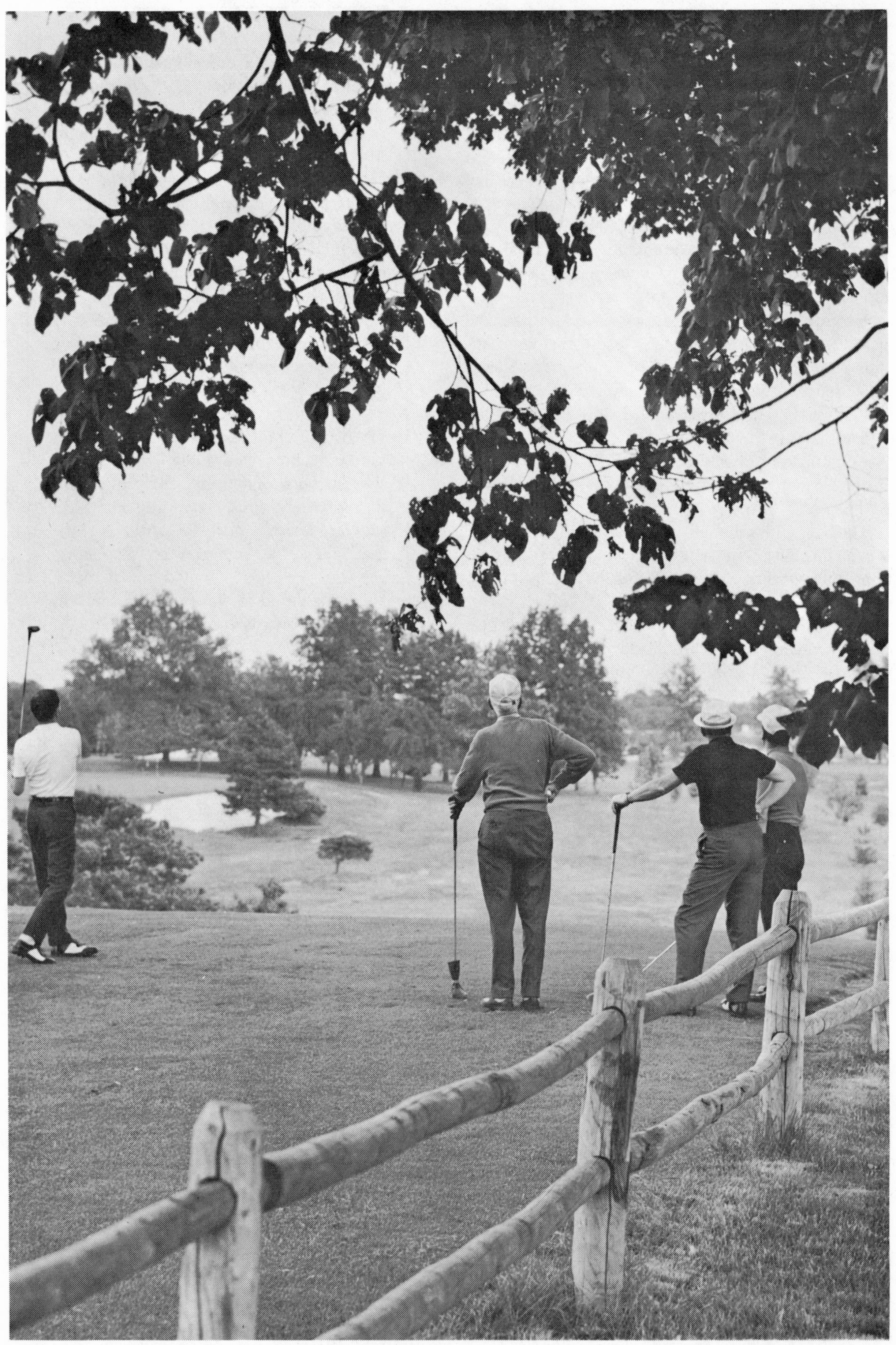

a point. The team with the rabbit in its possession at the end of the ninth hole is winner of that half, and the same is true of the second nine.

The "pool" bet is fairly common. Members of three or more foursomes make a separate $1 bet against each of the other players—11 bets in the case of three foursomes, 15 in the case of four.

The "take-out" is a Nassau bet in which the losers may, at their discretion, match the winners and pay double or nothing.

The "Checkers" bet is unique. When a player has lost a hole, he may elect to "jump." This means that the next hole is played for double the amount. In the event he challenges and wins, he has successfully "jumped," and the winner of the previous hole must, in addition to paying double, return to the challenger the money he lost on the last hole. If the challenger loses the "jump" hole, he pays double on it and does not recapture his loss from the previous hole.

A few hardy golfers in an Arizona club who don't want any publicity on it have a betting system for making their matches even that they call "Liquid Hazard." They play for $1 a hole, and the winner must down two shots of bourbon or Scotch before teeing off for the next. By their own admission, they have some rather ragged games.

The "Short Game" bet was created for novices and dubs at a Wisconsin club. The betting is for $1 a hole, but no strokes are counted until the player is on the green. The club pro says it is the only equalizer for erratic novice play that he's ever discovered. He says the bet has become popular with husband-and-wife golfers who play a fairly even game, because the husband nearly always has an edge in power.

The "Baccarat" is a Nassau bet in which the total score for the first nine, the second nine, and the overall score that ends in a 9 or the digit coming closest to nine wins $1, regardless of the Nassau bet. Winning can be offset by a score of 40 when the opponent has a score of 41. Losers can sometimes break even—and winners can sometimes double their winnings.

Assembling the freak bets in golf is virtually impossible, since every club has a few of its own. One club with a par-three hole has a traditional bet that is automatic, regardless of the betting on the round. A player who birdies this hole automatically collects $1 from other members of his foursome. It is understood by members without any stipulation that this bet applies under any and all circumstances.

While some of the betting variations at some clubs may seem stiff to the outsider, most of the money is traded back and forth by members who play regularly against each other. The bets are the spice of the game.

While every effort is made to keep golf a gentleman's game, it is not without its "hustlers," and some of them have made fabulous coups, particularly at plush resort hotel golf courses. The "hustler" specializes in playing resort courses and those that depend on paying guests for a substantial part of their revenue. At most of these, money is the major requirement for admission. The hustler knows his own capabilities and can size up an opponent in a few holes. His bets seem highly attractive, sometimes almost impossible for him to win. When he makes what looks like a losing wager, he knows what he's doing—and what he's doing is playing golf for all the money he can get.

Ted Craig, writing in *Golfer's Digest* warns golfers getting into money games to be sure they know what they're getting into. "Understand the betting," he advises. "It helps to know if the payoff is likely to be $150, particularly if you've only budgeted $10 for the week's golf."

The hustler's game usually calls for presses, and lots of them. *Golfer's Digest* says that many money golfers favor the "automatic" press in which the press goes into effect every time anyone loses a hole.

It explains their argot. Playing for "skins" means payment for beating all others on any hole. "Proxies" or "greenies" go to the person closest to the hole "in regulation." Skins and proxies are sometimes called "garbage," and are worth a stipulated amount, such as 50¢. Playing "carry-overs," any garbage that isn't won on one hole is carried over to the next.

Some bets call for double skins on birdies, five skins on eagles, and double proxies for reaching a par-five green in two strokes. A casual "25 skins for a hole-in-one" can be lethal if the bettor has a handicap on every hole.

When the press bets mount, winning the ninth and 18th holes becomes vital. A hustler's magnanimous

---

Bar Bet

A little old man who hangs around a bar on Lincoln avenue in Chicago pays for his drinks with an unusual bet. He offers to wager that he can drop an open pocketknife squarely into an open gin bottle from a height of at least six feet, above his own eye-level.

When he gets the bet, he sticks the knife blade into the top of a doorway so that the handle end is pointing downward. Then he holds a glass of water up to the handle of the knife far enough to get it thoroughly wet, and pulls it away.

A few drops of water trickle from the knife to the floor. He lines up the open gin bottle so that the water drops are directly centered in a line with the bottle's uncapped top.

Gently, carefully, he releases the blade from the wooden doorway, holding it in position between the fingers of his left hand. He releases the pressure of his fingers, and the knife drops into the bottle. Usually, the knife handle doesn't even touch the edges.

offer to "start you three up" can cost three more bets in the event that he wins all the presses.

Golfer's Digest tells about a favorite bet in Tucson, Arizona, called Seven-Up. The bet ends when any player in the foursome gets seven "plus" points for good putting or seven "minus" points for bad putting. "It sounds innocent enough," the publication says, "at 50¢ a point, until everyone starts paying or collecting from everyone else on the differentials between points." A player who goes out seven-minus and has to pay all the players who have plus points can lose much more than anticipated.

One legendary hustler who made all the fashionable Winter resorts did extremely well offering to bet that he could defeat an opponent using only his putter. The "putter" was somewhat different from most putters, and this player could use it as a driving iron, a mashie, a wedge—however he wished. Since he was a professional of tournament-play caliber and made a specialty of the one-club game, he had a gold mine until word of his prowess got around the country.

Some pros whose tournament victories have made them celebrities have a different kind of hustle. They know that wealthy amateurs want to play with them, and they won't set foot on the first tee unless the stakes are extremely high. Being able to brag that he has played against a famous pro is going to cost the affluent amateur money.

Nearly every private club has a few would-be hustlers who deliberately keep their handicaps high. Usually, they're soon discovered, and friendly bettors steer clear of them. The dangerous hustler is a stranger in the club, an unknown quantity. On public courses, he has a field day. Fortunately for his victims, the size of golf bets on public courses is normally lower than in private clubs.

Golf enthusiasts who bet with bookmakers on the outcome of professional tournaments and who band together to buy a player in a Calcutta are serious students of form and performance. Regardless of where bets are made with bookies, the odds and handicapping usually reach the bookmaker by way of Las Vegas. That they give him a "cushion" goes without saying.

Lovers of the game, as well as rules associations, try to keep obvious gamesmanship and gambitry out —not only because they want golf to maintain its status as a gentleman's game but because golf is a better game with lower scores when gambitry is missing.

It's frowned upon, it's deplored, but, unfortunately, it exists—and a golfer who is playing for money must know about it. GAMBLER'S DIGEST does not condone it any more than it condones loaded dice in a crap game, but the golf hustler is no gentleman, and he wins bets with it.

Flagrant and obvious distraction of a golfer who's making a play isn't tolerated anywhere, but some of the hustler's gamesmanship is subtle. For example, a hustler may praise an opponent to the skies—and talk him into trying the impossible. When the victim fails to achieve it, the hustler tells him how close he came, and talks him into trying it again.

One of the hustler's favorite tricks is to get an opponent's mind off the game with conversation. Golf requires concentration, and discussion of a subject that gets a player violently mad takes his mind off the game. So does talking about his hobbies or his family —anything about which he has strong feelings.

A golf pro who was something of a hustler in his less prosperous youth remembers a money player whose nickname was "Sniff." "The fellow had an annoying habit of making a quick, loud intake of breath through his nostrils," he says. "His sniffs were irritating enough at any time, but they were absolutely intolerable when you were putting or were at the top of your swing. The funny thing is, opponents never called him on it. I guess they thought it was a physical affliction he couldn't control. And what were they going to say? It would have sounded rather silly to protest, 'You're breathing too hard.'

"Sniff, himself, thought it was the best gimmick in existence. 'Any mannerism that annoys an opponent,' he told me, 'is worth at least a three or four handicap.' "

Mr. Odds-Maker's concern with golf bets is confined to tournament play, but the pro at a leading eastern club has a number of "best bets" for the player in a friendly game.

"The average player who bets on himself doesn't bet smartly," he says. "You can lose a Nassau and still make money by betting to your strength during the round. Bet side-bets to your strength. If you're good on the greens, bet on putts. If you're a power golfer, bet on tee shots.

"Equally important, bet to your opponent's weaknesses. If he's a poor putter, bet him that he won't sink a seven- or eight-foot putt. If his long game is

---

I'll Betcha!

Offer to bet anyone that he can't name or locate a desert east of the Mississippi in the United States and he'll tell you that there is no such thing.

At that point, offer to bet him that he's wrong and that there's a desert in, of all places, the state of Maine.

Unless he happens to be a resident of Maine, the chances are that he'll bet—and lose.

The Maine Desert is located in the village of Freeport, Maine. Source of the information is the Haskins Information Service. Better have some proof with you when you make the bet, because nobody will believe you.

weak, bet him that he won't get on the green in two on a par-four hole.

"Whenever he gets into trouble, apply the betting pressure. It makes getting out of trouble more difficult.

"If he's playing over his head, take advantage of it. Talk him into bets that require a continuation of the streak for him to win. If the hot streak continues, he'll become so over-confident that you can talk him into a bet he'll regret.

"If a man has an 80 average on a par-72 course, try to talk him into bets that require par golf to win. If he has a 90 average, bet him on every hole that he'll bogey it. If you're not good enough to beat him, don't bet on yourself, bet against him. Get him to bet on himself, in other words.

"Resist the temptation to make bad bets on yourself. Pride and rivalry are expensive destroyers of cool, calculated betting. Either bet to win or don't bet."

As to betting on tournament play, Mr. Odds-Maker says, "First, rate the entries on past performance, but don't stop there. Try to know the mental and physical condition of the top players. When a star golfer is off his game, it's usually no secret. And when a good golfer gets hot, the word gets around quickly. Your second rating is on mental and physical condition. Your third rating is on adaptability to the course where the tournament is being held. If it's a long course and he's weak on power, add a few points to his score. Do the same thing if he's a poor putter and the greens are tricky. If tough shots from tricky lies are his forte, give him an edge on a course that's loaded with tough hazards. If he occasionally hooks or slices and the rough is deep, add a couple of points against him. Every good pro occasionally finds a course that is made to order for him, and he murders it. Fourth, rate him on his reaction to pressure. Some excellent golfers come close, time after time, but always crack under pressure.

"When you've rated the contestants this way, you'll narrow the field considerably. Rate the few players still in contention on the basis of whether they're coming or going. Is their recent play showing steady improvement or is it slipping a little? Are they at the peak of their game or are they letting down, coasting? A player who struggles through to win a big major tournament by the skin of his teeth often has a letdown in his next tournament.

"The 'Man to Beat' technique is sometimes helpful. There are usually one or two players in a tournament who are the men the field must beat if they expect to win. Is anybody in the tournament ready to beat them?

"Today's caliber of play is so good that major tournaments are often a toss-up. In such cases, heavy betting on a favorite sometimes creates highly advantageous odds on other players whose chances are just as good as the favorite's."

MR. ODDS-MAKER'S BEST BET

Mr. Odds-Maker says, "Don't gamble at golf with anyone who just manages to beat you, who is always one stroke better, no matter how well you play. The chances are that your opponent is far better than you are."

Gazinta Golf

Throckmorton was a guest at the club.

His host said, "Charlie, we have a favorite club bet called the Gazinta. It's quite different from a Nassau and quite complicated to explain, but you'll get the hang of it as you play around the course. It has the Head Dragon, the Executive Dragon, the Assistant Dragon and the Tail Dragon. Each member of the foursome has a designation at the end of the game, based on his play. It's a lot of fun, and you'll catch on quickly. How about it?"

"Sure," agreed Throckmorton, a good golfer. At the end of the first hole, he was told, "Too bad you birdied that one, Charlie. On the first hole in Gazinta, high man wins and anyone with fewer strokes pays him a buck a stroke."

On the second hole, he was informed, "Anybody who gets a birdie must get another birdie on the next hole or pay double for every stroke over it.

By the 18th hole, some $80 down, he said, "This Gazinta is the craziest game I've ever seen. There's no rhyme or reason to the bets. They don't make sense."

"Oh, but they do," his host insisted. "Everything in Gazinta has one objective."

"What is it?" Throckmorton demanded.

His host smiled. "That the guest gazinta the locker room with his Tail Dragon."

TENNIS

With the leaps and bounds that professional tennis has taken in recent years, betting on pro tournaments would undoubtedly be heavy if it weren't for the fact that one player usually dominates the scene. Closer competition is necessary before wagering becomes as prevalent in the United States as it is in Australia.

Tennis rivals have made friendly bets with each other for years, and have even developed their own handicapping system in situations where one player is better than another.

Aside from betting with an opponent, considerable gambling has been done by "sponsors" of amateur

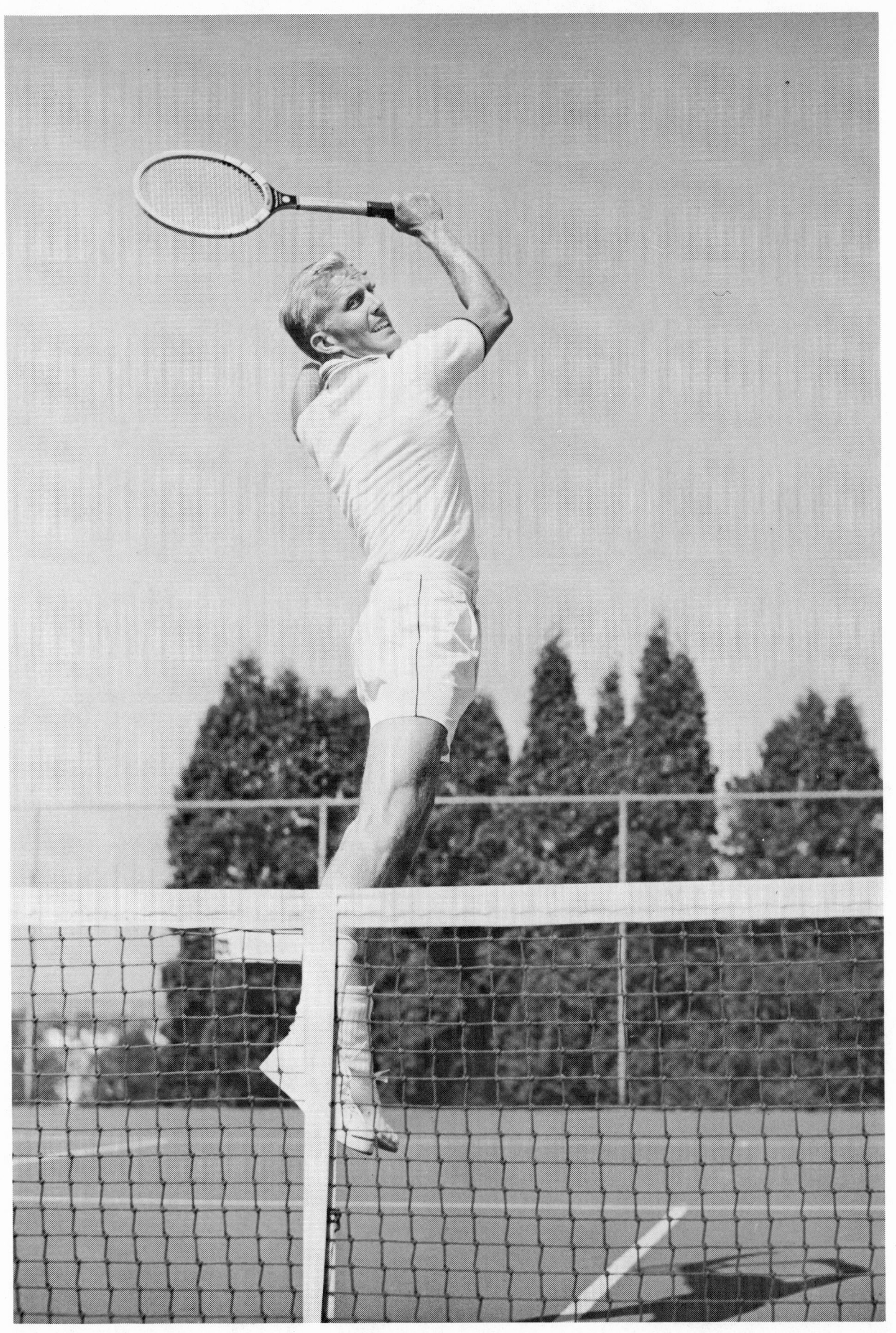

tennis players, nearly always without the knowledge of the contestants. Since the "sponsors" are invariably wealthy, and the rivalry is keen, these bets are sometimes substantial.

Public interest in wagering on tennis hasn't been sufficient to attract bookmakers in the United States, although "books" cover the sport in Australia, in Sweden and, occasionally, in France. The social status of the game has undoubtedly kept gambling at a low level, but the growing popularity of professional tennis may change that, eventually.

A tennis pro says, "In betting on tournament play, it's a rule of thumb to bet on the champion. Sure, you may lose, but you'll get a good run for your money.

"In a match between an amateur and a professional, always bet on the pro. Winning is his livelihood, not his hobby or avocation.

"In amateur tournaments, study the seeding. It makes it fairly obvious who the tennis moguls think will win. For a number of reasons, it's always easier for the top seeded players to win than it is for their opponents. When Althea Gibson first broke into tournament play, it seemed to me that she needed miracles to win. Maybe she was guilty of them, but I felt that the number of base-line faults called against her was, to put it mildly, extraordinary. Whether it's true or not, many amateur tennis players feel that the tennis powers have 'pet' players. Even if it's untrue, being regarded as a 'pet' is a strong psychological factor.

"In private play, if another player beats you consistently, face the bitter truth that he's better than you are and don't bet with him.

"Against an opponent of comparable skill, try to make him play your game rather than his own. If he's strong in the back-court, try to keep him close to the net. If he plays a 'soft' game, try to play a 'hard' game.

"Tennis is a 'social' game, and gambitry can often win. If you're playing a stuffed-shirt, be a roughneck. Against a mean, tough opponent, convey the idea that his behaviour simply isn't proper. Shame him or make him feel guilty and you've got him. If an opponent makes a vicious serve that you know you can't return, don't even try for it. Simply smile and ask, 'Do you want to call that serve a base-line fault or not? Just thought I'd ask.' Questioning plays and then being magnanimous about conceding them unnerves almost any opponent. I lost a close match to a tough opponent one time and after congratulating him said, 'You know, I'd like to play you again in a few days when I'm no longer plagued with this sore right ankle.' I got my money back on the return match.

"Gambitry is frowned upon in tennis, and there's often a fine line between psychology and unsportsmanlike conduct. Flagrant gambitry will ostracize a tennis player. Nevertheless, some of the top tennis stars have, either instinctively or with calculation, made subtle gambitry a strong weapon.

"One of the best bets in gambling on yourself at tennis is to use common-sense realism. Don't give your money away to better players. Every money tennis player I know has a few pigeons he cultivates —and beats with regularity. When he knows a competitor is too good for him, he doesn't bet."

MR. ODDS-MAKER'S BEST BET

Mr. Odds-Maker advises, "Never bet on anyone in tennis who is just recovering from an injury, no matter how minor. Always bet on someone who is playing consistently well in the tournament.

"Always take into consideration the surface on which the tournament is being played. Most players play better on a particular surface than on others."

TRACK AND FIELD EVENTS

One of the few places in sports where betting is practically non-existant is in track and field events. Footracing, high-jumping, shotput, pole vault, discus throw and similar contests of skill apparently hold no interest for most gamblers.

This can be attributed in part to the Olympic Games tradition, and the simon-pure attitude of the governing bodies that regulate such events. It may also be due in some measure to the betting fraternity's lack of attendance at track and field meets, most of which are sponsored by high schools, colleges and universities.

In the last decade of the nineteenth century and the first decade of the twentieth, professional footracers traveled the hinterlands, matching themselves against local favorites and wagering substantial sums on the outcome of the races. As the Amateur Athletic Union gained strength, it took a firm stand on such contests, ruling that the local boy who raced against the professional endangered his amateur standing. Before long, the professional sprinters and distance runners found themselves without competition and retired.

Today, peculiarly, the bettor whose activity at college football games is taken for granted is quickly

---

A New Deal

Sam Levinson tells about going into Lindy's for a late-night snack and being approached by a new waiter.

"Where's my regular waiter?" Sam asked.

"Your regular waiter ain't your regular waiter any more," the man replied. "He lost you to me in a crap game last night."

discouraged if he tries to wager on a track and field meet. The instant his betting activity attracts any official attention, he is ushered from the premises.

Smart Sam, a gambler who will gamble on anything, won't even attend track and field meets. "The last time I went to one," he says, "I offered to bet even money that a big, husky boy would put the shot farther on his second heave than on the first, and the people around me stared like I was some kinda freak. No action."

MR. ODDS-MAKER'S BEST BET

Mr. Odds-Maker feels that track and field meets would be among the easiest of all sports events to handicap. Barring injury, participants nearly always run true to performance. A human being who has developed the ability to run the 100-yard dash in 9.8 or a shot-putter who heaves the weight a certain distance will ordinarily be consistent. The best performances of competitors in every event are public knowledge, if they're good enough to attract attention.

BILLIARDS AND POOL

Billiards and pool are among the most scientific of all table games, requiring great skill and, when played by experts, leaving little to chance. Dating back to the fifteenth century, billiards achieved social distinction when the game became a favorite with the seventeenth century French court.

Because a good billiard or pool table is heavy, space-consuming and costly, the games were originally played mostly in public halls devoted to them, throughout the United States. The "pool hall" often became a hangout for town loafers and unsavory characters and was the gambling headquarters in many communities. Poker and dice games in "the back room," punch boards, "jar" numbers, pool tickets, raffles, and bookmaking not only augmented the proprietors' income but were often the major part of it, with pool and billiard tables as a legal "front."

The pool hustler has been immortalized in fiction and drama. He operated in almost every pool hall and had a level of skill that made his wagers more a confidence game than a gamble.

The games suffered from guilt by association.

There was nothing unsavory about either pool or billiards; it was the places where the games were played that brought censure from a community's better element. Many towns barred minors from the establishments, and the suggestion of a woman being present in them was unthinkable. The musical comedy, "The Music Man," illustrated the turn-of-the-century attitude with the song-recitative, "Trouble Right Here in River City."

The games were simply too good to be destroyed by unsavory associations. Tables in clubs and private homes won devotees, both male and female. Manufacturers of the tables were deeply concerned with the pool hall image and tried to improve it. They made, at the same time, an effort to stimulate the home and club market, and they conducted national and world tournaments at a high social and moral level.

Today, there is a type of pool and billiard establishment that the old pool hall habitue finds off-limits. It is clean, quiet, tastefully furnished and socially acceptable to both men and women. It is not a gambling house, and caters to lovers of the games. It has a hard row to hoe to overcome the stigma attached to the typical pool hall, but it is having a measure of success.

The pool hustler still exists, and so do many undesirable pool halls, but devotees of the games can play them in a good atmosphere.

Gambling on pool and billiards has always been prevalent. In South Africa, it is one of the two or three major forms of gambling.

Bar Bet

It's unbelievable, but there are people who don't know anything about dice who will bite on this bar bet, which was a favorite of the late Richard Himber, band leader.

"Throw a pair of dice while my back is turned," Himber would say, "and see what your point is. Got it? Now, turn the two dice completely over, so that both faces are against the table. What's your new point?"

Suppose the victim replied "Six."

Himber promptly announced, "Your original point was Eight." Turning around, he added, "and you threw a Six and Two."

All there is to it, of course, is that the top and bottom of a die will always add up to seven, no matter what point is thrown. The tops and bottoms of a pair of dice always add to 14. Turning around and seeing a Five and One, he knew immediately that the original throw was a Two and Six.

The combination of scientific knowledge and manual dexterity required to be a good player makes the games unique. The greatest players in the world admit that they still acquire new insight and new skill every day.

The felt-covered table has rubber "cushions" or "banks," and is usually ten by five feet. A ball, hitting one of the cushions, will rebound in accord with the physical law that "the angle of incidence equals the angle of reflection."

That is, the angles will be equal unless the ball has "English" on it. The "English" is a spin applied to the cue-ball by stroking it with the cue either to the right or left of center. "Draw" is applied to the cue ball by stroking it with the cue below center, and "follow" is applied by stroking it above center.

The amount of draw, English or follow depends on the touch of the player.

In both regular billiards and pocket pool, balls also carom off each other. Aiming the cue-ball precisely enough at another ball so that the rebound of both balls will move them exactly where the shooter wants them to go is a delicate art, complicated by English, draw and follow.

The object of all billiard games is to make the cue ball contact both of the other balls on the table. Three-cushion billiards, in which the cue ball must touch three cushions of the table before it completes a billiard, demands the ultimate in skill. Eighteen-inch balkline billiards is a game in which one of the object balls must be moved a certain distance on a shot, precluding the "nursing" of the object balls into a position where a number of billiards might easily be made.

In pool or pocket billiards, the table has six pockets, one at each corner and one mid-way along each long side. Most pool games are played with a "rack" of 15 object balls and a cue ball, and the object of the game is to put the object balls into the pockets. The commonest of the gambling games and the one requiring the least skill is "rotation" pool, in which the numbered object balls must be hit first in the order of their numbers. If a player hits the proper object ball—at the start of the game, the one ball, first and pockets another ball, he is allowed to score that ball. No balls may be scored unless the player hits the lowest number ball on the table first. "Call Shot," in which a player must specify what ball he will put into what pocket, is another popular gambling game, as is bottle pool.

A variant of pocket pool is "Snooker," probably the most popular gambling game in the group. It is played on a special table with smaller pockets which are rounded at the edges. There is a "rack" of 15 red balls and a group of colored balls which count from two through seven. A player must pocket a red ball, which counts one, before he is allowed to shoot for a ball of another color. A popular variation in

Success Story

A legend in a mid-west college community has it that a hobo rode the rods into the town, got a job as janitor in a disreputable, run-down pool hall, and blew his first week's wages in the pool hall crap game.

He was luckier, the second week. The story is that he cleaned every player in the game, including the pool hall proprietor, with total winnings of close to $7,000.

The pool hall owner eyed the pile greedily. "Tell you what I'll do," he proposed. "I'll put up the pool hall against your winnings."

The ex-hobo agreed. The pool hall owner picked up the dice, shook them vigorously, and rolled them out—a pair of sixes.

The ex-hobo took over the pool hall and, with a part of his cash winnings, cleaned it up. It was the beginning of a chain of clean, well-operated pool halls for college students, pool halls for young gentlemen. The ex-hobo soon became a well-to-do, important, respected member of the community.

And he wouldn't tolerate gambling in his establishments, although he, himself, bet huge sums of money on the college football teams.

Snooker is "Six Ball Wild," in which a player may shoot for the six ball at any time, out of its proper rotation. If he fails to pocket it, six points are deducted from his score. A good "position" player will work the six-ball and his cue-ball into position so that he may pocket it a number of times before missing.

Dick Westly says, "A good pool or billiard tournament is fun to watch and fun to bet on.The best players, the ones who have the skill to win, always stand out. Let their attitudes decide how you'll bet. There's as much gambitry in a big tournament as in bridge or gin or poker, and the good player who puts the Indian sign on another good player is a potential winner.

"Bet the seasoned pro against the skillful newcomer.

"A good 'position' player nearly always beats a dead-eye shooter. He doesn't make as many difficult shots as his opponent because he doesn't give himself tough shots. Faced with one, he tries to leave his opponent in the worst possible position instead of trying to make it. The sure-shot player is confident of his ability and often takes reckless chances. When he misses, he leaves the position player open for another long run.

"If you're going to bet on yourself in a friendly game, remember that playing a good game of pool or billiards is a profession. Face your limitations. Whatever you do, don't bet on yourself against a stranger—unless you happen to be a national champion.

"The average pool or billiard player makes the mistake of playing a strictly offensive game. At least half of the game is defense. Unless you have a shot you know you can make, play to give your opponent bad position. A 50-50 chance of making a shot which will score you one point is a bad gamble. Miss it and you give your opponent a chance for a run. Leaving your opponent so he can't make a point is always worth more than making a point, yourself.

"Study a masse shot carefully before you attempt it. Such a shot scatters object balls all over the table, which is fine if you make it. If you don't, the opportunity you give your opponent may lose the game for you.

"Summing up, make the shots you're reasonably sure you can make. When in doubt, concentrate on giving your opponent a bad 'leave'."

MR. ODDS-MAKER'S BEST BET

"Pool is a pressure sport. Many people choke up when the stakes are high. In professional tournaments or matches, the players often bet on themselves. When a player bets 'tough' money on himself, money he can't afford to lose, lay off. At the professional level, the game requires perfect touch and nerves of steel, and risking 'tough' money can make a great player crack.

"When betting on yourself in a friendly game, play on a table you are used to, and don't make the mistake of under-rating a player who always wins by attributing his victories to luck."

BOWLING

Bowling is one of the most popular participation sports in the United States and one of the most widely approved, played by both men and women for recreation and good exercise.

It probably stems from the old English game of skittles. The first recorded American match was on the Knickerbocker Alleys in New York City on January 1st, 1840. By 1875, bowlers from cities throughout the country held a convention to frame standard rules, and in 1895, the American Bowling Congress organized the sport.

The usual American bowling alley measures 60 feet from the head pin to the scratch line and is approximately three and a half feet wide. Ten pins are set up at the far end in a triangle with its apex toward the bowler, who is entitled to roll two balls at the pins, trying to knock them all down. Ten "frames" or turns for each player constitute a game.

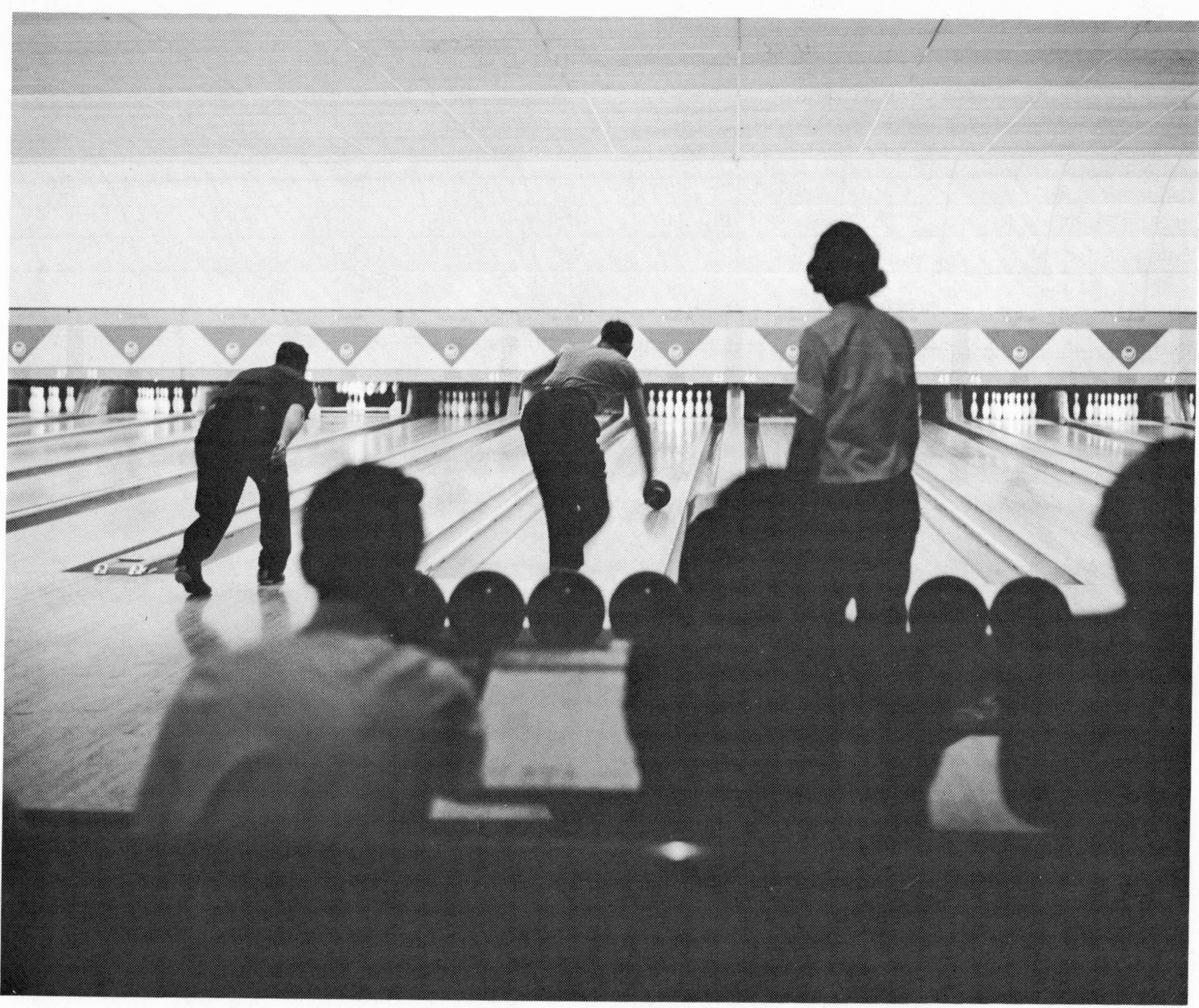

The only frame in which a player may roll three balls is the tenth, in the event he "strikes" or knocks down all ten pins with his first roll. In any frame in which a player "strikes," he adds the total of pins knocked down by his next two rolls to the ten already scored in that frame.

When all ten pins are knocked down by two rolls, it is called a "spare," and the player is entitled to add the number of pins knocked down with his next roll to the ten already scored. The most that can be recorded on a spare is 20, in the event that the next roll is a strike. The maximum to be scored in a frame by a strike is 30, in the event the next two rolls are also strikes.

Bowling is probably the most thoroughly organized sport in the country. The "league" is the backbone of it. There are men's leagues, women's leagues, industrial leagues, business and professional leagues, leagues of every conceivable kind. They meet at scheduled times, on specific days, with rival teams competing.

First air conditioning and then the automatic pin setter brought a phenomenal boom in bowling activity, and more people in the United States are bowling today than ever before.

Also, more people are gambling on the game. Since players gravitate into leagues containing bowlers of comparable skill, and since each bowler's average is carefully kept, a bettor has a good idea of his chances against another.

While individual bets between bowlers are common, a prize award system has evolved in bowling, with each bowler contributing to a kitty that is eventually divided according to rank. Prize money in many major tournaments consists in considerable part of entry fees. In one way, bowling is a sort of pari-mutuel gamble in which each bowler bets on himself or his team.

Television has stimulated professional bowling, and while it is impossible to estimate the amount of money bet on professional bowlers in match play, the amount must be considerable. Pools and parlays on bowlers are far from uncommon, and gambling of a type similar to golf's Calcutta is sometimes found in big tournaments.

Ed McGregor says, "Since bowling today is

mostly league and tournament participation, get into a league where you aren't over-matched. If you can find a league spot where the top team's average score is roughly your average score, you'll do fine.

"Betting against a bowler of your class, try to get him to bet on individual frames and try to parlay them. It takes four or five passes to win important money in a crap game, and getting four or five consecutive strikes and spares can give you the same kind of results. As in craps, hold the frame bets to a minimum until you win one, and then start betting your opponent's money against him.

"If you're a consistent bowler and your opponent goes all the way from 160 to 220, introduce him to 'Contract' bowling. You play against your league average. You pay a dime for every point under the 'contract' or league average and get a nickel for every point over. He does the same.

"Forget the pool in which high man on the team collects a dollar from each of the others. Make an individual bet of a buck with each of the other players on the team. If your average has you toward the top of your league, it's a much better bet. Only if you wind up in bottom position for the game does it really cost you.

"Don't bet on picking up a split. If somebody else wants to bet on it, take the bet."

"Bet on propositions where you have the edge. If you usually have fewer open frames than your opponent, bet him you'll mark in more frames than he will. If you're strong on spares but weak on strikes, bet on the number of spares.

"It's always easier to win bets on your opponent's weaknesses than on your own skill."

MR. ODDS-MAKER'S BEST BET

"Bowling is another pressure sport when the stakes are high. Alleys vary greatly. Some are fast, some slow, and all have different grooves. When you're betting on yourself, try to do it on your home surface, where you have the advantage of knowing the alley's idiosyncrasies." ♠

Hope springs eternal

Lotteries, legal or illegal, have always enjoyed popularity. The Romans made them a part of their Saturnalias and orgies, sometimes offering attractive slave girls as prizes. Various forms of lottery are as old as written history.

First conducted by individuals, lotteries found a ready market, whether the prizes were weird or practical, of little or great value, new or used. Merchants ran commodity lotteries in Holland in the 13th century, and Italian merchants soon followed, offering undesirable merchandise which they hadn't been able to sell.

Success of the commodity lotteries quickly brought protests from merchants who were trying to operate on a legitimate basis. The lottery, these business men complained, was unfair competition.

The first "modern" lottery and the first to offer money prizes, was instituted by the Italian government in 1530, and was called "Lotto." It began, as have most government-sponsored lotteries ever since, because the Italian government needed money.

Once other European countries saw the results of the Italian venture, they were quick to get on the bandwagon. France was in the lottery business within ten years, and found it such a quick, simple way to raise money for public improvements that it became a vital part of the French governmental economy. The French people had rebelled against the profligate spending of its ruling class, and collection of taxes had become increasingly difficult. The attractive bait offered by the government lotteries was so tempting that protests against paying for governmental extravagance were quickly forgotten.

Lottery as a means of money-raising soon spread to Spain, Germany, Austria and England, where Queen Elizabeth introduced the first British lottery in 1569.

From that time on, whenever a government has been pinched by a shortage in its treasury, one of the first suggestions has been, "Let's have a lottery."

It might be said, with some basis in fact, that the United States was founded on a lottery. In 1612, the Virginia Company turned to lotteries to finance the colonizing of the New World, with the blessing of King James I, who approved a lottery "in special favor for the present plantation of English colonies in Virginia." The lottery was extremely popular, with even the London church investing six pounds "to the profitte of our churche stocke in the lottery for the plantation of Vergenya and what benefit shall happen shall be for the good of our church."

The lottery brought the Virginia Company a profit of £29,000. The colonies recognized a good thing when they saw it. Bitter opposition to British taxes probably made even self-imposed taxes somewhat unpalatable, and the colonies quickly found lotteries to be a popular substitute. From 1744 until 1894, lotteries were used to raise funds in the New World for almost every conceivable purpose — churches, schools, bridges, turnpikes, public welfare, aid to the poor, munitions, and public buildings. During that period, there were more than 1,300 publicly sanctioned lotteries for one purpose or another, and everyone approved except the Quakers in Pennsylvania, who passed a law prohibiting lotteries and "such-like enticing, vain and evil sports and games" in 1682. They passed the law, but in 20 years were unable to enforce it, and Queen Anne rescinded it when she took the British throne in 1702.

King's College, which later became Columbia University, started with a New York licensed lottery in 1746, the first of several that raised money to get the school under way. A feud between the Presbyterians, who opposed the school, and the Anglicans, who favored it, brought attempts to divert the lottery funds from their avowed purpose. In 1756, the feud was at least partially settled and a semblance of harmony gained when legislation in New York gave half the funds raised from the King's College lottery to the city of New York for a "rest house" and jail.

Harvard University raised funds with a lottery in 1774, and in addition to the $18,000 raised by it for the Harvard building fund, invested in a block of tickets in its own lottery and won another $10,000.

I'll Betcha!

I'll bet you can't name the longest river in the United States," the bettor challenges, and everyone says, "The Mississippi."

The bettor shakes his head. "I'll bet you the Missouri river is longer than the Mississippi," he declares.

"Why, the Missouri is a tributary of the Mississippi," someone who knows his geography protests.

"Nevertheless, I'll bet you that the Missouri is longer than the Mississippi," the bettor insists. "Want to bet?"

The bets are made, and the challengers lose. The Missouri river is longer than the Mississippi. According to Webster's Geographical Dictionary, the Mississippi is 2,470 miles long to the head of the Passes. The Missouri is 2,475 miles long (or 2,723 miles including its tributaries to their ultimate source).

The school held two more drawings, in 1794 and 1805, to get money for additional buildings.

Among other early American colleges and universities that held building fund lotteries were Dartmouth, Yale, Williams and Brown.

An attempt to finance the American Revolution with a lottery failed. The Continental Congress authorized a drawing to raise $10 million, with $5 million in prizes. Tickets were offered at prices from $10 to $40. With only four million people in the country, including children, the plan was doomed to failure. Ten dollars was a substantial sum, and most of those who could afford to buy a ticket were Tories.

Swindles and confusion existed in the lottery field almost from the start. The *Loterie Royale* had done extremely well in France until the king and members of his court started to win the top prizes with a regularity that seemed to be contrary to the laws of chance. The bourgeoisie and even the peasants reached the conclusion that luck wasn't entirely responsible for the way the lottery was going, and the boom in ticket sales quickly fell off.

In 1823, Congress authorized a group of lottery agents to organize the Grand National lottery for the purpose of acquiring funds to beautify the far-from-beautiful Washington, D.C. Patriotic citizens all over the country responded to the appeal and bought tickets, probably close to a million of them. Drawings were held on the scheduled date and the winners were duly announced—but the prizes weren't awarded. The promoters had disappeared with the money and were never found. The ill-fated lottery not only failed to come up with funds to beautify Washington but actually cost the city $100,000. A man whose ticket had won $100,000 brought suit against Washington, fought it all the way to the Supreme Court, and got judgement for the full amount.

By 1830, there were numerous complaints of irregularities in various lotteries. A New York grand jury estimated in that year that there had been an average of one drawing a week for a 12-month gross of over $9 million. Three years later, the *Boston Mercantile Journal* investigated lotteries in eight seaboard states and published its findings. It asserted that more than 400 lotteries in 1832 had taken in more than $66 million, about five times the cost or running the U.S. Government at the time. Public opinion began to turn against the lotteries, and by 1840, they were illegal in Maine, Vermont, New Hampshire, Massachusetts, New York, New Jersey, Pennsylvania, Virginia, Ohio, Illinois and Louisiana.

Lotteries had been important in almost every phase of the new country's life. The Continental Congress had organized a lottery in 1776 for aid to soldiers suffering in the field, and General George Washington bought the first ticket. He later signed a bill issued by the first Congress for a $5 million lottery. In 1789, a lottery raised the funds to remodel the City Hall in New York for the first meeting of the Continental Congress.

Permission to hold lotteries had been responsible in the early years of the new country for paying off mortgages and for the capital to start small businesses.

A New York spinster, without a dowry, even proposed in 1747 that there be a lottery designed to provide "distressed widows and deserving virgins" with husbands.

Lotteries had played an important part in the moral, economic and sociological life of the country. The decline in their popularity probably began in 1790, with the appearance of professional lottery ticket brokers and contractors. Both groups exploited the lottery market for their own gain. The ticket brokers bought up huge blocks of tickets at cut-rate prices and peddled them all over the country for as much as the traffic would bear. By 1815, every town of over a thousand population had its ticket broker. The contractors assumed control and direction of lotteries. Largest among the contractors was Yates & McIntyre, who by 1823 owned all the New York lottery grants or at least held control of them. They controlled others as well, in other states. When the state of New York tried to stop the ticket-broker racket, more than 200 ticket shops locked up but continued to do business behind closed doors.

Stories of lottery swindles became common, and by 1840, the death knell for lotteries had been sounded.

The last major lottery of any consequence to be run in the United States for many years was the Louisiana Lottery, authorized by the Louisiana state legislature in 1868. The lottery company, a syndicate fronted by Charles T. Howard, agreed to pay $40,000 a year to the New Orleans Charity Hospital from a lottery with a monthly drawing, tickets to sell at 25¢ apiece. Howard lost no time in expanding the lottery. There were soon 50¢ tickets, and then a semi-annual prize of $600,000 on a $40 ticket, with a total yearly prize of $28 million. Agents operated all over the country. Howard became one of the most influential men in the state, if not in the country. Because of his operations, Congress passed a law barring lottery tickets and printed matter referring to lotteries from the U.S. mails. Much dissatisfaction with the lottery was heard in the Louisiana legislature, and a bitter battle developed between lottery and anti-lottery factions. When an anti-lottery governor was elected in 1892, Howard offered to turn over $1,250,000 annually to the state if the company's charter were renewed. The offer created a backlash of criticism from newspapers, clergymen and women's clubs, who accused the company of political corruption. President Benjamin Harrison delivered a special message to the U.S. Senate and House to affect the legislation barring lottery material from the mails, in which he charged that "the people of all the state are debauched and defrauded by the Louisiana Lottery."

The Louisiana legislature refused to renew the lottery company's charter and the drawing that had raised millions for its bosses while contributing only $40,000 to the hospital passed into oblivion. It had held power over many businesses and had spent millions to control legal agencies. It was to be the last legal lottery in the United States until 1963, when New Hampshire made a state lottery legal.

England somehow escaped the racketeering that brought U.S. lotteries into disrepute. The British football pools and "Bonds" lottery receive little criticism and operate with what appears to be scrupulous honesty. A strict check on operators, conducted by honest officials, is probably the answer.

The New Hampshire state lottery was closely followed by a New York state lottery. New Hampshire,

ALAS, POOR CHARLEY

The heart-rending story of Charley Cooper appeared in Newsweek Magazine of March 30, 1964. Charley, a clerk making roughly $30 a week as a clerk for the London Electricity Board, spent a Friday evening filling out a soccer pool card, working out 60 possible combinations, win, lose and draw, for the outcome of Saturday's major league soccer games. He bet a British penny, approximately 70 American cents, on each combination.

One of his penny bets won a tax-free fortune, the equivalent of $630,375.20 in American money. He immediately set aside £10,000 each for his three brothers, three sisters and his elderly "mum," with whom he lived in a bathless flat in London's working-class Bethnal Green section. He quit his job, bought a fine new umbrella and then considered buying a Rolls-Royce and a country cottage with plumbing.

There was so much money left, according to Newsweek, *that he consulted an investment expert. "Emerging from a two-hour conference," the magazine continued, "he admitted that although he should feel elated, he was the 'unhappiest man in Britain.'" He explained, "If it had been £2,000 or 20,000, I would have been happy, but this is too much for a man like me — much too much."*

first state to get into the lottery business in 70 years, tried hard to get started right. The Jusice, Treasury and Post Office departments were all called in and worked closely with the lottery commission and state general counsel to maintain legality and honesty.

Indications of the size of the first New Hampshire payoff came in 1964, with $2½ million to the state public school system. The U.S. Treasury was also enriched to the tune of $570,000 in taxes.

Buying a chance wasn't easy. Because transportation of tickets across state lines is illegal, there were no tickets. Prospective gamblers had to go to either of the state's two race tracks or one of its 49 state liquor stores. Upon payment of $3 for a chance, a clerk activated a machine which shoved forth a ticket on which the wagerer signed his name and address. The ticket then went back into the machine and issued a receipt.

There is a drawing whenever a million dollars worth of chances has been sold. Winners are notified by wire and their winnings are deposited to their name in a New Hampshire bank.

Revenue from the lottery was not initially up to expectations, and the New Hampshire legislature in 1967 approved the sale of chances in resort hotels and motels, and at fairs and public beaches where tourist traffic is heavy.

Despite the "take" being less than anticipated, *U.S. News & World Report* for Aug. 28, 1967, said, "The state still has been able to raise teachers' salaries, provide needed new books and other school equipment and raise budgets of local school districts. New Hampshire now is the only state in the country without a sales or income tax. Funds derived from the lottery are said by its supporters to preserve general tax funds for new highways and other improvements."

The state-sponsored New York lottery was approved by voters in a referendum on Nov. 8, 1966, and the lottery began in June of the following year. The first jackpot drawing was held beside the Fountain of Abundance in Central Park, with Guy Lombardo and a New York beauty queen as added attractions. *Newsweek* Magazine of Aug. 7, 1967, reported, "With six $100,000 jackpot prizes for winners in a $1,440,000 top winners' pool, the stage seemed all set for a splurge of publicity as the curtain rose for the state's first drawing. None of the grand prize winners even turned up for the ceremony and the finale flopped almost as badly as the lottery. State officials were miserable.

"Approved by voters in November, the state lottery was intended to meet the soaring costs of education. Governor Rockefeller suggested four drawings a year, Mayor Lindsay wanted eight. 'So the legislature compromised,' as one Albany veteran dryly observed, 'and agreed to have 12.' It was calculated that a monthly drawing would gross about $30 million, enough to net $198 million a year for the state's schools. The total take from the first month was under $7,000,000."

New York officials quickly learned that lottery publicity was a major problem, with federal anti-gambling laws preventing advertising of lotteries not only in newspapers but on radio and television. The state immediately went into billboard and poster advertising and hired a staff of sales representatives to work the state with a hard-sell. By the end of 1968, the *New Yorker* magazine's Talk of the Town commented that the state lottery had suffered from one trauma after another and quoted the *New York Times* as calling it a "gigantic fiasco."

Despite all the problems, New York officials worked diligently to promote the lottery. Police officials said that a vast market, people who regularly bet "numbers," regarded the payoff as too slow. The "Numbers" payoff was immediate, when it happened.

If the New York lottery had troubles, the Numbers Game didn't. Operating illegally in almost every large city of the country, it went merrily on its way

---

Bar Bet

The old grifter pulled a deck of cards from his pocket. "Boys," he said, "I've just learned a terrific new card trick." He fanned the deck and instructed one of the men at the bar to remove a card. Then he squared the deck, cut it, and offered the lower half of the cut for replacement of the selected card, on top. Rather obviously, he looked at the bottom card of the stock of cards that were deposited on top of the chosen card.

The men smiled tolerantly. Putting a known card on top of a selected card is probably the oldest and most widely known method of finding the chosen card. The trickster has only to find the card that was originally on the bottom of the deck and he knows that the chosen card is next to it.

The old grifter began turning cards from the top of the deck, face up onto the bar. The chosen card had been the six of spades, and he turned it up but went right on past it, turning up an eight of hearts, a seven of diamonds, a two of clubs and three or four other cards.

Then he stopped abruptly. "Mister," he said dramatically, his hands on the deck, "I'll bet you any amount of money you want to bet that the next card I turn over will be the card you selected."

He never failed to get at least a one-dollar bet. As soon as the bets were made, he put down the deck, reached into the pile of face-up cards, picked up the six of spades and turned it face down. As he'd guaranteed, the next card he turned over was the chosen card.

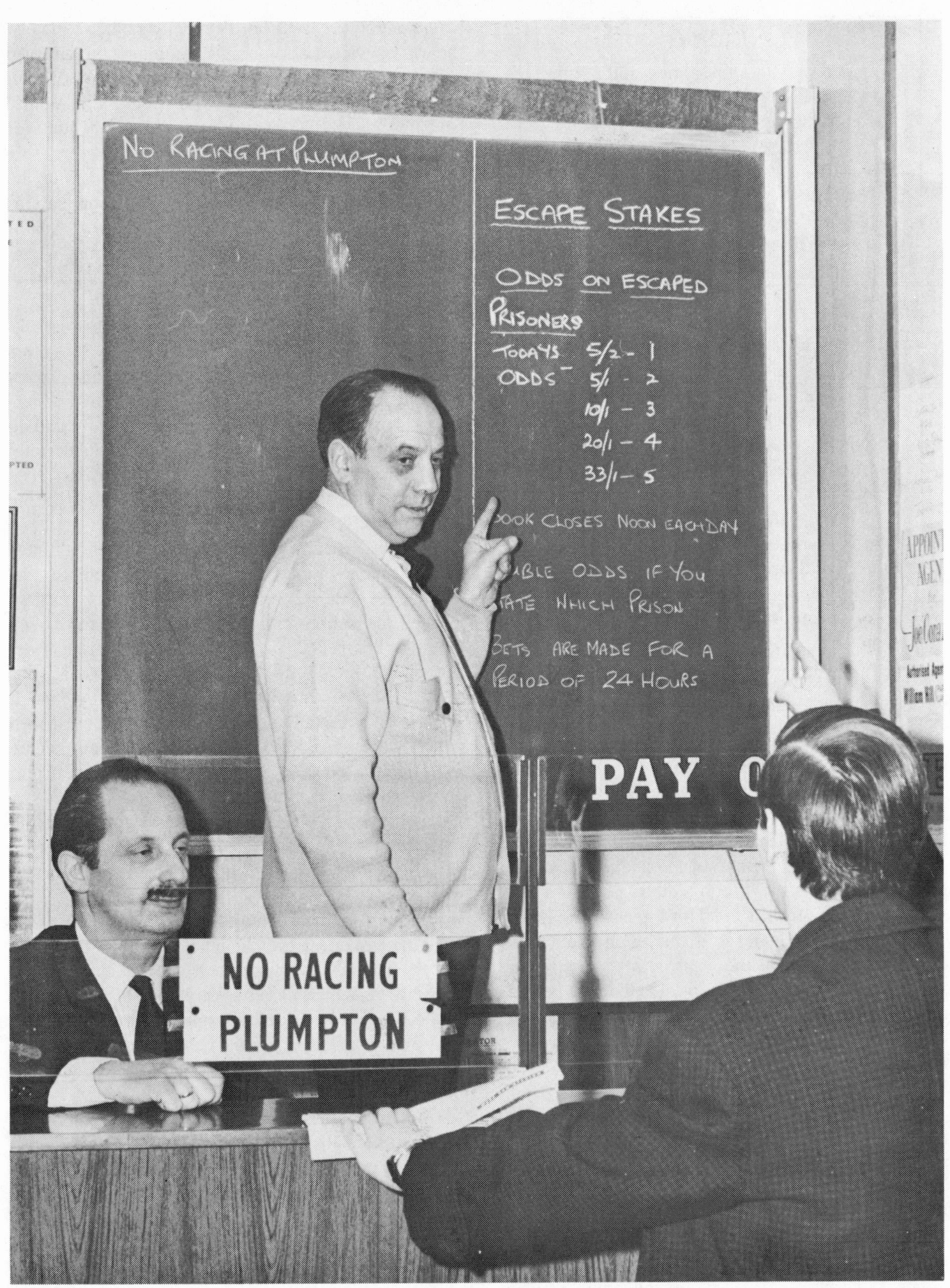

If you are having trouble getting an unusual bet down, try a British bookmaker. Maurice Davis, of Hendon, England, takes bets on jail escapees. The odds are doubled if you can name the prison where the escape takes place.

PUNCHY!

Some of the oldest old-timers still tell the story of "Punchy" Bell, who got rich in the ten years between 1910 and 1920 selling cash-prize punchboards for less than they cost him.

His sales "pitch" was brief. "The board costs you three bucks. It pays out $75 as a major prize and $25 in dollar and five-dollar prizes, and it takes in $250." He sold a minimum of five boards in every little town he passed through, and sold hundreds in larger cities.

The day after he sold the boards, his partner same to town and punched out the $75 winner on every board.

Punchy covered every state in the union, because, he explained, "It ain't a good repeat business."

"Most of the people who bought the boards were crooks," he added. "They didn't let their customers know that the $75 winner was already gone, and let 'em spend $250 with no chance of winning more than $25."

with an estimated 15 million bettors who "played the numbers" almost every day.

The first "Lotto" in Italy was really a form of the Numbers Game. Five senatorial candidates were selected by lot from the total roster of candidates and the public bet on the names of the five most likely to be selected. When the "Lotto" lottery started, it substituted numbers from 1 to 90 for the names.

The Numbers Game as it thrives in the United States today began in the eighteenth century in the London lottery office as a means of getting the pennies of all the people who couldn't afford lottery tickets. The players chose their own numbers in any way they liked, and winning numbers followed the order of numbers in the London lottery.

While the London lottery was operated for the benefit of charity, the "Numbers" take didn't go to similar sources. Minus the winner payouts, it went into the pockets of the lottery operators. Originally, the betting slips were called "insurance policies," which accounts for the "Policy Wheel" designation often used in the United States. As far back as 1880, policy shops were manipulating the numbers from which winners would be determined.

One Al Adams was boss of the policy racket for about 20 years, up until the turn of the century. By 1900, he had roughly 800 policy shops in New York City. He built a fortune from the operation and became a potent power in Tammany politics. Finally, he was convicted of running a gambling house, served 17 months in Sing Sing, and two years later, committed suicide. The crackdown by police and Adams' suicide slowed the operation to almost a halt for awhile.

But not for long. One of the problems with the Numbers Game had been that winning combinations could be "rigged." It had been charged that Al Adams often dictated to the Kentucky lottery, from whose winning number policy winners were determined, what numbers should be drawn.

The new regime in New York Policy got the brilliant idea of determining winners from the last three digits in the daily U.S. Treasury balance. This, players agreed, had little chance of being fixed. Another operator took the last three digits of the total daily trading on the stock exchange, while another took the total attendance at New York Yankee baseball games. The daily "handle" at specified race tracks was used during baseball's off-season.

Probably because residents of the area didn't have enough money for more expensive gambling, the Numbers Game got its first strong hold in Harlem. During the depression years of the 30's, the policy business boomed in distress areas, particularly Harlem and Chicago's Brownsville. The family that controlled the game in Chicago became wealthy enough to retire to a life of luxury. A banker for a big Harlem policy wheel, one Madame St. Clair, had an income of roughly a quarter of a million dollars a year and employed a private bodyguard.

Like any big, successful business, policy became organized. At the top were the operators. Then came the distributors, and at the bottom were the "runners" or agents.

Running in competition with the big, organized wheels were the little "independents," whose customers gathered every day to see the winning numbers drawn. Whenever a banker in one of these games found that any considerable sum of money was concentrated on one number, the ball bearing that number was surreptitiously removed before the drawing, to be replaced later.

Chinese policy, which had always been important to the chance-loving residents of America's Chinatowns, remained aloof from the "syndicates" that controlled other games, resisting "mergers" in spite of all threats.

Probably no gambling game in the world ever had as much superstition involved in it as the Numbers Game. Ever since the policy wheels began, "dream books" have been consistent best-sellers in Harlem book shops. The dream books claim to translate every conceivable type of dream into numbers. An apocryphal story tells of the Harlem resident who was hit by an automobile, managed to get the last three digits of the license, rushed to a numbers agent with a bet and won $5,000.

Many regular policy players actually have "systems" for determining their daily three-digit selections, with the systems based not only on dreams but on house street numbers, social security numbers, telephone numbers and the numbers assigned to race horses at various tracks.

If the players turn to superstition for aid, it's because they have nowhere else to turn. And if superstition lets them down, so what? Hasn't every other possible source of income?

During World War II, when many men went into war-allied industrial plants to escape the draft, the Numbers Game moved right in with them. Policy wheel bankers put agents into plant jobs, usually in janitorial or maintenance work that took them all through the plant. In Detroit, many of them got into the automotive unions and maneuvered to get elected shop stewards.

And when the Numbers Game moved into a plant, serious problems moved in, too, right along with it. Production declined, and workers spent more of their working hours on the Numbers Game than on the work they were being paid to do.

In 1948, the problem was so serious that Ford took drastic steps to solve it. During the year, Ford turned more than 50 Numbers operators over to the police for prosecution. Investigation revealed that one wheel in one Ford plant had grossed over $5 million, and three other Numbers operations had been selling policy slips to about 90,000 Ford workmen.

The size of the Policy wheel business almost automatically attracted organized crime syndicates, and people who believed in private enterprise and began a Numbers operation soon found themselves either in a partnership with gangsters or out of business.

Police in both New York and Chicago have, off the record, attributed the violent deaths of a number of hoodlums to their policy operations. Bosses of some of the wheels have always paid winners in a whimsical manner, setting different odds from day to day. One gangster is said to have lost his life because he didn't believe in paying off the winners at all, if it could possibly be avoided.

Investigators feel certain, from the evidence they've uncovered, that policy payoffs are a small part of the gross revenue. One estimate is that between a quarter and a third of the money collected is paid out again in prizes. The remaining 65 to 75 percent goes to the operators, who pay out part of it to the distributors and agents.

Investigators estimate that in New York City, alone, some 20,000 people are employed as Numbers runners. They bustle through Harlem and other depressed neighborhoods, collecting the nickels and dimes of both children and adults. Picked up by the police, they never have any idea of who employs them. "They aren't conning us about that, either," a policeman says. "One of the secrets of the racket's success is that the 'front' people never know who's next above them. Payoffs are handled by messengers who don't really know what it's all about. We've had plenty of cases where a runner or payoff man *wanted* to give us information to get himself out of a bad spot but simply didn't have it to give.

"At the economic level where the wheels operate, a job working for the policy boys is darned desirable. Putting the runners out of business doesn't even slow the operation; it's like trying to stop the flow of Niagara Falls with a paddle. For every runner who's nabbed, there are a dozen applicants eager to take his place.

"To stop policy, you'd have to stop the operators, the guys who bank the wheels. We think we know who they are, but trying to prove it in court is something else. They're always far enough removed so that we can't get any evidence that would be worth an indictment."

This same policeman has a theory to explain why the Numbers racket has been able to escape much of the criticism that is leveled against other illegal gambling.

"The average guy," he says, "looks at the Numbers game as kind of a joke. He thinks it's penny-ante stuff, with people betting nickels and dimes and quarters. He doesn't think it's really hurting anybody.

"What he doesn't know is that policy players get hooked on the racket. They start betting pennies, and

---

I'll Betcha!

"Here's an interesting little word game," the bettor said. "I'll bet you can't come up with a word that contains all the vowels—a,e,i,o,u—in order."

"Maybe there isn't any such word," his prospective victim countered.

"I'll give you one to start the game," the bettor said. "Then I'll come up with a second one. The first person who misses loses the bet. And to give you an added advantage, I'll even come up with the 'sometimes' vowel, y, in order, at the end of my word. You can start the game with the word, 'abstemious.' Do we have a bet?"

The victim agreed, and wrote down the word, "abstemious." The bettor immediately followed with the word, "facetious." "Oh, yes," he said, "I agreed to add the letter y." He changed the word to "facetiously."

The game was over. "Abstemious" and "facetious" are the only two words that contain the vowels in order. Many other words contain all the vowels, but not in the a,e,i,o,u order.

before long they're betting dollars—every day. They reach the point where they think it'd be tragedy to miss a day's bet, and they do whatever they have to do to get the buck to pay for a numbers slip. If policy could be stopped cold, I'll bet you that the number of muggings and purse-snatchings and petty thefts would go way down, too.

"And anybody who thinks the Numbers racket is penny-ante stuff is nuts. Over 15 million people buy policy slips every day. Some say the take runs to $6 billion a year. I'd guess that it's higher than that.

"Whether you disapprove of gambling or not," he continues, "has nothing to do with the continuation of the racket. For one thing, it's no gamble. On the operator's side, it's a sure thing. On the player's side, the odds are so heavy against him and the payoff is so ridiculously low, considering the gross, that it's much more like throwing money down the drain than it is like gambling.

"What a cop hates most about the policy wheels is the amount of money they pour into the crime syndicate. Every day the wheels operate, they give the syndicate more muscle. With six billion bucks a year, they've got power that's tough to beat."

Fifteen million numbers players couldn't care less about the sociological problems the game creates. The friendly neighborhood policy wheel is their club, one of the few bright spots in their social life. "Picking a number" is recreation in a day that has little else to offer. Win or lose, it creates some excitement. And it proves that it's possible to live on hope, since the policy player does exactly that, day after day.

Investigators who have been told by Harlem residents that over half of the community's economy depends on the Numbers game—probably 60 percent—have at first been incredulous, then shocked, and finally in agreement.

The traditional Numbers Game is big enough, but is greatly augmented by "Single-Action," a hectic game that disrupts the whole working day and produces three winning numbers in a few hours, every afternoon.

"Single-Action" draws devotees of the Free Enterprise system who go into business for themselves, confining their activities to a single block or, at the most, two. The bettor has three chances to win in one afternoon and the banker makes three profits.

The winning numbers are derived from the pari-mutuel payoffs at a designated race track, and the betting operates something like this. At the end of a stipulated early race, the pari-mutuel payoffs on a $2 ticket are added together for the win, place and show horses, six numbers in all and all of them three-digit numbers. In some Single-Action games, the figures for the first three races are added together. Let's say that the figures in the first race come to $33.60. Only the figures to the right and left of the decimal point are taken into consideration. The figure for the first race, then is 3.6. Let's say it's 2.8 for the second race and 4.2 for the third. When the three are added together, only the single number to the left of the decimal point is used. In this illustration, it's O, and that is the payoff number for the first action of the day.

Our independent business man goes into violent action the instant the number is determined. He must pay off any winners and pick up bets for the second go-round of the afternoon, which is based on the pari-mutuel payoffs on the fourth and fifth races. The third pay-off number is determined at the end of the track's daily racing program, on the balance of the races.

It's easy to see why our Free Enterprise numbers merchant has such a limited sphere of operations, having to cover every building in the block four times during the hectic afternoon, keeping track of all bets, figuring payoffs, and watching carefully to see that he isn't overloaded with bets on one particular number in any of the three rounds of betting.

Harlemites say that a Single-Action operator who is on the ball can gross a handle of $1,000 a day, out of which his profit will probably be $200. A less competent operator in a poor block can make a daily profit of $75 without half trying.

Some Harlem bars offer Single-Action operators free "office" space, on which they show a handsome profit. Players congregate to be at the source of the payoff, and drink while awaiting the results. If one happens to win, he usually buys a round of drinks for the house.

Runners for the more conventional three-digit Numbers Game keep 25 percent of the "take" for their commission, and a "control" to whom he passes the money takes off another 10 percent. The syndicate controlling the wheel pays winners out of the remaining 65 percent, in addition to handling overhead, an important item of which is "grease" or protection money.

I'll Betcha!

"One of my ancestors lived in the state of Franklin," the bettor remarked.

"In what country?" a listener asked.

"Why, in the United States, of course," the bettor replied.

"There's no state of Franklin in this country," the listener protested.

"There was when he was alive," the bettor maintained. "Do you want to bet that there never was a state of Franklin, named after Benjamin Franklin?"

After some deliberation, the listener made the bet—and lost. The state of Franklin was organized in 1784 and the name was later changed to Tennessee.

Anyone who plays the Numbers Game has odds of 1,000 to 1 against him, and the usual payoff runs from 600 to 1 to as low as 500 to 1—except in occasional instances where there is no payoff at all.

The runner is the most vulnerable part of the operation. The banker, who makes the most, is rarely touched and almost never convicted. One banker who merely set up and financed a policy operation was sued for divorce by his wife a few years ago, and she testified that her husband's share of the profits, which where mailed to him in Florida, always came to more than $200,000 a year.

Clyde B. Davis, in his book, *Something for Nothing,* published by J. B. Lipincott, is responsible for the statement that more people play the numbers than patronize any other form of gambling.

A Chicago police official is responsible for the "don't quote me" statement, "Ralph Nader says the Federal government doesn't have funds and manpower available to police the automotive industry or the soap business. How do you expect one city's police department to police anything as big as the policy racket? Whenever we make an arrest, I'll bet the Policy bosses are laughing at us. To be honest, I don't see how we'd ever get enough money and men to do an effective job. If the racket's ever killed, I think it'll be by the greed and crookedness of the policy bosses, not by the cops."

He points to what happened to lotteries in the United States in the 1890's. "It wasn't police action that killed them. They got into the hands of crooks, and the crooks put them out of business. Honest, legal lotteries conducted by the state or under government supervision are thriving all over the world. People will gamble on almost anything, until they know they're being cheated. Gamblers love to gamble, but they resent being taken as easy marks."

Don't the policy players know they're being cheated?

"They have a vague idea, sure, but when you get ten bucks back on a nickel policy slip, you're not mad at anybody. The odds are astronomically against the player and the payoffs are few, but the winners who hit get what looks to them like a big return, even if it's nowhere near what it should be.

"Remember that the 15 million policy players in the country are, for the most part, the least-educated members of our society, and the least privileged."

Does he think the Harlem policy players will eventually switch to the New York State Lottery?

"Not for a long time, if ever. It takes too much money, for one thing. A policy player can get into the game with whatever small coins he happens to have in his pocket. And remember, too, that the Numbers Game is a part of the social life of its players, a part of their *daily* social life. The lottery drawings aren't frequent enough to suit these people. On top of that, the lottery is supervised by 'the law,' and many policy players are scared to death of 'the law.' The lottery exists in another world, as far as they're concerned."

Does he think policy should be stopped?

"It should be replaced," he answers. "These people are going to find something to put a little pleasure into their lives. God knows, they need it. They play the numbers for fun, and they get a lot of enjoyment from it. Give them something that's more fun, within their price range, and they'll go for it. Unscrupulous as the policy operators are, I'd rather see these people buying their number slips every day for their kicks than see them turning to Heroin."

Does he think the New Hampshire and New York state lotteries will succeed?

"Yes. Don't forget that there hadn't been any legal lotteries in this country since the 1890's. It was like starting a new kind of business, and nobody antici-

Bar Bet

A bartender on Madison avenue in New York augments his tips with dollar bets on whether the date on a customer's dollar bill is odd or even. He almost never loses.

"I'll bet you the date on your dollar bill is an odd year," he says. "You prob'ly don't even know where to find the date, and it's a cinch I haven't seen it. You'll find it to the left of the signature on the bill. A buck bet, even money."

He guesses odd, and wins.

"It isn't a date," he confides. "It's a series number, and most of the bills in circulation are of the same series. The current series number on dollar bills is 1969, so I bet odd. If the guy happens to have an old bill he's been carrying around for years, I've still got an even-money bet."

Dice Stack

Don Alan, the television magician, can stack four dice into a pile while he's shaking them in a dice cup, so that when he removes the cup, the dice are piled up in a little tower. The only reason he doesn't stack five dice is that most leather dice cups aren't deep enough for that many dice to be piled into them.

There's no trick to it. He often does it with a water tumbler instead of a leather cup, so that viewers can see what happens. "You shake the dice hard," he says. "Then, when you put the cup on the table top, you give an additional hard shake, throwing the dice against the side of the cup. Once you acquire the knack, there's nothing to it—but getting that knack may take many hours of practice. And even when you can do it, it won't win any dice games for you."

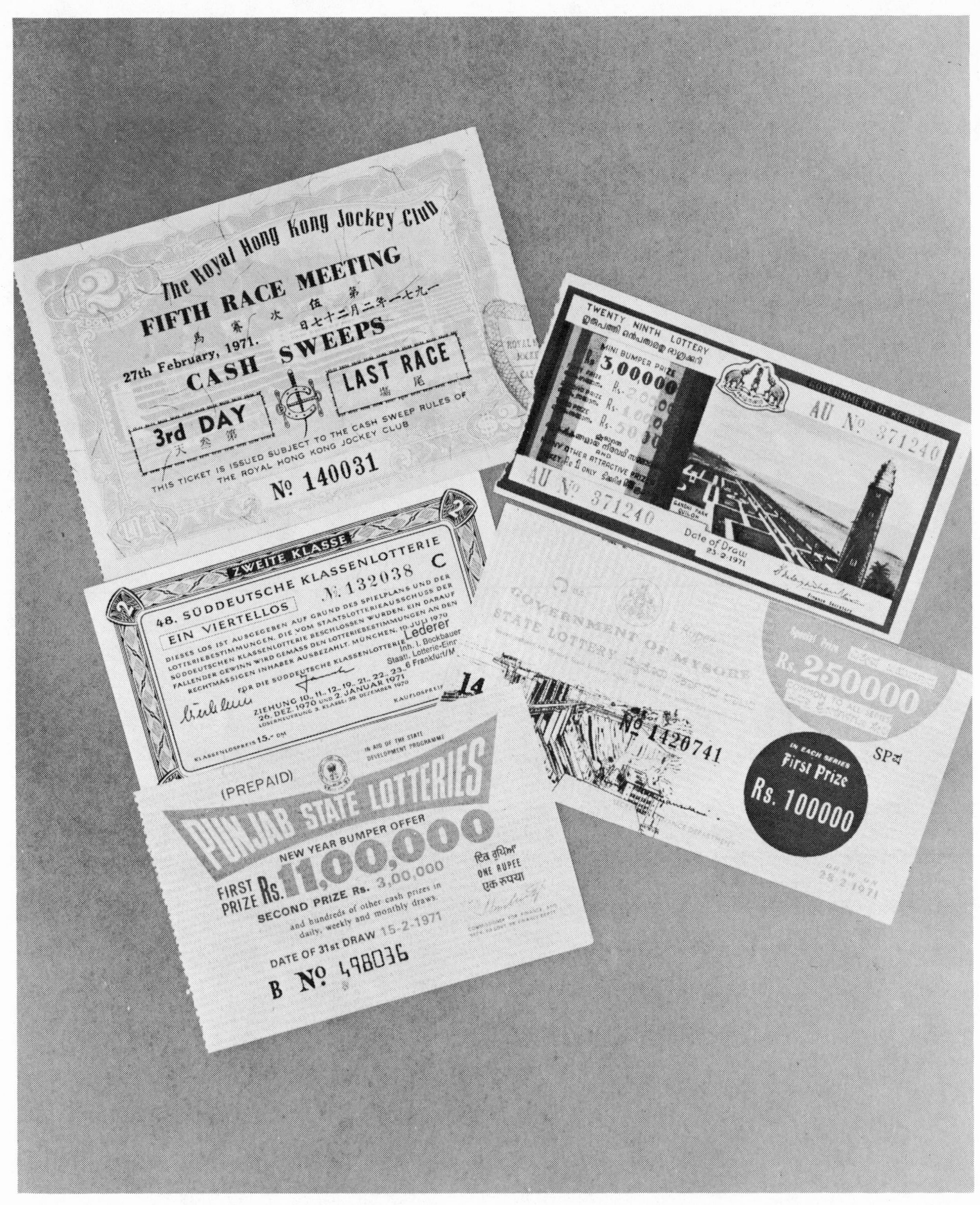

Ask the average American to name a country that has legalized lottery and he'll automatically come up with, "Ireland" (The Irish Sweepstakes). In actuality, lotteries are legal and common in many countries around the globe. They play an important part in the moral, economic and sociological life of a country.

pated the number and complexity of the problems. The Irish Sweepstakes had done a big business in this country for many years, and it had a tradition and romance built around it. And Irish Sweepstakes tickets were sold almost everywhere, despite their illegality.

"The New York and New Hampshire lotteries are state-controlled, and they can't violate state and national laws. Legally, they can't sell tickets outside of their own bailiwicks. If the Irish Sweepstakes had to confine their sales to Ireland, they'd go out of business. About four percent of their gross comes from sales within their own country."

Ask the average American to name a lottery and he'll automatically come up with, "The Irish Sweepstakes." Technically, it is the Irish Hospitals Sweepstakes and has been going since 1930, when the republic of Erie passed a law legalizing it. It is run by a private organization, Hospitals Trust, Ltd., and holds drawings three times a year, on the English Grand National and Cambridgeshire races and the Irish Sweeps Derby races. A number and the name of a horse are drawn simultaneously from two drums by Irish nurses, and every number that draws a horse wins a substantial prize, whether the horse starts or not. In recent years, the prizes have been changed to deal with the tremendous tax rap taken on gambling winnings. There are lots more winners, with smaller amounts. Where first prize used to be a flat $1 million, the top award in recent years has been $140,000, with a number of such amounts distributed.

Between 1893 and 1963, the only legal lottery that could be assigned to the United States was in the dependency of Puerto Rico. Until industry, attracted by the free commonwealth status of the island, moved in from the United States, the country was generally regarded as the "slum" of the Carribean, with much of the population destitute. The Puerto Rican Lottery contributes about $90,000 weekly to the commonwealth.

But the United States has been showing interest ever since 1957, when states began to legalize Bingo. There had been a movement afoot for 15 years to legalize "Bingo and raffles." One after another, 12 states legalized controled forms of Bingo and/or lotteries.

Churches, clubs and charities had been running illegal Bingo games and "raffles" for years, with only token protest from a militant few. While some may not approve, they are at least tolerant. In 1953, a bitter fight over legalization of bingo and raffles in New Jersey found the Advocate, official newspaper of the Roman Catholic archdiocese of Newark, stating, "It is not gambling but the abuse of gambling that involves an immoral act." A three to one vote made Bingo and raffles legal.

In 1957, the Bingo amendment in New York won by nearly 650,000 votes, and New York became the ninth state to go for Bingo.

Legal or not, Bingo is considered by many to be a great American pastime. The old Italian game of Lotto was played by American families in the 1800's and continued into the twentieth century. It has never changed much, and its simplicity is one of its merits. The players hold printed cards, with (in this country) numbers from 1 to 75. There are commonly five rows of five numbers each, 25 numbers in all on a card. All 75 numbers are contained in some kind of mixing device, and an operator draws them out, one at a time. A player covers each of his numbers that is called. The first player to cover a row of five numbers is the winner. In the commonest form of the game in this country, a row may run either across, up and down or diagonally. The player buys a card, each of which contains a different assortment of numbers.

Church and club bingo parties have long been a part of American life. The estimated "handle" of bingo games in the United States is estimated right around $2 billion.

When Great Britain legalized its lottery in 1960, it legalized Bingo, too, and the British went for it in a big way. Many "flicks" or movie houses that had fallen on hard times were quickly converted to Bingo halls, and business boomed. The British estimate is that there are about 13 million regular Bingo players, the preponderance of them female. The British expenditure on Bingo is said to run in the neighborhood of $70 million—a highly respectable neighborhood.

While the outcome of every Bingo game is pure chance, unless cheating is involved, the more avid players have their systems, and regard cards with certain combinations of numbers as "luckier" than others.

In some communities, churches or clubs have regular weekly Bingo sessions which serve not only as fund-raisers but are social events. In states where Bingo has not been made legal, clergymen and club presidents do not seem to be at all disturbed at the accustation of law-breaking. A mid-Westerner says, "I learned to gamble at church socials, and so did most of my friends. When we figured out how high the church 'vigorish' was, we quit playing Bingo and started shooting craps."

Playing Bingo for money is an easy step for housewives who have been competing for "table prizes" at card parties conducted by clubs and charities. The four women at a table pay $2 apiece for their party tickets and play bridge for a table prize that has probably been donated. Some women who loudly denounce gambling in all forms attend such parties regularly and would be shocked were anyone to accuse them of not practicing what they preach.

"It's for a good cause" has been the reasoning to

FAN TAN TOY

Fan Tan Toy ran a traveling Chinese Numbers game and gambling house in a tent during the period when the railroads employed thousands of Chinese laborers—at coolie wages—to lay the tracks joining the eastern and western sections of the United States.

Wherever he traveled, the lonely, transplanted coolies spent their long evening in his tent.

Fan Tan Toy suffered a fatal heart attack one evening, and there was enough money to send the body back to Toy's beloved China for burial.

The grandson of one of the coolies gambling in the tent at the time tells the story of how much money there was.

"My grandfather told me that there were over 100 men gambling at the time, including himself. The men went through Toy's personal possessions before notifying authorities, of whom they were frightened. They discovered close to $300,000 in gold and silver. Most of it, they reasoned, rightfully belonged to them and others like them. Each man took roughly $2,500 and pledged that he would always give financial aid to any Chinese who had worked on the railroad.

"With a start that was wealth beyond my grandfather's wildest dreams, he became a tremendously successful business man. And over the years, he staked 14 railroad coolies to a total of about $35,000, considering it an obligation."

justify many illegal gambling activities that are operated for sweet charity.

A perrenial fund-raising device is the "Las Vegas Night" party, usually operated by professionals who come in with gambling equipment, scenery and Western costumes. Those in attendance buy imitation money, usually fake hundred-dollar bills, which they bet on the various games. If they have any money left at the end of the evening, they can cash it in for the original purchase price. The difference between the fake money and the chips which are sold in casinos is hard to fathom, but guests at the parties would be shocked at such a suggestion.

Law enforcement men who are elected by public vote are always reluctant to crack down on any established and respectable community group, but they have stopped the "Las Vegas Nights" in some areas because of the outrageously high percentage of the "take" that goes to the non-charitable promoters.

The "raffle" is always with us. Probably the mildest form of raffle is "door prizes," offered by sponsors of meetings to promote attendance. Even little children are exposed to the "door prize" lure.

Sponsors may argue that the door prize is lagniappe, an extra thrown in to get a good turn-out, but if an admission is charged, the extra attendance comes from the universal urge to get something for nothing.

Frank, open, undisguised raffles to raise funds are common. Civic organizations, war veteran groups and churches have found raffling off a new car a sure-fire way to bring in money.

These raffles vary from small to gigantic. A college fraternity or sorority may raffle off a pocket radio, selling chances to its members, and an aggressive American Legion group may raffle off a Cadillac, a Buick and a Chevrolet to raise funds for a new clubhouse.

Raffles are a key part in nearly every "Benefit" party. Pretty girls circulate through the crowd, selling chances on anything from a painting done by one of the members to a mink coat or color TV set.

Interference with raffles from the law is almost unheard of, except where chances are sold by an individual for personal gain.

There's an old story about the untimely death of Wilbur Wallaby's fine riding horse.

"That horse cost you a lot of money," a friend observed. "Did you have it insured?"

"Nope," Wallaby replied cheerfully.

"Then it's quite a loss," the friend said.

"Oh, no," Wilbur told him airily. "I raffled it off. Sold 500 chances at a dollar apiece."

"But you can't raffle a dead horse," the friend protested.

"I only got one complaint," Wilbur said. "The guy who won was really mad, but I shut him up by giving him his dollar back."

While few raffles are as far out of line as Wilbur's, complaints about skullduggery are not unknown. Officals in some sponsoring organizations have been known to have the same phenomenal luck as the King of France had in his French National lottery.

Straight or rigged, raffles prosper everywhere.

The average purchaser of a ticket realizes that he is venturing his money on the longest long-shot known to man. Buying a $3 ticket in a lottery where the first prize is $500,000 and a million tickets are sold, he doesn't need to be much of a mathmetician to know that the chance of winning any prize, let alone the top one, is remote—a million to one against him.

It shouldn't demand much additional figuring to

convince him that the "vigorish" or "house take" is enormous, probably the heaviest to be found in any gambling operation except the Numbers Game.

Nobody forces him to buy a ticket. More often than not, he approaches a ticket seller and asks for one.

Hope springs eternal in the human breast. Sure, the chances are a million to one against him, but *somebody* is going to win. And nobody deserves good luck any more than he does.

If Fate is waiting to bless him, he'd be making the mistake of his life not to give her the opportunity. Other people get lucky, he reasons, and why shouldn't it happen to him?

Other factors may prompt his decision. The lure of something for nothing is the greatest ever offered. While the lottery or raffle prizes aren't exactly for nothing, if you want to get technical, they cost the winner *almost* nothing. If he loses, the money will never be missed. It isn't enough to be important. But if he wins! Man, just think of that great big, beautiful prize for free—or almost free.

Then, in the case of the lottery, this may be the Big Killing. He's never going to get rich from his job, he's concluded. At least, if he does, it will take a lifetime. Nope, working isn't the way to strike it rich. What he needs is one gigantic haul, one colossal coup. Winning the lottery could be it. How will he know if he doesn't try?

He buys a ticket, justifying the expenditure as being for a "good cause." He tells his friends, if they ask him, that he's well aware of the odds against him. He hasn't the slightest expectation of winning, he declares —and it's a lie. He *does* expect to win, and he has every bit as much chance as any other person who has bought a single ticket. Let people laugh at him, if they like. If this should turn out to be his lucky day, they'll laugh from the other side of the face.

"You don't sell lottery tickets," a man who has been connected with one declares. "You make them easily available to the greatest possible number of people. Oh, I suppose a ticket-seller persuades somebody here and there to take a chance, but the bulk of the tickets are bought, not sold, if you get the distinction. Have a big enough top prize, make it clear that your lottery is being run straight, make buying easy, and you'll have a winner."

If the get-rich-quick promise is unfulfilled for almost everyone who buys lottery tickets, it works for lottery sponsors.

New taxes or increases in old ones are decidedly unpopular with the public, particularly in depressed countries or areas. And nobody objects to a lottery except a few who do so on moral grounds.

Helping a government by purchasing lottery tickets is voluntary. Where taxes are forced down the public craw, like them or not, investment in a lottery ticket is entirely optional.

Perhaps nowhere was this point better illustrated than in the United States before and during the Revolutionary War. The war was *about* taxes levied by the Crown. Citizens of the New World hated them.

Historians pretty much agree that to get this New World functioning with and from heavy taxes would have been virtually impossible. Even taxes for bare necessities would have been paid grudgingly. As for taxes to get schools and colleges, forget them. Taxes for public buildings? Get along without them, or make do with what's already there.

The attitude toward lottery tickets was entirely different. The colonists weren't forced to buy them, and so they bought. They saw examples of the good works accomplished by lotteries all around them. Lotteries, they concluded, were all right. And it took many years of thievery and fraud to convince them otherwise.

New Jersey, the most recent entry in the legal state lottery derby in the United States, has profited from the earlier experiences of New Hampshire and New York. Where those two were disappointing at the outset to their sponsors, the New Jersey lottery got off to a flying start.

New Jersey recognized the drawbacks to its predecessors' lotteries. Buying a ticket hadn't been easy, quick or convenient, and the drawings were too infrequent. New Jersey corrected those two errors.

Furthermore, the advertising and promotion for the New York and New Hampshire lotteries had stressed the "worthy cause" angle. It had urged residents of the states to purchase tickets because the money would enable the states to offer more and better educational facilities, among other things. It was conservative advertising, cautiously executed.

New Jersey was realistic. Its advertising had a basic

Bar Bet

Almost everyone knows the old catch bet of pushing a half-dollar through a hole the size of a nickel. The hole in the card or piece of paper is placed over a pen or pencil, and the half-dollar is pushed along the bar with the pencil. The bettor, technically, is pushing the coin through the hole.

When everybody was wise to the gag, a bartender on Rush street in Chicago offered a variation. "I bet I can actually insert the half-dollar into the hole, moving it through the opening from one side of the paper to the other," he challenged.

He folded the nickel-size opening in half, folding the paper or card right across it. Then he put the coin beneath the opening, held one edge of the card or paper firmly with his left hand, and from the top, tugged the half-dollar through. The paper or card bends enough so that the trick can be done without tearing the opening.

"Get Rich Quick" appeal that prospective lottery ticket purchasers understood and liked. It was the appeal that, advertised or not, had made lotteries successful from the time of the first Italian *Lotteria*.

New York and New Hampshire officials admitted that they were watching the New Jersey operation closely and with great interest. Changes were anticipated.

For one thing, everyone seemed to agree that drawings must be frequent. There must be dates for specific drawings, and the greater their frequency, the better, so long as enough money could be taken in during the allotted time to make the lottery pay.

The greatest customer potential for the new state lotteries would come, they agreed, from the Numbers Game players, racing fans, and regular purchasers of sports pool and parlay cards. In all of these wagers, results and payoff are almost immediate. The economic status of this group, particularly of the Numbers player, makes immediacy not only highly desirable but the only thing that will prompt another gamble.

New Jersey's weekly drawing answers the "lack of frequency" objection. It also makes an important bid for the mass market in selling tickets for 50¢, where New York gets $1 and New Hampshire gets $3.

Also, the New Jersey ticket requires no paper-work on the part of the ticket buyer. Most gamblers vastly prefer that to the New York and New Hampshire tickets that call for the bettor to fill in his name and address.

Officials of at least 16 states are openly studying the three existing state lotteries with an eye to coming up with a satisfactory lottery arrangement in their own states.

Even while falling drastically short of expectations, the New York and New Hampshire lotteries have brought important revenue to their states. New Hampshire's drawings gross roughly four million dollars a year. New York sold $111 million in 1970.

All three state lotteries are hampered by federal and U.S. Postal regulations aimed at discouraging lotteries. Advertising in any medium that crosses state lines or goes through the mails is illegal, as is the interstate sale of tickets.

Whether they fulfill expectations or not, the state lotteries are financially helpful. As the New Hampshire Sweepstakes director puts it, "Our lottery may not solve the tax problem but it's just that much less the taxpayers will have to come up with."

One form of lottery that is almost sure-fire is the "Sweepstakes Drawing" conducted by reputable manufacturers to promote the sale of their goods.

These manufacturers and their advertising agencies are fully aware of the "something for nothing" appeal and they want to capitalize on it. The only catch is, they don't want to give their retail customers anything for nothing.

Making the purchase of an item necessary for a customer to participate in a lottery would violate the "consideration" part of lottery regulations. It would be giving the lottery operator money in return for goods and a chance at the prizes. The law says that is illegal.

And so, each lottery entry must be accompanied by a label from the product or "a reasonable facsimile thereof."

What constitutes a "reasonable facsimile"? Who *decides* what makes a facsimile reasonable? Does the drawing of the facsimile take time, talent and effort that make it a "consideration"?

It would be interesting to know how many "sweepstakes" lottery entries are accompanied by facsimiles rather than by actual labels from the products. For some reason, professional commercial contest promoters who often handle these promotions seem reticent about divulging this information.

We have briefly mentioned elsewhere in GAMBLER'S DIGEST the "lucky number" promotion which has become increasingly popular in recent years. The customer receives a multi-digit number, either in an advertisement or a mailing piece, and must visit a specified store or write to a certain address to determine whether or not his number is one of the winners. There are usually many, many prizes listed, some of great value and some, many more, "token" prizes.

Violent objections to such promotions have been expressed, on the ground that only a fraction of the advertised prizes are ever awarded. Since the holder of a lucky number must make himself known and must check contest rules before he wins anything and since only a fraction of those people who receive numbers ever take the trouble to investigate, the charge is probably true to some extent.

Another variation of this type of contest is used by publications as a circulation promotion. Prospective subscribers are sent a mailing piece describing the lavish prizes, together with an order blank. The

---

I'll Betcha!

"I'll give you two chances to name the most densely populated country in the world and bet you that you can't do it," the bettor offers.

The average person is sure that the most densely populated country is either China or India, but he isn't sure which. Given an opportunity to name both of them, he reasons that he can't lose, so he takes the bet.

Unless he's a rare exception, he loses. The most densely populated country in the world is the little principality of Monaco, the home of Monte Carlo. The whole country comprises 370 acres. The census of 1939 gave it a population of 24,000 and it's grown since then. There's no contest.

This shapely young lady is putting up the betting odds on the "Miss World" contest at a London betting parlour. "Miss Sweden" is the favorite at 7-to-1.

recipient of such a mailing piece must send in his lucky number, and two forms are provided—one in which he subscribes to the publication, and one in which he does not.

Again, it is argued by some that only a part of the prizes are ever awarded.

Mailings for such promotions probably run into the millions. Returns from the mailings are problematical, but it seems reasonable to assume that not all of the winning numbers will be returned.

That the contests are proiftable for their promoters seems self-evident, since they are continued, year after year.

The old "game of skill" contest in which participants were required to write an essay or "twenty-five words or less" about the product seem to have declined in favor of "drawings" or lotteries. One reason undoubtedly is that the "skill" contests require not only effort but capability.

Many newspaper circulation contests have as their only requirement that the would-be winner check the paper. Promoters of such contests argue that there is no "consideration," since people may come to the newspaper office and check a copy of the paper without buying it.

Postal officials are quick to admit that the line between illegal lotteries and legal "contests" is often so fine as to be almost invisible. Asked for an advance opinion on such promotions, the answer is nearly always opposed to them—but the answer is an opinion, not an order.

Some major companies which are active in "sweepstakes" of one kind or another hold no brief for them but can't see their way out. Competition, the head of one company admitted, forced his organization into the lottery arena and keeps it there.

A random poll of consumers indicates that most people do not regard the promotions as lotteries. "You don't pay for a chance," the usual explanation is. "Sure, you have to buy the product, but you pay the regular price for it."

Of 50 people questioned who had entered their names in such drawings, not one had ever submitted a "reasonable facsimile" in lieu of a product label. There seemed to be a universal understanding that this avenue of entry was strictly for legal purposes, to avoid a charge of lottery operation, and was not to be taken seriously by participants.

Actually, it is GAMBLER'S DIGEST's belief that anything even approximating a reasonable facsimile in such drawings would receive the same consideration as entries accompanied by box-tops or labels. Promoters aren't looking for legal difficulties.

An advertising agency contest expert has this to say about it. "The old slogan contest or short essay contest was cleaner. It was a contest of skill, with prizes awarded on the basis of merit, and nobody could call it a lottery. The trouble with it was that it didn't get the volume of entries our clients wanted. Even the people who have the talent to submit a good entry in a 'skill' contest won't take the time to do it. A lottery is different. Everybody figures his chances in a 'drawing' are just as good as anybody else's. If the prizes are attractive enough, people will buy products they neither want nor need in order to compete.

"In recent years, the tax situation has changed the complexion of drawings. Winners of $150,000 in cash discovered that what they had won was considerably less than advertised, after Uncle Sam took his cut. Today, you'll get far more action with a major prize of $12,500 a year income for life, or a new car every year for ten years, or something that doesn't take one overwhelming tax bite.

"As long as sweepstakes contests are permitted, they'll continue to thrive. Particularly when the economy is slow, such drawings are of real value to a manufacturer. They give sales a hefty shot in the arm. And I don't think they qualify as lotteries, at least in the way of the Irish Sweepstakes and similar operations. The customer doesn't buy a ticket to take a chance. He pays the standard price for merchandise and gets something extra, at no cost—a chance to win a big prize."

The subterfuge of paying for merchandise and getting a free chance has been used for years, long before the popularity of the prize drawing reached its peak. A slot machine was once marketed in which the customer inserted a coin in the slot for a ball of chewing gum or pack of mints, and got a free pull of the lever. Lottery tickets in various charity promotions have for years been, officially, receipts for a $1 donation to the charity. Legal experts are in fairly unanimous agreement that neither of these approaches would stand up in court, if put to a test of legality.

Legal or not, the "sweepstakes" do well, and will probably continue to stimulate business for their sponsors.

It is interesting to note that lotteries of various kinds, which for the most part have the longest odds against the gambler and have the highest house percentage against him, are popular all over the world.

Pools are also popular, but where the pool is privately conducted by a group of bettors in an office, the odds are usually as fair as they could possibly be. Some one person in the office is delegated to run the office pool on a major race or football game or other sporting event, and does so without recompense. Indeed, the person who runs the pool often gets stuck when somebody who "charges" his pool ticket forgets to pay, or when not all the tickets are sold. The office pool is popular, and deservedly so, since it gives the bettor a good run for his money and is fun for everyone participating.

Commercial pools, run by outsiders, are something

else. Nobody who buys a ticket in them has any way of knowing the amount of money put into the pool, and the returns to winners are often far short of what they should be, even allowing a good profit for the pool management.

In countries where such pools are run by the government or under government supervision, the returns are usually reasonable. Even under these conditions, however, they are not always a good gamble. London newspapers have commented from time to time that participants in the football pool in Great Britain often forfeit their winnings by not making out their pool entries properly. Apparently, the rules are followed to the letter, and it is possible for a winner to pick teams correctly without getting the expected return.

In the United States, sports parlay cards, which are illegal nearly everywhere, are extremely popular and do a landoffice business. Samples of both football and basketball parlay cards are illustrated.

Note the odds on them. They are nowhere near what they should be. One of the worst gambles the sportsfan can possibly get is the parlay card. He would be far better off to bet on individual games with a bookmaker.

Undoubtedly, one of the reasons for the sports parlay card's popularity is its simplicity. It is easy to buy and easy to fill in. The bettor doesn't even have to fill in the names of the teams he selects.

Lt. John J. Nolan of the Gambling section of the Chicago Police Department says, "The parlay cards are made up for almost all sports activities: baseball, football, basketball, hockey, etc. These cards are generally sold in taverns, factories, large office buildings, and in some cases, we have made arrests around high schools. Any place that offers a large sales potential in numbers of available people is used as a distribution point. In looking at the cards, one can see that they are, in most instances, directed toward weekend games.

"In most cases, the seller receives 25¢ of the money taken in on a card as his or her cut for making the sale. The amount bet on a card usually starts at $1 and goes up to $5. Amounts greater than $5 are usually bet with a sports bookie rather than on a parlay card."

He adds that "during the year 1970, there were extensive enforcement efforts (in Chicago) made by the Gambling Section of the Vice Control division in the area of parlay card gambling. As a result, there is very little activity in the sale and use of these cards at the present time."

For the police to keep sports parlay cards permanently out of circulation is a Herculean task. Salesmen are so numerous and the distribution is so widespread that hundreds of men would have to be assigned on a permanent basis to policing the sale of cards to achieve lasting and thorough results.

HIT OR FLOP?

Of all the wild gambles, financing a theatrical production is one of the most fascinating—at least, to anyone who has an interest in the theater.

Production costs rise, year after year, and more and more money is required to put a show on the boards. Flops are usually a total loss, but hit shows pay fantastic returns, sometimes returning many times the original investment.

An experienced theatrical producer with a good record never knows until after a show opens whether he has a smashing success, a so-so property or a dismal failure. One successful team with a string of smash hits on Broadway and on tour once ran an ad in *Variety* listing five flop shows they had produced, with the heading, "We Did It Before and We Can Do It Again."

With the cost of musical shows seldom running under half a million dollars, "angels" often have the opportunity to make investments as small as $100. Number of sets, size of cast and mechanical factors sometimes influence producers more than the "book," with investments being so high.

There's a Broadway legend about a producer who did a prosperous business producing dismal failures. His trick was selling 600 or 700 percent of the actual investment. He did fine until, unpredictably, he came up with a smash hit. Faced with a 700 percent payoff, he was ruined.

Conscientious police officials recognize the parlay card as one of the world's worst bets, with completely unfair odds to the bettor. On top of that, they feel that the sale of the money-grabbers is a crime syndicate operation. They also find particularly distasteful the fact that the cards appeal to sports-minded youngsters who are encouraged to buy them.

In many communities, police efforts to curb the sale are, unlike Chicago's, almost nil. Understaffed police forces have more serious law violations with which to cope and have a feeling that, at best, their efforts would accomplish little. Only when the sale of the cards is flagrantly open do they move in.

Without question, parlay cards are a business of great magnitude. With their enormous sale and the unreasonable payoffs to winners, the percentage of profit must be astronomical.

In many of the countries where association foot-

E–Z

93254

3	6
4	11
5	16
6	30
7	45
8	65
10	150
9/10	17

TIES LOSE

NOT TO BE

NAME ______
NO. TEAMS ______
AMT. ______

93254

E–

NOV.21, 22,1970

T V GAMES

1	OHIO ST.	2	MICHIGAN	+4
3	SO.CALIF.	4	U.C.L.A.	+6
5	FLORIDA ST.	6	KANSAS ST.	+3
7	WISCONSIN	8	MINNESOTA	+3
9	AIR FORCE	10	COLORADO	+4
11	RICE	12	T.C.U.	+4
13	OREGON	14	OREGON ST.	+4
15	OKLA.ST.	16	IOWA ST.	+4
17	NO.CAROLINA	18	DUKE	+6
19	PRINCETON	20	CORNELL	+6
21	N,WESTERN	22	MICHIGAN ST.	+6
23	YALE	24	HARVARD	+7
25	MISSOURI	26	KANSAS	+7
27	IOWA	28	ILLINOIS	+10
29	STANFORD	30	CALIFORNIA	+10
31	SO.CAROLINA	32	CLEMSON	+14
33	NO.DAME	34	L.S.U.	+14
35	PURDUE	36	INDIANA	+15
37	ARKANSAS	38	TEX.TECH	+17
39	NEBRASKA	40	OKLAHOMA	+20

SUNDAY

1	42	49ERS	-1
	44	N.ORLEANS	-1
	46	PITTSBURGH	+3
	48	ATLANTA	+6
	50	BUFFALO	+6
	52	SAN DIEGO	+7
	54	MIAMI	+7
	56	HOUSTON	+10
	58	BOSTON	+10
	60	GREEN BAY	+10

, 22, 1970

5	6	7	8	9	10
15	16	17	18	19	20
25	26	27	28	29	30
35	36	37	38	39	40
45	46	47	48	49	50
55	56	57	58	59	60
65	66	67	68	69	70

COLLLEGE BASKETBALL—SATURDAY, FEB. 27, 1971

1	Army	–2	2	Navy	–2
3	Mississippi	–2	4	LSU	–2
5	Missouri	–2	6	Nebraska	–2
7	No. Carolina	–4	8	Virginia	+3
9	Davidson	–4	10	Cincinnati	+3
11	Illinois	–4	12	Minnesota	+3
13	Kansas State	–4	14	Oklahoma St.	+3
15	Notre Dame	–6	16	St. John's	+5
17	Michigan	–6	18	Ohio State	+5
19	La Salle	–6	20	St. Joseph's	+5
21	Maryland	–6	22	West Virginia	+5
23	So. Carolina	–6	24	No. Carolina St.	+5
25	Texas Tech	–8	26	S.M.U.	+7
27	Iowa	–8	28	Wisconsin	+7
29	Jacksonville	–8	30	Houston	+7
31	Memphis State	–8	32	Wichita	+7
33	Wm. & Mary	–8	34	Richmond	+7
35	Drake	–10	36	St. Louis	+9
37	Ohio U.	–10	38	Toledo	+9
39	Purdue	–10	40	Michigan St.	+9
41	Dayton	–12	42	Xavier, O.	+11

1	2	3	4	5	6	7	8	9	10
11	12	13	14	15	16	17	18	19	20
21	22	23	24	25	26	27	28	29	30
31	32	33	34	35	36	37	38	39	40
41	42	43	44	45	46	47	48	49	50
51	52	53	54	55	56	57	58	59	60

SATURDAY, FEBRUARY 27, 1971

Parlay Cards courtesy
Chicago Police Department

ball or soccer is a big sport and where sale of the cards is legal, there is substantial revenue to the government as well as a more reasonable payoff to winners. In most of these countries, the operation is conducted as a "postal pool." Every week, bettors who have previously participated receive their parlay cards through the mail, mark their selections and return them, along with the amount of money they wish to wager. That this system tends to create habitual parlay card players is undeniable. So, however, is the fact that the vast sum of money wagered doesn't find its way into crime syndicate coffers.

Some European and South American sports fans have become expert sports handicappers as a result of their steady wagers and win small amounts of money rather consistently.

For a bettor in the United States to wind up ahead of the cards, he would have to be very good, indeed, in view of the short odds on payoffs when he is right. Winning is made even more difficult by the handicap which the pool operators attach to the teams.

Conservative estimates are that, depending on the number of winners a participant tries to pick, the pool operators wind up with from 35 to 80 percent of the money wagered.

The baseball pool tickets are an even worse bet than the football cards. With payoffs for either high or low total runs and with combinations of four or five teams, the bettor has from 36,000 to over 200,000 possible combinations. Estimates of operator "take" on the baseball tickets runs from 50 to 80 percent of the amount involved.

Some public officials are of the opinion that either football or baseball pool tickets or both are purchased by at least 50 million people during the two sports' seasons. Nearly that many are believed to play Bingo, but even with the high percentage of profit permitted in that game, players get a far better break than those who play the sports pools.

With incorrect odds, unreasonable handicaps, and ties canceling a parlay card's winning potential, the few bettors who win don't make much of a dent in the profits.

Punchboards and jar games are almost equally unfair. A story which GAMBLER'S DIGEST has been unable to either affirm or discredit is that the "jar games" in some lower-class pool halls, cigar stores and horse parlors are operated strictly for the casual or "drop-in" trade and never have any payoffs at all.

Only the most gullible and inexperienced gambler would be expected to participate in any of the above-mentioned come-ons. The fact is that their customers are not only numerous but steady.

WANNA BUY AN OIL WELL?

Oil wells, which at one time were considered the ultimate in wildcat gambles, are looked upon with favor today by some high-income speculators. With what modern oil geologists know, "dry" wells are no longer as prevalent as they once were, and the well that comes in strong pays a handsome profit.

Most independent wells are drilled by investment syndicates, with each member owning a piece of the action. In the event that a well fails to produce oil, the money put into it is a 100 percent tax write-off, unlike most gambling losses that cannot be written off in excess of gambling profits.

Oil well speculators find the Depletion Allowance particularly attractive. When an oil well is successful, a 22 percent depletion is allowed, which means that taxes on the income are levied against 78 percent of the amount instead of on the gross.

Water-flooding depleted wells in an attempt to reactivate them is another speculation which some gamblers find intriguing.

Even with all the adverse publicity they have received over the years, the carnival games still get a steady play. While there are unquestionably fewer rigged games or "flat joints" than in the salad days of traveling carnivals, the odds against the player make such "rigging" unnecessary. The alleged "games of skill" which have replaced many carnival wheels are even more impossible than the old games of chance.

Carnival auspices today, in most cases, forbid the double-up money games with which flat-joint operators fleeced victims of important money, and the operators must depend on a steady play instead of looking for "one big one" to take to the cleaners.

Big bets or small, the games are operated for the benefit of the men who run them and a customer's chance of beating them is almost infinitesimal.

With so many reasonable wagering propositions available, there can be only one answer as to why people continue to patronize the long-odds, little chance, unfair payoff gambles. Hope must, indeed, spring eternal in the gambler's breast. ♠

BOOK FOUR

THEY'RE OFF!

A complete look at horse-racing from the pari-mutuels and where the money goes through public selectors and their systems and on to money management at the track. The Winning System—the new, track-proven, Hussey method of handicapping thoroughbred and Standardbred horses.

They're off!

Why horse-racing is so often called "the sport of kings" is a mystery and will probably remain so. There haven't been many kings around in recent years, and those on the international scene seem to have interests and problems far afield from the bangtails. The patronage of royalty, it is generally admitted, wouldn't keep one modern racing plant in business. Since there are thriving race tracks in profusion in almost every country in the world, it becomes obvious that someone other than heads of state must like the sport.

The cold, hard fact is that horse-racing is the sport of gamblers. Around the world, every day, even on Sunday in many areas more money is bet on horses by more people than is wagered in any other way.

The original justification for racing, "improving the breed," has long since gone by the boards. From a strictly utilitarian standpoint, the horse is practically out of business, superceded by the automobile, the airplane, the tractor, motor-driven farm implements and even the bicycle and motorcycle.

Despite that undeniable fact, racing's prosperity increases every year, with more tracks, greater attendance and larger pari-mutuel handles.

During the 1970 season the total pari-mutuel handle for North American tracks was $4,332,272,195.00. That's right, more than $4 billion wagered on thoroughbreds by a record breaking attendance of 51,446,235. The 1970 racing calendar had 6,242 racing days with a total of 56,676 races. The largest average daily track pari-mutuel handle was $3,557,504 at Aqueduct.

Even earthquakes don't seem to shake horseplayers. On Tuesday, February 9, 1971, Los Angeles was hit by a disastrous 'quake that caused wholesale evacuation of large industrial and residential areas. Santa Anita, not being in the evacuated area, opened its doors for business as usual and better than 19,000 improvers of the breed came for the real action!

Racing is a thrilling sport to watch, as everyone will agree. But that isn't the reason for its popularity and prosperity. Almost every other sporting event that sells tickets to the public offers far more action than the 25 or 30 minutes of actual contest to be witnessed at a race track across a span of three or four hours.

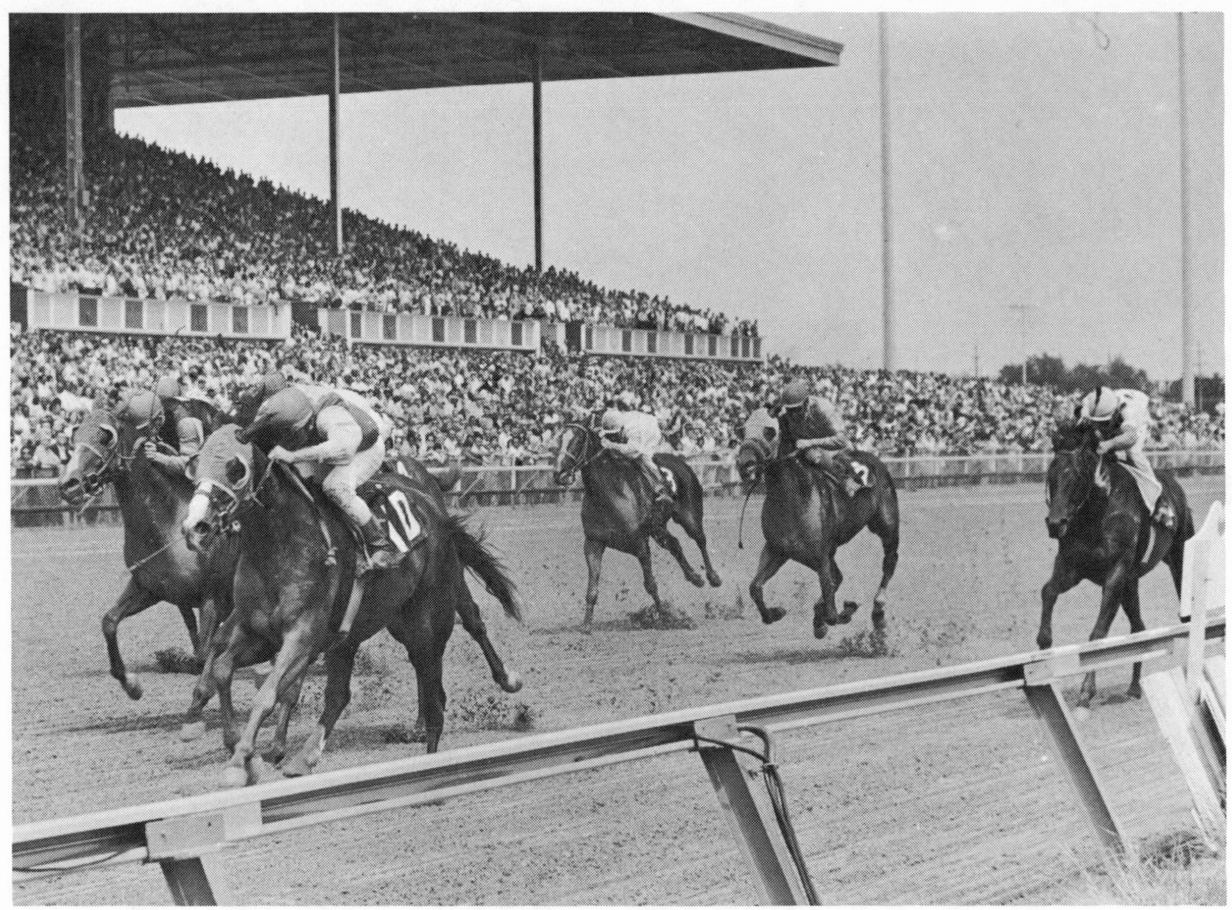

Photo courtesy Chicago Thoroughbred Enterprises, Inc.

The indisputable truth is that racing thrives because it is the most perfect, most unpredictable gamble ever devised by man.

Any racing enthusiast who cares to dispute that has only to ask himself what would happen to horse racing if wagering were eliminated from the sport. In the extremely rare instances where racing has tried to exist without pari-mutuels or bookies, it has gone out of business in short order.

It isn't the excitement of watching a thrilling race that makes the sport so successful, although the excitement is certainly there. But up until the advent of television and its airing of major racing events, hundreds of thousands of avid racing fans had never seen a race!

With the start of legal off-track betting (*O.T.B.*) in New York City even more racing fans will never have to go to the track to enjoy the thrill of the sport. The City fathers are aggressively promoting their new found source of revenue with posters: "Don't Ever Bet a Horse Named After Your Mother-In-Law. You Might Have to Split Your Winnings" and "Start a New Morning Routine—Coffee, Doughnut, and the Daily Double." And buttons that say, "There's a New Game in Town."

The excitement of trying to pick winners is what makes them racing enthusiasts, and the promise of a substantial return on a small betting investment is what will keep their enthusiasm at high pitch.

"Betting the horses" offers an almost ideal combination of science and luck. Records of past performance are available on every horse, and the bettor can check them. He can check the records of trainers. He can check the performance of the jockeys. He can make allowances for weight handicaps. He can find out whether or not a horse is a good "mudder." He can weigh the advantage of good post position. He can do extensive research on every starter in a given race. He can weigh the morning line odds, which tell him what the racing secretary thinks about each entry's chances of winning.

If the outcome of races were determined by the precise information that's available, no winner would ever pay more than the minimum $2.20 on a $2 ticket, and racing would be hard-pressed to survive.

Fortunately or unfortunately, payoffs aren't made on the basis of past performance. They depend entirely on what happens in a specific race not yet run, on a given day, at a stated time, under current conditions.

To the everlasting benefit of the sport, horses can't talk. They can't tell a bettor how they feel on the day

of a race. They can't let him know if they're tired, if they're sick, if they're irritable, if they've drunk too much water, if they've had a bad night in the stall, if they're annoyed by existing conditions. Most of all, they can't tell the bettor if they feel like running an all-out race.

There is no way to predict the kind of start a given horse will get. Nobody can know in advance if he will be boxed in by other horses at the time when he should make his big move. Nobody can predict a jockey's errors of judgment—and even the greatest are sometimes guilty of them. There is no way of foreseeing accidents, soft spots in the track, the breaking point of stamina that has up to then seemed endless, the horse's reaction to the bat under certain circumstances—dozens of imponderable factors.

Neither is there any way to know if the horse's owner is shooting for a win. Is the horse being "tested," is he being given a workout under racing conditions to observe his reactions, is it simply an exercise outing or do horse and jockey have instructions to win?

The above are a few of the many unknowns that make horse-racing the sport of gamblers. Favorites, over the years, have always won less than 35 percent of the races—and favorites inevitably pay short odds. A $2.20 win ticket on a sure-thing favorite doesn't even come close to making up for the inevitable $4 loss on two other sure-thing favorites.

And the horse player can't be absolutely sure what the payoff will be on his $2 ticket. A rush of last-minute betting on one horse will cause a sharp alteration in odds. On top of that, racing is the only gambling operation known to man in which the odds are determined *after* the race is run. After deduction from the total amount bet of a nice profit for the track and another nice profit for the state, the rest of the money is divided among the winners with mathematical fairness by a machine known as a "totalizator." Except in the case of a "minus pool," in which the great preponderance of wagering has been on one horse, the track ownership and state take a guaranteed profit from every losing and winning wager.

This "vigorish" or house percentage may vary from one state to another, but gamblers are generally agreed that, on the whole, it amounts to roughly 17 percent. It includes "breakage," which gives the track odd nickels and pennies in addition to the established percentage. A "breakage" for the track of 6¢ on a $2 ticket means that a $1,000 bettor gets $30 less than the proper pari-mutuel payoff after taxes and profit.

On top of this, a daily track handle of $2 million

doesn't mean that bettors have come to the track with $2 million, which they have wagered. Much, indeed most of the money that is wagered and won on the first race is re-bet on the second. A high percentage of winnings are reinvested seven or eight times throughout the day—and every time they go into the pari-mutuel pool, the inexorable 17 percent cut is taken.

A knowledgeable gambler who resents the 5 percent house "vigorish" in roulette says that betting the horses is no gamble at all.

And yet, horse players multiply. Why? Most of all, it has to be that interesting combination of science and luck involved in the wagering. Perhaps the exercise of knowledge for possible profit is another.

And the old saw that "all horse players die broke" is simply untrue. Nearly everyone knows a good, competent horse player who shows a yearly profit on his betting operations.

The late Pittsburgh Phil is an example. A cork cutter by trade, he rebelled against the drab monotony of his life. He became an expert, full-time horse player—and left an estate worth $3 million when he died. Edward W. Cole wrote a book, *The Racing Maxims and Methods of Pittsburgh Phil,* which has been republished as a Gambler's Book Club Turf Classic reprint.

The first regulated race meeting on North American soil took place in 1665, sponsored by the first English governor of New York, at Hempstead Plain. The track was called "Newmarket," named after an English race course. There had been horse-racing before that, but on the streets. There's argument among racing fans as to whether *Bulle Rock* or *Sparks* was the first thoroughbred horse in this country, but agreement that, whichever it was, it arrived some time around 1730.

By that time, racing was well established. Virginia had six tracks, and Maryland and New York had almost as many. Kentucky, which was eventually to get the better of Virginia as a racing stronghold, built its first track in 1797 at Lexington. That track was to give way to a replacement in 1828, and the second track was to continue until 1935. Most of the early-day plants had mile tracks, and the racing was done on grass.

The Union race course on Long Island had the first dirt track and was the first with rails. When it opened in 1823, it drew an opening day crowd of 60,000, with a betting handle of $1 million. The attraction was a three-heat race between *American Eclipse* and *Henry.* The latter horse, sponsored by visiting Southerners, won the first heat and lost the last two—but the Southerners bet on the first heat and kept their money in their pockets for the remaining two. *Henry* lost, but his backers won.

The Queen's Plate, at Woodbine in Toronto, is the oldest stake race in North America, and the Travers Stakes at Saratoga Springs, the oldest in the United States, is second.

Racing boomed. The first pari-mutuel betting came in 1871 at New York's Jerome Park. By 1940, pari-mutuel equipment was a part of every track, and the bookmakers had to conduct their operations off-course.

England started the breed of thoroughbreds when a stallion, *Byerly Turk,* was brought to the country in 1685. Of somewhere in the neighborhood of 200 sires in the first stud book, published in 1793, only three perpetuated themselves in racing history: *Byerly Turk, Darley Arabian* and *Godolphin Barb.* Every thoroughbred racing on every track at present can trace its ancestry back to one of these three sires. *Matchem,* foaled in 1748, became the only stallion which could continue the line of *Godolphin Barb;*

The attractive club house at Arlington Park, Arlington Heights, Illinois has helped make the Chicago area and the state of Illinois one of the top horse-racing areas of the country.

Packed stands at Sportsman's Park, Cicero, Illinois testifies to the popularity of harness racing in the Chicago area.

Herod, foaled in 1758, became the only direct stallion descendant of *Byerly Turk;* and *Eclipse,* foaled in 1764, became the sole stallion representative of the *Darley Arabian* line.

This makes *Matchem, Herod* and *Eclipse* the ancient grandfathers of today's thoroughbreds. *Man O' War* descended from the *Matchem* line. *Sir Archy,* one of the first great American thoroughbreds, often called the *Godolphin* of America, had *Herod* and *Matchem* blood lines on his dam's and sire's sides. *Fashion* was among the first American mares to distinguish herself, and she was descended from *Sir Archy. Boston,* one of the great American stallions in early racing history, was considered so superior that many owners would not even race their horses against him. *Lexington, Boston's* greatest son, ran the first major race against time, beating the 7:26 record for four miles held by *Lecomte.*

In discussing American thoroughbreds, one must start by admitting that they all go back to the original three British sires. The American strains are actually of English origin. The *Domino* strain, which produced such horses as *Equipoise, Alsab* and *Sarazen,* goes back to *Darley Arabian,* through *Eclipse.* The *Fair Play* strain, which has produced *Man O' War, Seabiscuit* and *Discovery,* among others, goes back to *Godolphin Barb. Ben Brusy,* head of another great American line, traces back to the *Byerly Turk.*

While racing's popularity knows no boundaries in the United States, it would have to be said that southern California and New York are the focal points. Hollywood Park and Santa Anita, along with a number of other good tracks, make southern California a factor of undeniable importance. Aqueduct and Belmont, of course, have determined the outstanding horses of a season often enough so that nobody can dispute their importance. Practically every important horse in the sport has raced at Belmont, and winning the Belmont Stakes is worth a respectable fortune to a horse's owner, not only because of the purse but because of the enormous stud fees that inevitably follow.

Since the Florida boom of the 20's, that state has moved up into the top brackets of racing, with Hialeah, Tropical Park and Gulfstream at the top of the state's list of tracks.

The Chicago area has made Illinois a top racing state, with Sportsman's Park, Washington Park and Arlington Park, particularly, one of the finest race courses and racing plants in the entire country. Its rich stake races attract top horses from all over the country, and at least one outstanding horse emerges from the Chicago racing season almost every year.

Maryland, with Pimlico, Laurel and Bowie, can't be overlooked in any list of important horse-racing states. All three tracks get an excellent class of contestants.

Kentucky, one of the nation's great breeding states, has tracks that can't be overlooked, Churchill Downs and Keeneland. The Churchill Downs reputation, stemming from the Kentucky Derby, still doesn't draw the impressive horses, day in and day out, to be found racing at other important tracks. Every racing fan wants to see at least one Kentucky Derby—and cringes at the carnival atmosphere and exhorbitant prices that prevail almost everywhere during Derby Week.

Governing bodies and agencies have made the sport what it is today.

The Jockey Club did yeoman service in regulating the registration of American thoroughbreds, and did much to save the sport of racing from disrepute at various times when bad track management threatened to give racing a black eye. It set up rigid rules for racing and insisted on their being followed to the letter.

The Thoroughbred Racing Association was founded in 1942, and brought a uniformity to racing conditions and regulations that had previously been lacking. Most of the best tracks in the country are

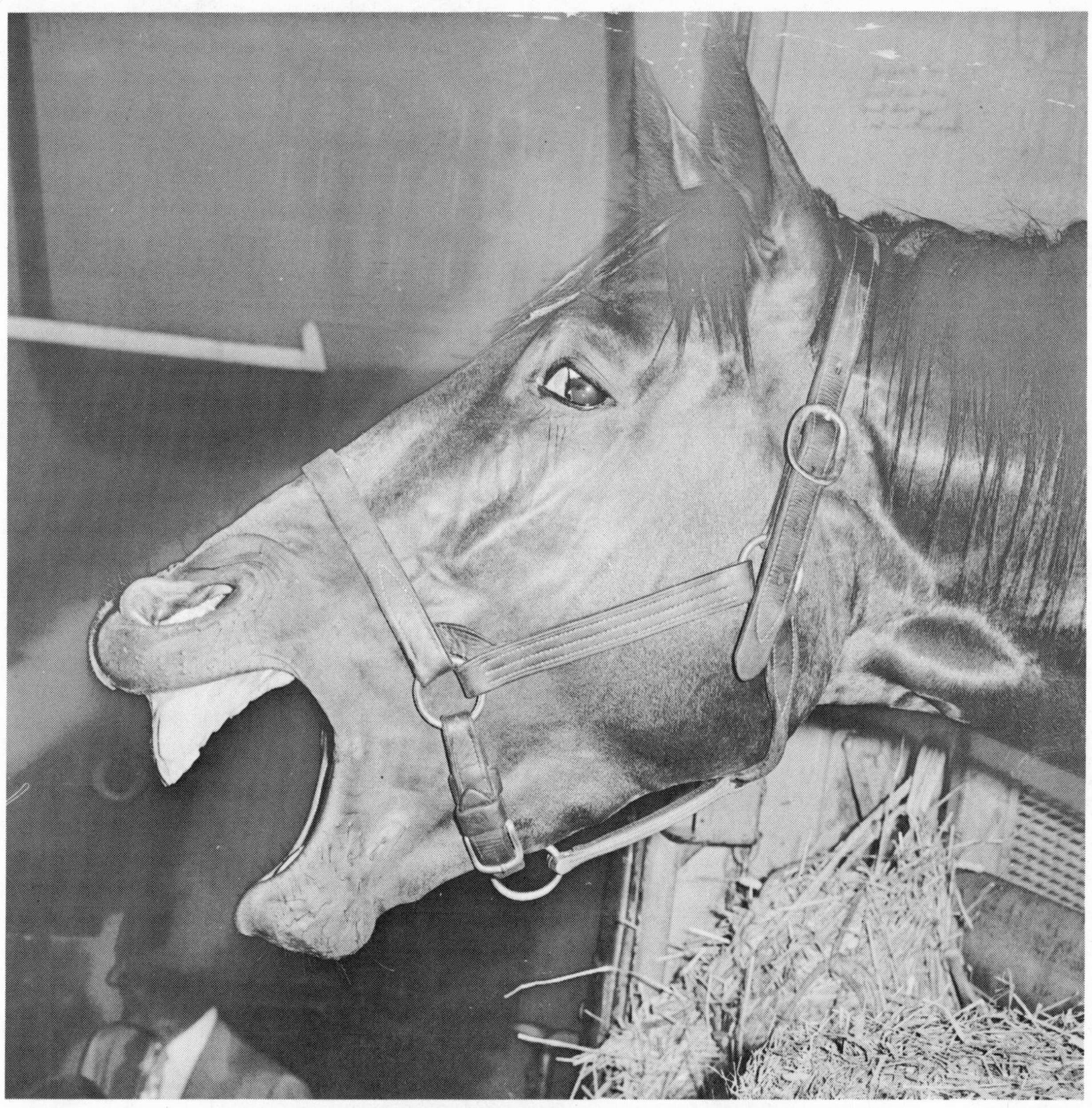

The price of stud fees has made syndication of a leading horse profitable. Back in 1955, Nashua was the basis of the first $1 million syndication deal.

members. Probably the most important single thing it did was to establish a long, strong arm, The Thoroughbred Racing Protective Bureau, with a former F.B.I. agent at the helm. The T.R.P.B. investigates all accusations and complaints of illegal procedures; it fingerprints everyone connected with the sport, with the intention of keeping out any criminal element. One of its most important innovations was to tatoo registration numbers inside the lips of horses. It also serves as an information bureau, and as a part of that duty keeps a special file on everyone in any way involved with racing who has any background of illegal operations, either inside racing or out.

While racing is more stringently regulated and supervised in the United States than anywhere else, it operates all over the world—even behind the Iron and Bamboo curtains.

With the popularity of racing, breeding had to become a major industry, and it grows more important and more affluent every year. Roughly a third of the American thoroughbreds spring from within a 50-square mile area around Lexington, Kentucky.

Breeding has become Big Business, with over 1500 breeding farms producing close to 18,000 foals every year. Stud fees, which in the early years of the century seldom ran over $1,000, have skyrocketed. A good brood mare is considered by many to be worth much more than a well-bred horse. While imported sires are still popular, American studs seem to have at least as good records. *Man O' War,* who came along before the astronomical stud fees, was at stud for over 20 years, 25 times a year. In today's economy, his stud fee would probably run in the neighborhood of $25,000, with a waiting line longer than he could possibly handle. Two of his sons won the Kentucky Derby, and *War Admiral* won the Triple Crown—The Kentucky Derby, The Preakness and the Belmont Stakes. His own record on the track was fabulous, with 9 to 10 the longest price he ever paid. In eight of his 11 races as a three-year old, he broke either world or track records.

Despite being one of the great horses of all time, the English Jockey Club would not register him as a thoroughbred, because his pedigree didn't meet English requirements on both sides.

One of the great tragedies of racing is that the immortal *Kelso,* winner of over $2 million in purses, was a gelding and consequently unable to be used for breeding purposes.

In general, Americans are said to breed more for speed and English for stamina. France breeds for the longer distances, as do most South American breeders. Some great racers, such as *Citation,* have been disappointing as sires.

In recent years, the price of stud fees has made syndication more and more popular. A group of sportsmen buy an outstanding stallion for the specific purpose of offering him at stud, with members of the syndicate getting a specific right to a certain number of stud services. The first really enormous syndication came in 1966 when *Kauai King,* winner of the Derby and Preakness, was syndicated for $2½ million dollars. *Nashua,* back in 1955, had been the basis of the first $1 million syndication deal. All records were broken when the late Charles W. Englehard's *Nijinsky* was syndicated for $5,440,000.

In any given year, one stallion—at most, two—dominates the stud market.

How do you become a successful breeder of racehorses? Nobody knows. One school of thought places greater stress on the selection of the brood mare than on the stallion. While many horses with notable blood lines have failed to get anywhere as racers, outstanding purse winners have always had superior ancestry.

If anyone becomes enough of a racing enthusiast to race a stable of horses, the chances are that he'll buy them, not breed them—and here again, the gamble is great. Every year at the Saratoga yearling sales, beautiful horses are bought for high prices. None of them have raced, and some of them never come close to justifying the prices paid for them. Conversely, some yearlings that turn out to be great money winners go for a song. As a yearling, *Count Fleet* was offered at an extremely low price. The 1971 Kentucky Derby winner—*Canonerro II*—sold at the Keeneland Auctions for only $1,500. The appearance of a yearling, most racing experts agree, means little.

The trainers of various horses receive much attention from the press. Most trainers are taciturn about their methods, but of those who talk, no two seem to agree on any ideal procedure. Most trainers, after breaking a horse and teaching him to gallop in a straight line, close to the rail, take the animals through a slow training process, conditioning them to the point where they can go at about half-speed for a full two miles. Once the horse is in good enough condition to do that, he is worked for speed for an extremely short distance, usually an eighth of a mile or furlong. The two-year old's workouts are generally slow and easy, not nearly as hard as those given older horses.

Once a horse is racing, trainers agree that there is no "standard" way to handle him. Horses have personalities as well as physical traits, and each combination demands special treatment.

The one thing that separates the men from the boys in the area of training is the expert trainer's ability to "pick the right spots" for his charges. In other words, he only puts his horse into races it has a good chance of winning, even if the spots happen to be cheap claiming races. When an expert trainer has a good horse, he nurses it along, trying to bring it to a peak for a big race.

Both trainers and professional handicappers are agreed on one thing—that most bettors at most tracks bet their money foolishly. With a pari-mutuel "vigorish" of roughly 17 percent reducing every dollar that goes through the ticket window by 17¢, it is only the preponderance of foolish betting that gives the knowledgeable bettor a chance of winning. Such a bettor generally plans on showing somewhere between 15 and 25 percent profit on a year's wagering—and often does it.

The hard-core bettor weighs the odds carefully. He knows that the pari-mutuel system encourages false favorites. The public takes a fancy to a horse that should be 15 to 1, bets heavily on it, and the odds plummet downward. In such instances, another horse that has a good chance of winning goes to the post as a bargain for the bettor.

But while an uneducated part of the racing public creates false favorites from time to time, the real long-shot is usually a long-shot for an excellent reason: he simply has no chance of winning. Nothing in his performance record indicates that he belongs against the competition he's facing. As a rule of thumb, very few horses that go to the post at 10 to 1 or more ever pay off.

How important is the jockey? Not nearly so important, apparently, as the average racing fan thinks. One great trainer incurred the enmity of all jockeys by stoutly maintaining that the horse accounted for 90 percent of the battle and the jockey for 10 percent at most.

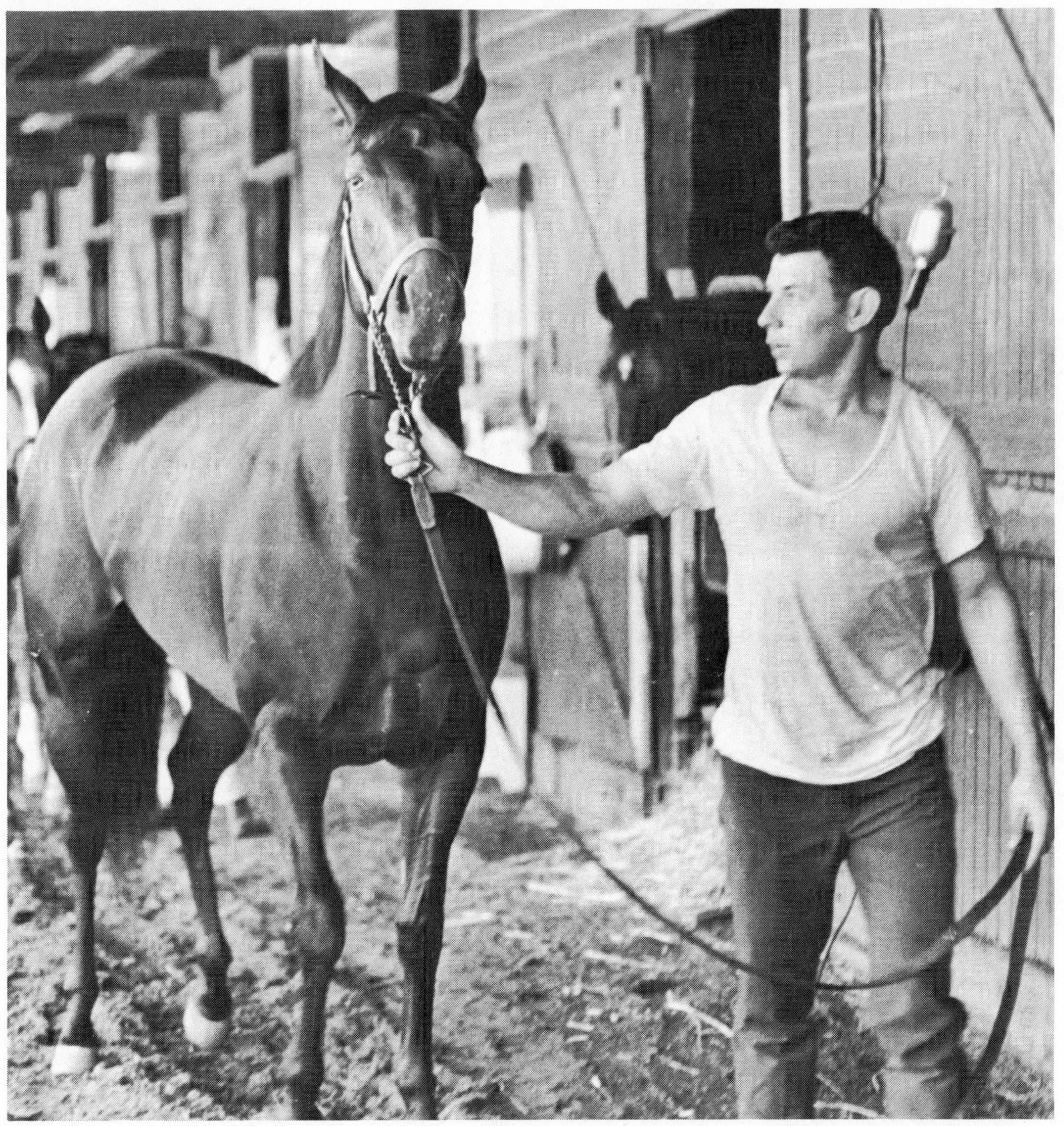

Trainers agree that there is no "standard" way to handle a race horse. Horses have personalities as well as physical traits, and each combination demands special treatment.

Many a racing fan has gone home from the track broke by pursuing the intriguing idea of betting on the jockey, not the horse. The great jockeys, the *winningest* ones, feel that they're doing very well, indeed, when they ride one winner out of five.

The horse is the thing—and not even the greatest of race horses are alike. Some are extremely delicate and injury-prone, while a *Kelso* can stand almost anything without getting hurt. Some have an inborn desire to win that prompts them to give everything they have in every race, while others of equal capability don't seem to care whether they win or not. Some are extremely friendly and some are vicious. Some otherwise great horses have eccentricities that almost brand them as insane. Some simply refuse to run off the pace, while others love to come from behind. A few champions have given their best only when challenged by a photo finish.

A horse's intelligence has been a subject for debate for years, and horse lovers become irate when anyone mentions to them that most encyclopedias list chimps, elephants and dogs as being superior in intellect.

Among the great race horses of all time, almost any authority would include *Man O' War, Count Fleet, Native Dancer* and *Citation*. *Whirlaway* may not have been great, but he gave racing fans a spectacular show

Photo courtesy Chicago Thoroughbred Enterprises, Inc.

Whatever else they may have, all jockeys are blessed with great courage. They know horses, and how to ride them to get the most out of them.

on every appearance. Ted Atkinson, a fine jockey, rates *Tom Fool* as the finest horse he ever rode. *Exterminator* was not only a great race horse but one of the most durable to ever hit a track. He won ten races against tough competition when he was seven years old and lived to an age of 30. *Hindoo, Salvator* and *Sysonby* were among the early-day greats. *Colin, Equipoise, Seabiscuit, War Admiral, Alsab, Stymie, Armed, Swaps,* and of course, the great money-winner, *Kelso.*

Among great races, one would have to include *Man O' War's* only upset, a loss to a horse named *Upset,* in 1919. Another upset would be *Alsab's* victory over *Whirlaway* in a match race in 1944. Probably the riders contributed as much excitement as the horses in the never-to-be-forgotten Kentucky Derby of 1933, with Don Meade up on *Broker's Tip* and Herb Fisher on *Head Play,* both slashing wildly at each other with their whips while they came down the stretch.

The first great match race to be seen by millions on television was the *Swaps-Nashua* race at the Washington Park meet in Illinois in 1955, with a winner-take-all purse of $100,000. Arcaro on *Nashua* went to the whip from the outset and crossed the finish line a good five lengths in front of *Swaps.*

One of the most thrilling match races of all times was the *Seabiscuit-War Admiral* race at Pimlico in 1938, in which *Seabiscuit* was challenged time after time by *War Admiral,* who raced head and head with him, only to be ridden down at the finish.

If great horses have been colorful, so have great jockeys. One of the marks of a great jockey is his dislike for losing. Among the all-time greats, most horsemen would include Earl Sande, George Woolf, Willie

Shoemaker, Walter Blum, Conn McCreary, Eddie Arcaro, Willie Hartack, Baeza, Ussery, Ycaza and Ismael Valenzuela. Whatever else they may have, they're all blessed with great courage. And while some of them may have had little formal schooling, they all have superior intelligence when it comes to their trade. They know horses, and know how to ride them to get the most out of them.

Probably every jockey makes mistakes, but what often look like errors or lapses aren't. Even the steadiest race horse isn't always predictable, and some great horses have made great jockeys look bad by performing in a way that nobody could have predicted.

The on-track bookies, once a colorful part of racing, are victims of the totalizator, the first version of which was invented by Pierre Oller in 1865. The modern totalizator is actually three complex units: a ticket issuing machine, the adding machines that are the backbone of the pari-mutuel operation, and the indicator, which relays last-second amounts bet and odds to the bulletin or tote board.

One of the greatest payoffs in pari-mutuel history was at Haddock Park in England in 1929, when a horse named Cooley paid 3409 to 1. In the same year, a horse named *Robledo* paid 3037 to 1 in a race in Shanghai, China. *Wishing Ring* at Latonia in 1912 paid $1885.50. *Man O' War* still holds the distinction of getting the consistently shortest odds; running three different times at 1 to 100.

While John W. "Bet-a-Million Gates" was widely heralded as the heaviest horse player of all time, the distinction probably belongs to Payne Whitney, who one afternoon casually lost a quarter of a million dollars on the first half of the card—and wound up the day with a $15,000 profit. Pittsburgh Phil, whose real name was George Smith, was certainly one of the big bettors—a highly successful one. Some of the plungers were more notorious than famous, such as Big Bill Dwyer, Little Ziggy Zweig and Arnold Rothstein. Rothstein once won $800,000 on a horse, *Sidereal,* at Aqueduct, on July 4th, 1921.

The Victorian Era was the time of horse-racing plungers, and the gigantic wagers will probably never be equaled again.

In the 1860's, the Marquis of Hastings owned a mare, *Lady Elizabeth,* that was racing against another horse, *Hermit,* the latter carrying odds of 66 to 1 in its favor. Hastings, in addition to backing his own mare heavily, made a huge book against *Hermit,* perhaps because of an intense enmity with Mr. Henry Chaplin, *Hermit's* owner.

Chaplin's winnings on the Derby in 1867 amounted to roughly $900,000, most of which came from the Marquis of Hastings, who had to borrow from a fashionable money lender in order to pay off. An interesting aftermath of the race is that Hastings died at the age of 24, the victim, according to his friends, of a broken heart.

The Duke of Hamilton, it was said, lost somewhere in the neighborhood of $5 million during his race betting career. His racing losses were so stupendous that he had to sell the pictures and art objects in Hamilton Palace. The sale brought him $2½ million dollars, enough to let him continue his losing ways at the track.

The legendary Pittsburg Phil bet heavily on many occasions, but admitted that the biggest coup he ever attempted didn't come off. The bettor had acquired a horse, *Parvenue,* which had not distinguished itself in any way. Phil gave careful attention to the animal's conditioning and training, and the horse showed remarkable improvement, so great that the bettor was convinced he could win in fast company.

He picked a spot for *Parvenue,* and then placed six men in New York pool halls with anywhere from $2,000 to $4,000 apiece to bet. He had additional men at the track. The pool hall bettors placed considerable of the money at 40 to 1, and the lowest price they got was 15 to 1. At the track, the lowest price was 12 to 1. Just before post time, with the horses on the track, it was discovered that one horse, *Dagonet,* should have had a much different impost from the one he was carrying, due to a mistake. After considerable debate, the stewards decided to scratch *Dagonet,* all bets were declared off, and a new book was opened on the race.

Since word of the heavy betting on *Parvenue* in the New York pool rooms had gotten around quickly, the new prices on *Parvenue,* Pittsburgh Phil's horse, were much lower than they had been. The best Phil got on any of his money was 12 to 1, and his men in New York and at the track were unable to get the total amounts of their previous bets down.

Parvenue won without working up much of a sweat, but Pittsburgh Phil's winning on the race were only $45,000.

At one time when Pittsburgh Phil suspected that some jockeys in some races weren't trying to win, he made a deal with Tod Sloan, a leading rider of the day. He agreed to pay Sloan $400 for every winner

---

Inside Story

Joe E. Lewis gets credit for the story about the chronic gambler who was finally committed to a mental institution in a desperate effort to cure him. "He'd been there three days," Joe says, when he set up a bookmaking operation. None of the inmates were allowed to have money, so they bet pebbles, and my friend almost got a corner on the pebble supply. One day a prospective horse-player came in with a huge rock and wanted to put it on a horse in the fourth at Hollywood Park. My friend turned the bet down cold and threw the guy out. The doctors asked him why, and he explained, 'He knows something'."

he rode, regardless of whether Phil had any money on the horse or not. Guaranteed by the deal that Sloan would be trying to win on every mount, Phil paid the jockey according to agreement—and in a month had netted himself between $70,000 and $80,000 betting on Sloan mounts. Sloan later attributed his rise as a jockey to the canny horse player.

Pittsburgh Phil was an expert horse handicapper, and carefully worked out the correct odds on every possible winner in a race. When the payoff odds were heavier than the correct odds, he bet heavily. "When a horse that should be 3 to 1 goes into a race at 8 to 1," he said, "you have a good bet." He also followed the Money Management rule of betting minimums during a losing streak and betting heavily "with the book's money in hand."

A highly successful horse player, he minimized crookedness in the sport. "There's not a tenth of one percent as much of it as you hear whispered," he said. "Most of the stories about fixed races are completely untrue. When a horse that should win runs out of the money, there can be a couple of dozen reasons for it—and crookedness is almost never the responsible one. When you start thinking about the possibility of crookedness in a race and weighing its possible effect on the outcome, you absolutely destroy yourself as a handicapper."

On many occasions, his handicapping showed more than one horse capable of winning a race—sometimes three or four so closely rated that the outcome would be a tossup. Asked how he decided which of the potential winners to bet, he replied, "That's easy. I don't decide and I don't bet. If a race is a tossup, I sit back and enjoy it without having a cent riding on the outcome. You know, there's no law says you have to bet on every race. I only make bets when I think I'm going to win."

He also minimized the possibility of "a killing" on a race. "Many killings are attempted," he observed, "but few are accomplished."

He regarded condition as of prime importance, and admitted that learning to judge it was extremely difficult. "Condition," he said, "has more to do with a horse winning or losing a race than the weight it carries. A high class horse couldn't win a race with a feather on his back if he is not in condition."

He held newspaper handicappers in low regard. "Deadlines make them pick their choices the day before the race," he said, "but that's not enough excuse for their mistakes. They just aren't first-rate handicappers. A really good handicapper wouldn't even think of giving his selections to a newspaper. Let's face it. If a man knows how to pick winners, he's not going to take a job telling other people how to bet. He'd have to be insane to do such a thing, and no good handicapper is nuts. Anybody who can pick winners with any consistency will do just what I've done—he'll keep quiet as a mouse about his choices and he'll bet 'em for all they're worth. What's more, he'll make so much money that he could buy any newspaper in the country—at which point, he'd hire his own inferior handicappers.

"If you want to make money betting on horses, don't expect anyone else to make your picks for you. The more money there is riding on a horse, the less it pays, and it's just plain common-sense economics that anybody who can pick winners isn't going to knock down his profits by letting anyone else in on a good thing. I've never in my life made money on the horses by following anybody else's advice, and I don't expect to.

"You have to do it, yourself. Everything's there for you to do it—past performance, condition of the track, the jockey who's going to be up, the records of the other horses in the race, the condition of every horse. It's all there—if you know how to read it.

"Most of the people who play the horses aren't too bright. They're looking for something for nothing. They either don't want to do the work required to pick winners or they don't know how. Any intelligent person who will regard it as a job, will use his brains, will go to any length to get the necessary information and will make a careful analysis of what he gets can pick

---

WHAT'S SO FUNNY?

Bernard J. Lasker, head of the New York Stock Exchange, apparently saw nothing funny in an Offtrack Betting Corporation promotional ad, the copy for which was disclosed by the betting corporation in advance of the campaign's release.

The ad copy said, "If you're in the stock market, you might find this a better bet."

"On behalf of more than 31 million shareholders," Lasker wrote to Howard Samuels, president of the offtrack betting corporation, "the exchange solemnly protests the ill-considered slogan . . . which infers an analogy between offtrack betting and investment in stocks."

Samuels, who received the protest on March 3, 1971, was prompt to reply. "On behalf of the 48,972 horses that raced in this country in 1970, I am sure that some of the horses feel they have been a better investment in the past few years than some of the investments on the New York Stock Exchange." He added that there was room for both the offtrack betting corporation and the stock exchange—and possibly a little humor—in the lives of New Yorkers. One small stock market investor who recouped his market losses with fortunate selections at the race tracks commented, "Lasker's right when he says there's no comparison between the two. Hypoed stocks don't get any saliva test."

winners. At least, he can pick enough winners to make money.

"The same thing happens to amateurs in horse racing that happens to amateurs in anything else. They get beaten.

"The best horse player in the world will make a mistake now and then. It's in the cards. But when a professional makes a mistake, he profits by it. He doesn't make the same mistake a second time.

"Don't think of betting on the horses as being an easy way to make a living, because it isn't. I make a lot of money at it, but I work hard. I put in long hours. I know how to apply information, and the reason I know how is because I've gone through a hard school. I love what I'm doing, and even when I'm out of bed at four o'clock in the morning to clock a secret workout of a horse, I enjoy it. There's a challenge that you won't find in many other lines of work—and the rewards for meeting challenges are big. But don't think I get my money easy. I work hard for it."

Asked why the bookmakers showed such tremendous profits on their operations, he had a quick answer. "Because most of the people who put down money with him don't know what they're doing. Good gambling, whether it's on dice or cards or horses, requires skill. Anybody who bets money on anything in the hope that luck will make him a winner is an idiot. When I was cutting corks, I had to know my business to make a living from my job, and the same thing's true of gambling.

"A poker player who studies the game, who learns all the percentages, who knows how to read his opponents, who knows when to bluff and when to run for cover, not only deserves to win but will inevitably win over the dub who depends on sheer luck. The same thing is true of betting on horses. If I'm not a better judge of horses than the bookie who's taking my bet, I don't deserve to win."

The odds against the various horses in a race that appear on the line are seldom correct, he observed. "When a long shot wins," he said, "it wasn't a long shot. It was ready and it was the right race, under the right conditions. The fact that few people recognized the truth was what created the false odds. The handicappers who say that a certain percentage of long shots win are really saying that they guessed completely wrong on that percentage of horses. When a horse deserves to be a long shot, it doesn't run in the money. Horse-racing isn't like Roulette, where luck will bring a certain number up on a spin of the wheel. A horse comes in first because it beats every other horse in the race, and not for any other reason. I've won lots of money on 20 to 1 shots—but it was the line that said they were 20 to 1, not me. I'd picked them as 2 or 3 to 1, and that's why I'd bet them. The fact that they won proved that I was right and the line was wrong."

The general opinion is that pari-mutuel odds have virtually eliminated the bettor of huge sums—at least, at the track.

One colorful character who remains—and one most racing fans would prefer to do without—is the tout. His continued existence is positive proof that new fans visit the tracks every day, because nobody familiar with the sport would listen to him, let alone bite on his implausible propositions.

The simple truth is that "inside information" isn't available. It stands to reason that anyone who had such information would keep it strictly to himself, to avoid ruining the odds on his horse.

Information allegedly handed out by one of the jockeys is most certainly suspect. Jockeys are traditionally and notoriously poor handicappers, so if the information actually comes from one of them, which is highly improbable, the bettor would be just as well off listening to a tout.

Really, the bettor doesn't need any inside information to win. All he has to do is a careful, accurate job of handicapping—and then have the horses run true to form.

Simple, huh?

Once only a break in the tedium of the county fair, harness racing now is an exciting spectacle witnessed by some 30 million paying fans last year.

THE START OF THE PARI-MUTUEL SYSTEM

Pierre Oller, the Parisian perfume shop owner, previously mentioned, who developed the first pari-mutuel calculating system in 1865, came up with eqiupment which bore little resemblance to today's complex calculating machine system—row upon row of tape-and-disc electronic marvels.

The American Totalisator Company handles all necessary maintenance for a track system and conducts an ongoing program of research and development to improve an almost perfect system. If you're interested, you can see the wheels spinning and lights flashing as the odds are swiftly computed and recomputed every 90 seconds. It is an incredible display of modern electronics.

As efficient and irreplaceable as these machines are now, many horse players were not enthusiastic about their introduction. Even though first seen in this country in 1870, they were not generally used until almost ten years later. It was hoped that they would be available for opening day at Churchill Downs in 1874 but bugs in the early machines and distrust on the part of the bettor kept their use a rarity until just befor World War I. At New York tracks, where bookies had more clout than elsewhere, the introduction of the pari-mutuel machine system was held up until just before World War I.

Interestingly enough it was not the tracks that were the prime movers for the pari-mutuel machine system, but rather the state and local authorities. This seems incongruous, until one considers that it is an almost infallible method of assuring that the proper taxes are being collected. Since every bet has to go through the machine and be recorded, there is no way for the track to "forget" any of the bets that have been made.

The fans, in general, resisted the introduction of the pari-mutuel because they felt it took some of the human element out of making a bet. Certainly it lessened the local color when the bookies were banished from the clubhouse lawn. It also reduced some "sharp shooting" and outright cheating at the track. Unfortunately, it also prevented a shrewd bettor from shopping around for odds. Proof of bettors' preference for the bookies was evident when pari-mutuels were in operation at some tracks and not at others. The tracks with bookies outdrew the pari-mutuel tracks. Indeed, some people still prefer to patronize their illegal neighborhood bookie rather than the recently legalized Off-Track Betting facilities in New York. The old time bookies laugh at the so-called "legal competition."

Today's pari-mutuel machines or "adding machines" are much more complex than is implied by their name. Calculations are performed in micro-seconds and electronically transmitted to the "tote" board as instantaneous information for the betting public. Each piece of equipment is put through a test run by the Chief Engineer and a crew of electricians and highly skilled mechanics each morning of a race meet. Back-up equipment is available in the event of any malfunction, and only a total power failure like the New York blackout can put them out of operation.

The total system, as previously noted, is threefold; the ticket seller's machines, the computational or "adding" machines and the information display unit or "tote" board. The two most familiar are the "tote" board and ticket selling machines. The least familiar is the central processing unit, the real brains of the set-up. This component takes in the data from the ticket seller's machines, digests it, makes the necessary calculations (not forgetting take and breakage) and then relays the information to the display unit—the "tote" board. The processing and display take place in micro-seconds and could even go faster. The bottleneck in the operation is the ticket seller's window. Most machines can turn out no more than one ticket per second. Because this is where the human element enters in, we must expect less efficient performance than from the machines.

"Tote" boards record only 12 positions. Normally, this is more than enough. However, some exceptionally popular and prestigious races attract huge fields,

---

"BET A MILLION"

Numerous stories have attempted to explain the origin of John W. Gates' nickname, "Bet a Million."

One story is that because of his great activity in the stock market, he wanted to acquire the reputation of being the world's biggest—and most successful—gambler. Certainly, he made spectacular and flamboyant bets that, somehow, were always recorded in the press. This version is that he suggested to a newspaper reporter that the reporter, assigned to cover Gates' gambling exploits, always refer to him in his news stories as John W. "Bet a Million" Gates.

Another story is that after winning over half a million dollars on his own horse at a race track, he was requested to limit future bets to a maximum of $10,000. Indignant, he is said to have wandered through the crowd at the track, offering any takers a million dollar bet on a single horse.

It is a matter of record that when "Bet a Million" publicity was no longer of any value to him, he quit gambling.

especially when the competition is wide open. The 1971 Kentucky Derby attracted more than 12 entries. What happens in such a case? Basically, the same procedure as when two or three horses owned or trained by the same person are entered as a betting unit—one ticket suffices for any one of the horses to win, place or show. A large field means that tickets one through 11 are sold on individual horses if there are no entries, and all horses with post positions 12 on up are covered as a "field" bet. That is, if you buy a ticket on the "field" to place and there are 18 horses in the race, you will collect if *any* of the horses in post positions 12 through 18 run second or better. In the '71 Derby, this became a great bargain, with the winning horse in the "field." However, prices at the mutuel often get extremely low when good horses appear in the field.

Tracks take great care to prevent counterfeiting of tickets. While it might look easier than counterfeiting money, don't try it. You aren't the first to have thought about doctoring today's losing ticket into tomorrow's winner. An unpleasant surprise awaits those who try, when the cashier tears and examines the ticket.

Some track chiselers have also tried to "late bet" the track. There is one old story that because the starting gate is ten to 20 yards behind the actual start of the race, if a front running horse got a good start, one observer could immediately signal a confederate standing at the $50 window. The latter could then tell the ticket seller to punch as many tickets as he could until the machine automatically locked. The catch is that the ticket seller's machine locks when the gate opens.

Stories about this system have popped up for years, but they are just part of the mythology. Even if the ticket machine didn't lock until the first horse passed the starting line, consider that a speedy thoroughbred covers ten yards in slightly over ½-second and 20 yards in not much more than one second. How much time would this allow for signaling and betting? Too little, say confirmed bettors who refuse to believe that the system has ever worked.

In the next section we will go into the mathematics of how the machines compute odds and payoffs.

WHERE THE MONEY GOES

Many professional gamblers in this country consider Roulette unbeatable because the house 0-00 combination increases the casino percentage on edge to 5 5/19 per cent. Craps and Blackjack are considered "best casino gambles" because the house edge is under two percent.

Any rail bird would welcome either house percentage as a boon. The race tracks currently take from 15 to 20 percent from the mutuel dollar before redistributing the funds. Taxes are largely responsible. While New York draws out the largest take, allowing the track less than one-third of the take and breakage, other states are not far behind. As operating expenses go up and taxes soar, the tracks receive smaller and smaller profits.

Some legislators seem to regard racing as an endless source of revenue, never considering that they may be killing the goose that's laying all their golden eggs.

The effect of this "take" is to reduce payoff odds and to make overlays more difficult to come by. For example, if there is a total of $100,000 in the win pool and $33,333 is bet on the favorite, the "true" odds are 2-1. A bettor would expect to get $2 back plus $4 profit, for a mutuel payoff of $6. Fat chance! Depending on the take, it will return anywhere from $4.80 to $5.20. And it's the bettor's profit that has been diminished.

Everybody agrees that states have a right to tax the tracks *as they would any corporation conducting legitimate business.* But they don't. Taxes levied on racing are higher than on any corporate tax structure. In addition, the inequities of the personal tax structure require a gambler to pay taxes on all winnings, but only to deduct losses to the extent of winnings. These are obvious injustices to gamblers, but the problem is to find a way to make horse bets pay off.

Before getting into the mechanics of calculating the win, place and show payoffs, let's define a few terms:

Mutuel handle or handle—*all money that goes through the pari-mutuel machines.*

Take—*the percentage withheld by the track to cover operating expenses, taxes and purses.*

Breakage—*the amount of money that is not returned in mutuel payoffs because it is in uneven amounts.*

While the first two are self-explanatory, the third term needs some clarifying. When the amount bet on a race shows a total win pool of $100,000, $15,000 is taken by the track (assuming we're in California, where the take is still 15 percent). Eighty-five thousand dollars is now left to be distributed to those people who have bought tickets on the winner. We see that $33,333 has been bet on the winner. This all goes back to holders of winning tickets. In addition, $51,667 ($85,000-$33,333) will be split up as profits. By dividing $33,333 into $51,667, it becomes evident that the true dollar odds of 2-1 ($33,333 out of $100,000) have been reduced to 1.550025 to one. Here is where breakage takes place. No one quibbles about the extra decimal points and would be happy to let the track keep the .000025 percent which occurs from calculation. Subtracting .000025 from 1.550025 leaves a nice round figure of 1.55 to one, which is 3.10 to two. Our mutuel payoff should be the original $2 invested (from $33,333) plus $3.10 (from

"What looks good in the fifth at Roosevelt?"

$51,667). The track could keep the breakage of .000025.

Instead, it legitimizes a larger cut by recalculating. The track says, "We don't pay off in 5¢ units, so for our purposes odds can't be stated in 5¢ units." In other words, they only recognize odds of 1.30 to one; 1.40 to one; 1.50 to one; 1.60 to one and so on. By this reasoning, they look again at the odds of 1.550025 to one and reduce them to 1.50, subtracting .050025 instead of .000025. Quite a percentage difference! Now the return is no longer $3.10 (1.55 to one), but $3.00 (1.50 to one). When the initial $2 bet is added, the winning ticket pays $5 instead of $5.10—not too much difference for a $2 bet, but a nice $10 lunch for a bettor with $200 on the winner. Also it is quite different from a $6 payoff on a "true" odds basis of 2-1, ($100,000 to $33,333).

This method of calculation adds about $12 million to New York state racing revenue each year, in addition to the previously mentioned large tax bite. With the sport taxed out of proportion, the dime breakage scheme is thoroughly disliked by many bettors who regard it as an insult to their intelligence.

The same procedure applies to calculations of place and show payoffs. Remember that money bet in each of the pools, win, place and show, is totally separate and can only be distributed among holders of those tickets. The previous example showed that the "take" is removed from the total amount of the win pool and the amount bet on the winning horse is divided into the amount bet on all other horses in order to find the $1 odds.

Let's look at what happens to the money in the place pool. The same factors of "take" and breakage work even more heavily against the bettor. Staying with the same example, if $100,000 were bet in the win pool, we would expect roughly $60,000 in the place pool, 15 percent of $60,000 is $9,000 for the "take," leaving $51,000 for redistribution. If $25,000 were bet on the *winning* horse to place and $16,000 bet on the runner-up to place (a relative long shot running second) that would mean the $25,000 plus $6,000—a total of $31,000 would be returned to holders of these tickets. This would leave $20,000 ($51,000-$31,000) to be split among the people with place tickets on the first horse and those with place tickets on the second horse. How is it split? Right down the middle! Ten thousand dollars for those who have place tickets on the winner and $10,000 for those who have tickets on the runner-up.

The same division occurs. Divide the $25,000 bet to place on the winner into the $10,000 available, and get .25. Without the insanity of dime breakage, this would be 1-4 odds (.25-1.00) or .50 to 2.00 for a place mutuel to 2.50. However, breakage reduces the .25 to .20, so the payoff becomes $2.40. In this case you can see that breakage alone, regardless of "take," reduces the profit from .50 to .40. This 10¢ on 50¢ is a healthy 20 percent lost.

The place ticket holders on the runner-up fare somewhat better, since dividing $6,000 into $10,000 produces dollar odds of 1.6667, which the track reduces to 1.60 to one. This in turn becomes 3.20 to two for a healthy place mutuel of $5.40. Without take and breakage, the prices would be better than double!

The show pool is merely more of the same. If the win pool was $100,000 and the place pool was $60,000, we would expect the show pool to be around $36,000. Fifteen percent of $36,000 is $5,400, leaving $30,600 to be redistributed. If $8,000 were bet on the winner, $2,000 on the runner-up (longshot, remember) and $5,600 on the third horse (second favorite), we give back $15,600 to show ticket holders and split $15,000 equally ($30,600-$15,600=$15,000), leaving $5,000 for each group: show ticket holders on the winner; show ticket holders on the runner-up; and show ticket holders on the number three horse. The same mathematics involve dividing $8,000 into $5,000 for dollar odds of .625 reduced to .60 and paying $3.20 for the winner to show. The runner-up divides $2,000 into $5,000 for dollar odds of 2.50 (no breakage this time!), and a show price of $7.00. The third horse divides $5,600 into $5,000 for dollar odds of .8928 (terrible breakage here!), reducing to .80 for $3.60 payoff. Let's look at this in perspective.

	win	place	show
Winner	5.00	2.40	3.20
Runner-up		5.40	7.00
Third horse			3.60

Does this look unusual? Indeed it does. Normally, the winner and runner-up do not pay more to show than to place. Why is this? Betting to place or show is like betting a Quinella. You're betting blind odds because you don't know who will share the place and show pool with you, a longshot or favorite. In this example, a shrewd bettor could look at the amounts bet in the place and show pool and cover his bet with a *show bet,* not a place bet. The reason is this: the winner was heavily bet ($25,000 out of $60,000) in the place pool, but underbet in the show pool ($8,000 out of $36,000). This does occur, and the sophisticated bettor with a fast slide rule can take advantage of the situation. The best rule is: Bet to win only! You know what your odds are and what your payoff will be. Place and show are mostly sucker bets. Leave them to Aunt Harriet.

Someone at this point will ask, "What about backing up my win ticket with *two* place tickets?" This type of hedge bet is common—and ridiculous. If you think the horse can win, go with him. If you don't, go to another horse who can. The same goes for across the board betting. Why take a chance on three low price horses causing low payoffs for all three positions? Place and show bets seldom make sense.

We mentioned earlier a related question on the point of hedging a bet: Betting more than one horse to win. So-called experts will tell you this is a bad idea because "you're betting against yourself." Not so. If you have narrowed the race down to only three horses and their post time odds are 6-1, 8-1 and 11-1, it's quite obvious you could bet all three and make money no matter which won. If you bet $20 on each of the three, you're investing $60. If the 6-1 wins, he returns $14 or $140 for $20, giving you $80 profit. If 8-1 wins paying $18, you're ahead $120. If the 11-1 wins paying $24, you've made $180. Maybe that's as it should be if you feel the 6-1 horse is not quite as good and your willing to sacrifice profit when he wins. But what if you view all three horses as equal and you'd like to equalize your payoff? You could do this by betting $15 on the 11-1; $20 on the 8-1 and $25 on the 6-1. In this manner your payoffs would be $180 if the 11-1 wins; $180 if the 8-1 wins, and

---

Unlucky Nag

A tout tipped Joe E. Lewis off that a certain horse was due. "I went to the stable," he said, "and I never saw a sorrier sight. That horse was so skinny a wind would have blown him away—and he looked hungry. I asked the stable boy what was wrong and he said, "Every morning, I toss a coin to see whether he gets his hay or I get my eye-opener, and that unlucky horse has lost six mornings straight."

$175 if the 6-1 wins. Congratulations, you have just reinvented the so-called "Dutch Book." It's not really known why this method is called the "Dutch Book," but it was effectively used by Arnold Rothstein to make money. In fact, it is sometimes called, "The A.R. System" after his initials.

While we don't recommend using the "Dutch Book" exclusively, it can be a powerful tool in those races where there are two or even three contenders that you find difficult to separate. The following table shows how to use this approach:

DUTCH TABLE

Total Bet Not to Exceed $50

Odds	Bet	Odds	Bet
3-5	$45.00	8-1	$8.00
4-5	40.00	9-1	8.00
1-1	35.00	10-1	6.00
6-5	34.00	11-1	6.00
7-5	32.00	12-1	6.00
3-2	30.00	13-1	6.00
8-5	28.00	14-1	5.00
9-5	26.00	15-1	5.00
2-1	24.00	16-1	5.00
5-2	22.00	17-1	4.00
3-1	20.00	18-1	4.00
7-2	18.00	19-1	4.00
4-1	16.00	20-1	4.00
9-2	14.00	21-1	2.00
5-1	12.00	22-1	2.00
11-2	10.00	23-1	2.00
6-1	10.00	24-1	2.00
		25-1	2.00

How To Bet

Any combination of horses that does not exceed $50.00 is acceptable.

For example: Horse A 11-1....$ 6.00
B 4-1.... 16.00
C 5-2.... 22.00
D 15-1.... 5.00

Total Bet....$49.00

If A wins and pays $24 you get $72 return on $49 investment for $23 profit.

If B wins and pays $10 you get $80 for $31 profit.

If C wins paying $7 you get $77 for $28 profit.

If D wins paying $32 you get $80 for $31 profit.

You could also bet a 7-5 and 4-1 combination for $48 or any number of horses at any odds as long as total does not exceed $50.

You can see that the system won't work for extremely short-priced horses. It's most effective in races where no favorite attracts strong support, and several contenders must be taken into consideration.

PUBLIC SELECTORS & SYSTEMS

At some time or another, every horseplayer wonders why the newspaper handicappers give their information away. If they're expert handicappers, why don't they just keep quiet and make a fortune? (Or for that matter, why don't we do that instead of writing this book?) The question is a legitimate one and deserves an answer. In our case, horse racing is a hobby, one which we enjoy and which makes us some money.

But primary occupations take precedence over hobbies. In addition, there are no entreprenurial tax advantages to gambling (except evasion and we don't like striped pajamas). Taxes on track winnings are prohibitively high and business expenses that would be allowed as part of any other enterprise are not even considered for gamblers by the I.R.S.

Another reason, especially for some of the newspapers and tout sheets, is that they may not be very good handicappers. Some sports writers are assigned to the task, while others have enthusiasm but lack knowledge. Study the results of the public selectors and you will find that few of them show a proft over an entire season.

This is not to say that all public selectors are poor handicappers. They're not. Some are highly skilled, dedicated professionals who find a real challenge in predicting tomorrow's performance from yesterday's results. Some, in fact, perform so well that it's hard to believe they are working under the handicaps the system places on them. Consider for a moment that the professional selector has no opportunity to pass a race as unplayable. You do (and we hope you will), and we do. But he does not. His newspaper needs a selection for every race—and sometimes, every race at several tracks. It's a sheer physical impossibility to handicap 18 or 27 races a day. In addition, he must perform this herculean task without the benefit of last minute scratches, last minute jockey changes, overweights, equipment changes or even a passing glance at the animal in the paddock. Further, he must rely on his own meticulously kept chart book, since the *Daily Racing Form* is not available when he must make his selections. The crowning blow is when he finds a good horse that should go off at 3-1 or better, the betting public takes his word for the horse's quality, and bets it down to 8-5. It's little wonder that even the Best Bets of most public selectors fail to show a profit—not because they don't win often enough but because they actually drive the odds down on their best selections.

Our suggestion is to use the public selectors cautiously, if at all. There's more pleasure in picking the horses yourself. That's what this game is all about.

Next to public selectors, the casual racegoer will

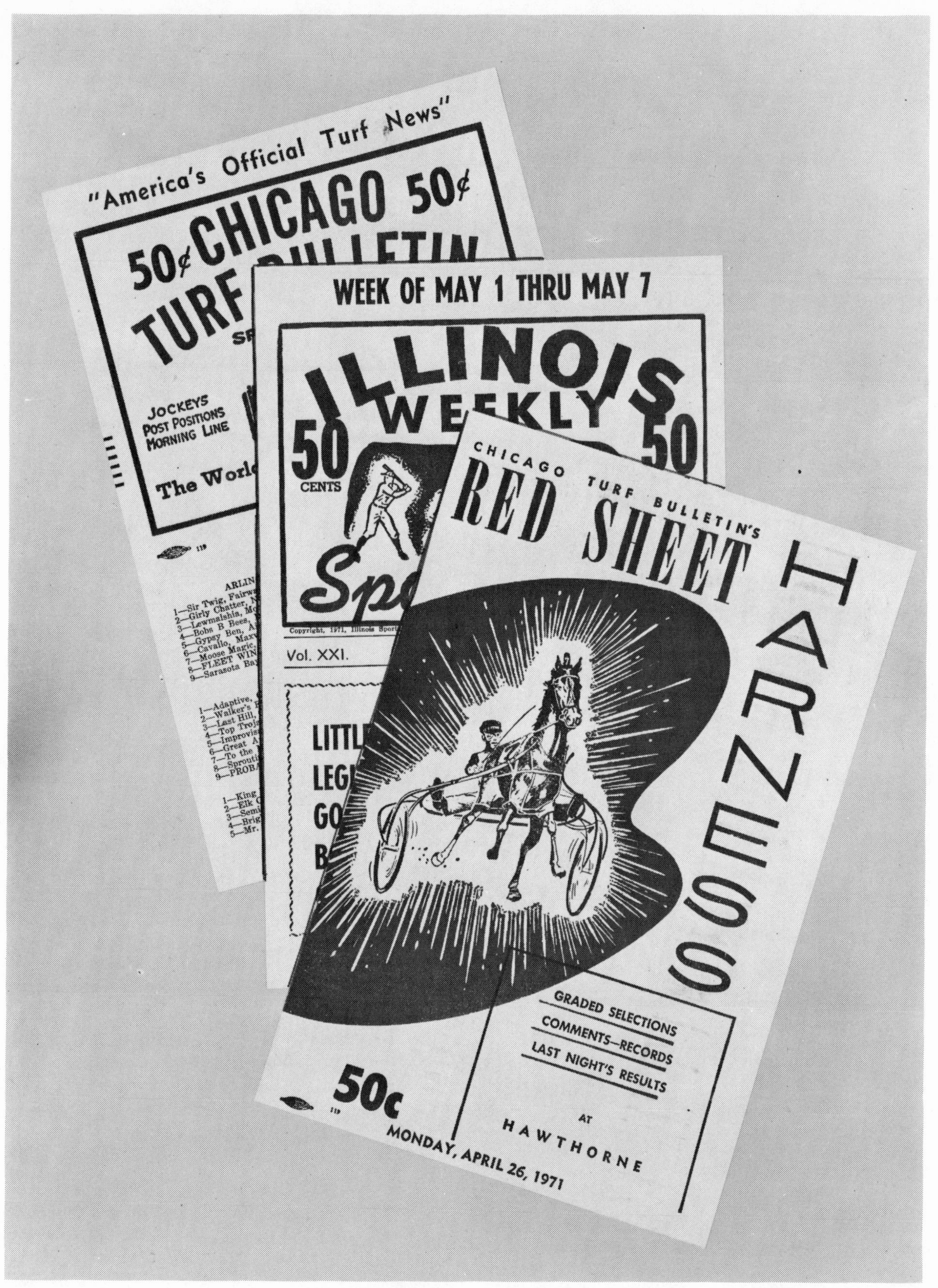

Courtesy Illinois Sports News

Some public selectors are highly skilled, dedicated professionals who find a real challenge in predicting tomorrow's performance from yesterday's results.

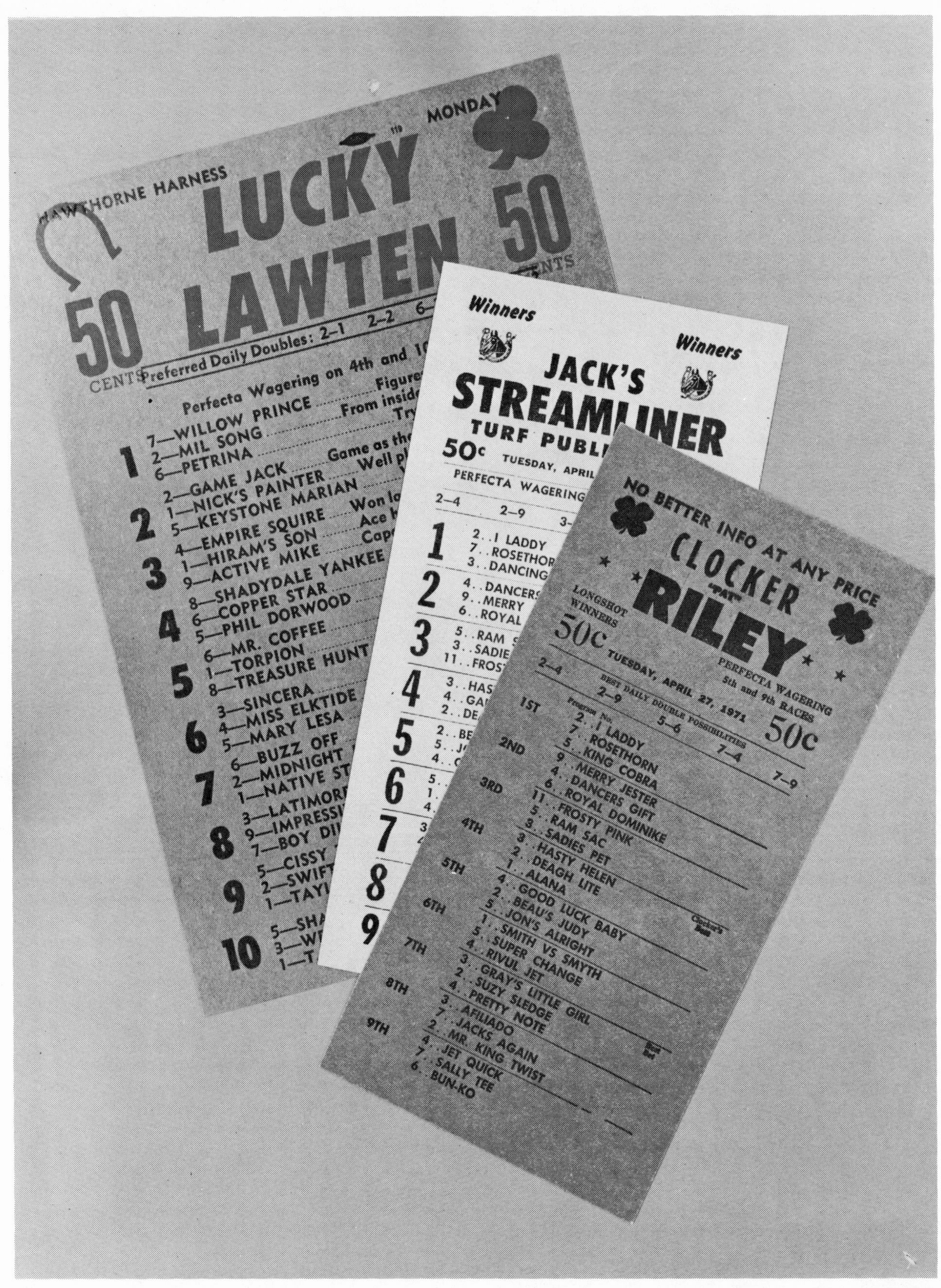

Courtesy Illinois Sports News

The public selector works under a great handicap in that he has no opportunity to pass a race as unplayable—he has to make a selection for every race, every day.

probably run into systems. Some can be good and quite profitable. Others are so ridiculous as to be laughable. If you have to play a system, look for one that suits your style, tinker with it a bit, try it out on paper and, *only* after it has shown a profit, try it out at the track. Most systems fail in one simple respect: they don't allow for judgment, and the people who use them never learn to make judgments. We hope that the system we show you in this book will help you become a better *handicapper,* not system player. Meanwhile we have gathered seven of the best systems we have ever seen. Each is based on a somewhat different premise, but on certain sound handicapping principles. Applying some judgments and modifying them to take into account your personal idiosyncracies (as your handicapping skills increase) could make any of the systems effective for you. Even if followed rigidly, without judgment, you'll be better off, simply because you'll be required to learn spot play by passing up certain races.

System #1
Easy Win

The horse that wins a race without over-extending itself is usually a great bet in its next outing. If the handicapper has kept result charts, it is easy to determine the manner in which the horse won, as the race is described as "won easily," "won handily (without heavy pressure)," "won going away." If result charts aren't available, we must rely on the past performance records, which aren't as accurate in that there is no precise information about the horse's performance. However, a last race like the following indicates that the animal won with so little difficulty that it should have plenty of energy left for another winning effort.

Jun 15-70^{6} Det 6f 1:11 ft 4¾ 116 1½ 1^{2} 1^{2} 1^{6} GADDIS KA^{2} 5000 93

Naturally, there are restrictions to using this system. The theory of the Easy Win is that the horse able to win in this manner is in top form, and we are going to capitalize on it in the next race. Therefore, we require that today's race is no longer than two weeks from the winning one. Actually, the best indication that a horse will be a repeater is when he is sent to the post within seven days of the easy win. Another consideration is the competition the animal faces in the next race. To avoid impossibly low odds, the trainer often enters his horse in a higher class race. Most experts allow a race horse to compete in a claiming race that is 20 percent higher than its last, so a jump from a $5,000 to a $6,000 claimer is permissible. Allowance races are harder to calculate, but consistency seems a reliable guide—our horse can move up in class to any level as long as its consistency (money earned) is as high as the highest rating in the race. If another horse has a higher consistency but is running at the wrong distance or is obviously in bad form, we will back the repeater.

System #2
The Consistent Horse

Because of the form cycle and the temperament of the thoroughbred animal, a truly consistent horse is like money in the bank. By combining this reliability with recent activity and eliminating fractious youngsters and tiring oldsters, there is a profitable system that can be developed. You won't get a lot of action from this system because this degree of reliability is rare in the racing world. In addition, most winners are favorites and don't pay exceptionally high prices. You will probably find most of your plays coming from allowance races and better class claiming races.

The rules are: In any race for three-year-olds and older, bet the horse who shows at least ten races in his past performance; has finished no worse than second in at least five of those outings; has won at least three of the races; has either raced and finished second or better in the last ten days or shows an exceptional workout in the last four days.

The only exceptions to this system are: If the animal is moving up more than 25 percent in claiming price—pass the race; if the horse is a filly against males—pass the race; if the horse is a three-year-old against older horses early in the year—pass the race; and if the horse is moving to a totally unfamiliar distance—pass the race.

This system has sound handicapping rules behind it and could find several really sound favorites a week, but no more.

System #3
Better Than The Favorite

In addition to the fact that favorites win roughly one of three races, it is also a fact that the second choice in the betting wins roughly one of five races. Sometimes the second choice can be an excellent overlay if the crowd is on a false favorite. The prices are rewarding with this system, and profits are available. Once again, bets arise no more than several times per week.

The rule is: In races of $5,000 or higher, bet the second choice on the "tote" board if the horse is a male; won its last race within the last two weeks; and the favorite either did not win its last race or the odds on the favorite are 6-5 or higher.

The exceptions to this rule are: If the second favorite is a three-year-old or older than eight and the favorite is a four-, five-, or six-year-old—pass the race; if the favorite is running a familiar distance and the second choice is running an unfamiliar distance—pass the race.

Following this system won't get you a lot of action, but will give the satisfaction of being right when the crowd is wrong.

System #4
When The Consensus Is Right

As we said earlier, many public handicappers are quite competent. This system is based on finding a horse that has been picked by a majority of public selectors and merits the selection. The horses spotted by this system are usually sound favorites and win a high percentage of their races. Consensus works best at major tracks where the handicappers devote the most time and attention. A feature of this system is that it finds about twice as many plays as the previously discussed systems.

So, for those of you who believe in the abilities of Sweeps, Hermis, Trackman and the others, here are the rules for a system based on the public selectors: In any race for three-year-olds and other, in classes of $5,000 or higher, play the Consensus choice if it is five points higher than the second place Consensus choice, and if the horse has had *both* one race and one workout within the last week.

As usual, the exceptions are to avoid playing fillies or mares against males, a horse running at a new distance, three-year-olds early in the year, or eight-year-olds against four-, five- or six-year-olds.

This system should put you on solid favorites by letting the professionals do most of your handicapping for you.

By playing any one or all in combination, these systems should accomplish two things: teach you the patience of spot play and show you the value of sound handicapping so that you can do it for yourself.

Photo courtesy Sportsman's Park, Cicero, Ill.

The form cycle and temperament of the Standardbred animal make a truly consistent horse like money in the bank.

THE WINNING SYSTEM

The Husseys, John and Anne, are an attractive young married couple, with a comfortable income from regular employment.

The Husseys have a hobby.

It's a profitable hobby that makes them a lot of money.

It's betting on the horses.

When the Husseys bet on the horses, they like to win. Sometimes they lose, but they wind up the year's betting with a handsome profit.

They make this profit by use of a method of handicapping they've worked out for themselves.

Their method of handicapping is not entirely original. They've taken various "systems" and discarded what they regarded as weaknesses, improved upon what they thought were strong points.

They have found voids in most handicapping systems and have tried to fill them.

They find horse handicapping an interesting if not always exact science, and they study it. They find the study fun—profitable fun.

They're not always right—and when they make mistakes, they try to profit from their errors. They don't make the same mistake twice.

In their development of their hitherto-unpublished handicapping system, they have used the race track as a nationwide laboratory, trying through trial and error to reach what they recognize must be an unobtainable goal—a perfect handicapping system.

They don't have it. They don't believe that anyone ever will have a perfect handicapping system.

What they have is, for them, a winning system. It wins more money than it loses—substantially more.

How much it will win for anyone else depends on the capability with which it is applied. Among other things, it depends on judgment—judgment backed with knowledge and experience. Like a computer, their system is no better than the information that's fed into it.

They say flatly that there's no such thing as a "get rich quick" scheme to beat the races. They have four basic premises that the would-be follower in their footsteps must accept before he even begins to learn their Winning System.

1. A knowledge of handicapping is essential.
2. Sometimes the rules don't apply.
3. Beating the horses on paper is a lot easier than winning at the track.
4. It takes money to make money.

The Husseys are not only good at using their system but are articulate about it, so let's permit them to explain it in their own words. From this point on through to the final summation of their horse-betting operation, they will give you their observations and findings—direct, one might say, from the Husseys' mouths.

A Knowledge Of Handicapping Is Essential

After more years of study and harder work than we ever put in through college, we have developed a library of over 30 books, a file of five years' back issues of Racing Forms and a thorough knowledge of what makes winning horses win and losing horses lose. To try to summarize this to such an extent that you can duplicate our efforts is like asking a chemist to give you a short course in Chemistry that would prepare you to work in the lab as a practicing chemist. A self-respecting chemist will tell you it can't be done.

If you are really serious about it, read everything you can get your hands on, especially the Tom Ainslie books, *Horse Sense, Science in Betting* and *Scientific Handicapping*. You don't have to be a veterinarian, but unless you know the difference between the normal healthy exuberance shown by a keyed-up thoroughbred and "fractiousness" or "rankness" you can misinterpret an awful lot of on-track post parade performance. Similarly, if you don't understand the difference between Starter Handicaps and true Handicap races, you will make quite a few errors in judgement. Also, when you understand the races, you will find yourself playing some maiden races, usually Maiden Special Wts. for two year olds, but passing most maiden races, certainly all low-price maiden claiming events for older horses. It's the knowledge of handicapping that can tell you the most important element—when a race is playable and when it should be passed as unplayable.

If, on the other hand, you're not that serious about it and enjoy racing as a sport and like to have some action going, then the rules we give you will be guidelines that will put you on sound favorites, catch an occasional longshot, and show you a way to handle "toss-up" races.

Sometimes The Rules Don't Apply

But if you're the rail bird who likes to spend some spare time learning something new, the rules we give you will help you to develop as a handicapper. You will end up adopting and modifying them for your own use. You may, for example, pick a horse in a maiden special weight event, even though the horse has never run the distance. Or you may stretch the one-month rule to include a classy horse whose past performance has shown he can maintain top form without racing frequently. These judgment decisions will be made on the basis of sound handicapping principles, even though they violate strict rules. For example, when should we consider a horse who raced 32 days ago? Or when to include a horse who finished 8¼ lengths off the pace? Obviously, there is nothing magical and mystical about 30 days or eight lengths. They are just arbitrary guidelines that tend to give solid choices, primarily because most winning horses share these characteristics.

For a principle, let's say we use these rules until you feel you have enough knowledge of handicapping to break them.

It's Easier To Beat The Horses On Paper Than To Win At The Track

Several factors make this true, not the least of which is the emotion in laying out actual cash. In addition, leaving your handicapping till you get to the track places you under an unusual time pressure, complicated by a noisy, excited atmosphere. If you can, have most of your decisions made at home so you can relax and enjoy the spectacle around you.

And don't let yourself be swayed by tips, touts or totes. If you have made a firm decision on a horse, stick to it. Probably this is the biggest difference between at the track and on the paper. There are no outside pressures on you when you sit comfortably at home. Also, don't change your handicapping rules at the track because of losses. Consistency is not only important in the horses' performance; it is important in *your* performance. If you feel your handicapping needs some changes, go home and work them out there. The place to experiment with new aircraft design is on the ground, in a wind tunnel with a model, not with a 747 full of passengers in the air.

Keep your emotions in check. Don't allow yourself the luxury of too much anger or too much good cheer (bottled or any other). Remember the pickpockets, pimps and penny-ante crooks. The track attracts them like maggots to a dead horse. The HBPA tries, but can't keep them all out.

It Takes Money To Make Money

One of the ways to help keep your emotions in check is to make sure that any single loss is unimportant to your overall program. The important attitude to maintain is that you expect a certain percent of profit over a time, but that you also expect losing races, losing days and maybe (God forbid) losing weeks.

The amount of a bet obviously depends on the bankroll, and the necessary bankroll is basic to the kind of performance you can display. But remember one thing, at the rate of track losses to state and local taxes, it is a cinch that prices will continue to go up. Right now, you can expect a day at the track to cost you $10 to $20, depending on your consumption of food and booze and on your frugality. And consider the $2 bettor who puts $18 through the mutual windows. Even if he achieves 50 percent return on investment (which is better than he should expect) his $9 winnings barely allow him to break even. Read the section on money management and let it sink home.

Now that we've made ourselves clear on a basic philosophy, let's get down to a discussion of the actual rules we've developed to make our system profitable for us. Some of them will be self-explanatory, and some will require clarification. We'll start with one that is, to us, elementary.

Elimination Rules

THIS TRACK RULE—Eliminate any horse that has not had one race at today's track. The race must have been run this season.

Thoroughbred racehorses are extremely sensitive. While some of them enjoy a change of scene and win their first race at a new track, most horses require a period of adjustment and don't show good form until they have raced several times at the new course. Furthermore, the surfaces of tracks vary. Some are soft and deep, which reduces speed; others are hard and firm, allowing greater speed but causing a tremendous impact, a disadvantage to horses with especially weak hooves. To avoid as many unknowns as possible, start by eliminating "first starters." The one exception is a horse competing in a stakes or handicap race, which draws the best racers in the country. Such a horse is accustomed to travel; it is often flown across country and raced after only a short rest.

DISTANCE RULE—Eliminate any horse that has not run today's distance at today's track.

The measure of distance in thoroughbred racing is the furlong (220 yards); there are 8 furlongs in a mile. Distances are divided into two categories: Sprints are races of 7 furlongs or less; a route is any race longer than 7 furlongs.

At most tracks, the distances vary from 3 furlong races for two-year-olds to 2½ mile endurance races. The most common sprint distance is 6 furlongs; the most common route is $1\frac{1}{16}$ mile.

Some of the very best horses are able to win both sprint and route races, but this is such a rare ability, that a horse will be eliminated from contention if it has never run today's distance. Peter Burrell, an authority on thoroughbred racing and breeding, made the following statement about horses and distance.

"Races are run at all distances from 5 furlongs to 2½ miles, requiring different types of horse, the sprinter being as different from the stayer (router) as a dairy cow from a beef cow.

"So high is the standard required today at each

distance that the individual horse has become specialized for that particular distance, and we must regard the horse which is top class at all distances as something of a freak.

"It is not difficult to breed sprinters, but it is an undisputed fact that the more speed one breeds into a horse, the less distance he stays, and with the stayers . . . one can breed them to stay further, but they then begin to lack the turn of speed so essential to the final dash to the winning post."

The distance elimination rule is a problem when the distance is decreased or extended by only ½-furlong or 110 yards. A good, fast 6 furlong sprinter can probably handle a 5½ or 7 furlong race. In most cases the horse will probably have run today's distance, and the race will appear in the past performance record.

If horses are suited to a certain distance, why are they often entered in races that are obviously not their distance, in which they perform wretchedly? In cheaper races, the trainer may enter a horse at the wrong distance so that its past performance record is deceptively bad. The ignorant bettor notes only that, in its last race, the horse finished tenth, 20 lengths behind the winner. In fact, this horse may be in peak form and when returned to the proper distance, it wins, paying a fantastic price. Some sprinters are entered in routes to develop stamina, while a router's speed is sharpened when it tries to keep up with the speedsters in a sprint.

CONSISTENCY RULE—Eliminate any horse whose consistency rating is not within 5 points of the highest rating, unless **the horse's speed rating is as high or one point lower than the highest speed rating.**

As usual, Handicap and Stakes races present a problem. Because of the vast difference in the quality of the competitors in these races, there may be a range of 50 points in the consistency ratings. Usually, other elimination rules will exclude the inferior horse from contention.

WHAT IS CLASS? Horsemen have equated class with speed, with breeding, and with intangibles, such as courage and stamina. Many people insist that a horse senses his class—that he will not compete with a superior animal, that he will beat inferior horses in spite of his condition. The most reasonable approach to this dilemma is that a horse's class is determined by the level of his performance and measured by the amount of money the animal has won. Because the size of the winner's purse increases with the quality of the race, we will use consistency (money won) as our guide. The variety of races offered at most tracks allows a horse to compete at his class level and, technically, to win enough money during the season to pay for his keep. Therefore, class is not constant. It is not unusual to find an ex-Stakes winner, now nearly crippled, running in the cheapest claiming races. *Stymie,* one of America's great racehorses, was claimed from a $1,500 race and went on to win $918,485. Cinderella horses appear rarely, but emphasize the importance of flexibility in calculating a thoroughbred's class.

Top Guarantee * **114** **B. g (1963), by We Guarantee—Rythmette, by Brown King.**
Breeder, A. L. Erwin (La.). 1971 5 1 0 0 $3,165
Owner, C. J. & L. Matherne. Trainer, S. Bearb. **$7,250** 1970 22 5 4 6 $17,596

Jan30-716FG	6 f 1:10⅘ft	13	122	48	611	816	816	TheallS2	Alw 79	SpeedyJake115 Ray'sLaw TicketBoss	8
Jan23-7110FG	1-40 1:41⅕ft	9½	122	41¼	32	52½	57¾	TheallS5	Alw 79	Karate114 Spider'sQueen LandingMan	8
Jan16-717FG	6 f 1:12⅗ft	20	112	46½	46	33	1h	TheallS6	Alw 86	TopGuarantee112 Karate Atchafalaya	11
Jan 9-714FG	6 f 1:13 m	20	114	66½	76	711	611	BourqueK1	Alw 73	H'rk theHer'ld120 R'y'sLaw L'nd'gM'n	7
Jan 2-717FG	6 f 1:13 gd	4	114	42	75¼	79½	611	SoirezW1	Alw 73	ThirtyDashes 110 Appoloquil Karate	9
Dec26-707FG	6 f 1:12⅖ft	6	113	52¼	51¼	32½	2no	SoirezW2	Alw 87	Ray'sLaw 113 Top G'r'ntee Atch'f'l'ya	8
Dec12-706FG	6 f 1:12 ft	3	114	54½	54½	810	79¾	TheallS6	Alw 79	LandingMan117 Karate SirRoderick	8
Dec 5-706FG	6 f 1:11 ft	4	115	62½	44½	34½	37	SoirezW6	Alw 87	H'k theH'r'd121 SirR'd'r'k T'pG'r'tee	10
Nov28-708FG	6 f 1:11⅘ft	17	116	43	42½	42¼	32	TheallS3	Alw 88	Alw'ysH're115 H'k theH'r'd T'pG'tee	7

Top Guarantee's consistency rating is 6. To obtain this rating, divide the amount of money won this year by the number of races the horse has run. If he has run fewer than five races this year, use the average of the two year total.

SPEED RULE—Eliminate any horse whose speed rating is not within five points of the highest rating.

SPEED—It is obvious the winner of the race is the horse who crosses the finish line in the fastest time. However, this winner is not necessarily the fastest horse in the race. The authors of *Scientific Handicapping* say, "It should be obvious that the horse which has previously run the best time will not always win a given race. The problem, of course, is to predict when the horse with the best speed will win. In such situations, speed in recent races is a most important factor in the selection of winners. True, other factors must also be considered. For example, class may be more important in a certain race than recent speed, and in another, weight may be a prime consideration." The weighing of the various factors is really the crux of handicapping. So, we must try to establish a reasonable speed rule to apply to each competitor and use it in conjunction with all handicapping factors.

WHAT IS THE SPEED RATING? In the past performance record, a horse receives a speed rating for each race he runs. The track's record time for each distance is 100. At the end of a race, one point is deducted for each 1/5-second that a horse finished slower than the record time. Theoretically it takes a horse 1/5-second to travel its own length, approximately ten feet, and five lengths per second is a convenient measurement. Actually, at top speed, a horse covers from six to seven lengths per second. If a horse breaks the record, his rating is greater than 100, but the new record is not effective until the start of the new season.

At Fair Grounds, the track record for 6 furlongs is 1:09.4/5. On January 30th, *Full Steam Ahead* ran 6 furlongs in 1:11 3/5, 9-fifths slower than the record time, earning a speed rating of 91.

A major problem in analyzing speed is that a race-

Full Steam Ahead * 117 B. g (1966), by Admiral's Voyage—La Lique, by Reneged.
Breeder. J. R. Cowden (Ky.). 1971 4 1 0 2 $3,054
Owner, C. & C. Stable, Inc. Trainer, J. H. Samuel. $7,250 1970 24 6 3 3 $15,907

Date	Dist.	Time	Track	Odds	Wt.					Jockey	Claim	Speed	Finishers	Field
Jan30-71 4FG	6 f	1:11 3/5	ft	9½	113	1h	2h	1h	1 1	MoyersL 7	7000	91	F'llSt'mAh'd113 Amb'rixB'i C'tch'rP't	7
Jan16-71 3FG	6 f	1:12 3/5	gd	4	114	5 2¼	3 3	7 8½	5 6	YoungJF 8	6250	80	Amb'rixBoi 116 R'si'sRogue Pr'ceG'l't	8
Jan 9-71 6FG	6 f	1:13 2/5	m	14	112	5 6¼	5 4½	3 4	3 8¼	YoungJF 7	7000	74	JayR'm116 L'd'yEv'ns'n FullSt'mAh'd	10
Jan 2-71 6FG	6 f	1:12 4/5	gd	9¾	113	7 3¼	5 3¼	4 4½	3 4	YoungJF 9	7000	81	LittleA.115 JayRoam FullSt'mAhead	11
Dec23-70 6FG	6 f	1:12	ft	3¾	115	4 1¼	2 1	3nk	1no	YoungJF 11	5000	89	F'llSt'mAh'd115 Limetime N'groBarro	12
Dec16-70 5FG	6 f	1:14	sl	5¾	112	2 1	3 1	2½	1no	YoungJF 4	5000	79	FullSt'mAh'd112 B'ttlePick Pollamber	12
Dec 5-70 4FG	6 f	1:12 1/5	ft	3¾	116	6 3½	6 3½	5 4½	5 5½	HolmesD 5	6500	82	Deadwood 114 Tudorfib Croydon	10
Dec 2-70 6FG	6 f	1:12	ft	4-5	▴117	3nk	1½	2 1	2no	Rub'coP 9	c5000	89	M.H.'sG'l'y115 F'lSt'mAh'd M't'rM'ha	12
Sep25-70 7HP	6 f	1:11	ft	5¼	119	1 1½	1h	2h	2h	Rubb'coP 8	6250	99	Cambrooke119 FullSt'mAh'd Charcap	9
Sep 7-70 5HP	6½ f	1:18	ft	3¼	115	2 2	1½	1 1	1h	SoirezW 6	5000	91	F'll SteamAhead115 Charcap Dr.J.Lee	10

horse is capable of running at top speed for appprox-imately 3/8 of a mile or 3 furlongs. In races for two-year-olds at the 3 furlong distance, we can rely on speed almost exclusively. However, in races beyond that distance we must consider the pace or the strategy of the race.

How will we use speed as an elimination rule? Many handicappers consider speed the most important factor in selecting winners. In some cases it is. In a rare race, one horse is clearly outstanding—it is in peak form, has the top consistency rating, is running its best distance, and is significantly faster than its competitors. This horse usually wins, but at miserable odds. Now what about the remaining eight races on the day's program? The first step is to find each animal's best speed rating for today's distance at this track. If the horse has not had a race on a fast track, add five points to the best speed rating on the off track. This is arbitrary, but unfortunately there are not reliable rules for each situation.

Although a horse's speed varies from race to race, most winning times are not more than one second or five points better than an animal's best time during the past six weeks. Only one in about 50 races is won by a horse whose winning form is not evidenced in the past performance record. After eliminations, there may be several horses whose speed and current form will get them to the winner's circle. Hopefully, the probable pace of the race will give one contender an edge.

If horses were machines and their performances constant, it would be easy to pick a winner, but not much fun. Racehorses run in definite form cycles—even the best horse in dull form performs dully. It is necessary to determine a horse's present form (physical condition) if we are to estimate his performance in today's race. Unfortunately, the horse can't tell us if he isn't up to par, but the past performance record should supply this information.

ONE MONTH RULE—Eliminate any horse that has not raced within one month of today's race.

Statistics prove the importance of recent activity in establishing current form. Two-thirds of all winners have had one race within the past 15 days; one-third of all winners have raced within the past seven days. Generally, a racehorse maintains his winning form for 30 days. This does not mean that he runs once a week and wins four races—horses rarely win two races in succession. However, for the 30-day period the animal is in sharp condition and able to compete the best that he is able. Again, the "Big" horses stay sharp for a longer time and often win after a month's layoff, but, for the common beast, we require a race within 30 days of today's race.

UNSOUND RULE—Eliminate any horse when the Past Performance notes that an animal "bled, ran sore, was lame" in its last race.

The horse may be perfectly sound for today's outing, but we will eliminate him. If the horse's past performance shows that he is clearly superior, has the highest consistency, best speed rating, etc., we may pass the race. But we will not take a chance on him.

NO WIN RULE—Except for maiden races, we eliminate any horse that has not won a race.

It is foolish to bet that an animal will do today, what it has been unable to do in the past. Again, some races are for such nags that the non-winner may look like a super-star. The best decision in this case is to pass the race.

WHAT IS FORM? Before covering the remaining three elimination rules, a discussion of form, the horse's present condition, is in order.

FORM—The past performance chart shown here is a good example of the form cycle.

JANUARY 20: Delbert ran an uneventful 6 furlong race. There is no evidence that he exerted himself; in fact, the two lengths gain in the stretch probably wasn't the result of increased speed but because other horses were slowing down. At any rate, he

7th Fair Grounds

6 FURLONGS. (Tudor Scott, Nov. 27, 1969, 1:09⅘, 3, 116.) Claiming. Purse $3,000. 4-year-olds and upward. 4-year-olds, 119 lbs.; older, 120 lbs. Non-winners of three races since Dec. 10 allowed 2 lbs.; two races since then, 4 lbs.; a race, 6 lbs. (Claiming races for $4,000 or less not considered.) Claiming price, $5,200.

COUPLED: LAZURE and ISPEEKFORMYSELF.

Delbert **116** B. g (1966), by Semi-pro—Errard You, by Errard King.
Breeder, Charlie Stuart Olds (Ind.). 1971 3 1 0 0 $1,680
Owner, W. A. Lofton. Trainer, J. R. Smith. $5,200 1970 5 0 0 2 $837

Feb 2-715FG	6 f 1:11⅘ft	6½	116	65½	63	3nk	12½	WhitedDE8	4500	90	Delbert116	FrenchWag'n	Rossi'sR'g'e	11
Jan26-716FG	6 f 1:11⅘ft	31	113	3nk	2h	3½	62¾	Val'zanF12	4500	87	Oc'nsAh'd116	M.H'sG'l'xy	R'nForD'dy	12
Jan20-715FG	6 f 1:11⅕ft	20	114	105¾	119	119¼	87¼	HolmesD1	5000	86	Croydon 114	DarkStarJr.	DoGoAbbey	12
Dec29-704FG	6 f 1:13⅕sy	4½	112	56½	33	32¼	35½	HolmesD4	2500	77	FrontRowSeat113	ComedySh'w	D'lb't	10
Feb14-703FG	1-40 1:41⅘ft	2½	115	34	37	36½	59½	WhitedDE1	6200	74	Frisked 111	Rush Home	Louk'sLick	7
Jan31-704FG	6 f 1:11⅘ft	20	116	32½	43	55	65½	MenardN4	7500	85	Deadwood110	FreeT'mble	F'ncyAff'r	7
Jan20-707FG	6 f 1:11⅗ft	19	118	53	31	41½	34	HolmesD8	7500	88	Com'on Along 116	Kendare	Delbert	8
Jan13-706F.G	6 f 1:14⅘hy	8¾	118	67	713	610	511	HolmesD3	7500	65	G'ttinOld118	J'ksAg'n116	Com'onAl'ng	8
Dec18-697F.G	6 f 1:12 ft	7¾	112	54½	65	67	75½	HolmesD3	9500	84	Jr's.Deck115	GentleGiant117	KemJr.	9

Jan 30 FG 3f ft :37⅖b **Jan 7 FG 5f ft 1:03b** **Dec 23 FG 4f ft :49b**

finished eighth, 7¼ lengths behind the winner.

JANUARY 26: In this race, *Delbert* showed marked improvement. Although his speed rating increased by only one point, 1/5 second, he managed to make the pace (stay with the leaders) for the first three calls of the race, and finished 2¾ lengths behind the winner. We are concerned with lengths behind, not position of finish, because there can be many horses bunched at the wire separated by only a few lengths. The important fact here is that the horse increased his speed at each stage of the race and maintained enough stamina to stay within three lengths of the winner at the finish. We cannot be accurate without the actual times for each call, but we can know that the speed today was greater than in the previous race and that the horse showed a great willingness to run—a sure indication of fitness.

FEBRUARY 2: The payoff. *Delbert* won this 6 furlong sprint by 2½ lengths in 1:11 4/5 seconds, which is three speed rating points faster than his last race. Most fans didn't recognize the improvement in this horse's form because they sent him off at odds of 6½ to 1 so that he paid $15 for a $2 ticket. It is possible that another horse had superior consistency, speed, etc., but *Delbert* should certainly have been considered a strong contender and the odds prove that he wasn't.

SEVENTH RACE
FG 44572
February 10, 1971

6 FURLONGS. (Tudor Scott, Nov. 27, 1969, 1:09⅘, 3, 116.) Claiming. Purse $3,000. 4-year-olds and upward. 4-year-olds, 119 lbs.; older, 120 lbs. Non-winners of three races since Dec. 10 allowed 2 lbs.; two races since then, 4 lbs.; a race, 6 lbs. (Claiming races for $4,000 or less not considered.) Claiming price, $5,200.
Value to winner $1,800; second, $600; third, $330; fourth, $180; fifth, $90. Mutuel Pool, $38,350.

Index	Horses	Eq't A Wt	PP	St	¼	½	Str	Fin	Jockeys	Cl'g Pr.	Owners	Odds to $1
44505FG2	—French Wagon	b4 114	8	2	2½	22	21½	1h	W Soirez	5200	River City Stable Inc	11.60
44505FG1	—Delbert	b5 116	1	6	6½	61	42	2h	D E Whited	5200	W A Lofton	4.10
44511FG2	—Lazure	b6 111	5	1	12½	14	15	34	A Richard5	5200	Mrs J A Behler	6.40
44511FG6	—Oceans Ahead	b5 116	3	3	35	31	3h	41	J Nichols	5200	H R Cournoyer	20.80
44348FG9	—Fantara	b3 111	4	5	8	71	65	5no	F Valdizan	5200	L Pike	24.10
44376FG4	—Jons Buddy	b5 114	6	4	41½	4h	51½	63	N Menard	5200	A Wellman	25.20
44321FG5	—Jay Roam	b6 116	7	7	71½	8	71	74	P Rubbicco	5200	M H Van Berg Stable Inc	1.00
44515FG6	—Es Kup	b4 111	2	8	5½	52	8	8	D Holmes	5200	J P Dorignac Jr	5.20

Time, :22, :45⅗, 1:11. Track fast.

$2 Mutuel Prices:			
8-FRENCH WAGON	25.20	8.20	5.20
1-DELBERT		4.60	3.80
5-LAZURE			4.80

B. c, by Conestoga—Pilleuse, by Vandale. Trainer, D. Cazaubon. Bred by R. Levi (Fla.).
IN GATE—3:50. OFF AT 3:50 CENTRAL STANDARD TIME. Start good. Won driving.
FRENCH WAGON bore in sharply at the start, raced nearest the pace throughout, closed determinedly along the outside and was up in the last stride. DELBERT finished with a rush between horses and just missed. LAZURE used superior speed to establish a long lead, began tiring leaving the eighth pole, and could not last. OCEANS AHEAD turned in a sharp effort. FANTARA closed mildly. JAY ROAM broke in a tangle, then was bothered as the winner cut over and failed to recover. ES KUP bean sluggishly and was not a threat.
Overweight—Es Kup, 3 pounds; Fantara, 3; French Wagon, 1.
Es Kup claimed by W. L. Roth, trainer A. J. Broussard. **Scratched—Ispeekformyself.**

FEBRUARY 10: Although *Delbert* didn't win this race, he showed ever better form than on February 2. He stayed with the leaders or close throughout and finished second by only a head. His time here was 1:11 flat, which gave him a speed rating of 94. The result chart states that he "finished with a rush between horses and just missed." In these last two races, *Delbert* has shown peak, winning form. It is possible that these efforts have depleted his energy, and that he will not have the stamina to compete as successfully in his next outing.

Naturally, each horse performs differently, and form cycles are rarely obvious, step-by-step progressions from win to win. Remember, though, that we have already eliminated most of the competitors, using our broader handicapping rules, and at this point should be working with only a few contenders. We will use the following rules to eliminate further.

EIGHT LENGTH RULE—Eliminate any horse that did not finish within eight lengths of the winner in its last race.

If a horse wasn't able to finish within eight lengths of the winner in his last race, he was either "out for exercise" (training for a future race) or in such dull form that we won't expect sufficient improvement today to allow him a win. The horse who doesn't perk up in the stretch is not interested in racing and won't compete until he shows some willingness to run. We allow one exception to this rule: If the horse did not finish within eight lengths of the winner, we do *not* exclude him if his speed rating is as high or one point lower than the highest in today's race.

LOSS IN THE STRETCH RULE—Eliminate any horse that in its last race lost more than ¾ lengths in the stretch.

The horse who loses ground in the stretch doesn't have the necessary stamina to maintain the terrific drive to the finish. There are many "alibis" for this failure. The horse may have been "boxed" with no racing room. The jockey may have blown it by allowing the horse to keep up a rugged pace in the backstretch, so that there was nothing left for the stretch drive. The horse may have been forced to run wide around the turn which added many yards to the distance. Most often though, the animal is in dull form and unable to make a bid in the stretch. Whatever reason applies, we must assume that he needs another race or two as sharpeners for a winning effort. The exception to this rule is that we don't exclude a horse on the loss-in-the-stretch rule if his speed rating is as high or one point lower than the highest.

FINISH IN THE MONEY RULE— Eliminate any horse that in its last race did not finish in the money (first, second or third).

This is a rather arbitrary rule, but at this point if we are left with more than one or two contenders, they must be fairly even. Our reasoning here is that the horse in the best condition has made an extra effort to gain some of the purse money in its last race, and therefore has shown a willingness to run, which indicates it will probably improve today. Again, we can't eliminate a horse if his speed rating is as high or one point higher than the highest.

Extra Points

Hopefully, we now have one horse who looks like a winner. However, there may be two, three, even four animals who refuse to be eliminated. This situation is always difficult, mainly because judgment enters here. Can the race be dutched? The answer is only evident a few minutes before the horses leave the gate, which doesn't leave any time for further handicapping if odds are too low for a dutch. Another frustrating factor is that we often develop hunches at this point. We may have overheard a conversation about Horse A's lameness today. The waiter's cousin is B's trainer, and invariably someone points out that the race is fixed —a charity event for C's owner who is in precarious financial straits.

It's extremely hard to be objective and ignore these authoritative statements. But if we have followed the Elimination Rules it would be foolish to blow it now, so we'll continue and use the "Extra Point" system.

THE JOCKEY—A successful American jockey is among the world's highest paid athletes. What is success? In one year, approximately 1,500 jockeys actually ride in races—500 of them never win. Two percent of these riders win nearly 20 percent of all races or ten times as many as would be expected.

A jockey is paid $50 for a winning ride, $40 for a second place, $30 for coming in third, and $25 for sitting on the horse as it runs around the course. In addition, he receives ten percent of the purse money. The majority of riders make about $5,000 a year; the successful ones do phenomenally well—ten percent of a $150,000 purse is not a bad payoff for a few minutes' work. Naturally, it's not that simple.

A good jockey works diligently. For some, it's almost impossible to maintain the necessary low weight —hours spent in steam rooms can make a jockey so weak that he can hardly climb on his mount. Most good riders don't have a weight problem; they are intelligent men, as well as talented. They must know their horse's running style and be able to anticipate what the competitors will do. Horseraces are often won by a nose; on rare occasions, the photo at the finish shows a dead heat.

The jockey must decide how he will get his horse out of the gate. If the animal is a front runner who must lead the pack and has drawn an outside post position, he must expend precious early speed covering the extra distance to the rail. The rider has to judge the pace accurately; if the speed is too fast, the horse must be held back to conserve energy for the stretch drive, not an easy task considering that the average thoroughbred weighs 1,000 pounds and reaches speeds of approximately 35 miles per hour. The jockey must keep the horse in the clear so that he won't be blocked when he's ready to make his bid. He also has to have the guts to push his animal through narrow openings without impeding other riders.

The apprentice jockey or "bug" is inexperienced, so in compensation is allowed a weight advantage of from 4 to 10 pounds, a significant reduction for most horses. It is almost impossible to determine if the weight factor offsets the bug's lack of racing experience.

Extra Point—Because the top jockeys have their pick of the best horses, we give an Extra Point to the horse whose jockey is in the top ten at the track. This information is given in the Daily Racing Form and also in the program. The horse receives an Extra Point if

his jockey is not in the top ten but has won with the horse at this track in the past.

WEIGHT—Technically, weight is the most important factor in handicapping because it has been used since the sport began in the attempt to equalize the competition in horseracing. In this country, the Track Handicapper or Racing Secretary, whoever creates the conditions for each race of the meet, uses the official Jockey Club Scale of Weights which sets guidelines for weights, according to the horse's age and the distance to be run. Since the object of weight assignment is to burden the horse with the best chance to win, it is difficult to judge the effect of weight on performance. However, horsemen agree, generally, on the following facts:

1. In a sprint, a horse carrying four extra pounds* is slowed 1/5 second, which means he loses a length.
2. At a mile, three extra pounds has the same effect.
3. At a mile and an eighth, two extra pounds are effective.
4. At a mile and a quarter, one pound is sufficient to slow the animal's speed by 1/5 second.

If the past performance chart shows that a horse has not been able to carry a certain weight successfully, we should not expect him to handle that or an increased amount today. We will use weight as an **Extra Point—If a horse is carrying 4 pounds less than his normal weight in a sprint race, he gets an Extra Point; if there is an 8 pound difference, he gets two points. The same Extra Points can be awarded for longer races using the "pounds for distance" list.**

However, Jockey Club, Racing Secretaries and pundits notwithstanding, let's look at some aspects of weight that are seldom considered.

First, the weight of a ½-ton animal can vary as much as 10 pounds, depending on his feeding and activity level. Yet the weight of the horse is never considered in handicapping.

Second, let's equate the horse and jockey to a man carrying a pack on his back. When a 1,000 pound horse increases his assigned weight from 110 to 115 pounds, it's the same as a 150 pound man running with a 16½ pound pack on his back being asked to increase it to 17¼ pounds. Is this extra ¾-pound going to be a significant factor? Try it and let us know, but we doubt if it will.

The point is, weight can be important, but let's not go overboard for a pound or two when the horse can sweat off that much during the paddock and post parade.

THE TRAINER—The least successful trainers are under tremendous pressures. Most of them are in desperate financial situations and can't afford to give a horse sufficient rest after a grueling race or time to fully recover from an injury. Because small owners must win as many purses as possible just to break even, and the track management must find the horses to fill nine or ten races a day, the trainer is forced to race a horse when it is not ready in a race that it has no chance to win. Often the horse that is run prematurely is permanently injured.

The successful trainer doesn't have these pressures. His owners are usually wealthy men who love and understand horses and can easily afford the upkeep of their animals. Thus the trainer has the great advantage of time necessary to develop each horse so that he can wait for a race in which his animal will have a good chance at the purse.

Extra Point—Naturally, the most talented trainers get the best horses, so we will give an Extra Point to the horse whose trainer is listed in the Top Ten at the track. This information is given in the Daily Racing Form and in the Track Program.

SEX—The Sex categories of thoroughbred racers are the following:

COLT—A male horse four years old or younger.
HORSE—A male horse five years old or older.
GELDING—A male horse, any age, that has been castrated.
RIDGLING—A male horse that has been partially castrated.
FILLY—A female horse four years old or younger.
MARE—A female horse five years of age or older.

The most important decision in the Sex category is if and when to back a female against male competitors. Women's Lib advocates may be offended, but a female must be significantly superior to merit financial support. There are valid reasons for this caution. A female is not as consistent because her sex cycle affects her performance. Also, she does not have the physical endurance of the male which means that often she cannot sustain the drive in the stretch. However, in many races a female is clearly the superior horse and usually pays an excellent price to win because most bettors aren't objective about her abilities. So although we must be careful about the female, we must recognize those instances when she is our Number One horse.

Another sex problem is the difficulty in deciding when to castrate a young horse. The gelding is the most reliable racehorse—even tempered and consistent. *Kelso* is probably the most famous of geldings, earning the "Horse-of-the-Year" title for an unprecedented five years (1960-1964), and winning $1,977,896 during his career. It's true that he may not have been a champion if he hadn't been castrated, but unfortunately, we will never know about his achievement as a sire.

Extra Points—A horse or colt receives one Extra Point. A gelding receives two Extra Points, and a female (against males) receives no extra point.

**The horse's normal weight is the number of pounds he carried in a race he won or in which he finished in the money.*

How Speed Ratings Are Compiled

Speed ratings are based on track records established prior to the current meeting. New track records set at the meeting now in progress will be used for compiling speed ratings at the next session at the same track. When a new track has its inaugural meeting or a new distance is being run, sufficient time will be allowed to compile records on which to base speed ratings. The track record will receive a standard rating of 100—thus, a horse equaling the record will have a speed rating of 100. For each one-fifth second slower than the track record one point is deducted. Therefore, the rating for a horse running his race two and one-fifth seconds slower than the track record receives a speed rating of 89 (100 minus 11).

EXAMPLE

Track record	**1:10**	**Rating figure**	**100**
Winner's time	**1:10⅕**	**Rating**	**99**
Time of second horse	**1:10⅗**		**97**
Time of third horse	**1:11**		**95**
Time of fourth horse	**1:11⅖**		**93**
Time of fifth horse	**1:11⅘**		**91**

One point (the equivalent of one-fifth second) is deducted from the rating for each length the horse is beaten. Thus, a horse beaten four-lengths in a six-furlong race run in 1:11 (rating of 100 where the track record is 1:10) is timed in 1:11⅘, receiving a speed rating of 91.

AGE—The official birthday of the thoroughbred race horse is January regardless of the date of his birth. As a yearling, the thoroughbred begins training, and usually starts his racing career as a two-year-old. A race horse reaches maturity at four years of age, and at five is considered at the peak of his career.

Because of the differences in a horse's abilities at various ages, the conditions of each race specify the age of the contenders. Two-year-olds haven't developed stamina or racing know-how so they must run short distances and cannot compete with older animals. Some three-year-olds are included in races with older horses, but they should be considered cautiously, until they have proved themselves, usually in late summer or fall. After five years of age, a horse is more susceptible to injury, and requires a longer time to recover from an especially hard race, which makes his performance less consistent.

Extra Point—The majority of races are for horses "four-years-old and upward" and we will give a horse an extra point if he is either four or five years of age.

THE WORKOUT—In addition to frequent races (at least one race in fifteen days), the trainer uses the workout to keep his horse in sharp condition. In handicapping, the workout is a definite indication that a horse is in serious training and in top form. Ideally, our horse will have worked every four or five days or three times within a 15-day period. A horse works in one of two ways: Breezing (b), he runs at his own speed without any pressure from the rider; handily (h), the horse runs with light pressure from the rider who uses his hands on the horse's neck to urge speed.

At distances to and including 5 furlongs, a horse works excellently if he covers a furlong in 12 seconds, breezing. If he is working handily, he should cover the distance of the workout in about 1 second less than the breezing time. For instance, the following are excellent times:

3 FURLONGS. 36 b; 35 h.
4 FURLONGS. 48 b; 47 h.
5 FURLONGS. 1.00 b; 59 h.

At distances more than 5 furlongs, the following times are excellent:

6 FURLONGS. 113 b.
7 FURLONGS. 1.27 b.
1 MILE. 1.42 b.

The following additional information about the workout is given in the past performance record.

(g) Horse began workout from the starting gate.
(tr.t) Horse worked on the training track, which is deeper than the main track surface and used for developing stamina.
(M.T.) Horse worked out on the main track.

Example of workouts listed in the *Daily Racing Form.*

FEBRUARY 11: Grand Native worked five furlongs on a fast track in one minute and one second, handily from the starting gate.

JANUARY 16: The horse ran five furlongs on a good (off) track in 1.04, breezing.

Extra Point—A horse receives an Extra Point for three workouts within the past 15 days if he has had one race in the last 15 days. (Workout times does not have to be excellent.) A horse receives an Extra Point for a workout the day before today's race if the time was excellent.

THE PADDOCK—Many excellent handicappers insist that after calculations such as speed, consistency, etc., have been made and we have a number-one

choice on paper, the decision about whether to bet this horse is made only after we have watched his performance in the paddock. It is necessary to get personal here and relate our experiences trying to use what we've "learned" about a horse's appearance before the race. As conscientious handicappers, we have faithfully visited the paddock before buying the ticket on our choice. On only two occasions did this horse look so pathetic that we passed the race; naturally, both horses won. These experiences may not be relevant, but they did teach us one lesson: We cannot judge from looking at a horse whether he is in stress. Each animal has its own style and temperament, and it seems that only a veterinarian can determine a horse with a problem so serious that it won't be able to run. However, since so many people claim success at the paddock stage of handicapping, we'll discuss some of the accepted indications of both good and poor form.

GOOD PADDOCK APPEARANCE—The horse in top shape who is eager to run is not excessively nervous or fractious. He is easily led by his groom and shows an interest in the fans at the rail. His coat gleams, his eyes are bright, his ears are forward. The walk is easy, not mincing and choppy. Naturally, he doesn't limp. (Again, we've sworn that a horse was lame who won a race easily.)

POOR PADDOCK APPEARANCE—Some horses are obviously in stress. They fight their groom every step, kicking, rearing, and tossing their heads. These horses may try to bite (savage) other horses. A sign of undue tension is excessive sweat (called washiness) which appears on the horse's neck and flank. Kidney sweat (white foam) may appear between the horse's rear legs. The nervous horse's ears jerk and may lie flat.

BANDAGES—Race horses have bandages for many different reasons, and it would be necessary to know whether a horse wears them for all races to determine their significance today. However, there are generally accepted facts about bandages. Tom Ainslie, author of *Ainslie's Complete Guide to Thoroughbred Racing* says, "Long bandages on the hind legs are often applied to give extra support. Muscles and ligaments held firmly together enable a horse to propel its weight forward with greater comfort. Long bandages on the forelegs are strong signs of tendon trouble where the horse can least tolerate it." Short bandages are a protection for the animal who "runs down" or tends to hit its ankles on the track's surface.

The only advice in the Paddock category is to pass a race if your choice exhibits all of the negative signs, especially if he continues his display of nervousness and irritability during the post parade to the starting gate.

Type Of Race

CLAIMING RACE—In a claiming race, any horse may be bought for the amount of money designated in the conditions of the race. The buyer must be a recognized horseman, usually defined as one who has a horse stabled at the racetrack. The prospective owner "claims" the horse before the race in the Racing Secretary's office. The result of the race does not affect the sale: If the horse is injured and must be destroyed, it is the new owner's responsibility. However, any money the horse wins goes to the previous owner.

Horseracing is no different than any sport, in that there is a vast difference in the skills of the performers. Claiming races allow owners to enter their animals in that class in which the contestants are fairly well matched, and each animal no matter how unsound should be able to find a level at which it can earn a purse. The owner of a $10,000 horse is forced to keep

'Points of Call' in Thoroughbred Charts

Following is a tabulation listing the "points of call" for the various distances in charts of thoroughbred racing:

Distance							
3 Furlongs	PP	Start				Str	Fin
3½ Furlongs	PP	Start	¼			Str	Fin
4 Furlongs	PP	Start	¼			Str	Fin
4½ Furlongs	PP	Start	¼			Str	Fin
5 Furlongs	PP	Start	3-16	⅜		Str	Fin
5½ Furlongs	PP	Start	¼	½		Str	Fin
6 Furlongs	PP	Start	¼	½		Str	Fin
6½ Furlongs	PP	Start	¼	½		Str	Fin
7 Furlongs	PP	Start	¼	½		Str	Fin
7½ Furlongs	PP	Start	¼	½		Str	Fin
1 Mile	PP	Start	¼	½	¾	Str	Fin
1 Mile 30 Yards	PP	Start	¼	½	¾	Str	Fin
1 Mile 70 Yards	PP	Start	¼	½	¾	Str	Fin
1 1/16 Miles	PP	Start	¼	½	¾	Str	Fin
1 1/8 Miles	PP	Start	¼	½	¾	Str	Fin
1 3/16 Miles	PP	Start	¼	½	¾	Str	Fin

Note: In races at 1 1/4 Miles or more, the start call is eliminated and the 1/4 mile call is substituted (as shown below):

Distance							
1 1/4 Miles	PP	¼	½	¾	1	Str	Fin
1 5/16 Miles	PP	¼	½	¾	1	Str	Fin
1 3/8 Miles	PP	¼	½	¾	1	Str	Fin
1 7/16 Miles	PP	¼	½	1	1¼	Str	Fin
1 1/2 Miles	PP	¼	½	1	1¼	Str	Fin
1 9/16 Miles	PP	¼	½	1	1¼	Str	Fin
1 5/8 Miles	PP	¼	½	1	1⅜	Str	Fin
1 11/16 Miles	PP	¼	½	1	1⅜	Str	Fin
1 3/4 Miles	PP	¼	½	1	1½	Str	Fin
1 13/16 Miles	PP	¼	½	1	1½	Str	Fin
1 7/8 Miles	PP	¼	½	1	1⅝	Str	Fin
1 15/16 Miles	PP	¼	½	1	1⅝	Str	Fin

Distances of 2 Miles, 2 Miles and 70 Yards, 2 1/16 Miles, 2 1/8 Miles, 2 3/16 Miles:

PP	¼	½	1	1¾	Str	Fin

Distances of 2 1/4 Miles, 2 5/16 Miles, 2 3/8 Miles, 2 7/16 Miles:

PP	¼	¾	1¼	2	Str	Fin

his at that level, because although it will be able to win and collect the purse in a $5,000 race, it will also be claimed.

The racing fan benefits from the claiming system because it eliminates certain unknowns. Technically, each horse in the race has a chance to win; at least, no animal has a staggering class advantage.

The conditions of the claimer vary. Some are limited to horses who have won only one race this season, or two or three, which provides additional opportunities for owners to find good spots for their horses. Generally the price of the claiming race varies from $2,500 to $25,000, although a few go as high as $75,000.

MAIDEN CLAIMERS—Horses eligible for the maiden claimers are the least talented animals at any track. A maiden is a horse that has never won a race. Maiden races for two years old don't fall in this "nag" category because the babies are just beginning their careers. However, maiden events for older animals are usually impossible to handicap even though we realize that one horse must win.

ALLOWANCE RACES—In an allowance race, horses carry various weights designated in the conditions. In order to give each contestant a *chance* at the purse, the horse with the best record, usually determined by the amount of money he has won, carries top weight which diminishes in relation to the animal's performance. At most tracks, allowance races are for animals that are too good to risk losing in a claimer and not good enough to compete with the big guys in the handicap and stakes events.

The purses in these races vary so greatly that in a low-price allowance, the horses are of the same quality as those in various claimers. In the higher allowance events, the horses are often being sharpened for important handicap and stakes races. Although some handicappers would never back a claiming horse running in an allowance race, the horse may actually be dropping in class. As we have indicated in the rules section on "consistency" it is the amount of money the horse has won in the past that determines class. So, if the newcomer at the allowance level has earned as much money as the other horses, he should be considered at his proper class level. This animal often goes off at excellent odds just because more bettors automatically assume that he is inferior.

Allowance Races for Two Year Olds—In the spring and early Summer, there are some excellent betting opportunities in these baby races. The distance is usually a 5 or 5½ furlong sprint, and speed is the primary handicapping factor. The two year olds are sound and eager to run, and are amazingly consistent, probably because they aren't yet hindered by injuries.

HANDICAP RACES—The handicap is a race in which the Track Handicapper, often the Racing Secretary, assigns weights according to *his* evaluation of the horse's ability to win. As in the allowance race, the purpose of varying the weights is to equalize the competitors. However, in the allowance, the weights are determined by the conditions.

STAKES RACES—Stakes Races, such as the Kentucky Derby, are held for the super-stars of the sport. In the stakes, short for Sweepstakes, the owners put up the purse money of which the winner takes the largest amount. Often the track adds a substantial amount (noted in the conditions as "$15,000 added") to insure that the very best horses will be entered. Because the owner has spent a significant amount, the bettor can be sure that each animal will make a good run for the purse. In some stakes events the horses carry same weights.

MAIDEN SPECIAL WEIGHTS—The Maiden Special Weight race is for non-winners who carry uniform weights designated by the Track Handicapper or Racing Secretary. These events are usually held for the better two year olds.

TURF RACES—Turf races are run on a grass course and may be claiming, allowance, handicap or stakes events.

ABBREVIATIONS FOR NORTH AMERICAN TRACKS

Abbreviations below designate tracks in DAILY RACING FORM entries and past performances.

AC	— Agua Caliente, Mex.	Hag	—*Hagerstown, Md.	SFe	— Santa Fe Downs, N. M.
Aks	— Ak-Sar-Ben, Neb.	Haw	— Hawthorne, Ill.	Sar	— Saratoga, N. Y.
Alb	— Albuquerque, N. Mex.	Hia	— Hialeah Park, Fla.	Sas	—*Saskatoon, Can.
Ali	—*Alliance, Neb. (Sandhillo)	Hol	— Hollywood Park, Calif.	ScD	— Scarborough Downs, Me.
AP	— Arlington Park, Ill.	HP	—*Hazel Park, Mich.	SD	—*Sawyer Downs, La.
Aqu	— Aqueduct, N. Y.	JnD	—*Jefferson Downs, La.	Sem	—*Seminole Downs, Fla.
Asc	—*Ascot Park, Ohio	Jua	— Juarez, Mex.	ShD	— Shenandoah Downs, W. Va.
AsD	—*Assiniboia Downs, Can.	Kee	— Keeneland, Ky.	Sol	—*Solano, Calif.
Atl	— Atlantic City, N. J.	LaM	—*La Mesa Park, N. Mex.	Spt	—*Sportsman's Park, Ill.
Ato	—*Atokad Park, Neb.	Lat	— Latonia, Ky.	SR	—*Santa Rosa, Calif.
BB	—*Blue Bonnets, Can.	LaV	— Las Vegas, Nev.	Stk	— Stockton, Calif.
BD	—*Berkshire Downs, Mass.	Lbg	—*Lethbridge, Can.	Suf	— Suffolk Downs, Mass.
Bel	— Belmont Park, N. Y.	LD	—*Lincoln Downs, R. I.	Sun	— Sunland Park, N. Mex.
Beu	— Beulah Park, Ohio	Lga	— Longacres, Wash.	Tdn	— Thistledown, Ohio
BF	—*Brockton Fair, Mass.	Lib	— Liberty Bell Park, Pa.	Tim	—*Timonium, Md.
Bil	—*Billings, Mont.	LnN	—*Lincoln State Fair, Neb.	TrP	— Tropical Park, Fla.
BM	— Bay Meadows, Calif.	Lrl	— Laurel Race Course, Md.	Tuc	—[2]*Tucson Turf Club, Ariz.
Bmf	— Bay Meadows Fair, Calif.	Mad	—*Madison, Neb.	TuP	— Turf Paradise, Ariz.
Bml	— Balmoral, Ill.	Mar	—*Marlboro, Md.	Was	— Washington Park, Ill.
Boi	— Boise, Idaho	Mch	—*Mitchell, Neb.	Wat	— Waterford Park, W. Va.
Bow	— Bowie, Md.	MD	—*Marquis Downs, Can.	Wey	—*Weymouth Fair, Mass.
Crc	— Calder Race Course, Fla.	Mem	—*Memorial Park, Colo.	Whe	—*Wheeling Downs, W. Va.
CD	— Churchill Downs, Ky.	Mex	—*Mexico City, Mex.	Win	—*Windsor Raceway, Can.
CdA	— Coeur d'Alene, Idaho	MF	—*Marshfield Fair, Mass.	WO	— Woodbine, Can.
Ceg	—*Calgary, Can.	MP	—*Miles Park, Ky.	YM	— Yakima Meadows, Wash.
Cen	— Centennial Race Track, Colo.	Mth	— Monmouth Park, N. J.		
Cka	—*Cahokia Downs, Ill.	Nar	— Narragansett Park, R. I.		**HUNT MEETINGS**
Cls	—*Columbus, Neb.	Nmp	—*Northampton, Mass.	Aik	— Aiken, S. C.
CT	—*Charles Town, W. Va.	NP	—*Northlands Park, Can.	AtH	— Atlanta, Ga.
Del	— Delaware Park, Del.	OP	— Oaklawn Park, Ark.	Cam	— Camden, S. C.
Det	— Detroit Race Course, Mich.	Pim	— Pimlico, Md.	DR	— Deep Run, Va.
Dmr	— Del Mar, Calif.	PJ	—*Park Jefferson, S. D.	Fai	— Fair Hill, Md.
Dov	—*Dover Downs, Del.	Pla	—*Playfair, Wash.	Fax	— Fairfax, Va.
ElP	— James C. Ellis Park, Ky.	Pln	— Pleasanton, Calif.	FH	— Far Hills, N. J.
EP	—*Exhibition Park, Can.	Poc	—*Pocono Downs, Pa.	Gln	— Glyndon, Md.
EvD	—*Evangeline Downs, La.	Pom	—*Pomona, Calif.	GN	— Grand National, Md.
FD	—[1]Florida Downs, Fla.	PM	— Portland Meadows, Ore.	Lex	— Lexington, Ky.
FE	— Fort Erie, Can.	Pmf	— Portland M'd'ws Fair, Ore.	Lig	— Ligonier, Pa.
Fer	—*Ferndale, Calif.	PP	— Pikes Peak, Colo.	Mal	— Malvern, Pa.
FG	— Fair Grounds, La.	PR	— Puerto Rico	Med	— Media, Pa.
FL	— Finger Lakes, N. Y.	Pre	—*Prescott Downs, Ariz.	Mid	— Middleburg, Va
Fon	— Fresno, Calif.	Ran	— Randall Park, Ohio	Mon	— Monkton, Md.
Fno	—*Fonner Park, Neb.	RaP	—*Raceway Park, Ohio	Mtp	— Montpelier, Va.
FP	— Fairmount Park, Ill.	RD	— River Downs, Ohio	Oxm	— Oxmoor, Ky.
GBF	—*Great Barrington, Mass.	Reg	—*Regina, Can.	Pur	— Purchase, N. Y.
GF	—*Great Falls, Mont.	Ril	—*Rillito, Ariz.	PW	— Percy Warner, Tenn.
GG	— Golden Gate Fields, Calif.	Rkm	— Rockingham Park, N. H.	RB	— Red Bank, N. J.
GM	—*Green Mountain, Vt.	Rui	—*Ruidoso Downs, N. Mex.	SoP	— Southern Pines, N. C.
GmP	—*Gresham Park, Ore.	SA	— Santa Anita Park, Calif.	Try	— Tryon, N. C
GP	— Gulfstream Park, Fla.	Sac	— Sacramento, Calif.	Uni	— Unionville, Pa.
Grd	—*Greenwood, Can.	Sal	—*Salem, Ore.	War	— Warrenton, Va.
GS	— Garden State Park, N. J.	San	—*Sandown Park, Can.	Wel	— Wellsville, Pa

*Indicates tracks less than one mile in circumference. [1]Formerly named Sunshine Park. [2]Formerly named Rillito.

A DAY AT THE TRACK

Now that all of the previous information has been digested, we're ready for our actual trip to the race track. Since this was written during the Winter, we have picked the Fairgrounds at New Orleans.

The day is Saturday, February 6, 1970. The weather is clear and the track fast, which is not always the case in New Orleans in February. A convenience of Fairgrounds is that it is an in-town track and is within a brisk walk or short cab ride from the best hotels in the area, including the world famous tourist center, the French Quarter.

With post time at 1:15, we have time for a late morning brunch and healthy walk to the track. By staying at one of the hotels that sells the *Racing Form,* we save ourselves the late night scurrying to the all-night newsstand on Friday night. Having the New Orleans Edition published in Chicago causes occasional problems when flights are delayed or some aberration of the postal service keeps the Form from arriving. Few irritations can match that of a horseplayer who can't get a Form for today's races. Anyway, today is one of the days that the Chamber of Commerce sings about, with temperature in the 70's and not a cloud in the sky. The *Daily Racing Form* was delivered at 9:00 a.m. on a tray with strong French Market coffee (including Chicory, of course,) and croissants with fresh butter. In New Orleans, you can go broke at the races and still die happy because of the food.

The first step after the coffee rinses out the cobwebs from a Friday night on Bourbon Street is to read the Form as you would any newspaper. It's positively amazing how many horseplayers only use the past performance charts. Occasional tidbits of information are contained in the columns about each track. For example, today's paper has an editorial about the Fairgrounds and near the bottom says "... with youth prevailing Wednesday as *Edomite* defeated Ardley Farm's *Island Chant. The two hooked at the far turn and battled it out the remainder of the distance."* While the result chart for the day shows *"Edomite* won in a stiff drive."

The point is that those two horses should be watched very carefully next time out. Few horses, certainly not $6500 claimers, can battle head to head for 3 furlongs around the turn and down the stretch, and have anything left. Chances are they are both burned out and will need several conditioning races before hitting top form again. This will have been verified if we see an unusually long lay-off before their next race. So we make a note of the fact and continue reading.

Today's feature is the 13th running of the Thelwa Stakes with $10,000 added. The race is for three year olds and should attract some of the best youngsters on the grounds. However, remember that all of these horses became three year olds just a month ago and are really still running off their two year old "baby race" form. In fact, several of the contenders have never run more than 5½ furlongs and ability to stretch out and last could be important. We make a note on the margin of the ninth race and finish reading the paper.

By this time, the second cup of coffee has taken effect and it is time to start in earnest.

The first race looks like a great way to start the day. It's a 6 furlong $3,000 claimer for three year olds, with weight allowance given for lack of winning performance since December 26th.

1st Fair Grounds

6 FURLONGS. (Tudor Scott, Nov. 27, 1969, 1:09⅘, 3, 116.)
Claiming. Purse $2,600. 3-year-olds. Weight, 120 lbs. Non-winners of three races since Dec. 6 allowed 3 lbs.; two races since then, 5 lbs.; a race, 8 lbs. Claiming price, $3,000.

Listed According to Post Positions

Ririmba **112** Dk. b. or br. g (1968), by Nadir—Miss Larimda, by Crafty Admiral.
Breeder, W. B. Robinson (Ky.). 1971 1 0 0 0 (—)
Owner, Audley Farm. Trainre, F. P. Aime III. **$3,000** 1970 14 1 1 1 $3,577

Jan 7-71 ^{2}FG	6 f	1:12⅕	ft	4¼	113	$3^{1\frac{1}{2}}$	2^{h}	5	7^{12}	MenardN	3000	76	M'd'aG.109 Z'D'g'l'gKid Ec'o in theD'l	12
Dec23-70 ^{1}FG	6 f	1:13⅖	ft	7¼	112	2½	3^{2}	$3^{1\frac{1}{2}}$	$6^{7\frac{3}{4}}$	MenardN^{2}	4500	74	Upsie 116 Touchland KutacrossShortie	12
Dec 9-70 ^{1}FG	6 f	1:12	ft	29	114	$5^{2\frac{1}{4}}$	$5^{7\frac{1}{2}}$	7^{9}	8^{12}	MenardN^{7}	4500	77	GalOGem 112 ApacheSignal SusanBea	12
Oct16-70 ^{3}Spt	6 f	1:14	ft	11	116	10^{17}	10^{12}	9^{11}	9^{12}	JonesK^{9}	5500	69	RegalCh'rg'r116 M'maMel T'mmysCar	10
Sep11-70 ^{1}Haw	6 f	1:12⅕	ft	6¾	118	3^{nk}	$4^{2\frac{1}{4}}$	10^{13}	12^{16}	Gallit'noG^{2}	5000	69	Wald 118 Easy Twist Count De Jo	12
Aug25-70 ^{4}Haw	6 f	1:11⅗	ft	1	▲118	1^{h}	1^{2}	4^{4}	$6^{8\frac{3}{4}}$	NicholsJ^{6}	6500	79	BimBuster 114 GoAbroad BigRiddle	6
Aug17-70 ^{3}AP	5½ f	1:05⅘	ft	7¾	115	2^{h}	2½	2^{5}	$7^{8\frac{3}{4}}$	NicholsJ^{6}	7500	77	BriteAxtion120 FastLegs BondMaiden	12
Aug 3-70 ^{7}AP	5½ f	1:07	ft	4	118	2^{2}	$4^{1\frac{3}{4}}$	$9^{9\frac{1}{2}}$	$10^{8\frac{3}{4}}$	Marq'ezC^{8}	7500	71	FastLegs118 BondMaiden Bedouee	12
Jly 27-70 ^{4}AP	5½ f	1:07⅕	ft	12	120	2^{1}	1^{h}	1^{h}	$1^{2\frac{1}{2}}$	M'q'zC^{8}	M7500	79	Ririmba 120 IrishPrince SmartBeauty	12

Jan 26 FG 4f ft :47⅕hg **Dec 19 FG 4f ft :49b**

8-LENGTH RULE (FINISHED 7th, 12 LENGTHS BEHIND THE WINNER.)

Touchland 107 B. g (1968), by Touchbutton—Sunesian, by Sun Again.
Breeder, M. N. Goodwin (Ohio). 1971 2 0 0 0 $168
Owner, G. Echols. Trainer, F. Behler. $3,000 1970 12 1 3 1 $4,232
Jan 8-716FG 6 f 1:14⅗sy 11e 111* 2h 2½ 34½ 813 RichardA3 6500 63 Sorta Like 112 Oiney's Pet Rivul Jet 11
Jan 1-716FG 6 f 1:15⅕hy 22 111* 32 32½ 35 48½ RichardA5 6000 64 Gal O Gem 115 Apache Signal Scootit 9
Dec23-701FG 6 f 1:13⅘ft 16 110* 3½ 1½ 2h 22½ RichardA6 4500 79 Upsie 116 Touchland KutacrossShortie 12
Dec16-703FG 6 f 1:14⅖sl 118 110* 42 33 9151214 Rich'rdA10 6500 63 RushAround112 Gal O G'm Ch'steBeau 12
Jly 1-703Suf 5 f :59⅘ft 41 114 42 42 53¾ 55¼ DrawdyT4 9500 87 Pride'sD'light110 God'rdK'te P'lyL'dd 7
Jun25-705Suf 5 f 1:00⅕ft 23 116 31 32 24 58¾ DrawdyT6 7500 82 Y'zzoKid115 PridesDel't K'nt'ckyGr'k 11
Jan 29 FG 5f ft 1:01b Jan 23 FG 4f ft :48b Jan 16 FG 4f gd :49⅗b

Loss in stretch rule (Lost more than 3/4 length in stretch.) (1.)

Capeson 107 Ch. g (1968), by Cape Grant—Wise Charge, by Fleet Feet.
Breeder J. C. Means, Jr. (Ark.). 1970 14 3 1 2 $5,544
Owner, Marbane Farm. Trainer, J. E. Leger. $3,000
Dec30-703FG 6 f 1:14 sl 51 110* 1012 1019 1021 1126 SibilleR4 6500 53 RushAround115 MissPluck BimBuster 12
Dec28-703FG 6 f 1:13⅗ft 9¼ 113 41¼ 55 76¾ 79 G'z'lesRD9 4500 72 Rulla theR'd115 E'syTwist CheironQ'n 12
Dec15-703FG 6 f 1:14⅗sy 11 111* 32 34 44 47 SibilleR8 5000 69 T. O. Said 112 You Test Em Madonna 12
Dec 9-701FG 6 f 1:12 ft 2½ 114 2h 35 35 611 YoungJF5 4500 78 GalOGem 112 ApacheSignal SusanBea 12
Dec 2-701FG 6 f 1:12⅗ft 4 112 34 23 31½ 26 YoungJF6 4500 80 LovelyOr'nt113 Capes'n WhiteL'dyGr'y 12
Aug 1-705EvD 6½ f 1:22⅗ft 4½ 112* 32 2½ 11 12 SibilleR9 7500 82 Capeson 112 Milk Queen Real Blonde 10
Jly 24-707EvD 6½ f 1:22⅘ft 27 120 57 56 55½ 57¼ SibilleR6 SplW 76 BillBlazer120 EightYear GatowHawk 8
Jly 17-709EvD 6½ f 1:22 sl 5¾ 110* 21½ 21 1h 3¾ SibilleR10 7500 83 RockyDay115 DragonBooty Capeson 10
Jly 2-709EvD 6½ f 1:24 ft 2½ ▲110* 11 11½ 75¼ 84½ SibilleR2 Alw 69 Super Change 112 Crafty Star Aleut 10
Jan 22 FG 5f ft 1:03b

One month rule (Last race December 30)

Noticia B 107 Ch. f (1968) by Bernburgoo—Novita, by Churrinche.
Breeder Mr & Mrs W. H. Bishop (Ill.). 1970 22 M 1 3 $4,600
Owner, W. H. Bishop Stable, Inc. Trainer, W. H. Bishop. $3,000
Nov18-703Spt 6½ f 1:21⅘sy 8¾ 117 31½ 45 66½ 715 PadronR7 Mdn 54 EasterOrder117 TyteM'rk't R'y'lCh'k'r 9
Nov11-704Spt 4 f :46⅗gd 6¾ 118 5 84½ 96½ 86¼ McC'rJW7 Mdn 86 MiniMiss118 GallaKing FifthWheel 10
Nov 4-703Spt 6½ f 1:21⅗sy 4¾ 117 64¼ 55 52¾ 54 McC'rJW10 Mdn 66 TyteVictory117 M'htyTytan D'leP'tive 10
Oct29-701Spt 6 f 1:15 sy 11 113* 24 25 25 25 WellsD6 M5000 71 Ch'mingTerry118 NoticiaB. Tarquinius 9
Sep25-703Haw 6 f 1:12⅘ft 14 106* 79 510 49 512 SpindlerL8 4000 73 W'fenAn'e112 Sm'hVsSm'h L'dyUrs'la 8
Sep17-703Haw 6 f 1:13⅘sy 3-2 ▲113 24 34½ 37 39½ Snyd'rD6 M4000 68 MacArthur 120 ColonelZora NoticiaB. 7
Sep14-703Haw 6 f 1:12⅘sy 23 117 76½ 59¼ 58 47¾ SnyderD2 Mdn 75 Pagmar117 BengalHead RedEmperor 8
Sep 5-704Haw 6 f 1:11⅗ft 39 114 68¾ 69½ 615 613 Belv'eEM1 7500 76 Q'n ofSpots119 F'rRabler's BimB'st'r 6
Sep 1-703Haw 6 f 1:12⅘ft 28e 114 612 614 611 56½ Belv'eEM5 5000 75 HastyHelen113 TrimB'le WolfenAnnie 11

This track rule (Has not had a race at Fair Grounds.)

Miss Aok 110 Ch. f (1968), by Time Tested—Glistnin Mission, by Omission.
Breeder, C. T. Houston (Ky.). 1971 2 0 0 0 (——)
Owner, W. T. Tschirhart. Trainer, J. Keefer. 1970 4 1 0 0 $2,200
Jan29-715FG 6 f 1:12⅕ft 116 116 31¾ 712 9211025 GalleyL2 6500 63 Ⓕ Upr'ht'M's115 Nas'm'sB'y M'dCatf'h 12
Jan 8-717FG 6 f 1:14⅗sy 50 113 75¾ 910 1028 1036 SoirezW4 6500 40 ⒻE'htWh'ls109 Manj'rrada Fl'w'rTh'f 10
May 5-703Was 4½ f :52⅘ft 3¾ 114 8 31 86¼ 912 Belv'eEM10 5000 R'dsideB'r114 G'd nHi Mich'le toM'k't 10
Apr30-705Was 4½ f :54⅗sy 10 111 1 15 15 11½ SpindlerL2 5000 Miss Aok 111 Good n Hi Roadside Bar 7
Apr20-705Was 4½ f :54⅕gd 47 114 3 711 813 820 Belv'leEM3 7500 Bet Jay Be 117 Ririmba Greybrook 8
Mar30-701OP 4 f :47 ft 53 117 11 11151121 918 CoxC11 Mdn 73 ⒻCrims'nK'ty117 GalOGem Oiney'sPet 12
Jan 19 FG 4f ft :50⅖bg Dec 29 FG 5f gd 1:03b Dec 22 FG 5f ft 1:02⅗b

8-length rule (Finished 10th 25 lengths behind winner.)

Isadoreable 107 Ch. f (1968), by World Traveler—Kitirick, by Air Rate.
Breeder, Clover S Farms (Tex.). 1970 10 2 0 0 $3,941
Owner, Clover S Farms. Trainer, W. R. Harp. $3,000
Dec29-702FG 6 f 1:14⅘sy 29 110 55½ 56 814 912 NiblickD4 5000 66 JudysDivid'd109 ProB'dit C'smicExp'n 12
Dec 9-701FG 6 f 1:12 ft 37 113 85¾ 811 810 711 MoyersL4 4500 78 GalOGem 112 ApacheSignal SusanBea 12
Dec 4-705FG 6 f 1:12⅘ft 45 114 63¾ 66¾ 9191014 HeathM9 6000 71 Sar Boy 120 Lady N. Amdor 12
Oct21-703HP 6 f 1:17⅕m 26 111* 1h 12 13 12 RichieS2 5000 68 ⒻIsadoreable111 EasyLancer YesBut 8
Sep23-703HP 4 f :47⅘ft 63 116 1 89 10191011 PerezR10 5000 81 ⒻSwing'gLisa113 D'dl'yQ'k L'taTr'bie 10
Sep10-703HP 6 f 1:13⅘ft 19 112 1h 44½ 617 623 ZakoorW3 5000 64 SingG'la112 Swing'gLisa M'n N Miz'n 6
Sep 1-702HP 6 f 1:15 ft 40 116 42½ 21½ 76 812 ZakoorW9 5000 67 ⒻOiney'sP't116, N'hv'leS'd TurnB't'n 10
Aug26-707HP 6 f 1:12 ft 24 112 46½ 612 719 731 C'mpb'lRJ4 Alw 63 Glorioso114 Buttonholer SecondP'sage 8
Aug14-707HP 6 f 1:14⅗ft 7½ 116 10131018 10231020 C'pbellRJ8 Alw 62 G'ld'nPromise122 Glorioso Butt'nhol'r 10
Apr29-704Det 4½ f :53⅘ft 6¾ 115 2 13 13 12 C'p'llRJ3 M5000 93 Isadoreable 115 Hi Skyer Artex 9

One month rule (Last race December 29.)

Fast Pickin 110 B. f (1968), by Cotton Pickin—Stephens Suzy, by Noble Creek.
Breeder, S. Robinson (Ark.). 1970 23 2 3 2 $3,162
Owner, E. Salvaggio. Trainer, J. F. Audibert. $3,000
Dec23-701FG 6 f 1:13⅘ft 96 114 77¼ 97 12161218 MayeuxR12 4500 64 Upsie 116 Touchland KutacrossShortie 12
Dec15-703FG 6 f 1:14⅗sy 94 112 56½ 67 65¾ 89 MayeuxR7 5000 67 T. O. Said 112 You Test Em Madonna 12
Dec 8-701FG 6 f 1:13⅘ft 43 114 45½ 612 78½ 89¼ M'yeauxR1 3200 74 CaminadaPass109 DirectLink H'd'sR'k 12
Nov17-704CT 6½ f 1:22 ft 15 111 2h 2½ 55½ 58 AderB2 3000 71 ScootersGleam120 Nil ItH'p OnceAr'd 9
Nov 2-704CT 4½ f :54⅗sy 3½ 114 3 22 43 42¼ AderB7 2500 84 ⒻSc'hH'hB'l113 B'dOleP'my Tip'ysP'e 10
Oct26-703CT 4½ f :53⅘ft 12 117 2 34½ 35½ 45¼ AderB9 2500 84 PrinceTozka117 M'ns'rK'no Skept'sm 9
Oct22-705CT 4½ f :54⅘m 4½ 119 5 3½ 11½ 21½ AderB3 2500 83 ⒻDebbie Babu 115 Fast Pickin Adria 9
Jan 22 FG 4f ft :49b

One month rule (Last race December 23.)

Balata 107 B. f (1968), by Royal Reason—Darin, by Golden Doubles.
Breeder, W. A. Anderson (Ky.). 1971 2 0 0 0 (——)
Owner, W. A. Anderson. Trainer, L. G. Howell. $3,000 1970 5 1 1 0 $3,635
Jan14-713FG 6 f 1:17 hy 27 111 69½ 817 913 67¼ HolmesD10 4500 57 Echo in theD'l 112 Z'D'g'l'gKid NaNu 11
Jan 8-717FG 6 f 1:14⅗sy 24 112 1h 53½ 57¼ 66 HolmesD9 6500 70 ⒻE'htWh'ls109 Manj'rrada Fl'w'rTh'f 10
Dec29-702FG 6 f 1:14⅘sy 13 112 74¾ 9111018 1118 CoxR10 5000 60 JudysDivid'd109 ProB'dit C'smicExp'n 12
Nov10-704Spt 6 f 1:15⅕sy 6¼ 115 44 31½ 21 11 CoxR1 M5000 75 Balata 115 Me Carla Bobby Gray 10
Nov 5-701Spt 6½ f 1:23⅗gd 7-5 ▲118 74½ 75 66½ 615 Ruyb'liJ4 M5500 47 SaltyTiger121 PinkieChief BobbyGray 10
Oct29-704Spt 6½ f 1:23 sy 7 115 42½ 32 21 2¾ Ruyb'liJ7 M5000 62 Rivul Jet 113 Balata Lady Hilda 9
Oct17-703Spt 6 f 1:14 ft 20 115 57¼ 58 611 57¾ CoxR9 M5000 73 Br'nLashes115 Sm'tEmper'r K'gB'dl'y 10
Dec 23 FG 5f ft 1:04b Dec 1 FG 4f gd :53⅗b

Contender

Lynnie Girl 107 Ch. f (1968), by Spring Sun—Pat and Lynn, by Doc Eggers.
Br., Mr. & Mrs. H. Mattingly (Ky.). 1970 7 2 0 2 $2,205
Owner, H. Buechner & S. L. Middleton. Trainer, J. Alohman. $3,000
Dec 2-701FG 6 f 1:12⅗ft 21 109* 14 13 21 711 RichardA1 4500 75 LovelyOr'nt113 Capes'n WhiteL'dyGr'y 12
Oct29-706Tdn 6 f ft 1 ▲119 14 21 2½ 32 FaticaF7 5000 0 Mother 111 Sue Pan Lynnie Girl 7
†Oct 29—No time available account failure of Teletimer.
Oct15-704Tdn 6 f 1:15⅘m 4½ 119 15 14 13 12 GaticaF3 4000 70 LynnieGirl 119 IndianBabeE. Wewaka 8
Oct 7-703Tdn 5½ f 1:08⅗gd 3½ 115 2h 1½ 12 12½ GaticaF6 M2500 77 LynnieGirl 115 Tomb'wl G'ldenC'm'd'r 8
Sep30-702Lat 6 f 1:14⅕ft 20 117 12½ 11½ 46 711 GaticaF9 M5000 66 RomanSpots120 Hesourpet Gotashot 11
Sep24-701Lat 5½ f 1:08⅘gd 19 116 14 14 2½ 36 GaticaF2 M2500 69 Lola Rush 111 Seezum Lynnie Girl 12
Sep15-703Lat 5½ f 1:07⅕ft 11 110 31½ 45½ 917 916 GaticaF1 2500 67 QuickCat 113 RashDarling Cleanse 11

One month rule (Last race December 2.)

(1.) Touchland was not eliminated on the 8-Length Rule because of the Off Track Factor.

Stacy Van **107** Ch. f (1968), by Beau Busher—Darling Darlene, by Knave.
Breeder, Mrs. W. Laycock (Ind.). 1971 . 1 M 0 0 (—)
Owner, W. Laycock. Trainer, J. R. Smith. $3,000
Jan29-715FG 6 f 1:12⅕ft 68 112 96¾101411211125 BroganC11 6500 63 Ⓕ Upr'htM's115 Nas'm'sB'y M'dCatf'h 12
Jan 21 FG 5f ft 1:04bg Jan 16 FG 5f gd 1:07b Jan 7 FG 4f ft :52⅗b

8-LENGTH RULE
(FINISHED 11th, 25 LENGTHS BEHIND.)

Solid Lark **115** Ch. g (1968), by Solid Lad—Town Maid, by Gay Town.
Breeder, Mrs. M. Salyer (Tex.). 1971 . 3 1 0 0 $1,578
Owner, W. Roberie. Trainer, J. R. Roberie. $3,000
Jan23-711FG 1 1/16 1:48⅕ft 11 113* 1h 55½ 32 613 BorelC5 3000 61 SnapTom 118 MarcyMia MajorYork 12
Jan16-711FG 1 1/16 1:48⅖gd 7½ 115§ 22 53½ 48½ 515 SamJ6 3000 58 Direct Link 118 Yes But Young Tiger 10
Jan 1-711FG 6 f 1:17⅕hy 2½ 115 83¾ 2½ 2½ 12 SamJ11 M4000 63 Solid Lark 115 Gottlieb David L. Van 12
Jan 20 FG 4f ft :49bg Dec 31 FG 3f m :40b Dec 24 FG 4f ft :48b

SPEED RULE
(AT THE 6-FURLONG DISTANCE, SOLID LARK DID NOT COME WITHIN 5 POINTS OF BALATA'S RATING—ADDING 5 POINTS TO THE OFF-TRACK RATING.) (2.)

(2.) SOLID LARK WAS NOT ELIMINATED ON 8-LENGTH RULE BECAUSE OF DISTANCE FACTOR.

Immediately, *Noticia B* is dismissed because of This Track rule. Also, looking at the dates of the last outing *Capeson, Isadoreable, Fast Pickin,* and *Lynnie Girl* are sent packing because of the One-Month rule. Next, the Eight-Length rule takes care of *Ririmba, Miss AoK* and *Stacy Van.*

Things are getting a little tougher now, but further searching shows that *Solid Lark* doesn't make the speed rule. This leaves us with *Touchland and Balata.* Now we decide whether we "dutch" these two or try to separate a solid choice. In this case, *Touchland* gets a black mark on Loss In The Stretch rule and *Balata* gets several Extra Points for showing the highest consistency rating, dropping four pounds for today's race and getting a speed rating of 80, which should be enough for $3,000 claimers.

Now that we have a Number One selection, we look at what the "professionals" say. Interestingly, Sweeps lists probability odds at 10-1 but Trackman picks *Balata* as the winner. Could get good odds on this one.

2nd Fair Grounds

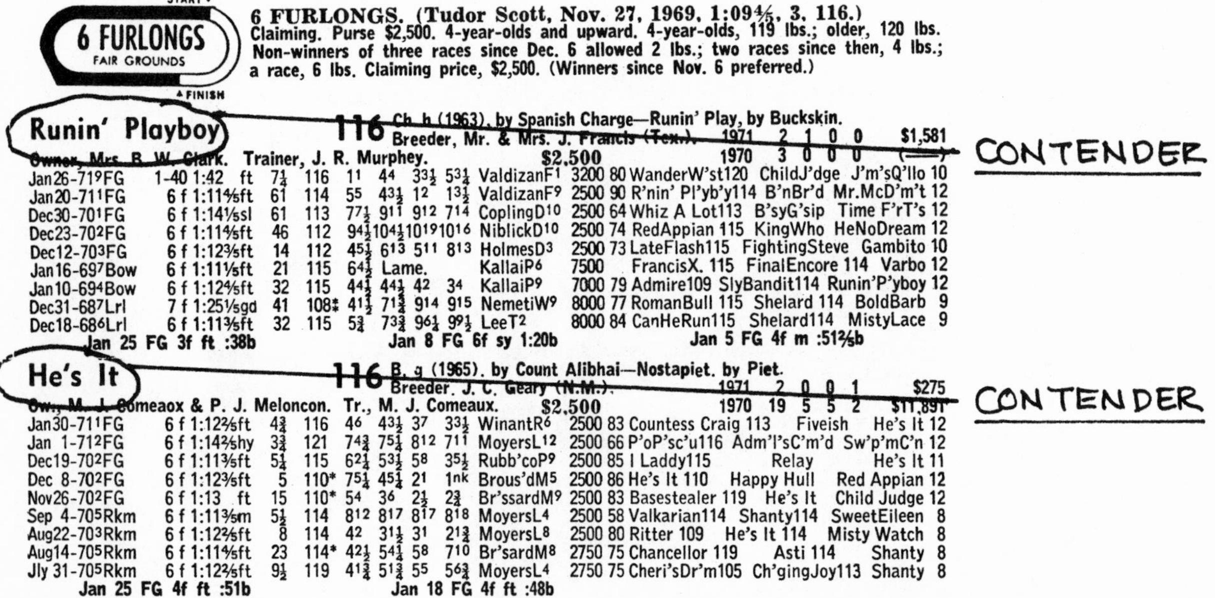
START
6 FURLONGS
FAIR GROUNDS
FINISH

6 FURLONGS. (Tudor Scott, Nov. 27, 1969, 1:09⅘, 3, 116.)
Claiming. Purse $2,500. 4-year-olds and upward. 4-year-olds, 119 lbs.; older, 120 lbs. Non-winners of three races since Dec. 6 allowed 2 lbs.; two races since then, 4 lbs.; a race, 6 lbs. Claiming price, $2,500. (Winners since Nov. 6 preferred.)

Runin' Playboy **116** Ch. h (1963), by Spanish Charge—Runin' Play, by Buckskin.
Breeder, Mr. & Mrs. J. Francis (Tex.). 1971 2 1 0 0 $1,581
Owner, Mrs. B. W. Clark. Trainer, J. R. Murphey. $2,500 1970 3 0 0 0 (—)
Jan26-719FG 1-40 1:42 ft 7¼ 116 11 44 33½ 53¼ ValdizanF1 3200 80 WanderW'st120 ChildJ'dge J'm'sQ'llo 10
Jan20-711FG 6 f 1:11⅘ft 61 114 55 43½ 12 13½ ValdizanF9 2500 90 R'nin' Pl'yb'y114 B'nBr'd Mr.McD'm't 12
Dec30-701FG 6 f 1:14⅕sl 61 113 77½ 911 912 714 CoplingD10 2500 64 Whiz A Lot113 B'syG'sip Time F'rT's 12
Dec23-702FG 6 f 1:11⅘ft 46 112 94½104½10191016 NiblickD10 2500 74 RedAppian 115 KingWho HeNoDream 12
Dec12-703FG 6 f 1:12⅗ft 14 112 45½ 613 511 813 HolmesD3 2500 73 LateFlash115 FightingSteve Gambito 10
Jan16-697Bow 6 f 1:11⅕ft 21 115 64½ Lame. KallaiP6 7500 FrancisX. 115 FinalEncore 114 Varbo 12
Jan10-694Bow 6 f 1:12⅘ft 32 115 44½ 44½ 42 34 KallaiP9 7000 79 Admire109 SlyBandit114 Runin'P'yboy 12
Dec31-687Lrl 7 f 1:25⅕gd 41 108‡ 41½ 71¾ 914 915 NemetiW9 8000 77 RomanBull 115 Shelard 114 BoldBarb 9
Dec18-686Lrl 6 f 1:11⅗ft 32 115 5¾ 73¾ 96¼ 99½ LeeT2 8000 84 CanHeRun115 Shelard114 MistyLace 9
Jan 25 FG 3f ft :38b Jan 8 FG 6f sy 1:20b Jan 5 FG 4f m :51⅖b

CONTENDER

He's It **116** B. g (1965), by Count Alibhai—Nostapiet, by Piet.
Breeder, J. C. Geary (N.M.). 1971 2 0 0 1 $275
Ow., M. J. Comeaox & P. J. Meloncon. Tr., M. J. Comeaux. $2,500 1970 19 5 5 2 $11,891
Jan30-711FG 6 f 1:12⅖ft 4¾ 116 46 43½ 37 33½ WinantR6 2500 83 Countess Craig 113 Fiveish He's It 12
Jan 1-712FG 6 f 1:14⅖hy 3¾ 121 74¾ 75¼ 812 711 MoyersL12 2500 66 P'oP'sc'u116 Adm'l'sC'm'd Sw'p'mC'n 12
Dec19-702FG 6 f 1:11⅗ft 5¼ 115 62¼ 53½ 58 35½ Rubb'coP9 2500 85 I Laddy115 Relay He's It 11
Dec 8-702FG 6 f 1:12⅗ft 5 110* 75¼ 45¼ 21 1nk Brous'dM5 2500 86 He's It 110 Happy Hull Red Appian 12
Nov26-702FG 6 f 1:13 ft 15 110* 54 36 2½ 2¾ Br'ssardM9 2500 83 Basestealer 119 He's It Child Judge 12
Sep 4-705Rkm 6 f 1:11⅗m 5½ 114 812 817 817 818 MoyersL4 2500 58 Valkarian114 Shanty114 SweetEileen 8
Aug22-703Rkm 6 f 1:12⅖ft 8 114 42 31½ 31 21¾ MoyersL8 2500 80 Ritter 109 He's It 114 Misty Watch 8
Aug14-705Rkm 6 f 1:11⅘ft 23 114* 42½ 54¼ 58 710 Br'sardM8 2750 75 Chancellor 119 Asti 114 Shanty 8
Jly 31-705Rkm 6 f 1:12⅖ft 9½ 119 41¾ 51¾ 55 56¾ MoyersL4 2750 75 Cheri'sDr'm105 Ch'gingJoy113 Shanty 8
Jan 25 FG 4f ft :51b Jan 18 FG 4f ft :48b

CONTENDER

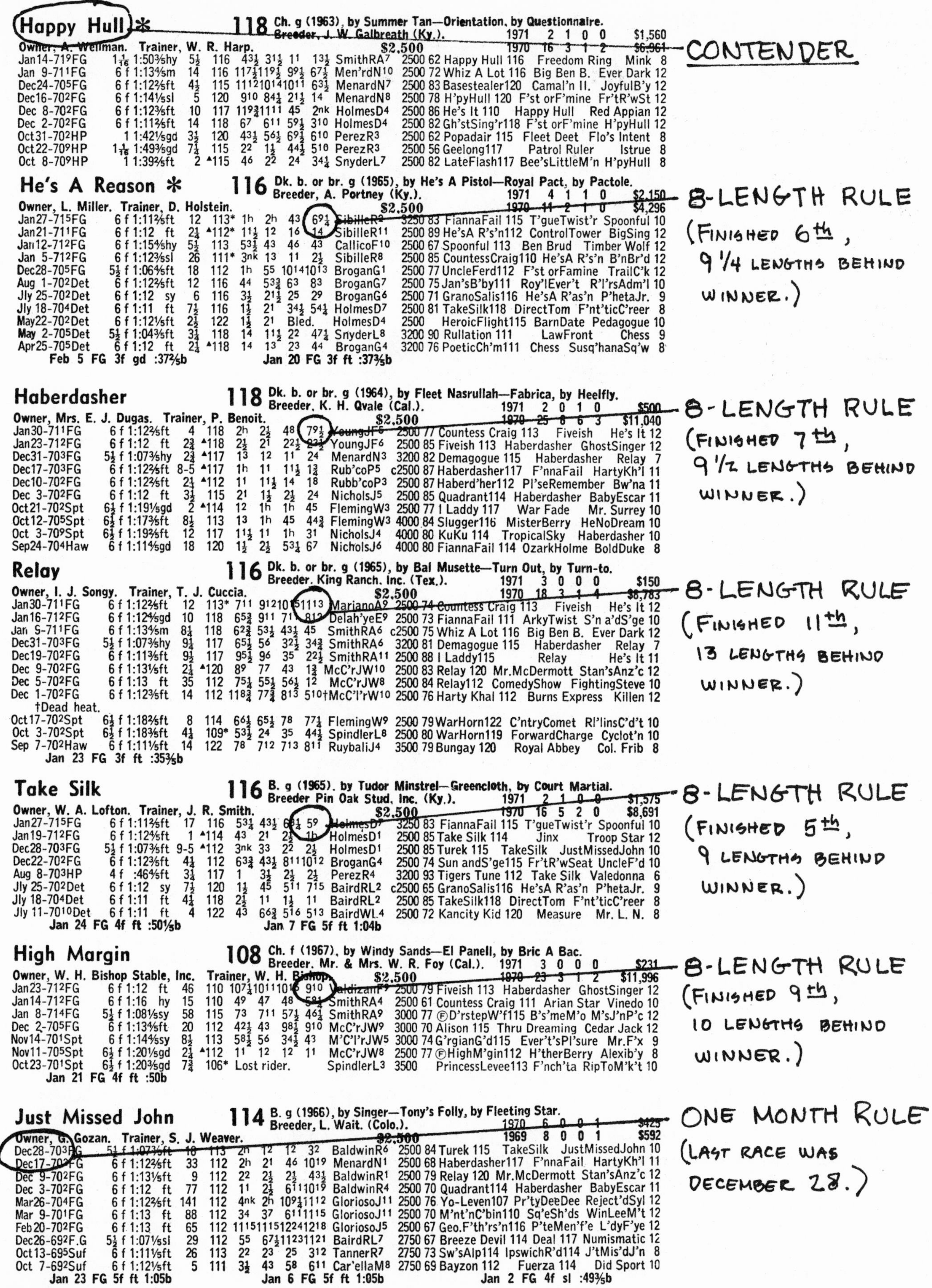

Happy Hull * 118 Ch. g (1963), by Summer Tan—Orientation, by Questionnaire.
Breeder, J. W. Galbreath (Ky.). 1971 2 1 0 0 $1,560
Owner, A. Wellman. Trainer, W. R. Harp. $2,500 1970 16 3 1 2 $6,961
Jan14-719FG 1 1/16 1:50⅗hy 5½ 116 43½ 31½ 11 13½ SmithRA7 2500 62 Happy Hull 116 Freedom Ring Mink 8
Jan 9-711FG 6 f 1:13⅘m 14 116 117½119½ 99½ 67½ Men'rdN10 2500 72 Whiz A Lot 116 Big Ben B. Ever Dark 12
Dec24-705FG 6 f 1:12⅖ft 4½ 115 111210141011 63½ MenardN7 2500 83 Basestealer120 Camal'n II. JoyfulB'y 12
Dec16-702FG 6 f 1:14⅕sl 5 120 910 84½ 21½ 14 MenardN8 2500 78 H'pyHull 120 F'st orF'mine Fr'tR'wSt 12
Dec 8-702FG 6 f 1:12⅗ft 10 117 119¾1111 45 2nk HolmesD4 2500 86 He's It 110 Happy Hull Red Appian 12
Dec 2-702FG 6 f 1:11⅗ft 14 118 67 611 59½ 310 HolmesD4 2500 82 Gh'stSing'r118 F'st orF'mine H'pyHull 12
Oct31-702HP 1 1:42⅕gd 3½ 120 43½ 56½ 69½ 610 PerezR3 2500 62 Popadair 115 Fleet Deet Flo's Intent 8
Oct22-709HP 1 1/16 1:49⅗gd 7½ 115 22 1½ 44½ 510 PerezR3 2500 56 Geelong117 Patrol Ruler Istrue 8
Oct 8-709HP 1 1:39⅘ft 2 ▲115 46 22 24 34½ SnyderL7 2500 82 LateFlash117 Bee'sLittleM'n H'pyHull 8

He's A Reason * 116 Dk. b. or br. g (1965), by He's A Pistol—Royal Pact, by Pactole.
Breeder, A. Portney (Ky.). 1971 4 1 1 0 $2,150
Owner, L. Miller. Trainer, D. Holstein. $2,500 1970 11 2 1 0 $4,296
Jan27-715FG 6 f 1:11⅗ft 12 113* 1h 2h 43 69¼ SibilleR2 3250 83 FiannaFail 115 T'gueTwist'r Spoonful 10
Jan21-711FG 6 f 1:12 ft 2¼ ▲112* 11½ 12 16 14 SibilleR11 2500 89 He'sA R's'n112 ControlTower BigSing 12
Jan12-712FG 6 f 1:15⅘hy 5½ 113 53½ 43 46 43 CallicoF10 2500 67 Spoonful 113 Ben Brud Timber Wolf 12
Jan 5-712FG 6 f 1:12⅗sl 26 111* 3nk 13 11 2½ SibilleR8 2500 85 CountessCraig110 He'sA R's'n B'nBr'd 12
Dec28-705FG 5½ f 1:06⅘ft 18 112 1h 55 10141013 BroganG1 2500 77 UncleFerd112 F'st orFamine TrailC'k 12
Aug 1-702Det 6 f 1:12⅖ft 12 116 44 53¾ 63 83 BroganG7 2500 75 Jan'sB'by111 Roy'lEver't R'l'rsAdm'l 10
Jly 25-702Det 6 f 1:12 sy 6 116 3½ 21½ 25 29 BroganG6 2500 71 GranoSalis116 He'sA R'as'n P'hetaJr. 9
Jly 18-704Det 6 f 1:11 ft 7½ 116 1½ 21 34½ 54½ HolmesD7 2500 81 TakeSilk118 DirectTom F'nt'ticC'reer 8
May22-702Det 6 f 1:12⅕ft 2½ 122 1½ 21 Bled. HolmesD4 2500 HeroicFlight115 BarnDate Pedagogue 10
May 2-705Det 5½ f 1:04⅗ft 3½ 118 14 11½ 22 47½ SnyderL8 3200 90 Rullation 111 LawFront Chess 9
Apr25-705Det 6 f 1:12 ft 2¼ ▲118 14 13 23 44 BroganG4 3200 76 PoeticCh'm111 Chess Susq'hanaSq'w 8
Feb 5 FG 3f gd :37⅖b Jan 20 FG 3f ft :37⅗b

Haberdasher 118 Dk. b. or br. g (1964), by Fleet Nasrullah—Fabrica, by Heelfly.
Breeder, K. H. Qvale (Cal.). 1971 2 0 1 0 $500
Owner, Mrs. E. J. Dugas. Trainer, P. Benoit. $2,500 1970 25 8 6 3 $11,040
Jan30-711FG 6 f 1:12⅖ft 4 118 2h 2½ 48 79½ YoungJF5 2500 77 Countess Craig 113 Fiveish He's It 12
Jan23-712FG 6 f 1:12 ft 2¾ ▲118 2½ 21 22½ 23½ YoungJF6 2500 85 Fiveish 113 Haberdasher GhostSinger 12
Dec31-703FG 5½ f 1:07⅗hy 2¾ ▲117 13 12 11 24 MenardN3 3200 82 Demagogue 115 Haberdasher Relay 7
Dec17-703FG 6 f 1:12⅖ft 8-5 ▲117 1h 11 11½ 1¾ Rub'coP5 c2500 87 Haberdasher117 F'nnaFail HartyKh'l 11
Dec10-702FG 6 f 1:12⅖ft 2¼ ▲112 11 11½ 14 18 Rubb'coP3 2500 87 Haberd'her112 Pl'seRemember Bw'na 11
Dec 3-702FG 6 f 1:12 ft 3½ 115 21 1½ 2½ 24 NicholsJ5 2500 85 Quadrant114 Haberdasher BabyEscar 11
Oct21-702Spt 6½ f 1:19⅕sgd 2 ▲114 12 1h 1h 45 FlemingW3 2500 77 I Laddy 117 War Fade Mr. Surrey 10
Oct12-705Spt 6½ f 1:17⅗ft 8½ 113 13 1h 45 44¾ FlemingW3 4000 84 Slugger116 MisterBerry HeNoDream 10
Oct 3-709Spt 6½ f 1:19⅗ft 12 117 11½ 11 1h 31 NicholsJ4 4000 80 KuKu 114 TropicalSky Haberdasher 10
Sep24-704Haw 6 f 1:11⅘gd 18 120 1½ 2½ 53½ 67 NicholsJ6 4000 80 FiannaFail 114 OzarkHolme BoldDuke 8

Relay 116 Dk. b. or br. g (1965), by Bal Musette—Turn Out, by Turn-to.
Breeder, King Ranch, Inc. (Tex.). 1971 3 0 0 0 $150
Owner, I. J. Songy. Trainer, T. J. Cuccia. $2,500 1970 18 3 1 4 $8,783
Jan30-711FG 6 f 1:12⅖ft 12 113* 711 912101 51113 MarianoA2 2500 74 Countess Craig 113 Fiveish He's It 12
Jan16-712FG 6 f 1:12⅘sgd 10 118 65¾ 911 711 812 Delah'yeE9 2500 73 FiannaFail 111 ArkyTwist S'n a'dS'ge 10
Jan 5-711FG 6 f 1:13⅘m 8½ 118 62¾ 53½ 43½ 45 SmithRA6 c2500 75 Whiz A Lot 116 Big Ben B. Ever Dark 12
Dec31-703FG 5½ f 1:07⅗hy 9½ 117 65½ 56 32½ 34¾ SmithRA6 3200 81 Demagogue 115 Haberdasher Relay 7
Dec19-702FG 6 f 1:11⅗ft 9½ 117 95½ 96 35 22½ SmithRA11 2500 88 I Laddy115 Relay He's It 11
Dec 9-702FG 6 f 1:13⅕ft 2¼ ▲120 89 77 43 1¾ McC'rJW10 2500 83 Relay 120 Mr.McDermott Stan'sAnz'c 12
Dec 5-702FG 6 f 1:13 ft 35 112 75¼ 55½ 56½ 1½ McC'rJW8 2500 84 Relay112 ComedyShow FightingSteve 10
Dec 1-702FG 6 f 1:12⅗ft 14 112 118¾ 77¾ 813 510†McC'l'rW10 2500 76 Harty Khal 112 Burns Express Killen 12
†Dead heat.
Oct17-702Spt 6½ f 1:18⅖ft 8 114 66½ 65½ 78 77¼ FlemingW9 2500 79 WarHorn122 C'ntryComet Rl'linsC'd't 10
Oct 3-702Spt 6½ f 1:18⅗ft 4½ 109* 53½ 24 35 44½ SpindlerL8 2500 80 WarHorn119 ForwardCharge Cyclot'n 10
Sep 7-702Haw 6 f 1:11⅕ft 14 122 78 712 713 811 RuybaliJ4 3500 79 Bungay 120 Royal Abbey Col. Frib 8
Jan 23 FG 3f ft :35⅗b

Take Silk 116 B. g (1965), by Tudor Minstrel—Greencloth, by Court Martial.
Breeder Pin Oak Stud, Inc. (Ky.). 1971 2 1 0 0 $1,575
Owner, W. A. Lofton. Trainer, J. R. Smith. $2,500 1970 16 5 2 0 $8,691
Jan27-715FG 6 f 1:11⅗ft 17 116 53½ 43½ 68½ 59 HolmesD7 3250 83 FiannaFail 115 T'gueTwist'r Spoonful 10
Jan19-712FG 6 f 1:12⅘ft 1 ▲114 43 21 2½ 1h HolmesD1 2500 85 Take Silk 114 Jinx Troop Star 12
Dec28-703FG 5½ f 1:07⅗ft 9-5 ▲112 3nk 33 22 2½ HolmesD1 2500 85 Turek 115 TakeSilk JustMissedJohn 10
Dec22-702FG 6 f 1:12⅗ft 4½ 112 63¾ 43½ 8111012 BroganG4 2500 74 Sun andS'ge115 Fr'tR'wSeat UncleF'd 10
Aug 8-703HP 4 f :46⅘ft 3½ 117 1 3½ 2½ 2½ PerezR4 3200 93 Tigers Tune 112 Take Silk Valedonna 6
Jly 25-702Det 6 f 1:12 sy 7½ 120 1½ 45 511 715 BairdRL2 c2500 65 GranoSalis116 He'sA R'as'n P'hetaJr. 9
Jly 18-704Det 6 f 1:11 ft 4½ 118 2½ 11 1½ 11 BairdRL2 2500 85 TakeSilk118 DirectTom F'nt'ticC'reer 8
Jly 11-7010Det 6 f 1:11 ft 4 122 43 66¾ 516 513 BairdWL4 2500 72 Kancity Kid 120 Measure Mr. L. N. 8
Jan 24 FG 4f ft :50⅕b Jan 7 FG 5f ft 1:04b

High Margin 108 Ch. f (1967), by Windy Sands—El Panell, by Bric A Bac.
Breeder, Mr. & Mrs. W. R. Foy (Cal.). 1971 3 0 0 0 $231
Owner, W. H. Bishop Stable, Inc. Trainer, W. H. Bishop. $2,500 1970 23 3 1 2 $11,996
Jan23-712FG 6 f 1:12 ft 46 110 107¼1011101 910 ValdizanF9 2500 79 Fiveish 113 Haberdasher GhostSinger 12
Jan14-712FG 6 f 1:16 hy 15 110 49 47 48 58½ SmithRA4 2500 61 Countess Craig 111 Arian Star Vinedo 10
Jan 8-714FG 5½ f 1:08⅕sy 58 115 73 711 57¼ 46¼ SmithRA9 3000 77 ⒻD'rstepW'f115 B's'meM'o M'sJ'nP'c 12
Dec 2-705FG 6 f 1:13⅘ft 20 112 42¼ 43 98¼ 910 McC'rJW9 3000 70 Alison 115 Thru Dreaming Cedar Jack 12
Nov14-701Spt 6 f 1:14⅘sy 8½ 113 58½ 56 34½ 43 M'C'l'rJW5 3000 74 G'rgianG'd115 Ever't'sPl'sure Mr.F'x 9
Nov11-705Spt 6½ f 1:20⅕sgd 2¼ ▲112 11 12 12 11 McC'rJW8 2500 77 ⒻHighM'gin112 H'therBerry Alexib'y 8
Oct23-701Spt 6½ f 1:20⅗gd 7¾ 106* Lost rider. SpindlerL3 3500 PrincessLevee113 F'nch'ta RipToM'k't 10
Jan 21 FG 4f ft :50b

Just Missed John 114 B. g (1966), by Singer—Tony's Folly, by Fleeting Star.
Breeder, L. Wait. (Colo.). 1970 6 0 0 1 $425
Owner, G. Gozan. Trainer, S. J. Weaver. $2,500 1969 8 0 0 1 $592
Dec28-703FG 5½ f 1:07⅗ft 18 113 2h 12 12 32 BaldwinR6 2500 84 Turek 115 TakeSilk JustMissedJohn 10
Dec17-702FG 6 f 1:12⅖ft 33 112 2h 21 46 1019 MenardN1 2500 68 Haberdasher117 F'nnaFail HartyKh'l 11
Dec 9-702FG 6 f 1:13⅕ft 9 112 22 2½ 2½ 43½ BaldwinR1 2500 79 Relay 120 Mr.McDermott Stan'sAnz'c 12
Dec 3-702FG 6 f 1:12 ft 77 112 11 2½ 6¹11019 BaldwinR4 2500 70 Quadrant114 Haberdasher BabyEscar 11
Mar26-704FG 6 f 1:12⅖ft 141 112 4nk 2h 109¼1112 GloriosoJ11 2500 76 Yo-Leven107 Pr'tyDeeDee Reject'dSyl 12
Mar 9-701FG 6 f 1:13 ft 88 112 34 37 6111115 GloriosoJ11 2500 70 M'nt'nC'bin110 Sq'eSh'ds WinLeeM't 12
Feb20-702FG 6 f 1:13 ft 65 112 11151115122411218 GloriosoJ5 2500 67 Geo.F'th'rs'n116 P'teMen'f'e L'dyF'ye 12
Dec26-692F.G 5½ f 1:07⅕sl 29 112 55 67½11231121 BairdRL7 2750 67 Breeze Devil 114 Deal 117 Numismatic 12
Oct13-695Suf 6 f 1:11⅘ft 26 113 22 23 25 312 TannerR7 2750 73 Sw'sAlp114 IpswichR'd114 J'tMis'dJ'n 8
Oct 7-692Suf 6 f 1:12⅘ft 5 111 3½ 43 58 611 Car'ellaM8 2750 69 Bayzon 112 Fuerza 114 Did Sport 10
Jan 23 FG 5f ft 1:05b Jan 6 FG 5f ft 1:05b Jan 2 FG 4f sl :49⅗b

CONTENDER
8-LENGTH RULE
(FINISHED 6th, 9 1/4 LENGTHS BEHIND WINNER.)
8-LENGTH RULE
(FINISHED 7th, 9 1/2 LENGTHS BEHIND WINNER.)
8-LENGTH RULE
(FINISHED 11th, 13 LENGTHS BEHIND WINNER.)
8-LENGTH RULE
(FINISHED 5th, 9 LENGTHS BEHIND WINNER.)
8-LENGTH RULE
(FINISHED 9th, 10 LENGTHS BEHIND WINNER.)
ONE MONTH RULE
(LAST RACE WAS DECEMBER 28.)

Nashell ✕ 108 B. f (1967), by Nashua Bell—Belleseem, by Bunty Lawless.
Breeder. C. L. Surgenor (Can.). 1970 9 1 0 0 $2,420
Owner, M. H. Van Berg Stable, Inc. Trainer, J. Van Berg. $2,500 1969 12 2 2 0 $4,180

```
Aug26-702HP    6½ f 1:20⅕ft  2   ▲110  13   11½  2h   53¾  BroganG5   2500 76 Relevant112  GoneMiss  Sw'tM'nh'tt'n 10
Aug15-707HP    6 f 1:14⅖ft   2¼  114   21   21½  22   43¾  BroganG2   3500 78 SongD've104  M'lieB'l'ro  ElkCityBoy 9
Aug 5-702HP    6½ f 1:19⅘ft  7¼  108   14   15   15   18   BroganG3   2500 82 Nashell 108  Gone Miss  Me'n Wag 10
Jly 24-702Det  6 f 1:12⅕ft   10  110*  31½  41½  66½  1110 Madd'kD10  2500 69 JoyGeorge 117  Edwinknill  MyRelease 12
Jly 3-7010Det  6 f 1:10⅘ft   7   114   11½  21½  25   515  BroganG1   3500 71 ⒻSpr'gH'sSpr'g114  Sw'tEva  M'lieB'o 6
Jun 8-703Det   6 f 1:12⅖ft   13  111   53½  59   615  615  SnyderL2   4000 63 Perretta 116  Burleson  Mr. Garfield 8
May19-706Det   6 f 1:13⅕ft   54  111   2h   72¾  98½  1111 LaylandW3  5000 63 Mr.MaePop116  Rellim'sChall  M'rchB'l 11
May 4-704Det   6 f 1:12⅕ft   18  111   42½  78   815  816  BroganG8   5000 63 CoolWink113  StarCollum  Bal'c'dTrade 8
Apr28-706Det   6 f 1:12⅕ft   9½  111   42½  95¾  107½ 119¼ SnyderL2   5000 70 JuniorD'ck111  R'lim'sCh'l  SniffinBilly 12
Nov 3-691Det   6 f 1:13⅘sm   6   115   2h   67½  717  718  SnyderL2   5000 53 Spr'gH'sSpr'g115  P'llyB.115  Mr.E.R. 8
      Jan 17 FG 4f ft :50b          Dec 24 FG 4f ft :50⅖b          Dec 18 FG 3f ft :36b
```

ONE MONTH RULE
(LAST RACE AUGUST 26.)

Okabush ✻ 114 B. g (1964). by Beau Busher—Okafai, by High Lea.
Br., W. K. Kesten & S. V. Scott (Ky.). 1971 3 0 0 0 $150
Owner, E. Domingue. Trainer, E. Terro. $2,500 1970 1 0 0 0 $150

```
Feb 2-712FG     6 f 1:12⅕ft    6¼   114   24   45   1219 1227 Gon'sRD12   2500 61 ComedySh'w118  Conspir'cy  B'nsExpr's 12
Jan13-712FG     6 f 1:15⅘sm    4    114   78¾  711  66½  710  Gon'sRD11   2500 60 LindaD.J.109  Sirt'rbance  Play ItRoyal 12
Jan 6-711FG     6 f 1:12⅖ft    4-5  ▲113  56   36   56½  42   G'z'lesRD1  2500 85 MarketSearch107  LindaD.J.  Royal T'r 12
Dec28-705FG     5½ f 1:06⅘ft   10   112   52¼  32   32   43¼  G'z'l'sRD10 2500 87 UncleFerd112  F'st orFamine  TrailC'k 12
Oct31-696Spt    6 f 1:14⅕sy    6½   116   59¼  55¼  58   65¼  Belv'leEM2  5000 75 N'co'sDr'm117  F'rw'rdCh'ge116  I L'dy 10
Oct23-699Spt    1 1/16 1:46⅕ft 3¾   119   21   1½   1h   24½  VieraH1     4000 78 TalentM'n117  Ok'b'sh119  WinAnOsc'r 8
Oct16-695Haw  Ⓣ 1 1:42⅘sf      8¼   118   21½  24   48   511  WinantR3    4500 56 Boffo122  PrinceMelaney116  LordCl'dy 7
Oct 7-696Haw  Ⓣ 7 f 1:27⅕yl    8¾   120   33   3½   11   11   WinantR2    4000 80 Okabush120  R'm'nLegend122  Allegiant 10
Oct 3-691Haw    6 f 1:11⅕ft    14   116   914  911  79½  65¼  WinantR2    5000 85 B't't'n120  WiseSt'd't122  TwoR'nH'ds 10
Sep24-695Haw  Ⓣ 1 1:40⅗sf      4¾   120   2h   12   21½  65¾  Bel'leEM8  c4000 62 TalentMan116  SkeeRuler116  D'tf'rme 10
Sep18-699Haw  Ⓣ 7 f 1:26⅕fm    4    116   14   13   2h   21   Belv'leEM7  4500 84 R'manLegend116  Okabush116  RunZag 10
      Dec 17 FG 3f gd :37⅗b          Dec 11 FG 3f ft :36⅘b          Dec 8 FG 4f ft :51⅕b
```

8-LENGTH RULE
(FINISHED 12th,
27 LENGTHS BEHIND.)

The second race is a good example of why Daily Doubles are so infrequently playable. After dumping *Just Missed John* and *Nashell* on the One-Month rule and shipping out *He's a Reason, Haberdasher, Relay, Take Silk, High Margin* and *Okabush* on the basis of the Eight-Length rule, we're stuck with three inseparable contenders: *Runin' Playboy, He's It* and *Happy Hull.* It's another 6 furlong for $2,500 potential baseball covers. It could be a matter of which of the three is still on four legs at the finish. These cheapies are the least predictable horses on the grounds and should always be viewed with caution.

Since we can't get any further now we'll wait to see what happens at the track.

In the third race, we get somewhat better horses at a $3,200 claiming price at 1$\frac{1}{16}$ mile for older horses, four years and upward. These have raced enough to show what they can do. Casual observation shows *Damaring* can be eliminated on This Track rule and *Control Tower* on the Distance rule. *Tennywood* and *Outrider* can't pass muster on the Eight-Length rule. Since *Stymeco* is still a maiden, he has no business in this race and *Pero Pescou* faltered for Loss In The Stretch. This leaves *Parmenio, James Quillo* and *Prince Saha'ed.* Closer examination of the speed ratings show that *Prince Saha'ed* has significantly better speed at the distance and can easily be justified as the best in the race. Once again a quick look at the Consensus shows *Prince Saha'ed* as the second consensus choice with one selector picking him first. Doesn't look like we'll get much in the way of odds, but should be a good bet.

The fourth race is a Starter Handicap for four year olds and up at 1$\frac{1}{16}$ miles. This is not to be confused with a high-class Stakes Handicap race. Rather, it is for horses normally racing in $3,500 claiming races. Since there are only seven horses in the race, our job is a lot easier. Brief examination of the post performance shows that *Dudes Finale* and *Ready Sport* don't pass the Eight-Length requirement and *Wee Willie* suffered from Loss In The Stretch. *Bum for Daddy* is easily seen to be lacking in Speed.

This leaves two strong contenders—*Mechief* and *Tantalio.* There seems to be no way to separate them. However, this is an Exacta race and we'll consider playing the Exacta both ways which requires tickets showing each horse winning and each horse placing. Or we may be able to "Dutch" these two if the odds are right (which is unlikely because all the public selectors have picked them). In any event, we can do no more now but wait to see what takes place at the track. One thing looks pretty certain—it's a two horse race.

Things are looking up now because the better horses are beginning to run. The fifth race is an allowance race with a $5,000 purse, at 6 furlongs. Looking closer, however, we see it is for Louisiana-bred horses, which means some of the top allowance horses at the track will not be eligible. This tends to depress the caliber of competition somewhat, so we handicap accordingly. *Mr. Reed* hasn't raced recently, so the One Month rule applies. *Bayou Bengal, Bill Blayer* and *Royal Pussycat* fail the Loss In The Stretch requirement, and once again we're down to weeding out potential contenders. However, *Real Blonde* doesn't have the Speed and *Frankie T* and *Jaymie M* don't make it because of the Finish In The Money rule.

This leaves *Oiney's Rule, Red's Story, Aleut, Garret Road,* and *Skycite*—far too many to work with, but we'll save the rest of the work for the track since we are just eliminating the obvious at this time.

The sixth race is another claimer but the $7,500

3rd Fair Grounds

1 1-16 MILES. (Tenacious, Feb. 14, 1959, 1:43, 5, 119.)
Claiming. Purse $2,700. 4-year-olds and upward. 4-year-olds, 119 lbs.; older, 120 lbs. Non-winners of three races since Dec. 6 allowed 2 lbs.; two races since then, 4 lbs.; a race, 6 lbs. Claiming price, $3,200.

***Parmenio II.** **118** B. g (1965), by Parsing—Nigromancia, by Nigromante.
Breeder, Haras Villegas (Peru). 1971 1 0 0 0 $78
Owner, M. H. Van Berg Stable, Inc. Trainer, J. Van Berg. **$3,200** 1970 27 5 5 4 $14,353
Jan 9-713FG 1 1/16 1:50⅖m 2 ▲118 6 6½ 7 2¾ 7 7 5 6¼ MoyersL8 3000 57 J. D.'s Pride 117 Ezekiel Rosehearty 8
Dec29-7010FG 1 1/16 1:49⅘sy 2 ▲115 1h 1 1 2 1 1 3 MoyersL1 2500 66 Parmenio II.115 IdentifyMe Inte'pt'n 9
Dec16-709FG 1-40 1:44⅘sl 2 ▲112 7 14 5 7½ 3 2 1 1 HeathM3 2500 69 Parmenio 112 Parar Top Bout 10
Dec 9-709FG 1 1/16 1:47⅗ft 6-5 ▲115 Fog. 2 2½ Whit'dDE6 2500 74 IdentifyMe115 Parmenio II. PaperBoy 10
Dec 1-709FG 1 1/16 1:47⅕ft 1 ▲115 5 6 1h 2 2 2¾ WhitedDE6 2500 78 Allentuck114 Parmenio II. StorageK'g 7
Nov10-706Spt 1 1-8 1:53 sy 3-2 ▲114 2 2 2 1½ 2 1 2 2½ HeathM2 2500 78 NoEmptyW'g'n117 P'm'nio II. N't'eR't 7
Nov 6-709Spt 1 1:42⅕gd 6¼ 114 3 5 3 3 3 2½ 2 1 HeathM2 2500 68 ParForSum114 Parmenio II. Fl'tDeet 8
Oct20-709Spt 1 1-8 1:53 sy 15 114 3 3½ 3 4½ 4 9 5 6½ JonesK5 2500 74 Tosinisbad122 Pallbearer SpaceJog 10
Sep26-7010Rkm 1⅛ 1:52⅖ft 85 110 8 9½ 9 35 9 39 9 31 CoxD8 H2750 48 Tantalio 125 Total Sum Hellenic Man 9
Sep16-709Rkm 1 1-8 1:54⅕m 5½ 110 4 6½ 6 32 6 29 6 27 MaffeoC4 H2750 43 Yarak113 Gobbler'sJewel RedSoxFan 6
Aug28-708LD 1 1:42 sy 8¼ 114 8 13 7 11 5 6½ 3 2¾ MichaudD6 2500 71 App'cept'n117 Mir'm'rCh'f P'm'nio II. 8
Jan 31 FG 4f ft :51b Jan 25 FG 4f ft :50b

Control Tower **113** Dk. b. orbr. g (1967), by Nade—Landing Lights, by First Landing.
Breeder, Mrs. H. S. Clark (Md.). 1971 2 0 1 0 $575
Owner, Mrs. H. S. Clark. Trainer, H. S. Clark. **$3,200** 1970 7 0 0 0 $435
Jan21-711FG 6 f 1:12 ft 8¾ 113 5 5 5 11 3 7 2 4 SmithRA3 2500 85 He'sA R's'n112 ControlTower BigSing 12
Jan 6-711FG 6 f 1:12⅘ft 12 112 7 12 6 8½ 4 5½ 5 4 MoyersL10 2500 83 MarketSearch107 LindaD.J. Royal T'r 12
Dec31-702FG 6 f 1:14⅘hy 60 112 12 16 10 16 7 14 5 8¼ MoyersL6 2500 67 L'tleS'laris112 C'mr'de inArms Gr'dNu 12
Dec19-701FG 6 f 1:12⅗ft 26 112 7 4¼ 10 11 8 7½ 10 9 TauzinL2 2500 77 Comr'de inArms112 ArkyTw't D'bleD'r 12
Dec15-706FG 5½ f 1:07 sy 32 112 10 13 11 15 11 17 12 14 MoyersL7 4500 75 Gall'tN'tions113 Fr'chW'g'n AwL'tsGo 12
Oct30-702Lrl 6 f 1:14 gd 19 114 3 5 5 8 10 20 11 15 P's'reWJ11 4000 65 B'ySpl'nd'r122 B'ckH'll'sMiss GerryT. 11
Oct 8-707Mar 6 f 1:15⅘ft 8¼ 116 4 4 6 6¼ 9 17 10 12 WalshE2 5000 75 Outtried113 Galligher PuntReturn 10
Sep 8-705Tim 7 f 1:29⅖ft 11 114 1h 3 1½ 2 4 4 5½ HowardR7 5000 77 DemonJack114 TryCharging BeCert'n 8
Aug31-708Tim 5¾ f 1:09⅘ft 8 112 3 1 2 3 3 6 4 8 HowardR6 5000 83 Parth'nK'g111 RoundJohn GoGoGr'ny 7
Aug21-707Tim 5¾ f 1:10 ft 45 110 6 2¾ 7 11 7 13 7 13 HowardR3 7500 77 TrickyNicky 114 GainesMills A-Ha 8
Oct31-695Lrl 6 f 1:12⅘ft 11 117 6 2¼ 9 8¼ 8 13 9 14 NelsonE12 7500 73 Ap'h t'eB'h113 C'n'd'nTh'd'r117 Gilzo 12
Sep 6-691Tim 5¾ f 1:11⅕ft 6¾ 117 3nk 1h 1h 1 1 BarnesR1 5000 84 C'ntr'lT'k'r117 Mr.J'hnL'gh114 M'sA'e 8

Pero Pescou **116** Dk. b. or br. g (1966), by Dog Fish—Noni Porter, by Dr. Harley.
Breeder, R. C. Schnorr (N. M.). 1971 3 1 1 0 $2,176
Owner, D. A. Harp. Trainer, W. R. Harp. **$3,200** 1970 5 2 0 1 $4,980
Jan20-719FG 1 1/16 1:46⅖ft 7¼ 116 2 1 4 2 2 1½ 4 2¼ WinantR3 c2500 81 Great Timing 114 Ezekiel Mink 8
Jan13-719FG 1 1/16 1:50⅘m 2½ ▲116 2 1 2 1 2 3 2no Rubb'coP1 c2500 61 Jim'sPr'tyGirl 109 P'roP'sc'u Nasc'l'n 8
Jan 1-712FG 6 f 1:14⅖hy 10 116 6 4¼ 6 5 2 3 1 8 Rubb'coP3 2500 77 P'oP'sc'u116 Adm'l'sC'm'd Sw'p'mC'n 12
Dec23-709FG 1 1/16 1:47 ft 8¼ 113 5 2½ 5 4½ 7 9 8 9 D'sO'xS10 c2500 71 Gobbler'sJewel 115 Killen CountMoore 11
Dec17-709FG 1 1/16 1:45⅗ft 41 114 4 4 2 1 3 12 6 15 DesOr'xS3 3200 72 Mechief 117 Great Timing Viet Nam 12
Dec 5-703FG 6 f 1:12 ft 115 115 7 7 7 9½ 8 15 7 8½ DesOr'xS12 4000 80 Prominence115 NegroB'ro DotD'tyDot 12
Nov28-706FG 6 f 1:11⅘ft 46 115 8 7¾ 6 7¾ 8 13 8 9¾ DesOr'xS9 4000 80 Tudorfib115 DotDittydot R'si'sRogue 11
Oct31-704Spt 6½ f 1:19⅘gd 15 116 6 4 5 4½ 4 1½ 3 4¼ Desor'uxS4 3750 75 Rose ofTudor115 H'lkaJet PeroPescou 10
Oct17-706Spt 1 1/16 1:45⅘ft 5¼ 116 2 3 2 3 4 5½ 6 5¾ JonesK8 c3500 79 NegroBarro118 YoungReaper Ravinia 8

Tennywood * **114** Ch. g (1965), by War Trouble—Royal Maam, by Royal Mustang.
Breeder, G. W. & J. Lancaster (Ky.). 1971 5 0 0 0 $90
Owner, W. H. Bishop Stables, Inc. Trainer, W. H. Bishop. **$3,200** 1970 16 2 2 1 $8,328
Jan28-716FG 1 1/16 1:45⅗ft 40 114 7 7½ 9 17 10 15 10 19 BairdRL5 4000 68 Stubzy 115 Limetime Pier d'Oro 10
Jan21-715FG 1-40 1:40⅘ft 9½ 113 4 6 4 7 7 9 8 17 BairdRL3 4000 72 Mechief 116 Stubzy Pier d'Oro 10
Jan14-715FG 1-40 1:44⅘hy 18 114 3 8 4 7 7 7¾ 5 16 SmithRA10 4000 53 Hillsub112 ReadySport Pitt'sL'stPick 10
Jan 7-715FG 1 1/16 1:46 ft 7¾ 114 2 5 3 5 8 14 8 14 SmithRA3 4000 71 Van 114 Ready Sport Child's Prince 8
Jan 2-712FG 6 f 1:13 gd 16 113 12 16 12 17 9 13 9 13 SmithRA3 4000 71 BigM'hS'm112 Ch'n'tP'k T'p of theD'k 12
Dec30-708FG 6 f 1:13⅕sy 13 112 9 4½ Rain 9 16 8 14 SmithRA10 5000 69 Rossi'sRogue112 N'groB'rro B'tlePick 12
Dec16-705FG 6 f 1:14 sl 14 112 12 12 12 11 7 7¼ 7 4 SmithRA9 5000 75 FullSt'mAh'd112 B'ttlePick Pollamber 12
Dec12-702FG 6 f 1:12⅖ft 14 112 8 7¼ 8 5¼ 9 7½ 7 5¾ McC'rJW10 4000 81 R'si'sRog'e112 Ch'tn'tP'rk D'tD'tyD't 12
Jun 9-709AP [T] 1 1/16 1:44⅕fm 6½ 114 5 8½ 2 5 2 3 1no MarquezC7 7000 88 Tennywood 114 Late Royal Silent Sea 8
Jun 3-706AP 1 1:38⅘gd 6 114 7 8 6 5¾ 4 6 4 7¼ MarquezC1 7000 60 BlackChapar'l 109 Resuello P's'y'sSp'l 8
Dec 8 FG 4f ft :50b

Stymieco **114** Ch. g (1965), by Quidico—Destymie, by Stymie.
Breeder, Live Oak Stable (Tex.). 1971 4 0 0 0 $318
Owners, Sharon Hild. Trainer, G. Hild. **$3,200** 1970 20 0 1 3 $3,184
Jan26-719FG 1-40 1:42 ft 37 113 5 3 7 6½ 5 4½ 4 2¼ SpindlerL3 3200 81 WanderW'st120 Child'Lage J'm'sQ'llo 10
Jan21-715FG 1-40 1:40⅘ft 22 113 9 10 5 7 9 11 9 18 SpindlerL7 4000 64 Mechief 116 Stubzy Pier d'Oro 10
Jan16-7110FG 1-40 1:42 ft 16 110 5 9 6 8 6 5½ 6 8½ Sp'dl'rL9 H3500 74 Tantalio117 DudesFinale WeeWillie 10
Jan 5-714FG 1 1/16 1:46⅗gd 15 114 6 5¼ 5 2¼ 4 4 4 2 SpindlerL1 3000 80 KingWho116 CountSash FreedomRing 9
Dec28-7010FG 1 1/16 1:49⅖ft 7½ 112 5 4 4 3½ 3 4 3 3½ SilvaW4 c2500 64 FreedomRing112 PaperBoy Stymieco 7
Dec18-709FG 1 1/16 1:47 ft 10 113 6 7½ 8 7¼ 7 8¾ 5 9 B'ldwinR7 c2500 71 Polly'sBounce104 Glow-St'r G'y Im'ge 12
Dec 8-702FG 6 f 1:12⅗ft 107 113 12 15 12 14 10 9½ 10 10 L'm'thR12 2500 76 He's It 110 Happy Hull Red Appian 12
Dec 3-702FG 6 f 1:12 ft 124 113 10 20 10 17 7 14 8 18 LambethR7 2500 71 Quadrant114 Haberdasher BabyEscar 11
May27-709Was 1 1:38⅗ft 6¼ 118 7 14 6 9 6 11 7 9¾ WinantR4 2500 78 Koala 113 Bookie Legal Aid 10

SPEED RULE
(78 SPEED RATING IS NOT WITHIN 5 POINTS OF PRINCE SAHA'ED'S 84 FOR THE DISTANCE.)

DISTANCE RULE
(HORSE HASN'T RUN THE DISTANCE.) (1.)

LOSS IN STRETCH RULE
(LOST MORE THAN 3/4 LENGTHS IN THE STRETCH RUN.)

8-LENGTH RULE
(FINISHED 10th, 19 LENGTHS BEHIND.)

NO WIN RULE
(STYMIECO HASN'T WON A RACE IN THE PAST 2 YEARS.)

(1.) WE CAN'T ASSUME THAT CONTROL TOWER HAS NEVER RUN THIS DISTANCE, BUT HE IS OBVIOUSLY BEST SUITED TO SPRINTS.

Outrider 114 B. g (1966), by Croque-Fer—Pony Tail, by Gee Whiz.
Breeder, Audley Farm (Va.). 1971 3 0 0 0 $84
Owner, Audley Farm. Trainer, F. P. Aime III. $3,200 1970 16 5 4 0 $13,750

Jan23-714FG 1-40 1:40⅕ft 5½ 112 36 38½ 51½ 618 TauzinL1 H3500 74 Mist'rRollins112 Building DudesFin'le 7
Jan16-7110FG 1-40 1:42 ft 8 112 812 814 811 57½ TauzinL3 H3500 75 Tantalio117 DudesFinale WeeWillie 10
Jan 2-714FG 1 1-8 1:54⅖gd 12 113 1h 31 58½ 614 JonesK3 H3000 58 Tantalio 113 SirVictor GreatPumpkin 6
Dec19-706FG 1-40 1:41⅕ft 2¾ ▲115 44½ 48½ 56½ 69¾ NicholsJ4 6200 77 Off to Market 109 Col. Frib Tudorfib 8
Dec 5-704FG 6 f 1:12⅕ft 12 114 98¾ 99½ 89½ 77½ BairdRL2 6000 80 Deadwood 114 Tudorfib Croydon 10
Oct30-709LD 1 1:39 ft 8-5 ▲112* 41½ 21½ 2½ 2½ RicciA5 7500 88 TapeDeck122 Outrider IThinkICan 7
Oct21-707LD 1 1:37⅗ft 9½ 109* 1½ 2h 42¼ 42 RicciA8 Alw 94 R'sell'sR'lah122 M't'nPine Oxf'dAc'nt 8
Oct14-707Rkm 1 1/16 1:46⅗ft 4½ 114 11 1h 11 2½ MaffeoC2 6000 77 AlarmKing115 Outrider TapeDeck 7

8-LENGTH RULE (FINISHED 6th 18 LENGTHS BEHIND WINNER.)

James Quillo 114 B. g (1966), by Cornell—Corinne T., by Jamestown.
Breeder, A. Gee (Okla.). 1971 2 0 0 1 $459
Owner, L. Robideaux, Jr: Trainer, L. Robideaux, Jr. $3,200 1970 27 2 7 5 $8,745

Jan26-719FG 1-40 1:42 ft 5½ 118 87¼ 88½ 66 31¾ NicholsJ8 3200 81 WanderW'st120 ChildJ'dge J'm'sQ'llo 10
Jan 8-7110FG 1-40 1:45⅖sy 3½ 115 21½ 23 23 42¾ NicholsJ1 3500 63 KingWho116 Big 'N Brassy Geelong 10
Dec 3-701FG 6 f 1:12⅕ft 9 117 87½ 87 64½ 31½ NicholsJ2 3200 86 WaysideInn115 Educator JamesQuillo 12
Nov28-706FG 6 f 1:11⅘ft 37 115 77¼ 99¾ 69½ 55 NicholsJ7 4000 85 Tudorfib115 DotDittydot R'si'sRogue 11
Nov 5-709Spt 1 1/16 1:49⅕gd 6½ 119 76 88½ 913 915 RayL7 c4000 53 Third Moon 114 Tony W. Salute John 9
Oct27-709Spt 1 1/16 1:46⅘ft 2½ ▲120 32½ 21½ 21½ 52¼ JonesK1 c3500 78 Y'gR'p'r116 Mr.M'chell Count'sJ.M.C. 10
Oct21-705Spt 1 1/16 1:48⅕gd 3½ 117 1½ 1½ 1h 12† JonesK2 3200 73 JamesQ'llo117 R'nForD'dy C't'sJ.M.C. 8
†Dead heat.
Dec 28 FG 3f ft :37⅗b

SPEED RULE (HORSE'S SPEED RATING IS NOT WITHIN 5 POINTS OF PRINCE SAHA'ED'S 84 FOR DISTANCE.)

Damaring 108 B. f (1967), by Saidam—Gotterdammerung, by Pinza.
Br., Mr. & Mrs. S. C. Register (Ky.). 1971 2 0 1 0 $720
Owner, E. Abadie. Trainer, T. Bougon. $3,200 1970 16 0 1 1 $1,892

Jan15-712TrP 1 1/16 1:45⅗ft 9 108* 88 96¾ 811 714 RichieS3 4000 60 Mont'rosso116 L'dsc'peP't'r SpiritsUp 12
Jan 5-7110TrP 1 1/16 1:47 ft 3¾ 113 54¾ 22 2½ 2¾ BreenR4 3500 66 ⒻBig andBr'ht115 Dam'ring Gam'r'te 11
Dec31-704TrP 1-70 1:44⅕ft 9½ 109* 76 69 49 39 Br'c'leVJr7 4000 67 ⒻTatting120 Up theStairs Damaring 11
Dec25-701TrP 1-70 1:44 ft 14 108* 53 46½ 46½ 29 Br'leVJr11 3500 68 ⒻCaptullus 113 Damaring Hilditchka 11
Dec19-702TrP 1 1/16 1:46 ft 4¼ 109* 67½ 56 57¼ 515 BreenR2 3500 57 Demost'nes III.116 W'rF'de J't'sSk'p'r 9
Dec11-702TrP 6 f 1:11⅕ft 9 110 811 78½ 77¼ 610 MacB'thD7 4500 72 Exhilarating 112 ShoeShine Southern 12
Oct21-703Kee 7 f 1:26⅗sy 15 110 99¼ 105½ 1012 1011 ArroyoH7 7500 64 D'nyM.116 DedicatedCh'ger ExoticB'd 11
Oct15-707Kee 6½ f 1:19⅖gd 11 117 913 914 913 78¾ Whi'dDE10 Alw 72 ⒻRunningBeauty117 MistyLil Timely 11
Sep23-707Haw 6½ f 1:18⅕sy 7¾ 110 814 811 66¼ 67 PerretC6 10000 76 Kammer 112 FortyWhacks AnneBallet 9
Dec 18 GP 4f ft :48⅘hg

THIS TRACK RULE (HAS NOT HAD A RACE AT FAIR GROUNDS.)

Prince Saha'ed 115 Dk. b. or br. g (1967), by Social Climber—Noble Princess, by Noble Hero. Breeder, F. D. Kohr (Fla.). 1971 1 0 0 0 $81
Owner, Cody Stable. Trainer, G. Geier. $3,200 1970 28 5 3 5 $13,491

Jan21-714FG 1 1/16 1:46⅕ft 2¼ ▲117 63¾ 53¼ 1h 12½†SmithRA8 c3500 84 PrinceS'ha'ed117 B'rn'dineB. St'yLine 12
†Disqualified and placed fifth.
Dec26-703FG 1-40 1:43⅕ft 4-5 ▲119 75½ 2½ 11½ 13½ BroganG5 3000 77 PrinceS'ha'ed119 Nascoll'n Dem'g'g'e 10
Dec19-703FG 1-40 1:41⅗ft 1 ▲119 75 46 21 2¾ HolmesD6 c3000 84 CarefulJuror110 Pr'ceS'ha'ed N'sc'l'n 10
Dec 8-705FG 6 f 1:11⅘ft 3¾ 115 76¾ 811 67 56¾ BroganG7 4200 83 EsKup111 GallantNotions S'nnyMiguel 12
Dec 1-707FG 6 f 1:12⅕ft 18 120 910 911 56 32¾ BroganG7 4500 85 ProudF'ce117 AwL't'sGo Pr'ceS'ha'ed 10
Nov12-706HP 6 f 1:16⅗sl 3½ 120 714 79¾ 66 1nk Rub'coP7 c3200 71 PrinceS'ha'ed120 Dr.H'ck'r Pride'sF'll 7
Oct26-707HP 6 f 1:12⅖ft 7¼ 122 915 99 710 56¾ HeimK8 3500 85 OldCup122 L'c'sO'Trig'r MillieBolero 9
Oct 8-701HP 6 f 1:13⅗ft 3 117 910 74¼ 52¾ 1½ S'ageJD6 c2500 86 PrinceSaha'ed117 Abraxas BeerCh's'r 10
Jan 19 FG 4f ft :50b Dec 25 FG 4f ft :50b

NUMBER 1 SELECTION

4th Fair Grounds

1 1-16 MILES. (Tenacious, Feb. 14, 1959, 1:43, 5, 119.) Pegasus Starter Handicap—Series No. 3. Purse $3,100. 4-year-olds and upward, starters for a claiming price of $3,500 or less in 1970-71, non-winners exceeding $4,000 in claiming and starter races since last starting for $3,500 or less.

COUPLED: TANTALIO and BUILDING.

***Tantalio** 120 B. h (1965), by Parsing—Tantioma, by Tantieme.
Breeder, Haras Villegas (Peru). 1971 2 2 0 0 $3,540
Owner, M. H. Van Berg Stable, Inc. Trainer, J. Van Berg. 1970 13 5 2 3 $13,310

Jan16-7110FG 1-40 1:42 ft 2 ▲117 1014 713 54½ 1¾ MoyersL8 H3500 83 Tantalio117 DudesFinale WeeWillie 10
Jan 2-714FG 1 1-8 1:54⅖gd 4 113 4nk 1h 1h 1nk MoyersL6 H3000 72 Tantalio 113 SirVictor GreatPumpkin 6
Dec19-7010FG 1 1/16 1:45⅖ft 3 116 76¾ 57¼ 59 54¼ NicholsJ2 H3000 84 BramblesBoy117 SirVictor WeeWillie 10
Dec 5-7010FG 1-40 1:41 ft 9-5 ▲119 613 512 49 45¼ MoyersL6 H3000 83 Ambi'rixBoi118 SirVict'r BramblesBoy 9
Nov28-7010FG 1-40 1:41⅗ft 2½ 120 34 32 31 2½ MoyersL1 H3000 84 Wee Willie 112 Tantalio Sir Victor 9
Oct17-7010Rkm 1⅛ 1:53⅘gd 3¼ 128 78¾ 56¼ 41¼ 2no RamosA3 H2750 72 Total Sum 112 Tantalio Asti 7
Sep26-7010Rkm 1⅛ 1:52⅖ft 9-5 ▲125 79 411 41¼ 11½ RamosA5 H2750 79 Tantalio 125 Total Sum Hellenic Man 9
Sep 5-7010Rkm 1 1/16 1:46 gd 2½ ▲126 2½ 2h 31½ 33 RamosA2 H2750 78 A-Ruse 128 Red Sox Fan Tantalio 10
Aug26-7010Rkm 1 1/16 1:45⅗ft 2¾ 122 75¾ 41½ 12 13½ RamosA9 H2750 87 Tantalio122 UncleHerbie HellanicMan 10
Jan 30 FG 5f ft 1:01b Dec 29 FG 5f gd 1:03b Dec 29 FG 5f gd 1:03b

CONTENDER

Dudes Finale 113 Ch. g (1964), by The Dude—Kirk Kriss, by Roi Rouge.
Breeder, Mr. & Mrs. A. H. Boyd (Ill.). 1971 3 0 1 1 $1,059
Owner, Cody Stable. Trainer, G. Geier. 1970 28 5 8 5 $18,125

Jan23-714FG 1-40 1:40⅕ft 2½ ▲114 514 617 412 310 Rub'coP3 H3500 82 Mist'rRollins112 Building DudesFin'le 7
Jan16-7110FG 1-40 1:42 ft 6½ 114 610 57 42½ 2¾ Rub'oP10 H3500 82 Tantalio117 DudesFinale WeeWillie 10
Jan 7-715FG 1 1/16 1:46 ft 10 118 69½ 77¾ 57 45¾ Del'yeE1 c4000 79 Van 114 Ready Sport Child's Prince 8
Dec31-7010FG 1-40 1:45⅖hy 22 116 77¼ 55½ 21 1no Delah'yeE2 4000 66 DudesFinale116 OneNightStand Van 10
Dec17-709FG 1 1/16 1:45⅗ft 7¾ 115 1215 99¼ 67 513 H'lm'sD11 c3200 74 Mechief 117 Great Timing Viet Nam 12
Dec12-7010FG 1 1/16 1:46⅕ft 9¾ 112 49 610 918 815 BroganG6 H3000 69 Br'mbl'sB'y114 Gr'tPumpkin SirVict'r 10
Nov26-703FG 1-40 1:42⅕ft 24 112 715 58¼ 5¾ 1½ BroganG4 5000 82 Dudes Finale 112 Mechief Sky Village 9
Nov12-708HP 6½ f 1:19⅘sl 12 115 813 818 718 413 BroganG5 A2500 69 Fl'tIrishman119 LongRoad Beaukawa 8

8-LENGTH RULE (FINISHED 3rd, 10 LENGTHS BEHIND WINNER.)

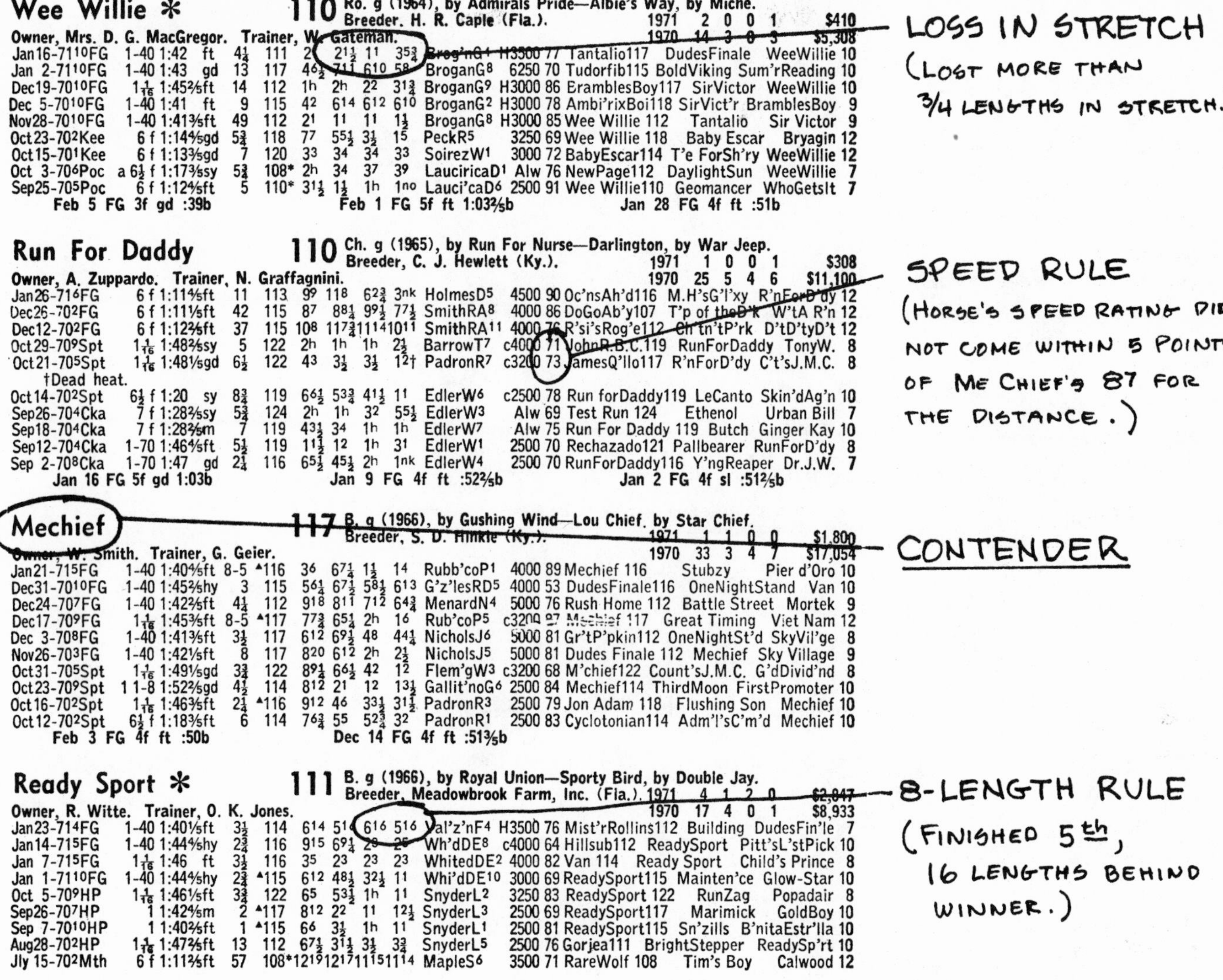


```
Wee Willie *               110 Ro. g (1964), by Admirals Pride—Albie's Way, by Miche.
                               Breeder. H. R. Caple (Fla.).          1971  2  0 0 1     $410
Owner, Mrs. D. G. MacGregor.  Trainer, W. Gateman.                   1970 14  3 0 3   $5,308
Jan16-71 10FG  1-40 1:42   ft   4¼  111  2   21½  11   35¾  Brog'nG1  H3500 77 Tantalio117   DudesFinale  WeeWillie 10
Jan 2-71 10FG  1-40 1:43   gd  13   117  46½ 711  610  58   BroganG8   6250 70 Tudorfib115 BoldViking Sum'rReading 10
Dec19-70 10FG  1 1/16 1:45⅖ft  14   112  1h  2h   22   31¾  BroganG9  H3000 86 EramblesBoy117  SirVictor  WeeWillie 10
Dec 5-70 10FG  1-40 1:41   ft   9   115  42  614  612  610  BroganG2  H3000 78 Ambi'rixBoi118 SirVict'r BramblesBoy 9
Nov28-70 10FG  1-40 1:41⅗ft    49   112  21  11   11   1½   BroganG8  H3000 85 Wee Willie 112   Tantalio   Sir Victor 9
Oct23-70 2Kee    6 f 1:14⅘gd    5¾  118  77  55½  3½   15   PeckR5     3250 69 Wee Willie 118   Baby Escar   Bryagin 12
Oct15-70 1Kee    6 f 1:13⅗gd    7   120  33  34   34   33   SoirezW1   3000 72 BabyEscar114 T'e ForSh'ry WeeWillie 12
Oct 3-70 6Poc  a 6½ f 1:17⅗sy   5¾  108* 2h  34   37   39   LauciricaD1 Alw 76 NewPage112  DaylightSun  WeeWillie 7
Sep25-70 5Poc    6 f 1:12⅘ft    5   110* 31½ 1½   1h   1no  Lauci'caD6 2500 91 Wee Willie110  Geomancer  WhoGetsIt 7
     Feb 5 FG 3f gd :39b             Feb 1 FG 5f ft 1:03⅖b              Jan 28 FG 4f ft :51b

Run For Daddy              110 Ch. g (1965), by Run For Nurse—Darlington, by War Jeep.
                               Breeder, C. J. Hewlett (Ky.).         1971  1  0 0 1     $308
Owner, A. Zuppardo.  Trainer, N. Graffagnini.                        1970 25  5 4 6  $11,100
Jan26-71 6FG     6 f 1:11⅘ft   11   113  99  118  62¾  3nk  HolmesD5   4500 90 Oc'nsAh'd116  M.H'sG'l'xy  R'nForD'dy 12
Dec26-70 2FG     6 f 1:11⅕ft   42   115  87  88¼  99½  77½  SmithRA8   4000 86 DoGoAb'y107  T'p of theD'k  W'tA R'n 12
Dec12-70 2FG     6 f 1:12⅖ft   37   115  108 117¾ 1114 1011 SmithRA11  4000 76 R'si'sRog'e112 Ch'tn'tP'rk  D'tD'tyD't 12
Oct29-70 9Spt  1 1/16 1:48⅖sy   5   122  2h  1h   1h   2½   BarrowT7  c4000 71 JohnR.B.C.119  RunForDaddy  TonyW. 8
Oct21-70 5Spt  1 1/16 1:48⅕gd   6½  122  43  3½   3½   12†  PadronR7  c3200 73 JamesQ'llo117  R'nForD'dy  C't'sJ.M.C. 8
    †Dead heat.
Oct14-70 2Spt    6½ f 1:20  sy  8¾  119  66½ 53¾  41½  11   EdlerW6   c2500 78 Run forDaddy119  LeCanto  Skin'dAg'n 10
Sep26-70 4Cka    7 f 1:28⅖sy    5¾  124  2h  1h   32   55½  EdlerW3     Alw 69 Test Run 124    Ethenol   Urban Bill 7
Sep18-70 4Cka    7 f 1:28⅖m     7   119  43½ 34   1h   1h   EdlerW7     Alw 75 Run For Daddy 119  Butch  Ginger Kay 10
Sep12-70 4Cka  1-70 1:46⅘ft     5½  119  11½ 12   1h   31   EdlerW1    2500 70 Rechazado121  Pallbearer  RunForD'dy 8
Sep 2-70 8Cka  1-70 1:47   gd   2¼  116  65½ 45½  2h   1nk  EdlerW4    2500 70 RunForDaddy116  Y'ngReaper  Dr.J.W. 7
     Jan 16 FG 5f gd 1:03b           Jan 9 FG 4f ft :52⅖b               Jan 2 FG 4f sl :51⅖b

Mechief                    117 B. g (1966), by Gushing Wind—Lou Chief, by Star Chief.
                               Breeder, S. D. Hinkle (Ky.).          1971  1  1 0 0   $1,800
Owner, W. Smith.  Trainer, G. Geier.                                 1970 33  3 4 7  $17,054
Jan21-71 5FG   1-40 1:40⅘ft   8-5 ▲116  36  67¼  1½   14   Rubb'coP1  4000 89 Mechief 116     Stubzy   Pier d'Oro 10
Dec31-70 10FG  1-40 1:45⅖hy     3   115  56¼ 67½  58½  613  G'z'lesRD5 4000 53 DudesFinale116  OneNightStand  Van 10
Dec24-70 7FG   1-40 1:42⅖ft     4¼  112  918 811  712  64¾  MenardN4   5000 76 Rush Home 112  Battle Street  Mortek 9
Dec17-70 9FG   1 1/16 1:45⅗ft 8-5 ▲117  77¾ 65¼  2h   16   Rub'coP5  c3200 87 Mechief 117   Great Timing  Viet Nam 12
Dec 3-70 8FG   1-40 1:41⅗ft     3½  117  612 69½  48   44¼  NicholsJ6  5000 81 Gr'tP'pkin112 OneNightSt'd  SkyVil'ge 8
Nov26-70 3FG   1-40 1:42⅕ft     8   117  820 612  2h   2½   NicholsJ5  5000 81 Dudes Finale 112  Mechief  Sky Village 9
Oct31-70 5Spt  1 1/16 1:49⅕gd   3¾  122  89¼ 66½  42   12   Flem'gW3  c3200 68 M'chief122  Count'sJ.M.C.  G'dDivid'nd 8
Oct23-70 9Spt  1 1-8 1:52⅖gd    4½  114  812 21   12   13½  Gallit'noG6 2500 84 Mechief114  ThirdMoon  FirstPromoter 10
Oct16-70 2Spt  1 1/16 1:46⅗ft   2¼ ▲116  912 46   33½  31½  PadronR3   2500 79 Jon Adam 118  Flushing Son  Mechief 10
Oct12-70 2Spt    6½ f 1:18⅗ft   6   114  76¾ 55   52¾  32   PadronR1   2500 83 Cyclotonian114  Adm'l'sC'm'd  Mechief 10
     Feb 3 FG 4f ft :50b             Dec 14 FG 4f ft :51⅗b

Ready Sport *              111 B. g (1966), by Royal Union—Sporty Bird, by Double Jay.
                               Breeder, Meadowbrook Farm, Inc. (Fla.). 1971  4  1 2 0   $2,847
Owner, R. Witte.  Trainer, O. K. Jones.                              1970 17  4 0 1   $8,933
Jan23-71 4FG   1-40 1:40⅕ft     3½  114  614 514  616  516  Val'z'nF4 H3500 76 Mist'rRollins112  Building  DudesFin'le 7
Jan14-71 5FG   1-40 1:44⅘hy     2¾  116  915 69¼  28   25   Wh'dDE8   c4000 64 Hillsub112  ReadySport  Pitt'sL'stPick 10
Jan 7-71 5FG   1 1/16 1:46  ft  3½  116  35  23   23   23   WhitedDE2  4000 82 Van 114   Ready Sport  Child's Prince 8
Jan 1-71 10FG  1-40 1:44⅘hy     2¾ ▲115  612 48½  32½  11   Whi'dDE10  3000 69 ReadySport115  Mainten'ce  Glow-Star 10
Oct 5-70 9HP   1 1/16 1:46⅕ft   3¾  122  65  53½  1h   11   SnyderL2   3250 83 ReadySport 122   RunZag   Popadair 8
Sep26-70 7HP       1 1:42⅘m     2  ▲117  812 22   11   12½  SnyderL3   2500 69 ReadySport117   Marimick   GoldBoy 10
Sep 7-70 10HP      1 1:40⅖ft    1  ▲115  66  3½   1h   11   SnyderL1   2500 81 ReadySport115  Sn'zills  B'nitaEstr'lla 10
Aug28-70 2HP   1 1/16 1:47⅖ft  13   112  67½ 31½  3½   3¾   SnyderL5   2500 76 Gorjea111  BrightStepper  ReadySp'rt 10
Jly 15-70 2Mth   6 f 1:11⅖ft   57   108* 1219 1217 1115 1114 MapleS6   3500 71 RareWolf 108   Tim's Boy   Calwood 12
```


tag indicates we're dealing with better horses again. This one is a 6 furlong for four year olds and up with weight allowances for performance.

Catcher Pat shows no wins in the past performance chart and is readily discharged. The Eight-Length rule takes care of *Top Guarantee,* while *Lodey Evenson* and *Salty Ruler* take a walk on the basis of speed. Our Finish In The Money rule gets rid of *Light Traveler,* leaving *Jokey, Full Steam Ahead, King Who* and *Tudor Fib.* While *Tudor Fib* could be eliminated on the rigid application of Loss In The Stretch, he has top speed and set the pace for the first three calls in his last race. We'll leave him in the running for now but he's on borrowed time for that loss in the stretch. Saving the rest of our handicapping of the sixth race for the track, we come to the seventh and another allowance.

This one is also for Louisiana-breds, four year olds and up so the same comments apply from the fifth race.

Our job is easier here and it looks like a pushover. Eight-Length rule takes out *Thirty Dashes, Always Here, Landing Man* and *Fast Rock.* Both *Tansy's Beau* and *Ray's Law* can't last through Loss In The Stretch, and Speed wipes out *Karate.*

Speedy Jake is easily best and will probably be the favorite but should be a good bet, anyway. No sense to the Exacta in this one.

The eighth race is another allowance but tougher competition because it's not restricted to Louisiana-bred horses.

Famed Prince has to go because he has not run at Fairground this season. We hate to see him go because he is a top horse, but rules are rules. *Tenacious Jr.* is at the wrong distance and so another good horse is eliminated. Speed dumps *Michigan Fall.* All the rest have to be left in for the final mathematics at the track.

The ninth race is the feature—*Thelma Stakes* for three-year-old fillies at 6 furlongs. As we saw earlier, *Bee Bee Dabo* has never run more than 5½ furlongs and we never bet that a horse will do something today

5th Fair Grounds

6 FURLONGS. (Tudor Scott, Nov. 27, 1969, 1:09⅘, 3, 116.) Allowances. Purse $5,000 (includes $2,500 supplement). 3-year-olds, accredited Louisiana-breds, non-winners of two accredited races since Nov. 25. Weight, 121 lbs. Non-winners of an accredited race since Nov. 25 allowed 3 lbs.; such a race since Aug. 25, 5 lbs.; a race since July 25, 8 lbs. (Maiden and claiming races not considered.)

COUPLED: SKYCITE and FOUR BAYOU PASS.

Bayou Bengal 121 Dk. b. or br. g (1968), by Iceberg II.—Agnes Pic, by Pictor.
Breeder, A. T. Gates (La.). 1971 2 0 0 0 (——)
Owner, A. T. Gates. Trainer, J. Y. Soileau. 1970 10 4 4 0 $15,054
Jan30-715FG 6 f 1:12⅕ft 13 121 7³¼ 5³½ 7³¼ 8⁵¼ CoplingD11 Alw 83 BullBayou 121 GarrettRoad Aleut 11
Jan16-714FG 6 f 1:13⅕gd 7¾ 120 3³ 6³ 8⁴½ 7⁴¾ SamJ3 Alw 78 Tall Tall 120 Skycite BullBayou 10
Dec26-709FG 6 f 1:11⅗ft 71 111 9³½ 8⁹ 10¹⁰11¹⁰ SamJ10 Hcp0 81 Alh'braGal 114 Windg'sh'r M'tiniAg'n 12
Dec10-706FG 6 f 1:13⅘ft 2 ▲122 9⁴½ 4³ 3²½ 1½ SamJ7 Alw 80 B'youB'g'l 122 S'perCh'ge Pr'dh'eB'y 13
Sep12-7011EvD 6½ f 1:22 gd 6-5 ▲123 3³ 1¹ 1¹½ 2nk SuireL12 HcpS 84 EightY'r119 BayouB'ngal TaniasM'gic 12
Sep 7-708EvD 6½ f 1:22⅖ft 3-5 ▲120 5³ 2² 1³ 1³ SuireL5 Alw 82 B'youB'g'l 120 Y't'ry'rs Id'l R'v'nC'j'n 8
Aug22-707EvD 6½ f 1:21⅘ft 2¼ 112 3⁴½ 3⁶ 2½ 1¹ SuireL3 Alw 85 BayouBengal 112 EightYear CraftyS'r 6
Aug15-705EvD 6½ f 1:21⅘ft 2-3 ▲115 5⁶ 3¹½ 1² 1² SuireL6 Alw 85 BayouBengal 115 Ee-Oo-Leven Aleut 9
Aug 1-709EvD 6½ f 1:21 ft 45 120 5²½ 3¹ 2½ 4³¼ Fr'm'nL5 ScwS 86 Mr. Reed 120 Toni Marie Eight Year 10
Jly 24-708EvD 6½ f 1:21⅕ft 3¼ 120 4¹½ 2½ 2³ 2⁴ SuireL2 SplW 84 B'ncyPrince120 BayouBengal Nashava 8
Jly 11-702EvD 5 f 1:00⅗gd 9¼ 117 8⁷¼ 4⁷ 2⁵ 2³½ SuireL8 AlwS 81 ToniMarie119 BayouB'gal DragonB'ty 10
Dec 22 FG 4f ft :49b Dec 8 FG 4f ft :51⅘b

LOSS IN STRETCH RULE (LOST MORE THAN 3/4 LENGTHS IN STRETCH.)

Real Blonde 113 Dk. b. or br. c (1968), by Real Change—Blonde Comet, by Blazing Comet.
Breeder, H. Gabriel (La.). 1971 3 0 1 0 $1,450
Owner, H. & R. Stable. Trainer, G. H. Horstmann, III. 1970 10 1 1 1 $2,642
Jan16-714FG 6 f 1:13⅕gd 21 112 9⁹¾ 9⁶½ 5²½ 5² CoxR4 Alw 81 Tall Tall 120 Skycite BullBayou 10
Jan 9-715FG 5½ f 1:07⅖m 3 115 7⁵¼ 7⁶ 5⁴½ 4⁹ WhitedDE6 Alw 78 RoyalPussycat 111 Skycite ToniMarie 12
Jan 2-715FG 6 f 1:13⅖gd 4½ 115 7⁷¼ 7⁶¼ 3¹½ 2¾ Whit'dDE10 Alw 81 BullBayou 113 RealBlonde FrankieT. 11
Dec25-706FG 6 f 1:13⅘gd 9 115 8⁷½ 9⁹¾ 5³¼ 2² WhitedDE8 Alw 78 BillBlazer112 RealBlonde GarrettRoad 12
Dec19-709FG 6 f 1:11⅘ft 15f 122 16¹⁴14¹⁹ 8¹¹ 6¹⁴ RinconR11 AlwS 76 Joey Bob 122 Duke of Padua Frankie T. 17
Sep12-7011EvD 6½ f 1:22 gd 9¼e 114 9¹² 7⁸ 7⁹½ 7⁷½ Fr'm'nL10 HcpS 76 EightY'r119 BayouB'ngal TaniasM'gic 12
Aug22-707EvD 6½ f 1:21⅘ft 22 113 5⁹½ 5¹¹ 4⁴ 4⁶ G'nz'lesRD1 Alw 79 BayouBengal 112 EightYear CraftyS'r 6
Aug 1-705EvD 6½ f 1:22⅖ft 25 108* 4²½ 4¹½ 3²½ 3⁴ RichardA4 7500 78 Capeson 112 Milk Queen Real Blonde 10
Jly 17-709EvD 6½ f 1:22 sl 9¾ 115 5⁷ 7⁴¾ 6⁸ 5⁶½ YoungJF8 7500 77 RockyDay115 DragonBooty Capeson 10
Jly 11-704EvD 5 f 1:01 gc 17 122 6²½ 7¹² 9¹⁶ 9¹² Gon'sRD4 AlwS 71 JaymeM.119 DeliberateSp'o NurseMe 10
Feb 4 FG 3f ft :37bg Jan 26 FG 7f ft 1:28⅖h Dec 31 FG 3f m :37b

SPEED RULE (HORSE'S SPEED RATING NOT WITHIN GARRETT ROAD'S 88.)

Frankie T. 113 Ch. g (1968), by Prince Nerida—Muffy, by Roman Sandal.
Breeder, F. Timphony (La.). 1971 2 0 0 1 $850
Owner, M. H. Van Berg Stable, Inc. Trainer, J. Van Berg. 1970 3 1 0 1 $4,354
Jan30-715FG 6 f 1:12⅕ft 10 113 8⁴¼ 6³½ 6³ 4²¼ HolmesD1 Alw 86 BullBayou 121 GarrettRoad Aleut 11
Jan 2-715FG 6 f 1:13⅖gd 3¼ 112 1¹ 1h 2h 3⁵¾ MoyersL1 Alw 76 BullBayou 113 RealBlonde FrankieT. 11
Dec29-707FG 5½ f 1:07⅕sy 4-5 ▲112 3² 3² 7⁸¾ 7⁴½ MoyersL12 6000 76 Ee-Oo-L'v'n115 Fl'meb'u St'gD'til'te 12
Dec19-709FG 6 f 1:11⅘ft 6 122 7³¼ 6⁴ 4⁸ 3⁸½ Rub'coP15 AlwS 81 Joey Bob 122 Duke of Padua Frankie T. 17
Jly 17-701Suf 5 f 1:01⅖gd 7-5 ▲120 3¹½ 2h 2½ 1¹¼ Moy'rsL9 M5500 84 FrankieT.120 KeyPose MiWench 9
Jan 25 FG 5f ft 1:05b

FINISH IN MONEY (HORSE FAILED TO FINISH IN THE MONEY.)

Aleut 113 B. c (1968), by Thirty Romans—More Cheers, by Isolater.
Breeder, R. W. Wilson (La.). 1971 2 1 0 1 $2,770
Owner, R. W. Wilson & R. N. Crews. Trainer, F. Behler. 1970 13 1 4 1 $3,875
Jan30-715FG 6 f 1:12⅕ft 11 113 6³¼ 8⁵½ 5² 3¹¼ Rubb'coP10 Alw 87 BullBayou 121 GarrettRoad Aleut 11
Jan 7-714FG 6 f 1:12⅘ft 4¾ 112 8³½ 5³½ 3³ 1nk SmithRA12 6000 85 Aleut112 ThirtyLight FavoriteWeaver 12
Dec25-706FG 6 f 1:13⅘gd 15 109* 7⁷½ 8⁸¼ 4³¼ 4⁴½ RichardA7 Alw 75 BillBlazer112 RealBlonde GarrettRoad 12
Dec19-708FG 6 f 1:13 ft 9e 122 2h 3nk 2h 6⁹¾ RichardA4 AlwS 74 Tall Tall 117 Garret Road Hawleys Pet 19
Dec10-706FG 6 f 1:13⅘ft 7¾e 114 6²¼ 6³¼ 8⁵¼10⁹ MenardN11 Alw 71 B'youB'g'l 122 S'perCh'ge Pr'dh'eB'y 13
Aug15-705EvD 6½ f 1:21⅘ft 3½ 115* 3³ 4²½ 3⁴ 3²½ RichardA8 Alw 82 BayouBengal 115 Ee-Oo-Leven Aleut 9
Aug 8-705EvD 6½ f 1:24⅗m 9-5 ▲115* 5⁴ 5⁷½ 3³ 2³ RichardA7 Alw 68 Ee-Oo-Leven118 Aleut RockitysJewel 10
Jly 25-702EvD 6½ f 1:21⅘ft 5½ 117 3² 3¹ 2² 2² RichardA7 Alw 83 DragonBooty107 Aleut EightWheels 10
Jly 11-701EvD 5 f 1:02⅕gd 8-5 ▲122 5²½ 5² 6³½ 6³ Gon'sRD2 AlwS 74 KatiesF'ly114 Str'gDistill'te WaKad'n 11
Jly 2-709EvD 6½ f 1:24 ft 7½ 114 3³ 4³ 2½ 3¾† RichardA3 Alw 73 Super Change 112 Crafty Star Aleut 10
†Placed second through disqualification.
Jan 22 FG 5f ft 1:02b Jan 16 FG 4f gd :49b Jan 2 FG 4f sl :52b

CONTENDER

Garrett Road 113 B. c (1968), by Hold the Fort—Ambling Annie, by Ambiorix.
Breeder, S. M. Paciera (La.). 1971 2 0 1 0 $1,300
Owner, J. Hingle. Trainer, F. Lodato. 1970 12 2 3 2 $9,201
Jan30-715FG 6 f 1:12⅕ft 24 113 10⁶¾ 7⁴½ 1½ 2nk CallicoF4 Alw 88 BullBayou 121 GarrettRoad Aleut 11
Jan 9-715FG 5½ f 1:07⅖m 11 112 11¹⁴12¹²11¹⁴10¹³ CallicoF10 Alw 74 RoyalPussycat 111 Skycite ToniMarie 12
Jan 2-715FG 6 f 1:13⅖gd 6½ 112 10¹⁰ 8⁷¼ 7²¾ 4⁵¾ CallicoF7 Alw 76 BullBayou 113 RealBlonde FrankieT. 11
Dec25-706FG 6 f 1:13⅘gd 2¾ 112 10⁹¾ 7⁶¼ 3³ 3³ CallicoF12 Alw 77 BillBlazer112 RealBlonde GarrettRoad 12
Dec19-708FG 6 f 1:13 ft 7f 122 15¹ 16¹² 6¹¾ 2⁵ CallicoP16 AlwS 79 Tall Tall 117 Garret Road Hawleys Pet 19
Dec10-708FG 6 f 1:11⅘ft 73 114 11⁶¾ 8⁵¼ 5⁹½ 4¹³ CallicoF9 Alw 77 JoeyBob115 Mr.Reed Duke ofPadua 12
Nov27-701FG 6 f 1:13 ft 29 119 9¹¹ 7¹¹ 5⁸½ 6¹¹ GloriosoJ9 6500 73 MissMarySue116 Amdor ValiantWind 12
Jly 24-706EvD 6½ f 1:21 ft 7 120 9⁸ 9⁸½ 8¹³ 5¹² Mart'zJ2 SplW 77 ToniMarie117 Mr.Reed Str'gDistillate 9
Jun 4-706Tdn 4½ f :55 gd 2½ 120 2 5³¼ 3³ 1nk MunsterL2 Alw 83 Garr'tRoad120 Fr't'rn'ly PhilsG'r'ntee 6
May22-706Tdn 5 f :59⅘ft 4½ 117 4³½ 4⁴½ 3⁵ 3½ MunsterL4 Alw 90 Adm'lsArg't120 G'tl'm'n'sD'l G'r'tR'd 8
May11-706Tdn 4 f :47⅗ft 3 ▲113‡ 4 4¹½ 5²¾ 2¹½ Hamm'dsR9 Alw 89 Ang'lR'q't'd113 G'r'tR'd G'tlem'n'sD'l 9
Jan 23 FG 5f ft 1:02⅗b Dec 17 FG 5f gd 1:04⅗b

CONTENDER

Oiney's Pet 108 Ch. f (1968), by Hasty Prince—Algie, by Reigh Count.
Breeder, Dr. C. W. Mattingly (La.). 1971 3 1 1 0 $2,640
Owner, C. & C. Stable, Inc. Trainer, J. H. Samuel. 1970 16 2 4 7 $9,076
Jan23-718FG 6 f 1:12⅗ft 14 114 8¹¹ 9¹² 9⁶¾ 5³½ YoungJF1 Hcp0 82 ⒻSkycite 119 Lady Fort Reds Story 14
Jan15-717FG 6 f 1:13⅕sl 1 ▲115 6⁷½ 2¹ 1¹ 1¹¼ Rub'coP6 c6000 83 Oiney'sP't115 Ap'heSign'l Nas'm'sB'y 7
Jan 8-716FG 6 f 1:14⅗sy 8-5 ▲115 6⁵ 6³¾ 5⁹ 2½ MoyersL4 6500 75 Sorta Like 112 Oiney's Pet Rivul Jet 11
Dec22-708FG 6 f 1:12 ft 4¼e 112 8⁸ 6⁵½ 5⁴¾ 3⁴ Rubb'coP10 Alw 85 ⒻEighthYear112 LadyFort Oiney'sPet 10
Dec 8-706FG 6 f 1:13 ft 2¾ 118 4³ 6⁴¼ 5⁶ 3⁴ MoyersL10 Alw 80 ⒻBackwater118 ThirtyL'ht Oiney'sP't 12
Nov 2-706HP 6 f 1:13⅘m 4½ 112 5⁹½ 5¹¹ 8²⁴ 7²⁹ SnyderL1 Alw 56 K'ght InArms115 M'tiniAg'n ProB'dit 8
Oct 9-703HP 6 f 1:13⅘ft 6-5 ▲114 5⁹½ 4⁸ 4⁶½ 3⁵¼ SnyderL3 Alw 80 ⒻUpright Miss 112 Jade Oiney's Pet 6
Sep25-708HP 6 f 1:13⅕ft 3½ 114 4⁵½ 4⁶½ 4⁶ 2nk SnyderL3 Alw 88 ⒻMissWaHoo111 Oiney'sP't M'nj'r'da 7
Sep18-704HP 6 f 1:15⅕hy 6 113 4⁴ 3³½ 3⁵ 2⁴ RubbiccoP5 Alw 74 SingGold111 Oiney'sPet SwiftOlympia 7
Jan 6 FG 4f ft :51b Dec 20 FG 3f ft :35⅗b Dec 12 FG 5f ft 1:02⅘bg

CONSISTENCY RULE (CONSISTENCY RATING NOT WITHIN 5 POINTS OF JAYME M.'s 15.)

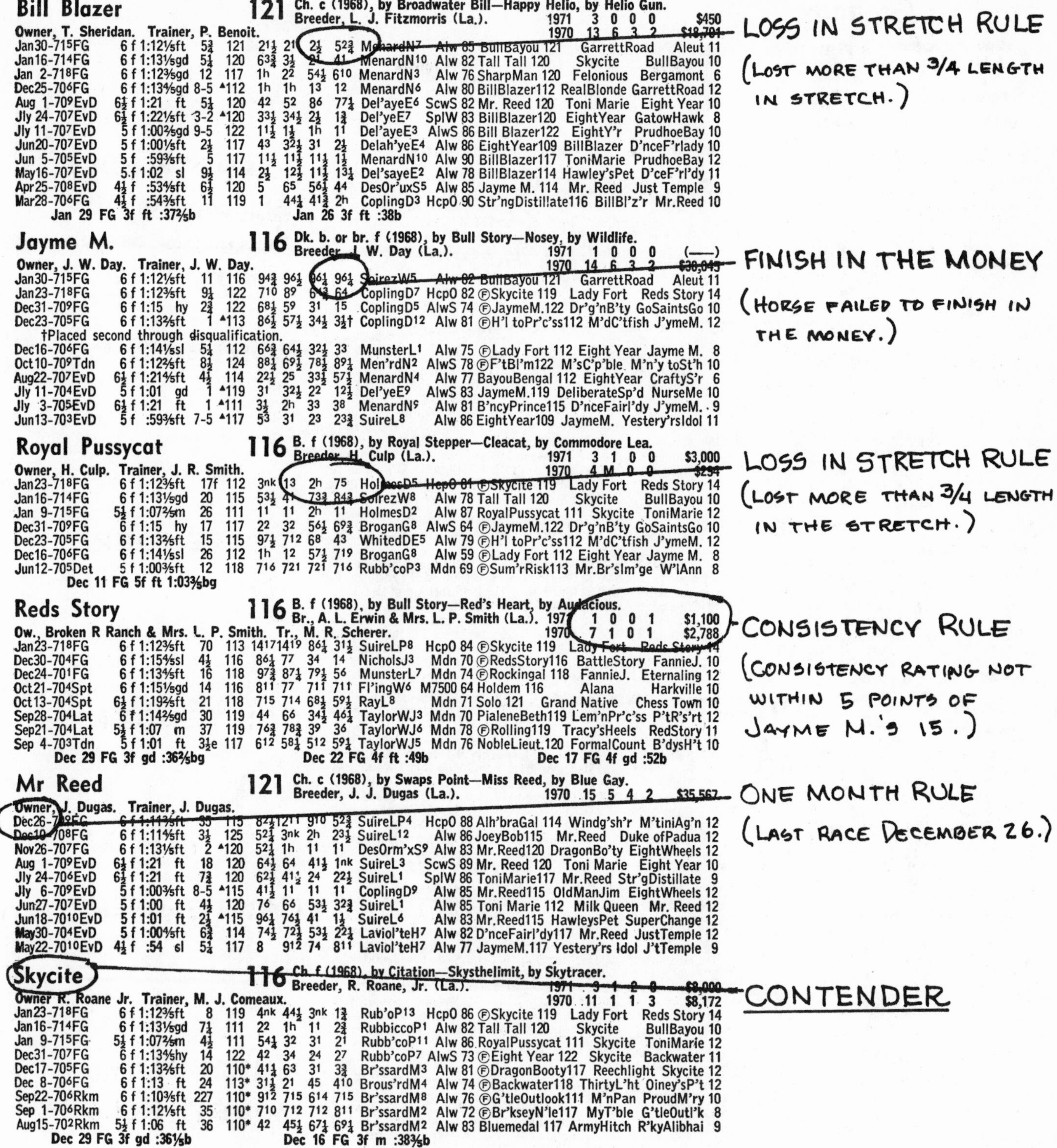
LOSS IN STRETCH RULE
(LOST MORE THAN 3/4 LENGTH IN STRETCH.)
FINISH IN THE MONEY
(HORSE FAILED TO FINISH IN THE MONEY.)
LOSS IN STRETCH RULE
(LOST MORE THAN 3/4 LENGTH IN THE STRETCH.)
CONSISTENCY RULE
(CONSISTENCY RATING NOT WITHIN 5 POINTS OF JAYME M.'S 15.)
ONE MONTH RULE
(LAST RACE DECEMBER 26.)
CONTENDER

Bill Blazer **121** Ch. c (1968), by Broadwater Bill—Happy Helio, by Helio Gun.
Breeder, L. J. Fitzmorris (La.). 1971 3 0 0 0 $450
Owner, T. Sheridan. Trainer, P. Benoit. 1970 13 6 3 2 $18,701

Jan30-715FG	6 f	1:12⅕ft	5¾	121	21½	21	2½	52¾	MenardN7	Alw 85	BullBayou 121	GarrettRoad	Aleut	11
Jan16-714FG	6 f	1:13⅕gd	5¼	120	63¾	3½	21	41	MenardN10	Alw 82	Tall Tall 120	Skycite	BullBayou	10
Jan 2-718FG	6 f	1:12⅗gd	12	117	1h	22	54½	610	MenardN3	Alw 76	SharpMan 120	Felonious	Bergamont	6
Dec25-706FG	6 f	1:13⅘gd	8-5	▲112	1h	1h	13	12	MenardN6	Alw 80	BillBlazer112	RealBlonde	GarrettRoad	12
Aug 1-709EvD	6½ f	1:21 ft	5¼	120	42	52	86	77¼	Del'ayeE6	ScwS 82	Mr. Reed 120	Toni Marie	Eight Year	10
Jly 24-707EvD	6½ f	1:22⅕ft	3-2	▲120	33½	34½	2½	1¾	Del'yeE7	SplW 83	BillBlazer120	EightYear	GatowHawk	8
Jly 11-707EvD	5 f	1:00⅖gd	9-5	122	11½	1½	1h	11	Del'ayeE3	AlwS 86	Bill Blazer122	EightY'r	PrudhoeBay	10
Jun20-707EvD	5 f	1:00⅕ft	2½	117	43	32½	31	2½	Delah'yeE4	Alw 86	EightYear109	BillBlazer	D'nceF'rlady	10
Jun 5-705EvD	5 f	:59⅗ft	5	117	11½	11½	11½	1½	MenardN10	Alw 90	BillBlazer117	ToniMarie	PrudhoeBay	12
May16-707EvD	5 f	1:02 sl	9½	114	2½	12½	11½	13¼	Del'sayeE2	Alw 78	BillBlazer114	Hawley'sPet	D'ceF'rl'dy	11
Apr25-708EvD	4½ f	:53⅘ft	6½	120	5	65	56½	44	DesOr'uxS5	Alw 85	Jayme M. 114	Mr. Reed	Just Temple	9
Mar28-706FG	4½ f	:54⅗ft	11	119	1	44¼	41¾	2h	CoplingD3	HcpO 90	Str'ngDistillate116	BillBl'z'r	Mr.Reed	10

Jan 29 FG 3f ft :37⅖b Jan 26 3f ft :38b

Jayme M. **116** Dk. b. or br. f (1968), by Bull Story—Nosey, by Wildlife.
Breeder, J. W. Day (La.). 1971 1 0 0 0 (——)
Owner, J. W. Day. Trainer, J. W. Day. 1970 14 6 3 2 $30,045

Jan30-715FG	6 f	1:12⅕ft	11	116	94¾	96½	96¼	96¼	SoirezW5	Alw 82	BullBayou 121	GarrettRoad	Aleut	11
Jan23-718FG	6 f	1:12⅗ft	9¼	122	710	89	64¾	64	CoplingD7	HcpO 82	ⒻSkycite 119	Lady Fort	Reds Story	14
Dec31-709FG	6 f	1:15 hy	2¾	122	68½	59	31	15	CoplingD5	AlwS 74	ⒻJaymeM.122	Dr'g'nB'ty	GoSaintsGo	10
Dec23-705FG	6 f	1:13⅖ft	1	▲113	86½	57½	34½	3½†	CoplingD12	Alw 81	ⒻH'l toPr'c'ss112	M'dC'tfish	J'ymeM.	12

†Placed second through disqualification.

Dec16-706FG	6 f	1:14⅕sl	5¼	112	66¾	64½	32½	33	MunsterL1	Alw 75	ⒻLady Fort 112	Eight Year	Jayme M.	8
Oct10-709Tdn	6 f	1:12⅖ft	8½	124	88¼	69½	78½	89¼	Men'rdN2	AlwS 78	ⒻF'tBl'm122	M'sC'p'ble	M'n'y toSt'h	10
Aug22-707EvD	6½ f	1:21⅘ft	4½	114	22½	25	33½	57½	MenardN4	Alw 77	BayouBengal 112	EightYear	CraftyS'r	6
Jly 11-704EvD	5 f	1:01 gd	1	▲119	31	32½	22	12½	Del'yeE9	AlwS 83	JaymeM.119	DeliberateSp'd	NurseMe	10
Jly 3-705EvD	6½ f	1:21 ft	1	▲111	3½	2h	33	38	MenardN9	Alw 81	B'ncyPrince115	D'nceFairl'dy	J'ymeM.	9
Jun13-703EvD	5 f	:59⅗ft	7-5	▲117	53	31	23	23¾	SuireL8	Alw 86	EightYear109	JaymeM.	Yestery'rsIdol	11

Royal Pussycat **116** B. f (1968), by Royal Stepper—Cleacat, by Commodore Lea.
Breeder, H. Culp (La.). 1971 3 1 0 0 $3,000
Owner, H. Culp. Trainer, J. R. Smith. 1970 4 M 0 0 $234

Jan23-718FG	6 f	1:12⅗ft	17f	112	3nk	13	2h	75	HolmesD5	HcpO 81	ⒻSkycite 119	Lady Fort	Reds Story	14
Jan16-714FG	6 f	1:13⅕gd	20	115	53½	41	73¾	84¾	SoirezW8	Alw 78	Tall Tall 120	Skycite	BullBayou	10
Jan 9-715FG	5½ f	1:07⅖m	26	111	11	11	2h	11	HolmesD2	Alw 87	RoyalPussycat 111	Skycite	ToniMarie	12
Dec31-709FG	6 f	1:15 hy	17	117	22	32	56½	69¾	BroganG8	AlwS 64	ⒻJaymeM.122	Dr'g'nB'ty	GoSaintsGo	10
Dec23-705FG	6 f	1:13⅖ft	15	115	97½	712	68	43	WhitedDE5	Alw 79	ⒻH'l toPr'c'ss112	M'dC'tfish	J'ymeM.	12
Dec16-706FG	6 f	1:14⅕sl	26	112	1h	12	57½	719	BroganG8	Alw 59	ⒻLady Fort 112	Eight Year	Jayme M.	8
Jun12-705Det	5 f	1:00⅗ft	12	118	716	721	721	716	Rubb'coP3	Mdn 69	ⒻSum'rRisk113	Mr.Br'slm'ge	W'lAnn	8

Dec 11 FG 5f ft 1:03⅗bg

Reds Story **116** B. f (1968), by Bull Story—Red's Heart, by Audacious.
Br., A. L. Erwin & Mrs. L. P. Smith (La.). 1971 1 0 0 1 $1,100
Ow., Broken R Ranch & Mrs. L. P. Smith. Tr., M. R. Scherer. 1970 7 1 0 1 $2,788

Jan23-718FG	6 f	1:12⅗ft	70	113	1417	1419	86¼	31½	SuireLP8	HcpO 84	ⒻSkycite 119	Lady Fort	Reds Story	14
Dec30-704FG	6 f	1:15⅘sl	4½	116	86¼	77	34	14	NicholsJ3	Mdn 70	ⒻRedsStory116	BattleStory	FannieJ.	10
Dec24-701FG	6 f	1:13⅘ft	16	118	97¾	87¼	79½	56	MunsterL7	Mdn 74	ⒻRockingal 118	FannieJ.	Eternaling	12
Oct21-704Spt	6 f	1:15⅕gd	14	116	811	77	711	711	Fl'ingW6	M7500 64	Holdem 116	Alana	Harkville	10
Oct13-704Spt	6½ f	1:19⅖ft	21	118	715	714	68½	59½	RayL8	Mdn 71	Solo 121	Grand Native	Chess Town	10
Sep28-704Lat	6 f	1:14⅖gd	30	119	44	66	34½	46¼	TaylorWJ3	Mdn 70	PialeneBeth119	Lem'nPr'c'ss	P'tR's'rt	12
Sep21-704Lat	5½ f	1:07 m	37	119	76¾	78¾	39	36	TaylorWJ6	Mdn 78	ⒻRolling119	Tracy'sHeels	RedStory	11
Sep 4-703Tdn	5 f	1:01 ft	3½e	117	612	58¼	512	59¼	TaylorWJ5	Mdn 76	NobleLieut.120	FormalCount	B'dysH't	10

Dec 29 FG 3f gd :36⅖bg Dec 22 FG 4f ft :49b Dec 17 FG 4f gd :52b

Mr Reed **121** Ch. c (1968), by Swaps Point—Miss Reed, by Blue Gay.
Breeder, J. J. Dugas (La.). 1970 15 5 4 2 $35,567
Owner, J. Dugas. Trainer, J. Dugas.

Dec26-70[illegible]FG	6 f	1:11⅗ft	35	115	82½	1211	910	52¾	SuireLP4	HcpO 88	Alh'braGal 114	Windg'sh'r	M'tiniAg'n	12
Dec10-708FG	6 f	1:11⅘ft	3½	125	52¼	3nk	2h	23½	SuireL12	Alw 86	JoeyBob115	Mr.Reed	Duke ofPadua	12
Nov26-707FG	6 f	1:13⅕ft	2	▲120	52¼	1h	11	11	DesOrm'xS9	Alw 83	Mr.Reed120	DragonBo'ty	EightWheels	12
Aug 1-709EvD	6½ f	1:21 ft	18	120	64½	64	41½	1nk	SuireL3	ScwS 89	Mr. Reed 120	Toni Marie	Eight Year	10
Jly 24-706EvD	6½ f	1:21 ft	7¾	120	62½	41½	24	22½	SuireL1	SplW 86	ToniMarie117	Mr.Reed	Str'gDistillate	9
Jly 6-709EvD	5 f	1:00⅗ft	8-5	▲115	41½	11	11	11	CoplingD9	Alw 85	Mr.Reed115	OldManJim	EightWheels	12
Jun27-707EvD	5 f	1:00 ft	4½	120	76	66	53½	32¾	SuireL1	Alw 85	Toni Marie 112	Milk Queen	Mr. Reed	12
Jun18-7010EvD	5 f	1:01 ft	2¼	▲115	96¼	76½	41	1½	SuireL6	Alw 83	Mr.Reed115	HawleysPet	SuperChange	12
May30-704EvD	5 f	1:00⅘ft	6¾	114	74½	72½	53½	22¼	Laviol'teH7	Alw 82	D'nceFairl'dy117	Mr.Reed	JustTemple	12
May22-7010EvD	4½ f	:54 sl	5¼	117	8	912	74	811	Laviol'teH7	Alw 77	JaymeM.117	Yestery'rs Idol	J'tTemple	9

Skycite **116** Ch. f (1968), by Citation—Skysthelimit, by Skytracer.
Breeder, R. Roane, Jr. (La.). 1971 3 1 2 0 $8,000
Owner R. Roane Jr. Trainer, M. J. Comeaux. 1970 11 1 1 3 $8,172

Jan23-718FG	6 f	1:12⅗ft	8	119	4nk	44½	3nk	1¾	Rub'oP13	HcpO 86	ⒻSkycite 119	Lady Fort	Reds Story	14
Jan16-714FG	6 f	1:13⅕gd	7¼	111	22	1h	11	2¾	RubbiccoP1	Alw 82	Tall Tall 120	Skycite	BullBayou	10
Jan 9-715FG	5½ f	1:07⅖m	4½	111	54¼	32	31	21	Rubb'coP11	Alw 86	RoyalPussycat 111	Skycite	ToniMarie	12
Dec31-707FG	6 f	1:13⅘hy	14	122	42	34	24	27	Rubb'coP7	AlwS 73	ⒻEight Year 122	Skycite	Backwater	11
Dec17-705FG	6 f	1:13⅖ft	20	110*	41¼	63	31	3¾	Br'ssardM3	Alw 81	ⒻDragonBooty117	Reechlight	Skycite	12
Dec 8-706FG	6 f	1:13 ft	24	113*	31½	21	45	410	Brous'rdM4	Alw 74	ⒻBackwater118	ThirtyL'ht	Oiney'sP't	12
Sep22-706Rkm	6 f	1:10⅗ft	227	110*	912	715	614	715	Br'ssardM8	Alw 76	ⒻG'tleOutlook111	M'nPan	ProudM'ry	10
Sep 1-706Rkm	6 f	1:12⅕ft	35	110*	710	712	712	811	Br'ssardM2	Alw 72	ⒻBr'kseyN'le117	MyT'ble	G'tleOutl'k	8
Aug15-702Rkm	5½ f	1:06 ft	36	110*	42	45½	67¼	69¼	Br'ssardM2	Alw 83	Bluemedal 117	ArmyHitch	R'kyAlibhai	9

Dec 29 FG 3f gd :36⅕b Dec 16 FG 3f m :38⅗b

6th Fair Grounds

6 FURLONGS. (Tudor Scott, Nov. 27, 1969, 1:09⅘, 3, 116.) Claiming. Purse $3,600. 4-year-olds and upward. 4-year-olds, 120 lbs.; older, 121 lbs. Non-winners of three races since Dec. 6 allowed 2 lbs.; two races since then, 4 lbs.; a race, 6 lbs. (Claiming races for $6,000 or less not considered.) Claiming price, $7,250; if for $7,000, allowed 2 lbs.

COUPLED: CIMMARON JET and SALTY RULER.

Top Guarantee * 114

B. g (1963), by We Guarantee—Rythmette, by Brown King.
Breeder, A. L. Erwin (La.). 1971 5 1 0 0 $3,165
Owner, C. J. & L. Matherne. Trainer, S. Bearb. $7,250 1970 22 5 4 6 $17,596

8-LENGTH RULE (FINISHED 8th, 16 LENGTHS BEHIND WINNER.)

Date	Dist	Time	Trk	Odds	Wt	1st	2nd	Str	Fin	Jockey	Class	SR	Finishers	Field
Jan30-716FG	6 f	1:10⅘	ft	13	122	48	611	8[illegible]	816	TheallS2	Alw	79	SpeedyJake115 Ray'sLaw TicketBoss	8
Jan23-7110FG	1-40	1:41⅕	ft	9½	122	41¼	32	2½	57¾	TheallS5	Alw	79	Karate114 Spider'sQueen LandingMan	8
Jan16-717FG	6 f	1:12⅗	ft	20	112	46½	46	3[illegible]	1h	TheallS6	Alw	86	TopGuarantee112 Karate Atchafalaya	11
Jan 9-714FG	6 f	1:13	m	20	114	66½	76	711	611	BourqueK1	Alw	73	H'rk theHer'ld120 R'y'sLaw L'nd'gM'n	7
Jan 2-717FG	6 f	1:13	gd	4	114	42	75¼	79½	611	SoirezW1	Alw	73	ThirtyDashes 110 Appoloquil Karate	9
Dec26-707FG	6 f	1:12⅖	ft	6	113	52¼	51¼	32½	2no	SoirezW2	Alw	87	Ray'sLaw 113 Top G'r'ntee Atch'f'l'ya	8
Dec12-706FG	6 f	1:12	ft	3	114	54½	54½	810	79¾	TheallS6	Alw	79	LandingMan117 Karate SirRoderick	8
Dec 5-706FG	6 f	1:11	ft	4	115	62½	44½	34½	37	SoirezW6	Alw	87	H'k theH'r'd121 SirR'd'r'k T'pG'r'tee	10
Nov28-708FG	6 f	1:11⅘	ft	17	116	43	42½	42¼	32	TheallS3	Alw	88	Alw'ysH're115 H'k theH'r'd T'pG'tee	7

Full Steam Ahead * 117

B. g (1966), by Admiral's Voyage—La Lique, by Reneged.
Breeder, J. R. Cowden (Ky.). 1971 4 1 0 2 $3,054
Owner, C. & C. Stable, Inc. Trainer, J. H. Samuel. $7,250 1970 24 6 3 3 $15,907

CONTENDER

Date	Dist	Time	Trk	Odds	Wt	1st	2nd	Str	Fin	Jockey	Class	SR	Finishers	Field
Jan30-714FG	6 f	1:11⅗	ft	9½	113	1h	2h	1h	11	MoyersL7	7000	91	F'llSt'mAh'd113 Amb'rixB'i C'tch'rP't	7
Jan16-71[illegible]FG	6 f	1:12⅗	gd	4	114	52¼	33	78½	56	YoungJF8	6250	80	Amb'rixBoi 116 R'si'sRogue Pr'ceG'l't	8
Jan 9-716FG	6 f	1:13⅖	m	14	112	56¼	54½	34	38¼	YoungJF7	7000	74	JayR'm116 L'd'yEv'ns'n FullSt'mAh'd	10
Jan 2-716FG	6 f	1:12⅘	gd	9¾	113	73¼	53¼	44½	34	YoungJF9	7000	81	LittleA.115 JayRoam FullSt'mAhead	11
Dec23-706FG	6 f	1:12	ft	3¾	115	41¼	21	3nk	1no	YoungJF11	5000	89	F'llSt'mAh'd115 Limetime N'groBarro	12
Dec16-705FG	6 f	1:14	sl	5¾	112	21	31	2½	1no	YoungJF4	5000	79	FullSt'mAh'd112 B'ttlePick Pollamber	12
Dec 5-704FG	6 f	1:12⅕	ft	3¾	116	63½	63½	54½	55½	HolmesD5	6500	82	Deadwood 114 Tudorfib Croydon	10
Dec 2-706FG	6 f	1:12	ft	4-5	▲117	3nk	1½	21	2no	Rub'coP9	c5000	89	M.H.'sG'l'y115 F'lSt'mAh'd M't'rM'ha	12
Sep25-707HP	6 f	1:11	ft	5¼	119	11½	1h	2h	2h	Rubb'coP8	6250	99	Cambrooke119 FullSt'mAh'd Charcap	9
Sep 7-705HP	6½ f	1:18	ft	3¼	115	22	1½	11	1h	SoirezW6	5000	91	F'll SteamAhead115 Charcap Dr.J.Lee	10

Jokey 109

Dk. b. or br. c (1967), by Curran'O—Oakville Gal, by Better Bet.
Breeder, A. J. Lambert (La.). 1971 3 1 0 0 $2,340
Owner, J. F. Guenther, Jr. Trainer, J. J. Loupe. $7,000 1970 10 3 3 1 $8,503

CONTENDER

Date	Dist	Time	Trk	Odds	Wt	1st	2nd	Str	Fin	Jockey	Class	SR	Finishers	Field
Jan29-716FG	6 f	1:11⅖	ft	13	119	42	21½	1½	11	YoungJF3	5000	92	Jokey 119 Sir Roderick Poetic Mae	11
Jan19-714FG	1-40	1:42⅖	ft	8¾	116	89¼	51¾	56	77¼	YoungJF7	5000	74	ChereSusan115 BitSub Mr.Pr'ceGinny	9
Jan12-716FG	6 f	1:14⅕	hy	7¾	119	108¾	98	612	712	YoungJF8	5000	66	Mr.Pr'eG'ny115 R'dS'fari T'p of t'eD'k	11
Dec23-703FG	6 f	1:12⅗	ft	7	112	55¾	32½	21½	1¾	YoungJF9	5000	86	Jokey 112 Mr.PrinceGinny Chuck'sLaw	12
Mar25-701FG	6 f	1:12⅕	ft	8½	117	611	59½	46	32½	YoungJF6	5000	86	Music Stepper 112 Iron Mike Jokey	12
Mar18-705FG	6 f	1:13⅘	sl	10	120	24	21½	31½	65½	YoungJF3	5000	75	PaulLouis120 IronMike I'm theJudge	12
Mar 6-704FG	6 f	1:13⅖	ft	2¼	▲115	79½	74¾	11	11	YoungJF2	3000	83	Jokey115 LouPaulette Thirty'sImage	11
Mar 2-703FG	6 f	1:12⅘	ft	3¼	117	32	35	35	23½	YoungJF5	3000	82	I'm the Judge 112 Jokey Eight Turns	9

Dec 18 FG 4f ft :48⅗bg

Tudorfib * 117

Dk. b. or br. g (1965), by Tudorich—Galafib, by Sir Gallahad III.
Breeder, T. Dunlap, Jr. (Ky.). 1971 3 1 1 0 $2,704
Owner, W. Smith. Trainer, G. Geier. $7,250 1970 11 2 1 1 $5,122

CONTENDER (1.)

Date	Dist	Time	Trk	Odds	Wt	1st	2nd	Str	Fin	Jockey	Class	SR	Finishers	Field
Jan28-718FG	1-40	1:40⅗	ft	4	117	1h	1h	3nk	56	Rubb'coP8	7500	84	Cl'syAdm'l 114 SkyV'l'ge Off toM'rk't	9
Jan20-717FG	6 f	1:10⅘	ft	2½	▲117	34	32	33	2nk	Rubb'coP8	6500	95	Sompn' LikeThat116 T'dorfib C's'rCire	8
Jan 2-7110FG	1-40	1:43	gd	14	115	13	15	15	16	Rubb'coP9	6250	78	Tudorfib115 BoldViking Sum'rReading	10
Dec19-706FG	1-40	1:41⅕	ft	3½	112	2h	21	22	36	Rubb'coP1	6200	81	Off to Market 109 Col. Frib Tudorfib	8
Dec 5-704FG	6 f	1:12⅕	ft	5¼	116	32	31½	2h	2nk	Rubb'coP1	6500	88	Deadwood 114 Tudorfib Croydon	10
Nov28-706FG	6 f	1:11⅘	ft	6-5	▲115	1h	13	13	11½	Rubb'coP5	4000	90	Tudorfib115 DotDittydot R'si'sRogue	11
Nov 7-706HP	6½ f	1:19⅖	gd	3¼	117	1h	1h	3nk	64¼	SnyderL7	5000	80	Charcap 117 Not So Li'l Wander West	8
Oct26-709HP	6 f	1:12	ft	2	▲114	12	12	12	12	SnyderL5	4000	94	Tudorfib 114 Pere Gai Mamselle Jess	8
Oct17-708HP	6 f	1:12	ft	6½	114	34½	35	47	69	SnyderL6	6500	85	SingingMark114 SaluteRic RoxannC.	8

Feb 5 FG 4f gd :51⅖b Jan 17 FG 4f ft :49⅕b Jan 10 FG 4f m :53b

King Who 113

B. h (1965), by Whodunit—King's Sweet, by Errard King.
Breeder, Ellis Farm (Ky.). 1971 3 3 0 0 $4,980
Owner, E. L. Talbot. Trainer, J. E. Broussard. $7,000 1970 22 2 4 4 $10,896

CONTENDER

Date	Dist	Time	Trk	Odds	Wt	1st	2nd	Str	Fin	Jockey	Class	SR	Finishers	Field
Jan27-716FG	6 f	1:11⅖	ft	27	115	79½	77	54¾	1nk	NicholsJ8	5000	92	KingWho 115 NegroBarro Lazure	12
Jan 8-7110FG	1-40	1:45⅖	sy	2½	▲116	11½	13	13	1¾	G'z'zRD6	c3500	66	KingWho116 Big 'N Brassy Geelong	10
Jan 5-714FG	1 1/16	1:46⅗	gd	11	116	43	11	13	12	Gon'lesRD9	3000	82	KingWho116 CountSash FreedomRing	9
Dec23-702FG	6 f	1:11⅘	ft	3¼	117	4nk	3nk	23	24	Val'zanF3	c2500	86	RedAppian 115 KingWho HeNoDream	12
Dec12-702FG	6 f	1:12⅖	ft	41	115	64¼	74¼	87	87¾	ValdizanF5	4000	79	R'si'sRog'e112 Ch'tn'tP'rk D'tD'tyD't	12
Oct15-702Spt	6 f	1:13⅖	ft	3½	114	74¼	41½	11	11½	PadronR5	c3200	84	KingWho 114 GoldBuggy SenorSly	10
Oct 8-706Spt	6 f	1:13⅖	sy	6¾	114	58	45	31	21	PadronR10	3200	83	Royal Abbey 114 King Who Bacchanal	10
Oct 3-709Spt	6½ f	1:19⅖	ft	3¼	▲114	44	67¼	914	94½	PadronR6	4000	76	KuKu 114 TropicalSky Haberdasher	10

Light Traveler 112

B. g (1966), by First Light—Track Traveler, by War Dog.
Breeder, P. W. Brady (La.). 1971 2 0 1 0 $950
Owner, Marie G. Krantz. Trainer, A. J. Broussard. $7,250 1970 16 4 1 2 $9,612

FINISH IN THE MONEY RULE (HORSE FAILED TO FINISH IN THE MONEY.)

Date	Dist	Time	Trk	Odds	Wt	1st	2nd	Str	Fin	Jockey	Class	SR	Finishers	Field
Jan30-716FG	6 f	1:10⅘	ft	8½	115	58¼	49	47½	56½	WhitedDE1	Alw	88	SpeedyJake115 Ray'sLaw TicketBoss	8
Jan 6-714FG	6 f	1:11⅖	ft	2½	109*	11½	11	1[illegible]	21¼	Rich'rdA1	c5000	90	T'k'tBoss114 LightTr'v'l'r B'kslapper	7
Dec26-707FG	6 f	1:12⅖	ft	32	110*	74	74½	77¾	67¾	RichardA5	Alw	79	Ray'sLaw 113 Top G'r'ntee Atch'f'l'ya	8
Dec12-706FG	6 f	1:12	ft	12	112*	32	43	56	69½	RichardA1	Alw	79	LandingMan117 Karate SirRoderick	8
Dec 5-706FG	6 f	1:11	ft	17	116	1h	34½	89½	915	RichardA3	Alw	79	H'k theH'r'd121 SirR'd'r'k T'pG'r'tee	10
Nov28-708FG	6 f	1:11⅘	ft	26	110*	2h	2h	2h	42	RichardA2	Alw	88	Alw'ysH're115 H'k theH'r'd T'pG'tee	7
Sep11-7010EvD	6½ f	1:21	ft	3-2	▲114*	22	32½	31½	22	RichardA7	Alw	87	Ol'piaVan119 L'htTr'v'l'r M'kToM'k't	7
Aug27-7010EvD	6½ f	1:21⅖	ft	4¼	109*	85½	44	43	63¼†	RichardA6	Alw	84	ErrantZephyr110 LadyFaye Darketta	9
Aug22-709EvD	6½ f	1:21⅘	ft	3	112*	21½	11	13	12	RichardA10	Alw	85	L'htTrav'l'r112 DitDotDash M'sCar'f'l	10

†Placed fifth through disqualification.

Jan 23 FG 5f ft 1:00⅘hg Dec 19 FG 4f ft :49⅖b

(1.) SEE TEXT — PAGE 207 AND PAGE 216

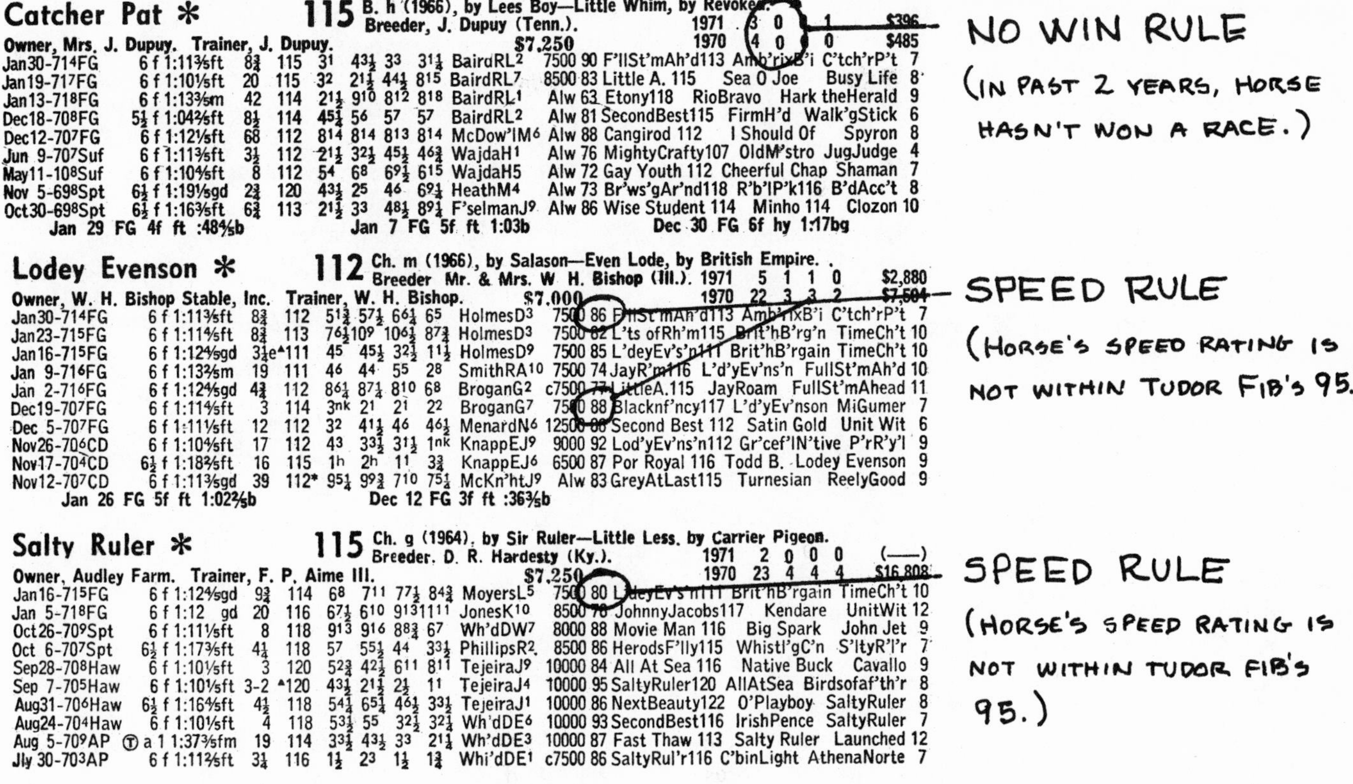

Catcher Pat ✻ **115** B. h (1966), by Lees Boy—Little Whim, by Revoked.

Breeder, J. Dupuy (Tenn.). 1971 3 0 1 $396

Owner, Mrs. J. Dupuy. Trainer, J. Dupuy. $7,250 1970 4 0 0 $485

Jan30-714FG	6 f	1:11⅗ft	8¾	115	31	43½	33	31¼	BairdRL2	7500	90	F'llSt'mAh'd113	Amb'rixB'i	C'tch'rP't	7
Jan19-717FG	6 f	1:10⅕ft	20	115	32	21¼	44½	815	BairdRL7	8500	83	Little A. 115	Sea O Joe	Busy Life	8
Jan13-718FG	6 f	1:13⅗m	42	114	21½	910	812	818	BairdRL1	Alw	63	Etony118	RioBravo	Hark theHerald	9
Dec18-708FG	5½ f	1:04⅖ft	8½	114	45¼	56	57	57	BairdRL2	Alw	81	SecondBest115	FirmH'd	Walk'gStick	6
Dec12-707FG	6 f	1:12⅕ft	68	112	814	814	813	814	McDow'lM6	Alw	88	Cangirod 112	I Should Of	Spyron	8
Jun 9-707Suf	6 f	1:11⅗ft	3½	112	21½	32½	45½	46¾	WajdaH1	Alw	76	MightyCrafty107	OldM'stro	JugJudge	4
May11-108Suf	6 f	1:10⅘ft	8	112	54	68	69½	615	WajdaH5	Alw	72	Gay Youth 112	Cheerful Chap	Shaman	7
Nov 5-698Spt	6½ f	1:19⅕gd	2¾	120	43½	25	46	69¼	HeathM4	Alw	73	Br'ws'gAr'nd118	R'b'lP'k116	B'dAcc't	8
Oct30-698Spt	6½ f	1:16⅗ft	6¾	113	21½	33	48½	89¼	F'selmanJ9	Alw	86	Wise Student 114	Minho 114	Clozon	10

Jan 29 FG 4f ft :48⅘b Jan 7 FG 5f ft 1:03b Dec 30 FG 6f hy 1:17bg

Lodey Evenson ✻ **112** Ch. m (1966), by Salason—Even Lode, by British Empire.

Breeder Mr. & Mrs. W H. Bishop (Ill.). 1971 5 1 1 0 $2,880

Owner, W. H. Bishop Stable, Inc. Trainer, W. H. Bishop. $7,000 1970 22 3 3 2 $7,504

Jan30-714FG	6 f	1:11⅗ft	8¾	112	51¾	57½	66¼	65	HolmesD3	7500	86	F'llSt'mAh'd113	Amb'rixB'i	C'tch'rP't	7
Jan23-715FG	6 f	1:11⅘ft	8¾	113	76½	109	106½	87¾	HolmesD3	7500	82	L'ts ofRh'm115	Brit'hB'rg'n	TimeCh't	10
Jan16-715FG	6 f	1:12⅘gd	3¼e	▲111	45	45½	32½	11½	HolmesD9	7500	85	L'deyEv's'n111	Brit'hB'rgain	TimeCh't	10
Jan 9-716FG	6 f	1:13⅖m	19	111	46	44	55	28	SmithRA10	7500	74	JayR'm116	L'd'yEv'ns'n	FullSt'mAh'd	10
Jan 2-716FG	6 f	1:12⅘gd	4¾	112	86¼	87¼	810	68	BroganG2	c7500	77	LittleA.115	JayRoam	FullSt'mAhead	11
Dec19-707FG	6 f	1:11⅘ft	3	114	3nk	21	21	22	BroganG7	7500	88	Blacknf'ncy117	L'd'yEv'nson	MiGumer	7
Dec 5-707FG	6 f	1:11⅕ft	12	112	32	41½	46	46½	MenardN6	12500	88	Second Best 112	Satin Gold	Unit Wit	6
Nov26-706CD	6 f	1:10⅘ft	17	112	43	33½	31½	1nk	KnappEJ9	9000	92	Lod'yEv'ns'n112	Gr'cef'lN'tive	P'rR'y'l	9
Nov17-704CD	6½ f	1:18⅖ft	16	115	1h	2h	11	3¾	KnappEJ6	6500	87	Por Royal 116	Todd B.	Lodey Evenson	9
Nov12-707CD	6 f	1:11⅗gd	39	112*	95¼	99¾	710	75¼	McKn'htJ9	Alw	83	GreyAtLast115	Turnesian	ReelyGood	9

Jan 26 FG 5f ft 1:02⅖b Dec 12 FG 3f ft :36⅗b

Salty Ruler ✻ **115** Ch. g (1964), by Sir Ruler—Little Less, by Carrier Pigeon.

Breeder, D. R. Hardesty (Ky.). 1971 2 0 0 0 (——)

Owner, Audley Farm. Trainer, F. P. Aime III. $7,250 1970 23 4 4 4 $16,808

Jan16-715FG	6 f	1:12⅘gd	9¾	114	68	711	77½	84¾	MoyersL5	7500	80	L'deyEv's'n111	Brit'hB'rgain	TimeCh't	10
Jan 5-718FG	6 f	1:12 gd	20	116	67½	610	913	1111	JonesK10	8500	78	JohnnyJacobs117	Kendare	UnitWit	12
Oct26-709Spt	6 f	1:11⅕ft	8	118	913	916	88¾	67	Wh'dDW7	8000	88	Movie Man 116	Big Spark	John Jet	9
Oct 6-707Spt	6½ f	1:17⅗ft	4¼	118	57	55½	44	33½	PhillipsR2	8500	86	HerodsF'lly115	Whistl'gC'n	S'ltyR'l'r	7
Sep28-708Haw	6 f	1:10⅕ft	3	120	52¾	42½	611	811	TejeiraJ9	10000	84	All At Sea 116	Native Buck	Cavallo	9
Sep 7-705Haw	6 f	1:10⅕ft	3-2	▲120	43½	21½	2½	11	TejeiraJ4	10000	95	SaltyRuler120	AllAtSea	Birdsofaf'th'r	8
Aug31-706Haw	6½ f	1:16⅘ft	4½	118	54¼	65¼	46½	33½	TejeiraJ1	10000	86	NextBeauty122	O'Playboy	SaltyRuler	8
Aug24-704Haw	6 f	1:10⅕ft	4	118	53½	55	32½	32¼	Wh'dDE6	10000	93	SecondBest116	IrishPence	SaltyRuler	7
Aug 5-709AP	Ⓣ a 1	1:37⅗fm	19	114	33½	43½	33	21¼	Wh'dDE3	10000	87	Fast Thaw 113	Salty Ruler	Launched	12
Jly 30-703AP	6 f	1:11⅖ft	3¼	116	1½	23	1½	1¾	Whi'dDE1	c7500	86	SaltyRul'r116	C'binLight	AthenaNorte	7

that it has never done in the past. Hence, she is dismissed for distance. The Eight-Length rule quickly disposes of *Flame Burgoo,* while the little maiden, *Boxing Miss,* is in over her head because of no win. Speed throws out *Toni Marie* and *Matchless Native,* while *Sweet Noise* falls to Loss In The Stretch.

This leaves *Little Sweeter, Eight Year* and the logical favorite, *Alhambora Gal.* We'll look at them more closely when we get to the track.

The final race today is at one mile and forty yards—a peculiarity of the Fairgrounds. For our purposes, we consider this as roughly the same as one mile. Similarly, when they run at one mile, 70 yards, we treat it as one mile and one-sixteenth. Why these unusual yardages, no one seems to know, but they are as peculiar to New Orleans as the Mardi Gras. Anyway, it looks like a good race with easy eliminations.

Distance takes care of *Kendare,* while Eight-Lengths knocks out *Barnacle B, Pointmenow* and *Rush Home.* Quickly running down the past races show *Limetiem* with Loss In The Stretch and Speed throwing out *Hillsub, Great Pumpkin* and *Out of the Trap.* This leaves *Sky Village* standing alone as our selection, although once again we'll probably be joined by all of the chalkies on the premises.

It promises to be a good afternoon, and we have left ourselves enough decisions to keep us busy between races. Now for the shower, shave and trip to the track.

All of the above eliminations have been made over two cups of coffee in a leisurely hour or so. We have what looks like four good selections: *Balata* in the first, *Prince Saha'ed* in the third, *Speedy Jake* in the seventh and *Shy Village* in the tenth. In addition, some last minute scratches could make the other races look good.

Since the croissants have taken the edge off hunger, we opt for a little exercise and leave for the track at 12:15. Once again having underestimated the New Orleans humidity, we arrive at the track about quarter to one, thoroughly wilted and vowing to take a cab in the future.

For $1.75 we get in the club house, and another $1.75 gets us upstairs to the Turf Club. Since we intend to have lunch here, we don't buy the reserved seat but head for the dining room instead. We get attention when we put out a fin for a table. Lagniappe is an old New Orleans custom, and they have elevated it to a fine art at the Fairgrounds.

While bribery is normally irritating, it is best to suppress the irritation at the track. Remember that old Devil Emotion. In addition, it is best to sit comfortably and make decisions in peace. This is difficult, if not impossible, to do while waiters are harassing you to make room for another party when you finish your lunch. So we pay up and figure to take it out of our winnings.

None of the scratches in the program help us any, but *Matchless Native* in the eighth is 3 pounds overweight. This is not surprising, since Whited has trouble getting to 115 but is extremely effective even at this weight. However, we have previously eliminated *Matchless Native* and see no reason to change our minds.

The first race is already decided so we have time to start working on the races wherein we have more than one contender. The first step now is to figure out the consistency ratings for all the contenders. This doesn't help a bit in the second or fourth race so we're left with our original contenders. However, Consistency gets rid of *Oiney's Rule* and *Red's Story* in the fifth, leaving *Aleut, Garrett Road* and *Skycite.* In the eighth, *Hark the Herald* drops out on Consistency, while *Loyal's Express* and *Tudor Scott* remain. Again we look wistfully at *Famed Prince,* but the rules say no.

Consistency didn't change things a lot but it used up 20 minutes and the horses are on the track for the first race. They look about as lively as you would expect $3,000 platers to look, but none seem lame or sore.

For some obscure reason, the public has made *Touchland* a 9-5 favorite with *Ririmba* second choice at 4-1. Our selection, *Balata,* is third choice sporting odds which are fluctuating between 8-1 and 9-1. In the last two minutes he drops to 5-1. This causes mixed emotions because we like the higher odds but the combination of last minute money and "underlay" position from 10-1 morning line add to our confidence. With $20 worth of win tickets we watch a clean start. *Capeson* sets an early fast pace of 22-1/5 but leaves his race at the quarter pole. *Fast Pickin'* slips through to take the lead on the inside with *Balata* sixth: at the turn *Ririmba* takes over the lead as *Balata* moves up to third. It is a great stretch drive and *Balata* makes it by a neck to return $13.80, $7.00 and $5.40. *Touchland,* the favorite, ran fifth and never threatened. We give *Cox* a few muttered curses for not making his move sooner, but all's well that ends well.

So the first race has put us well into the track's pocket and we're $118 ahead.

Now it is the steak sandwich instead of the chicken salad and we look more closely at the second race. It still looks like a toss-up so we break out the Dutch table and see if we can bet all three for $50. Fortunately, the public also has trouble establishing a solid favorite and the 3 minute odds are 5-2 on *He's It,* 9-2 on *Runin' Playboy* and 13-1 on *Happy Hull.* By betting $12 on *Runin' Playboy,* $22 on *He's It* and $6 on *Happy Hull* we cover all three contenders for only $40. If any one of them hits we are assured of a profit.

Once again, a good start, but racing luck takes

7th Fair Grounds

6 FURLONGS. (Tudor Scott, Nov. 27, 1969, 1:09$\frac{4}{5}$, 3, 116.)
Allowances. Purse $5,000 (includes $2,500 supplement). 4-year-olds and upward, accredited Louisiana-breds, non-winners of two accredited races since Nov. 25. 4-year-olds, 121 lbs.; older, 122 lbs. Non-winners of an accredited race since Nov. 25 allowed 3 lbs.; such a race since Aug. 25, 5 lbs.; a race since July 25, 8 lbs. (Maiden and claiming races not considered.)

COUPLED: TICKET BOSS and KARATE.

Fast Rock — 108

B. f (1967), by Bass Rock II.—Patricia O., by Manipur.
Breeder, P. W. Brady (La.). 1971 3 0 0 0 (—)
Owner, P. W Brady Trainer, W. H. Cochran. 1970 10 M 0 0 (—)

Date	Dist.	Time	Odds	Wt					Jockey	Class		Finish			Field
Jan19-71[1]FG	1 1-8	1:52$\frac{1}{5}$ft	69	108	6^{14}	10^{19}	9^{23}	[illegible]	RinconR4	2500	67	Parar 119	No Countess	Diabolic	12
Jan15-71[5]FG	6 f	1:14 sl	87	108	10^{16}	9^{16}	[illegible]	7^{14}	RinconR5	5000	65	RightSc'pe113	Ronr'm'n	Duke ofS'v'y	10
Jan 5-71[9]FG	$1\frac{1}{16}$	1:46$\frac{4}{5}$gd	63	110	9^{10}	11^{17}	9^{17}	9^{14}	RinconR7	2500	67	Parar 113	Diabolic	NoCountess	12
Dec25-70[2]FG	6 f	1:13$\frac{4}{5}$sl	66	109	12^{22}	12^{27}	11^{23}	9^{20}	RinconR4	3500	60	SeaBuoy 112	HardLick	ThruDreaming	12
Dec18-70[2]FG	6 f	1:13$\frac{4}{5}$ft	114	109	12^{15}	12^{16}	10^{17}	8^{10}	RinconR6	3500	70	Brushy 112	Teely Tooly	Hard Lick	12
Sep12-70[2]EvD	5 f	1:01 gd	21f	115	11^{11}	10^{8}	$6^{4\frac{1}{2}}$	6^{5}	DesOr'xS10	3500	78	MisKing109	BusySwaps	SaucePiquant	12
Sep 5-70[10]EvD	1	1:39$\frac{4}{5}$ft	$8\frac{1}{4}$	107	9^{12}	10^{20}	9^{20}	9^{23}	DavilleB10	2500	70	Interruption 117	Coal Pac	Uncle Clint	10
Aug28-70[9]EvD	5 f	1:01 ft	$8\frac{1}{4}$f	110	11^{15}	$11^{9\frac{3}{4}}$	$9^{3\frac{3}{4}}$	$9^{6\frac{1}{2}}$	PatinH6	2500	76	Orl'nsTess117	B'sySw'ps	Pr'ceRedbird	12
Aug21-70[9]EvD	$6\frac{1}{2}$ f	1:22$\frac{2}{5}$ft	70	117	10^{9}	9^{14}	7^{11}	7^{10}	GloriosoJ4	2500	72	Mo'n'sVal'ine115	Mr.Pr'eG'y	GetR'p'g	10

Feb 1 FG 4f ft :48$\frac{3}{5}$b Jan 29 FG 3f ft :37$\frac{4}{5}$b Dec 15 FG 5f sy 1:05b

8-LENGTH RULE

(HORSE FINISHED 7th, 14 LENGTHS BEHIND WINNER.)

Tansy's Beau — 118

Dk. b. or br. g (1967), by Banquet Beau—Tansy, by Ribot.
Breeder, H. Gabriel (La.). 1971 2 0 0 0 $150
Owner, H. & R. Stable. Trainer, L. Gabriel. 1970 8 3 2 1 $6,765

Date	Dist.	Time	Odds	Wt					Jockey	Class		Finish			Field
Jan16-71[7]FG	6 f	1:12$\frac{3}{5}$ft	$2\frac{3}{4}$	111	$6^{7\frac{1}{2}}$	$7^{9\frac{1}{2}}$	$4^{8\frac{1}{4}}$	$8^{6\frac{1}{4}}$	MenardN2	Alw	80	TopGuarantee112	Karate	Atchafalaya	11
Jan 9-71[4]FG	6 f	1:13 m	6	113	$7^{6\frac{1}{2}}$	$6^{5\frac{1}{2}}$	$5^{8\frac{1}{2}}$	$5^{7\frac{3}{4}}$	SmithRA2	Alw	76	H'rk theHer'ld120	R'y'sLaw	L'nd'gM'n	7
Dec26-70[4]FG	6 f	1:11$\frac{1}{5}$ft	11	115	$6^{4\frac{3}{4}}$	4^{5}	2^{5}	$2^{\frac{1}{2}}$	SmithRA8	Alw	92	R'y'lPl'ge117	T'sy'sBeau	Pr'e ofAsc't	8
Dec 2-70[7]FG	6 f	1:11$\frac{3}{5}$ft	15	113	5^{7}	5^{5}	4^{8}	$3^{2\frac{1}{2}}$	MoyersL3	9500	88	A Rom'nDr'g'n118	C'bDriv'r	T'nsy'sB'u	7
Nov27-70[2]FG	6 f	1:12$\frac{2}{5}$ft	$3\frac{3}{4}$	117	$5^{2\frac{1}{4}}$	2^{4}	$2^{\frac{1}{2}}$	$1^{2\frac{1}{2}}$	MoyersL8	4500	87	T'sy'sB'u117	Th'ty'sIm'ge	Mr.Pr'eG'ny	12
Sep12-70[9]EvD	$6\frac{1}{2}$ f	1:22 gd	21	113	3^{3}	2^{4}	$1^{\frac{1}{2}}$	1^{1}	YoungJF6	Alw	84	Tansy'sBeau113	ChereSusan	MoScope	10
Sep 3-70[10]EvD	7 f	1:30$\frac{1}{5}$m	17	108*	$6^{5\frac{1}{2}}$	6^{8}	6^{8}	6^{15}	RichardA4	Alw	60	Inez D. 116	Jay Val	Mo Scope	7
Aug29-70[9]EvD	5 f	1:01$\frac{2}{5}$m	9f	115	$9^{7\frac{3}{4}}$	$10^{6\frac{3}{4}}$	$10^{9\frac{1}{4}}$	$7^{3\frac{3}{4}}$	Del'sayeE8	Alw	77	Mr. Pratt 112	Music Stepper	Norgor	11
Aug20-70[5]EvD	5 f	1:00$\frac{4}{5}$ft	6-5	▲115	$2^{\frac{1}{2}}$	2^{h}	$1^{1\frac{1}{2}}$	1^{1}	Del'yeE11	Mdn	84	T'sy'sBeau115	S'd'nSh'd'w	C'mWaters	11
Aug13-70[2]EvD	5 f	1:01$\frac{2}{5}$ft	$3\frac{1}{2}$f	110*	3^{2}	$2^{\frac{1}{2}}$	1^{h}	$2^{\frac{1}{2}}$	Rich'dA8	M2500	80	ItsMeNow115	Tansy'sBeau	SaucePiq't	12
Jly 3-69[5]EvD	5 f	1:00$\frac{4}{5}$ft	$5\frac{1}{2}$	120	$9^{7\frac{1}{4}}$	$6^{8\frac{1}{2}}$	$5^{9\frac{1}{2}}$	4^{9}	Delah'veE7	Mdn	75	Fr'dlyR'f'nd120	HyMr.Br'ce120	RedJr.	12

Feb 4 FG 3f ft :35b Jan 4 FG 4f sy :48h Dec 19 FG 4f ft :48$\frac{3}{5}$b

LOSS IN STRETCH RULE

(HORSE LOST MORE THAN 3/4 LENGTH IN STRETCH.)

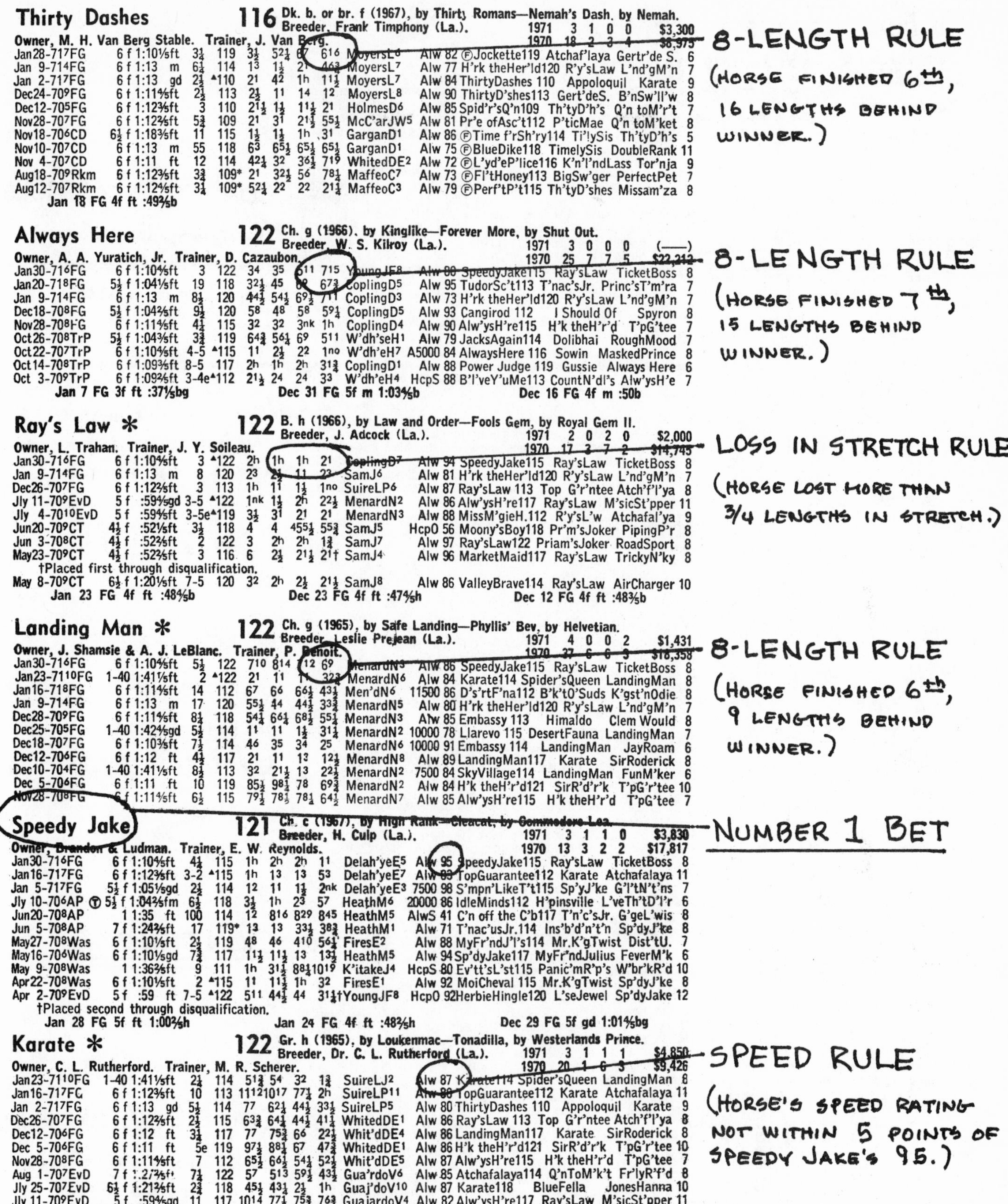

Thirty Dashes 116 Dk. b. or br. f (1967), by Thirty Romans—Nemah's Dash, by Nemah.
Breeder, Frank Timphony (La.). 1971 3 1 0 0 $3,300
Owner, M. H. Van Berg Stable. Trainer, J. Van Berg. 1970 18 2 3 4 $6,975
Jan28-717FG 6 f 1:10⅕ft 3½ 119 3½ 52½ 67 616 MoyersL6 Alw 82 ⒻJockette119 Atchaf'laya Gertr'de S. 6
Jan 9-714FG 6 f 1:13 m 6½ 114 13 1½ 2h 46¾ MoyersL7 Alw 77 H'rk theHer'ld120 R'y'sLaw L'nd'gM'n 7
Jan 2-717FG 6 f 1:13 gd 2½ *110 21 42 1h 11½ MoyersL7 Alw 84 ThirtyDashes 110 Appoloquil Karate 9
Dec24-709FG 6 f 1:11⅘ft 2½ 113 2½ 11 14 12 MoyersL8 Alw 90 ThirtyD'shes113 Gert'deS. B'nSw'll'w 8
Dec12-705FG 6 f 1:12⅗ft 3 110 21½ 1½ 11½ 21 HolmesD6 Alw 85 Spid'r'sQ'n109 Th'tyD'h's Q'n toM'r't 7
Nov28-707FG 6 f 1:12⅖ft 5¾ 109 21 31 21½ 55¼ McC'arJW5 Alw 81 Pr'e ofAsc't112 P'ticMae Q'n toM'ket 8
Nov18-706CD 6½ f 1:18⅗ft 11 115 1½ 1½ 1h 31 GarganD1 Alw 86 ⒻTime f'rSh'ry114 Ti'lySis Th'tyD'h's 5
Nov10-707CD 6 f 1:13 m 55 118 63 65½ 65¼ 65¼ GarganD1 Alw 75 ⒻBlueDike118 TimelySis DoubleRank 11
Nov 4-707CD 6 f 1:11 ft 12 114 42½ 32 36¼ 719 WhitedDE2 Alw 72 ⒻL'yd'eP'lice116 K'n'l'ndLass Tor'nja 9
Aug18-709Rkm 6 f 1:12⅗ft 3¾ 109* 21 32½ 56 78¼ MaffeoC7 Alw 73 ⒻFl'tHoney113 BigSw'ger PerfectPet 7
Aug12-707Rkm 6 f 1:12⅘ft 3¼ 109* 52½ 22 22 21¼ MaffeoC3 Alw 79 ⒻPerf'tP't115 Th'tyD'shes Missam'za 8
Jan 18 FG 4f ft :49⅗b

Always Here 122 Ch. g (1966), by Kinglike—Forever More, by Shut Out.
Breeder, W. S. Kilroy (La.). 1971 3 0 0 0 (—)
Owner, A. A. Yuratich, Jr. Trainer, D. Cazaubon. 1970 25 7 7 5 $22,213
Jan30-716FG 6 f 1:10⅘ft 3 122 34 35 611 715 YoungJF8 Alw 80 SpeedyJake115 Ray'sLaw TicketBoss 8
Jan20-718FG 5½ f 1:04⅕ft 19 118 32½ 45 69 67¾ CoplingD5 Alw 95 TudorSc't113 T'nac'sJr. Princ'sT'm'ra 7
Jan 9-714FG 6 f 1:13 m 8½ 120 44½ 54½ 69½ 711 CoplingD3 Alw 73 H'rk theHer'ld120 R'y'sLaw L'nd'gM'n 7
Dec18-708FG 5½ f 1:04⅗ft 9½ 120 58 48 58 59¼ CoplingD5 Alw 93 Cangirod 112 I Should Of Spyron 8
Nov28-708FG 6 f 1:11⅘ft 4½ 115 32 32 3nk 1h CoplingD4 Alw 90 Alw'ysH're115 H'k theH'r'd T'pG'tee 7
Oct26-708TrP 5½ f 1:04⅗ft 3¾ 119 64¾ 56¼ 69 511 W'dh'seH1 Alw 79 JacksAgain114 Dolibhai RoughMood 7
Oct22-707TrP 6 f 1:10⅘ft 4-5 *115 11 2½ 22 1no W'dh'eH7 A5000 84 AlwaysHere 116 Sowin MaskedPrince 8
Oct14-708TrP 6 f 1:09⅗ft 8-5 117 2h 1h 2h 31¾ CoplingD1 Alw 88 Power Judge 119 Gussie Always Here 6
Oct 3-709TrP 6 f 1:09⅘ft 3-4e*112 21½ 24 24 33 W'dh'eH4 HcpS 88 B'l'veY'uMe113 CountN'dl's Alw'ysH'e 7
Jan 7 FG 3f ft :37⅕bg Dec 31 FG 5f m 1:03⅘b Dec 16 FG 4f m :50b

Ray's Law * 122 B. h (1966), by Law and Order—Fools Gem, by Royal Gem II.
Breeder, J. Adcock (La.). 1971 2 0 2 0 $2,000
Owner, L. Trahan. Trainer, J. Y. Soileau. 1970 17 3 7 2 $14,745
Jan30-716FG 6 f 1:10⅘ft 3 *122 2h 1h 1h 21 CoplingD7 Alw 94 SpeedyJake115 Ray'sLaw TicketBoss 8
Jan 9-714FG 6 f 1:13 m 8 120 23 2½ 11 23 SamJ6 Alw 81 H'rk theHer'ld120 R'y'sLaw L'nd'gM'n 7
Dec26-707FG 6 f 1:12⅗ft 3 113 1h 1⅞ 1½ 1no SuireLP6 Alw 87 Ray'sLaw 113 Top G'r'ntee Atch'f'l'ya 8
Jly 11-709EvD 5 f :59⅘sgd 3-5 *122 1nk 1½ 2h 22½ MenardN2 Alw 86 Alw'ysH're117 Ray'sLaw M'sicSt'pper 11
Jly 4-7010EvD 5 f :59⅘ft 3-5e*119 3½ 31 21 21 MenardN3 Alw 88 MissM'gieH.112 R'y'sL'w Atchafal'ya 9
Jun20-709CT 4½ f :52⅕ft 3½ 118 4 4 455½ 55¾ SamJ5 HcpO 56 Moony'sBoy118 Pr'm'sJoker PipingP'r 8
Jun 3-708CT 4½ f :52⅖ft 2 122 3 2h 2h 1¾ SamJ7 Alw 97 Ray'sLaw122 Priam'sJoker RoadSport 8
May23-709CT 4½ f :52⅘ft 3 116 6 2½ 21½ 21† SamJ4 Alw 96 MarketMaid117 Ray'sLaw TrickyN'ky 8
†Placed first through disqualification.
May 8-709CT 6½ f 1:20⅕ft 7-5 120 32 2h 2½ 21¼ SamJ8 Alw 86 ValleyBrave114 Ray'sLaw AirCharger 10
Jan 23 FG 4f ft :48⅘b Dec 23 FG 4f ft :47⅘h Dec 12 FG 4f ft :48⅗b

Landing Man * 122 Ch. g (1965), by Safe Landing—Phyllis' Bev, by Helvetian.
Breeder, Leslie Prejean (La.). 1971 4 0 0 2 $1,431
Owner, J. Shamsie & A. J. LeBlanc. Trainer, P. Benoit. 1970 37 6 6 3 $18,358
Jan30-714FG 6 f 1:10⅘ft 5½ 122 710 814 712 69 MenardN3 Alw 86 SpeedyJake115 Ray'sLaw TicketBoss 8
Jan23-7110FG 1-40 1:41⅕ft 2 *122 21 11 11 32¾ MenardN6 Alw 84 Karate114 Spider'sQueen LandingMan 8
Jan16-718FG 6 f 1:11⅘ft 14 112 67 66 66½ 43¼ Men'dN6 11500 86 D's'rtF'na112 B'k'tO'Suds K'gst'nOdie 11
Jan 9-714FG 6 f 1:13 m 17 120 55½ 44 44½ 33¾ MenardN5 Alw 80 H'rk theHer'ld120 R'y'sLaw L'nd'gM'n 7
Dec28-709FG 6 f 1:11⅘ft 8½ 118 54¼ 66¼ 68½ 55¼ MenardN3 Alw 85 Embassy 113 Himaldo Clem Would 8
Dec25-705FG 1-40 1:42⅘sgd 5¼ 114 11 11 1½ 31¼ MenardN2 10000 78 Llarevo 115 DesertFauna LandingMan 7
Dec18-707FG 6 f 1:10⅗ft 7½ 114 46 35 34 25 MenardN6 10000 91 Embassy 114 LandingMan JayRoam 6
Dec12-706FG 6 f 1:12 ft 4½ 117 21 11 13 12½ MenardN8 Alw 89 LandingMan117 Karate SirRoderick 8
Dec10-704FG 1-40 1:41⅘ft 8½ 113 32 21½ 13 22¼ MenardN2 7500 84 SkyVillage114 LandingMan FunM'ker 6
Dec 5-704FG 6 f 1:11 ft 10 119 85½ 98¼ 78 69¾ MenardN2 Alw 84 H'k theH'r'd121 SirR'd'r'k T'pG'r'tee 10
Nov28-708FG 6 f 1:11⅘ft 6½ 115 79¼ 78¾ 78¼ 64¼ MenardN7 Alw 85 Alw'ysH're115 H'k theH'r'd T'pG'tee 7

Speedy Jake 121 Ch. c (1967), by High Rank—Cleacat, by Commodore Lea.
Breeder, H. Culp (La.). 1971 3 1 1 0 $3,830
Owner, Brandon & Ludman. Trainer, E. W. Reynolds. 1970 13 3 2 2 $17,817
Jan30-716FG 6 f 1:10⅘ft 4½ 115 1h 2h 2h 11 Delah'yeE5 Alw 95 SpeedyJake115 Ray'sLaw TicketBoss 8
Jan16-717FG 6 f 1:12⅗ft 3-2 *115 1h 13 13 53 Delah'yeE7 Alw 83 TopGuarantee112 Karate Atchafalaya 11
Jan 5-717FG 5½ f 1:05⅕gd 2½ 114 12 11 1½ 2nk Delah'yeE3 7500 98 S'mpn'LikeT't115 Sp'yJ'ke G'l'tN't'ns 7
Jly 10-706AP Ⓣ 5½ f 1:04⅘fm 6½ 118 3½ 1h 23 57 HeathM6 20000 86 IdleMinds112 H'pinsville L'veTh'tD'l'r 6
Jun20-708AP 1 1:35 ft 100 114 12 816 829 845 HeathM5 AlwS 41 C'n off the C'b117 T'n'c'sJr. G'geL'wis 8
Jun 5-708AP 7 f 1:24⅘ft 17 119* 13 13 33¼ 38¾ HeathM1 Alw 71 T'nac'usJr.114 Ins'b'd'n't'n Sp'dyJ'ke 8
May27-708Was 6 f 1:10⅘ft 2½ 119 48 46 410 56¼ FiresE2 Alw 88 MyFr'ndJ'l's114 Mr.K'gTwist Dist'tU. 7
May16-706Was 6 f 1:10⅕gd 7¾ 117 11½ 11½ 13 13¼ HeathM5 Alw 94 Sp'dyJake117 MyFr'ndJulius FeverM'k 6
May 9-708Was 1 1:36⅗ft 9 111 1h 31½ 88¼1019 K'itakeJ4 HcpS 80 Ev'tt'sL'st115 Panic'mR'p's W'br'kR'd 10
Apr22-708Was 6 f 1:10⅘ft 2 *115 11 11½ 1h 32 FiresE1 Alw 92 MoiCheval 115 Mr.K'gTwist Sp'dyJ'ke 8
Apr 2-709EvD 5 f :59 ft 7-5 *122 511 44½ 44 31½†YoungJF8 HcpO 92HerbieHingle120 L'seJewel Sp'dyJake 12
†Placed second through disqualification.
Jan 28 FG 5f ft 1:00⅗h Jan 24 FG 4f ft :48⅗h Dec 29 FG 5f gd 1:01⅘bg

Karate * 122 Gr. h (1965), by Loukenmac—Tonadilla, by Westerlands Prince.
Breeder, Dr. C. L. Rutherford (La.). 1971 3 1 1 1 $4,850
Owner, C. L. Rutherford. Trainer, M. R. Scherer. 1970 20 1 6 3 $9,426
Jan23-7110FG 1-40 1:41⅕ft 2½ 114 51¾ 54 32 1¾ SuireLJ2 Alw 87 Karate114 Spider'sQueen LandingMan 8
Jan16-717FG 6 f 1:12⅗ft 10 113 11121017 77¼ 2h SuireLP11 Alw 86 TopGuarantee112 Karate Atchafalaya 11
Jan 2-717FG 6 f 1:13 gd 5½ 114 77 62¼ 44½ 33¼ SuireLP5 Alw 80 ThirtyDashes 110 Appoloquil Karate 9
Dec26-707FG 6 f 1:12⅗ft 2½ 115 63¾ 64¼ 44½ 41¼ WhitedDE1 Alw 86 Ray'sLaw 113 Top G'r'ntee Atch'f'l'ya 8
Dec12-706FG 6 f 1:12 ft 3¼ 117 77 75¾ 66 22½ Whit'dDE4 Alw 86 LandingMan117 Karate SirRoderick 8
Dec 5-706FG 6 f 1:11 ft 5e 119 97½ 88¼ 67 47¾ WhitedDE1 Alw 86 H'k theH'r'd121 SirR'd'r'k T'pG'r'tee 10
Nov28-708FG 6 f 1:11⅘ft 7 112 65½ 66¼ 54¼ 52¼ Whit'dDE5 Alw 87 Alw'ysH're115 H'k theH'r'd T'pG'tee 7
Aug 1-707EvD 7 f 1:27⅖ft 7¼ 122 57 513 59¼ 43¼ Gua'rdoV6 Alw 85 Atchafalaya114 Q'nToM'k't Fr'lyR'f'd 8
Jly 25-707EvD 6½ f 1:21⅘ft 2¾ 118 45¼ 43¼ 2½ 1h Guaj'doV10 Alw 87 Karate118 BlueFella JonesHanna 10
Jly 11-709EvD 5 f :59⅘sgd 11 117 1014 77¼ 75¾ 76¾ GuajardoV4 Alw 82 Alw'ysH're117 Ray'sLaw M'sicSt'pper 11
Jan 31 FG 5f ft 1:02⅕b Jan 15 FG 3f hy :37⅖b Dec 24 FG 4f ft :48⅘b

8-LENGTH RULE
(HORSE FINISHED 6th, 16 LENGTHS BEHIND WINNER.)
8-LENGTH RULE
(HORSE FINISHED 7th, 15 LENGTHS BEHIND WINNER.)
LOSS IN STRETCH RULE
(HORSE LOST MORE THAN 3/4 LENGTHS IN STRETCH.)
8-LENGTH RULE
(HORSE FINISHED 6th, 9 LENGTHS BEHIND WINNER.)
NUMBER 1 BET
SPEED RULE
(HORSE'S SPEED RATING NOT WITHIN 5 POINTS OF SPEEDY JAKE'S 95.)

8th Fair Grounds

6 FURLONGS. (Tudor Scott, Nov. 27, 1969, 1:09⅘, 3, 116.) Allowances. Purse $4,800. 4-year-olds and upward, non-winners of three races other than maiden, claiming, starter, optional or Louisiana-bred since Oct. 6. 4-year-olds, 120 lbs.; older, 121 lbs. Non-winners of a race other than maiden or claiming since Dec. 6 allowed 3 lbs.; such a race since Nov. 6, 5 lbs.; a race since Oct. 6, 8 lbs.

COUPLED: TENACIOUS JR. and DOCTOR BROCATO; ROLL AND TOSS and LOYAL'S EXPRESS; VICS TURN and STORM VELOCITY.

Hark the Herald * 118 B. h (1965), by Royal Stepper—Lost Chord, by Loser Weeper.
Breeder, R. T. & C. H. Dolese (La.). 1971 3 1 1 1 $4,466
Owner, R. T. Dolese. Trainer, A. Barrera. 1970 22 5 7 3 $27,370
Jan30-718FG 6 f 1:11⅗ft 6½ 119 75¾ 77¼ 43 2h NicholsJ6 Alw 92 Reig'gC't114 H'k t'eH'r'ld L'y'l'sExp's 8
Jan13-718FG 6 f 1:13⅗m 3½ 117 62¾ 54½ 21 33 NicholsJ3 Alw 78 Etony118 RioBravo Hark theHerald 9
Jan 9-714FG 6 f 1:13 m 3-5 ▲120 33½ 32 31½ 13 NicholsJ4 Alw 84 H'rk theHer'ld120 R'y'sLaw L'nd'gM'n 7
Dec23-708FG 6 f 1:10⅖ft 9-5e▲118 32 34 33 54¾ NicholsJ3 Alw 92 Sunburn 115 Port Digger Loyal Yet 10
Dec 5-706FG 6 f 1:11 ft 2-3 ▲121 3nk 1½ 11½ 16 NicholsJ10 Alw 94 H'k theH'r'd121 SirR'd'r'k T'pG'r'tee 10
Nov28-708FG 6 f 1:11⅘ft 1-2 ▲115 1h 1h 1h 2h NicholsJ1 Alw 90 Alw'ysH're115 H'k theH'r'd T'pG'tee 7
Nov 5-708HP 6 f 1:13⅘m 5 115 55¼ 42½ 34 21¼ HolmesD3 Alw 84 J'ieD'c'th'n112 H'k theH'ld L'y'sExp's 7
Oct29-708HP 6½ f 1:17⅘sy 5 115 43 44 37 29 PerezR5 Alw 83 L'y'l'sExp'ss112 H'k theH'ld Syn'gism 8
Oct20-708HP 6½ f 1:19 gd 8-5 ▲112 2½ 11 12 1no HolmesD2 Alw 86 H'rk theH'r'ld112 J.P.McC'thy Picoso 7
Jan 26 FG 3f ft :37b Dec 19 FG 3f ft :36b

Tenacious Jr. 112 B. c (1967), by Tenacious—Errcountess, by Errard King.
Breeder, Mrs. J. W. Brown (Ky.). 1971 1 0 1 0 $840
Owner, Mrs. J. W. Brown. Trainer, A. Richard. 1970 7 4 1 1 $35,310
Jan20-718FG 5½ f 1:04⅕ft 3-2 120 62¾ 55¼ 34 24 WhitedDE4 Alw 99 TudorSc't113 T'nac'sJr. Princ'sT'm'ra 7
Jly 8-708AP 7 f 1:22⅘ft 1-2 ▲121 65 55 413 413 Whi'dDE3 AlwS 77 C'lt'wnCat121 Mr.K'gTw't Cl'sicT'k't 6
Jun20-708AP 1 1:35 ft 3 114 612 44 35 26 Whi'dDE1 AlwS 80 C'n off the C'b117 T'n'c'sJr. G'geL'wis 8
Jun 5-708AP 7 f 1:24⅘ft 2½ 114 57¼ 46 11½ 16 Whit'dDE2 Alw 80 T'nac'usJr.114 Ins'b'd'n't'n Sp'dyJ'ke 8
Mar 9-709FG 1-40 1:40⅘ft 7-5 117 34 32½ 1½ 1¾ WhitedDE4 Alw 89 TenaciousJr.117 Herbalist PaganKing 7
Feb21-709FG 1 1/16 1:44⅕ft 2½ ▲115 56½ 47 43 34½ Wh'dDE6 HcpS 89 Act'nGetter117 Herbalist Tenac'sJr. 14
Feb16-707FG 6 f 1:13⅗sy 4-5 ▲120 2½ 11 11½ 14 WhitedDE2 Alw 82 TenaciousJr.120 J'geSeym'r Dent'nt'n 6
Feb 6-706FG 6 f 1:12⅘ft 9-5 ▲118 75½ 22 13 13½ Whit'dDE2 Mdn 86 Tenac'usJr.118 Purch'ser L'trecsS'sta 12
Feb 5 FG 3f gd :35⅖h Feb 1 FG 4f ft :48b Jan 28 FG 3f ft :35⅖b

Loyal's Express 118 B. g (1966), by Moonlight Express—Loyal's Dream, by Gray Dream.
Breeder, Mr. & Mrs. D. Waters (Okla.). 1971 2 0 1 1 $1,488
Owner, W. H. Bishop Stable, Inc. Trainer, W. H. Bishop. 1970 23 7 3 3 $22,825
Jan30-718FG 6 f 1:11⅗ft 3 122 52¾ 52½ 53½ 3¾ WhitedDE4 Alw 91 Reig'gC't114 H'k t'eH'r'ld L'y'l'sExp's 8
Jan 6-717FG 6 f 1:10⅘ft 9-5 ▲115 61½ 42 31 2nk Whi'dDE3 18000 95 S'c'ndB'st112 L'yl'sExpress Embassy 8
Dec26-706FG 6 f 1:10⅘ft 6-5 ▲120 55¼ 54½ 34 1¾ Whi'dDE7 14000 95 L'y'l'sExp's 120 S'ndB'st B'ck'tO'S'ds 7
Dec17-707FG 6 f 1:11⅕ft 1 ▲121 43 32 2h 23¼ WhitedDE9 Alw 89 LoyalYet114 Loyal'sExpress FirmH'nd 9
Dec 9-706FG 6 f 1:11⅕ft 4-5 ▲120 42½Fog. 55½ 44 Wh'dDE1 20000 89 Ass'pt'n 116 FinalEnc're St'rmV'l'city 10
Dec 1-708FG 6 f 1:10⅕ft 2½ 120 24 2½ 13 16 WhitedDE3 Alw 98 Loyal'sExpress 120 LoyalYet BonBon 8
Nov18-707CD 7 f 1:24 ft 3 120 31 3nk 1½ 2½ Br'f'ldD7 14000 86 Engl'hD'c'r114 L'y'l'sExp's G'd'nB't'ns 7
Nov 5-708HP 6 f 1:13⅘m 4-5 ▲115 22 21 23 33½ SnyderL7 Alw 82 J'ieD'c'th'n112 H'k theH'ld L'y'sExp's 7
Oct29-708HP 6½ f 1:17⅘sy 3½e 112 1½ 11 14 19 SnyderL1 Alw 92 L'y'l'sExp'ss112 H'k theH'ld Syn'gism 8
Oct17-707HP 6½ f 1:18⅕ft 3¼ ▲114 57¼ 44 31 1nk Ret'leD3 c11500 90 Loyal'sExpress114 RoseAg'n Jarullah 9

Famed Prince 113 Dk. b. or br. h (1966), by Bolinas Boy—Neshanic, by Princequillo.
Breeder, Farnsworth Farms (Fla.). 1971 19 4 5 1 $39,209
Owner, H. Peltier. Trainer, J. O Meaux. 1969 12 3 5 0 $22,890
Aug22-708Haw 6 f 1:14⅗ft 3½e 118 1118 1119 912 85¼ NicholsJ6 HcpS 96 TrustyPro113 BarelyOnce Fl'idaRoyal 11
Aug12-708AP 7 f 1:21⅗ft 1e 118 56½ 56½ 58 69¾ PerretC8 HcpS 86 Barely Once 116 Trusty Pro Listado 8
Jly 25-708AP Ⓣ 1 70 1:38⅘fm 2½e 122 711 66 55¼ 54½ Wh'dDE3 Alw 102 P's theB'dy114 K'ry'sTime Acl'm'do II. 9
Jly 18-708AP 1 1:36⅗ft 3½e 115 85¾ 1h 12 2h GavidiaW8 HcpS 78 Doc'sT.V.114 FamedPr'ce Str'ngStr'g 12
Jly 6-708AP Ⓣ5½ f 1:02⅗fm 5 119 74¾ 62¾ 76 64¾ PerretC10 HcpS 97 Ch'fSunD'nce115 Tr'styPro Am'nVic'y 10
Jun27-706AP 7 f 1:21⅗ft 6½ 122 56½ 32½ 11 14¼ GavidiaW3 Alw 94 F'm'dPr'ce122 Am'c'nVict'y K'ry'sT'e 7
Jun10-706AP 1 1:34⅘ft 1 ▲117 34 2h 12 11½ GavidiaW5 Alw 87 Famed Prince 117 Sedoval Remoto 6
May30-705AP 5½ f 1:03⅕ft 2½ 114 38 34½ 47 55 GavidiaW1 Alw 94 Trusty Pro 112 Barely Once Loco Kid 7
May16-707Was 6 f 1:10 gd 2-3 ▲117 2h 1½ 12¼ 14½ GavidiaW1 Alw 95 Fam'dPrince117 Col'r'doC'y S'nH'lm't 6
May 2-707Was 6 f 1:09 ft 11 115 47 41¾ 21½ 2¾ G'vidiaW2 HcpS 99 FleetWing121 Fam'dPrince CoupL'd'g 5
Apr18-707Was 6 f 1:09⅘ft 2½ ▲114 62¾ 41 2h 1nk RosierD5 Alw 97 F'm'dPrince114 L'ghingBill BluntM'n 12
Mar28-708FG 6 f 1:11 ft 2¾ 116 44½ 35 23 21½ WhitedDE7 Alw 93 TrustyPro120 FamedPrince GageLine 8
Feb 5 FG 3f gd :35h Jan 30 FG 4f ft :46⅗h Jan 23 FG 4f ft :48⅗b

Tudor Scott * 121 Dk. b. or br. g (1966) by Tudor Minstrel—Bethany, by Jet Pilot.
Breeder, Canaan Farm (Ky.). 1971 2 1 0 1 $3,048
Owner, S. Gray & S. Parise. Trainer, S. Parise. 1970 5 2 1 1 $27,978
Jan20-718FG 5½ f 1:04⅕ft 4-5 ▲113 11½ 14 14 14 BairdRL2 Alw 103 TudorSc't113 T'nac'sJr. Princ'sT'm'ra 7
Jan 6-718FG 5½ f 1:04⅗ft 1-2 ▲114 2h 21½ 2½ 33½ BairdRL3 Alw 97 Cangirod117 Assumption TudorScott 8
Dec30-709FG 6 f 1:12 sy 3-5 ▲115 1h 12 13 21 BairdRL2 Alw 88 Port Digger 115 TudorScott Sunburn 7
Apr 4-706Kee 6 f 1:10⅖ft 2¾ ▲122 97¼118 109¼ 87¼ Whi'dDE9 HcpS 84 Paderoso 115 True North Blade 11
Feb14-709FG 6 f 1:10⅖ft 3-5e▲125 53 42 11 12 Wh'edDE4 HcpS 98 TudorScott125 I ShouldOf GageLine 9
Jan17-709FG 6 f 1:11 ft 2-5 ▲123 31½ 11 11½ 1¾ BairdRL6 Hcp0 95 TudorScott123 I Sh'ldOf St'mVelocity 6
Jan 1-707TrP 6 f 1:07⅘ft 8-5 ▲120 11 13 11½ 32¼ BairdRL5 HcpS 97 G'dg'tMan116 Adv'ceP'ty115 T'd'rSc't 13
Dec13-698F.G 6 f 1:11⅗gd 1-2 ▲120 67½ 45 11½ 11½ RayL9 Alw 93 TudorSc't120 Doc'sT.V.117 St'mV'l'ty 9
Nov27-698F.G 6 f 1:09⅘ft 2½e 116 11 15 16 15 B'rdRL3 Hcp0 101 TudorScott116 Ornatan114 SatinGold 13
Feb 2 FG 5f ft 1:01b Jan 29 FG 4f ft :49b Jan 16 FG 4f gd :49b

Loyal Yet * 120 Ch. g (1967), by Count Amber—Mrs. Coonjine, by Errard King.
Breeder, Dr. A. F. Polk, Jr. (Ky.). 1971 3 1 0 0 $3,288
Owner, J. P. Dorignac, Jr. Trainer, J. Dorignac III. 1970 14 2 2 2 $8,556
Jan21-718FG 1-40 1:40⅗ft 2½ 121 11½ 11½ 11 13 HeathM5 Alw 90 Loyal Yet121 Mak'gN'se C'l'ssC'rage 10
Jan15-719FG 5½ f 1:05⅘sl 3½ 120 66½ 68 58½ 55½ HolmesD1 Alw 89 Spyr'n120 Ch'p'gneCarol A R'nDr'gon 7
Jan 7-718FG 1-40 1:41 ft 2½ 119 12 1h 11 43 HolmesD7 Alw 85 Pr'ce ofAs't119 Cl'mW'ld C'rel'sC'r'ge 8
Dec30-709FG 6 f 1:12 sy 11 119 58 57 59 410 HolmesD3 Alw 79 Port Digger 115 TudorScott Sunburn 7
Dec23-708FG 6 f 1:10⅖ft 3½ 119 74¼ 68¼ 68¼ 34¼ WhitedDE1 Alw 93 Sunburn 115 Port Digger Loyal Yet 10
Dec17-707FG 6 f 1:11⅕ft 5½ 114 53 52¼ 1h 13¼ HolmesD4 Alw 93 LoyalYet114 Loyal'sExpress FirmH'nd 9
Dec 1-708FG 6 f 1:10⅕ft 2 ▲114 59¼ 56¼ 35 26 HolmesD4 Alw 92 Loyal'sExpress 120 LoyalYet BonBon 8
Nov26-705FG 6 f 1:11⅘ft 11 115 59¼ 36 1h 15 Wh'dDE8 10000 90 LoyalYet115 CabDriver A R'm'nDr'g'n 9
Oct 3-707Spt 6½ f 1:18 ft 15 114 78¼ 713 711 79 DesOr'xS9 Alw 79 Mr.K'gTwist121 V'g'sP'c's W'tz'gBee 9
May20-708Was 6 f 1:09⅘ft 6¾ 112 72½ 74¾ 79¾ 713 FiresE6 Alw 83 Mr.KingTwist112 Cocoinea BeachGlow 7
Dec 11 FG 4f ft :48⅕h

CONSISTENCY RULE

(CONSISTENCY RATING IS NOT WITHIN 5 POINTS OF TUDOR SCOTT'S 45.)

DISTANCE RULE

(HORSE HASN'T RUN 6 FURLONG DISTANCE AT THIS TRACK THIS YEAR.)

CONTENDER

THIS MONTH RULE

(LAST RACE AUGUST 22.)

CONTENDER

CONSISTENCY RULE

(CONSISTENCY NOT WITHIN 5 POINTS OF TUDOR SCOTT'S 45.)

```
Storm Velocity              113 B. h (1966), by Petare—Miss Velocity, by Spy Song.
                                Breeder. Meadowbrook Farm, Inc. (Fla.). 1971  3 0 0 0   $771
Owner, M. H. Van Berg Stable, Inc.  Trainer, J. Van Berg.               1970 24 3 4 7 $23,737
 See chart of yesterday's ninth race.
Jan23-717FG   6 f 1:10⅘ft  3½  115  6²¼ 6⁴¼ 5⁴½ 4¹   TauzinL4 c15000 94 O'Playboy112 S'cn'dBest DesertFauna  9
Jan13-718FG   6 f 1:13⅗m   6   118  4²  2²½ 3²½ 4⁴½†MoyersL6   Alw 76 Etony118   RioBravo   Hark theHerald  9
   †Dead heat.
Jan 6-717FG   6 f 1:10⅘ft  5¾  116  7²½ 3¹  5¹¼ 4²¼ V'dizanF6  20000 93 S'c'ndB'st112  L'yl'sExpress  Embassy  8
Dec23-708FG   6 f 1:10⅖ft  3   119  2²  2⁴  2³  4⁴¼ MoyersL6    Alw 93 Sunburn 115   Port Digger   Loyal Yet 10
Dec 9-706FG   6 f 1:11⅕ft  3½  118  2¹½Fog. 3³ 3⁴   MoyersL5  20000 89 Ass'pt'n 116 FinalEnc're St'rmV'l'city 10
Sep30-707Haw  6 f 1:10⅕ft  8½  119  1½  2h  1h  1½  FiresE1     Alw 95 StormVel'city119 Dr.Gr'ne Danc'gL'te  7
Sep19-707Haw  6 f1:09⅖ft  14   117  3²½ 4⁴½ 4⁴½ 5⁵¼ FiresE2     Alw 94 Int'sitivo117  Insub'din't'n  FilthyRich  8
Sep 4-707Haw  6 f 1:10⅕ft  2¾  122  4²  6³¼ 6⁸  5⁴½ FiresE1     Alw 90 DancingLate117 Gadg'tMan SirRealist  7
     Dec 9 FG 4f ft :49⅗b
Michigan Fall               115 Dk. b. or br. f (1967), by Kentucky Pride—Fallaha, by Sayani.
                                Breeder, Crimson King Farm (Mich.).     1971  1 1 0 0  $5,787
Owner, W. A. Lofton.  Trainer, J. R. Smith.                             1970 12 4 1 1 $10,816
Jan 9-719FG   6 f 1:13⅗m  11   112  7⁶¼ 7⁶½ 4⁴  1²   MenardN9  HcpS 81 Ⓕ Michig'nF'll 112 Fr'cesFl'r G'ldR'gs  9
Dec28-708FG   6 f 1:12⅗ft  3   112  4⁴  4³  2h  1no  MenardN1    Alw 86 Ⓕ Michig'nF'l 112 ClearAm'r Fabolina  6
Dec11-708FG   6 f 1:11⅖ft 91   109  7⁷¾ 8¹¹ 9¹⁰ 8²½ MenardN8    Alw 89 SpottedLine 115  O'Playboy  Herbalist  9
Sep23-708HP   1 1:38⅘ft    5   110  4⁵  3²½ 3⁴½ 3⁵¾ PerezR5    HcpO 83 Hayalong119 Hunt'rsCr'k Michig'nFall  7
Aug19-709HP   1 1/16 1:48⅘m 3¼ 114  5⁶½ 2½  1¹  1³  PerezR8    6000 70 Michig'nF'l 114 B'tleShot Child'sPr'ce 10
Aug 6-705HP   1 1:40⅗ft   3½e  111  4⁶½ 2⁴  1h  1³  PerezR8    4500 80 Ⓕ Michig'nF'l 111 M'g'nLina Mariaz'l  8
Jly 4-704Det  6 f 1:11⅖ft  6½  108  7³¾ 7⁴¼ 6⁵¾ 4⁸  HuvalK8   c6500 75 TropicalJudge116 Perretta Sn'finBilly  8
Jun24-708Det  6 f 1:11⅘ft  4½  106* 6³  5²¾ 3²  2¹½ HuvalK3    6500 79 Hull'sP'ck113 Michig'nF'll Mich'nLina  9
Jun15-707Det  6 f 1:13 m  10   115  3²½ 2¹½ 2½  1¾  WaltB10    5000 75 MichiganFall 115 WildTiger  Perretta 10
     Jan 31 FG 5f ft 1:02b        Jan 27 FG 5f ft 1:02⅕b        Jan 22 FG 4f ft :50b
```

CONSISTENCY RULE

(CONSISTENCY RATING IS NOT WITHIN 5 POINTS OF TUDOR SCOTT'S 45.)

SPEED RULE

(SPEED RATING NOT WITHIN 5 POINTS OF LOYAL'S EXPRESS' 95.)

over and *Happy Hull* gets boxed in without racing room. Shifting our loyalties to *He's It* at the half we see we're in great shape. At the turn we know things are good because *He's It* turns on the speed and the only horse with a chance to catch him is *Runnin' Playboy.* The latter closes well but is no threat to *He's It,* who takes all the chalk for an easy five-length win. A good price for a favorite, he pays $7.60, $4.80 and $3.00. Our eleven $2 tickets are worth $83.60 and we only put up $40. Adding another $43.60 we are now $161.60 ahead after the first two races.

Surely some reader who is infatuated with *Sweet Dee Dee* will mention that for the price of three tickets we could have wheeled *Balata* in the first with all three contenders in the second and picked up a fat $96.00 double. Be our guest. The double is not our meat and we only play it when we've got all long-shot contenders in both races. Since *He's It* was the favorite, there was no way to know before the first race what the fickle public might do in the second race. Besides, we hate to lose both races when we could have a winner in one and a loser in the other.

Winning the first two earns a drink, and since the sun is now well over the yardarm, it's turning out to be a beautiful day.

The third race was one of our easier selections and still looks good. The public decides to agree with us and ignore the professional handicappers. They establish *Prince Saha'ed* as a 2-1 favorite over *Outrider* at 5-2. Not much early speed leaves all entrants except *Pero Pescou* with a final effort. *Tennywood* provides some anxious moments as he makes a strong middle pace down the backstretch, but rounding the turn *Prince Saha'ed* justifies the public confidence and wins ridden out by nine lengths under no urging.

But this time, we're wondering if we're still asleep after a night of New Orleans hospitality. We are reassured by the cashier who looks questioningly as we cash our ticket. With *Prince Saha'ed* paying 6.60, 3.80 and 3.20, we add another $46 to our account for a total profit of $207.60.

The fourth race brings us back to reality when we realize we have yet to decide on a choice between *Tantaljo* and *MeChief*. As we feared, the public is also aware of the nature of this race and sets the price at 6-5 on *Tantaljo* and 2-1 on *MeChief*. While normally we would just pass this race as unplayable, today with track money in our pocket we do the unforgivable and buy a $10 Exacta ticket on number 1-5 and on 5-1.

The gods of the racetrack overlook the breach of conduct and indeed it is a two-horse race with *Tantaljo* outrunning *McChief* in the stretch. The exacta pays only $12.60 because so many people recognized it, but that is enough to add another $43 profit. Guiltily we cash our ticket, vowing never to play the sucker bets again—but knowing, as gamblers, that we probably will.

The fifth race is now upon us and once again no choice is possible. *Aleut, Garrett Road* and *Skycite* are as close as we can get to a selection. But the masses of tourists and occasional fans help us. For some unfathomable reason they put the tag of 2-1 favorite on *Mr. Reed,* who has not raced in over a month. Ignoring our three contenders, they present us with a classic example of "Dutching" effectiveness. With *Aleut* at 18-1, *Garrett Road* at 7-1 and *Skycite* at 4-1, we look at the table and buy seven $2 tickets on *Skycite,* five $2 tickets on *Garrett Road* and two $2 tickets on *Aleut,* for a total investment of $28. Again the rules pay off as *Aleut* and *Garrett Road* run 1-2 to return $39.40, $18.00 and $10.00. The favorite, *Mr. Reed,* finishes fourth but looks good doing it. He probably needed this conditioning after his layoff and could be a threat next time. We make a note to watch him. With another $50.80 added to our bulging bank account, we show a profit of $301.40 for the day. And we're only half-way through the card.

The sixth race gives us our first "I shoulda" for today. We mentioned that *Tudor Fib* could have been eliminated on the Loss In The Stretch rule, but we let him stay because of his speed. When the public made him a 9-5 favorite, we decided he should stay in contention. As a result, we had to buy $26 worth of tickets on him in addition to $12 on *Full Steam Ahead,* who went to the post at 9-2 and $8 each on *Jokey* and *King Who,* both at 10-1. This cost us profit when *King Who* won and paid $22.80, $7.40 and $4.80. Our four tickets returned $91.20 but the unnecessary investment of $26 on *Tudor Fib* reduced our profit to $37.20. We "shoulda" kicked out *Tudor Fib* and had a nice Dutch book. Still, we're $338.60 ahead and that is not bad.

Again in the seventh race, the public makes one of its great errors. In establishing *Ray's Law* as the 6-5 favorite, they allow our Number One selection, *Speedy Jake,* to get off at 5-2. Because he is such an obvious choice and had been ignored by the public, we aren't even tempted by the Exacta on this race. The favorite makes one bid at the half and catches *Speedy Jake* briefly after our selection had made the early pace. But *Speedy Jake* lives up to his name and runs *Ray's Law* into the ground to win by an easy 5 lengths. Paying $7.40, $5.00 and $3.00, he contributes another $54 to our roll.

With profit of $392.60 so far we should probably go back to the hotel. But that's not what gambling is all about. So we stay for the eighth.

It's another "I shoulda." Having to eliminate *Famed Prince* has us in a nervous seizure but sticking to the rules, we Dutch *Loyal's Express* at 11-1 for $6 and *Tudor Scott* at 6-5 for $34. Our punishment for betting the Exacta in the fourth is to watch *Famed Prince* romp home over the field. We can't be sure, but think he sneered at us as they led him away from the winners circle. Subtracting this $40 loss we're still $352.60 ahead.

The featured Thelma Stakes looks a little better. *Alhambra Gal,* the 2-1 favorite dances excitedly around the track and looks every bit a champion. Once again, we're struck by the beauty of these top quality young animals, especially when compared with the $2,500 oats-ovens in the early races. In addition to the favorite, we have *Little Sweeter* at 6-1 and *Eight Year* at 8-1 as contenders, and betting $24, $10 and $8 respectively, we have a great $42 Dutch, including the favorite.

After some trouble getting these high spirited youngsters into the gate, the starter does an excellent job of getting a fair start. *Bee Bee Dabo,* the 5 furlong whiz, blazes the first quarter in 21-4/5 before she burns out and has to be eased. As expected, *Alhambra Gal* takes command at the half and has things pretty much her own way, but in the stretch *Matchless Native* comes on strongly between horses to win going away. So much for the classic Dutch. Taking another look at our bank shows $310.60, due to the $42 loss.

The last race is about as expected. *Sky Village* settles on the Tote board as a 2-1 favorite. Except that it's the last race, where the afternoon plungers were trying to get even with longshots, and if three favorites had not already won today, thus scoring off the "law of average" players, *Sky Village* would go at about 3-1. We feel pretty good about this since it is seldom you get a really sound favorite at 2-1. Again it is like the textbooks say. *Sky Village* is never more than six lengths off the pace, moves up steadily and wins ridden out. Whited never touches the bat to him.

It is now 5:45 in the afternoon and we tip our waiter, pay our bill and summarize our day. With *Sky Village* paying $6.00, $3.60 and $2.80, our $20 bet shows a $40 profit, making our total profit for the

9th Fair Grounds

6 FURLONGS. (Tudor Scott, Nov. 27, 1969, 1:09⅘, 3, 116.) Thirteenth running THELMA STAKES. Allowances. $10,000 added. Fillies. 3-year-olds. By subscription of $25 each which shall accompany the nomination; $250 additional to start with $10,000 added of which $2,000 to second, $1,500 to third, $700 to fourth, $300 to fifth. Weight, 122 lbs. Non-winners of $20,000 allowed 3 lbs.; $10,000, 5 lbs.; two races other than maiden, optional or claiming since Nov. 26, 8 lbs.; $1,625 other than maiden, optional or claiming since Nov. 26, 10 lbs. The owner of the winner to receive a trophy. Closed with 22 nominations.

Little Sweeter **112** Ch. f (1968), by Above the Law—Dash o' Sugar, by Condiment. CONTENDER

Breeder, Mrs. J. M. Branham (Tenn.). 1971 1 1 0 0 $2,280

Owner, M. H. Van Berg Stable, Inc. Trainer, J. Van Berg. 1970 21 7 4 1 $17,618

Jan14-71[7]FG	6 f	1:14⅘hy	2½	110	1^{h}	2^{4}	2^{3}	$1^{1\frac{1}{4}}$	MoyersL[1]	14500	75	LittleSweeter110 R'dR'd Mitch'sLine	6
Dec28-70[7]FG	6 f	1:11⅘ft	6-5	▲111	3^{nk}	1^{1}	1^{5}	1^{8}	MoyersL[5]	10000	90	LittleSweeter111 N'sh'va Ren'g'dsJoy	6
Dec17-70[6]FG	6 f	1:12⅕ft	5¼	113	4^{6}	$4^{5\frac{1}{2}}$	4^{3}	$4^{1\frac{1}{4}}$	MoyersL[1]	Alw	87	ⒻChouCroute113 Tan'sMagic Cruline	9
Nov16-70[6]CD	6 f	1:12⅗gd	4¼	118	8^{7}	6^{6}	$3^{\frac{1}{2}}$	2^{h}	GarganD[8]	8000	83	CountsNest119 LittleSweeter Ravailla	8
Nov 6-70[5]CD	6 f	1:11⅗ft	8-5	▲119	$8^{9\frac{1}{4}}$	$7^{4\frac{1}{4}}$	$6^{6\frac{1}{4}}$	$6^{5\frac{3}{4}}$	WhitedDE[7]	8500	82	OldFitz122 CapitalStar ManyRibbons	9
Oct 2-70[6]Rkm	6 f	1:12⅖ft	9-5	▲119	6^{4}	$4^{3\frac{1}{2}}$	3^{2}	3^{2}	MoyersL[4]	10000	80	CraftyP'ts119 Terpsichor'n L'tleSw't'r	7
Sep25-70[6]Rkm	6 f	1:11⅘ft	2¼	112	4^{4}	2^{1}	1^{1}	$1^{2\frac{3}{4}}$	MoyersL[4]	8500	85	LittleSweeter112 Thunder Classy St'p	8
Sep 4-70[4]Rkm	6 f	1:12⅖m	3	119	$3^{2\frac{1}{2}}$	2^{2}	$2^{1\frac{1}{2}}$	$4^{3\frac{1}{2}}$	MoyersL[6]	10000	78	ScotchQue119 MummyBoop Thunder	6

Feb 5 FG 4f gd :49b **Jan 24 FG 5f ft 1:02⅖b**

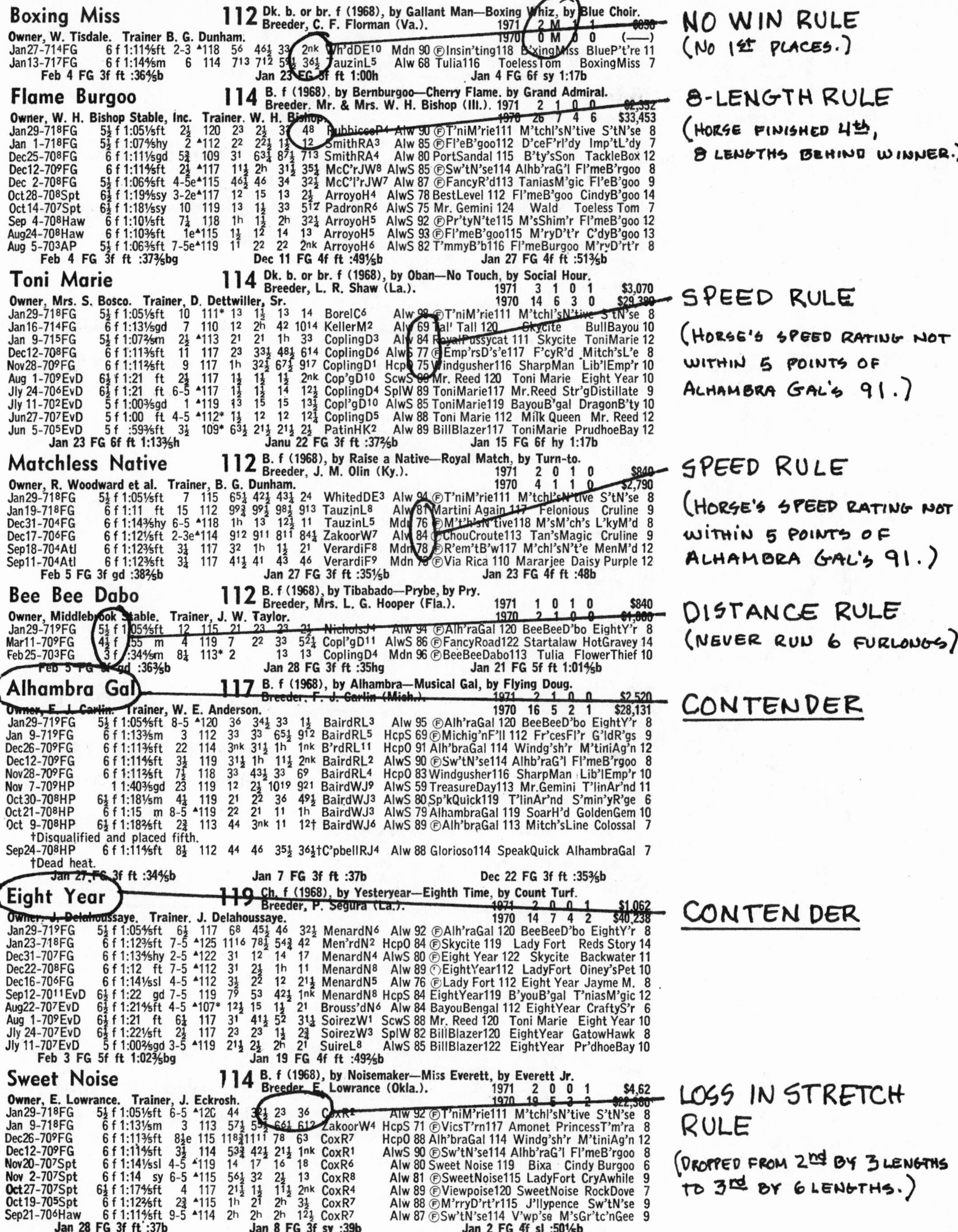

Boxing Miss 112 Dk. b. or br. f (1968), by Gallant Man—Boxing Whiz, by Blue Choir.
Breeder, C. F. Florman (Va.). 1971 2 M 1 1 $830
Owner, W. Tisdale. Trainer B. G. Dunham. 1970 0 M 0 0 (—)
Jan27-71⁴FG 6 f 1:11⅘ft 2-3 ▲118 56 46½ 33 2nk Wh'dDE¹⁰ Mdn 90 Ⓕ Insin'ting118 B'xingMiss BlueP't're 11
Jan13-71⁷FG 6 f 1:14⅘m 6 114 7¹³ 7¹² 5¹¹ 36½ TauzinL⁵ Alw 68 Tulia116 ToelessTom BoxingMiss 7
Feb 4 FG 3f ft :36⅘b Jan 23 FG 5f ft 1:00h Jan 4 FG 6f sy 1:17b

NO WIN RULE
(NO 1ST PLACES.)

Flame Burgoo 114 B. f (1968), by Bernburgoo—Cherry Flame, by Grand Admiral.
Breeder, Mr. & Mrs. W. H. Bishop (Ill.). 1971 2 1 0 0 $2,352
Owner, W. H. Bishop Stable, Inc. Trainer, W. H. Bishop. 1970 26 7 4 6 $33,453
Jan29-71⁸FG 5½ f 1:05⅕ft 2½ 120 23 2½ 37 48 RubbicoP⁴ Alw 90 Ⓕ T'niM'rie111 M'tchl'sN'tive S'tN'se 8
Jan 1-71⁸FG 5½ f 1:07⅘hy 2 ▲112 22 22½ 1½ 12 SmithRA³ Alw 85 Ⓕ Fl'eB'goo112 D'ceF'rl'dy Imp'tL'dy 7
Dec25-70⁸FG 6 f 1:11⅗gd 5¾ 109 31 63¾ 87¼ 7¹³ SmithRA⁴ Alw 80 PortSandal 115 B'ty'sSon TackleBox 12
Dec12-70⁹FG 6 f 1:11⅘ft 2½ ▲117 11½ 2h 31½ 35½ McC'rJW⁸ AlwS 85 Ⓕ Sw'tN'se114 Alhb'raG'l Fl'meB'rgoo 8
Dec 2-70⁸FG 5½ f 1:06⅘ft 4-5e▲115 46½ 46 34 32½ McC'l'rJW⁷ Alw 87 Ⓕ FancyR'd113 TaniasM'gic Fl'eB'goo 9
Oct28-70⁸Spt 6½ f 1:19⅘sy 3-2e▲117 12 15 13 2½ ArroyoH⁴ AlwS 78 BestLevel 112 Fl'meB'goo CindyB'goo 14
Oct14-70⁷Spt 6½ f 1:18⅕sy 10 119 13 1½ 33 51⅞ PadronR⁶ AlwS 75 Mr. Gemini 124 Wald Toeless Tom 7
Sep 4-70⁸Haw 6 f 1:10⅕ft 7¼ 118 1h 1½ 2h 32½ ArroyoH⁵ AlwS 92 Ⓕ Pr'tyN'te115 M'sShim'r Fl'meB'goo 12
Aug24-70⁸Haw 6 f 1:10⅗ft 1e▲115 1½ 12 14 13 ArroyoH⁵ AlwS 93 Ⓕ Fl'meB'goo115 M'ryD't'r C'dyB'goo 13
Aug 5-70³AP 5½ f 1:06⅗ft 7-5e▲119 11 22 22 2nk ArroyoH⁶ AlwS 82 T'mmyB'b116 Fl'meBurgoo M'ryD'rt'r 8
Feb 4 FG 3f ft :37⅗bg Dec 11 FG 4f ft :49⅕b Jan 27 FG 4f ft :51⅗b

8-LENGTH RULE
(HORSE FINISHED 4th, 8 LENGTHS BEHIND WINNER.)

Toni Marie 114 Dk. b. or br. f (1968), by Oban—No Touch, by Social Hour.
Breeder, L. R. Shaw (La.). 1971 3 1 0 1 $3,070
Owner, Mrs. S. Bosco. Trainer, D. Dettwiller, Sr. 1970 14 6 3 0 $29,390
Jan29-71⁸FG 5½ f 1:05⅕ft 10 111* 13 1½ 13 14 BorelC⁶ Alw 98 Ⓕ T'niM'rie111 M'tchl'sN'tive S'tN'se 8
Jan16-71⁴FG 6 f 1:13⅕gd 7 110 12 2h 42 10¹⁴ KellerM² Alw 69 Tal' Tall 120 Skycite BullBayou 10
Jan 9-71⁵FG 5½ f 1:07⅖sm 2½ ▲113 21 21 1h 33 CoplingD³ Alw 84 RoyalPussycat 111 Skycite ToniMarie 12
Dec12-70⁸FG 6 f 1:11⅗ft 11 117 23 33½ 48½ 6¹⁴ CoplingD⁶ Alw 77 Ⓕ Emp'rsD's'e117 F'cyR'd Mitch'sL'e 8
Nov28-70⁹FG 6 f 1:11⅘ft 9 117 1h 32½ 67½ 9¹⁷ CoplingD¹ Hcp0 75 Windgusher116 SharpMan Lib'lEmp'r 10
Aug 1-70⁹EvD 6½ f 1:21 ft 2½ 117 1½ 1½ 1½ 2nk Cop'gD¹⁰ ScwS 90 Mr. Reed 120 Toni Marie Eight Year 10
Jly 24-70⁶EvD 6½ f 1:21 ft 6-5 ▲117 1½ 1½ 14 12½ CoplingD⁴ SplW 89 ToniMarie117 Mr.Reed Str'gDistillate 9
Jly 11-70²EvD 5 f 1:00⅗gd 1 ▲119 13 15 15 13½ Copl'gD¹⁰ AlwS 85 ToniMarie119 BayouB'gal DragonB'ty 10
Jun27-70⁷EvD 5 f 1:00 ft 4-5 ▲112* 1½ 12 12 12¼ CoplingD⁵ Alw 88 Toni Marie 112 Milk Queen Mr. Reed 12
Jun 5-70⁵EvD 5 f :59⅗ft 3½ 109* 63½ 21½ 21½ 2½ PatinHK² Alw 89 BillBlazer117 ToniMarie PrudhoeBay 12
Jan 23 FG 6f ft 1:13⅗h Janu 22 FG 3f ft :37⅖b Jan 15 FG 6f hy 1:17b

SPEED RULE
(HORSE'S SPEED RATING NOT WITHIN 5 POINTS OF ALHAMBRA GAL'S 91.)

Matchless Native 112 B. f (1968), by Raise a Native—Royal Match, by Turn-to.
Breeder, J. M. Olin (Ky.). 1971 2 0 1 0 $840
Owner, R. Woodward et al. Trainer, B. G. Dunham. 1970 4 1 1 0 $2,790
Jan29-71⁸FG 5½ f 1:05⅕ft 7 115 65½ 42½ 43½ 24 WhitedDE³ Alw 94 Ⓕ T'niM'rie111 M'tchl'sN'tive S'tN'se 8
Jan19-71⁸FG 6 f 1:11 ft 15 112 99¾ 99½ 98½ 9¹³ TauzinL⁸ Alw 81 Martini Again 117 Felonious Cruline 9
Dec31-70⁴FG 6 f 1:14⅗hy 6-5 ▲118 1h 13 12½ 11 TauzinL⁵ Mdn 76 Ⓕ M't'h'sN'tive118 M'sM'ch's L'kyM'd 8
Dec17-70⁶FG 6 f 1:12⅕ft 2-3e▲114 9¹² 9¹¹ 8¹¹ 84¼ ZakoorW⁷ Alw 84 Ⓕ ChouCroute113 Tan'sMagic Cruline 9
Sep18-70⁴Atl 6 f 1:12⅗ft 3¼ 117 32 1h 1½ 21 VerardiF⁸ Mdn 78 Ⓕ R'em'tB'w117 M'chl'sN't'e MenM'd 12
Sep11-70⁴Atl 6 f 1:12⅗ft 3¼ 117 41½ 41 43 46 VerardiF⁹ Mdn 78 Ⓕ Via Rica 110 Mararjee Daisy Purple 12
Feb 5 FG 3f gd :38⅖b Jan 27 FG 3f ft :35⅕b Jan 23 FG 4f ft :48b

SPEED RULE
(HORSE'S SPEED RATING NOT WITHIN 5 POINTS OF ALHAMBRA GAL'S 91.)

Bee Bee Dabo 112 B. f (1968), by Tibabado—Prybe, by Pry.
Breeder, Mrs. L. G. Hooper (Fla.). 1971 1 0 1 0 $840
Owner, Middlebrook Stable. Trainer, J. W. Taylor. 1970 2 1 0 0 $1,800
Jan29-71⁹FG 5½ f 1:05⅘ft 12 115 21 23 23 2½ NicholsJ⁴ Alw 94 Ⓕ Alh'raGal 120 BeeBeeD'bo EightY'r 8
Mar11-70⁹FG 4½ f :55 m 4 119 7 22 33 52¼ Copl'gD¹¹ AlwS 86 Ⓕ FancyRoad122 Startalaw HotGravey 14
Feb25-70³FG 3 f :34⅘m 8½ 113* 2 13 13 CoplingD⁴ Mdn 96 Ⓕ BeeBeeDabo113 Tulia FlowerThief 10
Feb 5 FG 3f gd :36⅗b Jan 28 FG 3f ft :35hg Jan 21 FG 5f ft 1:01⅘b

DISTANCE RULE
(NEVER RUN 6 FURLONGS)

Alhambra Gal 117 B. f (1968), by Alhambra—Musical Gal, by Flying Doug.
Breeder, F. J. Carlin (Mich.). 1971 2 1 0 0 $2,520
Owner, F. J. Carlin. Trainer, W. E. Anderson. 1970 16 5 2 1 $28,131
Jan29-71⁹FG 5½ f 1:05⅘ft 8-5 ▲120 36 34½ 33 1½ BairdRL³ Alw 95 Ⓕ Alh'raGal 120 BeeBeeD'bo EightY'r 8
Jan 9-71⁹FG 6 f 1:13⅗m 3 112 33 33 65½ 9¹² BairdRL⁵ HcpS 69 Ⓕ Michig'nF'll 112 Fr'cesFl'r G'ldR'gs 9
Dec26-70⁹FG 6 f 1:11⅗ft 22 114 3nk 31½ 1h 1nk B'rdRL¹¹ Hcp0 91 Alh'braGal 114 Windg'sh'r M'tiniAg'n 12
Dec12-70⁹FG 6 f 1:11⅘ft 3½ 119 31½ 1h 11½ 2nk BairdRL² AlwS 90 Ⓕ Sw'tN'se114 Alhb'raG'l Fl'meB'rgoo 8
Nov28-70⁹FG 6 f 1:11⅘ft 7½ 118 33 43½ 33 69 BairdRL⁴ Hcp0 83 Windgusher116 SharpMan Lib'lEmp'r 10
Nov 7-70⁹HP 1 1:40⅗gd 23 119 12 2½ 10¹⁹ 9²¹ BairdWJ⁹ AlwS 59 TreasureDay113 Mr.Gemini T'linAr'nd 11
Oct30-70⁸HP 6½ f 1:18⅕m 4½ 119 21 22 36 49½ BairdWJ³ AlwS 80 Sp'kQuick119 T'linAr'nd S'min'yR'ge 6
Oct21-70⁸HP 6 f 1:15 m 8-5 ▲119 22 21 11 1h BairdWJ³ AlwS 79 AlhambraGal 119 SoarH'd GoldenGem 10
Oct 9-70⁸HP 6½ f 1:18⅘ft 2¾ 113 44 3nk 11 12† BairdWJ⁶ AlwS 89 Ⓕ Alh'braGal 113 Mitch'sLine Colossal 7
†Disqualified and placed fifth.
Sep24-70⁸HP 6 f 1:11⅘ft 8½ 112 44 46 35½ 36½†C'pbellRJ⁴ Alw 88 Glorioso114 SpeakQuick AlhambraGal 7
†Dead heat.
Jan 27 FG 3f ft :34⅘b Jan 7 FG 3f ft :37b Dec 22 FG 3f ft :35⅗b

CONTENDER

Eight Year 119 Ch. f (1968), by Yesteryear—Eighth Time, by Count Turf.
Breeder, P. Segura (La.). 1971 2 0 0 1 $1,062
Owner, J. Delahoussaye. Trainer, J. Delahoussaye. 1970 14 7 4 2 $40,238
Jan29-71⁹FG 5½ f 1:05⅘ft 6½ 117 68 45½ 46 32½ MenardN⁶ Alw 92 Ⓕ Alh'raGal 120 BeeBeeD'bo EightY'r 8
Jan23-71⁸FG 6 f 1:12⅗ft 7-5 ▲125 11¹⁶ 78½ 54¾ 42 Men'rdN² Hcp0 84 Ⓕ Skycite 119 Lady Fort Reds Story 14
Dec31-70⁷FG 6 f 1:13⅘hy 2-5 ▲122 31 12 14 17 MenardN⁴ AlwS 80 Ⓕ Eight Year 122 Skycite Backwater 11
Dec22-70⁸FG 6 f 1:12 ft 7-5 ▲112 31 2½ 1h 11 MenardN⁸ Alw 89 Ⓕ EightYear112 LadyFort Oiney'sPet 10
Dec16-70⁶FG 6 f 1:14⅕sl 4-5 ▲112 3½ 22 12 21½ MenardN⁵ Alw 76 Ⓕ Lady Fort 112 Eight Year Jayme M. 8
Sep12-70¹¹EvD 6½ f 1:22 gd 7-5 119 79 53 42½ 1nk MenardN⁸ HcpS 84 EightYear119 B'youB'gal T'niasM'gic 12
Aug22-70⁷EvD 6½ f 1:21⅘ft 4-5 ▲107* 12½ 15 1½ 21 Brouss'dN⁶ Alw 84 BayouBengal 112 EightYear CraftyS'r 6
Aug 1-70⁹EvD 6½ f 1:21 ft 6½ 117 31 41½ 52 31¾ SoirezW¹ ScwS 88 Mr. Reed 120 Toni Marie Eight Year 10
Jly 24-70⁷EvD 6½ f 1:22⅕ft 2½ 117 23 23 1½ 2¾ SoirezW³ SplW 82 BillBlazer120 EightYear GatowHawk 8
Jly 11-70⁷EvD 5 f 1:00⅖sgd 3-5 ▲119 21½ 2½ 2h 21 SuireL⁸ AlwS 85 BillBlazer122 EightYear Pr'dhoeBay 10
Feb 3 FG 5f ft 1:02⅗bg Jan 19 FG 4f ft :49⅖b

CONTENDER

Sweet Noise 114 B. f (1968), by Noisemaker—Miss Everett, by Everett Jr.
Breeder, E. Lowrance (Okla.). 1971 2 0 0 1 $4,62
Owner, E. Lowrance. Trainer, J. Eckrosh. 1970 19 5 3 2 $22,380
Jan29-71⁸FG 5½ f 1:05⅕ft 6-5 ▲120 44 32½ 23 36 CoxR² Alw 92 Ⓕ T'niM'rie111 M'tchl'sN'tive S'tN'se 8
Jan 9-71⁸FG 6 f 1:13⅕m 3 113 57½ 53¾ 66½ 6¹² ZakoorW⁴ HcpS 71 Ⓕ VicsT'rn117 Amonet PrincessT'm'ra 8
Dec26-70⁹FG 6 f 1:11⅗ft 8¼e 115 118¾11¹¹ 78 63 CoxR⁷ Hcp0 88 Alh'braGal 114 Windg'sh'r M'tiniAg'n 12
Dec12-70⁹FG 6 f 1:11⅘ft 3½ 114 53¾ 42½ 21½ 1nk CoxR¹ AlwS 90 Ⓕ Sw'tN'se114 Alhb'raG'l Fl'meB'rgoo 8
Nov20-70⁷Spt 6 f 1:14⅕sl 4-5 ▲119 14 17 16 18 CoxR⁶ Alw 80 Sweet Noise 119 Bixa Cindy Burgoo 6
Nov 2-70⁷Spt 6 f 1:14 sy 6-5 ▲115 56½ 32 2½ 13 CoxR⁸ Alw 81 Ⓕ SweetNoise115 LadyFort CryAwhile 9
Oct27-70⁷Spt 6½ f 1:17⅘ft 4 117 21½ 1½ 11½ 2nk CoxR⁴ Alw 89 Ⓕ Viewpoise120 SweetNoise RockDove 7
Oct19-70⁵Spt 6 f 1:12⅗ft 2¾ ▲115 1h 21 2h 3½ CoxR⁷ Alw 88 Ⓕ M'rryD'rt'r115 J'llypence Sw'tN'se 9
Sep21-70⁶Haw 6 f 1:11⅘ft 9-5 ▲114 2h 2h 2h 12½ CoxR⁷ Alw 87 Ⓕ Sw'tN'se114 V'wp'se M'sGr'tc'nGee 9
Jan 28 FG 3f ft :37b Jan 8 FG 3f sy :39b Jan 2 FG 4f sl :50⅕b

LOSS IN STRETCH RULE
(DROPPED FROM 2nd BY 3 LENGTHS TO 3rd BY 6 LENGTHS.)

10th Fair Grounds

1 MILE & 40 YARDS. (Mike's Red, March 18, 1967, 1:38⅗, 5, 116.) Claiming. Purse $3,400. 4-year-olds and upward. 4-year-olds, 119 lbs.; older, 120 lbs. Non-winners of three races since Dec. 6 allowed 2 lbs.; two races since then, 4 lbs.; a race, 6 lbs. (Claiming races for $5,000 or less not considered.) Claiming price, $6,500.

COUPLED: POINTMENOW and SIR VICTOR; GREAT PUMPKIN and TONY W.

Limetime **114** Ch. h (1965), by Star Performance—Limealee, by Limestone.
Breeder, Leonard & Barry (Tex.). 1971 2 0 1 0 $600
Owner, E. A. Barielle. Trainer, M. J. Comeaux. $6,500 1970 20 2 1 1 $4,692
Jan28-71⁶FG 1 1/16 1:45⅗ft 4 115 42½ 41¼ 13 2nk Wh'dDE4 c4000 87 Stubzy 115 Limetime Pier d'Oro 10
Jan20-71⁵FG 6 f 1:11⅕ft 6½ 115 83¾ 98½ 75 64¾ Whit'dDE9 5000 88 Croydon 114 DarkStarJr. DoGoAbbey 12
Dec30-70⁸FG 6 f 1:13⅕sy 3¾ 117 119½Rain 67½ 67½ SoirezW4 c5000 75 Rossi'sRogue112 N'groB'rro B'tlePick 12
Dec23-70⁶FG 6 f 1:12 ft 33 115 52¾ 54½ 1h 2no SoirezW1 5000 89 F'llSt'mAh'd115 Limetime N'groBarro 12
Nov27-70⁴CD 6½ f 1:18⅘ft 9 117 42 33 48½ 56¼ SpencerS4 6000 80 Yar 114 Big Trouble What A Roman 10
Nov17-70⁴CD 6½ f 1:18⅖ft 5½ 118 52¾ 65½ 64½ 42¾ Mang'loM2 6000 85 Por Royal 116 Todd B. Lodey Evenson 9
Nov11-70⁶CD 7 f 1:26⅕sm 10 118 65½ 57 32 13 TauzinL10 4500 76 Limetime118 SharpMixture Turfbound 11
Oct31-70³CD 6 f 1:12⅕ft 23 112 67½ 45½ 12 1¾ TauzinL6 3750 85 Limetime112 WhatAR'm'n Misd'c'pt'n 12
Jan 16 FG 3f gd :37⅖b Dec 29 FG 3f gd :36⅘b Dec 17 FG 4f gd :51⅕b

LOSS IN STRETCH RULE
(FROM 1st BY 3 LENGTHS TO 2nd BY A NECK.)

Barnacle B. **114** Ch. g (1966), by Neptune—Hokey Pokey, by Apache.
Breeder, Mrs. W. O. Bridge (Mich.). 1971 3 0 1 0 $788
Owner, B. Ales. Trainer, R. Heitzmann, Jr. $6,500 1970 21 5 3 1 $15,625
Jan30-71¹⁰FG 1 1/16 1:45⅗ft •2½ ▲111 35 56 618 713 Rubb'coP1 6250 74 BigMouthSam115 Gallamiss Hillsub 8
Jan 9-71¹⁰FG 1-40 1:44⅖sm 3½ 114 12½ 11 12 22 Rubb'coP6 6250 69 Sw'tManh'ten113 B'rnacleB. SkyVil'e 8
Jan 2-71⁶FG 6 f 1:12⅘gd 10 115 52½ 74¼ 66 56 Rubb'coP4 7500 77 LittleA.115 JayRoam FullSt'mAhead 11
Dec26-70⁵FG 6 f 1:12⅗ft 2½ ▲114 52¼ 31 21 32¾ Rubb'coP6 7500 83 Kendare 114 CimarronJet BarnacleB. 7
Dec10-70⁴FG 1-40 1:41⅕ft 8-5 118 1h 11½ 23 512 Rubb'coP5 7500 75 SkyVillage114 LandingMan FunM'ker 6
Dec 5-70⁵FG 1 1/16 1:45⅖ft 3¼ 118 22 11 2½ 2½ HolmesD3 7500 87 TakeOver 115 BarnacleB. FunMaker 9
Nov28-70⁴FG 6 f 1:11⅘ft 3 119 3nk 1h 2½ 23½ RubbiccoP6 7500 86 Embassy114 BarnacleB. JenniferBlue 6
Nov 7-70⁷HP 6 f 1:14 gd 4¼ 117 2½ 23 35 46¼ SnyderD3 8000 78 LongRoad114 Corky ofClinton DoyleG. 7
Oct28-70⁸HP 6 f 1:12⅕ft 5 114 76¼ 87¼ 811 87¼ PerezG7 9000 86 SingingMark114 CimarronJet Mejor 8
Oct19-70⁵HP 1 1:38⅕ft 14 114 11½ 11 11½ 1nk PerezR5 8000 92 BarnacleB.114 Br'mblesBoy TexasGlen 8
Jan 22 FG 3f ft :37b Dec 22 FG 4f ft :49⅘b

8-LENGTHS RULE
(HORSE FINISHED 7th BY 13 LENGTHS.)

Sky Village **116** B. g (1964), by Pure Village—Sky Ramp, by Skytracer.
Breeder, F. Fancher (Ky.). 1971 5 0 2 2 $2,516
Owner, J. P. Dorignac, Jr. Trainer, J. Dorignac, III. $6,500 1970 22 2 1 8 $14,478
Jan28-71⁸FG 1-40 1:40⅗ft 3¾ 115 610 513 56¼ 24 HolmesD7 7000 86 Cl'syAdm'l 114 SkyV'l'ge Off toM'rk't 9
Jan21-71⁶FG 1-40 1:40 ft 4¼ 117 68½ 54½ 44½ 3¾ Whit'dDE3 7500 92 B'ldVik'g114 M'm'sH'meN'w SkyV'ge 10
Jan14-71⁶FG 1 1/16 1:49⅗hy 5½ 116 711 65 56 2h HolmesD6 7500 67 M'k'gN'se113 SkyVill'ge M'm'sH'eN'w 7
Jan 9-71¹⁰FG 1-40 1:44⅖sm 2¼ ▲116 717 65¾ 57 32 HolmesD3 6250 69 Sw'tManh'ten113 B'rnacleB. SkyVil'e 8
Jan 2-71¹⁰FG 1-40 1:43 gd 8-5 ▲117 1020 1021 814 47 HolmesD5 6250 71 Tudorfib115 BoldViking Sum'rReading 10
Dec24-70⁸FG 1 1/16 1:45⅖ft 9-5 ▲117 820 88¾ 42 32 WhitedDE5 7500 86 TakeOver117 Gr'tPumpkin SkyVillage 8
Dec10-70⁴FG 1-40 1:41⅕ft 4¼ 114 617 614 44½ 12½ HolmesD6 7000 87 SkyVillage114 LandingMan FunM'ker 6
Dec 3-70⁸FG 1-40 1:41⅗ft 8-5 ▲112 827 823 612 31¾ HolmesD8 5000 83 Gr'tP'pkin112 OneNightSt'd SkyVil'ge 8
Nov26-70³FG 1-40 1:42⅕ft 3 112 925 715 61¾ 32 HolmesD2 5000 80 Dudes Finale 112 Mechief Sky Village 9
Oct 9-70⁷Spt 1 1/16 1:47⅗m 7½ 116 814 815 68 68½ DesOr'uxS6 8000 67 BusyLife120 Central Sq're Caes'rCire 8
Oct 2-70⁷Spt 1 1:39⅕ft 9½ 116 815 75¾ 22 32½ DesOr'xS8 7000 81 BusyLife 118 StaysDream SkyVillage 8
Feb 3 FG 3f ft :36⅗b Jan 27 FG 3f ft :36⅗b Dec 31 FG 3f m :38⅖b

NUMBER 1 BET

Pointmenow **114** Ch. h (1964), by Point of Order—Passing Glance, by Basileus II.
Breeder, J. Dobkin (Ill.). 1971 2 0 0 0 (——)
Owner, J. C. Dobkin. Trainer, C. Scott. $6,500 1970 18 0 1 0 $2,875
Jan28-71⁸FG 1-40 1:40⅗ft 15 115 919 921 71 78¾ HeathM1 7500 81 Cl'syAdm'l 114 SkyV'l'ge Off toM'rk't 9
Jan 7-71⁷FG 1-40 1:41⅕ft 4½ 116 67 66½ 67½ 64¼ HeathM2 7500 83 T'keOv'r120 M'm'sH'eN'w Off toM'k't 6
Dec28-70⁹FG 6 f 1:11⅘ft 38 113 820 820 818 812 HeathM6 Alw 78 Embassy 113 Himaldo Clem Would 8
Dec23-70⁸FG 6 f 1:10⅖ft 106 115 1017 1018 1017 1013 HeathM4 Alw 84 Sunburn 115 Port Digger Loyal Yet 10
Nov21-70⁸Spt 1 1-8 1:50⅗ft 14 108 612 615 718 715 Spindl'rL7 HcpS 78 R'y'lH'rm'ny129 T'ribleTig'r HighRov'r 7
Nov11-70⁸Spt 1 1:39⅗gd 8 113 825 813 712 513 HeathM1 HcpS 69 Jaimsie 114 Judge Tytus Bold Colonel 8
Oct14-70⁸Spt 1 1:38⅕sy 16 114 813 812 715 717 HeathM6 Alw 72 ElegantHeir119 SteelPike ClassicT'k't 8
Oct 7-70⁸Spt 1 1/16 1:44⅖ft 6 116 716 79 67 66¼ HeathM1 Alw 86 But Sure 122 Pago Moon Fast Thaw 8
Sep29-70⁷Haw 1 1/16 1:43⅖ft 11 111 711 614 59 21¼ HeathM1 Hcp0 85 ButSure116 Pointmenow M'ss'uriGent 7
Feb 5 FG 3f gd :38⅗b Feb 2 FG 4f ft :50⅗b Jan 27 FG 3f ft :37⅕b

8-LENGTH RULE
(HORSE FINISHED 7th BY 8¾ LENGTHS.)

Out of the Trap **114** Ch. h (1966), by Crimson Satan—One Clear Call, by Gallant Man.
Breeder, E. V. Benjamin, Jr. & 1971 5 1 0 1 $2,118
R. C. Crisler (Ky.). 1969 14 4 2 1 $13,606
Owner, J. A. Sider, Sr. Trainer, G. H. Gleber, Jr. $6,500
Feb 4-71⁶FG 1-40 1:41⅗ft 8¼ 114 22 1½ 14 14 Belv'leEM6 4000 85 O'toft'eTr'p114 OneN'tSt'd Th'dM'n 10
Jan28-71⁶FG 1 1/16 1:45⅗ft 5 114 32 11 43¼ 57¼ ZakoorW10 4000 80 Stubzy 115 Limetime Pier d'Oro 10
Jan19-71⁷FG 6 f 1:10⅕ft 4½ 115 65 54 34 410 Belv'eEM3 8500 88 Little A. 115 Sea O Joe Busy Life 8
Jan13-71⁸FG 6 f 1:13⅗m 21 114 84¼ 68¼ 79 714 HeathM2 Alw 67 Etony118 RioBravo Hark theHerald 9
Jan 5-71⁸FG 6 f 1:12 gd 17 116 56½ 55 55½ 87 Belv'leEM8 8500 82 JohnnyJacobs117 Kendare UnitWit 12
Oct15-69⁶Kee 7 f 1:24⅖ft 9-5 ▲114 51¾ 1h 14 12½ WhitedDE4 Alw 86 Out of theT'p114 RioB'vo114 H'pyM'm 7
Oct 9-69⁶Kee 1 1/16 1:44 ft 5¼ 118 55¾ 22 22 23½ WhitedDE7 Alw 82 Tripsville118 Out oftheT'p118 JugJ'ge 7
Sep 5-69⁸A.P 5½ f 1:04 sy 11 112 55½ 47 59 69 PinedaA2 Hcp0 86 Cr'gForM'e115 L'coKid120 D'kSt'rK'g 7
Dec 19 FG 3f ft :37⅗b

SPEED RULE
(SPEED RATING NOT WITHIN 5 POINTS OF SKY VILLAGE'S 92.)

Great Pumpkin * **114** B. g (1966), by Amber Morn—My Cinderella, by Mighty Story.
Breeder, Preston Madden (Ky.). 197- 3 0 0 1 $785
Owner, W. A. C. Stable. Trainer, W. A. Cervini, Sr. $6,500 1970 23 3 8 2 $11,057
Jan28-71⁸FG 1-40 1:40⅗ft 6½ 115 49 412 44¼ 44½ SilvaW2 7500 85 Cl'syAdm'l 114 SkyV'l'ge Off toM'rk't 9
Jan23-71⁵FG 6 f 1:11⅘ft 9½ 114 1010 97 63¼ 44 SilvaW5 7500 86 L'ts ofRh'm115 Brit'hB'rg'n TimeCh't 10
Jan 2-71⁴FG 1 1-8 1:54⅖gd 7¾ 115 2h 2h 2h 31¾ SilvaW2 H3000 70 Tantalio 113 SirVictor GreatPumpkin 6
Dec24-70⁸FG 1 1/16 1:45⅖ft 12 114 35 42 1h 22 SilvaW2 7500 86 TakeOver117 Gr'tPumpkin SkyVillage 8
Dec12-70¹⁰FG 1 1/16 1:46⅕ft 15 115 610 33 22 22 SilvaW1 H3000 82 Br'mbl'sB'y114 Gr'tPumpkin SirVict'r 10
Dec 3-70⁸FG 1-40 1:41⅗ft 38 112 57 33 1h 11½ SilvaW3 5000 85 Gr'tP'pkin112 OneNightSt'd SkyVil'ge 8
Nov28-70¹⁰FG 1-40 1:41⅗ft 60 112 511 824 717 613 SilvaW4 H3000 72 Wee Willie 112 Tantalio Sir Victor 9
Oct10-70¹⁰HP 1 1:38⅘ft 36 112 79¾ 77¾ 46 44¾ SilvaW3 H2500 84 Semi-Phade123 AmbiorixBoi LongR'd 7
Oct 3-70¹⁰HP 1 1-8 1:52⅖ft 13 114 715 813 612 512 SilvaW3 H2500 76 Semi-Phade 121 Tonga Base OleHub 8
Jan 21 FG 4f ft :47⅗h Dec 10 FG 4f ft :52⅕b

SPEED RULE
(BEST SPEED AT DISTANCE NOT WITHIN 5 POINTS OF SKY VILLAGE'S 92.)

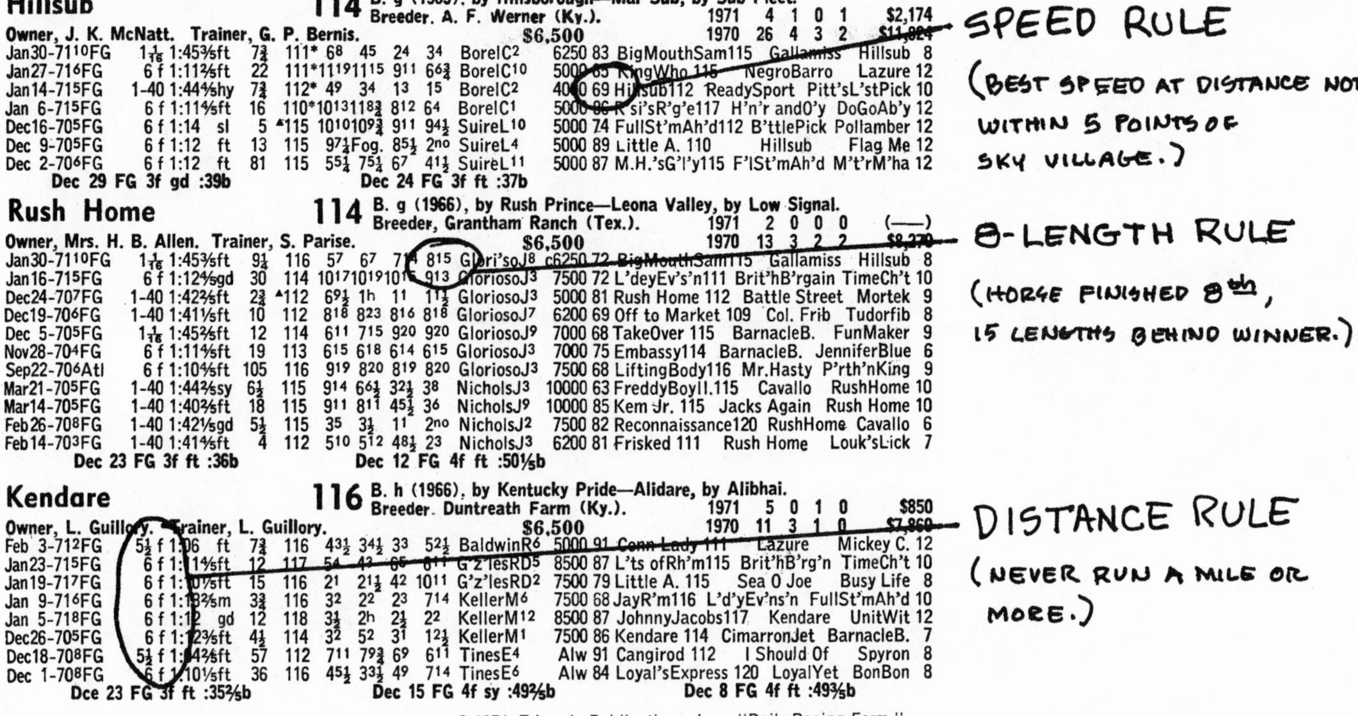

Hillsub — 114 — B. g (1965), by Hillsborough—Mar Sub, by Sub Fleet.
Breeder. A. F. Werner (Ky.). — 1971 4 1 0 1 $2,174
Owner, J. K. McNatt. Trainer, G. P. Bernis. — $6,500 — 1970 26 4 3 2 $11,824

Jan30-71 10FG 1 1/16 1:45 3/5 ft 7¾ 111* 6 8 4 5 2 4 3 4 BorelC 2 6250 83 BigMouthSam115 Gallamiss Hillsub 8
Jan27-71 6FG 6 f 1:11 2/5 ft 22 111* 11 19 11 15 9 11 6 6¾ BorelC 10 5000 83 KingWho 115 NegroBarro Lazure 12
Jan14-71 5FG 1-40 1:44 4/5 hy 7¾ 112* 4 9 3 4 1 3 1 5 BorelC 2 4000 69 Hillsub112 ReadySport Pitt'sL'stPick 10
Jan 6-71 5FG 6 f 1:11 4/5 ft 16 110* 10 13 11 8¾ 8 12 6 4 BorelC 1 5000 86 R'si'sR'g'e117 H'n'r andO'y DoGoAb'y 12
Dec16-70 5FG 6 f 1:14 sl 5 ▲115 10 10 10 9¾ 9 11 9 4½ SuireL 10 5000 74 FullSt'mAh'd112 B'ttlePick Pollamber 12
Dec 9-70 5FG 6 f 1:12 ft 13 115 9 7¼ Fog. 8 5½ 2 no SuireL 4 5000 89 Little A. 110 Hillsub Flag Me 12
Dec 2-70 6FG 6 f 1:12 ft 81 115 5 5¼ 7 5¼ 6 7 4 1½ SuireL 11 5000 87 M.H.'sG'l'y115 F'lSt'mAh'd M't'rM'ha 12
Dec 29 FG 3f gd :39b — Dec 24 FG 3f ft :37b

Rush Home — 114 — B. g (1966), by Rush Prince—Leona Valley, by Low Signal.
Breeder, Grantham Ranch (Tex.). — 1971 2 0 0 0 (—)
Owner, Mrs. H. B. Allen. Trainer, S. Parise. — $6,500 — 1970 13 3 2 2 $8,270

Jan30-71 10FG 1 1/16 1:45 3/5 ft 9¼ 116 5 7 6 7 7 14 8 15 Glori'soJ 8 c6250 72 BigMouthSam115 Gallamiss Hillsub 8
Jan16-71 5FG 6 f 1:12 4/5 gd 30 114 10 17 10 19 10 15 9 13 GloriosoJ 3 7500 72 L'deyEv's'n111 Brit'hB'rgain TimeCh't 10
Dec24-70 7FG 1-40 1:42 2/5 ft 2¾ ▲112 6 9½ 1 h 1 1 1 1½ GloriosoJ 3 5000 81 Rush Home 112 Battle Street Mortek 9
Dec19-70 6FG 1-40 1:41 1/5 ft 10 112 8 18 8 23 8 16 8 18 GloriosoJ 7 6200 69 Off to Market 109 Col. Frib Tudorfib 8
Dec 5-70 5FG 1 1/16 1:45 2/5 ft 12 114 6 11 7 15 9 20 9 20 GloriosoJ 9 7000 68 TakeOver 115 BarnacleB. FunMaker 9
Nov28-70 4FG 6 f 1:11 4/5 ft 19 113 6 15 6 18 6 14 6 15 GloriosoJ 3 7000 75 Embassy114 BarnacleB. JenniferBlue 6
Sep22-70 6Atl 6 f 1:10 4/5 ft 105 116 9 19 8 20 8 19 8 20 GloriosoJ 3 7500 68 LiftingBody116 Mr.Hasty P'rth'nKing 9
Mar21-70 5FG 1-40 1:44 2/5 sy 6½ 115 9 14 6 6½ 3 2½ 3 8 NicholsJ 3 10000 63 FreddyBoyII.115 Cavallo RushHome 10
Mar14-70 5FG 1-40 1:40 2/5 ft 18 115 9 11 8 11 4 5½ 3 6 NicholsJ 9 10000 85 Kem Jr. 115 Jacks Again Rush Home 10
Feb26-70 8FG 1-40 1:42 1/5 gd 5½ 115 3 5 3½ 1 1 2 no NicholsJ 2 7500 82 Reconnaissance120 RushHome Cavallo 6
Feb14-70 3FG 1-40 1:41 4/5 ft 4 112 5 10 5 12 4 8½ 2 3 NicholsJ 3 6200 81 Frisked 111 Rush Home Louk'sLick 7
Dec 23 FG 3f ft :36b — Dec 12 FG 4f ft :50 1/5 b

Kendare — 116 — B. h (1966), by Kentucky Pride—Alidare, by Alibhai.
Breeder. Duntreath Farm (Ky.). — 1971 5 0 1 0 $850
Owner, L. Guillory. Trainer, L. Guillory. — $6,500 — 1970 11 3 1 0 $7,860

Feb 3-71 2FG 5½ f 1:06 ft 7¾ 116 4 3½ 3 4½ 3 3 5 2½ BaldwinR 6 5000 91 Conn Lady 111 Lazure Mickey C. 12
Jan23-71 5FG 6 f 1:11 4/5 ft 12 117 5 4 4 3 6 5 8 11 G'z'lesRD 5 8500 87 L'ts ofRh'm115 Brit'hB'rg'n TimeCh't 10
Jan19-71 7FG 6 f 1:10 1/5 ft 15 116 2 1 2 1½ 4 2 10 11 G'z'lesRD 2 7500 79 Little A. 115 Sea O Joe Busy Life 8
Jan 9-71 6FG 6 f 1:13 2/5 m 3¾ 116 3 2 2 2 2 3 7 14 KellerM 6 7500 68 JayR'm116 L'd'yEv'ns'n FullSt'mAh'd 10
Jan 5-71 8FG 6 f 1:12 gd 12 118 3½ 2 h 2½ 2 2 KellerM 12 8500 87 JohnnyJacobs117 Kendare UnitWit 12
Dec26-70 5FG 6 f 1:12 3/5 ft 4½ 114 3 2 5 2 3 1 1 2½ KellerM 1 7500 86 Kendare 114 CimarronJet BarnacleB. 7
Dec18-70 8FG 5½ f 1:04 2/5 ft 57 112 7 11 7 9¾ 6 9 6 11 TinesE 4 Alw 91 Cangirod 112 I Should Of Spyron 8
Dec 1-70 8FG 6 f 1:10 1/5 ft 36 116 4 5½ 3 3½ 4 9 7 14 TinesE 6 Alw 84 Loyal'sExpress 120 LoyalYet BonBon 8
Dce 23 FG 3f ft :35 2/5 b — Dec 15 FG 4f sy :49 2/5 b — Dec 8 FG 4f ft :49 3/5 b

day $350.60. Since our total bets only amounted to $304 we more than doubled our money. Totaling our expenses we see:

Racing Form and Program	$1.00
Admission for two	7.00
Bribe for table	5.00
Lunch for two	9.75
Six drinks	9.00
Waiter's tip	3.00
TOTAL	$34.85

Roughly, $17 per person. Which, incidentally, is why the $2 bettor can't win. The expenses of the track eat up too large a portion of his winnings and secondly, he can't manipulate a Dutch book. He's tempted to shoot at longshots to build his bankroll and he's constantly trying to catch up. He'd be better off staying at home until he saves enough to make his bets effective.

In any case, our day was successful, more successful than normal. Actually, the five races using the Dutch technique were about average. We bet $40 on the second, $28 on the fourth, $54 on the fifth, $40 on the eighth, and $42 on the ninth for a total of $204 invested. It returned $253.60 or $49.60 profit, which is pretty much in line with the 25-30 percent profit we normally show. But the additional $43 profit from the Exacta was an unexpected windfall and winning four for four on our individual selections is better than we usually fare.

The truth is, if we had not been trying to get action, we would have bet no more than three or four races. This is the most intelligent way to bet if you go to the track every day. But the casual horseplayer who goes on weekends and holidays doesn't like to miss the action by passing a race, and our Saturday outing was designed to show you can combine action with intelligent horseplaying.

On these pages we have reproduced the past performance charts from this day and made our notes so you can follow the entire procedure.

MR. ODDS-MAKER'S BEST BET

Mr. Odds-Maker says, "When the payoff odds on a horse that has a good chance of winning are substantially better than the true odds, you have a Best Bet in horse racing. All you need is a better ability to estimate race horses than the general betting public has. For that matter, if you're a superior handicapper and understand money management, you don't need any advice from me. There are handicappers and money managers who show a profit on their bets, thanks to sheer ability."

Photo courtesy Pimlico Race Course, Baltimore, Md.

Above—The Clubhouse Turn, 1966 Preakness, as Stupendous *(8), outside, assumes the lead over* Kauai King *(3).* Kauai King *was the winner in the second fastest Preakness ever run. The first Preakness was run at Pimlico in 1873. Below—Golden Gate Fields, home of the California Derby, was built in 1940. Not shown in this photo is the new 9/10 mile turf course that has been constructed in the infield.*

Photo courtesy Golden Gate Fields, Albany, Calif.

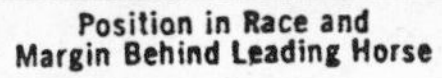

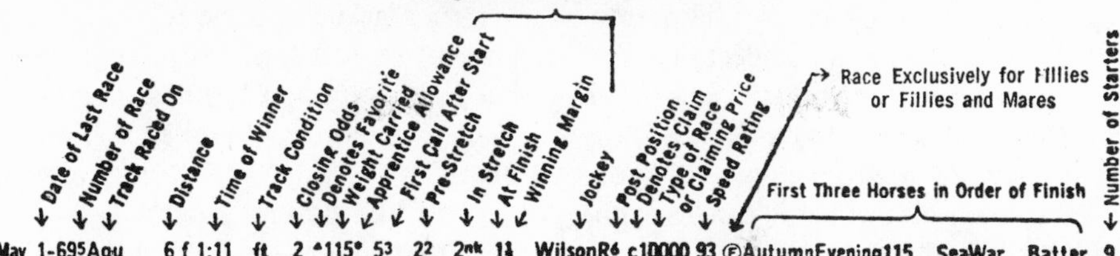

Note: The position in the race for "first call after start" is as follows: In races at 5 1-2 furlongs or more the first call is at the quarter mile; at 5 furlongs, it is at the three-sixteenths; at less than 5 furlongs it is at the start.

FAIR GROUNDS speed ratings are based on track records in effect prior to the opening of this meeting, November 26, 1970.

*** Fair Mud Runner. × Good Mud Runner. ⊗ Superior Mud Runner.**

MONEY MANAGEMENT

Before going into any of the positive aspects of money management, here's some sound advice: STAY AWAY FROM *ANY* Progressive Betting systems on the horses. There are not only sound, logical reasons for this but an important mathematical one. A progressive betting system, to be effective, must know odds and payoff of each future independent event, must rely on randomness of occurrence, and must have a predictable estimate of occurrence over a stated period of time. The race track provides none of these elements. It does, however, provide other compensations that are more important. For example, at the track you don't bet against a shrewd professional gambler as you do in casino games. You bet against Aunt Harriet and her cookie-jar money. And Aunt Harriet shows us she is wrong two out of three times because the favorite, that she and all the other $2 bettors establish through the mutuel, wins only about one-third of the time.

Don't be lured by parlays, double-ups, due-columns or any other type of money manipulation. Pick a level that fits your temperament, your bank book and your handicapping performance. Remember that you can make 20 percent profit in many different ways, but each way requires a different type of money management. For example, let's look at two different characters going to the track. They each handicap in roughly the same way but each wants a different kind of horse. "Chalk Charlie" waits for the sure thing. He cashes eight of ten bets that he makes, but his average odds are only one to two. When he gets even money on a horse he considers it a longshot. "Longshot Larry," on the otherhand, bets the same number of races (maybe even the same races, strangely enough) but he only takes a trip to the cashiers' windows one out of ten times. When he does, though, his chubby fist is clutching a ticket with an average of 11-1. How do these two guys make out? Exactly the same in the long run. Charlie wins 80 percent of his bets, so if he bets 20 races with $100 on each he invests $2,000; if he wins 16 out of 20 at average odds of 1-2 $(3 payoff) he gets back $2,400. This is $400 profit on $2,000 invested so he makes 20 percent on his money.

Meanwhile, Larry bets $100 on the same 20 races and finally hits two of his 11-1 winners. He also gets back $2,400 for his $2,000 invested and achieves the same rate of profit. What's the difference? Well, since Charlie visits the cashier so much more frequently, he doesn't run into the long strings of losses that sometimes cause Larry to contemplate homicide against horse, jockey and trainer. In the final analysis, Charlie will multiply his starting bankroll faster because he can start with larger bets. How does this work? Well, consider that they both have $1,000 to start. The probability that Charlie will lose five straight races is extremely small, since he wins 80 percent of his bets. So, being very conservative, he bets 10 percent of his bank (which would allow him ten straight losses—inconceivable, when he picks 80 percent winners!) At starting bets of $100 and showing a 20 percent rate of profit, in 50 races he doubles his initial $1,000.

At the same time, Larry looks at his past handicapping record and sees he has sometimes gone as long as 25 bets without a winner. He has to consider the possibility of 50 straight losses (since he wins only 10 percent of his races) to provide the same margin of safety that Charlie has! This means he can only bet $20 per race. In order to double his initial bankroll of $1,000 he will have to bet 250 races. It takes him five times as long as Charlie to double his money.

Obviously, these two are extreme cases, chosen to illustrate a point. That point is: don't neglect favorites simply because of price. Remember that a horse with a 90 percent probability of winning is a good healthy overlay at even money! As a handicapper, it's your job to know when an even money bet is a steal at the price and when it's all the Aunt Harriets who sent a true 2-1 horse down to ridiculous odds.

One method of determining the necessary bankroll needed to sustain a given level of bet is simply to take the longest run of losses that you have ever experienced and triple that figure. While there are complex statistical calculations based on highly sophisticated mathematics, we have found that the simpler method of tripling your longest string of losses works equally well. For example, in our handicapping methods and spot-play techniques we have restricted our own activity to "Best Bets." Occasional visitors to the track may require more action than we get and therefore have to count on lower percent of winners and longer runs of losses. Our handicapping turns up an average of one "Best Bet" and two "Dutch Book" bets per day. Normally we cash two out of every three bets (roughly 70 percent wins) and our longest string of losses went for three days or seven races. At the same time somebody who was betting five races a day might have had as many as 15 straight losses in those three days and a person who bets every race could have torn up 27 tickets during a three-day losing period. So while we need to accommodate roughly 20 losses in our bankroll, a less conservative player may need a bank that can afford 50 losses.

Working strictly on our figures we notice seven losses, multiply by three and see our bankroll should contain 21 bets. For ease of computation, we reduce this to 20 and now bet 1/20 or 5 percent of our bankroll. This means that in order to make $5 bets we need $100; for $20 bets we need $400; for $50 bets, $1,000. We never recommend betting less than $5 because expenses at the track make it impossible to show a profit on $2 bets.

This necessary capital is something that most bettors don't give enough attention. Perhaps it's the psychology of the gambler's personality or the looseness of the track atmosphere, but horse players attempt things at the track that they would never do anywhere else. We have a friend who owns a tavern on the Near North Side in Chicago. After several visits to the track with him, he asked, "Why is it I pick most of the same horses you do and still wind up losing?" So we attempted to explain Money Management to him. We asked what percent profit he expected to make on all the money that passed through his till on a Saturday. He estimated 20 percent. We then asked him whether he thought he knew horse racing or the tavern business better. He agreed, that though he was a pretty fair handicapper, he knew the tavern business better because it was his livelihood. We then asked why he felt he should make a larger percent of profit on his money going through somebody else's till in a business that was not his primary interest than from other people's money going through his till in a business that he knows well. He replied that he had never thought of it in those terms, but now that he had, he would be willing to show a 10 to 15 percent profit on all his bets. Since he is a heavy bettor, this would be a significant amount. Next we looked at the average amount he bet (which varied from $20 to $200) and determined what size bankroll he needed. His handicapping performance is quite good and he specializes in horses that go off around 5-2, 3-1, 7-2 or 4-1. He seldom plays a favorite, but doesn't go for longshots, either. However, he has had stretches of up to 14 losers. This meant that he should accommodate about 45 losses in his bankroll or could bet roughly 2 percent of his bankroll on each race. When he saw that he should be willing to put up $5,000 in order to make $100 bets, he lost interest in the whole idea. The last time we saw him at the track, he said that he had taken some of our Money Management ideas to heart and was no longer trying to turn $500 into $5,000 on one afternoon, but was willing to settle for 20 percent profit and come home with $100 profit. *But* he had ignored the basic principle of having enough bankroll to sustain a *constant* bet level. As a result, if he had three losses early in the day at $100 bets, he would cut back his bets to $50 or $20 in the next races. You can easily see what happened. When he lost, he lost big, but when he won, he won small. Obviously, our entire discussion of Money Management had been wasted. He'll probably go on betting as usual and wind up losing. It's a good thing he runs his tavern with better Money Management.

What are the principles then that should guide your Money Management? The first and most obvious is not to bet more than you can afford to lose. Nobody can do his best work while threatened with eviction, divorce or jail. Similarly, financial pressure puts a real burden on your handicapping, and emotion has no place in horserace handicapping and betting.

Second, look closely at your handicapping style and how you like to bet. If you really like the thrill of longshots and lots of action, at least don't con yourself. Be ready to admit that you'll pay for these thrills in reduced rate of profit and increased length of losing streaks. If you still want to enjoy yourself, you can still show a profit, even if it isn't as steady and as rapid as that of the more conservative spot player.

Third, establish a separate "betting fund." This helps in several ways, one of which is that you don't have to account for missing paychecks when a drought occurs. Also, it gives you a ready evaluation of how well you are doing. It's easy to remember winners,

12,762-1, he collects!

NEW ORLEANS (AP)—There was just the simple announcement over the public address system at the New Orleans Fair Grounds that a $2 bet had just paid off $25,527.

They had to announce it over the loudspeaker because they can't fit a sum like $25,257 into the flashing lights on the tote board.

The collective gasp from the crowd of 7,000 was a mixture of astonishment, delight and envy.

"I WAS SO shocked all I could think about was getting home," said Calvin McManus, a 21-year-old Navy veteran of Viet Nam who now works as a bus boy in a New Orleans restaurant. He held the winning ticket yesterday.

McManus, wearing a floppy hat left over from his Navy days, arrived at the horse race track "with only $10 to bet and that $2 on the exacta was my first bet of the day."

The first exacta was the fourth race. To win an exacta, the bettor must pick the winner and the second place finisher.

McMANUS WAS the only one at the track who managed to turn that trick in the fourth race. For one thing, Mae W. S., the horse he picked to win, was such a long shot she paid $281.60.

The horse he chose for second, Driprint, hadn't inspired much confidence either, paying $17.40 to place.

The winning combination was 11 and 1.

The exacta payoff was a record for horse tracks in North America. The previous high was $9,224 last Nov. 14 at Lincoln Downs.

forget losers and feel you're running "about even, maybe a little ahead." If all the people who describe their track performance that way really did that well there would be nothing but minus pools at race tracks. Keep an *accurate* evaluation of how well you do and go back over your losers during the winter when the tracks are closed. Maybe you'll even find some patterns emerging that will help next season's performance.

Fourth, bet a constant amount on each race. If it is a percent of bankroll, you will find your bets increasing as your bankroll increases. In our case we start a season with $2,000 and begin betting at the $100 level. When the bankroll hits $2,500 we bet $125; when we hit $3,000 we bet $150, and on up the ladder in $500 jumps.

Perhaps at this point we should mention a "safety valve" approach that beginning handicappers might use. Because we know our performance and have kept voluminous records over the years, we never decrease our bets when losses occur. We are confident that we will not hit 20 straight losses and therefore can sustain any losing streak at 5 percent bets*. A more conservative player may decide to decrease his bets when he loses and increase when he wins, thereby extending his bankroll even further. For example, if we were to start with $2,000 and lose $100 on two races we would now have a bankroll of $1,800 and a 5 percent bet would be $90. If we lost two more, our bank would now be $1,620 so our new bet level would now be $80. While this is a perfectly acceptable and highly recommended method of Money Management, we don't like to be quite that pessimistic. Besides, if you have correctly anticipated your bankroll and bet level, you won't need this additional margin of safety. But by all means, if you're not sure, estimate on the conservative side.

While we're on the topic of Money Management, let's keep in mind that each person who goes to the track is a unique individual. He has certain interests in common with all of the patrons, but he also has individual traits, wants and needs. These individual peculiarities are the things that make one person a longshot fancier, another person a chalk player; one person a rigid system follower, another person an individual handicapper. These psychological components of a person's make-up should not be thwarted. The rule here is simple: find the type of action that you feel most comfortable with. If you're a night person, don't get up early in the morning to do your handicapping; try to do most of it the night before. If you really like longshots, try to keep off the impossible ones, but find a method of play that picks up some longshots. If long losing streaks make you nervous, try betting on solid favorites. There is a method of

*Ed. Note: Quite differerent from the Money Management system outlined in *11 Ways to Win At All Games,* page 23.

EXACTA-LY BIG

One of the hottest developments in turf betting is the Exacta, a bet on two horses to finish first and second in a specified race. Both attendance and pari-mutuel handle have gone up wherever and whenever the Exacta has been added to the betting routine.

The long odds that have made the Daily Double so popular have created instant interest in Exacta bets. Any wager that may pay off as much as $8,000 on a $5 ticket is bound to get a big play, even when the odds against the bettor are astronomical.

Some bettors pick the favorite to win and a long-shot to place—not that they think the long-shot will come in but because the payoff will be juicy if it does. Others link a pair of long-shots in combination. Serious handicappers sometimes buy an Exacta ticket on their No. 1 and No. 2 selections in the hope that the return will be higher than it would be on individual bets—which it usually is.

A California track executive says, "The public loves that 1,000 to 1 payoff, even when it happens to somebody else. If you were to guarantee bettors a $6.00 return on a $5.00 ticket—a sure thing—you wouldn't get anywhere near the action you get by offering an almost impossible bet with a 100 to 1 payoff."

spot play that can be comfortable for everyone. But do try to restrain yourself from betting every race. Some are just too unpredictable. If you still need a lot of action, maybe you can develop two separate bankrolls. One can be reserved for your "flyers," where you bet a constant proportion but at a much lower level, and another can be your main fund, for use where you expect to make your profit. No two people are exactly alike, and what works for one may not work for another.

The same principle applies to the great sucker bets such as Quinellas, Exactas, Perfectas, Big Q, Big P and the queen of them all, "Sweet Dee Dee"—the Daily Double. If you keep one fact in mind, you'll hate them as much as we do: every penny that goes into any of these special pools is money that has no chance of going into the regular win, place or show pools. It reduces the action of the main pools and allows the odds to be more easily distorted. The only consolation that you as an intelligent horseplayer have is that the money in those pools is dumb money, anyway, and would probably have gone into the show pool where we wouldn't get a shot at it.

However, much as we may dislike these "blind odds" bets, they are here to stay and getting more popular year by year. (This should tell us something about the nature of our competition.) Since we should at least make some attempt to cope with them, let's take them one at a time.

The Daily Double is usually run on the first and second races of the day. Normally the cheapest hides at the track compete in these early events, some of whom can barely make it to the track. Usually either the first or second race is a Maiden event where none of the beasts has ever been able to win anything. In addition, since cheap animals are more plentiful than expensive ones, both fields normally look like a cavalry charge with 12 milkwagon rejects trying to stay one length ahead of the dogfood company. Not only do the rules state that you have to pick not one, but both of the winners of these maypole dances, but you are not even allowed to know what the odds are on either of the horses nor on the pair. This is somewhat like a poker player having to call or raise a hand without being allowed to know how much is in the pot. If this kind of event sounds attractive to you, you shouldn't be reading this book; you should be out playing the slot machines and Keno.

Remember that it is quite rare for a Daily Double to pay significantly more than a Parlay on the same two horses would have paid, and in a Parlay you may only lose one half of the bet and still win the other half. If you have to play the first two races, (and most of the time at least one is unplayable) play them as a Parlay, not as a Daily Double.

Quinellas are somewhat different and sometimes make sense. More frequently, they don't. If you have determined through your handicapping that only two horses stand a chance of winning and you can't separate them, in most instances it is safer to "Dutch" these two horses than to bet them as a Quinella. Keep in mind that by "Dutching" both horses to win, you are only betting that one of them will win and even if the other one throws his rider, refuses to run or breaks down, you still have the win. On the other hand the Quinella makes you dependent on the performance of both animals and if one gets blocked and runs third your whole bet is lost. Also if it is really a two-horse race, other people will have noticed it, and Quinella prices have a distressing habit of being quite low when two favorites finish one-two.

Since Perfecta and Exacta ask an additional risk on your part, that is predicting the precise *order* of finish for the first and second horse, the payoffs are usually greater, but not enough to offset the additional risk. Keep in mind that a bet is only a good bet when the payoff is commensurate with the risk. When the risk is too high or the payoff too low, it's a good time to pass the race.

The Big Q and Big P add one other backbreaker to your task. They ask you to pick *both* the winner and the place horse in *two* consecutive races and the Big P further requires the precise order of finish. Having found no challenge in the Daily Double or simple Perfecta, they now display true genius by asking you to combine these two tasks. No wonder payoffs sometimes exceed $25,000.

The net effect of all these sucker bets is to drive the good handicapper to despair while bringing Cousin Emma and Uncle Bob to the track for their once a year outing. This increases attendance and handle, and that's what the tracks need to survive.

Just as a closing note on these "boob bets," let's mention the 5-10 at Caliente. In Tijuana, they have another method of getting a paycheck away from the sailors of San Diego. Try picking the winners in six consecutive races (5 thru 10)! The payoffs here have exceeded $200,000 and attract a lot of border traffic for Mexican tourism. As a bettor, we need not even comment on the 5-10.

Yonkers Raceway, a half-mile night harness racing track, has a crowd capacity of 42,000 plus parking for 9,400 cars. It was here in 1962 that the first $3 million one-night "handle" in trotting history was recorded—35,677 persons bet $3,191,020.

Photo courtesy Sportsman's Park, Cicero, Ill.

IN HARNESS

Once only a break in the tedium of the county fair, harness racing now is an exciting spectacle witnessed by some 30 million paying fans last year. Americans have made this the fastest growing spectator sport in the U.S. The attractions are great: year-round, air-conditioned in summer, heated-in-winter, spectator facilities; night-time programs; synthetic all-weather race course surfaces; speed; noise; pari-mutuel betting; and last but not least, horses—Standardbreds that are fast, colorful and fun to watch.

Standardbred racing, in general, differs from flat or thoroughbred racing in just two basic areas. A Standardbred pulls or hauls a sulky and driver instead of carrying a jockey, and the Standardbred may not run, canter or gallup, but must pace or trot. The differences become instantly apparent to any flat railbird who makes his first trip to a harness raceway. Other differences, not quite so conspicuous, will be covered later.

Like the thoroughbred, the Standardbred traces his lineage back to the seeds of the *Byerly Turk, Darby Arabian* and *Godolphin Barb*. Early forebears of the modern Standardbred were crossed with horses and mares that not only worked well in harness, but had a desirable gait. Back in those days when the Standardbred was developing, the harness horse and buggy was a prime mode of transportation. One doesn't have to reach too far into his imagination to picture the country doctor coming upon a farmer heading for town and with a casual nod of agreement to the crack of whips, racing down to the big oak at the ford in the stream. Soon those horses that were fastest were sought out to cover mares that showed similar traits. These and their offspring competed at fairs, with barnstorming itinerant "pros," and finally the sport began to grow.

This period of growth was a period of evolution for the breed. Blood from outside the thoroughbred ranks produced a gentler horse, a stronger, more durable horse, and, may every handicapper get down on his knees and thank the patron Saint of horseplayers, a more predictable horse.

Blood pedigree is the absolute, prime consideration

to the horseman who is seeking to enlarge his stable. He won't even look at a horse whose pedigree he hasn't studied. Then he seeks out the horse that has the best general conformation, stance, and joints—joints that can take the tremendous stresses required of a winning pacer or trotter.

Blood tells! Consider *Adios,* the greatest sire of all time. Bred at the late Leo C. McNamara's Two Gaits Farm in what is now Carmel, Indiana, sired by *Hal Dale* out of E. J. Baker's (St. Charles, Ill.), *Adios Volo,* foaled in 1940, sold as a yearling for $2,100 to Tommy Thomas of Cleveland, Ohio; this great horse, during his 25-year life, sired animals that have earned their owners more than $19,000,000.00. The next closest sire is *Bull Lea,* thoroughbred.

Adios, a pacer, was sold in turn to Del Miller for $35,000. At the age of 18, T. B. Shepherd bought him for $500,000. He syndicated out two-thirds of *Adios* a year later for $333,333, Del Miller buying back one-half of the syndication.

Adios was a pacer; so how does he differ from a trotter? A pacer's right foreleg and right hindleg move in tandem, (the same with the left side). Most pacers wear hopples, leather harness straps that connect these legs, restricting any other movement. A trotter is exactly the opposite, right foreleg moving with left hindleg, left foreleg with right hindleg, without leg harness. To the spectator a pacer has a delightful side to side rolling gait, the trotter, a jouncy, bouncy gait.

"For the improvement of the breed" is not a phrase to be scoffed at among Standardbred horsemen. Major races, true classics, are held every year and are well attended in spite of the fact that no betting, pari-mutuel or otherwise, is permitted. The Hambletonian at DuQuoin, Ill. and The Fox Stake at Indianapolis are just two examples of where betless fans cheer their favorites on with the same hullabaloo they would if their wallets depended on the result. The Standardbred horseman can point proudly, and rightly so, to events like these.

If breeding were the only requirement for selecting the winning horse in a race, all the handicapper would need to insure trips to the cashier's window would be the stud book. Yet, one of the old but true maxims of harness racing is: a good horse with a poor driver will lose to a fair or average horse with a good driver.

How do you handicap the horse and the driver? First, as in our winning thoroughbred system, a knowledge of handicapping is a must. Purchase and study the *Daily Racing Form* or the *Morning Telegraph* and the program at the raceway. Driver performances are reported in most programs; if not, good supplementary sheets like the *Illinois Sports News* can provide this data. But before we can handicap a race, we must take the track into consideration.

Most harness races are one mile, but most race courses aren't mile tracks. Therefore shorter, half-mile, five-eighths-mile, eleven-sixteenths-mile, three-quarter-mile and thirteen-sixteenths-mile tracks cause the handicapper to adjust his figuring to accommodate the length of the track. On shorter tracks more turns are made; there are no long stretches. Post, and later rail position, are critical, due to the turns. A horse that must stay *parked out* on just one turn is traveling many feet farther than a horse on the rail, and when one considers that many races are won by inches, those extra feet on the turns could make the difference between winning and losing. Shorter tracks with tighter turns are also harder on the horses. Flying hooves and sliding sulkies cause injury, confusion and sometimes panic.

More turns with shorter stretches also slow winning times. So a horse that has done respectable miles on the mile tracks will not necessarily do well on a five-eighths-mile course. His time is always slower on the short track.

Mile tracks have always been the favorite of the horsemen, but not so with track managements. The operators feel the short track is more exciting for the spectator. The horses start right in front of the grandstand, come around and then race away again for another circuit to finish in front of the grandstand. The spectators love those four tough turns. And what the spectator loves, track management adores. So if you are used to mile tracks and you are making your first visit to a ½-mile oval, don't tear up your tickets when the horses come around the first time with your selection well back. Cheer him on. They have to go around one more time!

Some of the leading harness tracks are:

One Mile—Du Quoin State Fair, Du Quoin, Ill.
Hawthorne, Cicero, Ill.
Bay Meadows, San Mateo, Cal.
Washington Park, Homewood, Ill.
Latonia Raceway, Florence, Ky.
The Red Mile, Lexington, Ky.
Wolverine Raceway, Livonia, Mich.
Scarborough Downs, Scarborough, Maine

13/16-Mile—Assiniboria Downs, Winnepeg, Man.

3/4-Mile—Cahokia Downs, East St. Louis, Ill.
Vernon Downs, Vernon, N.Y.

11/16-Mile—Raceway Park, Toledo, Ohio

5/8-Mile—Sportsman's Park, Cicero, Ill.
Pompano Park, Pompano Beach, Fla.
Liberty Bell Park, Adelphia, Pa.
Brandywine Raceway, Wilmington, Del.
Scioto Downs, Columbus, Ohio
Laurel Raceway, Laurel, Md.
Blue Bonnets, Montreal, Que.

1/2-Mile—Maywood Park, Maywood, Ill.
Roosevelt Raceway, Westbury, N.Y.
Suffolk Downs, East Boston, Mass.
Yonkers Raceway, Yonkers, N.Y.
Balmoral Park, Crete, Ill.
Audubon Park, Henderson, Ky.
Saratoga Harness, Saratoga Springs, N.Y.

BETTING:

Kinds of Bets

To Win	You collect win money if your horse finishes **first** only.
To Place	You collect place money if your horse finishes **first or second.**
To Show	You collect show money if your horse finishes **first, second, or third.**
Combination	You collect win, place, and show money if your horse finishes first; place and show money if he's second; show money if he's third.
Daily Double	This applies only to the first and second races. You select one horse to win from each race. They **both** must win. The daily double generally offers a handsome payoff.
*Quinella	To win, you must select the first two finishers in a race, regardless of order of finish.
*Big Q	To win, you must select the first two finishers in one race, and exchange these winning tickets for a second winning combination in the next race.

*Quinella and Big Q betting operate only on specially announced races. Consult your program to see if and when these bets are in effect.

HOW TO READ THE TOTE BOARD:

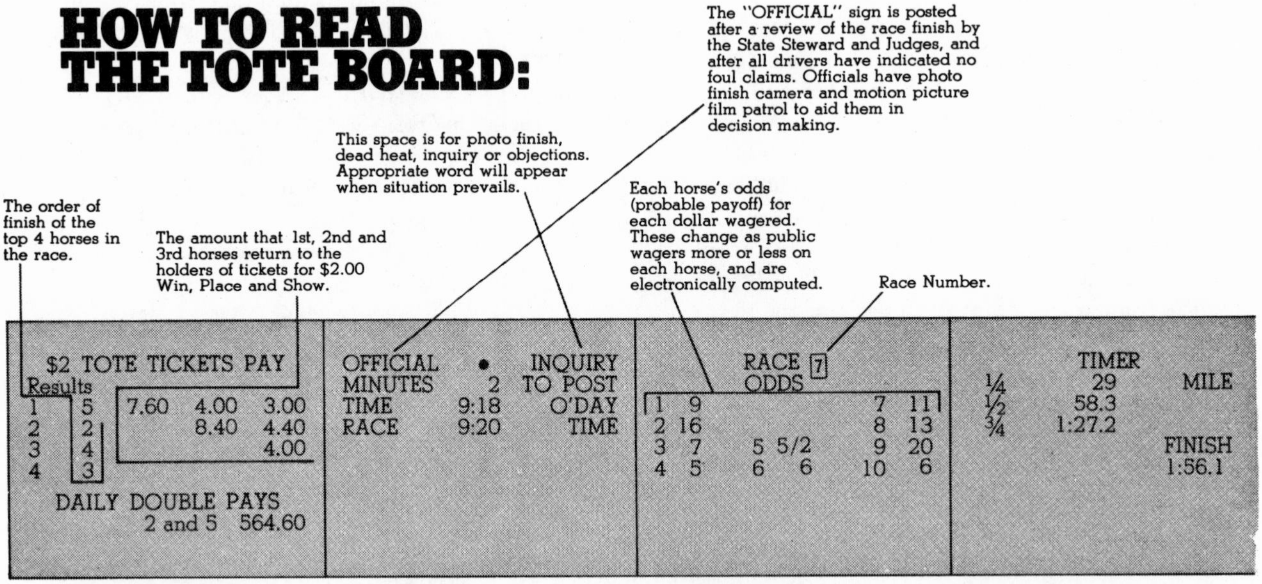

The "OFFICIAL" sign is posted after a review of the race finish by the State Steward and Judges, and after all drivers have indicated no foul claims. Officials have photo finish camera and motion picture film patrol to aid them in decision making.

This space is for photo finish, dead heat, inquiry or objections. Appropriate word will appear when situation prevails.

The order of finish of the top 4 horses in the race.

The amount that 1st, 2nd and 3rd horses return to the holders of tickets for $2.00 Win, Place and Show.

Each horse's odds (probable payoff) for each dollar wagered. These change as public wagers more or less on each horse, and are electronically computed.

Race Number.

$2 TOTE TICKETS PAY

Results				
1	5	7.60	4.00	3.00
2	2		8.40	4.40
3	4			4.00
4	3			

DAILY DOUBLE PAYS
2 and 5 564.60

OFFICIAL • INQUIRY

MINUTES	2	TO POST
TIME	9:18	O'DAY
RACE	9:20	TIME

RACE 7
ODDS

1	9			7	11
2	16			8	13
3	7	5	5/2	9	20
4	5	6	6	10	6

TIMER

1/4	29	MILE
1/2	58.3	
3/4	1:27.2	
		FINISH
		1:56.1

HOW THE TOTE WORKS:

Parimutuel wagering is a system in which the public makes the odds by the amounts it bets, and the track merely serves as a stakeholder. The bettor never bets against the track—only against other bettors, and in fact the term parimutuel means "to wager among ourselves." The system is not as complicated as it appears at first sight.

After a small amount is deducted as the state and track share (16 per cent), the remainder is redistributed to the public.

Up-to-date totalisator systems provide the bettor with foolproof computations of correct odds and payoffs. The totalisator—often referred to as the tote—actually functions as a huge cash register which automatically registers and displays odds and payoffs.

The bettor purchases a ticket from a seller, who punches out tickets on electronically controlled keys. Each key is connected to the control or tote room, and bets are totalled automatically to provide frequent flashes of odds to bettors. Before the horses leave the starting gate, keyboards are automatically locked to prevent anyone betting after the race is started.

Here is the way the above win pool would be calculated:

Horse No. 5 won the race. From the $100,000 the calculator deducts 16% in track and state commissions, as required by law. The net pool of $84,000 is then split into two parts—the amount

PLACING YOUR BET:

1. Go to the proper window for purchasing tickets. For example: If you want to bet $10 on a horse to win, go to the $10 win seller rather than buying 5 tickets at the $2 win window.

2. Please try to have the exact amount of money for your wager.

3. Ask for your ticket by first saying the program number of your selection, and then the number of tickets you want. For example: "number 7, once, or number 6, four times."

4. Examine your tickets carefully before leaving the window. No tickets can be exchanged after the sale is completed.

5. When you win, pick up your money as soon as possible at a cashier's window of the same face value as your ticket.

APPROXIMATE PAYOFF FOR A $2.00 WIN TICKET

1-9	$ 2.20	8-5	$ 5.20
1-5	$ 2.40	9-5	$ 5.60
2-5	$ 2.80	2-1	$ 6.00
3-5	$ 3.20	5-2	$ 7.00
4-5	$ 3.60	3-1	$ 8.00
1-1	$ 4.00	7-2	$ 9.00
6-5	$ 4.40	4-1	$10.00
7-5	$ 4.80	9-2	$11.00
3-2	$ 5.00	5-1	$12.00

Total amount wagered to PLACE. Holders of Place Tickets on 1st and 2nd horses each receive share of Place Pool. Numbers show dollars wagered on individual horses to place.

Total amount wagered to SHOW. Holders of Show Tickets on 1st, 2nd and 3rd horses each receive share of Show Pool. Numbers show dollars wagered on individual horses to show.

Total amount wagered to WIN. Numbers show dollars wagered, on individual horses, to win.

Message board

Condition of track—as set by the State Steward and Judges.

SPORTSMAN'S PARK
THE IN-TOWN TRACK
HOME OF THE AMERICAN NATIONALS

WIN POOL 100,000

1	8000			7	7000
2	5000			8	6000
3	10000	5	22000	9	4000
4	14000	6	12000	10	12000

PLACE POOL 50,000

1	3000			7	3000
2	4000			8	2000
3	4000	5	12000	9	2000
4	5000	6	10000	10	5000

SHOW POOL 25,000

1	2000			7	1000
2	2500			8	800
3	2500	5	6000	9	1200
4	3000	6	4000	10	2000

TRACK FAST:

wagered on the winner, $22,000 and what is left, $62,000 The odds are then determined by dividing the $62,000 by the $22,000

If, in making this division, the resulting figures come out with odd cents over a dime, the odd cents are known as "breakage." Illinois law specifies that payoffs be made to the dime, and the breakage or odd pennies over the dime are divided for the convenience of handling between the track and the state.

In our example, when $62,000 is divided by $22,000 it comes out to $2.81 for each dollar bet. The one cent (breakage) is disregarded and the odds are $2.80 to $1.00.

Doubled for a $2 ticket, this becomes $5.60 plus the $2.00 wagered which is also returned to the winning bettor, so the payoff would be 5 to 2 or $7.60 for each $2 bet on number 5 to win.

The place price is determined by subtracting the amount bet on the win and place horses from the net pool. The remainder is divided in half and allotted to each horse. From this point, prices are computed as the win pool. The show pool is computed in the same way as place, except that the money available is divided equally on the first three horses.

WHAT IS THE MORNING LINE?

The morning line is the opinion of an experienced handicapper and oddsmaker as to the possible estimated payoff on each entry, should it win. This is in the program, and is the first set of odds posted on the tote-board before a race.

Courtesy Sportsman's Park, Cicero, Ill.

With the tighter quarters and rougher racing conditions of the short tracks, driver skill and luck are more important than ever. Since good drivers, like good crapshooters, tend to be luckier than poor ones, make the driver's past performance an important part of your handicapping, with points being added on the short track. Couple a good driver with a good horse and a good post position. Some winning post positions exceed others by more than 300 percent. Get the right combination and you have a bet that will be hard to beat.

In the very next race, there may be several good drivers guiding as many good horses from some pretty good post positions, plus some average to fair drivers with some pretty fair horses. A bad post position doesn't mean that the horse can't win, so what have you got? You've got a harness race! And you've got a real handicapping job on your hands.

Handicapping

At the risk of being repetitive, the *Daily Racing Form* or *Morning Telegraph* and a track program are absolute musts. Past Performance charts of thoroughbreds and Standardbreds are basically similar in appearance, yet have important differences.

Where's that mention of breeding in the past performances? Simple. It isn't there—just the immediate parentage noted above the owner's name. Breeding has been discussed and argued as long as there have been horsemen. Breeding and bloodlines will tell, no argument, but it will not tell enough for one particular race, one particular day, at one particular track. There are thousands of well bred horses racing against each other every day, so unless it's a dead heat, all horses but one will lose every race. What you want to do is pick that *one* that has the best chance of winning that next race you are about to bet. The only way this predicting of the future can be done is through careful analysis of what has been done in the past. As in our winning system for thoroughbreds, there's no reason to expect a Standardbred to do something he has never been able to do before. This does not mean he won't, they do, and they will. It means that no handicapper can forecast it with any hope of making it an even irregular habit. When faced with having to pick a horse from a bunch of horses that have never won before, just skip this maiden and take a little extra time figuring the next bettable race. It's tough enough picking the fastest animals without trying to select the least slow critter from eight or nine other slow ones.

Since harness races are jockeyless, a driver's weight has little effect on his horse's speed on dry track. So without jockeys, two types of races do not appear on Standardbred programs, the Handicap and the Allowance. Other races are similarly-conditioned; Maiden, non-winners of $5,000, etc., 2 year olds, three year olds, etc.; Claiming Races (allowances may be granted here but only on claiming price); Stake Races.

Free for Alls and Invitationals are races that are

Photos courtesy Sportsman's Park, Cicero, Ill.

With the tighter quarters and rougher racing conditions of the shorter tracks, driver skill and luck are more important than ever.

EXPLANATION OF DAILY RACING FORM'S PAST PERFORMANCES
(For Harness Racing)

ORDER OF FINISH

Date of last race
Number of race
Track raced on
Distance of race
Leader's time at ¼
Leader's time at ½
Leader's time at ¾
Time of winner
Condition of track
Cl'ng odds *Den'tes favorite
Position at quarter
Position at half
Position at three quarter
Lengths behind leader
Position in stretch
Lengths behind leader
Official finish position
Lengths behind winner
Driver
...st position
Class of race
Horse's actual time
Winner
Second

Feb22-70^{6}Spk⅝ 1 :31^{3}1:03^{2}1:37^{3}2:07^{2}ft 5½ 1^{0} 1x 2½ 2^{1}½ 2^{1}½ BusseD^{1} c5000 2:07⅘ MissGaiety D'?byRaid

The following explanation tells how to read a past performance line in Sportsman's Park past performances. The line begins with the month, date and year. The superior figure which follows indicates the race number in which the horse last competed with the track Spk⅝ (abbreviation for Sportsman's Park) and distance of race. All tracks listed are ½ mile, except where superior figure after track abbreviation indicates different distance. Fractional times of the race list the time of the leader at the ¼, ½ and ¾ and then the time the winner was clocked. Past performances of race: at 6 furlongs or less show fractional time at the quarter and half-mile in addition to final time. Races longer than customary mile distance show fractional time at the quarter half-mile and mile in addition to final time. Condition of the track and the closing odds then follow. The actual chart of the horse is next posted. The calls are at the ¼, ½, ¾, head of stretch and official finish position. Lengths behind the leader are listed at the ¾ pole, stretch and finish. Following the chart calls comes the driver with the superior figure indicating post position of the horse. Next is the class of race which is fully defined in the section Classification System used at Sportsman's Park. Following this is the horse's actual individual time. Next are the names of the horses placed first and second by the judges.

Abbreviations for track conditions are: ft—fast, gd—good, sy—sloppy, sl—slow, m—muddy, hy—heavy. Explanation of symbols: *—favorite, x—broke, ix—interference break, ex—equipment break, e—entry, f—field, †—indicates footnote. ^{0}—indicates horse "parked out" for more than ¼ mile. c—horse was claimed out of that race for amount specified, im—impeded.

‡ Before horse's name indicates horse races without hopples. ⊗ After horse's name indicates horse won on other than a fast or good track.

Above each horse's name in the past performances is his Best Winning Time at one mile and the track, month and year mark was set. No record indicates that the horse did not win at this distance during 1970 or 1971. Enclosed in parentheses immediately to the right of the horse's best time are his lifetime earnings through the 1970 season. A horse's best win time may be earned in either a purse or non-purse race; however, it may not be earned in a time trial or in a qualifying race without post race testing.

Qualifying races are not competitive and will not be included in the starts of a horse for 1970 or 1971, but are merely used to determine the manner of a horse and its ability to complete the course within the time standards set by the judges for the class in which the horse will compete.

made up of the very best horses racing for top purses. There are no weights to be considered, and since most sulky races are for the mile, distance is of minor importance.

It is now time to list the basic rules of handicapping Standardbreds.

Hussey Standardbred System

1. **This Track Rule**
2. **Time (Speed) Rule**
3. **Seven Week Rule (Condition)**
4. **Pace Rule**
5. **Driver Rule**
6. **Post Position Rule**
7. **Consistency Rule**
8. **No Break Rule**
9. **Class Rule**
10. **No Win Rule**

1. This Track Rule—As cited earlier, there is a vast difference in track lengths. Today's horses must have had at least three races at today's track.

2. Time (Speed) Rule—Today's horses must show good competitive speed. Remember to check competition's speed versus track size. Not finishing more than 3/5 of a second, three lengths behind the winner in its last or next to last race is important.

3. Seven Week Rule—We have extended the thoroughbred one-month rule to seven weeks for Standardbreds because this breed stays in form longer. Refer to One Month Rule for detailed discussion.

4. Pace Rule—Today's horses must show the ability to overcome an early fast pace or finish in the fastest time while setting the early fast pace. The former can be deceiving due to the fact the horses in a harness race may enjoy a drafting effect, similar to that seen in automobile racing, when leading horses are bunched directly in front of the horse in consideration. If the past performances show something like 5¾, 4^{1}, 4½, the animal may be enjoying an easy time of lower wind resistance, and not really keeping or moving up to pace.

5. Driver Rule—A good horse with a poor driver will lose to a fair or average horse with a good driver. This is especially true on the shorter raceways. Heavy traffic on four turns requires skillful maneuvering and split second timing if an opportunity presents itself. The local race program gives past driver performances, including percentages. Check the percentages.

KEY TO SYMBOLS, ABBREVIATIONS IN PAST PERFORMANCES

FOREIGN BRED HORSES

•Preceding the name of the horse indicates foreign-bred. (No notation is made for horses bred in Canada, Cuba or Mexico.)

TODAY'S CLAIMING PRICES

Claiming prices for horses entered today appear to right of trainer's name, directly over "type of race" listing in past performances.

MUD MARKS

*—Fair mud runner X—Good mud runner
⊗—Superior mud runner

COLOR

B.—Bay Blk.—Black Br.—Brown Ch.—Chestnut
Gr.—Gray Ro.—Roan Wh.—White
Dk. b. or br.—Dark bay or brown
(Lt. before color denotes Light)

SEX

c—colt h—horse g—gelding rig—ridgling
f—filly m—mare

PEDIGREE

Each horse's pedigree lists, in the order named, color, sex, year foaled, sire, dam and grandsire (sire of dam).

BREEDER

Abbreviations, if any, following breeder's name indicates the state, place of origin or foreign country in which the horse was foaled.

RECORD OF STARTS AND EARNINGS

The horse's racing record for his most recent two years of competition appears to the extreme right of the name of the breeder. This lists the year, number of starts, wins, seconds, thirds and earnings. The letter "M" in the win column of the upper line indicates the horse is a maiden. If the letter "M" is in the lower line only, it indicates the horse was a maiden at the end of that year.

DISTANCE

a—preceding distance (a6f) denotes "about" distance (about 6 furlongs in this instance).

TURF COURSES

Ⓣ—before distance indicates turf (grass) course race.
[T]—before distance indicates inner turf course (races run beginning March 1, 1970).

TRACK CONDITIONS

ft—fast fr—frozen gd—Good sy—sloppy
sl—slow m—muddy hy—heavy

Turf course races, including steeplechase and hurdles:
hd—hard fm—firm gd—good yl—yielding sf—soft
Note: tt in place of track condition, indicates the Tartan Track in use at Tropical Park. The condition of this synthetic strip is fast at all times.

CLOSING ODDS

2 •favorite 2e—entry 15f—mutuel field

APPRENTICE OR RIDER WEIGHT ALLOWANCES

§-3 lbs. •-5 lbs. ‡-7 lbs. ‡-8 lbs. ∴-10 lbs. ‡‡-11 lbs.

ABBREVIATIONS USED IN POINTS OF CALL

no—nose h—head nk—neck

POST POSITION

Horse's post position appears after jockey's name—WilsonR4

RACE CLASSIFICATIONS

10000—Claiming race (eligible to be claimed for $10,000). Note: The letter "c" preceding claiming price (c10000) indicates horse was claimed.
M10000—Maiden claiming race (non winners—eligible to be claimed).
10000H—Claiming handicap (eligible to be claimed).
O10000—Optional claiming race (entered NOT to be claimed).
10000O—Optional claiming race (eligible to be claimed).
Mdn—Maiden race (non-winners).
AlwM—Maiden allowance race (for non-winners with special weight allowance for those having started in a claiming race).
Alw—Allowance race.
HcpO—Overnight handicap race.
SplW—Special weight race.
Wfa—Weight-for-age race.
Mtch—Match race.
A10000—Starter allowance race (horses who have started for claiming price shown, or less, as stipulated in the conditions).
H10000—Starter handicap (same restriction as above).
S10000—Starter special weight (restricted as above). Note: Where no amount is specified in the conditions of the "starters" race, dashes are substituted as shown below.
A— H— S—

STEEPLECHASE AND HURDLE RACES

[S—Steeplechase [H—Hurdle race

STAKES RACES

AlwS—Allowance stakes.
HcpS—Handicap stakes.
ScwS—Scale weight stakes.
SpwS—Special weight stakes.
WfaS—Weight-for-age stakes.
50000S—Claiming stakes (eligible to be claimed).

INVITATIONAL RACES

InvH—Invitational handicap.
InvSp—Invitational special weights.

RACES EXCLUSIVELY FOR FILLIES, MARES

Ⓕ—Immediately following the speed rating indicates races for fillies or fillies and mares (effective May 1, 1969).

SPEED RATING

This is a comparison of the horse's time with the track record established prior to the opening of the meeting. The track record is given a rating of 100 and one point is deducted for each one-fifth second slower than the record. When a horse breaks the track record, one point is added to the par 100 for each one-fifth second faster than the record. One-fifth of a second is considered the equivalent of a beaten length.

No ratings are given for hurdle or steeplechase events, for races of less than three furlongs, for races where the horse's speed rating is less than 25.

NOTE: Speed ratings for new distances are computed and assigned when adequate time standards are established. At Caliente, Mexico, which operates throughout the year, rating changes are made whenever a track record is broken.

EACH HORSE'S MOST RECENT WORKOUTS APPEAR DIRECTLY UNDER THE PAST PERFORMANCES

For example, July 30 Bel 3f ft :38b indicates the horse worked on July 30 at Belmont Park. The distance of the trial was three furlongs over a fast track and the horse was timed in 38 seconds, breezing. The following abbreviations are used to describe how each horse worked:

b—breezing d—driving e—easily g—worked from stall gate h—handily o—all out
u—eased up bo—bore out ro—ran out
trt following track abbreviation indicates horse worked on training track tc—turf course
TR—Trial race HC—Hillside course

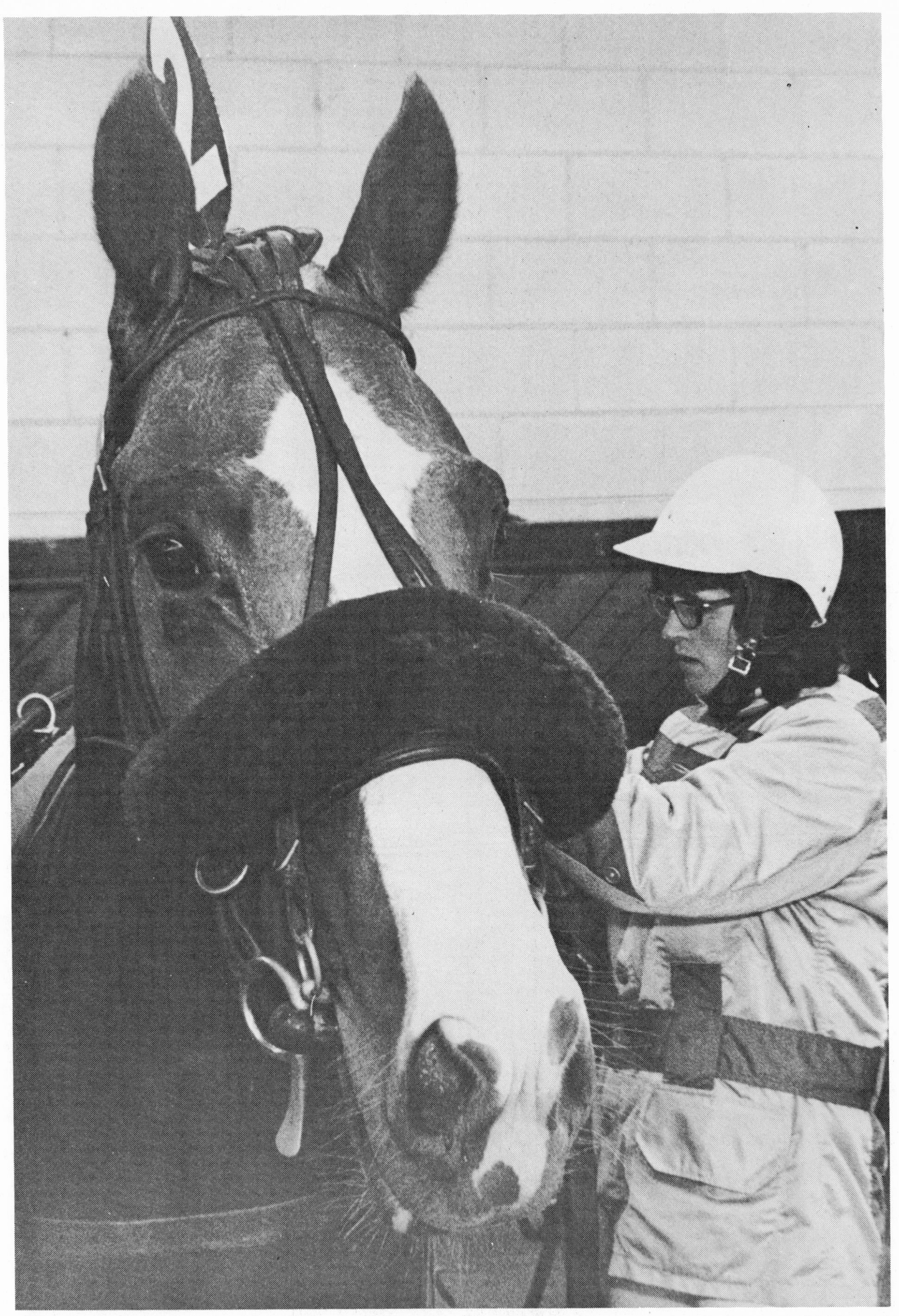

Photo courtesy Sportsman's Park, Cicero, Ill.

Photo courtesy Sportsman's Park, Cicero, Ill.

Harness horses enjoy a drafting effect, similar to that seen in automobile racing, when leading horses reduce wind resistance and create a partial vacuum for horses immediately behind.

6. Post Position Rule—On some non-banked tracks, post position may be the deciding factor between contending selections. This can also affect selections on banked short courses. However, poor post position should never cause the elimination of a horse and driver that are of clearly superior caliber.

7. Consistency Rule—Consistent earnings, consistent efforts within class, indicate a potential winner. A large step down in class, 40-50 percent, may make this the fastest horse in his new-found company. A step up in class requires not just consistency but significant signs of improvement.

8. No Break Rule—Trotters and Pacers must either trot or pace. They cannot run, canter or gallop. This is known as breaking gait. If a horse broke, it is so indicated in his past performances with an X at the position, call, where the break occurred. The driver must take the horse to the outside, causing no interference, and get him back on gait. The horse may not gain ground breaking. The race is not automatically lost, but precious time is, and wins after breaks are rare. A chronic breaker should be quickly eliminated from contenders. Young, green horses tend to break more often than more experienced animals. A break may not be solely the fault of the animal. Trash blowing in front of a horse, a sulky bump, broken tack, another horse breaking or an injury may cause breaking. Because a horse has broken recently does not mean that he should be bumped from contention. If possible, find out what made him break, then proceed with your evaluation.

9. Class Rule—Beware of an over-matched horse unless he is showing good improvement. The trainer may just want him out for the exercise with his betters. See Consistency Rule.

10. No Win Rule—A horse cannot be expected to do what he has never done before. Conversely, winning horses and drivers tend to keep on winning. Eliminate non-winners unless the non-winner is taking a big step down in class, where his previous times qualify him under the Time (Speed) Rule.

It is understood that if while watching warm-ups you notice that your selection seems unsound, your second best contender should be the one on which you place the bet. If there is no clear-cut second best, the race should be passed.

Now that you have read the Hussey Standardbred System Rules, we will show you how they are applied and how they work.

We picked a cloudy Saturday afternoon to spend at Sportsman's Park, in Cicero, Ill. Late March is usually cold around Chicago, but we were pleasantly surprised when the temperature rose to 44 degrees. The date was the 27th and we did not have 2-7 or 7-2 in the double.

We had bought the *Daily Racing Form* at the corner newstand early that morning. This gave us ample time to eliminate most non-contenders before leaving for the track. We arrived about an hour early for the 2:00 pm post time. Cold gray afternoons are delightful at a race track if your surroundings are warm and bright. The Saddle and Sulky Restaurant is both so that's where we headed after purchasing a program at the gate. Our table had a good view of the track,

LEADING DRIVERS AT SPORTSMAN'S PARK

Standings list drivers through Thursday, March 25, 1971

Computed With the Universal Driver Rating System Win 9 Points, Place 5 Points, Show 3 Points

Driver	Wt.	Age	Sts.	1st	2nd	3rd	Avg.
Robert Farrington	155	42	152	21	21	24	.268
Joe Marsh Jr.	125	37	99	20	13	12	.315
Gene Valland'h'm	157	30	87	19	6	11	.299
Harry Burright	180	55	84	17	16	9	.344
Dwayne Pletcher	190	40	60	11	8	5	.285
Johnny Blevins	175	35	65	11	4	3	.219
Ken Vander Sch'f	185	38	31	10	5	3	.444
Ivan Sugg	250	28	30	10	2	6	.437
Philip Milburn	170	35	84	10	16	4	.241
Glen Kidwell	160	49	25	9	3	4	.480
Marc Grenier	195	24	44	8	8	5	.321
Connel Willis	190	37	82	8	8	15	.213
Bruce Nickells	175	42	19	7	3	1	.474
Joseph Vollaro	118	43	27	7	2	1	.313
Raymond Tripp	195	45	16	6	1	3	.465
William Beckley	150	26	24	6	5	3	.407
Ray J. Gillilan	140	30	25	6	2	4	.338
Jessie Willis	175	34	31	6	4	2	.287

Winning Post Positions

1st	2nd	3rd	4th	5th	6th	7th	8th	9th	10 & Over	Total
47	38	33	38	53	39	35	23	16	1	323*

*Includes three dead heats for win.

Winning favorites: 32 per cent.
Favorites in the money: 67 per cent.

so we settled down to check if any of our selections had been scratched. Happily, none had been. The track was good. Next step—take a look at the leading drivers' chart in the program.

It comes as no surprise to Midwesterners like us that Bob Farrington is heading the list. Joe Marsh, Jr. is right up there, too. Vallandingham, Burright, Pletcher, Blevins and Vander Schaaf are all good men. In fact, all except Milburn, Connel Willis and Farrington are winning good percentages of their races. And these three are redeemed by their strong place and show records. So we are faced with the prospect of choosing from the best of the leading top drivers, plus from the other gentlemen each individual race will throw at us.

Winning Post Positions appear directly below the driver list.

We note that the inside rail position has almost three times as many winners as the outside spot and that PP5 is even better. Sportsman's Park is a ⅝-mile track, so post position does not have an effect.

Our drinks and sandwiches arrive. We quickly review our decision to pass up the first race. We feel that none of the horses are showing enough speed. The fastest horse, *Miss Dillon's Son,* has the lowest-rated driver. Nor are the horses that have dropped in class—*Keeper's Kid, Diane D. Adios* and *Lady Softie*—showing much promise. *Keeper's Kid* is the opening favorite, but his 2:10 2/5 win eight days previous wasn't impressive. The other favorite, *Shadydale Yankee,* has been the beaten favorite on his last three outings.

Right before post-time we agree that we'd hold onto our money, but if we were longshot players *Diane D. Adios* would get the nod, because of the post position, the 22-1 odds and drop in class.

Diane D. Adios did win and paid $47.80, $18.20 and $7.60. Number 4 horse *Mr. Debonair* placed, paying $9.20 and $4.80. *Keeper's Kid* paid $2.80 to show.

The second race is a one-mile pace for 8-year-olds and up. A $4,000 claimer with *Lang's Filly* and *Carlen Dirty Bird* in for $4,800. It's the second half of the Daily Double.

We tend to agree with the Trackman's selection of *Amosson's P.J.* Although we are violating the No Win Rule, this horse has by far the best speed. He has also shown this speed against more expensive horses. He looks to be in good condition and seems to be coming into form. *Pipe Of Peace* is also a contender with a win two weeks ago. Post Positions 3 and 8 may make a difference. *Amosson's P.J.'s* speed should tell. We consider a Dutch on the pair since our $20 budget for the first race wasn't used but decide to save the twenty in case we need it later. The crowd starts to get on the *Pipe Of Peace* odds. The odds on *Amosson's P.J.* move up to 4-1, then 5-1. Just as we leave the seller's window with two $10 tickets, the odds move again to 6-1.

Amosson's P.J. wins in 2:08 3/5, paying $14.40, $7.20 and $4.00, with *Lang's Filly* paying $6.00 and $3.40 to place and *Pipe Of Peace* paying $3.20 to show.

One race, one bet and a payoff of $144. Not a bad start. Now we can spare that extra twenty from the first race and maybe try a likely Dutch. Lucky holders of the 5-8 Daily Double tickets earned $392.80 for each $2 invested.

The third race was also a one mile pace. Three-year-olds and up, claiming price $5,000, except *Lydia's Girl,* in for $6,000.

We disagreed with the Trackman on this one, feel-

Love Walked Out

Toots Shor tells about a friend of his who gave up gambling at the insistence of the girl of his dreams. But after he reformed, he didn't marry her. He told Toots why. "Any dame who'll gamble on keepin' a guy like me away from the horses and the crap tables permanently ain't too bright."

ONE MILE PACE — 1st RACE (afternoon program) — Purse $2,600

(FIRST HALF OF DAILY DOUBLE)

Claiming. Claiming price $3,500. 3-year-olds and up.
Keeper's Kid, Diane D. Adios, Lady Softie in for $4,200; rest for $3,500.

PLEASE ASK FOR HORSE BY PROGRAM NUMBER

1 (8-1)
2:10 (Aur, '70) ($2,327) — Driver—JAMES PERRIN. Trainer, D. Perrin (54-5-7-5—.195) — Maroon-Gold-Blue
Stormy Bob — Gr. g (1962), by Phil Bob—Stormy Envy, by Schuey Hanover. 1971 10 0 2 1 $1,428
Owner, Leland F. Janke, Oxford, Wis. 1970 19 2 2 6 $2,327

```
Mar19-71 1Spk⅝  1 :31 2 1:05 3 1:38 2 2:10 2 gd 6½ 3 3 4 3 7 6½ 8 7 PerrinJ1 3500 2:11⅘ Keeper'sKid CherylF'd'r Sn'kyJohn
Mar11-71 1Spk⅝  1 :32 1:05 1:38 2:09 3 gd 26 2 3 3 3 2 2 2¾ PerrinJ3 3500 2:09⅘ Wildw'dAnn St'rmyBob Sn'kyJohn
Mar 3-71 10Spk⅝ 1 :30 2 1:04 2 1:37 2:08 4 ft 8¼ 4 4 5 5 6 4½ 7 7½ PerrinJ1 3500 2:10⅖ Elberta'sBoy PatriciaDale RushOn
Feb25-71 10Spk⅝ 1 :30 4 1:03 2 1:35 2 2:07 2 ft 21 x4 4 7 20 6 20 6 21 PerrinJ5 3500 2:11⅗ Dr. Farr Pat's Dee Air Venture
Feb16-71 10Aur  1 :32 3 1:10 2 1:45 2:19 1 sy 3¾ 2 2 0 2½ 4 2 4 5¾ PerrinJ1 2500 2:20⅖ Ka'sCityK'y Cardam'n Gr'gTheGr't
Feb 6-71 2Aur   1 :32 1 1:05 1 1:37 4 2:10 4 ft 3 2 2 3 1½ 4 2 5 5½ PerrinJ1 2500 2:12 T'rpid'sG'ld Fr'kyL'ss Elb'rta'sB'y
```

2 (3-1)
2:07⅘ (Spk⅝, '70) ($8.055) — Driver—KEN VANDER SCHAAF. Trainer, L. Fox (31-10-5-3—.444) — Gold-Black
Keeper's Kid ⊗ — B. g (1967), by Keeper's Gay Boy—Direct Choile, by Jasper Hanover. 1971 11 1 1 1 $2,553
Owner, Leroy Fox, Sandwich, Ill. 1970 26 1 4 2 $5.795

```
Mar19-71 1Spk⅝  1 :31 2 1:05 3 1:38 2 2:10 2 gd 2½ ▲1 2 1 1¼ 1 3 1 3 VanderSchaafK5 4200 2:10⅖ Keeper'sKid CherylF'd'r Sn'kyJohn
Mar10-71 1Spk⅝  1 :31 1 1:04 1:35 2 2:08 4 ft 3 x9 9 8 13 7 7 6 7 FoxL3 4200 2:10⅕ ShiawayG'se Tantaliz'r BuzzEagle
Mar 5-71 1Spk⅝  1 :30 3 1:01 4 1:34 3 2:07 ft 4¾ 4 4 5 5 6 5½ 3 2 VanderSchaafK4 4200 2:07⅖ Reed'sMichael YukonEric K'p'sKid
Feb27-71 1Spk⅝  1 :31 2 1:05 2 1:37 2:10 1 ft 8½ 3 4 4 2½ 3 1 2 1 VanderSchaafK3 4200 2:10⅖ Andy'sEddie K'p'r'sKid PaintAway
Feb23-71 2Spk⅝  1 :32 2 1:04 1 1:34 4 2:09 1 gd 45 4 0 5 5 16 5 15 6 10 VanderSchaafK9 4200 2:11⅕ FlashieRuth Amigo'sHeir HavaD'te
Feb20-71 3AurA  1 :33 3 1:06 4 1:40 4 2:16 1 sy 7¾ 2 0 4 0 5 5 4 4½ 4 5¾ VanderSchaafK5 3000 2:17⅖ PrivateBill SuccessSp'rt OzarkBob
```

3 (8-1)
2:04⅘ (Was1, '70) ($50,095) — Driver-Trainer—RON WEINBERG (12-0-2-1—.120) — Blue-Black
Ryan's Pride — Br. g (1962), by Star's Pride—Lady Peg, by Scotland. 1971 9 0 1 0 $906
Owner, Weinberg & Weiss; Glenwood, Chicago, Ill. 1970 24 6 0 1 $10,206

```
Mar20-71 1Spk⅝A 1 :31 4 1:05 1 1:36 2 2:09 4 ft 23 7 7 7 7½ 6 4 2 1 WeinbergR5 3500 2:10 KosherDill Ry'n'sPride SatinGr't'n
Mar10-71 2Spk⅝  1 :31 2 1:04 4 1:36 2:08 1 ft 34 9 9 9 7½ 9 8 9 8¼ WeinbergR8 3500 2:09⅘ PhilDorw'd TopGene Shady'leY'kee
Mar 1-71 2Spk⅝  1 :32 1:04 1:35 2:07 2 ft 12 x9 9 9 14 9 14 9 12 WeinbergR1 3500 2:09⅘ Ruthl'sG'ge D'm'teQu'n K'ghtSc'p
Feb22-71 2Spk⅝  1 :32 2 1:07 1:40 2:12 4 sy 25 5 6 7 7½ 8 8½ 8 17 WeinbergR1 4000 2:16⅕ MerrieKiwi Sh'dy'leY'kee LouisHal
Feb12-71 8BmlP  1 :33 1 1:07 2 1:40 2 2:14 gd 17 4 5 4 3¼ 4 4½ 4 11 WeinbergR3 4000 2:16⅕ MissInd'nBr'k St'dyBill G'n'r'lJoy
Feb 5-71 8BmlP  1 :32 1 1:06 1:37 2 2:11 1 ft 31 4 8 8 6½ 7 5 6 6½ WeinbergR2 4000 2:12⅗ Qu'n'sR'cr't Str'ghtT'lk TrueH'b'r
```

4 (10-1)
2:06⅕ (Haw1, '70) ($19,675) — Driver—HARRY BURRIGHT. Trainer, E. Jefferson (84-17-16-9—.344) — Blue-Gold
Mr. Debonair ⊗ — B. g (1964), by Solicitor—Cerise, by Tar Heel. 1971 5 0 0 0 $546
Owner, Arlene Jefferson & T. Davies; Chicago, Worth, Ill. 1970 31 5 2 3 $8,041

```
Mar20-71 1Spk⅝A 1 :31 4 1:05 1 1:36 2 2:09 4 ft 8¾ 2 2 3 1½ 2 2 4 2½ BurrightH6 3500 2:10⅖ KosherDill Ry'n'sPride SatinGr't'n
Mar12-71 1Spk⅝  1 :32 1 1:05 3 1:37 2 2:09 2 ft 6 6 7 7 4½ 5 7½ 5 5 BurrightH4 3500 2:10⅖ K'sasCityK'ty Gol'nD'ze Belr'kBen
Mar 6-71 1Spk⅝  1 :32 2 1:08 1 1:40 1 2:14 4 sy 8¼ 2 2 1 2x 4 3½ 4 2½ BurrightH3 3500 2:15⅖ Tantalizer Succ'ssSport CraftyBill
Feb27-71 2Spk⅝A 1 :30 1 1:02 3 1:33 3 2:07 3 ft 15 4 3 6 7 8 11 8 16 BurrightH2 3500 2:10⅘ Hi Buster Point Adios Rush On
Feb23-71 2Spk⅝  1 :32 2 1:04 1 1:34 4 2:09 1 gd 17 5 4 4 13 4 13 7 11 BurrightH3 3500 2:11⅖ FlashieRuth Amigo'sHeir HavaD'te
Dec22-70 10Aur  1 :33 1:07 3 1:41 2 2:14 2 sl 4 x8xx8 8 8 8di. BurrightH2 2500 SoFiann DangerousSteve Pat'sDee
```

5 (12-1)
2:13⅘ (Aur, '71) ($203) — Driver-Trainer—DARYL BUSSE (60-5-6-2—.150) — Gray-Red
Diane D. Adios — Br. m (1964), by Noble Adios—Mountain Goose, by Goose Bay. 1971 11 1 1 0 $910
Owner, Marion & Louis DeFilippis; Chicago, Ill. 1970 0 0 0 0 (——)

```
Mar18-71 2Spk⅝  1 :32 2 1:06 1:39 4 2:12 1 sy 19 7 7 7 5 8 6 7 9½ BanksS4 4200 2:14⅕ Dolly'sCinndy KellyDirect All Nose
Mar 9-71 1Spk⅝  1 :30 3 1:04 2 1:37 2:08 4 ft 13 5 5 7 4½ 9 9½ 9 7¾ BusseDa3 4200 2:10⅖ Rush On Gustomar Paula Brown
Mar 4-71 1Spk⅝  1 :30 4 1:04 1:36 3 2:08 2 ft 15 4 0 1 x1½ 8 19 8 16 BusseDa9 4200 2:11⅗ Gustom'r MissDil'n'sSon Wil'dAnn
Feb27-71 5Spk⅝A 1 :30 4 1:06 1 1:36 4 2:09 1 ft 13 5 5 5 6½ 6 14 6 12 BusseDa3 nw3500 2:11⅗ KitseyHano'r Pick'l'sPride Apache
Feb20-71 4Aur   1 :31 4 1:05 1:40 2:14 3 sl 3-2 ▲6 4 0 6 13 7 11 7 24 BusseDa1 nw2000 7071 2:19⅖ DonPasquale Just'yStar OttaDo
Feb16-71 7Aur   1 :33 1 1:09 3 1:44 2:18 3 sy 3-5 ▲2 2 2 1 2h 2½ BusseDa6 nw1000 2:18⅘ MissL'kyC'k DianeD.A's DonnieA's
```

6 (6-1)
2:09⅕ (May, '70) ($10,923) — Driver-Trainer—STANLEY BANKS (94-4-10-14—.154) — White-Purple
Pat's Dee — B. g (1961), by Spencer Camp—Miss Pronto Key, by Long Key. 1971 14 2 5 2 $4,350
Owner, Buchen & Davis; St. Augustine, Avon, Ill. 1970 7 2 0 2 $1,964

```
Mar18-71 10Spk⅝ 1 :33 1 1:08 1 1:40 3 2:12 sy 7¾ 4 4 4 4½ 5 7 5 3¾ BanksS2 4000 2:12⅘ Whizmor Hot Deck Hi Buster
Mar13-71 1Spk⅝  1 :30 4 1:04 2 1:36 3 2:08 1 ft 6½ 2 0 1 2½ x8 13 8 13 BanksS9 3500 2:10⅘ Q'n'sNav'jo Dia'nteQ'n Kni'tSc'mp
Mar 6-71 1Spk⅝A 1 :30 4 1:03 1 1:35 1 2:09 3 sy 5¼ 5 4 3 5½ 2 3½ 2¾ BanksS9 3500 2:09⅘ R.J.M. Pat's Dee Crystal Chief
Mar 3-71 2Spk⅝  1 :31 1:02 3 1:34 1 2:08 2 ft 2¼ ▲2 2 2 4 2 2½ 2¾ BanksS1 3500 2:08⅗ Sportster Pat's Dee All Nose
Feb25-71 10Spk⅝ 1 :30 4 1:03 2 1:35 2 2:07 2 ft 17 1 1 1 1½ 2h 2 3 BanksS8 3500 2:08 Dr. Farr Pat's Dee Air Venture
Feb23-71 2Spk⅝  1 :32 2 1:04 1 1:34 4 2:09 1 gd 21 9 9 8 20 7 17 4 8¼ BanksS8 3500 2:10⅘ FlashieRuth Amigo'sHeir HavaD'te
```

7 (6-1)
2:06⅖ (Was1, '70) ($16,049) — Driver-Trainer—DESMOND O'DONOHOE (13-0-1-0—.043) — Green-White
Miss Dillon's Son — Ch. g (1961), by Clarkspur—Miss Dillon Dewey, by Widow's Chief. 1971 13 2 5 2 $4,091
Owner, Desmond O'Donohoe, Crete, Ill. 1970 6 1 0 2 $1,678

```
Mar17-71 1Spk⅝  1 :30 1 1:03 3 1:36 4 2:08 1 ft 14 9 9 8 6¼ 7 5 4 2¾ O'DonohoeD8 3500 2:08⅘ Solvig AirVenture DangerousDude
Mar10-71 1Spk⅝  1 :31 1 1:04 1:35 2 2:08 4 ft 7¾ 7 7 4 9½ 5 3 4 4 O'DonohoeD2 4200 2:09⅗ ShiawayG'se Tantaliz'r BuzzEagle
Mar 4-71 1Spk⅝  1 :30 4 1:04 1:36 3 2:08 2 ft 8½ 5 5 4 2 2 1 2 2½ O'DonohoeD1 3500 2:09 Gustom'r MissDil'n'sSon Wil'dAnn
Feb20-71 5BmlP  1 :33 3 1:09 1:41 1 2:13 ft 5¼ 4 4 6 7½ 5 8 5 5½ O'DonohoeD3 3000 2:14⅕ Li'leB'byThor Talaria VolcanicG'ge
Feb13-71 3BmlP  1 :32 1 1:05 1:38 2:10 3 ft 5¼ 6 6 4 7 4 4½ 3 3½ O'DonohoeD4 3000 2:11⅖ Pal'rC'hC'n Blueb'ry M'sDil'n'sSon
Feb 6-71 1BmlP  1 :32 2 1:04 2 1:37 1 2:10 1 ft 3½ 10 2 2 2 2 1½ 1 1 MilburnP5 2500 2:10⅕ MissDillon'sSon Amri AdiosWayne
```

8 (7-2)
2:03⅘ (Was1, '70) ($17,801) — Driver-Trainer—GENE VALLANDINGHAM (87-19-6-11—.299) — Red-White-Blue
Shadydale Yankee — Br. g (1961), by Yankee Scott—Adele Chief, by Chief Abbedale. 1971 6 1 1 1 $2,392
Owner, Neil M. Kelly, Elgin, Ill. 1970 21 6 4 4 $12.498

```
Mar20-71 1Spk⅝A 1 :31 4 1:05 1 1:36 2 2:09 4 ft 1 ▲5 5 2½ 5 3½ 5 3¼ VallandinghamG2 3500 2:10⅖ KosherDill Ry'n'sPride SatinGr't'n
Mar10-71 2Spk⅝  1 :31 2 1:04 4 1:36 2:08 1 ft 6-5 ▲1 1 1 1 2½ 3 3 VallandinghamG6 3500 2:08⅘ PhilDorw'd TopGene Shady'leY'kee
Mar 2-71 10Spk⅝ 1 :31 2 1:04 1:35 3 2:07 2 ft 9-5 ▲x6 0 6 0 4 5½ 6 11 8 13 VallandinghamG8 4000 2:10 NobleYates Lydia'sGirl Cumberl'nd
Feb26-71 10Spk⅝ 1 :30 1 1:06 4 1:38 2 2:11 1 gd 3-2 ▲6 0 3 0 1 1¼ 1 1 1 1½ VallandinghamG7 4000 2:11⅕ ShadydaleY'kee TrueHarbor GoMo
Feb22-71 2Spk⅝  1 :32 2 1:07 1:40 2:12 4 sy 5¾ 1 3 0 2½ 2nk 2 1½ VallandinghamG6 4000 2:13⅕ MerrieKiwi Sh'dy'leY'kee LouisHal
Jan 9-71 7Aur   1 :30 4 1:02 3 1:34 1 2:07 1 ft 5½ 3 3x 6 19 6 23 6di. VallandinghamG1 4000 Friskim Old Blue Gerry's First
```

9 (12-1)
2:11⅖ (BmlP, '70) ($27,106) — Driver—JERALD GREVENGOED. Trainer, W. Stahl (34-2-2-6—.150) — Gold-Black
Lady Softie — Blk. m (1961), by Marlin Hanover—Wilmington's Lady, by Wilmington. 1971 6 0 1 0 $850
Owner, Wm. H. Stahl, Somonauk, Ill. 1970 17 2 1 2 $2,274

```
Mar18-71 2Spk⅝  1 :32 2 1:06 1:39 4 2:12 1 sy 19 6 6 0 6 3½ 6 4½ 4 3½ GrevengoedJ3 4200 2:13 Dolly'sCinndy KellyDirect All Nose
Mar 8-71 2Spk⅝  1 :30 2 1:03 1 1:35 2:07 2 ft 20 8 8 7 6½ 6 5½ 6 7¾ GoveiaH6 3500 2:09 Dolly'sC'ndy K'ns'sCityK'ty Tal'ria
Mar 1-71 2Spk⅝  1 :32 1:04 1:35 2:07 2 ft 39 7 7 7 11 6 11 6 10 GoveiaH8 4200 2:09⅖ Ruthl'sG'ge D'm'teQu'n K'ghtSc'p
Feb24-71 1Spk⅝  1 :32 3 1:07 3 1:38 2 2:09 3 ft 11 4 5 5 5½ 5 7 4 7¼ GoveiaH2 4200 2:11 Torpid'sGold Gol'nDaze Wild'dAnn
Feb18-71 8BmlP  1 :32 2 1:06 3 1:39 4 2:11 3 ft 12 5 2 0 2 1½ 2 2½ 2 5 GoveiaH6 2750 2:12⅗ AdiosWayne LadySoftie Houdaille
Feb15-71 7BmlP  1 :32 2 1:06 2 1:39 3 2:13 2 ft 6½ 7 7 8 5 8 4½ 7 2 GoveiaH4 2750 2:13⅘ Zal Free Choice Carol Row Gil
```

Trackman's Selections—2 8 6

ONE MILE PACE **2nd RACE (afternoon program)** **Purse $2,800**

(SECOND HALF OF DAILY DOUBLE)

Claiming. Claiming price $4,000. 3-year-olds and up.
Lang's Filly, Carlen Dirty Bird in for $4,800; rest for $4,000.

PLEASE ASK FOR HORSE BY PROGRAM NUMBER

2:06⅘ (H.P⅝, '70) ($18,306) Driver-Trainer—IVAN SUGG (30-10-2-6—.437) **Green-Gray-White**

Reed's Michael — **B. g (1965), by Reed's Knight—Michael Monica Lee, by Michael S.** 1971 8 1 0 0 $1,524
Owner, Sugg, Myers, Cook, Leigh, Deshler, Carey; Kenton, Ohio. 1970 37 8 3 3 $10.749

5-1 **1**

Mar19-71^{2}Spk⅝ 1 :31^{1}1:04^{4}1:36^{3}2:09 gd 3¾ 4 4 1^{nk} 1^{nk} 4$^{4\frac{1}{4}}$ SuggI^{2} 4000 2:09⅘ Hobby'sCh'r Br'nRang'r M'rieKiwi
Mar11-71^{10}Spk⅝ 1 :32^{3}1:05^{4}1:39^{3}2:10^{3}gd 7 2 3 2$^{\frac{3}{4}}$ 5$^{2\frac{1}{4}}$ 7$^{5\frac{1}{2}}$ SuggI^{8} 5000 2:11⅘ GeneH'v'ns Mr.LakeC'y King'sRaid
Mar 5-71^{1}Spk⅝ 1 :30^{3}1:01^{4}1:34^{3}2:07 ft 6 6 5 4$^{4\frac{1}{2}}$ 2$^{\frac{1}{2}}$ 1$^{1\frac{1}{2}}$ SuggI^{3} 3500 2:07 Reed'sMichael YukonEric K'p'sKid
Feb27-71^{2}Spk⅝ 1 :30^{3}1:06^{3}1:36^{3}2:10^{4}ft 36 10 1 4$^{7\frac{1}{2}}$ 7^{6} 8^{9} SuggI^{7} 4000 2:12⅗ ElD'nyP'g's Lang'sFilly Tact'lTom
Feb24-71^{2}Spk⅝ 1 :31^{3}1:04^{4}1:36^{4}2:08^{2}ft 29 4 6 4$^{2\frac{1}{2}}$ 8$^{6\frac{1}{2}}$ 9^{7} SuggI^{1} 4500 2:09⅘ RicoBay Mic'yAdios West'n'sJef'ry
Feb16-71 W.R⅝ 1 :29^{4}1:03^{1}1:35^{2}2:07^{2}ft 73 1 2 4 5$^{2\frac{1}{2}}$ 7di. SuggI^{8} 5000 RogerRock Becky'sPride Pr'ceG'ry

2:06⅗ (Nfld, '70) ($2,799) Driver-Trainer—LARRY GREGORY (19-3-4-3—.327) **Gray-Orange**

Lang's Filly — **B. f (1967), by Lang Hanover—Scotch Enough, by Scotch Valley. Ow.** 1971 12 0 2 4 $2,471
Lee R. Figgins, Leonard D. Jones; S. Pasadena, Pico Rivera, Calif. 1970 27 1 2 3 $2.799

8-1 **2**

Mar20-71^{1}Spk⅝ 1 :31^{1}1:03^{1}1:35^{1}2:07^{3}ft 19 7 7 4$^{2\frac{1}{2}}$ 3$^{\frac{1}{2}}$ 3$^{1\frac{1}{2}}$ GregoryL^{9} 4800 2:08 UncleSm'ge Mic'yAd's Lang'sFilly
Mar13-71^{2}Spk⅝A 1 :30^{1}1:02^{1}1:34^{2}2:06^{2}ft 6½ 8 8^{0} 6$^{3\frac{1}{2}}$ 6$^{6\frac{1}{2}}$ 6^{7} GregoryL^{7} 4800 2:07⅘ Br'kAbbe West'n'sJ'f'y Gr'tCredit
Mar 5-71^{2}Spk⅝ 1 :31^{3}1:04^{3}1:36 2:07 ft 8¼ 7 7 6$^{6\frac{1}{2}}$ 7$^{7\frac{1}{2}}$ 7$^{5\frac{1}{2}}$ GregoryL^{7} 5400 2:08⅕ Gerry'sFirst HadAKing RushTime
Feb27-71^{2}Spk⅝ 1 :30^{3}1:06^{3}1:36^{3}2:10^{4}ft 8¼ 7 8^{0} 5^{8} 4$^{3\frac{1}{2}}$ 2^{1} GregoryL^{5} 4800 2:11 ElD'nyP'g's Lang'sFilly Tact'lTom
Feb22-71^{2}Spk⅝ 1 :32^{2}1:07 1:40 2:12^{4}sy 6¾ 6 5^{0} 5$^{3\frac{1}{2}}$ 5^{3} 4$^{3\frac{1}{2}}$ GregoryL^{3} 4800 2:13⅗ MerrieKiwi Sh'dy'leY'kee LouisHal
Feb12-71 B.M^{1} 1 :31^{2}1:04^{2}1:36^{3}2:07 ft 7¼ 6 4 2 2^{3} 2$^{1\frac{1}{4}}$ GregoryL^{8} 4350 2:07⅕ JoeRichard LangsFilly T'x'sFr'ght

2:05 (Was^{1}, '70) ($27,722) Driver—EDWARD DORN. Trainer, D. Allen (32-5-5-3—.274) **Gold-White**

Pipe of Peace — **B. g (1962), by Morris Eden—Grattan Dillon, by Dillon Hall.** 1971 8 1 1 2 $3,026
Owner, M & A Stable, Chicago, Ill. 1970 18 7 2 3 $11.580

6-1 **3**

Mar22-71^{10}Spk⅝ 1 :31^{3}1:05 1:37^{2}2:09^{2}ft 3¼ 8 8 8^{4} 7^{5} 3$^{3\frac{1}{2}}$ DornE^{6} 4000 2:10⅕ HiSkipper LouisHal Pipe ofPeace
Mar13-71^{1}Spk⅝A 1 :30^{1}1:00^{1}1:33^{2}2:06 ft 2¾ 7 7 7$^{4\frac{1}{2}}$ 2^{nk} 1$^{2\frac{1}{2}}$ DornE^{3} 3500 2:06 Pipe of P'ce Jack'sL'd'g Tr'nc'rL'l
Mar 5-71^{1}Spk⅝ 1 :30^{3}1:01^{4}1:34^{3}2:07 ft 3¾ ▲9 9 8^{9} 7^{6} 6^{3} DornE^{8} 3500 2:07⅗ Reed'sMichael YukonEric K'p'sKid
Feb27-71^{1}Spk⅝ 1 :31^{2}1:05^{2}1:37 2:10^{1}ft 9-5 ▲8 7 8^{6} 6^{3} 4^{2} DornE^{7} 3500 2:10⅗ Andy'sEddie K'p'r'sKid PaintAway
Feb22-71^{1}Spk⅝ 1 :33^{1}1:09^{1}1:43^{4}2:15^{2}sy 8-5 ▲4 4 4$^{2\frac{1}{2}}$ 2$^{2\frac{1}{2}}$ 3$^{5\frac{1}{4}}$ DornE^{2} 3500 2:16⅖ Go Mo Hi Buster Pipe of Peace
Feb 4-71 B.M^{1} 1 :32^{3}1:04^{4}1:36^{3}2:07^{3}ft 4¼ 5 6 5 6^{3} 5$^{2\frac{3}{4}}$ DornR^{5} 3500 2:08⅕ RicoBay SengaLuDean Bl'ckAmigo

2:09⅘ (Spk⅝, '71) ($39,084) Driver-Trainer—JOHNNY BLEVINS (66-11-4-3—.219) **White-Blue-Black**

Kosher Dill — **B. g (1961), by Diller Hanover—Midinette, by Alemite.** 1971 12 2 1 2 $2,552
Owner, Johnny L. Blevins, Palos Heights, Ill. 1970 5 0 0 0 (——)

8-1 **4**

Mar20-71^{1}Spk⅝A 1 :31^{4}1:05^{1}1:36^{2}2:09^{4}ft 27 1^{0} 1 1$^{\frac{1}{2}}$ 1^{2} 1^{1} BlevinsJ^{9} 3500 2:09⅘ KosherDill Ry'n'sPride SatinGr't'n
Mar12-71^{1}Spk⅝ 1 :32^{1}1:05^{3}1:37^{2}2:09^{2}ft 9½ 3^{0} 1 1^{1} 7^{9} 7$^{5\frac{1}{2}}$ BlevinsJ^{5} 3500 2:10⅗ K'sasCityK'ty Gol'nD'ze Belr'kBen
Mar 6-71^{1}Spk⅝ 1 :32^{2}1:08^{1}1:40^{1}2:14^{4}sy 14 7 7 7^{8} 6$^{6\frac{1}{2}}$ 5$^{2\frac{1}{2}}$ BlevinsJ^{7} 3500 2:15⅖ Tantalizer Succ'ssSport CraftyBill
Mar 3-71^{2}Spk⅝ 1 :31 1:02^{3}1:34^{1}2:08^{2}ft 16 9 9 9^{22} 7^{16} 6$^{8\frac{3}{4}}$ BlevinsJ^{6} 3500 2:10⅕ Sportster Pat's Dee All Nose
Feb25-71^{2}Spk⅝ 1 :30^{3}1:02^{4}1:35^{4}2:08 ft 14 6 6 3^{2} 4^{6} 5$^{3\frac{1}{2}}$ BlevinsJ^{1} 3500 2:08⅘ NikkSh'r't'n BuzzEagle Suc'ssSp't
Feb18-71^{8}Aur 1 :33^{2}1:10 1:45^{3}2:21^{1}sy 6 8 8 3^{8}ex4^{10} 3^{16} BlevinsJ^{3} nw1000^{7071} 2:24⅖ Continental BelrockBen KosherDill

2:07⅕ (Spk⅝, '70) ($6,931) Driver—CHRIS BORING. Trainer, M. Schanks (50-5-8-8—.253) **Green-White**

Rush On — **Blk. g (1966), by Check Up—Iosola K., by Athlone Iosola Guy.** 1971 6 1 0 2 $2,264
Owner, John Varvisotis, Evergreen Park, Ill. 1970 12 2 3 0 $4,525

6-1 **5**

Mar25-71^{10}Spk⅝ 1 :30^{4}1:02^{4}1:34^{4}2:07^{1}ft 4½ 6 6 7$^{9\frac{1}{2}}$ 4$^{6\frac{1}{2}}$ 4$^{2\frac{1}{2}}$ BoringC^{4} 4000 2:07⅘ HiBuster KellyDirect DollyJean
Mar16-71^{9}Spk⅝ 1 :31 1:04 1:37 2:08^{2}ft 5¼ 9 8^{0} 7$^{4\frac{1}{2}}$ 5^{5} 5$^{3\frac{3}{4}}$ KnoxR^{9} c4000 2:09⅕ Private Bill Doctor B. Louis Hal
Mar 9-71^{1}Spk⅝ 1 :30^{3}1:04^{2}1:37 2:08^{4}ft 4¼ 8 8^{0} 6$^{4\frac{1}{2}}$ 6^{6} 1^{1} KnoxR^{4} 3500 2:08⅘ Rush On Gustomar Paula Brown
Mar 3-71^{10}Spk⅝ 1 :30^{2}1:04^{2}1:37 2:08^{4}ft 2 ▲7 7 6$^{6\frac{1}{2}}$ 5$^{3\frac{1}{2}}$ 3^{2} KnoxR^{6} 3500 2:09⅕ Elberta'sBoy PatriciaDale RushOn
Feb27-71^{2}Spk⅝A 1 :30^{1}1:02^{3}1:33^{3}2:07^{3}ft 22 8 8 8$^{9\frac{1}{2}}$ 7^{6} 3$^{5\frac{1}{2}}$ KnoxR^{9} 3500 2:08⅘ HiBuster PointAdios RushOn
Feb23-71^{10}Spk⅝ 1 :31^{1}1:05^{1}1:37^{2}2:10^{2}gd 30 8 9 9^{12} 8^{15} 7^{11} KnoxR^{7} 4000 2:12⅗ Q'n'sPalef'e TimelyC'd'r Tact'lTom

2:10⅕ (Aur, '70) ($6,914) Driver-Trainer—CHARLES McDERMOTT (30-2-3-1—.133) **Red-White-Blue**

Coalmont Fritz ⊗ — **B. g (1966), by Set Sail—Dinah Knight, by Knight Dream.** 1971 13 1 0 4 $2,586
Owner, Pershall, Harper & Sutton; LaPorte, Valparaiso, Ind. 1970 32 4 2 4 $4,138

10-1 **6**

Mar20-71^{2}Spk⅝A 1 :30^{1}1:03^{2}1:34^{1}2:08 ft 14 4^{0} 6^{0} 3$^{4\frac{1}{2}}$ 9^{11} 9^{12} McDermottC^{8} 4500 2:10⅖ YatesBoy Torpid'sGold Wes'n'sJ'y
Mar13-71^{4}Spk⅝A 1 :31^{2}1:03^{4}1:35^{4}2:05^{3}ft 30 8 7 4^{2} 4^{1} 3$^{2\frac{3}{4}}$ McDermottC^{8} 5000 2:07⅕ JayCouns'l Ev'n'gSky Coalm'tFritz
Mar 6-71^{3}Spk⅝ 1 :31^{1}1:04^{3}1:35^{4}2:10^{1}sy 15 5 5 4$^{5\frac{1}{2}}$ 6^{6} 6^{10} McDermottC^{6} 5000 2:12⅕ Tartar ShadySideBill GustoLobell
Mar 1-71^{4}Spk⅝ 1 :32 1:04^{4}1:37^{2}2:08 ft 9¼ 3 1 1$^{\frac{3}{4}}$ 2^{nk} 4$^{3\frac{3}{4}}$ McDermottC^{1} 5000 2:08⅘ Ad'sMickey AllKeyedUp M'keyAd's
Feb19-71^{9}BmlP 1 :32 1:06^{2}1:39^{2}2:13 sy 9½ 4 5 5$^{3\frac{1}{4}}$ 2$^{1\frac{1}{2}}$ 3$^{1\frac{1}{4}}$ PershallP^{2} 5000 2:13⅕ DickCouns'l JayCouns'l Coal'tFritz
Feb15-71^{6}BmlP 1 :31^{2}1:05^{1}1:37^{3}2:09^{4}ft 18 3 3 3^{2} 2$^{1\frac{1}{2}}$ 3^{1} PershallP^{3} nw3500^{7071} 2:10 W'thyRew'd Pr'c'sP'na Coal'tFritz

2:07⅕ (Cka¾, '70) ($18,513) Driver-Trainer—STANLEY BANKS (94-4-10-14—.154) **White-Purple**

Louis Hal — **Blk. g (1962), by Purdue Hal—Lulu Belle, by Worthy Boy.** 1971 12 3 1 2 $3,662
Owner, Victory Lane Farm, Inc., Dwight, Ill. 1970 18 4 0 1 $3,940

6-1 **7**

Mar22-71^{10}Spk⅝ 1 :31^{3}1:05 1:37^{2}2:09^{2}ft 11 6 7 7$^{3\frac{1}{4}}$ 5$^{3\frac{1}{2}}$ 2$^{2\frac{1}{2}}$ BanksS^{5} 4000 2:10 HiSkipper LouisHal Pipe ofPeace
Mar16-71^{9}Spk⅝ 1 :31 1:04 1:37 2:08^{2}ft 7 6 6 8^{5} 4$^{4\frac{1}{2}}$ 3^{3} BanksS^{3} 4000 2:09 Private Bill Doctor B. Louis Hal
Mar 9-71^{1}Spk⅝ 1 :30^{3}1:04^{2}1:37 2:08^{4}ft 8-5 ▲3 3 3$^{2\frac{1}{2}}$ 2^{3} x4^{2} BanksS^{1} 3500 2:09⅕ Rush On Gustomar Paula Brown
Mar 3-71^{5}Spk⅝ 1 :32^{1}1:06^{1}1:37^{4}2:09^{1}ft 22 6 8^{0} 8^{7} 6$^{4\frac{1}{2}}$ 5$^{3\frac{3}{4}}$ BanksS^{2} 5000 2:10 Queen'sP'f'ce B'bbl'gBr'ke RicoB'y
Feb26-71^{5}Spk⅝ 1 :31^{2}1:05^{3}1:36^{1}2:09^{2}gd 11 6 6 6$^{7\frac{1}{2}}$ 6^{17} 6^{14} VallandinghamG^{7} 5000 2:12⅕ JohnnyAtom G'stoL'b'll Jilt'rL'b'll
Feb22-71^{2}Spk⅝ 1 :32^{2}1:07 1:40 2:12^{4}sy 7¼ 4^{0} 1 1$^{\frac{1}{2}}$ 1^{nk} 3$^{3\frac{1}{2}}$ BanksS^{9} 4000 2:13⅗ MerrieKiwi Sh'dy'leY'kee LouisHal

2:07⅘ (Spk⅝, '70) ($4,952) Driver-Trainer—WALTER PAISLEY (68-6-9-10—.211) **Green-White**

Amosson's P. J. — **B. g (1963), by Will Direct—Chalidale Anne, by King's Ransom.** 1971 4 0 0 1 $572
Owner, Evans & Welch; Crystal Lake, Ill. 1970 4 1 0 2 $2,164

7-2 **8**

Mar22-71^{10}Spk⅝ 1 :31^{3}1:05 1:37^{2}2:09^{2}ft 3 5^{0} 4^{0} 4$^{1\frac{1}{4}}$ 3^{2} 5^{4} PaisleyW^{7} 4000 2:10⅕ HiSkipper LouisHal Pipe ofPeace
Mar13-71^{10}Spk⅝ 1 :31^{1}1:03 1:34^{1}2:05^{3}ft 3¾ 4 4 5^{5} 6^{3} 7$^{3\frac{1}{2}}$ PaisleyW^{5} 6000 2:06⅖ Rainmaker TimelyGold Lydia'sGirl
Mar 9-71^{10}Spk⅝ 1 :31^{4}1:03^{2}1:38^{1}2:09^{4}gd 2½ ▲2^{0} 2 3^{1} 4$^{1\frac{1}{2}}$ 3$^{4\frac{1}{2}}$ PaisleyW^{7} 6000 2:10⅘ Dr'mBus'r Whaleb'ne Am's'n'sP.J.
Mar 1-71^{5}Spk⅝ 1 :32 1:04^{1}1:35^{4}2:06^{4}ft 18 8 8 8$^{9\frac{1}{2}}$ 7^{7} 7$^{7\frac{1}{2}}$ PaisleyW^{8} 6000 2:08⅖ Queen'sRecruit KingSelka Mose
Mar 7-70^{4}Spk⅝A 1 :29^{4}1:02 1:32^{3}2:05^{2}ft 8½ 8 8 8$^{4\frac{1}{2}}$ 5^{3} 4^{2} WelchR^{5} 6000 2:05⅘ Fr'styAbbe MissM'phy'sW'y F.E.V.
Feb28-70^{10}Spk⅝ 1 :32^{1}1:04^{4}1:36^{2}2:07^{4}ft 4½ 3 3 3$^{3\frac{1}{2}}$ 2^{1} 1^{2} WelchR^{3} 4000 2:07⅘ Am'n'sP.J. HavaDate Q'n'sRingl'r

2:12⅗ (Aur, '71) (——) Driver—PHILIP MILBURN. Trainer, S. Buch (84-10-16-4—.241) **Blue-Gold**

Carlen Dirty Bird — **B. f (1967), by Dusty Jerry—Birdie D. Thoughts, by Deep Thoughts.** 1971 10 3 2 0 $2,812
Owner, W. & T. Stewart; Plainfield, Ill. 1970 0 M 0 0 (——)

10-1 **9**

Mar23-71^{10}Spk⅝ 1 :31^{2}1:07 1:38^{4}2:10 ft 7 5 5 6$^{4\frac{1}{2}}$ 6$^{6\frac{1}{2}}$ 4$^{7\frac{1}{2}}$ WillisN^{5} nw3500 2:11⅗ MarineHan'r Emma'sKid TopperTy
Mar17-71^{10}Spk⅝ 1 :31^{4}1:04 1:35^{1}2:06^{4}ft 13 7 7 4$^{3\frac{1}{2}}$ 4^{5} 5$^{5\frac{1}{2}}$ PaisleyW^{4} 6000 2:08 Ch'ceyRub'n Gerry'sFirst K'g'sR'd
Mar 6-71^{4}Spk⅝A 1 :32^{4}1:08 1:38^{4}2:11^{4}sy 17 1 2 2^{3} 2^{6} 4^{5} PaisleyW^{8} nw3500 2:12⅘ Apache All Keyed Up Edwin Yates
Mar 2-71^{5}Spk⅝ 1 :32 1:03^{4}1:35^{1}2:06^{2}ft 11 8 8 8^{11} 7^{14} 7^{16} PaisleyW^{8} fnw2250L 2:09⅗ LaurelW'y DionnaDiller LovinLuLu
Feb 8-71^{8}Aur 1 :34 1:08 1:41^{3}2:14^{3}ft 2½ ▲2 2 1^{h} 1^{2} 1$^{5\frac{1}{2}}$ PaisleyW^{2} nw1750^{7071} 2:14⅗ C'l'nD'tyBird J'stlySt'r H'n'stR'k't
Feb 4-71^{8}Aur 1 :33^{1}1:08^{3}1:45 2:19^{2}sy 3 5 6 5^{4} 4^{8} 2^{10} PaisleyW^{6} nw1500 2:21⅖ L.A.P'rk'r C'rl'nD'tyB'd L'yBl'kB'd

Trackman's Selections—8 1 3 **Scratched—HYPATIA.**

ONE MILE PACE — 3rd RACE (afternoon program) — Purse $3,200

Claiming. Claiming price $5,000. 3-year-olds and up. Lydia's Girl in for $6,000; rest for $5,000.

PLEASE ASK FOR HORSE BY PROGRAM NUMBER

1 (6-1)
2:05 2/5 (Spk5/8, '70) ($19,134) Driver-Trainer—DAN SHETLER, JR. (19-1-3-3—.193) Purple-Gold-White
Mickey Adios ⊗ B. g (1965), by Ellen's Adios—Ann Mary, by Mitimac. 1971 5 1 2 1 $3,384
Owner, Linda June Sechel, Maywood, Ill. 1970 25 1 3 6 $6,737
Mar20-711Spk5/8 1 :3111:0311:3512:073ft 4 6 6 64 2h 21 PaisleyW5 c4000 2:07 4/5 UncleSm'ge Mic'yAd's Lang'sFilly
Mar13-713Spk5/8 1 :31 1:0341:3622:064ft 2¼ 6 6 44¾ 43 66 PaisleyW6 5000 2:08 Rico Bay Disneyland Sassy Kid
Mar 6-714Spk5/8 1 :3321:0831:4112:134sl 3½ 50 1 1½ 12 12 PaisleyW6 5000 2:13 4/5 MickeyAdios NobleYates Whizmor
Mar 1-714Spk5/8 1 :32 1:0441:3722:08 ft 3 10 2 2¾ 1nk 3¾ PaisleyW6 5000 2:08 1/5 Ad'sMickey AllKeyedUp M'keyAd's
Feb24-712Spk5/8 1 :3131:0441:3642:082ft 13 10 2 32 31½ 2nk PaisleyW9 4500 2:08 2/5 RicoBay Mic'yAdios West'n'sJef'ry
Dec12-7010Aur 1 :3211:0521:3842:12 sl 3½ 5 5 43 31½ 23½ PaisleyW2 4000 2:12 4/5 DoctorS. MickeyAdios VoloHonor

2 (8-1)
2:03 3/5 (Was1, '70) ($31,642) Driver-Trainer—JOHN WOLFE (37-1-2-9—.138) Green-White-Brown
Shady Side Bill Ch. g (1964), by Hi Lo's Tweed—Misty Counsel, by Chief Counsel. 1971 10 0 3 0 $2,120
Owner, Malcolm & Jeannette Dinsmore, Hebron, Ind. 1970 37 8 5 8 $17,713
Mar18-719Spk5/8 1 :31 1:0441:38 2:094sy 8¼ 10 1 11½ 1h 66½ WolfeJ9 5000 2:11 1/5 R.J.M. Jay Chief Sno Van
Mar12-7110Spk5/8 1 :3031:0231:3432:063ft 7½ 1 1 11½ 32½ 76¾ WolfeJ8 6000 2:08 Scotty'sLeader Shadydale RedClay
Mar 6-713Spk5/8 1 :3111:0431:3542:101sy 17 1 1 11½ 2h 22 WolfeJ4 5000 2:10 3/5 Tartar ShadySideBill GustoLobell
Feb26-715Spk5/8 1 :3121:0531:3612:092gd 6¼ 1 1 2½ 57 58 WolfeJ4 5000 2:11 JohnnyAtom G'stoL'b'll Jilt'rL'b'll
Feb22-714Spk5/8 1 :3131:06 1:39 2:121sy 20 1 1 1nk 33½ 55¾ WolfeJ9 6000 2:13 2/5 WorthyH'rN. McC'ryM'sile SnoVan
Feb13-714BmlP 1 :3131:0341:37 2:102ft 7 2 1 11 1h 62¾ WolfeJ3 5500 2:11 Green'sSt'r Babbl'gBr'ke SassyKid

3 (12-1)
2:07 3/5 (LouD, '70) ($9,313) Driver-Trainer—DESMOND O'DONOHOE (13-0-1-0—.043) Green-White
Banker Paul B. h (1965), by Adios Paul—Banker Girl, by Hector Prim. 1971 9 0 0 1 $265
Owner, Desmond O'Donohoe, Crete, Ill. 1970 33 3 4 4 $4,413
Mar20-712Spk5/8 1 :3141:0631:3642:084ft 36 7 8 88 99 64 O'DonohoeD6 5000 2:09 3/5 SassyKid Even'gSky Samp'nFrisco
Mar12-7110Spk5/8 1 :3031:0231:3432:063ft 27 2 2 65½ 918 9di. O'DonohoeD4 6000 Scotty'sLeader Shadydale RedClay
Feb17-716BmlP 1 :3241:0741:3932:121ft 20 6 6 67½ 65 64 O'D'hoeD7 nw35007071 2:13 HalryG'ne FairsideM'd'le TammyR.
Feb12-713BmlP 1 :3141:05 1:3912:131gd 29 7 6 52½ 52 32¾ O'D'hoeD7 nw25007071 2:13 4/5 GratefulLover ManorHope B'k'rP'l
Feb 3-718BmlP 1 :3141:06 1:38 2:102ft 13 5 6 78 79 78½ O'D'hoeD7 nw30007071 2:12 1/5 BillyBobAd's Gr't'n'sB'nie LaAnita
Jan28-716BmlP 1 :31 1:0321:3612:102gd 11 7 70 55 35 59¾ O'D'hoeD6 nw35007071 2:12 2/5 St'dyMoran SandyElk'n Ruth'sLad

4 (7-2)
2:07 3/5 (D.D5/8, '70) ($67,663) Driver-Trainer—CHARLES McDERMOTT (30-2-3-1—.133) Red-White-Blue
Mil Song ⊗ B. g (1961), by Patrick Song—Camoed Martina, by Santios. 1971 11 5 1 0 $7,192
Owner, C. McDermott & H. Brooks; Chicago Heights, Crete, Ill. 1970 10 1 5 0 $3,554
Mar20-712Spk5/8 1 :3141:0631:3642:084ft 2¾ 4 40 21¼ 11 43 McDermottC1 5000 2:09 3/5 SassyKid Even'gSky Samp'nFrisco
Mar13-7110Spk5/8 1 :3111:03 1:3412:053ft 3¾ 7 50 44 42½ 95¾ McDermottC6 6000 2:06 4/5 Rainmaker TimelyGold Lydia'sGirl
Mar 6-715Spk5/8A 1 :3221:0721:3842:104sy 8-5 •2 1 11½ 11¼ 1½ McDermottC5 6000 2:10 4/5 MilSong BethAHal Sp'rkl'gDiam'd
Mar 1-715Spk5/8 1 :32 1:0411:3542:064ft 5¼ 6 50 53½ 52 41 McDermottC4 6000 2:07 Queen'sRecruit KingSelka Mose
Feb 9-716BmlP 1 :31 1:0341:37 2:091ft 2 •20 1 1½ 1½ 1¾ McDermottC6 5000 2:09 1/5 MilSong King'sRaid Donna'sCape
Feb 5-719BmlP 1 :32 1:06 1:3732:094ft 9-5 •5 30 1no 2no 21 McDermottC5 5000 2:10 DickCounsel MilSong Donna'sCape

5 (6-1)
2:04 (Hol1, '70) ($18,917) Driver-Trainer—ROBERT FARRINGTON (152-21-21-24—.268) Red-Gray
Atlas N. ⊗ B. g (1963), by Johnny Globe—Floreate, by U. Scott. 1971 5 0 0 0 $576
Ow., Seibert & Farrington Stables, Inc.; Cincinnati, Richwood, Ohio. 1970 25 3 2 3 $9,837
Mar20-713Spk5/8 1 :3041:0341:3542:08 ft 4 •3 3 53 65½ 75 FarringtonR3 5500 2:09 Gold Mound Go Mo True Harbor
Mar12-7110Spk5/8 1 :3031:0231:3432:063ft 4¼ 6 6 55 44½ 44½ FarringtonR5 6000 2:07 3/5 Scotty'sLeader Shadydale RedClay
Mar 6-715Spk5/8A 1 :3221:0721:3842:104sy 9½ 1 2 21½ 31½ 43½ FarringtonR9 6000 2:11 3/5 MilSong BethAHal Sp'rkl'gDiam'd
Feb26-712Spk5/8 1 :3031:0511:3722:102gd 4½ 7 7 65 54 87¾ PaisleyW5 6000 2:12 McCr'yMissile TimelyG'ld MilesD's
Feb22-715Spk5/8 1 :33 1:0931:4212:143sy 5¾ 9 70 42½ 56½ 611 FarringtonR9 7500 2:16 4/5 DutchDi'ct Mic'ySup'e Mary'sD'wn
Dec19-70 Hol1 1 :33 1:0511:37 2:062gd 6¾ 6 6 5 34½ 33¾ FarringtonR6 6000 2:07 1/5 Dre'mBuster SaraPaiinter AtlasN.

6 (6-1)
2:05 3/5 (Spk5/8, '70) ($82,964) Driver-Trainer—KEN VANDER SCHAAF (31-10-5-3—.219) Gold-Black
Evening Sky ⊗ B. g (1960), by Sky Raider—Evening Silk, by Genoa. 1971 15 4 6 1 $8,398
Owner, Ken Vander Schaaf, Sandwich, Ill. 1970 28 4 3 3 $9,955
Mar20-712Spk5/8 1 :3141:0631:3642:084ft 7½ 2 3 54 42½ 22 VanderSchaafK9 5000 2:09 1/5 SassyKid Even'gSky Samp'nFrisco
Mar13-714Spk5/8A 1 :3121:0341:3542:063ft 2½ •1 2 1no 1h 22 VanderSchaafK5 5000 2:07 JayCouns'l Ev'n'gSky Coalm'tFritz
Mar 6-714Spk5/8 1 :3321:0831:4112:134sl 2 •4 5 53 43 42¾ SheelyD3 5000 2:14 2/5 MickeyAdios NobleYates Whizmor
Mar 1-7110Spk5/8 1 :3121:0431:3632:081ft 2¾ 2 3 53 42½ 2¾ VanderSchaafK4 5000 2:08 2/5 GustoLobell EveningSky KarenGray
Feb24-7110Spk5/8 1 :3221:0531:3812:093ft 3 3 4 42 3½ 1no VanderSchaafK1 5000 2:09 3/5 EveningSky Profast AllKeyedUp
Feb20-717Aur 1 :3311:0721:42 2:152sl 2½ •6 6 41 21 13 VanderSchaafK8 4000 2:15 2/5 EveningSky NewRule Justacatch

7 (6-1)
2:07 1/5 (Spk5/8, '70) ($17,899) Driver-Trainer—EUGENE WASZAK (35-1-8-3—.184) White-Blue-Gold
Hi Brewer B. g (1964), by Hi Hill—Erla Direct, by Direct Brewer. 1971 5 0 1 0 $1,280
Owner, J. Genovese & E. Waszak; Franklin Park, Chicago, Ill. 1970 37 3 2 3 $6,302
Mar20-713Spk5/8 1 :3041:0341:3542:08 ft 21 6 7 65½ 53½ 51¾ WaszakE5 5500 2:08 2/5 Gold Mound Go Mo True Harbor
Mar13-713Spk5/8 1 :31 1:0341:3622:064ft 15 4 4 55 64½ 55½ WaszakE2 5000 2:08 Rico Bay Disneyland Sassy Kid
Mar 6-7110Spk5/8 1 :3111:0511:3642:122sl 20 30 3 33 21½ 21 WaszakE5 5000 2:12 3/5 Profast Hi Brewer Friskim
Feb27-713Spk5/8 1 :3111:0431:3542:093ft 49 4 4 97½ 98½ 97¼ WaszakE6 5000 2:11 Scotty'sL'der Fl'm'gPink Whizmor
Feb23-719Spk5/8 1 :3121:0531:3822:112gd 40 2 3 43 33 53¼ WaszakE1 5000 2:12 Tartar DeaconDarl't'n GeneHavens
Dec28-706Aur 1 :32 1:0521:3642:083ft 28 3 3 31 31½ 43¾ WaszakE2 4000 2:09 3/5 Big David Old Blue Whizmor

8 (10-1)
2:07 3/5 (Spk5/8, '71) ($5,710) Driver-Trainer—WAYNE SHORT (42-5-2-8—.209) Purple-White
Uncle Smudge ⊗ B. g (1964), by Uncle Sam—Sakkara, by Demon Hanover. 1971 12 3 1 2 $4,270
Owner, J. T. Russell, Huntsville, Ala. 1970 20 2 0 2 $3,085
Mar20-711Spk5/8 1 :3111:0311:3512:073ft 14 10 2 53 52 11 ShortW3 4000 2:07 3/5 UncleSm'ge Mic'yAd's Lang'sFilly
Mar13-712Spk5/8 1 :3111:0241:3432:063ft 19 5 50 55½ 916 920 ShortW3 4500 2:10 3/5 Active George Go Mo Yates Boy
Mar 6-713Spk5/8 1 :3111:0431:3542:101sy 18 70 60 99 917 918 ShortW3 5000 2:13 4/5 Tartar ShadySideBill GustoLobell
Mar 1-714Spk5/8 1 :32 1:0441:3722:08 ft 7 5 5 54 76½ 78½ ShortW3 5000 2:09 4/5 Ad'sMickey AllKeyedUp M'keyAd's
Feb24-7110Spk5/8 1 :3221:0531:3812:093ft 4½ 40 1 2h 2h 41¼ ShortW3 5000 2:09 4/5 EveningSky Profast AllKeyedUp
Feb11-71 B.M1 1 :3131:03 1:35 2:05 ft 7¼ 5 5 6 65½ 31½ McClimansR3 c4000 2:05 1/5 W'thyP'c'gTime ElD'nyP'g's U'eS'e

9 (5-1)
2:04 (Det1, '70) ($18,858) Driver-Trainer—A. GEORGE SHAW (43-6-4-2—.207) Blue-White
Lydia's Girl B. m (1965), by Farvel—Lydia's Way, by Direct Way. 1971 12 1 3 3 $5,010
Owner, A. George Shaw, Summit, Ill. 1970 31 3 4 7 $8,931
Mar22-714Spk5/8 1 :31 1:03 1:3422:081ft 2 •1 2 21 2¾ 1nk GrenierM3 c6000 2:08 1/5 Lydia'sGirl PrivateBill R'thl'sG'rge
Mar13-7110Spk5/8 1 :3111:03 1:3412:053ft 2¼ •2 2 21¼ 21 32¼ GrenierM4 7200 2:06 Rainmaker TimelyGold Lydia'sGirl
Mar 8-715Spk5/8 1 :3011:0141:3222:052ft 4½ 2 2 21¼ 21¼ 2½ GrenierM3 6000 2:05 3/5 Dr. Farr Lydia's Girl Rico Bay
Mar 2-7110Spk5/8 1 :3121:04 1:3532:072ft 4½ 1 1 12 12 2nk GrenierM5 4800 2:07 2/5 NobleYates Lydia'sGirl Cumberl'nd
Feb13-71 B.M1 1 :32 1:0411:3542:053ft 3 4 4 3 33¼ 44¼ GrenierM8 4200 2:06 2/5 Gon'sM'ryF. Bl'kAmigo S'ngaM't'n
Feb 5-71 B.M1 1 :3021:03 1:3512:06 ft 6½ 3 2 3 31½ 84 LongoG1 6000 2:06 4/5 Id'na'sF'ith FrancisQu'ry SilverJ'ck

Trackman's Selections—4 9 5

ing that *Mil Song's* last two outings were very poor efforts, with finishes of 3 lengths and 5¾ lengths behind the winner. We hesitated to violate the Time (Speed) Rule. We dropped *Banker Paul* quickly because of the No Win Rule. *Shady Side Bill* with indifferent speed was dropped along with *Mickey Adios,* who had been beaten by *Uncle Smudge* on their last outing. *Atlas N.,* because of Farrington and PP5, was briefly considered, but he was also discarded due to 5, 4½, 3½, 7¾, 11 and 3¾ length losses. *Uncle Smudge* did win last time out, but not in this class of race. He hadn't done well when he was with today's class. *Evening Sky* was right on the edge of the Time (Speed) Rule and had won, but not handily, at Sportsman's. *Mickey Adios* had beaten him three weeks earlier and *Mickey* has already been eliminated. Scratch *Evening Sky*. That leaves just one remaining contender—*Lydia's Girl*. She hadn't raced from PP9 in her last six races and she hadn't done well from PP8. She had also been claimed on her last race and had a new driver-trainer. Best to wait and see. We decided to pass this one and try for the fourth. The chart shows you that the Trackman was right.

THIRD RACE—1 MILE. PACE. Claiming price $6,000-$5,000. Purse $3,200. Mutuel Pool $106,607.

Horse	¼	½	¾	Str	Fin	Driver PP	Odds
Mil Song	7	7	$2^{1\frac{1}{2}}$	$1^{\frac{1}{2}}$	$1^{2\frac{1}{2}}$	C McDermott^{4}	4.40
Shady Side Bill	1	1	1^{5}	2^{5}	2^{1}	J Wolfe^{2}	9.70
Atlas N.	8	8	$8^{1\frac{1}{2}}$	4^{1}	3^{nk}	R Farrington^{5}	5.60
Mickey Adios	5	5	$6^{\frac{1}{2}}$	$3^{\frac{1}{2}}$	4^{2}	D Shetler Jr^{1}	6.70
Evening Sky	9	9	9	6^{1}	5^{5}	K Vander Schaaf^{6}	2.60
Lydia's Girl	4^{0}	4	$4^{\frac{1}{2}}$	7^{h}	6^{h}	A G Shaw^{9}	4.10
Uncle Smudge	2^{0}	2	3^{1}	5^{1}	7^{1}	W Short^{8}	10.90
Hi Brewer	3	3	$5^{\frac{1}{2}}$	8^{2}	8^{6}	E Waszak^{7}	20.10
Banker Paul	6	6	$7^{\frac{1}{2}}$	x9	9	D O'Donohoe^{3}	24.70

Time, :31⅖, 1:03⅕, 1:35⅖, 2:07⅗. Track good.

The fourth race was relatively easy to handicap. Only two horses stood out because of the Class Rule. Both *Whalebone* and *Gene Time* had taken big steps down in class. *Gene Time* had the speed to overcome PP9. *Whalebone's* driver wasn't exactly hot, but maybe PP5 would help. If we had been short on funds we probably wouldn't have kept *Whalebone,* due to speed and driver, but we were flush from the second race, so we Dutched *Whalebone* and *Gene Time* to win.

Whalebone ran out of the money, finishing fourth. *Gene Time* paced a 2:08 1/5, not one of his better times, but good enough to win and pay $20.80, $8.60 and $6.40. One and one-half lengths back was *Sassy Kid,* paying $5.60 and $4.20. *Sampson Frisco* paid $7.40 to show.

Our net on the race, after deducting the $20 win ticket on *Whalebone* and our $20 investment on *Gene Time,* came to $168. Quite a payoff from coupling the two classiest horses in the race. We still can't figure how the crowd let that one get by. Three hundred ninety-two dollars total profit and still six races to go.

The fifth and next race claimed for $7,000, except for *Chancey Tzana,* in for $8,400. Here again we Dutched, selecting *Dr. Farr* and *Chancey Tzana.* Class Rule again made it easy, but this time both horses were moving steadily up in class, moving in leaps compared to their competition. *Chancey Tzana's* times look super-fast, but check again. The 2:03 3/5 and 2:04 2/5 were on a fast mile course at Washington. But her early and later Sportsman's efforts are the fastest past performances we've seen yet today. The No Win Rule is waived because she just raced once this year and finished show. Her driver is tops in the race and PP6 is not going to hurt this flying filly.

Farrington is just too tough to bet against when he's behind a good horse, and *Dr. Farr* has all the necessary credentials: speed, recently claimed back by one of the sports' truly great trainer-drivers, consistent, good pace, this track and has even won from PP8, which is the second worst post position.

This shapes up to a dream Dutch. We're $392 ahead and this is where the action is. We decide to round off the bet to an even $100 each, to win.

Right from the start it's *Dr. Farr* and *Chancey Tzana,* pacing 1 and 2 at the ¼, at the ½, at the ¾. Then *Dr. Farr* loses it in the stretch. *Chancey Tzana* hangs in there and right in front of our eyes beats off a good move by *Adios Mickey* to win by one-half length!

Chancey Tzana pays a handsome $8.60, $5.60 and $3.80; *Adios Mickey* $7.60 and $5.40; *Shadydale* $5.60 to show.

The total bet cost us $200. Deduct that from *Chancey Tzana's* winnings of $430, and we still profit $230 from the race, besides getting our $200 bet back. So we now stand as winners of $522.

The sixth race is a conditioned one mile pace for three-year-olds and up that are non-winners of $8,000. *Gomer Hanover, Grey Fitzgerald, Andy's William* and *Golden Butler* are dropped because of the Time (Speed) Rule, losing by wide margins their last times out. *Hoosier Goose,* although capable of speed, has shown a tendency to break. Note two breaks in the last four races. *Peachiedean* seems to be dropping in form and was beaten by the Trackman's favorite, *Maedean Frisco,* last time out. Granted, it was a close race on a sloppy track, but the condition factor eliminates her. Although *Kimpam* has speed, it hasn't shown on this track. Post Position, Driver, This Track and No Win Rule eliminate *Kimpam. Maedean Frisco* and *Timothy Parker* show about equal speed in recent efforts. *Timothy Parker's* PP5 is good, but his recent breaks cloud his past. Maybe Burright, his driver, can maintain his gait and get a repeat win out of him. *Maedean Frisco* lost badly last time out under the same driver from an almost equal post position. We decide Driver and Post Position will have to rule here. Non-winners of low monies force us to bet conservatively on this one. Our $20 win ticket

Photo courtesy Sportsman's Park, Cicero, Ill.

Watching warm-ups can help select or reject a contender.

ONE MILE PACE **4th RACE (afternoon program)** **Purse $3,600**

Claiming. Claiming price $6,000. Illinois owned preferred. 3-year-olds and up.
Direct Emlen, Whalebone, Gene Time in for $7,200; rest for $6,000.

PLEASE ASK FOR HORSE BY PROGRAM NUMBER

2:04⅖ (Was^1, '70) ($28,024) Driver—JOE MARSH, JR. Trainer, A. Fields (99-20-13-12—.315) Gray-Blue-Red
Sassy Kid B. h (1963), by Kimberly Kid—Soucy Hanover, by Bill Gallon. 1971 7 1 0 2 $2,590
Owner, John Wolff, Paw Paw, Ill. 1970 22 7 2 2 $11,866
5-1 **1**
Mar20-71^{2}Spk⅝ 1 :31^{4}1:06^{3}1:36^{4}2:08^{4}ft 2¼ ▲8 6^0 4^{3½} 3^{1½} 1^2 MarshJJr^7 5000 2:08⅘ SassyKid Even'gSky Samp'nFrisco
Mar13-71^{3}Spk⅝ 1 :31 1:03^{4}1:36^{2}2:06^{4}ft 7½ 9 9 8^{7½} 5^4 3^{2¾} MarshJJr^8 5000 2:07⅖ Rico Bay Disneyland Sassy Kid
Mar 6-71^{5}Spk⅝A 1 :32^{2}1:07^{2}1:38^{4}2:10^{4}sy 12 9 9 9^{6½} 6^9 6^8 MarshJJr^7 6000 2:12⅖ MilSong BethAHal Sp'rkl'gDiam'd
Feb27-71^{10}Spk⅝ 1 :31 1:04^{3}1:34^{2}2:06^{4}ft 10 8 8 5^5 5^{3½} 5^{5½} MarshJJr^8 6500 2:08 W'thyH'n'rN. LadyWood Sen'rMite
Feb19-71^{9}BmlP 1 :32 1:06^{2}1:39^{2}2:13 sy 5¾ x8 8 8 8 8di. DolbeeJ^8 6000 DickCouns'l JayCouns'l Coal'tFritz
Feb13-71^{4}BmlP 1 :31^{3}1:03^{4}1:37 2:10^{2}ft 7¾ 7 5^{0}x7^{5¼} 5^{2¼} 3^2 DolbeeJ^7 6000 2:10⅘ Green'sSt'r Babbl'gBr'ke SassyKid

2:07⅗ (Spk⅝, '70) ($21,311) Driver—JAMES MORRISSEY. Trainer, J. Ozak (17-1-2-7—.261) Green-White-Yellow
Mr. Lake County ⊗ Ch. g (1965), by Nyland Hanover—Orpha Star, by The Widower. 1971 8 0 2 1 $2,601
Owner, James Morrissey, Chicago, Ill. 1970 30 3 4 2 $8,799
5-1 **2**
Mar20-71^{3}Spk⅝A 1 :30 1:02^{4}1:34 2:07 ft 13 3 4 3^4 2^1 2no MorrisseyJ^1 6000 2:07 GypsyG'se Mr.LakeC'y Ch'c'yTz'na
Mar11-71^{10}Spk⅝ 1 :32^{3}1:05^{4}1:39^{3}2:10^{3}gd 9½ 7 7 3^{¾} 1^{1½} 2^h MorrisseyJ^5 5000 2:10⅗ GeneH'v'ns Mr.LakeC'y King'sRaid
Mar 4-71^{9}Spk⅝ 1 :31 1:04^{1}1:34^{4}2:07 ft 12 4^0 1 3^{1½} 3^1 6^{4½} MorrisseyJ^7 5000 2:08 Dr.Farr ChanceyRuben ElD'nyP'g's
Feb26-71^{5}Spk⅝ 1 :31^{2}1:05^{3}1:36^{1}2:09^{2}gd 4½ 2 2 1^{½} 2^{½} 4^3 MorrisseyJ^3 5000 2:10 JohnnyAtom G'stoL'b'll Jilt'rL'b'll
Feb22-71^{10}Spk⅝ 1 :32^{4}1:07 1:40 2:14^{2}sy 13 1 1 1^{1½} 1^{nk} 3^1 MorrisseyJ^6 5000 2:14⅗ Rainm'k'r Flam'gPink Mr.LakeC'ty
Feb 2-71^{6}Aur 1 :32^{2}1:06^{1}1:38^{2}2:09^{4}ft 4¾ 6 6 6^6 6^5 6^5 MorrisseyJ^5 5000 2:10⅘ Gerry'sFirst Y.Bridge EveningSky

2:07⅗ (Brd⅝, '70) ($13,158) Driver-Trainer—MARC GRENIER (44-8-8-5—.321) Red-White-Gold
Direct Emlen Blk. m (1964), by Direct Rhythm—Miss Dorothy Goose, by Goose Bay. 1971 3 2 0 0 $3,160
Owner, J. Nyssen, Santa Barbara, Calif. 1970 31 2 1 12 $6,320
6-1 **3**
Mar16-71^{3}Spk⅝ 1 :31 1:04^{1}1:36^{2}2:07^{4}ft 13 4 4 2^{nk} 1^1 1^{nk} GrenierM^2 6000 2:07⅘ DirectEm'en Petrina FlamingPink
Mar10-71^{5}Spk⅝ 1 :30^{3}1:04 1:36^{4}2:07^{2}ft 19 1^0 2 5^4 6^{12} 5^7 GrenierM^7 6000 2:08⅘ TrueHarbor Y.Bridge FlamingPink
Feb22-71 L.B⅝ 1 :33 1:05^{2}1:38^{4}2:12^{1}gd 30 2 3 2 2^{¾} 1^{nk} RathboneL^4 6000 2:12⅕ Dir'ctEmlen Mickey'sF'ly Sen't'rR.
Nov24-70 D.D⅝ 1 :30^{3}1:03 1:35^{4}2:09^{3}ft 4¼ 1 2 2 5^{3½} 6^{12} StoltzfusA^7 3600 2:12 FranBrown QueenOregon KashGail
Nov14-70 D.D⅝ 1 :30 1:01^{3}1:34^{1}2:06^{1}ft 8½ 2^0 1 2 8^{3¾} 8^{9¼} StoltzfusA^8 3600 2:08 S'n't'rFr'k G'rg'naM'mie Mr.D'gF'e
Nov 5-70 D.D⅝ 1 :30^{3}1:02 1:33^{1}2:05^{2}ft 4¼ 1 2 3 3^2 4^{4½} StoltzfusA^3 4800 2:06⅖ B.T.June Lightn'gTime FriskyStar

2:05 (Det^1, '70) ($17,844) Driver-Trainer—WALTER PAISLEY (68-6-9-10—.211) Green-White
Mary's Pretty Boy Blk. g (1965), by Elby Hanover—Miss Anna Dale, by Mr. Dale. 1971 13 2 1 2 $4,140
Owner, Paisley Enterprises, Inc., Plainfield, Ill. 1970 45 7 4 9 $12,127
8-1 **4**
Mar18-71^{9}Spk⅝ 1 :31 1:04^{4}1:38 2:09^{4}sy 3¾ 6 6 7^{10} 6^{6½} 8^{6½} PaisleyW^8 5000 2:11⅕ R.J.M. Jay Chief Sno Van
Mar 8-71^{5}Spk⅝ 1 :30^{1}1:01^{4}1:32^{2}2:05^{2}ft 5½ 4 4 5^8 5^7 4^{2½} McDermottC^1 c5000 2:06 Dr. Farr Lydia's Girl Rico Bay
Mar 3-71^{3}Spk⅝ 1 :32^{1}1:04^{4}1:36^{1}2:08^{2}ft 8-5 ▲2 2 2^{1½} 1^{½} 1^{1½} SuggI^7 c4000 2:08⅖ Mary'sPr'tyBoy GoMo D'n'yS'pson
Feb25-71^{9}Spk⅝ 1 :32^{4}1:07^{2}1:38^{4}2:10 ft 16 6 1 1^{1½} 1^{2¼} 1^1 SuggI^5 4000 2:10 Mary'sP'tyB'y Justac'h Mona'sNite
Feb16-71 W.R⅝ 1 :30^{4}1:05^{1}1:37^{1}2:08^{4}ft 6¼ 4 7 6 5^{3¾} 4^{5¾} SuggI^4 4000 2:10 Andy'sRod Mr.Flyaway BingoTime
Feb11-71 W.R⅝ 1 :32^{3}1:05^{4}1:37^{1}2:09 ft 8¾ 6 6 6 5^{6¾} 6^9 SuggI^4 4000 2:10⅘ Maud'sCh'mp D'leDeeD'm G'yDir't

2:08⅕ (May, '70) ($10,219) Driver-Trainer—FRED RATHGEBER (37-1-5-5—.147) Green-Gold-Black
Whalebone ⊗ B. g (1967), by Addio Byrd—J's Ann Dean, by Seattle Dean. 1971 6 0 2 0 $2,307
Owner, Ray G. Holtman, Quincy, Ill. 1970 26 3 3 5 $7,378
6-1 **5**
Mar23-71^{9}Spk⅝ 1 :30^{1}1:01^{1}1:33^{3}2:07 ft 6½ 8 7 4^6 5^5 5^5 RathgeberF^5 8400 2:08 B't'eSt'rN. Try'sFirst Sp'kl'gSt'ne
Mar13-71^{4}Spk⅝ 1 :30^{4}1:04^{4}1:37^{1}2:08^{1}ft 4¾ 4^0 3^0 2^2 2^{½} 2^{nk} RathgeberF^5 7200 2:08⅕ Nob'eYates Whalebone KarenGray
Mar 9-71^{10}Spk⅝ 1 :31^{4}1:03^{2}1:38^{1}2:09^{4}gd 8 6 5 4^{1½} 3^1 2^2 RathgeberF^2 7200 2:10⅕ Dr'mBus'r Whaleb'ne Am's'n'sP.J.
Mar 4-71^{4}Spk⅝ 1 :30^{3}1:04^{4}1:36 2:06^{3}ft 19 x9 9 9^{14} 9^{16} 9^{14} RathgeberF^7 8400 2:09⅖ Sen'rMite BuenoT'po Deac'nDarl'n
Feb27-71^{7}Spk⅝ 1 :31 1:06^{2}1:36^{1}2:08^{3}ft 16 8 8 8^{5½} 8^{6½} 8^{12} RathgeberF^8 9000 2:11 Mary'sD'wn Gr'c'nAd's B'noT'mpo
Feb23-71^{5}Spk⅝ 1 :33 1:06^{1}1:38 2:09^{4}gd 16 7 7 6^{5½} 5^5 4^{3¾} RathgeberF^7 9600 2:10⅗ SkyHawk BillDoyle LatimoreHan'r

2:05⅖ (Spk⅝, '70) ($23,499) Driver-Trainer—JAMES HERMAN (12-2-1-0—.213) Blue-White-Gold
Rainmaker ⊗ B. g (1964), by Muncy Hanover—Gray Sky, by Follow Up. 1971 13 3 2 1 $5,998
Owner, Charles J. Daly, Chicago, Ill. 1970 28 3 3 7 $8,285
7-2 **6**
Mar23-71^{9}Spk⅝ 1 :30^{1}1:01^{1}1:33^{3}2:07 ft 6 6^0 5^0 6^8 7^{8½} 6^7 HermanJ^9 7000 2:08⅖ B'tleSt'rN. Try'sFirst Sp'kl'gSt'ne
Mar13-71^{10}Spk⅝ 1 :31^{1}1:03 1:34^{1}2:05^{3}ft 7¾ 1 1 1^{1½} 1^1 1^{1½} HermanJ^1 6000 2:05⅗ Rainmaker TimelyGold Lydia'sGirl
Mar 5-71^{10}Spk⅝ 1 :31^{4}1:04^{4}1:36^{3}2:08 gd 3¼ 2 2 2^{nk} 2^{1½} 2^1 HermanJ^3 5500 2:08⅕ KingGene Rainmaker SirThomas
Feb26-71^{2}Spk⅝ 1 :30^{3}1:05^{1}1:37^{2}2:10^{2}gd 4¾ 4^0 1 1^{1½} 3^{2½} 5^{4¼} HermanJ^9 6000 2:11⅕ McCr'yMissile TimelyG'ld MilesD's
Feb22-71^{10}Spk⅝ 1 :32^{4}1:07 1:40 2:14^{2}sy 7 4 4 4^3 3^{2¼} 1^1 HermanJ^9 5000 2:14⅖ Rainm'k'r Flam'gPink Mr.LakeC'ty
Feb13-71^{10}Aur 1 :31^{4}1:05 1:38 2:10^{2}ft 2 ▲1 1 1^2 1^1 2^1 HermanJ^8 5000 2:10⅗ Profast Rainmaker H'rySc'ryWick

2:07⅖ (Rich, '70) ($19,842) Driver-Trainer—WAYNE SHORT (42-5-2-8—.209) Purple-White
Berkey Ch. h (1965), by Stephen Smith—Chalidale Jewel, by Brother 1971 11 1 3 1 $3,914
Harmony. Owner, Christy Doonan, Reynolds, Ill. 1970 47 7 7 11 $9.604
12-1 **7**
Mar20-71^{3}Spk⅝ 1 :30^{4}1:03^{4}1:35^{4}2:08 ft 26 8 8 9^8 7^6 6^2 ShortW^7 5500 2:08⅖ Gold Mound Go Mo True Harbor
Mar13-71^{4}Spk⅝ 1 :30^{4}1:04^{4}1:37^{1}2:08^{1}ft 19 3 4 5^4 6^{3½} 7^{4¼} ShortW^4 6000 2:09 Nob'eYates Whalebone KarenGray
Mar 9-71^{10}Spk⅝ 1 :31^{4}1:03^{2}1:38^{1}2:09^{4}gd 8 3 3 5^{2½} 8^{10} 9^{14} ShortW^4 6000 2:12⅗ Dr'mBus'r Whaleb'ne Am's'n'sP.J.
Mar 2-71^{7}Spk⅝ 1 :32^{3}1:05^{3}1:37^{3}2:08^{4}ft 10 6 6 7^6 8^9 7^{5¾} ShortW^3 6000 2:10 RexG. McCrearyMissile G'ldMound
Feb27-71^{4}Spk⅝ 1 :29^{3}1:03^{3}1:34^{2}2:09^{1}ft 5½ 6 6 6^9 4^3 1^{¾} WillisJ^5 c5500 2:09⅕ Berkey Gold Mound Sno Van
Feb22-71^{4}Spk⅝ 1 :31^{3}1:06 1:39 2:12^{1}sy 5 4 5 4^{2½} 5^4 7^{7½} WillisJ^2 6000 2:13⅘ WorthyH'rN. McC'ryM'sile SnoVan

2:04⅘ (Haw^1, '70) ($29,059) Driver-Trainer—GEORGE HARDIE (8-0-0-1—.043) Black-Gold
Sampson Frisco Br. h (1960), by Sampson Hanover—Margy Frisco, by Frisco Dale. 1971 4 0 0 1 $544
Owner, Aronowitz, Jr. & Hardie; Albany, N. Y.; Oak Lawn, Ill. 1970 35 1 2 3 $5,455
10-1 **8**
Mar20-71^{2}Spk⅝ 1 :31^{4}1:06^{3}1:36^{4}2:08^{4}ft 19 5 5 7^6 6^5 3^{2¼} HardieG^2 5000 2:09⅕ SassyKid Even'gSky Samp'nFrisco
Mar13-71^{3}Spk⅝ 1 :31 1:03^{4}1:36^{2}2:06^{4}ft 20 7 7 6^6 8^{5¾} 7^6 HardieG^7 5000 2:08 Rico Bay Disneyland Sassy Kid
Mar 6-71^{10}Spk⅝ 1 :31^{1}1:05^{1}1:36^{4}2:12^{2}sl 26 8 8 7^{12} 6^{14} 5^6 HardieG^7 5000 2:13⅗ Profast Hi Brewer Friskim
Feb26-71^{2}Spk⅝ 1 :30^{3}1:05^{1}1:37^{2}2:10^{2}gd 54 6 6 7^{5½} 8^{8½} 7^{6¼} HardieG^1 6000 2:11⅗ McCr'yMissile TimelyG'ld MilesD's
Dec19-70 Hol^1 1 :30^{4}1:03^{3}1:35^{2}2:05^{1}gd 29 5 5 7 8^{15} 8^{13} HardieG^3 5000 2:07⅘ CousinAnn BoyTrust Balmacraig
Dec11-70 Hol^1 1 :31^{1}1:02^{1}1:34 2:04^{4}ft 46 4^0 2 4 10^{7¾}10^{11} HardieG^9 5000 2:06⅘ MiMargarita Lornaway OrbitMan

2:04⅖ (Hol^1, '70) ($11,731) Driver—CONNEL WILLIS. Trainer, W. Feld (82-8-8-15—.213) Red-White-Green
Gene Time Blk. g (1967), by Time to Play—Brenda Frisco, by Bond Hanover. 1971 3 0 0 0 $484
Owner, William & Betty Feld; Chicago Ridge, Ill. 1970 28 2 5 3 $10,592
8-1 **9**
Mar20-71^{3}Spk⅝A 1 :30 1:02^{4}1:34 2:07 ft 13 6^0 1 1^3 1^1 5^{2¾} WillisC^7 7200 2:07⅗ GypsyG'se Mr.LakeC'y Ch'c'yTz'na
Mar 9-71^{6}Spk⅝ 1 :32^{4}1:05^{3}1:38^{4}2:09^{3}gd 9 8^0 7^0 5^{3½} 7^{5½} 7^{9¼} WillisC^8 8400 2:11⅖ RangerRic'd B't'eStarN. Vo't'nL'g
Mar 2-71^{9}Spk⅝ 1 :30^{4}1:04^{4}1:35^{3}2:07^{3}ft 11 4 4 4^6 5^5 4^5 WillisC^1 8400 2:08⅗ CiscoWils'n Idlewh'sV'r S'dyElk't'n
Dec19-70 Hol^1 1 :31^{3}1:04 1:36 2:05^{2}gd 8 1 1 1 2^h 3^{3¼} WilliamsJ^6 7500 2:06 FrancisP.Adios Act'nBoy G'neTime
Dec12-70 Hol^1 1 :30 1:01^{2}1:33^{1}2:03^{2}ft 6¼ 10 10 10 10^9 7^9 WilliamsJ^9 7500 2:05⅕ Fr'cisP.Ad's B'witc'gG'die P'coC'lo
Dec 4-70 Hol^1 1 :30^{4}1:03^{3}1:35^{4}2:05^{2}ft 3¼ ▲2 2 3 3^{2½} 3^4 WilliamsJ^8 7500 2:06⅕ WesternRaider OrbitM'n GeneTime

Trackman's Selections—6 2 1

ONE MILE PACE **5th RACE (afternoon program)** Purse $3,800

Claiming. Claiming price $7,000. 3-year-olds and up. Chancey Tzana in for $8,400; rest for $7,000.

PLEASE ASK FOR HORSE BY PROGRAM NUMBER

8-1 — 1

2:01⅗ (Was1, '70) ($19,038) Driver—EDWARD DORN. Trainer, D. Allen (32-5-5-3—.274) Gold-White
Shadydale ⊗ B. g (1961), by Fallacy—Young Conova, by Young Charles. 1971 4 0 1 0 $1,095
Owner, M. & A. Stables, Inc., Chicago, Ill. 1970 25 5 5 4 $11,219

Mar20-7110Spk⅝ 1 :3011:0231:3442:054ft 8¾ 6 6 65½ 45½ 57 DornE3 7500 2:07⅕ Idlew'lesVictor BuenoT'po Dr.Farr
Mar12-7110Spk⅝ 1 :3031:0231:3432:063ft 17 4 4 32½ 21½ 22 DornE1 6000 2:07 Scotty'sLeader Shadydale RedClay
Mar 6-716Spk⅝A 1 :31 1:0411:36 2:083sy 24 5 5 67 710 718 DornE9 6500 2:12⅕ MilesDares McC'yM'sile BethExp's
Feb24-714Spk⅝ 1 :3031:0241:3512:063ft 12 30 40 610 621x7di. DornE7 7000 OldBlue MajorBreeze HappyOtto
Nov 4-705May 1 :3041:0241:3512:074gd 27 7 8 88 89½ 818 AllenD6 8000 2:11⅘ JestLess BumperGuy Laurinda
Oct 3-706Was1 1 :3041:0311:3632:06 ft 34 10 2 21½ 54½ 911 AllenD9 9000 2:08⅕ HarryT.Hill Tommyjon Laurinda

10-1 — 2

2:05⅘ (Was1, '70) ($10,098) Driver-Trainer—JACK WILSON (9-0-1-0—.062) Blue-Gray-Red
Illini Don ⊗ Ch. h (1964), by Don Adios—Pretty Penny, by Cold Cash. 1971 7 0 0 1 $442
Owner, John M. Wilson, lessee, Fairfield, Ill. 1970 22 3 5 4 $8,084

Mar19-714Spk⅝ 1 :32 1:0521:3632:084gd 23 7 7 86½ 88 88 WilsonJ1 7000 2:10⅖ Dr'mBuster OldBlue Latim'reHan'r
Feb20-719AurA 1 :3421:0841:4222:162sy 4½ 5 6 63½ 52½ 55¾ WilsonJ1 nw65007071 2:17⅗ Bal'rd'sBandit PlutoHal CarryMan
Feb13-718Aur 1 :3311:0611:3822:10 ft 13 4 5 52½ 42 35 WilsonJ1 nw60007071 2:11 Chemung Co Check Illini Don
Feb 6-719Aur 1 :3111:0331:36 2:083ft 48 6 6 75½ 85½ 56½ WilsonJ7 7000 2:10 W'thyH'v'rN. OldBlue Sp'k'gD'm'd
Jan30-717Aur 1 :3231:0721:4012:112ft 25 8 8 87 85½ 74½ WilsonJ7 7000 2:12⅖ OldBlue W'thyH'n'v'rN. M'hic'nG'd
Jan23-715Aur 1 :3111:0441:37 2:081ft 11 4 4 63½ 53 65 WilsonM4 7000 2:09⅕ SaraBeth DutchDir't W'thyH'n'rN.

8-1 — 3

2:05⅘ (Was1, '70) ($23,777) Driver-Trainer—EUGENE WASZAK (35-1-8-3—.184) White-Blue-Gold
Timely Gold B. h (1964), by Guinea Gold—Miss Good Time, by Good Time. 1971 5 0 2 0 $2,038
Owner, J. Genovese & E. Waszak; Franklin Park, Chicago, Ill. 1970 26 3 4 2 $10,484

Mar23-715Spk⅝ 1 :3041:0431:3612:08 ft 9 6 6 74½ 75 63¼ WaszakE3 7000 2:08⅘ VoltanLong LadyWood J'nnyAtom
Mar13-7110Spk⅝ 1 :3111:03 1:3412:053ft 16 3 3 33½ 32 21½ WaszakE2 6000 2:06 Rainmaker TimelyGold Lydia'sGirl
Mar 6-715Spk⅝ 1 33 1:0541:3732:13 sl 14 70 70 67 53 43¾ WaszakE6 6000 2:13⅘ GypsyGoose Andy'sRussell SnoVan
Feb26-712Spk⅝ 1 :3031:0511:3722:102gd 19 5 5 53½ 22 21½ WaszakE2 6000 2:10⅘ McCr'yMissile TimelyG'ld MilesD's
Feb22-714Spk⅝ :3131:06 1:39 2:121sy 22 6 6 54½ 74½ 66 WaszakE3 6000 2:13⅘ WorthyH'rN. McC'ryM'sile SnoVan
Dec 5-7010May 1 :31 1:0231:3512:072ft 9½ 7 7 86½ 76 710 WaszakE6 5000 2:09⅗ BethExpress T.T.Pilot GoldMound

8-1 — 4

2:06⅕ (Was1, '70) ($26,996) Driver-Trainer—JOHN SEARLE (25-3-3-4—.240) Green-Gold
Adios Mickey B. h (1963), by Adios Dream—Lucy F., by Siskiyou. 1971 5 2 0 0 $3,299
Owner, Marjorie Albrecht & J. Searle; Princeton, Ill. 1970 27 1 2 4 $5,460

Mar23-715Spk⅝ 1 :3041:0431:3612:08 ft 7¾ 7 7 64 64 52½ SearleJ4 7000 2:08⅗ VoltanLong LadyWood J'nnyAtom
Mar16-714Spk⅝ 1 :32 1:0531:3712:08 ft 8¾ 8 8 97 87 44 SearleJ7 7000 2:08⅘ MilesDares ErlaB.Win PolarBear
Mar 8-717Spk⅝ 1 :3121:0511:3532:062ft 20 8 8 73½ 74 63¾ SearleJ8 8000 2:07⅕ Rex G. Cisco Wilson Mary'sDawn
Mar 1-714Spk⅝ 1 :32 1:0441:3722:08 ft 6¼ 6 6 64 51 1¾ SearleJ5 5000 2:08 Ad'sMickey AllKeyedUp M'keyAd's
Feb23-711Spk⅝ 1 :3011:04 1:3632:094gd 14 5 5 53 52 12 SearleJ9 3500 2:09⅘ AdiosMick'y Kni'tSc'p Ruthl'sG'ge
Dec15-70 Hol1 1 1/16 :32 1:0431:36 2:142ft 3½ 5 7 9 76½ 42½ SearleJ3 3000 2:14⅘ NuLu TexasFreight BlackAmigo

6-1 — 5

2:04⅘ (Spk⅝, '70) ($21,735) Driver-Trainer—STANLEY BANKS (94-4-10-14—.154) White-Purple
Deacon Darlington B. g (1965), by Adios Express—Sulky Girl, by Judy's Creed. 1971 4 0 1 1 $1,708
Owner, Victor Galanga, New Philadelphia, Ohio. 1970 36 6 4 6 $13,482

Mar23-715Spk⅝ 1 :3041:0431:3612:08 ft 6 5 5 31½ 21 41½ BanksS6 7000 2:08⅖ VoltanLong LadyWood J'nnyAtom
Mar13-715Spk⅝ 1 :3011:0121:34 2:061ft 6¾ 8 70 32 32 53¾ BeckleyW7 c7000 2:07 WillowPrince Try'sFirst MissGift
Mar 4-714Spk⅝ 1 :3031:0441:36 2:063ft 13 40 4 2½ 2½ 33 BeckleyW9 7000 2:07⅕ Sen'rMite BuenoT'po Deac'nDarl'n
Feb23-719Spk⅝ 1 :3121:0531:3822:112gd 3½ 4 4 2¾ 1½ 2nk BeckleyW2 5000 2:11⅖ Tartar DeaconDarl't'n GeneHavens
Dec26-709BmlP 1 :32 1:0431:3642:092ft 4 x8 7 x85¼ 8 8di. BeckleyW7 6000 WillCreed BattleLine JerilynnAdio
Dec19-707BmlP 1 :3231:0631:3722:101ft9-5 ▲4 40 1no 11 2h MilburnP3 6000 2:10⅕ Jeril'nAdio D'c'nD'l'gt'n R'y'lR'ck

5-1 — 6

2:06 (Spk⅝, '70) ($8,417) Driver—DWAYNE PLETCHER. Trainer, G. Kidwell (60-11-8-5—.285) White-Black
Chancey Tzana B. f (1967), by Painter—Miss Carol, by High Volo. 1971 1 0 0 1 $432
Owner, Chancey Acres & G. Kidwell; Kenosha, Wis.; Marengo, Ill. 1970 21 3 1 4 $8,207

Mar20-713Spk⅝A 1 :30 1:0241:34 2:07 ft 3 ▲2 3 66½ 52 3¾ KidwellG3 7200 2:07⅕ GypsyG'se Mr.LakeC'y Ch'c'yTz'na
Aug 7-704Was1 1 :3021:0211:3342:04 ft 9½ 1 3 32½ 32½ 31½ KidwellG8 fmnw400070 2:04⅗ J'sticeSlo MissL'yFar'l Ch'ceyTz'a
Jly 28-706Was1 1 :3031:0221:33 2:024ft 21 1 1 11¼ 31½ 54 Kidw'lG2 fmnw60006970 2:03⅗ HeleneHano'r BabyTears DuMeans
Jly 18-704Spk⅝ 1 :31 1:0341:3442:041ft 30 7 7 42 41¼ 53¼ KidwellG6 n4R 2:04⅗ GoodLegend Colorama H.A.Knight
Jly 11-704Spk⅝ 1 :3031:03 1:34 2:04 ft 28 7 8ix86½ 54 57 KidwellG5 n4R 2:05⅖ Edge'dBr't SurfBoard GoodLeg'nd
Jly 3-705Spk⅝ 1 :3041:0321:3332:041ft 19 3 4 53½ 58 57¼ Kidw'llG1 nw18002-6970 2:05⅘ M'n'naHill W't'n'sJ'y M'j'ticB'leG.

8-1 — 7

2:04⅘ (Haw1, '70) ($39,213) Driver—PHILIP MILBURN. Trainer, J. Cisna (84-10-16-4—.241) Blue-Gold
John L. Purdue Br. g (1965), by Purdue Hal—Sissy C., by Lieut. Commander. 1971 1 0 0 0 (—)
Owner, Royal-Wyn Stable, Springfield, Ill. 1970 21 1 2 1 $5,470

Mar17-716Spk⅝ 1 :3041:04 1:3532:061ft 28 2 3 41½ 85½ 86¼ MilburnP2 8000 2:07⅖ SissySassy Pr'c'sL'd R'ng'rRich'rd
Dec26-70 BmlP 1 :3041:0241:35 2:09 ft 3¾ 8 8 715 712 715 MilburnP8 nw500070 2:12 AlbertLee St'dyPr'ce Qu'n ofAmb'y
Dec12-705BmlP 1 :3321:0441:3642:093ft 2½ ▲6 6 74½ 62½ 41¾ MilburnP5 nw650070 2:10 **Biggs** Robert David Fonda Dares
Dec 7-706May 1 :30 1:02 1:3332:051ft 14 1 2 21½ 31½ 33 MilburnP4 nw600070 2:05⅘ Rod'sF'ler CarryMan JohnL.P'due
Dec 2-709May 1 :3141:0411:3532:071ft 4¼ 1 1 2h 42½ 64½ WillisC5 nw550070 2:08⅕ West'rn'sJ'k Li't'gMiss Sams'nCr'd
Nov19-708May 1 :3031:0341:36 2:071ft 10 50 30 68¼ 712 720 WillisN8 nw600070 2:11⅕ StartingGate VoltanLong Rozella

5-2 — 8

2:05⅖ (Spk⅝, '71) ($4,551) Driver-Trainer—ROBERT FARRINGTON (152-21-21-24—.268) Red-Gray
Dr. Farr Blk. g (1966), by Tar Lad Hill—Bethel's Belle, by Lieut. 1971 5 4 0 1 $5,768
Commander. Owner, Farrington Stables, Inc., Richwood, Ohio. 1970 29 1 2 4 $4,551

Mar20-7110Spk⅝ 1 :3011:0231:3442:054ft 2¼ ▲10 1 21½ 22 33½ FarringtonR7 7500 2:06⅗ Idlew'lesVictor BuenoT'po Dr.Farr
Mar 8-715Spk⅝ 1 :3011:0141:3222:052ft 2½ ▲1 1 11¼ 11½ 1½ GuerraH5 c5000 2:05⅖ Dr. Farr. Lydia's Girl Rico Bay
Mar 4-719Spk⅝ 1 :31 1:0411:3442:07 ft 11 10 3 2½ 11 11½ GuerraH8 5000 2:07 Dr.Farr ChanceyRuben ElD'nyP'g's
Feb25-7110Spk⅝ 1 :3041:0321:3522:072ft 2¼ 2 2 21½ 1h 13 PaisleyW4 c3500 2:07⅖ Dr. Farr Pat's Dee Air Venture
Feb20-7110BmlP 1 :3111:0341:3712:103ft 8-5 ▲7 7 63 52 11¼ FarringtonR4 2500 2:10⅗ Dr.Farr PowerCrater BlackBeard
Dec19-70 Hol1 6 f :29 1:002 1:324gd 7¼ 5 4 4 22½ 21 FarringtonR10 2000 1:33 GamePick Dr.Farr GeneHughes

10-1 — 9

2:04⅗ (Hol1, '70) ($85,386) Driver-Trainer—JOHN WOLFE (37-1-2-9—.138) Green-White-Brown
‡Bomber Bay Br. h (1961), by Bomber Down—Rose Anna, by Frisco Dale. 1971 5 0 0 0 $380
Owner, John Wolfe, Whiting, Ind. 1970 31 2 3 4 $10,459

Mar20-7110Spk⅝ 1 :3011:0231:3442:054ft 24 8 8 88½ 69½ 69 WolfeJ9 7500 2:07⅗ Idlew'lesVictor BuenoT'po Dr.Farr
Mar12-717Spk⅝ 1 :3011:0111:3412:06 ft 27 5 5 53¼ 63 75¼ WolfeJ7 8500 2:07 Mary'sDawn M'htyLoyal W'yH'rN.
Mar 4-714Spk⅝ 1 :3031:0441:36 2:063ft 16 5 5 55½ 55 55 WallW3 c7000 2:07⅗ Sen'rMite BuenoT'po Deac'nDarl'n
Feb27-717Spk⅝A 1 :3121:07 1:3732:09 ft 12 2 3 21½ 33½ 56½ WallW3 7500 2:10⅘ ToothPick Mick'ySup'me H'pyOtto
Feb22-715Spk⅝ 1 :33 1:0931:4212:143sy 14 8 5ix912 813 713 PaisleyW8 7500 2:17⅕ DutchDi'ct Mic'ySup'e Mary'sD'wn
Dec19-70 Hol1 1 :31 1:0141:33 2:033gd 39 7 7 7 65¾ 43½ WallW6 8500 2:04⅕ Sc'tysC'lt S'ntEst'pheA. Fr'ghtM't

Trackman's Selections—8 6 5

ONE MILE PACE 6th RACE (afternoon program) Purse $3,600

Conditioned. Non-winners of $8,000 in 1970-1971. 3-year-olds and up.

PLEASE ASK FOR HORSE BY PROGRAM NUMBER

6-1 1
2:07⅘ (Spk⅝, '71) ($2,933) Driver—WALTER PAISLEY. Trainer, E. Calvert (68-6-9-10—.211) Green-White
Peachiedean B. f (1967), by Knox Hanover—Solicitor's Peach, by Solicitor. 1971 13 3 2 2 $5,308
Owner, Carunchia & Gunsallus; Kendallville, Ind. 1970 24 2 5 4 $2,418
Mar15-71³Spk⅝ 1 :31²1:07²1:39 2:11³sy 4¼ 4 4 6⁴ 5²½ 3nk Bur'tH³ fmnw12000⁷⁰⁷¹ 2:11⅗ M'deanFr'co Kits'yH'v'r P'ch'dean
Mar10-71⁷Spk⅝ 1 :32¹1:05¹1:36⁴2:07¹ft 6¼ 4 4 4³½ 3¹½ 2² BurrightH⁴ nw1500²L 2:07⅗ JimBl'ks'ne Peachied'n ForbesTime
Mar 3-71⁴Spk⅝ 1 :32⁴1:05³1:36²2:07⁴ft 8¾ 2 2 3² 3¹ 1¾ BurrightH² fmnw6000 2:07⅘ Peachiedean RipplingWave TeeToo
Feb25-71⁵Spk⅝ 1 :33¹1:07 1:38²2:09⁴ft 30 2 2 2² 2¹½ 2¹ BurrightH⁶ n3R 2:10 PeterBrown Peachied'n Ins'ntLob'l
Feb18-71⁵BmlP 1 :31¹1:04 1:37²2:08³ft 22 1 1 3¹½ 5²½ 7⁸¾ HarryJ⁸ nw3250⁷⁰⁷¹ 2:10⅖ Gene Havens Rare Event Joe Byrd
Feb12-71⁷BmlP 1 :34¹1:09 1:43¹2:15⁴gd 3½ 3 3 3¹ 3¹½ 1¹ ParkerRo¹ nw400² 2:15⅘ Peachiedean GeneHavens S'nicDel

8-1 2
2:07⅖ (Hol¹, '70) ($10,314) Driver-Trainer—DEL CRONK (24-1-1-3—.106) Green-Gray
Gomer Hanover ⊗ Br. h (1966), by Gamecock—Golden Flame, by Hoot Mon. 1971 11 0 3 1 $2,674
Owner, Menlo Stable, El Monte, Calif. 1970 17 3 0 1 $5,274
Mar13-71⁶Spk⅝ 1 :29⁴1:02²1:34 2:05 ft 36 6 8⁰ 9⁷½ 8⁸ 8⁶¾ CronkD¹ nw9000⁷⁰ 2:05⅖ Swift Duke Doctor C. Noble Scot
Mar 6-71⁸Spk⅝A 1 :30 1:03 1:34⁴2:07⁴sy 36 7 7 9¹⁷ 9²¹ 9¹⁹ CronkD⁸ nw10000⁷⁰⁷¹ 2:11⅗ NobleScot MonasByrd ChuckFarr
Feb27-71⁶Spk⅝A 1 :30 1:05⁴1:37³2:10¹ft 6½ 7x 7 7 7 7di. CronkD³ nw1400⁸ Cecelia MightyLoyal BillyClipper
Feb15-71 B.M¹ 1 :30³1:02³1:33²2:03⁴ft 8½ 7 8 8 5⁸ 5⁶¾ CartnalK⁵ Cond 2:05⅕ FargoRich'd Top'lAdios Nev'daJ'ck
Feb11-71 B.M¹ 1 :32³1:04²1:35 2:04¹ft 7 5 4 2 2¹ 5²½ CronkD⁵ Cond 2:04⅘ P't'rP'kins E'sterL'cky L'dyAb'd's
Feb 4-71 B.M¹ 1 :34³1:07³1:39 2:07²ft 5½ 2 2 2 2¹½ 2h CronkD² Cond 2:07⅖ S'ndraK'yA. Gom'rH'v'r C'sc'deC'f

8-1 3
2:05⅕ (Haw¹, '70) ($10,575) Driver-Trainer—JOHN FITZGERALD (5-1-1-0—.311) Green-Gray-Black
Grey Fitzgerald Gr. m (1965), by Blue Steel—June Mite, by Volomite. 1970 33 2 2 4 $7,560
Owner, Joseph F. Fitzgerald, Valparaiso, Ind. 1969 20 4 4 1 $3,015
Dec18-70⁸BmlP 1 :32²1:07²1:38⁴2:10⁴ft 14 6 7 8⁴¾ 8⁴¾ 8⁶½ FitzgeraldJ⁸ nw7500⁷⁰ 2:12⅕ ArmbroH'z'rd Liv'niaBoy F'rv'letta
Dec 7-70⁸May 1 :32¹1:04²1:38 2:09¹ft 31 3 4 8⁴½ 6⁴½ 5³½ FitzgeraldJ⁶ nw7000⁷⁰ 2:10 VoltanLong FondaDares C'ntryBoy
Nov27-70⁹May 1 :31⁴1:05¹1:40²2:14 sy 26 7 7⁰ 6⁵½ 6⁸ 6¹² FitzgeraldJ⁶ nw8000⁷⁰ 2:16⅘ RosedaleAd's St't'gGate B'lyClip'r
Nov 6-70⁸May 1 :31⁴1:02³1:34²2:06³ft 6 5 5 6³½ 6⁵ 6³½ Fitzg'ldJ² fmnw7600⁷⁰ 2:07⅖ L'tleM'sE'n W'd'eAn'aT'x Em'aG'y
Oct30-70⁹May 1 :31 1:03¹1:33⁴2:06 ft 5¾ 4 4 8⁸ 8⁶ 8⁶¼ FitzgeraldJ¹ nw8000⁷⁰ 2:07⅕ TimmieWin ForbesTime Farmont
Oct 2-70¹⁰Was¹ 1 :29 1:01 1:34 2:03⁴ft 9¾ 4 4 4⁵ 4³½ 3³ FitzgeraldJ³ nw6000⁷⁰ 2:04⅖ BabyT'rs GunTagF'bes GreyFitz'd

6-1 4
2:07⅖ sl (B.M¹, '71) ($4,514) Driver-Trainer—MARC GRENIER (44-8-8-5—.321) Red-White-Gold
Andy's William ⊗ Br. g (1966), by Worthy Mon—Good Sister, by Scottish Pence. 1971 10 2 1 2 $3,988
Owner, A. B. Hanson, Santa Maria, Calif. 1970 19 2 2 3 $3,524
Mar19-71¹⁰Spk⅝ 1 :30⁴1:02⁴1:34²2:08 gd 3 1 3 3² 6⁴ 9⁸¼ GrenierM³ nw1400²L 2:09⅗ Dellv'leF'cy Light'gMiss Garv'kH'r
Mar13-71⁶Spk⅝ 1 :29⁴1:02²1:34 2:05 ft 20 2 4 5²½ 5³½ 5³ GrenierM⁴ nw9000⁷⁰ 2:05⅗ Swift Duke Doctor C. Noble Scot
Mar 6-71⁶Spk⅝ 1 :30⁴1:05²1:37⁴2:11¹sl 2½ ▲2 2 2¹ 1¹ 1¹ GrenierM⁴ nw1450L 2:11⅕ Andy'sWil'm Ham'dW'y Fr'coClem
Feb27-71⁴Spk⅝A 1 :31²1:04 1:34³2:08⁴ft 3¾ 2 4⁰ 2½im5⁸ 6⁶¾ GrenierM² nw1400L 2:10⅕ LovinLuLu T'klaAd'sB. FriscoClem
Feb10-71 B.M¹ 1 :31¹1:02³1:32³2:03³ft 25 2 1 6 7¹¹ 8¹⁴ GrenierM⁸ nw6000⁷⁰⁷¹ 2:06⅖ F'rgoRich'rd F'stSign'l FinalCount
Feb 4-71 B.M¹ 1 :34³1:07⁴1:39 2:07¹ft 2¾ x7 5 5 7¹⁸ 7¹⁷ GrenierM⁵ nw6000⁷⁰⁷¹ 2:10⅘ S'draK'yA. G'm'rH'n'v'r C'sc'deC'f

6-1 5
2:05⅗ (Was¹, '70) ($5,848) Driver—HARRY BURRIGHT. Trainer, B. Ranquist (84-17-16-9—.344) Blue-Gold
Timothy Parker Blk. g (1967), by Parker Byrd—Miss Harwood, by Lieut. 1971 3 1 0 0 $1,956
Commander. Owner, Robert Ranquist Jr., Palos Heights, Ill. 1970 10 3 3 1 $5,848
Mar19-71⁶Spk⅝ 1 :31²1:04³1:35⁴2:08¹gd 8½ 5 6 7³ 5¹ 1h BurrightH² nw7000⁷⁰⁷¹ 2:08⅕ Tim'yP'k'r Mel'yWar'r Fre'n'sC'ce
Mar15-71⁵Spk⅝ 1 :31²1:05⁴1:36¹2:09²sy 4¼ x9 9 9¹⁷ 9¹⁷ 9²⁰ BlevinsJ¹ nw15000⁷⁰ 2:13⅖ Rosed'leCh'f R'y'lC'val'r Sist'rD'll
Mar 8-71⁶Spk⅝ 1 :32 1:05 1:36 2:07⁴ft 5¾ 6 7 8⁵ 5¹ 4¹ BlevinsJ³ nw6000⁷⁰⁷¹ 2:08 M'resF'xyG't J.C.St'my Ch'fR'time
Dec19-70⁵BmlP 1 :32 1:04³1:36³2:08⁴ft 2¾ x2⁰ 8 x8²³ 8¹⁷ 8²³ RanquistB³ nw5000⁷⁰ 2:13⅖ GoodPolicy LibertyF'ld St'dyPrince
Dec12-70⁶Aur 1 :32³1:05³1:38²2:10⁴sl 6-5 ▲2 2 2h 1½ 2½ BlevinsJ² op1800 2:11 Bock Timothy Parker Great Grant
Nov30-70⁹May 1 :32 1:02⁴1:34⁴2:06²ft 2¾ 3 3 3² 2²¼ 2³ BlevinsJ¹ nw5000⁷⁰ 2:07 CarryMan Tim'yPark'r Smok'gH'se

5-1 6
2:04⅘ (Cka¾, '70) ($18,095) Driver-Trainer—AUBREY PETTY (28-3-6-5—.286) Maroon-Black
Hoosier Goose Blk. g (1964), by Goose Win—Congressional Ann, by Congressional. 1971 4 0 0 1 $829
Owner, Ralph R. Sprinkle, Linton, Ind. 1970 28 2 3 2 $6,889
Mar18-71⁵Spk⅝ 1 :31⁴1:04³1:37³2:09¹sy 12 7 7⁰ 8⁴½ 9¹²x9¹⁶ PettyA⁹ nw1400⁸ 2:12⅖ TimmieWin AdiosSenor Paint'rTi'e
Mar13-71⁵Spk⅝A 1 :30⁴1:02²1:34¹2:05 ft 4½ 6 6 5³½ 3¹½ 4² PettyA³ nw12500⁷⁰⁷¹ 2:05⅖ Dick Duane Arturo Mai Tai
Mar 2-71⁶Spk⅝ 1 :32¹1:03⁴1:34⁴2:06 ft 15 7 7 6⁴½ 5³½ 5¹¾ Bur'ghtH⁶ nw12000⁷⁰⁷¹ 2:06⅖ DillerVolo Colorama EasyFaith
Feb24-71⁶Spk⅝ 1 :32¹1:05²1:36²2:08 ft 3½ 1 1 1¹½ 1½ x2¹† FalknerJ² nw1400⁸ 2:08⅕ Ch'k'teT'to Casc'eCh'f Hoos'rGoose
†Disqualified and placed third for lapped-on break at the wire.
Sep29-70⁹Was¹ 1 :29⁴1:01 1:34²2:04 ft 4¾ 4 4 4³ 3¹½ 4¹½ PettyA² 9000 2:04⅕ PeakTime Mic'ySup'me St'yB'keN.

7-2 7
2:05 (F.P¹, '70) ($11,680) Driver—CONNEL WILLIS. Trainer, W. Feld (82-8-8-15—.213) Red-White-Green
Maedean Frisco ⊗ Blk. m (1964), by Frisco's Choice—Lassie Dean, by Seattle Dean. 1971 7 4 1 0 $3,825
Owner, William & Betty Feld; Chicago Ridge, Ill. 1970 21 5 3 1 $2,532
Mar20-71⁵Spk⅝ 1 :31²1:04³1:36¹2:07 ft 2¾ 1 2 4²½ 7¹² 7¹¹ WillisC³ nw10000⁷⁰⁷¹ 2:09⅕ Rip'gWave Den'nDick'y Od'teAdios
Mar15-71³Spk⅝ 1 :31²1:07²1:39 2:11³sy 3¼ 2 2 3² 3¹½ 1nk WillisC¹ fmnw12000⁷⁰⁷¹ 2:11⅗ M'deanFr'co Kits'yH'v'r P'ch'dean
Mar 6-71 F.P¹ 1 :30²1:04⁴1:36 2:07 ft 4¾ 2 3 3 1nk 1no CollarC² w3000 2:07 Maed'nFrisco Ad'sJulia Inst'tC'dit
Feb26-71 F.P¹ 1 :33 1:06⁴1:39 2:10²gd 2½ ▲1 2 2 1½ 1³¾ HofstraR¹ nw3600⁷⁰⁷¹ 2:10⅖ M'deanFrisco Popl'rD'sy L'cyBird
Feb20-71 F.P¹ 5 f :29⁴1:01³ 1:16²gd 3½ 2 1 1 2nk 2³¾ HofstraR² w3000 1:17⅕ L'tleShyst'r M'd'nF'co L'tleB'eA's
Feb16-71 F.P¹ 1 :31³1:05²1:37⁴2:09¹ft 2½ 2 3 3 1½ 1¹ HofstraR² Cond 2:09⅕ MaedeanFrisco Printeena BeDirect

8-1 8
2:04⅖ (PmP⅝, '70) ($13,226) Driver-Trainer—STANLEY BANKS (94-4-10-14—.154) White-Purple
Golden Butler B. h (1966), by Adios Butler—Golden Blade, by Gene Abbe. 1971 2 0 0 0 $340
Owner, Victor Ga'anga, New Philadelphia, Ohio 1970 29 2 1 1 $6,839
Mar20-71⁴Spk⅝ 1 :30²1:03¹1:35⁴2:07³ft 17 6 6 7⁴½ 6⁵ 5⁴½ BanksS³ nw1400⁸ 2:08⅖ MaiTai DonaldByrd CrystalKlata
Mar15-71⁵Spk⅝ 1 :31²1:05⁴1:36¹2:09²sy 36 5 8 8⁸½ 8⁷ 5⁹½ BanksS² nw15000⁷⁰ 2:11⅖ Rosed'leCh'f R'y'lC'val'r Sist'rD'll
Dec 4-70⁹May 1 :32 1:04²1:37 2:08 ft 16 7 8 8¹¹ 8¹⁴ 8²² RoseboomW³ nw8000⁷⁰ 2:12⅖ JetBro Wil'wBr'kSc't MoeWest'rn
Nov24-70⁸May 1 :30³1:02¹1:33⁴2:05²ft 20 8 8 8¹¹ 7¹⁴ 7¹⁴ AckermanJ⁸ nw7500⁷⁰ 2:08⅕ Diam'dJoeN. J.J.Byrd J'nnyFoster
Nov17-70⁶May 1 :30 1:00²1:32¹2:04⁴ft 14 7 8 7³½ 6³ 4⁴½ AckermanJ⁶ nw7500⁷⁰ 2:05⅗ Gay Pam Conniption Moe Western
Nov13-70 May 1 :31 1:04²1:36²2:08²ft N.B. 4⁰ 4⁰ 2¹½ 2¹ 2no ClicknerC⁵ Qua 2:08⅖ JohnL.Purdue GoldenB'tl'r S'syKid

12-1 9
2:08⅕ (Nfld, '70) ($18,373) Driver-Trainer—DESMOND O'DONOHOE (13-0-1-0—.043) Green-White
Kimpam Ch. m (1964), by Irish—Meadow Wick, by Meadow Gold. 1971 1 0 0 0 (—)
Owner, Desmond O'Donohoe, Crete, Ill. 1970 12 1 2 1 $2,342
Mar20-71⁵Spk⅝ 1 :31²1:04³1:36¹2:07 ft 19 5 5 6⁴½ 8¹² 8¹¹ O'Don'eD² nw10000⁷⁰⁷¹ 2:09⅕ Rip'gWave Den'nDick'y Od'teAdios
Oct28-70⁶May 1 :31²1:05²1:38 2:10⁴gd 2½ ▲3 4 3¹½ 3¹ 2½ O'DonohoeD¹ nw3000⁷⁰ 2:11 Capt'nThorpe Kimpam Gr't'nGr't'n
Oct 5-70⁹Was¹ 1 :30³1:02¹1:34²2:06²ft 7½ 6⁰ 4⁰ 5⁵½ 7¹½ 6³ O'DonohoeD⁵ nw4000⁷⁰ 2:07 VoltanL'g Ros'd'leAdios Ch'pyTime
Sep26-70²Was¹ 1 :31 1:03³1:35⁴2:05⁴ft 4 3 2⁰ 1½ 1h 5⁴ O'DonohoeD⁴ nw4000⁷⁰ 2:06⅗ R'ngeL'ss R's'd'leAd's C'mp'sM't's
Sep19-70²Was¹ 1 :30¹1:01²1:32⁴2:03³ft 19 4 4 3¹½ 2²½ 2½ O'DonohoeD¹ nw4000⁷⁰ 2:03⅘ GunTagF'rbes Kimpam M'l'dyW'r'r
Sep10-70⁷Was¹ 1 :30 1:02⁴1:34²2:04¹ft 52 8 8 8⁷½ 8⁸ 5⁷¾ O'DonohoeD⁸ nw4000⁷⁰ 2:05⅘ Tommyjon GunTagForb's FreePass

Trackman's Selections—7 6 5

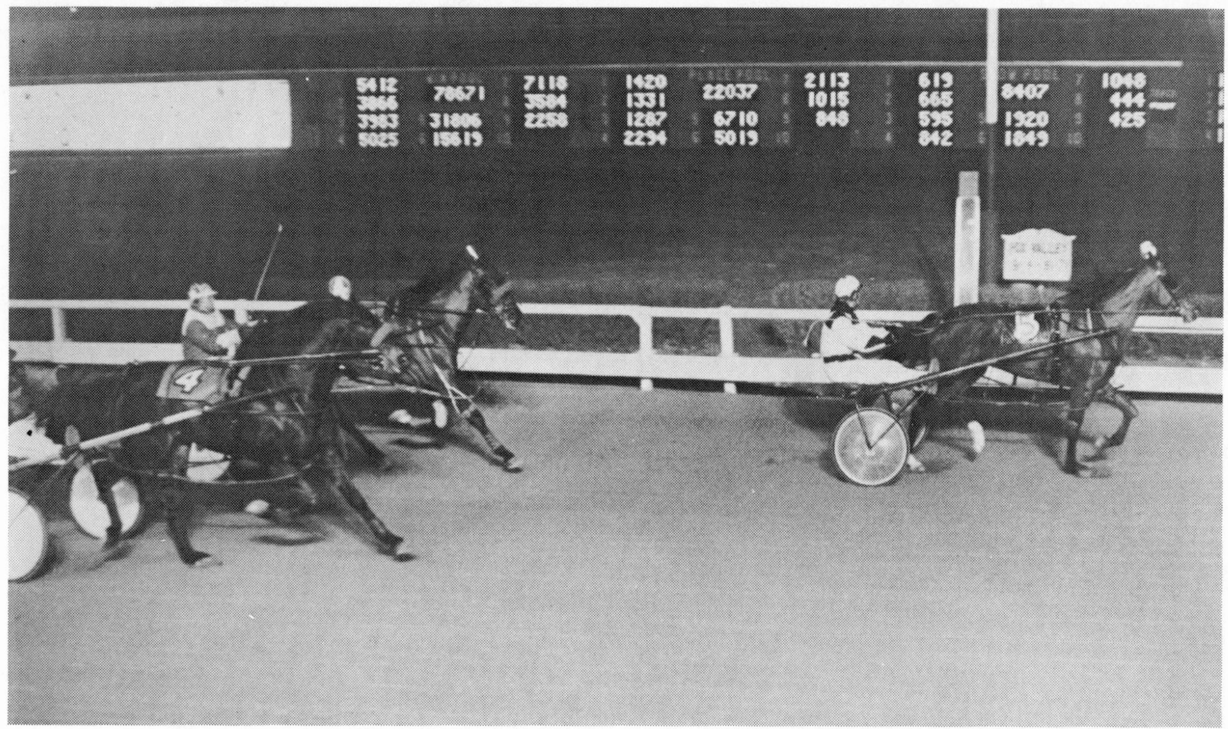

Photo courtesy Sportsman's Park, Cicero, Ill.

A horse that has not won a race cannot be expected to do what he has never done before. Conversely, winning horses and drivers tend to keep on winning.

on *Timothy Parker* pays $6.40, $4.60 and $3.60. The place horse *Golden Butler* pays $9.60 and $7.60, *Hoosier Goose's* show price is $4.20. Our profit is $44 after deducting the ticket price. Four winnings in four tries; we can hardly believe it. But the system is working and we're not about to complain with $566 in profits in our pockets.

Race number seven was an $8,000 claiming for three-year-olds and up. *Spen Filter* is in for $9,600.

Prior to coming to the track we had scratched *Spen Filter,* feeling he was trying to run in overly rich company. The program confirmed this and showed that his driver had the poorest record in the race. The No Win Rule dropped number 6, *Adam Ike,* and even though he was coming down slightly in class, he had put forth no recent efforts, losing his last races by 9¼, 3½, 11, 4¾, 15 and 13 lengths, respectively. *Cascade Chief* was also being soundly trounced and seemed way of his class.

Cisco Wilson had been the beaten favorite the last two times out and we felt his condition would continue to worsen. *Senator Mite* looked about the same as *Cisco Wilson,* besides having the worst post position.

Worthy Hanover N. had lost to the Trackman's favorite just a week ago and gave us no reason to believe it wouldn't happen again, though he was the biggest money winning horse in the race, with the top driver.

We dropped *Co Check* with the Time (Speed) Rule. Last two efforts were not impressive. Paisley's win with him wasn't exactly a record breaker on a slow track. *Miles Dares* seemed to be rounding into form, but his 2:08 on a fast Sportsman's track would not put him in front of *Impressive Time.*

Impressive Time seemed to be the bet, with good recent speed, good driver and post position. And for once, the crowd agreed with us. He was definitely the favorite, with even money odds. Normally we would leave this one alone considering the percentage of return versus the risk involved. But we were well ahead for the day and plunged on a $20 winning ticket.

Well, it had to stop sometime; *Impressive Time* almost made it—but not quite. *Senator Mite* paid $3.20 and $2.60, but not to us. The show horse was number 7, *Worthy Hanover N.,* paying $3.

Now we were $502 ahead, having just lost $20. It had been close and we felt that we had picked the best horse in the race. You can't win 'em all.

It was drink time again, so we ordered another

Happy Horse!

Joe E. Lewis tells about the fellow who, "got a handler to give a horse a big shot of bourbon one day just before it was going to race. The horse was a dog, at 20 to 1 the fellow figured to make a killing. Unfortunately, the horse didn't win, but he was the happiest nag on the track."

ONE MILE PACE **7th RACE (afternoon program)** **Purse $4,200**

Claiming. Claiming price $8,000. 3-year-olds and up. Spen Filter in for $9,600; rest for $8,000.

PLEASE ASK FOR HORSE BY PROGRAM NUMBER

7-2 1
2:04⅕ (Spk⅝, '70) ($13,699) Driver-Trainer—AUBREY PETTY (28-3-6-5—.286) **Maroon-Black**
Impressive Time B. h (1966), by Right Time—Rosemary Brook, by Miller Brook. 1971 5 1 0 2 $3,532
Owner, Vornado Stables, Niles, Ill. 1970 11 2 4 2 $9,657
Mar19-715Spk⅝ 1 :3141:0431:3532:074gd3-5 *6 6 42 21¼ 11 PettyA6 8500 2:07⅘ Imp'veTime Q'n'sC's'rt W'thyH'rN.
Mar13-718Spk⅝A 1 :3031:0221:33 2:034ft 3 6 6 44½ 41½ 31¾ PettyA5 10000 2:04⅕ Auth'ntic WillCreed Impr'siveTime
Mar 6-717Spk⅝ 1 :3221:0731:38 2:102sl 3½ 5 5 56 47½ 34 WillisC4 10000 2:11⅕ SkyHawk PoppaRex Impr'siveTime
Mar 1-719Spk⅝ 1 :3041:0321:3512:051ft 3½ 2 2 55¾ 78 711 MilburnP1 12000 2:07⅖ TinaKnox SpeederPick Fr'tyFr'ght
Feb24-719Spk⅝ 1 :3221:04 1:3632:071ft 3¼ 2 4 32 31½ 42 BurrightH6 12000 2:07⅗ Len'eCreed MissC'tTime ClearBr'k
Jly 6-708Spk⅝ 1 :3031:0231:33 2:032ft 3¾ 9 9 96 53 2no PettyA9 14400 2:03⅖ Sp'derPick Impr'siveT'e Pet'rG'se

4-1 2
2:05 (Haw1, '70) ($73,185) Driver-Trainer—PHILIP MILBURN (84-10-16-4—.241) **Blue-Gold**
Cisco Wilson ⊗ B. h (1961), by Ed Wilson—Kissimee, by The King Direct. 1971 4 2 1 0 $4,830
Owner, Jack G. Zuzak, Akron, Ohio. 1970 34 5 7 5 $18,604
Mar17-716Spk⅝ 1 :3041:04 1:3532:061ft 8-5 *6 9 84½ 74½ 52½ FarringtonR4 c8000 2:06⅘ SissySassy Pr'c'sL'd R'ng'rRich'rd
Mar 8-717Spk⅝ 1 :3121:0511:3532:062ft 9-5 *4 4 41½ 21 21 FarringtonR3 8000 2:06⅗ Rex G. Cisco Wilson Mary'sDawn
Mar 2-719Spk⅝ 1 :3041:0441:3532:073ft 1 *6 6 58 33½ 11 FarringtonR3 7000 2:07⅗ CiscoWils'n Idlewh'sV'r S'dyElk't'n
Feb25-714Spk⅝ 1 :30 1:0321:3512:062ft 9-5 *4 4 41½ 2½ 1no BanksS1 6000 2:06⅖ CiscoWil'n Queen'sRec't KingSelka
Dec21-70 Hol1 1 :3211:0441:37 2:08 sl 9-5 *3 3 5 2¾ 1¾ FarringtonR2 5000 2:08 CiscoWilson ElD'yP'g's's East'rL'y
Dec17-70 Hol1 1 :30 1:0221:33 2:023ft 15 4 4 5 22 22¼ FarringtonR1 5000 2:03 ValsPl'b'y CiscoWils'n ElD'yP'g's's

8-1 3
2:05⅗ (Haw1, '70 ($10,255) Driver—WALTER PAISLEY. Trainer, W. Klopp (68-6-9-10—.211) **Green-White**
Co Check ⊗ B. g (1966), by Check Up—Co Princess, by Bay Prince. 1971 9 1 2 1 $2,980
Owner, William Klopp, Batavia, Ill. 1970 32 2 4 4 $8,276
Mar 8-717Spk⅝ 1 :3121:0511:3532:062ft 6 1 1 1nk 11 52¾ MilburnP1 8000 2:07 Rex G. Cisco Wilson Mary'sDawn
Mar 2-716Spk⅝ 1 :3211:0341:3442:06 ft 26 5 5 75½ 64½ 62¼ PaisleyW3 nw120007071 2:06⅖ DillerVolo Colorama EasyFaith
Feb20-713Aur 1 :3221:0631:4132:15 sl 4 4 4 31½ 2½ 1nk PaisleyW4 nw85007071 2:15 CoCheck OldBlue FancyBoy
Feb13-718Aur 1 :3311:0611:3822:10 ft 9¾ 1 2 31 21 22¼ PaisleyW5 nw60007071 2:10⅗ Chemung Co Check Illini Don
Feb 6-713Aur 1 :3141:05 1:3722:092ft 9-5 *5 50 31½ 41¼ 2¾ PaisleyW5 nw27507071 2:09⅗ Even'gPl'sure CoCh'ck Gilm'reCh'f
Jan30-715Aur 1 :32 1:0231:3432:081ft 37 8 8 818 810 814 HermanJ7 nw50007071 2:11 JohnnieCrain RusKing SallyBrooks

8-1 4
2:06⅕ (F.P1, '71) ($7,019) Driver—NELSON WILLIS. Trainer, J. Graham (42-0-4-8—.116) **Maroon-Gray-White**
Spen Filter Br. g (1967), by Filter—Joan Spencer, by Spencer. 1971 7 3 0 0 $1,518
Owner, Herman Graham Stock Farm, Salem, Ill. 1970 0 0 0 0 (——)
Mar19-717Spk⅝ 1 :31 1:0421:36 2:08 gd 10 x8 60 74½ 78½ 712 GrahamJ7 st6000 2:10⅖ HammondWay SkipperHal Ajax
Mar12-71 F.P1 1 :32 1:0441:3512:031ft 4½ 2 2 2 2½ 11 GrahamJ1 nw40007071 2:06⅕ SpenFilter PoplarDaisy BeDirect
Mar 5-71 F.P1 1 :33 1:07 1:39 2:101ft 2¾ x8 8 7x 8 8di. GrahamJ1 nw17507071 DavyPilot MightyBoone Classy
Feb25-71 F.P1 1 :3211:0221:3422:10 gd 2 *1 1 1 13 14 GrahamJ2 nw20007071 2:10 SpenFilter HighWidow BigJimAd's
Feb18-71 F.P1 1 :37 1:0841:4222:132gd6-5 *x6 6 6 6 6di. GrahamJ4 nw15007071 EmoByrd Mino'sAllen Classy
Feb13-71 F.P1 1 :3141:0511:3642:09 gd3-5 *70 30 1 1½ 44½ GrahamJ7 nw15007071 2:09⅘ Key ofTime EmoByrd SeaBow

6-1 5
2:02⅕ (PmP⅝, '70) ($14,566) Driver-Trainer—JOHNNY BLEVINS (65-11-4-3—.219) **White-Blue-Black**
Miles Dares ⊗ Ch. h (1966), by Meadow Gene—Dottie Reed, by Knight Dream. 1971 10 2 1 1 $4,658
Owner, Leroy Stone, Chicago Heights, Ill. 1970 32 6 3 3 $11,701
Mar16-714Spk⅝ 1 :32 1:0531:3712:08 ft 3½ 10 1 11¼ 11½ 12½ BlevinsJ4 7000 2:08 MilesDares ErlaB.Win PolarBear
Mar 6-716Spk⅝A 1 :31 1:0411:36 2:083sy 2¼ 4 1 11½ 11 11 BlevinsJ2 6500 2:08⅗ MilesDares McC'yM'sile BethExp's
Feb26-712Spk⅝ 1 :3031:0511:3722:102gd 20 9 9 87½ 76½ 33½ BlevinsJ7 6000 2:11⅕ McCr'yMissile TimelyG'ld MilesD's
Feb13-714Aur 1 :3311:0631:3922:112ft 5 30 30 810 89 814 BlevinsJ7 nw30007071 2:14⅕ RedWeas'l LoBoJoe Dolly'sCinndy
Feb 6-718Aur 1 :3341:0821:41 2:124ft 9½ 7 7 76½ 77 77½ BlevinsJ8 nw55007071 2:14⅖ F'ncyB'y K'per'sD't'r B'rtha'sD'l't
Jan30-719AurA 1 :33 1:0621:3912:113ft 3¾ 4 40 42½ 63½ 74½ BlevinsJ4 nw50007071 2:12⅗ M're'sFoxyG't VoltanL'g FancyBoy

12-1 6
2:02⅘ (Spk⅝, '70) ($29,738) Driver-Trainer—MICHAEL JONES (13-1-2-0—.162) **Red-White**
Adam Ike ⊗ B. g (1963), by Adam Frisco—Glowmir, by Lew Hanover. 1971 4 0 0 0 $210
Owner, Michael Jones, El Paso, Tex. 1970 29 4 4 3 $17,372
Mar19-715Spk⅝ 1 :3141:0431:3532:074gd 16 30 30 2¾ 32½ 8¾ JonesM8 8500 2:09⅗ Imp'veTime Q'n'sC's'rt W'thyH'rN.
Mar12-717Spk⅝ 1 :3011:0111:3412:06 ft 17 3 3 2½ 1½ 53½ JonesM4 8500 2:06⅘ Sm'k'yBl'ze Wil'wB'kSc't M'rB'ze
Mar 3-717Spk⅝ 1 :3031:0311:3412:064ft 28 30 20 32½ 33½ 811 JonesM6 9000 2:09 Mary'sDawn M'htyLoyal W'yH'rN.
Feb27-718Spk⅝A 1 :3111:0531:3622:10 ft 11 2 3 31½ 53 64¾ JonesM2 10000 2:11 Farmont HedgeA'leJ'n Card'lH'rN.
Nov24-70 Hol1 1 :31 1:0131:3222:012ft 28 2 2 2 34 915 JonesM1 8500 2:04⅖ HiramsBay HappyHal Mary'sDawn
Nov14-70 Hol1 1 :2931:00 1:3142:02 ft 27 5 3 1 11½ 813 JonesM1 8500 2:04⅗ UplandQueen HiramsBay HappyHal

5-1 7
2:03 (Spk⅝, '70) ($62,761) Driver-Trainer—GENE VALLANDINGHAM (87-19-6-11—.299) **Red-White-Blue**
Worthy Hanover N. ⊗ Ch. g (1958), by Garrison Hanover—Bright Banner, by Colossal. 1971 11 4 3 3 $9,158
Owner, Neil Kelly, Elgin, Ill. 1970 23 8 5 2 $18,001
Mar19-715Spk⅝ 1 :3141:0431:3532:074gd 2¾ 4 4 52½ 62½ 31¼ VallandinghamG3 8500 2:08 Imp'veTime Q'n'sC's'rt W'thyH'rN.
Mar12-717Spk⅝ 1 :3011:0111:3412:06 ft 8-5 *10 2 31½ 42 32 VallandinghamG6 8500 2:06⅖ Mary'sDawn M'htyLoyal W'yH'rN.
Mar 5-71'7Spk⅝ 1 :30 1:0041:3232:033ft 1 *3 3 2½ 2h 21½ MarshJJr2 c7500 2:04 Mose W'thyH'n'v'rN. ComoHan'v'r
Feb27-7110Spk⅝ 1 :31 1:0431:3422:064ft 2 2 2 31½ 2½ 12½ VanderSchaafK2 c6500 2:06⅘ W'thyH'n'rN. LadyWood Sen'rMite
Feb22-714Spk⅝ 1 :3131:06 1:39 2:121sy9-5 *2 2 2nk 11¼ 11 VanderSchaafK7 6000 2:12⅕ WorthyH'rN. McC'ryM'sile SnoVan
Feb13-719Aur 1 :3321:07 1:39 2:104ft 4½ 4 5 74 86½ 62¼ SheelyD4 op3000 2:11⅕ Lacatime Sky Hawk Bear Green

15-1 8
2:06 (AsD1⅛, '70) ($9,288) Driver-Trainer—ROBERT FARRINGTON (152-21-21-24—.268) **Red-Gray**
Cascade Chief Br. g (1963), by Lumber Jack—Far West, by General Todd. Ow., 1971 11 0 4 1 $3,740
Farr'ton Sta., Inc.-Arnold Cattle Co., Inc.; Richw'd Ohio; G'nsea, Ill. 1970 23 4 2 4 $2,857
Mar20 7110Spk⅝ 1 :3011:0231:3442:054ft 8¼ 5 5 55ix825 8di. PaisleyW2 c7500 Idlew'lesVictor BuenoT'po Dr.Farr
Mar12-715Spk⅝ 1 :3011:0331:3542:064ft 8¾ 8 8 85 58 58½ WillisC8 nw15008 2:08⅗ Ajax Long Gone Farvel Miss
Mar 4-716Spk⅝ 1 :3111:0511:3722:08 ft 4¾ ix9 9 9 9 9di. WillisC6 nw1300L TeckleAd'sB. FastSig'l Lon's'eLou
Feb24-716Spk⅝ 1 :3211:0521:3622:08 ft 2 *2 2 21¼ 2½ 31† WillisC4 nw14008 2:08⅕ Ch'k'teT'to Casc'eCh'f Hoos'rGoose
†Placed second through disqualification.
Feb13-71 B.M1 1 :31 1:0231:3322:03 ft 6 4 4 5 43 21½ WilliamsR4 6500 2:03⅕ H'lryAbbe C'sc'deC'f Linc'nL'dB'k

6-1 9
2:06⅗ (Spk⅝, '71) ($17,047) Driver—CONNEL WILLIS. Trainer, O. George (82-8-8-15—.213) **Red-White-Green**
Senator Mite ⊗ Blk. g (1965), by Dominionmite—Hue B. Donna, by Hal Senator. 1971 13 3 1 2 $6,681
Owner, Otis George, Chicago, Ill. 1970 32 5 3 1 $10,516
Mar19-715Spk⅝ 1 :3141:0431:3532:074gd 9½ 1 1 1¾ 11¼ 42¾ MilburnP1 8500 2:08⅖ Imp'veTime Q'n'sC's'rt W'thyH'rN.
Mar12-717Spk⅝ 1 :3011:0111:3412:06 ft 11 2 1 1½ 31¾ 43½ MilburnP5 8500 2:06⅘ Mary'sDawn M'htyLoyal W'yH'rN.
Mar 4-714Spk⅝ 1 :3031:0441:36 2:063ft 2 *1 1 1½ 1½ 11 MilburnP1 7000 2:06⅗ Sen'rMite BuenoT'po Deac'nDarl'n
Feb27-7110Spk⅝ 1 :31 1:0431:3422:064ft 10 10 1 11 1½ 32½ WolfeJ6 6500 2:07⅖ W'thyH'n'rN. LadyWood Sen'rMite
Feb22-715Spk⅝ 1 :33 1:0931:4212:143sy 13 3 4 2¾ 34½ 45½ WolfeJ2 7500 2:15⅘ DutchDi'ct Mic'ySup'e Mary'sD'wn
Feb16-718BmlP 1 :3141:05 1:3722:11 ft 8½ 8 80 66½ 84½ 73½ DolbeeJ8 c6000 2:11⅘ MissGift GustoLobell StraightTalk

Trackman's Selections—1 2 7

ONE MILE PACE **8th RACE (afternoon program)** Purse $6,000

Conditi:ned. W:nners of $10,0C0 or more in 1970-1971. 3-year-olds and up.

PLEASE ASK FOR HORSE BY PROGRAM NUMBER

3-1 — 1

2:01⅕ (Was1, '70) ($30,147) Driver-Trainer—DWAYNE PLETCHER (60-11-8-5—.285) White-Black
Well To Do Ch. g (1966), by Majestic Hanover—Moon Wick, by Attorney. 1971 4 2 1 0 $6,:00
Ow., S. Lieberman-Dw. Pletcher; Skokie, Ill.; Shipshewana, Ind. 1970 32 1 5 8 $13,837
Mar16-718Spk⅝ 1 :3131:06 1:3612:06 ft 2¼ ▲4 4 32 52½ 52 Pletc'rDw2 w100007071 2:06⅖ TrueDeeD'ne Kni'tDesire HarkWon
Mar11-717Spk⅝ 1 :3131:05 1:3712:07 gd 2¾ ▲4 4 42 3½ 1nk Pletc'rDw3 w100007071 2:07 WellToDo BeagleBoy KnightDesire
Mar 5-718Spk⅝ 1 :3121:0321:3422:043ft 3 10 1 11 11 14 PletcherDw8 nw17502L 2:04⅗ WellToDo Br'dm'nG'rge R'reEv'nt
Feb26-717Spk⅝ 1 :3131:0521:3642:084gd 6¾ 5 5 64¼ 32 22½ Pl'tc'rDw4 nw175007071 2:09⅖ DillerVolo WellToDo Tommyjon
Dec 1-705May 1 :30 1:02 1:34 2:051ft 22 7 7 62 35 33 GordonC8 w800070 2:05⅘ VictoryDart R.Dir'ctW'y W'llToDo
Nov25-705May 1 :3111:0211:34 2:06 ft 15 8 20 2nk 2½ 61½ GordonC5 w1000070 2:06⅖ Tom'sChoice TimeCl'k R.Dir'ctWay

6-1 — 2

2:01⅗ (Hol1, '70) ($30,645) Driver-Trainer—ROBERT FARRINGTON (152-21-21-24—.268) Red-Gray
Taylor Creek Br. g (1965), by Ohio Time—Jane Farr, by The Mutineer. Owner, 1971 4 2 1 1 $6,648
Farrington Sta., Inc.-Galanga; Richwood, New Philadelphia, Ohio. 1970 29 11 6 4 $27,772
Mar10-719Spk⅝ 1 :3031:0511:3532:06 ft 1 ▲4 20 1½ 1h 11 FarringtonR6 17500 2:06 TaylorCr'k FlashOnP'k FrostyFr't
Mar 4-717Spk⅝ 1 :3131:04 1:3442:053ft 3-2 ▲30 4 64 64½ 21 FarringtonR8 16000 2:05⅘ FlashOnP'k Tayl'rCr'k TheGr'mbl'r
Feb27-719Spk⅝A 1 :3111:0531:3642:08 ft 4 4 5 52¼ 43½ 32½ PaisleyW8 w100007071 2:08⅗ Kni'tD'sire Les'aSkyR'r Tayl'rCr'k
Feb20-716BmlPA 1 :31 1:0221:3412:062gd8-5 ▲3 4 33½ 33 1¾ FarringtonR2 pr4500 2:06⅖ TaylorCr'k Kni'tDesire JimBl'ks'ne
Dec21-70 Hol1 1⅛ :3131:0331:3442:213sl 2¾e x4 1 2 43½ 65 AckermanD8 Cond 2:22⅗ St'l'gAdios FranklinJ'w'll B'dyTime
Dec18-70 Hol1 1 :3121:0231:3412:034sy 3¼ 7 5 5 34½ 21¼ FarringtonR6 14000 2:04 HiramsBay TaylorCr'k FlashOnP'k

5-1 — 3

2:04⅕ (W.R⅝, '70) ($38,701) Driver-Trainer—CHRIS BORING (80-5-8-8—.253) Green-White
Knight Desire ⊗ Br. h (1965), by Reed's Knight—Attorney's Desire, by Attorney. 1971 9 1 3 2 $8,410
Ow., E. W. Ross & Viola & Jack Foehr; Grand Blanc, Linden, Mich. 1970 41 6 8 2 $23,175
Mar16-718Spk⅝ 1 :3131:06 1:3612:06 ft 5 3 3 42½ 32 2nk BoringC3 w100007071 2:06 TrueDeeD'ne Kni'tDesire HarkWon
Mar11-717Spk⅝ 1 :3131:05 1:3712:07 gd 13 1 2 31¼ 41 3nk BoringC7 w100007071 2:07 WellToDo BeagleBoy KnightDesire
Mar 6-719Spk⅝A 1 :3131:0611:3842:101sy 7¾ 2 6 86 75¼ 61¾ BoringC5 w100007071 2:10⅗ Mt.AiryBill LaronM'd'n Tom'sCh'e
Feb27-719Spk⅝A 1 :3111:0531:3642:08 ft 2½ 2 3 31 21 1h BoringC1 w100007071 2:08 Kni'tD'sire Les'aSkyR'r Tayl'rCr'k
Feb20-716BmlPA 1 :31 1:0221:3412:062gd 4¾ 2 30 22 21½ 2¾ PershallP1 pr4500 2:06⅗ TaylorCr'k Kni'tDesire JimBl'ks'ne
Feb13-716BmlP 1 :3111:05 1:3632:083ft 9¼ 3 4 31 41½ 4¾ PershallP3 hp5000 2:08⅘ ChiefG.D'ct CafineKid JimBl'kst'ne

4-1 — 4

2:01 (Was1, '70) ($83,364) Driver—CONNEL WILLIS. Trainer, W. Feld (82-8-8-15—.213) Red-White-Green
‡Cleo's Dream B. g (1965), by Adios Cleo—Knight Lassie, by Knight Dream. 1971 2 0 1 1 $2,122
Owner, William & Betty Feld; Chicago Ridge, Ill. 1970 38 9 7 6 $37,426
Mar20-719Spk⅝A 1 :3131:0431:3512:06 ft 3½ 5 5 57½ 44½ 31 WillisC5 w100007071 2:06⅕ HighCard ShiawayDr'm Cleo'sDr'm
Mar11-716Spk⅝ 1 :3021:0221:3322:042gd 2¾ 6 1 31½ 22 2no WillisC4 23000 2:04⅖ Eurahead Cleo's Dream Bill Blaine
Mar 4-71 Spk⅝ 1 :31 1:0411:3442:063ft N.B. 3 1 11½ 12 13½ WillisC4 Qua 2:06⅗ Cleo'sDr'm P'ck'tAd'm J'mieAc's
Previous races with hopples.
Dec19-70 Hol1 1 :3011:0111:32 2:014gd 18 6 6 6 77¼ 74¼ ShortW4 w1000070 2:02⅗ AdiosPo!e W'ltzinaH'me C'nT'rCh'f
Dec10-70 Hol1 1 :2931:0021:3222:02 ft 20 2 4 5 64½ 73¾ ShortW1 20000 2:02⅘ ByeByeR'q'r B'ddyTime B'tl'qB'u

5-1 — 5

1:59⅖ (Hol1, '70) ($75,034) Driver—ROBERT WILLIAMS. Trainer, F. Redden (16-3-1-2—.264) Purple-White
Eurahead Ch. h (1965), by Widower Creed—Eura Mae, by Cardinal Prince. 1971 12 1 2 2 $9,653
Owner, B. N. Redden, Mayfield, Ky. 1970 20 6 1 3 $24,450
Mar20-719Spk⅝A 1 :3131:0431:3512:06 ft 5¾ 6 6 69½ 55 41½ WilliamsR7 w100007071 2:06⅖ HighCard ShiawayDr'm Cleo'sDr'm
Mar11-716Spk⅝ 1 :3021:0221:3322:042gd 4 1 4 11½ 12 1no MarshJJr5 24000 2:04⅖ Eurahead Cleo's Dream Bill Blaine
Mar 6-717Spk⅝A 1 :3021:0341:3632:093sy 2 10 1 11½ 1nk 54 WillisC6 24000 2:10⅖ Bil:Blaine LittleC'sar Vict'y'sHorn
Feb27-719Spk⅝ 1 :2931:0521:3522:061ft 2½ ▲5 5 55½ 69½ 612 WillisC4 in7500 2:08⅗ Cafine Kid Ballard's Boy Cecil T.
Feb23-718Spk⅝ 1 :3231:0631:3732:082gd7-5 ▲3 5 63½ 41¼ 31¾ WillisC1 in6000 2:08⅘ ShiawayLad MagicTime Eurahead
Feb13-71 B.M1 1 :3031:0141:3232:012ft 2 1 1 1 11½ 41 WilliamsR5 in10000 2:01⅗ Am'coT's Sc'tishD'sign B'tlingB'u

5-1 — 6

1:58⅗ (Lex1, '70) ($25,623) Driver—MAX LYNCH. Trainer, B. Nickells (13-3-5-2—.496) Maroon-Blue
Waycount Hanover B. c (1967), by Sampson Hanover—Waydear, by Dazzleway. 1971 2 0 0 0 $200
Owner, Lyons & Gascoigne; Aurora, Hudson, Ohio. 1970 28 12 8 1 $25,623
Mar20-71 PmP⅝ 1 :30 1:0131:3112:014ft 6¾ 6 6 6 64 56¼ NickellsW6 w7500 2:03 KnoxPatch Colonial Prestwick
Mar13-71 PmP⅝ 1 :2921:0041:31 2:002ft 7¾ 5 5 6 54¼ 58½ NickellsW4 w7500 2:02 KnoxPatch H.W.Expr's Wint'rDean
Oct 7-70 Lex1 1 :293 :5831:29 1:58 ft 3-2e▲2 2 2 31 33¼ NickellsW1 w5000 1:58⅗ P'pl'rM'rk M'yM'h'neB'tl'r W'tH'r
Oct 7-70 Lex1 1 :292 :5821:2841:583ft 2e 1 2 3 3¾ 1¾ NickellsW5 w5000 1:58⅗ W'yc'tH'n'v'r M'ryM'neB'r P'rM'k
Sep29-70 Lex1 1 :292 :59 1:30 2:001ft 2¼ 2 5 2 2½ 2h NickellsW4 w2000 2:00⅕ BeAlert Wayc'tH'n'v'r N'bleK'tT'e
Sep29-70 Lex1 1 :3111:0221:33 2:014ft 9-5 1 2 4 22 2¾ NickellsW8 w2000 2:02 M'mie'sK'ht Wayc'tHan'r BeAlert

6-1 — 7

2:01 (Was1, '70) ($24,369) Driver—JOE MARSH, JR. Trainer, H. Brown (99-20-13-12—.315) Gray-Blue-Red
Nardin's Dream B. g (1967), by Lehigh Hanover—Kakie Knight, by Knight Dream. 1971 4 1 1 0 $3,590
Owner, Donner Packing Co., Milwaukee, Wis. 1970 31 5 5 2 $19,262
Mar20-716Spk⅝A 1 :31 1:04 1:3512:06 ft 5½ 6 6 42 3nk 11½ MarshJJr4 nw17502-10 2:06 Nardin'sDr'm RailTime RightLane
Mar11-717Spk⅝ 1 :3131:05 1:3712:07 gd 5½ 5 5 63 76 77¼ BurrightH4 w100007071 2:08⅖ WellToDo BeagleBoy KnightDesire
Mar 5-719Spk⅝ 1 :3111:0411:3522:052ft 9-5 ▲6 6 65 55½ 53¼ MarshJJr6 4y7800 2:06 SwiftD'ke Aks'lH'v'r Shiaw'yDr'm
Feb25-718Spk⅝ 1 :3121:05 1:3622:06 ft 4-5 ▲6 50 2½ 1¾ 22½ MarshJJr6 nw200007071 2:06⅗ Be'gleBoy Nar'n'sDr'm DustyH.F's
Dec12-70 Hol1 1 :2911:0031:3042:001ft 3¼ 9 9 7 612 69¼ WilliamsR9 nw2500070 2:02 DownTownLobell Forli Niag'raAce
Dec 5-70 Hol1 1 :2921:00 1:31 2:004ft 9-5 ▲7 7 7 88 41½ WilliamsR4 nw2500070 2:01⅕ Springt'eCh'r Swat'ra M'nt'nSc't

Trackman's Selections—1 4 5

OFF AND RUNNING

After a major and lengthy expenditure of sweat, nerves and money, the New York City Off-Track Betting Commission got under way on April 8th, 1971, with the opening of two off-track betting operations, one in Grand Central Station and the other in Forest Hills, Queens.

Howard Samuels, president of the Off-Track Betting Corporation, breathed a sigh of relief. Following a year of planning, he had gone through seven false starts, and the off-track betting operation had acquired a pre-opening debt of five and a half million dollars.

Unlike the opening of the New York State lottery, the OTB opening was a great success. Instead of the opening day total of $10,000 which Samuels had predicted, the handle was $66,098. Bettors at Grand Central formed 100-deep lines in front of the ten betting windows, and nobody was permitted to join the lines a full two and a half hours before closing time. Betting was only on night racing at one track, and Samuels said agreement must be reached with New York's day tracks to assure success of the operation. He predicts a city net of $160 million in three years, with 100 legal betting places in New York City.

Many gamblers remained skeptical, firm in the belief that horse players would stick with their favorite illegal bookies in large numbers. Samuels, however, had been conservative in his predictions, and insisted that legal off-track betting will bring substantial aid to the city coffers.

round and turned to our morning selections for the Eighth Race.

This race contained the biggest purse winners we had seen so far, the conditions being that all contestants must have won $10,000 or more in 1970-71. It was for three-year-olds and up. *Waycount Hanover* could be eliminated by the This Track Rule, but his Florida times were most impressive. We would hold him in reserve since he had a red-hot driver.

Well To Do hadn't done well on his last outing and might still be smarting. His speed wasn't bad and he had a good spot on the rail. His driver was good. But his last loss on a fast track created enough doubt to drop him.

Taylor Creek had Farrington, plus was showing good form. Definitely a contender.

Knight Desire looked to be improving. He didn't have quite the speed of his current opposition. He was dropped.

Cleo's Dream was dropped due to declining condition and lowest-rated driver.

Eurahead had speed but not against this company. Drop *Eurahead.*

Nardin's Dream was dropped due to poor showings, Speed Rule and because of his races on March 5, 11 and earlier.

We now had two contenders: *Taylor Creek,* with Farrington, in good form; and *Waycount Hanover* held in reserve. Speed versus the This Track Rule was now the problem. Maybe we could bet around it.

Both horses were attractive plays from an odds standpoint. We figured final odds would probably average out at 4-1 and no less than 3-1. *Waycount Hanover* carried the best price. We'd done well on our earlier Dutch and felt we'd do it again, although this race compared in no way with the clear cut superiority of our combination in the 5th.

Twenty dollar win tickets on each paid off.

EIGHTH RACE—1 MILE. PACE. Winners of $10,000 in 1970-71. Purse $6,000. Mutuel Pool. $116,720.

Horse	¼	½	¾	Str	Fin	Driver PP	Odds
Waycount Hanover	1^0	1	$3\frac{3}{4}$	3^2	$1^{1\frac{1}{2}}$	M Lynch^6	8.00
Cleo's Dream	5	4^0	2^2	1^{nk}	2^1	C Willis^4	3.80
Taylor Creek	4	5	$6\frac{1}{2}$	$6\frac{1}{2}$	3no	R Farrington^2	4.90
Well To Do	3	3	7	5^1	4no	Dw Pletcher^1	5.30
Knight Desire	2	2	5^1	$4^{1\frac{1}{2}}$	5no	C Boring^3	4.00
Eurahead	6	6^0	1^{nk}	2^{nk}	6^2	R Williams^5	2.70
Nardin's Dream	7	7	4^1	7	7	J Marsh Jr^7	11.20

Time, :31$\frac{2}{5}$, 1:04$\frac{2}{5}$, 1:34$\frac{4}{5}$, 2:04$\frac{4}{5}$. Track good.

($2 Mutuels Paid)			
6-Waycount Hanover	$18.00	$ 7.60	$ 4.20
4-Cleo's Dream		5.00	3.20
2-Taylor Creek			3.40

We netted $160 on this one and felt almost godlike with our powers of prescience. Five hundred and two dollars plus $160 makes $662, an excellent day so far.

The Ninth race is a derby preview for three-, four-, and five-year-olds with the eight leading money winners in contention, as well as any dash winners not among the eight leading winners on the Pontiac, Pottawatomie and Black Hawk divisions of the Midwest Series. They are pacing the mile for a $10,000 purse.

True speed will count a lot in this race. We drop *Hammond Way* while still at breakfast—No Speed. *Miss Amscot's Janie* and *Ajax* fall to the same rule. *Worsham's Warrior* falls to a combination of Driver and Consistency and Form Rules. We felt that even with Farrington, *Doctor C* does not have the speed of *Slope's Skipper* and *Culver Cadet. Slope's Skipper* is showing good form and consistency.

Culver Cadet violates the This Track Rule and his driver does not have Busse's experience.

Slope's Skipper is our choice at $20 to win. He

ONE MILE PACE | **9th RACE (afternoon program)** | **Purse $10,000**

DERBY PREVIEW. 3-, 4- and 5-year-olds. The eight leading money winners as well as any dash winners not among the eight leading money winners of the Pontiac, Pottawatomie and Black Hawk divisions of the Midwest Series.

PLEASE ASK FOR HORSE BY PROGRAM NUMBER

6-1 — 1

2:02⅕ (Hol1, '70) ($8,710) Driver-Trainer—ROBERT FARRINGTON (152-21-21-24—.268) Red-Gray

Doctor C. B. g (1966), by Amortizor—Roberta Giers, by R. K. Giers. Ow., Farrington Sta., Inc.-Arnold Cattle Co., Inc.; R'hw'd, O.; G'n's'o, Ill. 1971 3 0 1 1 $1,881 / 1970 23 8 0 3 $7,110

Mar20-718Spk5/8A 1 :30 1:0131:32 2:05 ft7-5e▴2 1 1½ 2½ 4²¼ FarringtonR1 st7000 2:05⅖ W'sh'm'sW'r Gr'nAdios MoeW'st'n
Mar13-716Spk5/8 1 :2941:0221:34 2:05 ft 2¼ 8 50 42 43 2¹½ FarringtonR3 nw900070 2:05⅗ Swift Duke Doctor C. Noble Scot
Mar 3-716Spk5/8 1 :3121:04 1:35 2:062ft 3½ 5 5 713 58½ 36 FarringtonR5 n4R 2:07⅗ Str'ngByrd Ch'ck'y'teT'to D'ct'rC.
Nov14-70 Hol1 1 :3021:0041:3122:011ft 8½ 9 8 7 914 86¾ Farringt'nR8 nw1700070 2:02⅘ SpringtimeCheer S'w'ra Adi'sP'le
Nov 4-70 Hol1 1 :31 1:02 1:33 2:021ft 5½ 5 5 4 32 11¼ Farringt'nR5 nw1250070 2:02⅕ DoctorC. StarfireH'n'v'r C'nT'rCh'f
Oct27-70 Hol1 1 :3131:0231:34 2:024ft 25 9 9 9 78½ 54¾†Farringt'nR8 nw1000070 2:03⅘ TheFooler AbbeChance C.K.Adios

6-1 — 2

2:06⅘ (Spk5/8, '71) ($5,115) Driver-Trainer—WILBUR BEATTIE (2-1-0-1—.667) Green-White

Ajax B. g (1967), by Adios Cleo—Little Judy, by John Dillard. Owner, Apex Stable, Fowlerville, Mich. 1971 2 1 0 1 $2,420 / 1970 22 4 3 5 $4,745

Mar19-717Spk5/8 1 :31 1:0421:36 2:08 gd3-2 ▴20 1 1nk 1nk 31 BeattieW6 st6000 2:08⅕ HammondWay SkipperHal Ajax
Mar12-715Spk5/8 1 :3011:0331:3542:064ft 7¼ 2 2 2¹¼ 14 13 BeattieW2 nw15008 2:06⅘ Ajax Long Gone Farvel Miss
Nov28-70 Nor 1 :3211:0621:39 2:111gd 13 2 2 2 2½ 1²½ BeattieW5 nw500070 2:11⅕ Ajax CarolChief J.W.Creed
Nov21-70 Nor 1 :3031:0311:3522:063ft 19 3 3 3 2½ 2²½ BeattieW5 Cond 2:07 CarolChief Ajax O.K'sLaura
Nov14-70 Nor 1 :3111:05 1:3832:122sl 18 7 7 6 32 4²¼ BeattieW7 nw400070 2:12⅘ O.K'sLaura G'dPolicy V'sta'sB'yL'n
Nov 2-70 Nor 1 :3211:0731:3942:111sl 27 2 4 7 64½ 411 BeattieW6 nw400070 2:13⅗ Sudan'sCom't O.K'sLaura C'rdin'lJ.

7-2 — 3

2:03⅗ (Spk5/8, '71) ($5,403) Driver-Trainer—DARYL BUSSE (60-5-6-2—.150) Gray-Red

Slope's Skipper B. c (1968), by Meadow Skipper—Countess Frost, by Good Time. Owner, Daniel S. Seymour, Elkhorn, Wis. 1971 3 2 1 0 $4,550 / 1970 8 3 2 2 $5,043

Mar19-719Spk5/8 1 :3131:04 1:3412:052gd5-5 ▴50 1 12 11 21 BusseDa8 st6000 2:05⅗ Q'kerByrd Slope'sSkip'r Cul'rCad't
Mar 5-716Spk5/8 1 :3031:0021:3212:033ft3-5 ▴10 1 12½ 15 13½ BusseDa6 nw1500L 2:03⅗ Sl'pe'sSkipp'r P't'rBr'n P'd'saL'y
Feb25-716Spk5/8 1 :3011:03 1:3512:051ft1-2 ▴1 1 11 12 1nk BusseDa1 n3R 2:05⅕ Slope'sSkip'r Rip'gW've Andy'sL't'r
Sep 9-706Was1 1 :3131:0211:3242:033ft 2¾ 40 2 2½ 11 1no BusseD8 n3R 2:03⅗ Slope'sSkip'r EmmaGr'y Pil'tRec'd
Aug18-705Was1 1 :30 1:0011:3122:014ft 2 7 7 44 22 2³½ BusseD3 n3R 2:02⅗ S'yHeel Slope'sSkipper SkipperHal
Aug 7-705Was1 1 :3121:0141:34 2:04 ft 1 ▴6 6 63½ 15 17½ BusseD5 nw2000 2:04 Slope'sSkip'r TidyFr'ght FairGinny

8-1 — 4

2:06⅗ (Nfld, '70) ($5,734) Driver—CONNEL WILLIS. Trainer, R. Kline (82-8-8-15—.213) Red-White-Green

Hammond Way ⊗ Ch. g (1967), by Waylay—Martha Washington, by Gene Abbe. Owner, Kline, Aptilon & Weisbach; Sharon, Wis.; Chicago, Ill. 1971 3 1 1 0 $3,825 / 1970 18 9 2 0 $5,303

Mar19-717Spk5/8 1 :31 1:0421:36 2:08 gd 5¾ 5 4 2nk 2nk 11 WillisC1 st6000 2:08 HammondWay SkipperHal Ajax
Mar12-715Spk5/8 1 :3011:0331:3542:064ft 6¼ 7 7 63½ 918x9di. KlineR5 nw15008 Ajax Long Gone Farvel Miss
Mar 6-716Spk5/8 1 :3041:0521:3742:111sl 11 3 3 32½ 42½ 21 KlineR3 nw1450L 2:11⅖ Andy'sWil'm Ham'dW'y Fr'coClem
Dec19-708Aur 1 :3121:0331:3612:082ft 12 6 6x 817 820 8di. KlineR5 op2000 Dr.Conway Rod'sFooler YankeeOak
Dec12-703Aur 1 :32 1:0531:3922:133sl 4¾ 7 40 2nk 1½ 2½ KlineR4 nw5000 2:13⅘ Mr.C'b'llo H'm'ndW'y K'yst'neG'ce
Dec 5-704May 1 :3111:0311:3522:072ft 8½ 20 1 2½ 43 48 KlineR5 nw500070 2:09 Duane'sGold RobertDavid Winston

6-1 — 5

2:05 (Spk5/8, '71) ($10,711) Driver—ROBERT AUMSBAUGH. Trainer, S. Stucker (12-1-0-4—.194) Blue-White

Worsham's Warrior ⊗ Ch. g (1966), by Merrie Adioson—Lynn Direct, by Chief Abbedale. Owner, Emanuel Worsham, Tippecanoe, Ind. 1971 1 1 0 0 $3,500 / 1970 13 1 2 2 $4,674

Mar20-718Spk5/8A 1 :30 1:0131:32 2:05 ft 24 4 40 2½ 1½ 1½ AumsbaughR10 st7000 2:05 W'sh'm'sW'r Gr'nAdios MoeW'st'n
Jly 20-706Spk5/8 1 :2941:0231:3312:024ft 39 5 7 76 717 725 Aums'hR2 nw18002-6970 2:07⅘ ZhivagoN. Ch'fG.Dir'ct GrandBr'ks
Jly 4-708Spk5/8 1 :3031:0331:3422:041ft 14 20 1 3¹½ 78 79¾ AumsbaughR7 n4R 2:06⅕ PoplarMark GoodLeg'd Edge'dBr't
Jun19-7010Spk5/8 1 :3011:0141:3312:042ft 3½ 4 5 4²½ 5¹½ 2h AumsbaughR2 n3R 2:04⅖ W.E. L'r'mie W'sh'm'sW'r'r S.O.S.
Jun11-705Spk5/8 1 :3111:0311:3322:024ft 4 2 2 2¹½ 21 3⁷½ AumsbaughR1 n4R 2:04⅖ Edg'dBr't Ch'ceB'tl'r Wors'm'sW'r
Jun 4-707Spk5/8 1 :31 1:0141:3342:043ft 7 10 3 52 41 2¾ Aums'hR6 nw150006970 2:04⅘ HarkWon Wors'm'sW'r FunNFr'lic

4-1 — 6

2:05⅖ (Was1, '70) ($3,566) Driver—JOE MARSH, JR. Trainer, E. Clum (99-20-13-12—.315) Gray-Blue-Red

Right Good ⊗ Ch. c (1968), by Right Time—Wayfield, by King's Counsel. Owner, Sho-Mor Stable, Park Ridge, Ill. 1971 3 2 0 1 $4,550 / 1970 8 1 3 1 $3,566

Mar22-719Spk5/8 1 :29 1:01 1:3122:031ft9-5 ▴3 3 2¹¼ 3²½ 31 MarshJJr1 st5000 2:03⅖ Michig'nM'k Br'dm'nG'ge RightG'd
Mar15-719Spk5/8 1 :3141:05 1:3632:11 sy 2 ▴8 60 4³½ 1nk 11 MarshJJr4 st5000 2:11 RightGood Breadm'nG'rge RusKing
Mar12-714Spk5/8 1 :3111:0331:36 2:063ft 5 5 5 42 21 11 HankinsJ1 n2R 2:06⅗ RightGood AprilHope BelowZero
Oct 2-702Was1 1 :31 1:0321:3522:052ft 5½ 10 1 1¹¼ 1nk 22 MarshJJr9 nw300070 2:05⅘ NobleChoice RightG'd J'my'sBlaze
Sep22-706Was1 1 :3411:0611:3842:084sl 1 ▴5 20 2¹½ 22 29 MarshJJr6 n2R 2:10⅗ Overshad'w RightGood ShareCrop'r
Sep17-705Was1 1 :30 1:0141:3422:053ft 1 ▴1 2 3¹½ 1¾ 2no MarshJJr5 nw2000 2:05⅗ Edg'dK'ne RightGood MissInd'nB'k

6-1 — 7

2:04⅕ (Det1, '70) ($7,201) Driver-Trainer—JIM McGARTY (1-0-0-1—.333) Green-White

Culver Cadet B. g (1966), by Greentree Adios—Culver Wick, by Gene Abbe. Owner, J. R. Laneville, Dodgeville, Wis. 1971 7 1 3 1 $7,635 / 1970 17 8 5 0 $6,486

Mar19-719Spk5/8 1 :3131:04 1:3412:052gd 2½ 4 5 3²¼ 33 32 McGartyJ3 st6000 2:05⅘ Q'kerByrd Slope'sSkip'r Cul'rCad't
Mar13-71 W.R5/8 1 :29 1:0111:33 2:041ft 5½ 4 3 4 4¹¾ 2h McGartyJ2 hp7500 2:04⅕ RobbieNorth CulverCadet AdiosP'le
Mar 6-71 W.R5/8 1 :30 1:0211:34 2:05 ft 10 4 5 3 3¹¼ 4½ McGartyJ2 hp5500 2:05 BlazePick WalvisBay DarnVita
Feb 6-71 W.R5/8 1 :2941:01 1:3222:034ft 4½ 20 2 2 21 44 McGartyJ6 hp5000 2:04⅗ VerityKid StormyDuke T.J'sSh'ron
Jan30-71 W.R5/8 1 :3111:0521:3612:08 ft 5 4 4 6 5¹¾ 2½ McGartyJ3 hp5000 2:08 DarnVita CulverCadet T.J'sSharon
Jan23-71 W.R5/8 1 :3141:0631:3542:061ft 11 2 2 4 4²½ 2¹¾ McGartyJ1 hp5000 2:06⅗ RobbieNorth CulverC'det P.B.Abbe

8-1 — 8

2:08⅗ (BmlP, '71) ($1,950) Driver-Trainer—WILLIAM BECKLEY (24-6-5-3—.407) Blue-Gold

Miss Amscot's Janie B. f (1967), by Halcitas Jimmy—Miss Amscot, by Amscot. Owner, Eddie M. Wilborn, Alexandria, Ind. 1971 9 4 2 1 $6,517 / 1970 28 8 6 2 $1,950

Mar22-719Spk5/8 1 :29 1:01 1:3122:031ft 4¼ 4 4 55 46½ 47 BeckleyW2 st5000 2:04⅗ Michig'nM'k Br'dm'nG'ge RightG'd
Mar15-717Spk5/8 1 :3031:03 1:3542:094sy 2¾ 20 2 2¹¼ 2¹½ 1nk BeckleyW4 st5000 2:09⅘ M'sAm't'sJ'nie Ch'tteT'to Ins'tCr't
Mar 8-718Spk5/8 1 :3131:0321:3332:032ft 5¾ 1 2 22 23 23 BeckleyW3 st3500 2:04⅗ Ap'loRex M'sAm't'sJ'nie G'meJ'ck
Feb22-716Spk5/8 1 :3221:07 1:39 2:121sy 5½ 3 4 35½ 56½ 64¾ BeckleyW6 nw1400L 2:13⅕ Str'ngByrd VerneW'st'rn DanFr'co
Feb13-718BmlPA 1 :3231:06 1:3842:114gd6 5 ▴20 20 1h 1h 2nk BeckleyW4 nw47507071 2:11⅘ Cry'lKl'a M'sAm't'sJ'ie Fr'kyL'mie
Feb 6-714BmlP 1 :3141:0341:3532:083ft 2½ 4 30 1¹½ 1¹½ 1²½ BeckleyW2 nw35007071 2:08⅗ MissA's't'sJ'ie Cry'lK'ta St'dyD'be

Trackman's Selections—3 6 7

ONE MILE PACE **10th RACE (afternoon program)** Purse $10,000

DERBY PREVIEW. 3-, 4- and 5-year-olds. The eight leading money winners as well as any dash winners not among the eight leading money winners of the Pontiac, Pottawatomie and Black Hawk division of the Midwest Series.

PLEASE ASK FOR HORSE BY PROGRAM NUMBER

1 (12-1)
2:05 (Atl⅝, '70) ($8,209) Driver—NELSON WILLIS. Trainer, R. Rombola (42-0-4-8—.116) Maroon-Gray-White
Moe Western B. c (1967), by Darn Flashy—Cady Song, by Gay Song. 1971 6 1 0 3 $3,424
Owner, Bahcall & Weisenthal; Maywood, Ill.; Hollywood, Fla. 1970 30 6 4 5 $8,209
Mar20-718Spk⅝A 1 :30 1:0131:32 2:05 ft 51 6 6 53¾ 42½ 32 WillisN9 st7000 2:05⅖ W'sh'm'sW'r Gr'nAdios MoeW'st'n
Mar10-717Spk⅝ 1 :3211:0511:3642:071ft 15 6 6 87½ 77 79¼ WillisN6 nw15002L 2:09 JimBl'ks'ne Peachied'n ForbesTime
Jan30-716BmlPA 1 :3221:0711:4012:123ft 5½ 4 4 43¼ 31½ 31¾ WillisN3 w65007071 2:13 Farmont Brew'rsChips MoeW'st'rn
Jan23-716BmlPA 1 :3031:0341:3722:102ft 5 20 1 11 12½ 32¼ WillisC6 w65007071 2:10⅘ EyreNav'h Br'w'sChips MoeW'st'rn
Jan16-716BmlP 1 :31 1:0331:35 2:071ft 8¼ 2 3 32 33 46½ WillisC1 in3500 2:08⅖ JohnnyFoster JetBro Mr.Painter
Jan 9-719BmlP 1 :3311:0631:3912:114ft 2¾ 3 1 11 11 1½ WillisN2 w65007071 2:11⅘ MoeWestern EyreNav'rch Sunglow

2 (6-1)
2:01⅗ (Hol1, '70) ($10,614) Driver-Trainer—ROBERT FARRINGTON (152-21-21-24—.268) Red-Gray
Easy Faith B. g (1967), by Easy Adios—Amosson's Faith, by Prince Richard. 1971 5 1 2 2 $5,650
Ow., Farrington Sta., Inc.-Arnold Cattle Co., Inc.; R'hw'd, O.; G'o, Ill. 1970 14 9 3 1 $10,614
Mar20-717Spk⅝ 1 :31 1:0331:3522:062ft 2½ 4 4 33 31 21 FarringtonR1 st7000 2:06⅗ PocoPilot EasyFaith TimeHonored
Mar17-717Spk⅝ 1 :3141:0411:36 2:06 ft 6-5 •20 2 22 21 21 Far't'nR6 nw20002-7071 2:06⅕ M're'sF'xyG't EasyFaith D'c'sJ'rry
Mar10-718Spk⅝ 1 :3011:02 1:3242:044ft 4-5 •10 2 11 12 1h Farrin'nR4 nw130007071 2:04⅘ EasyFaith Laur'lWay JohnnyFost'r
Mar 2-716Spk⅝ 1 :3211:0341:3442:06 ft 1 •4 4 53½ 42 3nk Farrin'nR2 nw120007071 2:06 DillerVolo Colorama EasyFaith
Feb24-717Spk⅝ 1 :3111:0311:3342:044ft 1 •2 3 43½ 32½ 32½ FarringtonR4 nw19008 2:05⅖ Dean'sT's're Hic'yAd'nis EasyFaith
Dec11-70 Hol1 1 :3011:0111:3242:02 ft 6-5 •4 4 3 22½ 22½ Farringt'nR2 nw200007O 2:02⅖ PleasantLadN. EasyFaith D'ctT'off

3 (10-1)
2:05⅖ (Spk⅝, '70) ($10,871) Driver-Trainer—JACK ACKERMAN (11-0-0-1—.030) Black-Gold
Time Honored B. c (1967), by Good Time—Fleet Star, by Ensign Hanover. 1971 3 0 0 1 $840
Owner, Messenger Stable, Chicago, Ill. 1970 26 4 4 3 $10,841
Mar20-717Spk⅝ 1 :31 1:0331:3522:062ft 13 10 2 21½ 1½ 34 AckermanJ6 st7000 2:07⅕ PocoPilot EasyFaith TimeHonored
Mar13-717Spk⅝ 1 :30 1:0121:33 2:023ft 22 3 5 53½ 66½ 613 AckermanJ1 4y7800 2:05⅕ C.V.Thor FranklinJ'w'l AkselHan'r
Mar 5-71 PmP⅝ 1 :3111:0141:32 2:02 ft 36 7 7 7 77¾ 68¼ FisherH4 Cond 2:03⅗ Afric'nSt'r J'zyAdmir'l OB'd'ntP'k
Nov28-705May 1 :31 1:0311:36 2:072gd 4¾ 1 1 21¼ 32 32¼ AckermanJ1 nw100007O 2:08 SenatorGlib JohnJefry TimeH'n'red
Nov21-705May 1 :31 1:02 1:3322:041ft 22 3 3 43½ 43 62½ AckermanJ1 w100007O 2:04⅘ Luciano Franadio HiddenPleasure
Nov14-704May 1 :3121:0731:4032:124gd 8 1 1 11 11 11 AckermanJ5 nw90007O 2:12⅘ TimeHon'd ForbesTime Yond'rPr's

4 (5-2)
2:03⅘ (Spk⅝, '71) ($1,640) Driver—DWAYNE PLETCHER. Trainer, G. Kidwell (60-11-8-5—.285) White-Black
Apollo Rex ⊗ B. g (1968), by Duane Hanover—Adioo Bye Bye, by Bye Bye Byrd. 1971 3 3 0 0 $6,750
Owner, Evans & Wannebo; Crystal Lake, Ill.; Fall Brook, Calif. 1970 4 2 1 1 $1,640
Mar22-716Spk⅝ 1 :31 1:0231:3242:043ft 1-5 •40 1 12 12 11½ KidwellG6 st5000 2:04⅗ ApolloRex GameJ'ck Ch'k'y'teT'nto
Mar15-714Spk⅝ 1 :3041:0631:3632:102sy 2-5 •4 1 16 112 17 KidwellG3 st5000 2:10⅖ Apollo Rex Fast Signal Strider
Mar 8-718Spk⅝ 1 :3131:0321:3332:032ft 1 •20 1 12 13 13 KidwellG7 st3500 2:03⅖ Ap'loRex M'sAm't'sJ'nie G'meJ'ck
Jly 7-708Spk⅝ 1 :3211:0331:34 2:041ft 3-2 •5 5 54 3½ 21 KidwellG2 st5000 2:04⅖ NibbleTar ApolloRex PatTaylor
Jun17-70 Spk⅝ 1 :3231:0541:3512:053ft N.B. 60 20 1nk 11 12 KidwellG5 2y300 2:05⅗ ApolloRex Mr.Rebel QuakerByrd
Jun10-70 Spk⅝ 1 :32 1:05 1:3512:05 ft N.B. 3 1 13 15 110 KidwellG1 2y300 2:05 ApolloRex Mr.Rebel TommyLobell

5 (6-1)
2:04⅕ (PmP⅝, '71) ($2,406) Driver—JOE MARSH, JR. Trainer, O. Hileman (99-20-13-12—.315) Gray-Blue-Red
Apache ⊗ B. c (1967), by Lehigh Hanover—Quilla Byrd, by Poplar Byrd. 1971 8 4 1 2 $6,452
Owner, Ken Hirsch, St. Mary's Ohio. 1970 12 3 1 1 $1,292
Mar22-718Spk⅝ 1 :3131:0431:3642:072ft 7 1 1 12 12 11 MarshJJr5 st5000 2:07⅖ Apache Dean's Treasure D. Judge
Mar15-718Spk⅝ 1 :32 1:0611:3722:094sy 3½ 1 1 12½ 12 24 MarshJJr4 st5000 2:10⅗ D. Judge Apache Calories
Mar 6-714Spk⅝A 1 :3241:08 1:3842:114sy 7-5 •6 30 13 16 13 MarshJJr5 n2R 2:11⅘ Apache AllKeyedUp EdwinYates
Feb27-715Spk⅝A 1 :3041:0611:3642:091ft 6-5 •40 4 43½x42x 32 MarshJJr5 nw3500 2:09⅗ KitseyHano'r Pick'l'sPride Apache
Feb 3-71 PmP⅝ 1 :31 1:0241:35 2:053ft 2½ 1 2 1 12 1¾ HuberLJr2 Cond 2:05⅗ Apache SirH'rv'yPick FreightLady
Jan20-71 PmP⅝ 1 :31 1:03 1:3432:07 ft 1 •7 7 6 42½ 32 HuberLJr6 Cond 2:07⅖ ButternutLad CusterAdios Apache

6 (6-1)
2:05⅕ (Lat1, '70) ($4,710) Driver-Trainer—HARRY BURRIGHT (84-17-16-9—.344) Blue-Gold
Majestic Dream B. c (1967), by Majestic Hanover—Sultry Nite, by Knight Dream. 1971 3 2 0 0 $4,450
Owner, Kenneth L. Wildman, West Allis, Wis. 1970 19 3 3 1 $4,074
Mar22-717Spk⅝ 1 :30 1:0321:3412:061ft 8-5 •3 3 11½ 12 11½ BurrightH4 st5000 2:06⅕ M'j'sticDr'm JimB'ks'ne Inst'tC'dit
Mar15-718Spk⅝ 1 :32 1:0611:3722:094sy 3¾ 5 5 32½ 45 48½ BurrightH10 st5000 2:11⅘ D. Judge Apache Calories
Mar 9-717Spk⅝ 1 :3311:06 1:3722:082gd 3¾ 1 1 11 11 11¼ BurrightH5 nw5500 2:08⅖ MajesticDream PocoPilot TeeToo
Oct22-70 Nor 1 :3041:04 1:3622:072ft 6½ 4 4 2 2½ 21 SinaidA3 Cond 2:07⅗ CyndiP'r Maj'ticDr'm T.J'sSharon
Oct15-70 Nor 1 :3031:0331:3722:083ft 8¼ 8 8 8 87 77¼ SinaidA8 nw45007O 2:10 Van'sAd'w'y BillC'lith Midn'tJ'h'e
Oct 6-70 Lex1 1 :301 :5831:2831:583ft 71 7 7 6 87½ 813 SinaidA2 nw65007O 2:01⅘ N'bleK'htT'e Add'air Spr'gt'eCh'r

7 (5-1)
2:03⅕ (W.R⅝, '71) ($228) Driver-Trainer—SHELDON GOUDREAU (3-2-0-1—.778) Red-Gold
D. Judge ⊗ Br. c (1968), by Gamecock—Silent Shadow, by Shadow Wave. 1971 9 7 1 1 $7,825
Ow., John E. Riggs, Jr. & Sharon E. Riggs; Livonia, Mich. 1970 4 M 0 0 $228
Mar22-718Spk⅝ 1 :3131:0431:3642:072ft 3-5 •7 8 65½ 34½ 31½ GoudreauS8 st5000 2:07⅘ Apache Dean's Treasure D. Judge
Mar15-718Spk⅝ 1 :32 1:0611:3722:094sy 8-5 •4 4 44 22 14 GoudreauS2 st5000 2:09⅘ D. Judge Apache Calories
Mar 9-719Spk⅝ 1 :31 1:0231:3612:092gd 9-5 •8 8 78 44 14 GoudreauS5 nw4000 2:09⅖ D.Judge FriscoMcK'o Ward'nllimo
Feb28-71 W.R⅝ 1 :3231:0711:3912:094ft 9-5 3 3 3 21¼ 2½ GoudreauS3 nw65007071 2:09⅘ J.P.Bristol D.Judge RebelRolly
Feb23-71 W.R⅝ 1 :3221:0611:3732:104ft 3-5 •7 7 7 74¼ 1½ GoudreauS7 nw41007071 2:10⅘ D.Judge KeithD'ctSt'ne Br'tJ'h't'n
Jan27-71 W.R⅝ 1 :3241:0541:38 2:103ft 4-5 •7 7 4 42 11½ GoudreauS5 nw3000 2:10⅗ D.Judge TaskMaster RedEye

8 (9-2)
2:04⅖ (Spk⅝, '71) ($9,006) Driver—JAMES PERRIN. Trainer, D. Perrin (54-5-7-5—.195) Maroon-Gold-Blue
Poco Pilot B. g (1968), by Knight Pilot—Gramp's Girl, by Scottish Pence. 1971 3 2 1 0 $5,775
Owner, Carson L. Perrin, Beloit, Wis. 1970 16 5 2 3 $9,006
Mar20-717Spk⅝ 1 :31 1:0331:3522:062ft 6-5 •7 7 54 2½ 11 PerrinJ7 st7000 2:06⅖ PocoPilot EasyFaith TimeHonored
Mar12-719Spk⅝ 1 :3121:0311:3332:042ft 3 5 5 12 16 18 PerrinJ2 3y5000 2:04⅖ Poco Pilot Real Blast Pedo
Mar 9-717Spk⅝ 1 :3311:06 1:3722:082gd 5¾ 5 5 52½ 32 21¼ PerrinJ6 n3R 2:08⅗ MajesticDream PocoPilot TeeToo
Sep10-70 Sandwich—Finished 3-2 in two non-wagering races in 2:11⅗ and 2:09⅘, good (Da. Insko).
Sep 7-70 Mendota—Finished 3 in one non-wagering race in 2:12⅘, good (Da. Insko).
Aug30-70 Henry—Finished 2-6 in two non-wagering races in 2:07⅘ and 2:08⅕, good (S. Banks).

Trackman's Selections—4 8 7

Photo courtesy Sportsman's Park, Cicero, Ill.

There are thousands of well bred horses racing against each other every day, so unless it's a dead heat, as above, all horses but one will lose every race.

leads all the way, except in the stretch, where it really counts. *Doctor C* pays $15.80, $8.80 and $6 to lucky ticket holders. *Ajax* pays the biggest place money of the afternoon at $13.80 and $10.80. *Miss Amscot's Janie* earns her backers $10.20 for show, the largest payoff. Our profit for the day is reduced to $642.

The afternoon program has just one race left, a mile pace for a $10,000 purse. Conditions are the same as they were for the last race.

Moe Western is dropped by Time (Speed) Rule,

MR. ODDS-MAKER'S BEST BET

"Stick with the top drivers even though it is reflected in shorter prices. For the handicappers, the time of the last quarter in a trotter's last race is very important."

having lost his last two races by more than two lengths. *Time Honored* falls to the same ax. *D. Judge, Majestic Dream* and *Apache Man* also drop from contention due to Speed. *Poco Pilot* has beaten *Easy Faith,* but only by a length. Post Position didn't seem to have much effect then, so we won't count it now. We give the nod to *Easy Faith* over *Poco Pilot* because of Farrington's superior driving ability. Number 4, *Apollo Rex,* has shown more consistency and speed than *Easy Faith.* Pletcher, his driver, is doing well.

We put $20 down to win on *Apollo Rex.* He is soundly beaten after breaking at the ½. Without the break, we might have had another winner. Well, $622 isn't a bad day's work. And we won more races than we had any right to expect.

We toast our success with one last drink, promising ourselves an early return to Sportsman's Park, a pleasant place to spend Saturday afternoon. ♠

STANDARD TRACK ABBREVIATIONS AND SPEED RATINGS

Track.	Abbrev.	Time.	Track.	Abbrev.	Time.
Atlantic City	Atl$^{5/8}$	2:04⅕	Latonia	Lat^{1}	2:03
Audubon	Aud	2:05⅗	Laurel	Lau$^{5/8}$	2:03⅕
Aurora	Aur	2:07	Lebanon	Leb	2:06⅖
Balmoral Park	BmlP	2:06	Lexington	Lex^{1}	2:01⅖
Batavia	Btva	2:05⅕	Liberty Bell	L.B$^{5/8}$	2:03
Bay Meadows	B.M^{1}	2:04	Louisville Downs	LouD	2:05⅖
Blue Bonnets	B.B$^{5/8}$	2:03⅕	Maywood	May	2:05
Brandywine	Brd$^{5/8}$	2:02⅗	Monticello	M.R	2:05⅕
Buffalo	B.R	2:05⅕	Northfield	Nfld	2:05
Cahokia	Cka$^{3/4}$	2:04⅕	Northville	Nor	2:05
Columbus	Cols	2:05⅕	Ocean Downs	O.D	2:05⅖
Delaware	Dela	2:04⅗	Pocono Downs	PcD$^{5/8}$	2:03⅕
Detroit (Wolverine)	Det^{1}	2:03⅖	Pompano Park	PmP$^{5/8}$	2:03⅖
Dover Downs	D.D$^{5/8}$	2:04⅖	Raceway Park	R.P$^{11/16}$	2:04⅗
DuQuoin	DuQ^{1}	2:02⅖	Richelieu Park	Rich	2:04⅘
Fairmount Park	F.P^{1}	2:03⅗	Rockingham	Rock	2:05⅘
Foxboro (Bay State)	Fox$^{5/8}$	2:03⅘	Roosevelt Raceway	R.R	2:04⅗
Freehold	Fhld	2:04⅗	Rosecroft	RcR	2:05⅕
Gator Downs	G.D	2:05⅖	Sandwich	Sand	
Georgetown	Grgtn	2:05⅖	Santa Anita	S.A^{1}	2:02⅖
Goshen (Historic)	Gosn	2:05	Saratoga	Stga	2:04⅗
Green Mountain	GmP$^{5/8}$	2:05⅖	Scioto Downs	ScD$^{5/8}$	2:03
Greenwood	Grd$^{5/8}$	2:04	Sedalia	Sed^{1}	2:03
Hamilton	H.R	2:06⅖	Sportsman's Park	Spk$^{5/8}$	2:03⅘
Harrington	Harr	2:05⅖	Springfield	Spr^{1}	2:02⅖
Hawthorne	Haw^{1}	2:03⅘	Suffolk Downs	S.D	2:06⅖
Hazel Park	H.P$^{5/8}$	2:04	The Meadows	Mea$^{5/8}$	2:03⅕
Hinsdale	Hin	2:06⅕	Vernon Downs	V.D$^{3/4}$	2:01⅘
Hollywood	Hol^{1}	2:01⅘	Washington Park	Was^{1}	2:03⅕
Indianapolis	Ind^{1}	2:02⅖	Wheeling Downs	W.D	2:05⅗
Jackson	Jack	2:07	Windsor Raceway	W.R$^{5/8}$	2:03⅖
			Yonkers	Y.R	2:05

All tracks are ½-mile, except where superior figure indicates different distance.

Of harness racing, Mr. Odds-Maker says, "Stick with the top drivers even though it is reflected in shorter prices."

BOOK FIVE

GAMBLING AROUND THE WORLD

Gambling thrives all over the world and to prove it GAMBLER'S DIGEST takes you on a visit to the famous casinos from Monte Carlo to Macao off the China Mainland

Gambling around the world

A statement made years ago by some Arctic explorer that Eskimos don't gamble has gained acceptance by repetition and the stature of the man who originally made it.

Maybe the Eskimos he came in contact with didn't gamble—or maybe they didn't gamble with *him*. There'd be little point in gambling with anyone who didn't have some good seal steak or blubber or something equally valuable to wager against them.

Of course, while Alaska was once known for its gambling halls, no Eskimo casino has ever received any publicity.

If it's true that Eskimos don't gamble, they must be the only people in the world with that distinction. When Australians will gamble huge sums on Monopoly and the Irish will bet heavily on a game of dominoes, it's safe to assume that you'll find some form of gambling anywhere you go.

Of course, some of it may be illegal. Students of gambling suspect that *most* gambling is illegal, although a person who's determined not to break any laws can find some form of legal gambling almost anywhere. Almost.

For all practical purposes, China may be considered the fountainhead of modern gambling. We know that the Chinese were gambling 300 years before Christ, and many of the casino and private games played today throughout the world are of Chinese origin.

The Chinese have always been among the most enthusiastic gamblers, and wherever they have gone, they have taken their native gambling games with them. A peculiar (to us) kind of mysticism is attached to gambling by the Chinese, and gambling games and gambling devices have been used for many centuries to foretell the future. To most Chinese, gambling is an integral part of life.

Today, the Chinese Communist regime regards gambling as a subversive activity. While open gambling is forbidden by law, it is hard to believe that private gambling has been curtailed in a country that had six-sided dice in the third century and had the first version of the Shell Game, played with three sea shells, hundreds of years before any similar game was known in other parts of the world.

Wherever Chinese have gone, they have taken with them their Fan-Tan game and their own ancient Numbers game, as well as many other games, some with romantically beautiful and poetic names.

Legislation has never completely stopped gambling anywhere else in the world and it is unthinkable that the traditionally most enthusiastic of all gamblers would allow even the heavy arm of Communist law to curtail their unquenchable penchant for wooing the Goddess of Chance. Visitors behind the Bamboo Curtain report that finding a drink of water and finding a friendly game are of about equal difficulty.

Gambling in India dates back almost as far as in China, with dice a popular game as early as 200 B.C. In addition to wooden and ivory cubes, gamblers in India shot dice with the nut of the vibhitaka fruit—a nut approximately the size of a hazelnut and having five facets.

Ancient India was full of gambling dens which were under state control and paid heavy taxes. Today, such places are illegal. The fine for operating one, however, is the equivalent of $21 in American money. Horse racing is the major gambling outlet, with race tracks in every major city. Dice games have never lost their popularity, and card games are equally attractive to the Indian populace. Even the dog races get a big play. Dice have always had a mystic symbolism in India and were used at least 1,000 years ago to foretell the future. They also played a part in the Indian's love life.

Ancient Egypt was another stronghold of gambling, the favorite games being a kind of draughts and a game played with dice sticks. Dice became popular at roughly the same time they enjoyed the favor of Chinese gamblers. Gambling casinos exist in the United Arab Republic, but Arab nationals can't patronize them. They are not even allowed inside the establishments, and a potential gambler must produce a passport or other evidence of foreign citizenship. As far as legal gambling is concerned, Egyptians must content themselves with on-track horse race betting and, oddly, betting on pigeon shooting.

Of the ancient gambling Meccas, only Greece retains its status as a heavy-gambling country where almost every form of gambling is legal under certain conditions.

The state runs a national football pool, as well as a state lottery that has five drawings a year. Betting on horse races can be done at the tracks through the totalizator or elsewhere with bookmakers.

Penny-Arcade type games such as pinball are licensed, and gambling on them is popular and legal in cafes and clubs throughout the country.

Deluxe casinos are located at Rhodes and Athens under the supervision of a board of five government officials. The Greeks have long been regarded as among the world's most competent gamblers. Normally an emotional race, they play the casino games in a cool, unemotional way—although Greek "worry beads" can sometimes be seen in the free hand of a Greek gambler when the stakes are high.

Mention gambling casinos anywhere in the world and the one that is most frequently mentioned is Monte Carlo. Other casinos may have more to offer, but Monte Carlo has the fame and the name. While gambling is the backbone of the little principality's economy, Monaco has more going for it per square foot than any other country in the world. Princess Grace Rainier, the former Grace Kelly, an American movie star of real stature, is by no means Monaco's only international claim to fame.

It has beauty, charm, dignity and grandeur, the last authentically aristocratic resort from a long-gone era. Even the non-gambler recognizes that it is unique. That a country consisting of only 370 acres has been able to stay alive at all is something of a miracle. It has not only stayed alive but has thrived while consistently refusing to popularize and cheapen itself.

Futile, misguided attempts to establish Monaco as a gambling center began in 1856, but it wasn't until Francois Blanc, a Parisian financier, took over in 1863 that much happened. Blanc built a new casino and a luxury hotel, the Hotel de Paris, and began to build a new town around the casino. Prince Charles named the area Monte Carlo in 1866. When a new railway began operating between Monte Carlo and Nice in 1870, Blanc was ready for Monte Carlo's boom. Among other inducements to gamblers, he removed the 00 from the Roulette wheels, substantially reducing the house advantage.

After his death in 1877, his son took over, continuing the expansion and improvement, much of which had been planned by the elder Blanc.

A decade after the son's death in 1922, a private gambling club was moved into a place next to the casino. A "Summer Casino" is a recent addition to the scene, but the Winter Casino is the heart of Monte Carlo. It is a huge, ornate building, loaded with marble and mirrors, as well as crystal chandeliers. In addition to three night clubs, it contains a theater that was designed by Charles Garnier, designer of the Paris Opera House. It was in this sumptuous setting that Serge Diaghilev introduced the Ballet Russe de Monte Carlo in 1911. Top ballet troupes are still to be seen there in June and during the Christmas and Easter holiday seasons. The Orchestre National de l'Opera de Monte Carlo accompanies the ballet and operas, in addition to giving concert performances.

Attractions for non-gamblers have not been overlooked. There's the Monte Carlo Rally in Winter and the Grand Prix auto race in May, as well as interna-

The Bettmann Archive

The main salon at Monte Carlo, circa 1890.

tional tennis tournaments and yachting regattas. The beaches are excellent, and Alpine ski trails are only a couple of hours away by car in winter.

The Palais de Prince, a palace with parts of it dating from the thirteenth century, is open to tours in the summer whenever Prince Rainier and Princess Grace aren't there. The Changing of the Guard ceremony takes place every noon.

The aquarium is one of Europe's finest, and the Jardin Exotique, high above the sea, has one of the world's outstanding collections of cacti.

It is the casino, however, that is Monte Carlo's magnet. The rooms where the hoi polloi gambles are known, perhaps contemptuously, as "the kitchen," but the big money shows up in the *salles privee,* in some of which there is no house limit on bets.

Admission to "the kitchen" is about half what it is to the *salles privee,* and the play is small-time, probably accounting for about a fourth of the house "take." "The kitchen" recognizes that the tourist trade wants to see Monte Carlo and wants to gamble there—but what the tourist trade gets is a far cry from the *salles privee.*

The wealthy international gambling set is kept aloof, by its own wishes. Aristotle Onassis, husband of the former Jacqueline Kennedy and one of the wealthy men of the world, is said to have the controlling shares in Monte Carlo, and his frequent presence, along with his wife, certainly adds to the glamour of the place. Add Prince Rainier and Princess Grace, and Monte Carlo has a combination of "names" with which no casino in the world can compete.

The casino is well, if almost primly, conducted. Entertainment is generally less flamboyant than in other casino areas, but there is plenty of it and it is good. The casino help is superbly trained, and the security against cheating on either side is maximum. Even the casino police are policed.

Monte Carlo's success was unquestionably responsible for the return of casino gambling to France, where it had been illegal since roughly the middle of the nineteenth century. Casino gambling was legalized early in the twentieth century, and Biarritz, Cannes, Deauville, Le Touquet and Nice immediately acquired casinos of their own. France today has somewhere in the neighborhood of 150 casinos, and those along the French coast are among the most lavish.

The Deauville casino is the heart of the resort. It stands out as the most important building and gives the impression of catering to the affluent, which it does. The play is for high stakes, not so much because of high minimums but because the backbone of the casino's patronage *wants* to wager heavily.

The French Coast casinos, as Biarritz, Cannes, Le Touquet and Nice as well as at Deauville, are fashionable gambling places, drawing from an elite clientele.

France, however, has casinos to appeal to gamblers in all walks of life. In addition to them, France has *cercles,* clubs restricted to members, in which baccarat and poker are the main activities. Some 30 of the *cercles* are in Paris, and they seem to get a good play.

Pari-mutuel gambling on horse and dog races is legal, and there are official off-track pari-mutuel betting places which place all bets at the tracks. The *tierce,* in which the bettor picks three horses to win, place and show in a designated race rivals the American Daily Double in popularity.

The Lotterie Nationale holds drawings once a week, and a few charity lotteries are permitted.

While bookmaking and football pools are illegal, the French have ample opportunity to exercise their gambling enthusiasm in legal outlets. French policing.

Great Britain, and London, particularly, boomed as a gambling center immediately following the 1960 Betting and Gaming Act which legalized gambling "clubs." Clubs popped up everywhere, some excellent, some dubious and some downright bad. The Gaming Act legalized them but did little to regulate them and an undesirable element was immediately attracted by what it regarded as a license to steal.

The better clubs were, for all practical purposes, gambling casinos. A unique part of the Gaming Act stipulated that chances in any game must be identical for all players and that no percentage of the "handle" could be taken out by the house.

By 1969, Britain had 1,200 gambling casinos—more than could be found in any other country, with a total gross handle of somewhere between £500 and £600 million a year and gross profits of around £100 million.

Great Britain had headaches as well as casinos, since there was no official control, only token supervision and less than token taxation. By 1968, the British government saw evidence that an American criminal element sometimes referred to as The Syndicate, had started to move in. American law enforcement officials confirmed their suspicions.

A new Gaming Act was passed in 1968, with a Gaming Board to license, limit and supervise casino gambling. The board was headed by Sir Stanley Raymond, former chairman of British Rail, and it immediately showed signs of muscle and know-how. Predictions were that the number of casinos in central London would drop from 30 to as few as six or seven. The new Gaming Act did not go into effect until the summer of 1970. The average British citizen who put his gambling money into pools and betting shops had no idea how big casino gambling had become. The six-floor Play Club had tables on nearly every floor, with play 24 hours a day, seven days a week, and was considered one of the best because of self-imposed regulation which was lacking in many of the others.

Six months after the Gaming Act of 1968 went into force, the *London Times* for February 8, 1971, carried an assessment of the act's effect, written by Norman Fowler, Conservative MP for Nottingham South. "A chill wind is blowing through the green baize world of gaming clubs and casinos," he wrote. "A few clubs have already closed down their gaming activities. Others say they will be driven out of business unless the next Budget alters the basis for raising the gaming duty."

Of the 710 clubs that applied for certificates of consent under the new act, certificates were granted to 165. Of these, seven did not apply for a license, and licenses were granted to only 128.

Gambling license duties were sharply upped, with the Playboy Club, at the top of the list, paying £250,-000 a year. Several others paid well over £100,000. Crockford's, the oldest name in British gambling, was among the missing.

Central London clubs seemed to be better able to cope with the new Gaming Act than others. Curzon House Investments, which runs Curzon House and the Palm Beach casinos, showed a profit of over £300,000 for the first six months of the act's existence, and applied to reopen Crockford's and an International Sporting Club on the site of the defunct Colony Sporting Club.

One of the first effects of the new act, aside from the important one of eliminating crooked clubs, was to get rid of poorly operated ones. Another is the regulation of house percentage. Roulette now has a house percentage of about two percent; Craps has only one percent; and the Baccarat percentage is slightly under one percent.

The over-supply of casinos under the 1960 Gambling Act had put clubs into such stiff competition with each other that the "gambling junket," in which plane-loads of foreigners were brought in for the sole purpose of gambling, resulted. Many of the big gamblers who participated in these junkets were found to have strong underworld connections, and the British government hopes that the sharp reduction in clubs will eliminate the hoodlum junketeers.

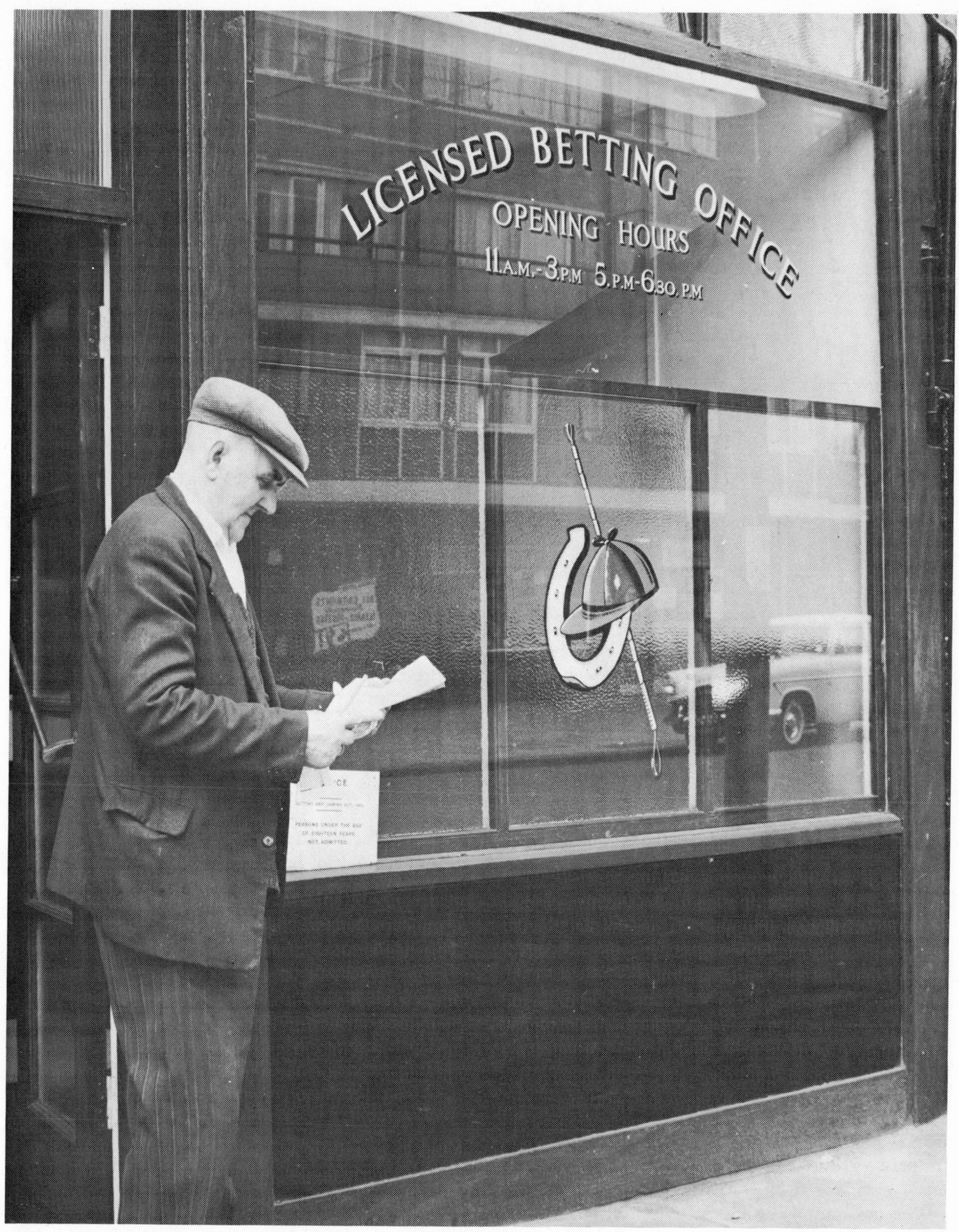

The British Betting and Gaming Act of 1960 legalized gambling clubs and betting shops. Pictured is the Charlie Mayer betting shop in Caledonia Road, London.

Guests play Boule in one of the gaming rooms at the London Playboy Club.

Great Britain, under the new act, has gaming inspectors, who are being carefully trained but have no previous experience with gambling.

The Playboy Club has 40,000 members, of whom roughly 32,000 avail themselves of the club's gambling facilities. The Victoria Sporting Club in London's Edgeware Road, has 13,000 members. The Palm Beach Club has 10,000 members and Curzon House Club has 3,000. Mecca has seven gambling clubs, including Sportsman's, in Tottenham Court Road, London.

Late London Report—Great Britain's 1968 Gaming Act is bringing a "gentler but more permanent" prosperity to the casino business, The *London Sunday Telegraph* of April 4, 1971, reports.

With the granting of ten more licenses in January, 1971, the Gaming Board brought the total of London casinos to almost 30. Crockfords, whose French owners were refused a license and left, the International Sporting Club, the New Casanova and the Knightsbridge Sporting Club, not yet licensed, are all planning to open but must first prove that there is a demand.

Sir Stanley Raymond, head of the Gaming Board, is generally credited with doing a fine job of cleaning them up. The board has the power to put any of the lavish clubs out of business at the turn of a card. Its inspectors visit most clubs about twice a month, unannounced.

One rule they are enforcing is the 48-hour rule, which requires new members to wait two full days after applying for admission before they gamble or even enter the club. Owners of casinos don't like the rule, which they feel will discourage tourist business.

With all the restrictions and supervision, the big, well-conducted clubs are doing as well as ever, perhaps even better.

Small clubs outside the large cities are suffering from the new regulations, and some of them may have to close.

The 1968 Gaming Act set up complicated—and lengthy—regulations covering all forms of gaming. This detailed information is available from the British Information Services, London, upon request for the booklet, *Control of Gambling in Britain*.

Totalizator betting on horses in Great Britain is big, with greyhound racing a poor second, football pools a fair third, and Bingo a distant fourth. Over half of the legal betting, about $1½ billion, is on the

A scene from Crockford's, the oldest gambling club in Great Britain.

horses. By comparison, the activity in Premium Bonds, the British Lottery, is small.

Legal bookmaking seems to have been encouraged rather than deterred by the 1968 Gaming Act. The large betting shop chains continued to grow, with Ladbroke's aiming at 1,000 shops by 1975. Independent bookmakers complain that betting shops abound to such an extent that the competition is too much for them.

Millions of British bet regularly every week on the football pools, and they are a healthy form of revenue, since a third of the gross take goes to the government. Many bettors send in pool forms which cannot possibly win because of their failure to conform with the rules.

Many of Britain's 1,500 bridge clubs were bitter over the new gaming act, with its requirement that they pay a £1,000 licensing fee and a yearly renewal fee of £200.

Great Britain apparently learned a bitter lesson—that you cannot permit gambling to "just grow." It mushroomed, Sir Stanley Raymond admits, to the point where control was imperative.

Intimations and even open charges that American gangsters were affiliated with British casinos had become frequent.

Sir Stanley was well aware of them. "In an industry where there is so much loose money, hot money and big money about, there is *bound* to be a criminal fringe or a criminal element, and this is why we must have this continuous attack. . . . Parliament and the Home Office would never have stated that one of the objects of setting up the Board was to rid the industry of its criminal element if they had not good reason to believe that there was a criminal element to be got rid of. I am not underestimating the significance of the Mafia in this connection."

He points out that there are at least six different casino areas in London. Mayfair and the West End are quite different. South London and North London present different problems, too. East London and suburban London have their own unique problems, as do Birmingham, Liverpool and Manchester. The casinos of Glasgow are dissimilar to those of Edinburgh.

"The British mix," Sir Stanley says, "is part of the problem," a problem he is determined to solve.

There are even problems with Bingo, he says, mostly with housewives who intend to spend a relatively small amount on the game and wind up losing £9 or £10 on casino games. He is convinced that there must be a complete separation between Bingo and what is sometimes called hard gambling.

English visitors who find Great Britain's new Gaming Act restraining may take an air-hop to the Isle of Man, where instant gambling and easy credit, both forbidden in England, are available. The island is outside the gaming board's jurisdiction.

Its casino is in a new million-pound hotel, the first new building for 50 years in a mile-wide stretch of boarding houses. It is a first-class hotel, built because the applicants for a casino permit were told they would be refused unless they also built a hotel to attract tourist business. The government collects taxes of somewhere in the neighborhood of £35,000 a year, and the casino management reported that it expected 500,000 visitors during the 1971 season.

Ireland's big gambling promotion is the Hospitals Sweepstakes. Football pools and casinos are illegal, and only carnival-type games in which the gamble is about equivalent to a dime are sanctioned. In view of tight restrictions on other gambling, it is odd that booking on horse and dog races is perfectly legal. There are more than 100 race meets a year, and night greyhound racing. In the charming Irish pubs throughout Ireland, dominoes continue to be the most popular private betting game, as much a part of Irish life as Irish whiskey.

Horse and dog race betting vie for Austria's gambling money, with betting both at the track and with off-track bookmakers. Nearly eight times as much money is bet through bookmakers as goes through the pari-mutuel windows at the tracks. There are two large race tracks handy to Vienna, and smaller tracks throughout the country.

Gambling casinos welcome visitors in Salzburg, Seeboden, Kitzbühel, Vienna, Bad Gastein and Baden.

Lotteries are an important part of Austrian gambling, with a number of popular ones either controlled by the state or licensed by them.

There's plenty of night life of a kind to be found only in Austria, including the *bauernstubes* in the smaller towns, where friendly games sometimes compete with singing and dancing.

Italy's state lottery is Europe's oldest. It holds a drawing every week and continues to be one of the most popular lotteries in the world. The government also controls football and horse-racing pools, and sanctions totalizator betting on horse and dog races.

While casino gambling is forbidden in most parts of Italy, casinos operate with government approval in Venice, San Remo, St. Vincent and Campion, with a stiff government tax.

In West Germany, gambling casinos operate in many spas and resort communities, with a stipulation that players must be over 21 years old. The Baden-Baden casino is over 200 years old. While the town was always famous as a health resort, the casino made it Germany's fashionable watering (and wagering) resort. With substantial improvements in the last two decades, it is a favorite gathering place for wealthy European gamblers. The country has many small casinos and the unique *spielhallen,* junior-type casinos that specialize in slot machines and hold little interest for the tourist.

The state lotteries draw by far the largest part of West Germany's gambling money, with football pools second and horse-racing third in popularity. Well over 1,000 lottery offices and many thousands of betting establishments operate with legal sanction.

As for East Germany, one world traveler and gambling enthusiast remarked, "Getting in and out of the country is too big a gamble."

The big gambling game in Switzerland is *boule,* an odd form of Roulette which has existed for about 200 years. Numbers from One to Nine appear twice on the wheel, 18 numbers in all. The wheel doesn't spin, but the ball is rotated around the edge of the bowl. Number Five replaces 0 as the house number, and since it appears twice, the house percentage is about 12¼ percent. Money bet on individual numbers pays off seven to one. Betting on odd or even numbers is an even-money bet. Two groups of four numbers each also pay even money. The maximum bet is the equivalent of about $1.20, and boule casinos are to be found in Arosa, Bad Ragas, Baden, Berne, Brunnen, Davos, Geneva, Lausanne, Locarno, Lucerne, Montreux and St. Moritz. Since the maximum wager is so low and minimums are even lower, gambling tourists can have a lot of fun without losing much money.

Private lotteries and betting on the horses are illegal in Switzerland, but football pools have government sanction, and charity lotteries operate with government sanction.

Gambling—at least, legal gambling, is of comparatively minor importance in the Scandinavian countries. Denmark has a state football pool. Horse-race betting, to be legal, must be done at government-controlled tracks through totalizators. A few slot machines and roulette wheels operate on a nickel-and-dime basis. The only place aside from sport gatherings where gambling is permitted is at the Marienlyst hotel in Elsinore.

Gambling is not permitted in Norway, and the amount spent on lotteries, football pools and horse-race betting is small by world standards.

Sweden shows far more interest in gambling than either Denmark or Norway, with betting on the horses, either at the track or through bookmakers, coming close to the $100 million mark. Football pools and a national lottery add another $100 million. Over 200 casinos operate inside the country, mostly in *stads-*

hotels. Maximum bets are small, and winnings must be spent within the establishments.

In Finland, private betting is illegal. Government-controlled football pools, lotteries and horse-race betting thrive, and give the government an income of over $20 million annually. Roulette for small stakes is permitted in some restaurants.

Bullfighting is, of course, Spain's greatest spectator sport, and while gambling on it is technically illegal, wagering does happen. The season usually runs from April to October, and every town of any size has its bullring. Madrid and Barcelona usually have the major bullfighting events.

Jai-Alai, or *Pelota,* is played the year 'round at frontons in the major cities, and soccer draws huge crowds from September through May. Betting on both sports is heavy. Greyhound races draw well, too, as does cockfighting. Government lotteries enjoy a big play.

Portugal's government-supervised gambling casinos operate in specific localities. On-track betting at the races is legal, as are authorized football and other sports pools. There is a national lottery. One of the most colorful casinos is at the Portuguese colony of Macao, off the Chinese mainland, about 40 miles away.

The Estoril casino is a beautiful building in a beautiful location. Estoril bills itself as Europe's sunniest resort. The new casino, modern in architectural style, has huge windows overlooking palm-fringed flower gardens and the ocean. It has games to appeal to gamblers from all over the world: Roulette, Boule, French Bank, Chemin-de-Fer, Baccarat, Baccarat punto-banco, Blackjack, Chuck-a-Luck, Craps—and the inevitable slot machines. It is open from three o'clock in the afternoon to three o'clock in the morning, all year.

There's dining and dancing every evening in the Grand Salon restaurant, which features an international menu as well as a Portuguese cuisine, as well as spectacular floor shows.

Espina, another important coastline beach, has a large casino and casino-theater among its many attractions. Povoa de Varsim, still another great seaside resort, has a picturesque and luxurious casino overlooking the ocean, excellent hotel accommodations and unique restaurants that specialize in regional dishes.

Figueira da Foz, an Atlantic seaside resort in the center of Portugal, claims to have the best beach in the country, which it advertises as "The Beach of Brightness." In addition to gambling, the Grande Casino Peninsular offers a music hall, dancing, evening social parties and a midnight cabaret. The visitor gets mild climate, the sea, the mountain ranges of Beira, and gambling, all in one attractive package. There's bullfighting, too, of course, as there is everywhere in Portugal.

All Portuguese casinos are a part of the country's resort life, designed to attract important tourist trade.

Going from Portugal to Poland is an alliterative if unlikely trip. In Poland, the *toto lotek,* the national lottery, is the big gamble. The same organization that runs it runs the football pools. Horse-race betting is state-supervised, and a peculiar Numbers game gets a big play.

A state lottery and state-controlled pools are the only gambling in Czechoslovakia. The same situation exists in Hungary, except that cafe patrons are permitted to play cards for money in certain licensed eating places, with a strict limitation as to the size of bets.

While Bulgaria has strict laws against all forms of private gambling, gambling casinos are being operated in the resorts on the Black Sea. They are, for the most part, prosperous. A realistically-operated state lottery attracts a heavy play by listing as prizes such hard-to-get items as automobiles, dwellings and major appliances.

Yugoslavia's principal gambling attractions are its busy gambling casinos. The Hotel Esplanada Inter-Continental in Zagreb has a most attractive one. Most of the casino gambling is done in resort towns, by resort patrons. About a dozen such communities have thriving casinos.

Private gambling is a *nyet-nyet* in Russia, but the Soviet Republic runs a profitable lottery. If any tourist should be fortunate enough to win, he would be faced with a serious problem—the rubles cannot be taken out of the country.

Russia also receives some revenue from totalizator betting on horse races, but bets are limited to two rubles. Most of the races are trotting races, and there are no place or show bets at the Russian tracks. Russian newspapers hardly acknowledge the existence of horse racing and apparently are not permitted to carry

---

I'll Betcha!

"Which end of the Panama Canal is farther east, the Atlantic end or the Pacific end?" the bettor asked.

"Why, the Atlantic end, of course," his prospective victim answered.

The bettor shook his head. "I'll bet you're wrong," he said.

He got a bet, and won. The Pacific end of the Panama canal, strange as it seems, is about 27 miles east of the Atlantic end.

"It's one of those bets," the bettor says, "where you get no takers if you simply offer to bet that the Pacific end of the Canal is east of the Atlantic end. You have to trap your victim into declaring that the Atlantic end is east of the Pacific end. Once he's taken a stand, he'll bet on it."

either handicaps or racing results. While the government permits race betting and collects a small revenue from it, the sport is not encouraged.

In addition to all its scenic charm, Belguim has gambling casinos at Knokke-Le Zoute, Blankenberge, Ostend, Namur, Chaudfontaine, Middelkerke, Spa and Dinant, as well as swinging night clubs and some of the best food to be found anywhere in the world.

The little independent commonwealth of Malta has some excellent new hotels, and the Malta Hilton and Malta Sheraton are both conveniently close to the Dragonard Palace Casino in St. Julian's. There's betting on horse races every Sunday from October to June, Lotto games every week, and a government lottery every three months.

You can even gamble when you're on the rocks—at least on the rock, the Rock of Gibraltar. There's a gambling casino right next door to the Rock Hotel. Packed within 2¼ square miles is plenty of night life, the Rock and its Barbary apes leading their uninhibited lives, a Moorish castle built in 1333, the Gibraltar Museum, and duty-free shopping.

Going to the North American continent, Canada forbids practically all gambling except betting on the horses. This is said by many Canadians to have greatly encouraged and increased illegal gambling in private clubs.

Nowhere else in the world is the gambling "handle," both legal and illegal, as high as in the United States.

Beautiful, well-conducted race tracks with fine physical plants are spread across the land, along with some of poorer quality, and do a staggering business. The private clubs at some of the tracks would be a credit to any plush resort, and mass accommodations are often superior, too.

A trend toward state lotteries, discussed in detail elsewhere in this book, has been sparked by New Hampshire, New York and New Jersey.

Nevada is the only state to permit casino gambling. Aside from horse-racing, Bingo and a few minor items, most gambling is illegal in most parts of the country, yet the amount wagered in the United States continues to grow.

Gambling's popularity is attested by Nevada, with its monopoly on casinos within the continental limits of the country. Las Vegas has more first-class casino-hotels than anywhere else in the world. It has the greatest dollar volume of casino business. Counting Casino Center, it is doubtful if even London can top it in the number of full-scale casinos operating the year around and doing substantial business. Add the casino activity at Reno and Lake Tahoe and you have, without any contest, the legal gambling capitol of the universe.

Most of the casinos on the Las Vegas strip are multi-multi-million dollar investments. Most operate in conjunction with superb resort hotels or motels and offer the finest night club entertainment that ever greeted a demanding audience.

The Las Vegas gambling plants have been refurbished in recent years by the aid of Big Business money. With so much action not only inside the casinos but in building, remodeling, buying and selling, it would be virtually impossible for Las Vegas to stand still.

When Las Vegas citizens aren't talking about a proposed new hotel-casino, they are probably discussing one that is currently being built or completely remodeled. At least, they will have a rumor about new money taking over. Anything that is written about the current Las Vegas scene runs the risk of being obsolete before the printed words are off the presses.

In the last few years, there has been an astonishing attempt to upgrade and improve downtown Casino Center. Much money has been poured into remodeling existing downtown casinos and hotels, and building is booming. Observers do not feel that Casino Center will ever challenge the Strip for supremacy, but there is no question about its efforts to improve itself.

The same observers have been shaking their heads ever since the Circus Circus opened in 1968, certainly the only casino of its kind in the world and a $15 million investment. One of its points of difference is that it is not a part of a hotel, and the big question in the experts' minds is whether or not a casino can "make it" without a hostelry.

The Circus Circus, designed by the same Jay Sarno who designed Caesar's Palace, features circus entertainment, with superb aerial acts swinging over the heads of the gamblers.

While the place's inspiration may have come from Ringling-Barnum, it has also drawn on the old traveling carnival. In addition to the standard games found in other casinos, the Circus offers old carnie games in new dress. There are also "girlie" and peep shows, but these are not made available to the young and tender customers who visit the place with their parents.

There is no argument about the Circus Circus drawing family trade, but some casino entrepeneurs predicted that it would also draw camp-ground and tourist court business to the discouragement of more profitable traffic.

The Showboat casino and hotel has found family business lucrative. Located away from both The Strip and downtown Casino Center, The Showboat has done well enough to encourage its management to expand. What looks like a glorified paddlewheel showboat of the 90's offers attractions that would make an old-time showboat owner have a nervous breakdown. With all its attractions and its sponsoring of special events, the casino is still what keeps the Showboat cruising.

One of the newest and most grandiosely elegant of Las Vegas attractions is Caesar's Palace, referred to by some wags at the time of its construction as "The Barnum-Hilton." Designed by the same Jay Sarno who created the physical form of the Circus Circus, it represents lavishness at its most overwhelming. There are 700 rooms and suites, along with the Circus Maximus and the Bacchanal Room, two dining rooms that gourmets regard with reverent awe. The casino is on the same scale and in the same style as the rest of the establishment.

The Tropicana, even without the drawing power of its casino, would certainly qualify as one of the great luxury hotels to be found anywhere. So, for that matter, would the Desert Inn, the Sands and the Sahara. The Flamingo and the Dunes are in the same class. Anyone who saw the film, "Bob and Carol and Ted and Alice" has had at least a casual glimpse of the Riviera, which has a great deal more to offer than meets the eye in its brief background appearance in the film. First, there was the Last Frontier, which was followed by the New Frontier. The current Frontier might be called the new-new Frontier, because it is entirely new, and excellent.

Kirk Kerkorian's International Hotel began construction with the intent of topping everything else around, with a swimming pool said to be the largest body of water in Nevada, aside from Lake Meade, a huge International Theater and an 800-seat legitimate theater intended for the presentation of Broadway shows. The International has 1,500 rooms and is said to have cost Kirk Kerkorian at least $50 million. In contrast to Howard Hughes, Kerkorian has been labeled Las Vegas' "visible" millionaire. Kerkorian has had the casino that began Strip gambling activity, the Flamingo, for three or four years.

Although the Las Vegas Chamber of Commerce doesn't like reminders of it, the Strip and the Flamingo were started by one Benjamin "Bugsy" Siegel, a notorious hoodlum who was written out of the Las Vegas story by bullets in 1947—not, Las Vegas public relations men point out, in Nevada but in Beverly Hills, California.

Kerkorian, an Armenian who got his start in the airline business, is said to own or control somewhere in the neighborhood of 20 percent of the gambling capitol's hotel accommodations.

Del Webb was the contractor who built the Flamingo. He later got into the casino and hotel business, himself, with the Thunderbird, the Saraha and the Casino Center Mint, not to mention the Sahara-Tahoe.

Webb is credited with arousing the interest of Howard Hughes, whose current investments in Las Vegas are probably somewhere in the neighborhood of a quarter of a billion dollars, including the Desert Inn, the Frontier, the Sands, the Castaways, the Silver Slipper, and, by no means least, the Landmark.

The Landmark is the star of a story that could happen only in Las Vegas. Following its completion, it stood idle and empty when its owners were refused a permit to operate it as a hotel and casino. It had the distinction of being the tallest building on the Strip and a $17.3 million fiasco. When Howard Hughes bought it, one Las Vegas observer remarked, "It makes sense. Only Howard Hughes could afford to own it."

Hughes is said to have spent at least $3½ million to correct obvious deficiencies in the Landmark. The kitchens were designed in an impractical manner that made food men mumble, the lighting system was erratic, and the plumbing was unbelievably bad. One of the most serious problems was lack of sufficient elevators—or any place to put them. Hughes, undaunted by the many deficiencies, got the Landmark open, which was considered by many to be a major achievement.

The Mint, in downtown Casino Center, is the Landmark's only challenger for height. Twenty-six stories tall, its glass-enclosed restaurant, Top o' the Mint, gives diners a wonderful view of the Las Vegas scene.

The Mint also is unique in giving gambling lessons. Roughly 1,000 customers every month take the course in "Winning Fundamentals of Gambling," in which three popular games are explained and students gather at gaming tables for the addition of practice to theory. Another unique promotional feature offered by The Mint is "The Other Side of the Coin," a guided tour that reveals many aspects of casino operation.

Downtown Casino Center, with its earthier approach to gambling, is said by students of the Nevada operations to be doing extremely well, attracting tremendous crowds of hard-core gamblers who may spend less at the tables in one evening but spend it more steadily than Strip patrons.

The show rooms and night clubs on the Strip have seldom broken even. They are costly shills, designed to draw the type of customers who will give the casinos a big play.

The competition for talent is both keen and wild, since there aren't enough Frank Sinatra, Dean Martin, Danny Thomas, Barbra Streisand, Jerry Lewis type performers to go around. The International was reported to have paid Streisand well over half a million dollars for four weeks as its opening star.

One problem is that many of the biggest "draws" in entertainment are rock singers and groups whose main appeal is to a youthful segment of society that isn't even allowed to patronize the casinos. These "names," casino owners say, would actually drive their best customers away instead of bringing them in.

The Stardust found warm, live flesh a fine substitute for big names when it introduced the Lido de Paris show to its customers. The spectacular production has found a second home in Las Vegas, as has the Folies Bergere show, staged by the producers of the Paris edition. The Folies has kept the Tropicana hotel from worrying about the dearth of stellar names. The Dunes knew a good thing when its management saw it, and the Casino de Paris has become a standard attraction there. Weekly budgets for these shows probably runs over the $50,000 mark, and management thinks they're bargains at the price.

The Desert Inn, not wanting to glut the market with another lavish French revue and working on the theory that female epidermis doesn't have to be Gallic to hold appeal, came up with a Broadway-type revue of equal magnitude and lavishness, *Pzazz*. It, too, was a smash.

Big Names are still booked into the Las Vegas spots in profusion, and they still draw—but so do the spectacular revues.

Even the cocktail lounges, where the tariff is a paltry drink minimum, compete heavily for name performers and acts.

New York City's somewhat tarnished Broadway doesn't like to admit it, but it simply cannot compete with Las Vegas in the area of top night-club entertainment. Its current supremacy is in the legitimate theater, and Las Vegas cheerfully concedes the serious drama laurels to the eastern seaboard metropolis.

Reno remembers when it was *the* gamblin' town, and it works hard to live up to its slogan, "The Biggest Little City in the World." The Ponderosa and Harrah's are first-class hotels, with or without gambling.

The new 24-story Harrah's, completed in October of 1969, was built over the casino, which never stopped operations for a minute during the 18 months of construction. It is loaded with innovations, and its convention center can seat 1,300 people, banquet style. An interesting part of the Harrah operation is the Harrah automobile collection, number 1,400 automobiles, 1,000 of them on display and the rest being restored at the rate of 20 or 30 a year.

William F. Harrah claims his gambling operation is the second largest in the world, second to Howard Hughes who, Bill Harrah concedes, became Number One by his acquisition of Harold's Club in Reno.

Harold's Club must be the champion billboard advertiser of all gambling enterprises, has for years been one of the most profitable, and may have just claims for its self-appointed title of the world's largest gambling casino.

Visitors to Reno get a huge kick out of watching Chinese gamblers playing their own distinctive games at the New China Club.

Reno now considers Lake Tahoe almost a part of its establishment, and there is no question but what the Tahoe skiing facilities and summer resort water sports have brought loads of business to Reno. Tahoe, however, has its own gambling, and plenty of it.

The new Kings Castle, a $20 million hotel-casino in Tahoe's Incline Village, opened in 1970, a 500-room mod-medieval pleasure palace with a Tudor theme. The hotel employees wear mini-mod Paris-designed medieval costumes that look like they've come straight from Camelot. The place was built and is operated by the same Nate Jacobson who built Caesar's Palace in Las Vegas.

Jacobson sponsors a $52,000 snowmobile Grand Prix race meet, to back up the skiing, and is making an all-out bid for family business, with a special youth center, open from ten in the morning 'til midnight.

Harrah's Tahoe is adding an 18-story hotel on the site of its present casino and theatre restaurant on the South Shore of the lake, with 522 rooms and a three-tiered parking facility to handle about 450 cars.

Lake Tahoe offers the gambler almost unlimited recreation facilities, Winter or Summer. Skiing, snowmobiling, skating, sledding, tobogganing, sleigh rides and hiking in the Winter, exceptional hunting and fishing, horseback riding, hiking, water skiing, boating, sailing, golf and scenic trips to historic landmarks, ghost towns, waterfalls, museums and the TV filming location of *Bonanza,* the Ponderosa Ranch, are all attractions.

Reno, which for years competed with Las Vegas on Las Vegas' terms—come and gamble—is now taking a new approach in its bid for gamblers' patronage. Colorful desert and snow-capped mountains, beautiful lakes, scenic grandeur, outdoor sports of every kind, the historical west—plus gambling—has a sales appeal that seems to be working, as evidenced by the building activity.

Both Reno and Tahoe offer the wayfaring gambler good food and good entertainment, with the larger

---

Bar Bet

"Here's an interesting little trick I just learned," the beer drinker said to the man standing next to him at the bar.

He buttoned the neighbor's top suit-coat button and then put a rubber band around the botton, giving it a couple of twists.

"All right," he said. "I'll bet you now that you can't take off your coat alone."

After considerable discussion, the bet was accepted. The fellow removed the rubber band from the button without the slightest difficulty, unbuttoned the top button of his coat and started to remove his arms from the sleeves.

As he did so, the beer drinker began taking off his own coat.

"I get it," the victim said sheepishly. "I didn't take my coat off alone. Your took yours off at the same time." He frowned. "But what did the rubber band have to do with it?"

"Window dressing," the beer drinker replied. "For some strange reason, it induces people to bet."

places going after Big Name attractions and getting them.

Aside from Nevada, the two most popular places for American casino gamblers to gather are the Bahamas and Puerto Rico.

For the east coast, particularly Floridians and Florida vacationers, a taste of gambling is available in the colorful Bahamas, a pleasant boat trip or quick plane jaunt from Miami.

The Lucaya-Freeport casinos are the closest. The Lucayan hotel casino is just off the hotel beach, and although called the Monte Carlo, bears little resemblance to that gambling institution. El Casino, farther inland, claims to be the largest gambling casino in the western hemisphere. It is not lavish or pretentious, and its size does nothing for the warmth that most casino management strives to acquire. Both places give the impression of being heavily policed.

The casino on Paradise Island in Nassau enjoys a beautiful tropical setting and has more of an air of luxury. Perhaps, too, Nassau's local color and traditions make a difference.

Natives of the Bahamas are strictly forbidden to gamble in either the Paradise Island or Lucaya-Freeport Casinos. They are for the tourists.

Puerto Rico is making a big play for North American gambling dollars. In addition to pari-mutuel horse-race betting and weekly state lottery drawings, there are casinos in most of the major hotels. The casinos are a cross between Nevada and Monte Carlo, but in neither class as far as big-money gambling is concerned. There's a $100 limit at the Craps and Blackjack tables and a $180 limit on an even-money bet at Roulette. One major reason for the low limit is said to be a desire to keep unsavory state-side characters from taking much interest in the Puerto Rican gambling scene.

Local gambling house rules give the Puerto Rican casinos a slightly heavier percentage against the player than Nevada takes. One of the more practical rules is that drinks may not be served to players.

The Caribe Hilton's casino is one of the largest and best-run. The Puerto Rican Sheraton casino is smaller, which has its advantages during the long off-season. Among other San Juan casinos are those in the San Jeronimo Hilton, the Condado Beach, the San Juan and La Concha.

The Conquistador in Fajardo is a 390-room hotel situated on several levels of a mountainside, with a funicular railway and tram cars instead of elevators. Lou Puro, operator of both El Conquistador and the San Juan, has a problem in that El Conquistador is a considerable distance from San Juan. Drop-in trade doesn't exist, and natives aren't permitted inside gambling casinos.

The hotel does turn-away business during the four-month Winter season, without conventions or groups—but must bring in players from the outside to keep the casino going during the other eight months of the year.

Planeloads of prospective players are sold on "executive packages," once called "gambling junkets," and brought in from the United States, with varying degress of success. Sometimes, a group that's flown in isn't interested in gambling, but Puro says that going out after business during the long off-season is vital.

His hotel and others in San Juan must buy "name" entertainment both in and out of season, because of the intense competition.

The strict government regulations limiting the size of bets unquestionably keep some big gamblers from choosing Puerto Rico as a playground, and every casino fights hard for a profitable share of the business. For all practical purposes, they must get it during a four-month span. As for the little extra "edge" their rules give them over Nevada casinos in some games, they point out that they need it to continue in business.

Tourist gamblers find spirited wagering on Saturdays and Sundays in the San Juan cockfights and at the horse races. The ultimate in action is to be found at the bullfights, which run from mid-December to May.

Antigua, an independent member of the British Commonwealth, offers Craps, Blackjack, Roulette and the unavoidable slot machines in its casino in the Holiday Inn.

Forget about gambling in Barbados, Bermuda and the Cayman Islands. Havana's once bustling casino activity is a thing of the past. There's livelier action in the Dominican Republic, where casinos operate highly in the El Embajador and Chantilly hotels. There are also weekly lotteries, and pari-mutuel wagering at the Perla Antillana track.

Haiti is certainly exotic enough to satisfy any tourist, with its voodoo tradition, La Citadelle and Sans Souci Palace. It is the oldest Negro republic in the world, and it needs the gambling dollars of tourists. There's casino gambling at the International Casino, and lotteries help to keep the economy going. The casino has floor shows on Wednesdays and Saturdays. Cockfighting is a popular gamble for the natives.

Jamaica's horse-race gambling is both pari-mutuel and legal off-track wagering. A government lottery offers a weekly first prize of about $24,000.

The island of Curacao has gone for casino gambling in a big way. There are casinos in the Inter-Continental, Flamboyant Beach, Holiday Inn and Hilton hotels, as well as in the nearby Aruba Carribean, Aruba Sheraton and Hotel Bonaire in Aruba.

Pari-mutuel horse-race betting and a national lottery that holds drawings every two weeks are the popular gambles in Trinidad, the home of Angostura Bitters.

The Virgin Islands aren't quite virginal as far as

gambling is concerned, but almost so. The one legal gamble is a monthly lottery.

Mexico has outlawed most forms of gambling, but there's pari-mutuel betting on horse-racing and Jai-Alai games, as well as a national lottery every Monday, Wednesday and Friday. There are even girls' teams in Jai-Alai. From December to March, the gambling instinct reaches its peak when bull-fights occupy every Sunday afternoon. The Plaza Mexico is the world's largest bull ring. The gambler touring Mexico who wants the experience of betting on cockfights must first find them.

Cockfighting is popular and wagering on them is heavy in Nicaragua. The main form of legal gambling is a government lottery, with profits going to Nicaraguan hospitals.

Panama is gambling territory. Casinos do a good business nightly at El Panama, El Continental and La Siesta hotels. The national lottery has drawings twice a week, and there's pari-mutuel betting at the race track. Bullfighting adds to the gambling fever in season, and cockfighting draws wagers all year long on Sundays, Mondays and holidays at the Club Gallistico.

Gambling thrives in many parts of South America. There are weekly lotteries in Argentina, and pari-mutuel horse-racing at Palermo and San Isidro. Casinos in Bariloche, Mar del Plata, Necoches, Miramar, Rio Hondo and a few other cities do a good business.

Bolivia has banned all forms of gambling except its state lottery. Brazil has a federal lottery with twice-weekly drawings and permits both on and off-track betting on the horses. Most forms of gambling are illegal, including one of the most active and profitable, the Numbers game, which hangs on outside the law.

Chile's foremost gambling casinos are in summer resort areas, at Vina del Mar and Arica. Roulette, Baccarat and Chemin-de-Fer get the big play. Seven race tracks do good business with pari-mutuel betting. The Concepción University lottery and the national lottery get substantial patronage.

From January to May, visitors to Ecuador will find casino gambling at the beach resorts on Salinas, Punta Carnero and Playas. All year long, casinos operate at the Hotel Inter-Continental Quito, the Hotel Humboldt and Hotel Colon in Quito, as well as in the Hotel Cimas, the Hotel Atahualpa and El Terminal night club in Guavaquil. There's pari-mutuel betting on the horses, at the equivalent of 25¢ a ticket. *Pelota de Guante* or glove-ball is a popular sport that attracts bettors. Bullfights run only occasionally. As in so many South American countries, there is a national lottery.

Peru has lots of lotteries, and the *polla,* a horse-racing pool that gets a big play. Bullfighting gives the gambler something to do on Sunday afternoons from January to April, and there's cockfighting on Saturdays, Sundays and holidays at the Coliseo de Sandia. Private clubs have illegal gambling, such as crap games, and Bingo is legal when run by authorized charities.

Uruguay has lots of casinos, and the night life of the country revolves around them, particularly during the summer. Among the better ones are those in the Parque and Carrasco hotels in Montevideo and those at the smart beach resorts. There's pari-mutuel betting on the horses, and, of course, a national lottery. *Pelota vasca* is similar to Jai-Alai, and is a big attraction for bettors. The casinos are cosmopolitan, and so are the restaurants, which feature superb dishes from around the world, including North American cuisine. A really excellent dinner costs anywhere from $3 to $4, including good local wine. Punta del Este, among the most famous resorts in South America, has numerous casinos, and they are the heart-blood of the night life.

Venezuela has no casinos, but lots of horse players. The "5 y 6" is a six-horse parlay that sells lots of tickets and ordinarily has a heavy payoff. Everywhere you go, you find municipal and state lotteries which have drawings at least once a week.

Cockfighting is a big gambling sport in the smaller towns and week-end cockfight cards run all day long on the weekends.

Night life in Caracas is expensive, with the tariff in the more elegant clubs higher than in spots of similar quality in the United States. Most of the entertainers must be imported, and there are no casinos to underwrite the overhead. In one smart French night spot, a cow is paraded through the room several times nightly to remind the customers that milk is "also" available to the thirsty.

As a rule of thumb, the best "buys" in night life in South America are to be found in the vicinity of gambling casinos. Gambling and night clubs seem to have an affinity for each other, and each is advantageous to the other.

Even where and when it is illegal, gambling in South America is done with a verve and enthusiasm. The South American zest for wagering approaches that of the Chinese. For the most part, their gambling is happy, even gay. Lotteries are a part of South American life, and even the poorest somehow find the money for regular purchase of inexpensive lottery tickets. In many cases, the lottery is their one hope for affluence. In some parts of South America, baseball is a growing outlet for the gambling urge. Regardless of legal restrictions, the South American finds ways to wager.

Legal gambling is light in the Middle East. Lebanon has a good gambling casino, the Casino du Liban, 12 miles north of Beirut on a drive that is scenically pleasing. The games are similar to those in Monte Carlo, and the casino's night club features an excellent dinner and European floor show, with prices that are pleasantly modest. Pari-mutuel betting is a part of the racing scene at Beirut's track, every Sunday afternoon.

A good deal of the gambling in Turkey is done privately. The country has pari-mutuel horse-racing and a national lottery, but no casino gambling.

Asia has always had gambling, but much of it today is under-cover and illegal.

The casino in Cambodia is strictly for the tourist trade, and the government makes sure of that by forbidding citizens of Cambodia to patronize the place. The only legal form of gambling offered them is the state lottery.

Hong Kong has pari-mutuel horse-racing and lotteries. Macao, six square miles of Portuguese territory on the China mainland, is one of the most colorful settings for casino gambling in the world, and is 40 miles away from Hong Kong, attainable by either ferry boat or hydrofoil. Sidewalk Mah-Jongg sessions are commonplace, with the players oblivious to the Chinese merchants in the crowded streets. Loud, brassy casinos operate next to quiet Buddhist temples. One new hotel, the Lisboa, has two casinos, and its room rates for double occupancy run less than $15 a night. Other new hotels have even lower rates. In addition to the casinos, there are excellent night clubs with good entertainment. Other gambles are greyhound racing, and Portuguese-style bullfighting.

The only country in the world where more money is bet on bicycle racing than on horse racing is Japan. Bicycle tracks operate in every major city, and the betting handle runs close to $200 million a year.

Bar Bet

The stranger pointed to an unopened bottle of brandy displayed on the back-bar.

"Bartender," he said, "I'll bet you five bucks I can drink a full jigger of brandy out of that bottle without breaking the seal, pulling the cork, breaking the bottle or tampering with it in any way."

The bartender thought it over, asked a few questions, and made the bet.

The stranger threw some money on the bar and said, "Before I try to win the bet, give me a shot of brandy." The bartender poured it and put it on the counter. "Now," the stranger said, "give me that bottle."

The bartender handed him the sealed brandy bottle. The stranger turned it upside down, poured the jigger of brandy into the cup-like indentation in the bottom of the bottle, and then tossed it off. He had drunk a full jigger of brandy out of the bottle without breaking the seal or doing any tampering. He had also won five dollars.

"Only certain brands of liquor have that indentation in the bottom," he warned the bartender. "Be sure you have that kind of a bottle before you try to win your money back."

Horse-racing is a poor second, and Japanese bettors also put their money on motorboat and motorcycle racing.

Government-sponsored lotteries get some play, but the gambling craze that took Japan by storm was a game called *Pachinko,* which burst onto the scene about twenty years ago and soon grew to a point where *Pachinko* houses were to be found everywhere.

Any tourist looking for exotic forms of gambling can wager on fishfighting and cockfighting in Thailand. The more prosaic can bet on the horses and buy lottery tickets. Most popular of private gambling games are Mah-Jongg and Dominoes, both with legal sanction.

In Africa, there are gambling casinos in Egypt in both Cairo and Alexandria, as well as betting on the horse races in both places.

Kenya has a 23-day horse-racing season, with wagering. Lotteries are legal, but of little importance. The big new gambling item is the casino at Nairobi, offered as an attraction for tourists.

Morocco has the gambling casino of Mohammedia, about 15 miles from Casablanca, the Casino of Tangier and the Casino of Marrakesh. There is also wagering at the dog and horse tracks. The casino night clubs, as in most places where casinos operate, are inexpensive and have good shows.

The Casino Africa gets lots of action at Accra, in Ghana. For the gambler who wants something else, there are a national lottery, horse-race betting, football pools, card games and Craps.

Nigeria offers just about every form of gambling, without state control, but football pool operators need a federal license.

Tunisia has the Casino Belvedere in Tunis, where Baccarat and Roulette are the "hot" games. There's also pari-mutuel betting on horses.

The handle of Tanganyika's lotteries and football pools is insignificant.

South Africa's only legal betting is on-track horse-racing through totalizators. Nevertheless, gambling thrives—particularly, gambling with cards and the game of Craps. South Africa's gambling regulations in the past have stipulated that gambling of any kind is illegal for black people.

There's always a way around gambling restrictions, even a legal way—and even if you're in South Africa. The South African or the tourist in the country who wants some no-nonsense casino gambling without danger of being arrested for law violation simply goes to Johannesburg and grabs a plane flight for Mbabane, Swaziland.

It's a short hop, and no visa is needed.

Mbabane has a mild climate, with a year-round temperature of from 60 to 70 degrees, and the gambling-bent visitor heads immediately for the Royal Swazi hotel and spa, part of the Holiday Inn chain, seven miles south of Mbabane.

It's a beautiful, modern luxury hotel, and there's a championship 18-hole golf course—but that isn't what prompted the trip.

Right inside the hotel, so that the gambler doesn't even have to expose himself to sunshine and fresh air, is the Royal Swazi gambling casino, a beautiful room where the action is high, wide and handsome.

Roulette, Blackjack and Chemin-de-Fer are the major games, and all get a heavy play from the hotel guests. The atmosphere is pleasant, the gambling is good, and life is so easy that most visitors find it difficult to leave.

Swaziland hopes that South Africa continues its restrictions against casino gambling, since the restrictions give the little country far more business than it would otherwise enjoy.

When a gambler who wants to impress his fellow-bettors can say, "One of my favorite casinos is the Royal Swazi. Where? Why, I thought everyone knew about it. It's in the Royal Swazi hotel and spa, near Mbabane, in Swaziland, and it's really elegant," he can lay long odds that nobody's going to top him. One visitor started what is probably the world's most exclusive gambling club, the SBP—more formally known as the Swaziland Blackjack Players.

In what can best be designated as the "Pacific" area, Australia is big on gambling. Horse-racing has betting either through the totalizators or through licensed bookmakers. One Sydney track can take care of 100,000 spectators, and there are three others. Trotting races take place on Friday nights, and greyhound racing on Saturday nights. Melbourne also has four race courses, one of which, Flemington, has a straight six furlongs for six-furlong races. The famous Melbourne Cup is run at Flemington on the first Tuesday in November. Football, played under Australian rules, attracts as many as 120,000 people.

Poker machines, a type of slot machines with the reels bearing pictures of playing cards, are highly popular in New South Wales, probably the only place in the world where they get any impressive play.

Probably the most important and significant addition to Australian gambling is the comparatively new casino in Hobart.

Horse racing is the biggest gambling attraction in New Zealand, with pari-mutuel betting. A unique feature is that bets may be placed not only at the tracks but through Totalizator Agency Board offices throughout the country.

Guam bets heavily on cockfighting and *carabao* races. New Caledonia has a short horse-racing season.

In the Phillipines, cockfighting is the most popular gamble, without any contest. Cockfight cards are weekly events, and the betting reaches fever pitch. Jai-Alai games bring out the money, too, and there is horse racing every Saturday and Sunday at San Lorenzo and Santa Ana. Baseball and basketball bring out additional wagering money.

Gambling thrives all over the world, and wherever it is restricted, the major objection is not so much to gambling as to (a) either the people who control it, or (b) the people who participate in it to excess.

Whenever unscrupulous people have gained control of legal gambling, public opinion has been outraged and an anti-gambling wave has formed. The Louisiana Lottery, for example, was conducted in such a flagrantly bad way that lotteries, once extremely popular in the United States, were declared illegal. It took the country nearly 80 years to get over the lottery scandals.

Today, state lotteries are definitely on their way back. New Hampshire, New York and New Jersey have them in operation and other states are giving them serious consideration. A need for more state funds, particularly in the area of education, has legislators looking desperately for additional sources of income, and the lottery is one answer.

The game of Bingo is already well on its way toward national legality and respectability. Illinois, which has resisted all efforts to make Bingo legal, is re-examining the situation. A new State Superintendent of Education in one state has just publicly announced that he is recommending Bingo as a means of saving private and parochial grade and high schools which are in precarious financial condition throughout the state. About a dozen states which have already legalized the game seem to be happy with it.

Off-track horse-race betting has been illegal almost everywhere. The city of New York has seen the millions and millions of dollars funneled into the pockets of bookies and has put itself into the bookmaking business. Success of the venture is by no means certain, but all the other states with pari-mutuel betting are watching the experiment with great interest.

I'll Betcha!

"Which of the two Lord's Prayer's in the Bible do they recite in your church?" the bettor asked.

"Why, there's only one Lord's Prayer," his listener replied.

"I'll bet you there are two Lord's Prayers in the Bible," the bettor insisted.

"There's only one prayer that's commonly accepted as the Lord's Prayer," the listener said.

"I'll bet I can show you a Lord's Prayer in two different places in the Bible and you'll admit that both are commonly accepted," the bettor maintained. He got his bet, and won it.

The Lord's Prayer appears twice in the Bible, in Mathew VI and St. Luke XI. Since it is the same prayer, the challenger has to admit that each is commonly accepted.

A few years ago, astute politicians would have blanched at the idea of suggesting legalized gambling casinos in their states. Casinos for Atlantic City and New York are now being seriously discussed.

Observers of the gambling scene feel that the first casinos on the Eastern seaboard may not appear in either of those places, but in Florida. They are unanimous in their belief that Nevada's monopoly on legal casino gambling will not continue. Let any other state declare casinos legal, they say, and a wave of casinos in resort areas all over the country will follow. Many superb resort areas, they point out, have natural scenic, climate and location advantages which have been overcome by Nevada's open gambling. Most important, they sense a change of public attitude toward gambling—a willingness to at least tolerate if not accept.

The change of attitude is by no means confined to the United States. England's Gambling Acts of 1960 and 1968 signalled an increase in legal gambling throughout the world. Criticism of legal gambling's growing popularity has been much less than anticipated.

The underworld that controls illegal gambling is violently opposed to its being made lawful and consequently coming under government regulation, with a part of its revenue going into government coffers. Illegal gambling revenue has furnished a large part of the financing for organized crime, and underworld bosses don't like to lose it.

In addition to being a major source of revenue for organized crime, gambling has been a much safer field of operation than other lucrative areas. Illegal gambling operations are regarded by gamblers in "closed" states as almost a form of public service. The general public looks upon bookies, football and baseball pools, parlay cards, floating crap games and other gambling in a far different light than it regards organized prostitution and the sale of narcotics. Even many courts regard gambling with a sort of tolerance, inflicting token fines as punishment for the immensely profitable operations that go merrily and prosperously on their way without much worry about serious legal crackdowns.

Public concern over an alliance between law enforcement officers and organized crime has grown in recent years, and adds impetus to the trend toward legal gambling, controled or supervised by government.

Moral and ethical viewpoints have undergone a change. "If people are going to gamble, which they obviously are," a New York legislator argues, "it is certainly more moral for them to gamble legally than illegally. And it is certainly far better from society's standpoint to have them contributing a small part of their gambling funds to public welfare than a larger part to the perpetuation of the crime syndicate. To divert money from organized crime and channel it into lowering our oppressive tax burden and improving our schools is highly moral, in my opinion."

Gambling, both legal and illegal, is on the increase. The population explosion accounts for part of it, but so do higher stakes. An observer at the Arlington Park race track in the Chicago area says, "The $2 horse player is practically a thing of the past. Most of the minimum tickets are now $10 and up."

The Numbers Game take is said to have not only been unhurt by economic showdowns, but to have gone sharply up. A police sergeant stationed in a slum area says, "You'd be giving the poor devils in the blight areas the break of their lives if the Numbers Game could be taken over by the government. They'd at least get a fair shake—a run for their money. Even if the government took 50 percent of the gross, the players would get a whale of a lot better return than they do now—and the profit could be used to help the people who buy the Policy tickets. God knows, they need help."

From the casual gambler's viewpoint, legalized gambling would be a great boon. Legal gambling is, for the most part, honest. In every country where it exists, it is supervised and regulated. Illegal gambling is quite a different story. While there are honest illegal operations, much illegal gambling is conducted by underworld characters who regard the customer as a victim and will take every possible dishonest advantage of him.

Perhaps the ill-fated experiment with Prohibition in the United States has pertinent bearing on the question of legal gambling.

The legal sale of intoxicating liquors had created problems. Some people drank too much. Some spent more than they could afford on liquor.

Then Prohibition came along. The sale of liquor passed into the hands of the criminal element. Prices on liquor skyrocketed and quality went dismally down. Drinking increased. The underworld, with a bonanza from the sale of liquor, was able to buy public officials. It created a crime syndicate that was the most

---

I'll Betcha!

"I can hardly wait for the earth to get farther away from the sun so that we'll have warmer weather," the bettor remarked.

"You've got that all wrong," a listener said. "It's warmer when the earth is close to the sun than when it's farther away."

"I'll bet you that the earth is closer to the sun in Winter than it is in Summer," the bettor offered, and the listener quickly took the bet.

He lost. In the United States, the earth is nearer the sun in Winter than in Summer. The U.S. Weather Bureau will confirm the statement.

powerful underworld organization in history. People went blind from fusel oil. Less fortunate ones died. Teenagers, who had never before been able to buy liquor, ruined their stomachs on rot-gut booze. Gangsters fought to take over lucrative areas, and machine gun killings became common.

Through it all, hoodlums became wealthy, and so entrenched in their power that law enforcement officials found it virtually impossible to touch them.

When the situation became completely intolerable, Prohibition was repealed and the sale of liquor was again legalized. Alcohol still presented social problems, but they paled into insignificance when compared to the problems of prohibition. The quality of liquor went up and the price went down.

John Q. Public found life with legal liquor far more satisfactory than Prohibition. Government generally operated in his interest, where the crime syndicate had operated solely for its own profit, to the exclusion of consideration for the customer.

The same gangster element that controlled liquor during Prohibition days now controls most illegal gambling in the United States. It has grown wealthier, wiser, and much more deadly. Through its enormous profits, it has branched out into legitimate business, bringing to it the same objectionable tactics it has always used outside the law.

Every day that the crime syndicate is permitted to control most forms of gambling throughout most of the United States, it strengthens its position and perpetuates its most objectionable features. It operates not only without consideration for the casual gambler, but without mercy.

Every piece of state legislation that legalizes any form of gambling and puts it under governmental regulation not only weakens the crime syndicate but helps the honest citizen.

Since a movement toward more widespread legal gambling is already under way, it is reasonably safe to assume that the gambling locales mentioned here will be substantially augmented during the coming year. Gambling has always existed and nobody's ever been able to stop it. As long as millions of people throughout the world are going to do it, anyway, current thinking is, "Let them gamble without breaking the law."

Whether you depend on a horseshoe, a four-leaf clover, a rabbit's foot or a shamrock, GAMBLER'S DIGEST wishes you luck. ♠

MR. ODDS-MAKER'S SUM-UP

Mr. Odds-Maker says, "The key to becoming a successful gambler is Money Management. Learn how to control your money, and do it. Everyone of probability guarantees it.

"But when you make 50 bets, win 25 and lose 25, and show a profit, then you've become successful. You've learned how to apply the one great secret of every good gambler."

A gambling memory

Bert "Kid" Valance was one of six names he used from the turn of the century up until about 1930, when he retired. He is now a hale and hearty 89 years old, clear of eye, steady of hand, slender almost to the point of frailty. He has a heavy mane of snow-white hair, good carriage and the impressive manner of a retired dignitary.

He has lived in Denver for a good many years in a comfortable but unpretentious little home. A woman comes in once a week to do the housecleaning, and he eats all of his meals except breakfast in restaurants. His funds have dwindled over the years to the point where he now has about $50,000 left.

"I can remember a good many years when I spent that much," he says, "but one of the nice things—and there are few of them—about growing old is that the older you get, the simpler your wants become. I watch television, I read, I take a five-mile walk every day, and I spend considerable time with a few old yokels who have formed an octogenarian club. Some of 'em are downright senile, and not one of 'em knows my past. I've told 'em I was in the investment business, handling other people's money, which is as close to the truth as I care to come.

"I never smoked, but I drink four ounces of good bourbon every evening before dinner. The older I get, the less liquor it takes to give me a glow. I still enjoy looking at a pretty girl, but that's all—just looking—and maybe remembering. The kind of penny-ante gambling I see around here bores the daylights out of me. Betting the horses has never interested me. For one thing, I can't shuffle a deck of horses—and for another, the 'vigorish' on the pari-mutuels is too high. Some of the members of the octogenarian club are big Bingo fans, but Bingo's a game for 'Marks,' old women and suckers. When you know you're being systematically taken, it's no fun.

"I feel pretty good, maybe because I get plenty of exercise and sleep. The one thing I know is wrong is that my mind wanders. I can recall every detail of something that happened 60 or 70 years ago, but it's hard to remember the news in yesterday's paper. And I ramble when I get to talking—jump from pillar to post."

Kid Valance was one of the last of the great gamblers—crooked gamblers, that is. He fleeced victims from one end of the country to the other, and went outside the United States for expeditions on ocean liners and trips to Mexico, most of them highly successful.

Why did he retire in 1930?

"The big money was gone," he explained. "The

Depression took it out of circulation, and it never came back. Then, too, what folks today call 'communications' improved by leaps and bounds. It got so that if you fleeced a mark in some little burg out in the sticks, police all over the country had a description of you within a couple of days, along with a report on how you'd operated.

"And the marks were getting too smart. Too much was written about crooked gambling, and too many prospects either read it or heard about it. Nearly everybody who got into a game with a stranger was suspicious and on the alert. The saps, the suckers, the innocent rubes were all but gone. The few people who had ready cash weren't risking it, even when they had what they thought was a sure thing. The stock market has shown them that sure things can go bust, and that what looks good on the surface may be all front with nothing behind it.

"After the crash, you had to hunt for marks, which was something I'd never had to do before. There were plenty of gullible people around, but you had to find one who could put up some money. And sometimes after you'd spent time and money in the buildup, he got frightened away before you could take him for the big killing.

"Prospects were so few that crooked gamblers often found themselves trying to hustle each other. Part of the buildup was to have a good front, looking well-heeled but naive. If you put on a good act, some alert hustler was bound to spot you and go to work on you. We decided we should wear some kind of identification to keep from wasting time on each other, but nothing ever came of it.

"I found a live one, a Nebraska banker who still had plenty of money. He was the larcenous type, and they're always the easiest to take. I only got him for $10,000, but he screamed like it was a million. Of course, he'd been unloading stocks and bonds on his customers for years at inflated, fictitious values, and he'd sold his customers who looked to him for financial advice on real estate that was greatly over-priced. The real estate, incidentally, was his, and the profit was his.

"Well, he brought fraud charges against me and had me picked up before I could get out of town. I wasn't much worried, because he didn't have a shred of evidence of fraud. But it turned out that he had something better. He had the judge in his hip pocket. I was brought before the judge who had always okayed all his real estate and stock deals and who had gotten him appointed as executor of all kinds of estates. As far as that judge was concerned, the banker's loss of $10,000 was proof of fraud. After giving me a long lecture, he sentenced me to a year in jail, which was a new experience—I didn't like it one damned bit. The worst that had ever happened to me up to that time was a $1,000 fine, which wasn't too hard to take. But that jail sentence was poison. During the eight months I was actually behind bars, I had time to do a lot of thinking. I had close to $400,000 cached in banks, stocks and bonds and other investments around the country—considerably more in government bonds than in banks, thank goodness. The depression was getting worse, and I could see opportunities for anyone who still had money to pick up some nice propositions.

"And the handwriting was on the wall. If I continued to operate as a hustler when I got out, I'd get picked up again, sure as shooting. Like I say, the cops were in touch with each other. I'd be a marked man, too, which meant I'd be watched, wherever I went.

"If the rewards had stayed as high as they'd been in the 1920's, I'd have been tempted to continue, but they'd dwindled to the point where they weren't worth the risk.

"When I got out, I invested in some distress property. You could hardly miss at the time with that kind of operation. Everybody knew that real estate prices were far too low, but not many had the cash to do anything about it. I did.

"I'd made my stake during times when income taxes meant nothing. It paid plenty in taxes later on, most of it in capital gains—but I guess I've got no complaints. Most of the crooked gamblers I knew who stayed with it died broke, or close to it.

"Some of the smarter hustlers sat back and waited for the good old days to return, but they were due for a lifetime wait. I never happened. Marks with enough money to make taking them worthwhile had become too sophisticated."

How had he become a crooked gambler?

"When I was 18 years old," he said, "I had a job working in a grain elevator. I wanted to get enough money to go to college, and getting it at $15 a week was no easy trick. There was a guy in the town running a crap game in his hotel room every Saturday night. You rolled the dice out across the carpet in the room, and I lost my whole week's pay in about ten minutes, the first night I got into the game. The same thing happened for three straight weeks.

"I didn't know it at the time, but the guy who ran the game was 'Mudcat' Mooney, one of the slickest mechanics who ever conned a sucker out of his bankroll.

"After I'd lost $45, which was a fortune to me, I noticed that Mooney was always the big winner. Either he knew something I didn't know or he was cheating.

"With all the innocence and brashness of a punk kid, I went to see him, and I told him that I wanted to learn to shoot craps as well as he did and would pay for instructions.

"He was studying me all the time I was talking, trying to come to a decision. A good gambler is always

a great student of human nature and can size up a possible mark in a few seconds. Mooney made up his mind about me.

" 'Kid,' he said, 'you could shoot craps against me from hell to breakfast and never beat me. Nobody who gets into my game can beat me if I want to win.' I asked him if he was using loaded dice, and he laughed at me. 'Hell, no,' he said. 'Anybody who uses gimmicks in a gambling game is living more dangerously than I ever want to live.' He explained to me that gimmicks were mechanical devices that enabled a crook to cheat.

" 'Whenever there's a gimmick in a game,' he said, 'there's always a chance that it will be spotted. And if it *is* spotted, you're dead. When I say you're dead, I mean exactly that. Somebody puts a bullet into you, or a knife—and I don't want either one. I use skill—nothing else. Kid, you've been the victim of the old blanket roll.'

"That didn't mean anything to me until he showed me what the blanket roll was. On any soft surface like a blanket or thick carpet, it's possible to control the roll of an honest pair of dice. It's all in the way you hold 'em and release 'em.

"He showed me how to hold the dice, how to make it sound like I was shaking them, and how to release them. I wasn't very good at it, but he commented that I had a perfect pair of hands for a hustler. 'You've also got a face like a choir boy,' he said. 'Maybe I can show you how to get that money for college. You go home and practice the blanket roll until you think you're good at it. Then come back here and get into the game, but bet with the marks, not with me.'

"It took me three weeks, all my spare time, to reach a point where I thought I could control the dice. I went back to Mudcat's game and won $150 in the first five minutes I had the dice. After that, everybody laid off of me. They decided I was too hot. I wound up the evening about $250 ahead, which was almost as much as I'd make in 17 weeks at my job.

"Mudcat was unhappy with me, though. 'You're a quick study, kid,' he told me, 'and you got a good pair of mitts. But you violated the first rule of gambling. You scared off the marks. Never, never, go out to kill 'em.Treat 'em gently, lead 'em along, encourage 'em, and bring 'em up to the point where they're ready for the big blow, where they'll gamble their bundle. Then smash 'em and get out. You got greedy too soon and scairt 'em off before there was any big money showing.'

"The next thing he showed me was how to run up a couple of hands with an overhand shuffle of a deck of cards. 'Running up one good hand isn't enough,' he told me. 'If you've got the only good hand in the game, you'll get no takers. When you can run up *three* good hands, you're ready to play cards for money. Three good hands, but yours is the best.'

"He was dead set against marked cards. 'Sure, some gamblers get away with using them,' he told me, 'but they're fools. There's always some way to spot a marked deck, and if one of your marks is smart enough to catch it, you're in bad trouble. I once saw a guy killed in New Orleans for dealing from a marked deck. The mark riffled the deck and saw the dots dancing around on the backs of the cards. Without any warning, he pulled a revolver and shot the hustler right through the heart. He didn't get into any trouble over it, either. The other players in the game all testified that the hustler drew on him and he shot in self-defense. I coulda sworn otherwise, but if I'da done it, I'da been dead the next day. They'da prob'ly found my body in an alleyway some place in the French quarter.'

"After a couple of weeks practicing run-ups with an overhand shuffle, he gave me a little paperback book, *Expert at the Card Table*. 'This book,' he said, 'is the card hustler's Bible. If you ever learn to do even half the moves in the book well enough to get by with 'em, you'll be one of the greatest card sharps in the business.'

"He showed me how to do a card crimp that he called the Mooney crimp, his own invention. It was so delicate that not even another card hustler ever detected it. In all my years in the business, I only ran across three gamblers who used the Mooney crimp. In a few hands of play, you could mark every face card in the deck so you could spot it—and nobody else could. You couldn't be accused of playing with marked cards, and yet you made any deck a marked deck. It's still the greatest way to mark cards that's ever been invented.

"Once I'd mastered the Mooney crimp, he taught me how to deal seconds and bottoms—and that took months to get, even with such an expert teacher. He was a tough taskmaster, and demanded that every move be perfect.

" 'One mistake in most businesses isn't too important,' he told me, 'but you're gonna be in a racket where one mistake is fatal. Until you can deal seconds or bottoms perfectly, without the slightest fear of getting caught, don't try to do it. With the Mooney crimp and a good second and bottom deal, you can beat any card player who ever held a hand—but you've gotta be able to do the moves perfectly. Absolutely without a flaw. If you goof, nobody's gonna be interested in your apologies.'

"Once he had me handling a deck of cards like a pro, he taught me something that very few gamblers can do. He taught me how to handle a deck of cards clumsily. 'Don't be a Fancy Dan dealer,' he warned me. 'Handle those cards like a big, clumsy ox, like you couldn't pull any fast ones if your life depended on it. Most card sharps handle the pasteboards like a sleight-of-hand performer doing an act, and that's all wrong, the worst thing you can do.'

"Believe me, once you could make a deck of cards

sit up and say Mama, learning to handle them like you didn't know anything about shuffling was no easy trick—but it was sure a good one, and it paid off.

"Mudcat had been in town about six months when he told me one Wednesday afternoon to pack my clothes and be ready to leave town late Saturday night. I didn't know what he was talking about. 'The big killing is set for Saturday night, kid,' he told me, 'and it may not be too healthy for me to hang around any longer than I have to after it's over. You're going with me. You're gonna work for me, and I'll make you rich.' He gave me instructions on my part in the Saturday night blowoff, and I agreed to leave town with him."

Valance's story of the first major coup in which he participated may seem crude almost to the point of incredibility, but it worked.

"Mooney had given me $500, with instructions to bet it against him, in amounts of not more than $25 at a time, and to lose it, which I did. When it was gone, I screamed bloody murder about not being able to afford that heavy a loss. Mooney smiled at me and said, 'I'll tell you what I'll do, kid. I'll take the dice and you can bet any amount you like against me—no limit. If I win, I'll let the winnings ride, not dragging one thin dime. And I'll keep leaving everything in the pot until I lose. Is that fair enough?' I answered, as I'd been told to do, 'It's more than fair, Mr. Mooney—only my money's gone. I'm cleaned, and you know it. You wouldn't make that kind of a proposition to the rest of the men in this game.'

"Mooney shook his head. 'That's where you're wrong, kid. The same deal goes for everybody in this room—and Mr. Swanson and Mr. Garner probably have more money in their kicks than I have.' Swanson was the cashier at the bank and Garner was the town's leading real estate man. They were the two biggest gamblers in the area. Swanson asked quickly if Mooney was on the level, and Mooney said he sure was. Garner put $1,000 on the line and handed Mooney the dice. Swanson peeled another thousand off a big roll of bills. 'Remember,' he said to Mooney, 'you let your winnings ride until you lose.' Mooney nodded, but added, 'Or until you can't cover all the money I'm betting.' Garner thought that was a big joke. 'That'll be the day, Mooney,' he said.

"Well, Mooney took the dice and shook 'em hard. At least, it sounded that way. He rolled a natural seven. I've never seen anybody better at the blanket roll than he was, and he'd had six months of practice on that particular surface. 'Well, boys,' he said, 'there's four grand to cover. Get it up.' They shelled out $2,000 apiece, and Mooney rolled another seven. 'Eight thousand to cover,' he said, without any expression in his voice. They put another $4,000 apiece on the line, and you could see that their rolls were getting thin. This time, Mooney rolled out a five-two. 'Sixteen grand to cover,' he said.

"Garner grabbed the dice. 'Just a minute,' he said. 'I want to look at these dice.' Mooney grinned. 'Look 'em over all you like. Do you wanta cover the 16 grand or don't you?'

"Garner got a glass of water and dropped the dice into it seven or eight times. The dice were as honest as could be; only the shooter was crooked. He and the banker talked alone over in a corner of the room for a minute, and Garner said, 'Swanson's going out to get us some more money. It won't take long.' Mooney nodded. 'Go right ahead. Just don't ask me to take any paper. Only cash.' Swanson left the room and Garner held onto the dice until he returned.

"He puffed out his chest like a pouter pigeon as he said, 'We've now got $30,000 apiece, Mooney, and if that isn't enough, there's more where this came from.' He gave half the money to Garner, and they put $16,000 on the line. This time, Mooney rolled out a four-three.

"He picked up the dice and said, 'Thirty-two grand to cover, boys.' They shelled out $16,000 apiece, and Mooney rolled a six, a five and another six. 'You had me sweating there for a minute, boys,' he said. 'Sixty-four thousand to cover.'

"Neither of the big bettors said a word for a few seconds, and then Swanson said, 'We've only got $6,000 apiece.' Mooney smiled and reminded him, 'You said there was plenty more where that came from.' Swanson gulped and turned to Garner. 'How about it, you want me to get you another $30,000?' Garner nodded, and Swanson left again. He came back with $60,000, and they covered the $64,000 that was on the line.

"Mooney shook the dice and rolled out a five-deuce. 'A hundred and twenty-eight thousand to cover, gentlemen,' he said. 'Do you have to leave again?'

"The sweat stood out all over Swanson's face. 'I can't get any more,' he said. 'That's it. We're both overdrawn as it is. There's something funny going on here.' Mooney shook his head. 'I've only made six passes,' he said, 'and there've been times when I was hot that I've made 13 or 14. My offer stands, gentlemen. I said I'd let everything ride until I crapped out or until you couldn't cover me any more.'

"Garner was shaking. 'How about taking our checks?' he asked. Mooney laughed. 'After Mr. Swanson just said both of you are overdrawn? No, thanks.' He began stuffing the $128,000 into his pockets.

"Garner hadn't given up. 'You tricked us,' he said. 'You gave us the idea that you'd keep shooting until we won. You made it sound like we couldn't lose.' 'I don't know how it sounded to you,' Mooney said, 'but I know what the deal was, and so does everybody else in this room.' I nodded, and then so did everybody else. Mooney shrugged his shoulders. 'Well, it seems that the game is over for the evening.' I walked to the door as Mooney'd told me to do, and everybody else followed, Swanson and Garner last.

"I met Mooney at the livery stable 20 minutes later. He'd bought a horse and rig, and we left town. We drove to a nearby town that was a railroad terminal, where Mooney sold the horse and rig to the livery stable proprietor for half what it was worth, and we took a train that eventually got us to Chicago.

"We stayed at the old Sherman House for a few days, living like kings, and Mooney drove home a point he'd made earlier. 'Kid,' he said, 'you saw how I nursed those two marks along for nearly six months. If I'd tried to take 'em for $126,000 the first week I hit town, what chance do you think I'd have had? None! Always remember, the buildup is half the battle—and don't get greedy 'til you're ready to make that final big hit.'

"We went from Chicago to some sleepy little bayou towns around New Orleans where Mooney had heard the pickings were easy. They were, but there wasn't enough money around unless you went into New Orleans, and Mooney wouldn't do it. I think he'd been in some kind of trouble there and was afraid of being remembered.

"When we went out to Montana and Wyoming, Mooney switched from the blanket roll to poker. He never switched in a cold deck and he never used marked cards. Heck, he didn't have to. We never roomed together, and I usually hit a town a few days before he did, and won a little money. Then Mooney came in and took it way from me. We got it established quick that there was bad blood between us, which was all part of the buildup. In a game with six or seven players, I usually made the haul on Mooney's deal and he made it on mine.

Mooney was real liberal with me, and I made more money than I'd ever dreamed there was. But I noticed right off that Mudcat worked the sticks, never the big cities, and I soon figured out why. He lacked the personal polish, the class, to get into fast company. Men of genuine importance were out of his league in every way except at gambling. I began going to the town libraries during the day when there was nothing to do, and in Sioux City, Iowa, I even took a course in French. Later on, I learned Spanish. I knew that if I wanted to play with real gentlemen, I had to learn to act like one and talk like one.

"I worked with Mooney for over two years before I struck out on my own, and I played the role of a young hair-brained playboy who had inherited a fortune and loved to gamble. It was funny to watch other card hustlers and dice mechanics trying to move in on me—until they found I was a member of the fraternity. Wherever I went, I tried to get in with a young, fast crowd, which was easy to do—and getting their money was like taking candy from a baby. Most of the young sons of wealthy fathers had no business gambling for anything bigger than pennies, but they'd lose $5,000 or $10,000 without batting an eyelash, and come back for more. Some of the playboys always told their fathers how good I was, and some of them nearly always decided to teach me a lesson. An Oklahoma oil man whose son had lost $20,000 to me decided to take me to the cleaners, and it was the biggest single evening's haul I ever made—180,000 nice, big dollars. I almost had to laugh when he paid off and told me, 'Son, I been around long enough to spot a crooked gambler from clean across the room—and I know you ain't a cheat. You're just plain too good for me—or for anybody else around here.'

"I liked working the trains, because you could work fast. You had to, if you wanted to make important money. Sometimes, I didn't even bother to pick a mark who looked like money. I'd just walk into the smoker and announce, 'Boys, I may look like I'm not dry behind the ears yet, but I've got $100 says I'm the best poker player on this train.' There were always at least three or four travelers who wanted me to prove it—which I did.

"I worked one train pretty often, a run between Chicago and New York. The conductor was going to stop me, the second time I took the trip, so I made him a silent partner. He'd tip me off on the well-heeled passengers and even drop the word to some of 'em that a poker game was getting under way in the club car or in my bedroom. For a while, I think he made more out of me than the railroad paid him.

"I had one real interesting experience on his train. A well-dressed, elderly man wearing a diamond ring that must have been worth 5,000 bucks got into the game. He claimed to be a New York financier. I soon noticed that whenever he dealt, I got an unusually good hand—but he got a little better one. I watched him closely and saw right away that he held the deck in a mechanic's grip when he dealt—a pretty good tipoff that he wasn't the gentleman he professed to be.

"I bet my hands on his deal, letting him take me for $10 or $20 each time. The crimps he'd put into the cards were so glaring it was almost funny. There were five players in the game, and during the course of the next four hands after his deal, I had plenty of chance to change the crimps without being detected. When his deal came, he shuffled, had the cards cut, and dealt. When he looked at his hand, the funniest expression came over his face I've ever seen in a card game. He stared at that hand, and began to sweat. He didn't know what to do. His cards weren't at all what they were supposed to be. I bet on three eights, and he folded like an accordion. When my deal came, I deliberately dealt him a royal flush in Spades. He stared at it, looked at me and bet a dollar. A couple of players stayed, but I folded. He hauled in his measley pot, got up and left the game. That was exactly what I wanted him to do, and he got my message. Before the game was over, I'd won $1,100, which isn't a bad day's work.

"The more poker I played, the less I cheated. I always let the first few hands run their natural course, without any attempt at fast stuff, and I found that most amateur poker players let you know what they're holding by the way they act. A good deal of the time, all I did was give the Mooney crimp to the four Aces. If on top of being a better poker player than the others in the game you always know where the four Aces are, you've got an edge that's pretty hard to beat. Only when I was playing for the big kill, a carefully built setup to take a mark for a big bundle, did I resort to sure-thing tactics. Since I'd played straight right up to that point, nobody was on the lookout for any funny business when it finally came.

"I found early in the game that giving the impression you'd had more to drink than you could handle was a big asset. The other players figured they were in a position to take advantage of you—and it was surprising how easily you could sneak quick peeks at the hands on either side of you under the guise of having had too much to drink and not paying proper attention to your own hand. The tipsiness fit in well, too, with my playboy role.

"A fellow who went under the name of Cornball Jason had the funniest drunk act I ever saw, and he lived high on it. He'd stagger into a saloon, apparently almost at the point of passing out, lurch up to the bar and pull a deck of cards from his pocket. 'I'm Cornball Jason,' he'd announce in a thick voice, 'and I'm one of the greatest card cheats that ever lived, so whatta you think about that? I can deal crooked hands like no other gambler in the world. The best, see? I deal you a hand that's good enough to make you bet everything you got on it, but I always deal myself a better one. I'll show you how it works.' He'd have spotted a likely victim at the bar by this time, and he'd give the cards a couple of clumsy shuffles, letting a card or two drop. 'Oops,' he'd say, almost falling down as he picked up the cards and put them back in the deck, 'I hope I didn't mess this up.' He'd hand the deck to his victim. 'Cut the cards,' he'd order. Everybody at the bar was interested by this time, and most of the onlookers were amused. Once the cards had been cut, he'd deal out two hands of five-card draw, all butterfingers. The victim would pick up his cards and see that he held four Kings. 'I bet you got a good hand, huh?' Cornball would ask. 'You always gotta give the sucker a good hand or he won't bet.' He'd wave his own hand around while he was explaining this, so that everybody in the place could see he held a full house, three jacks and a pair of aces. 'All right,' he'd continue, 'this is five-card draw. How many cards you want?' The victim would either stand pat or draw one card. 'Now, before I draw, before I even look at my hand, I'll bet you any amount you wanta bet that I'll have you beat. I'll bet that way because I've got a sure thing. I know I'll have you beat because I know what cards you'll have and what cards I'll have—and I know mine will be better. I'll cover anything up to $1,000. How about it?'

"He pulled a big roll of bills from his pocket, waving it in one hand and his cards in the other. Everyone at the bar reasoned that the drunken bum had made a grievous miscalculation, giving the other fellow the cards he was supposed to hold. He seldom got takers for less than $100, and sometimes got the entire $1,000 covered.

"Once the money was up, he discarded his three Jacks, drew three cards, and turned-up his hand—four Aces and a deuce. He picked up the money, shook his head in bewilderment and observed, 'I just can't understand why anybody will bet with a gambler who admits he's crooked and tells 'em exactly what he's gonna do.' He lurched for the door, staggered around the corner and walked quickly away, now cold sober.

"He worked with a stacked deck and only had to make one move that required the slightest skill, depending on whether the victim drew a card or not. If he didn't, Cornball got the one indifferent card off the top of the deck to leave the pair of Aces as the first two cards of his draw.

"He told me that, surprisingly, the 'Drunken Deal' as he called it worked much better in cities than in the sticks. He'd done a lot of thinking about it and his only explanation was that the small town hicks often felt sorry for the poor drunk and didn't want to take advantage of him. He'd work every bar in a city, one after the other, and then move on.

"I loved working the river boats on the Mississippi. It was a pleasant, easy life and the money was plentiful. Some of the wealthy Southerners were real gamblers. Unfortunately, some of them were also extremely hot-headed. I usually acquired a Southern drawl the minute I boarded one of the boats, because they were less suspicious of a Southerner than a Northerner. One of my problems was my youth. Where the young Southern hot-heads who lost their money would have respected the age of an older man, they invariably wanted to fight me when I took them to the cleaners. And it would have looked extremely fishy for a young fellow like me to have a bodyguard—as if I was expecting trouble. My final solution to the problem was to avoid beating the young Southern dandies and take money only from the older men. It was hard to pass up such easy pickings, but after I'd been beaten up a few times, I convinced myself that letting them break nearly even was the only wise thing to do.

"One wealthy old Southern gentleman who was traveling on one of the boats was a rabid poker enthusiast. He even resented having to take time away from the poker table to eat. He bet rather conservatively and his game was so sound that it was hard to take him for the big roll he was carrying. I finally ran up a hand on him—a full house, Aces on sixes, and dealt myself four nines. He made a modest opening bet and I immediately raised him $100. He studied his hand briefly, and said 'I'll see you,' putting $100 into the pot. Of course, I had him beaten, but when he showed his hand, I said, 'If I'd had a hand like that, I'd have raised you to Kingdom Come.' He smiled blandly and answered, 'Son, these two hands just confirm what my old daddy always preached to me. He told me never to get greedy in a poker game, just to string along and be content with winnin' a little money. He told me that sure as shootin,' if I tried to take advantage of another player, I'd lose my shirt.'

"It brought something home to me. The mark has to have the killer instinct, want to take you for all you've got, or you can't take him for much. The amateur poker player who loses the most is the one who's the greediest. Let him think he has a sure thing and he'll try to get you to bet every penny you have. It's the player of that type who was my meat. You might say, my Chateaubriand.

"One of the things that kept me from having a guilty conscience about weaning the marks away from their money was that they were eager to take every advantage, fair or foul, that they could possibly get. If you inadvertently exposed one of your cards, they'd make the most of it. If you made the slightest error, they'd call you on it and take the pot.

"Every once in a while, you'd run across one who would try to cheat—and his efforts were usually laughable. My policy was always to let a fellow think he was getting away with it—and then cut him to ribbons with some real professional cheating that was far beyond anything he ever dreamed of.

"On one of the old river boats, I once got into a two-handed game of five-card stud with a prosperous-looking young man who pulled his own deck of cards from his pocket and suggested playing.

"He let me make the first deal, and it was apparent just from a riffle shuffle that I had a marked deck of cards in my hands—not only a marked deck but a miserably crude one. What it amounted to was that he knew the value of my down card. On his own deal, his style of play was an immediate tipoff as to whether he had me beat or not, and if he thought he had, I didn't argue with him. On my deal, however, I overhand shuffled and ran up hands where it would look like he had me beaten until each of us was dealt his last card. I did my heavy betting after the third face-up card was dealt, and I'd run up the hands so that by reading my down card, he was sure he had me. On the fourth face-up card, of course, he knew that he'd lost—and I took him for $2,500 in a few hours, playing with his marked deck that I couldn't read. When he finally quit, he walked out onto the deck and threw his cards into the river. I innocently asked him why, and he told me, 'Those cards were bad luck,' and stalked away.

"I once got into a poker game in a neighborhood hotel on Chicago's North Side. I'd played for several evenings, winning nice money, before I learned that I'd been playing with members of the old prohibition syndicate. I continued to play, and continued to win—although I was careful not to win so much that I'd make anybody angry. From what I later discovered, the men in that game were tough nuts, with two of them having been charged with murder, but they were convivial and gentlemanly when they played poker. They played for relaxation and to kill time, and they were making enough money so that a fairly stiff loss didn't bother them. Not one of them ever tried to cheat, and I suppose they felt that no outsider would ever have the audacity to try any fast ones against them. One evening, a burly young man stopped by for a brief conference with one of the players. After he'd left, one of the players mentioned that the fellow's name was Al Brown. It was several years before I learned that the visitor had undoubtedly been Al Capone. After I'd been a consistent winner in this game, one of the players asked me if I'd be interested in running a poker casino setup in Cicero, Illinois, but I quickly declined. The reason for the offer, the fellow explained, was that the 'take' from the operation was lighter than they thought it should be, and they were suspicious of the casino manager. It didn't sound to me like a job that had much future in it."

Strangely, Valance said that he always enjoyed participating in a crooked game of any kind much more than in a straight one. "A straight game with players of equal ability gets down to sheer luck," he explained, "and you might as well be flipping coins. If the players aren't of equal ability, which is true most of the time, you can win without half trying—and that's extremely boring. Frankly, there's an excitement about a crooked game that can't be duplicated. You're playing dangerously, almost literally staking your life on your ability to cheat the marks. You need steady nerves and a lot of sheer guts. And more than anything else, you need skill. One miscue and you're washed up. Playing under those circumstances was really exciting.

"Unfortunately, you seldom played under those circumstances, because you didn't need to take chances. To put it simply, you could win without cheating. And you didn't want to create the slightest question of your integrity until you were ready for the Big Kill.

"The Big Kill was always the ultimate in excitement for me. I'd put in a lot of hours and sometimes invested considerable money bringing the marks along to the point where I thought they were ready to be cleaned out. I always had everything planned in advance and knew exactly what I was going to do. However, things almost never worked out exactly as planned. Something nearly always happened that called for a quick change of strategy, approach or method during the play. I had to make a quick decision under those circumstances, and I knew that the decision better be right. At times like that, gambling was the most fun for me.

"Most of the stories you hear about cold decks are pure poppycock. Ringing a cold deck into a game isn't easy, and it's always dangerous. Since I always followed Mudcat Mooney's advice about never using mechanical gimmicks of any kind, including such things as holdouts or bugs to hold a cold deck in readiness for the switch, cold-decking was extremely difficult.

"One time I had to use a cold deck. I wanted to keep two wealthy marks in the game right to the finish, both thinking they had sure winning hands, and I wanted to get three other players out early, to avoid cluttering the action. This meant setting up six hands—30 cards—and the balance of the deck, so that nobody could accidentally draw a hand that would beat mine. Now, I can run up three hands in a riffle shuffle if I have to, but six hands and the rest of the deck? Nope. Not me. So I set up a deck carefully, put a good crimp in the bottom card and cut the crimped card to about the middle. I put this deck in the drawer of the telephone table, along with a couple of others and a pencil. I gave the hotel switchboard operator a $10 bill, along with instructions that exactly two minutes after I asked for room service, she should call me, ask for me by name if anyone else answered, and stay on the line until I hung up.

"When I was ready for the Big Kill, I noticed, just before the cards were gathered up from the preceding hand, that we needed more ice. I called room service and ordered it. Then I went back to the table and gathered the cards as deliberately as possible. I began a thorough riffle shuffle, and accidentally dropped a couple of cards onto the floor. The player sitting to my right, one of the two marks I hoped to take, picked them up and handed them to me. I stopped shuffling to joke about my clumsiness, gave the cards an overhand shuffle, and then several more riffles. The phone rang, and I jumped up, cards still in hand, and lunged for it. 'This may be an important call I've been expecting,' I said, and the players watched me go to the phone and pick it up from the cradle with my left hand, the cards clearly in sight in my right. 'A call for whom?' I asked. Pause. 'Operator, why wasn't I given the call earlier? I see. Did he leave a number? Good. Just a second while I get a pencil.' With my left hand holding the phone, I opened the drawer of the phone table with my right, reached in, dropped the deck of cards I'd been holding, picked up the stacked deck and a pencil and withdrew my hand, closing the drawer. I copied a number on a slip of paper and repeated it to be sure I had it right. Then I hung up. 'He's waited this long; he may as well wait 'til the game is over,' I said as I came back to the table. I sat down, gave the deck a false riffle shuffle which didn't disturb the order of a single card, and offered it to the mark for a cut. He cut, obligingly, to the crimped card, which meant I didn't have to do a sleight known as the pass to get it to the bottom, and I dealt.

"Every move I made had been completely natural. If anyone had remembered that I opened the drawer with the deck in my hand, an examination would have shown three decks of cards in the drawer, none of them stacked. Nobody could have proved a thing. I won $34,000 on that one cold-deck deal, which made all the preparation worth doing.

"I reached the conclusion early in my career that the simplest way of cheating is nearly always the best. The more complicated an operation becomes, the more chance there is of getting caught.

"I've seen gamblers using shiners to read the faces of cards, and I wouldn't be caught dead with one. Why? For the simple reason that if I were caught, that's how I'd soon be—dead.

"I never even liked to use a slick Ace, which is practically indetectable. If I wanted a locator card, I broke diagonally opposite corners of a card, as close to the corner as possible. A slight riffle would make that card show its whereabouts with a snap, every time, and nobody in the game could say how the card had been damaged or who had done it. Actually, nobody ever noticed it.

"A card sharp by the name of Dodo Verzani once showed me a dealing move where you tossed out the cards by gripping them between the first and second fingers of the right hand and flipping them out across the table. The move enabled you to lift up the rear corner of any card you dealt with your thumb and spot its identity. It was a beautiful move, but it depended on a flourish, a tricky way of dealing, and that wasn't my style, so I only used the move on rare occasions.

"One of the most beautiful moves I ever saw was taught to me by this same man. In draw poker, you noted the cards in your discard and remembered them in order. Since you were the dealer, your discard cards went on top of the discard pile. You usually used the move when all you had was a pair. You dealt yourself three cards after discarding. If one of them matched with one or more of the cards in your discard, you gathered up the discard pile before you added your new cards to the two you held, holding your draw between the right thumb and forefinger and the discard pile between your other fingers and your palm. In making a move to throw the discard pile aside, you switched one or two of your draw cards for one or two of the cards you had just discarded. Your hand was making a broad, sweeping motion in tossing the discards aside, and the card switch was a very small motion. Done with any speed at all, it was impossible to detect. If anyone had accused me of doing it, I'd have invited him to try such a thing and he'd have decided his accusation was completely ridiculous. I've gotten many a full house or two pairs with that move and I was always tempted to use it, even when I didn't need to, because I liked it so much."

He did the move four or five times, and the GAMBLER'S DIGEST interviewer wasn't able to detect the slightest irregularity. He chuckled. "When you can make up your hand from eight cards instead of five, it gives you somewhat of an advantage over your opponents," he observed.

"San Francisco used to be a great town for card hustlers," he said. "The action was always fast, and the losers usually took their losses with good grace. Los Angeles was a bad town. It had too many amateur crooks who didn't know their business and scared off prospective suckers from getting into big games. I played one time with a big star of the old silent films, and he was one of the crudest, most obvious card cheats I ever saw. Everybody who played against him knew what he was doing, but he was such a poor poker player that he couldn't even win with his flagrant cheating. I was warned before I got into my first game with him that I shouldn't call him, for the excellent reason that he swung enough power in the L.A. area to make bad trouble for anyone he disliked.

"Well, he should have disliked me plenty, because I took him for over $5,000, letting him think that he'd rung in a stacked deck on me. I top-palmed a single card from the top of the deck when I cut, carefully cutting to the card he had crimped, and then added the palmed card to the top of the deck as I shoved it back to him for dealing. He got so flustered when he picked up the hand I was supposed to have that he lost his head completely and played the rest of the evening like an idiot child.

"There have always been capable card hustlers and incompetent ones. To start with, the lousy ones have never learned the fine art of poker. Usually, they depend on marked decks, and they soon get caught. A good card hustler never gets caught, because even if you suspect what he's doing, there's never any concrete evidence that could lay him low. To accuse a man of dealing the second instead of the top card is easy, but to prove that he did it is impossible. See what I mean?

"Another reason why the good hustler doesn't get caught is that he only cheats when cheating pays. He lulls your suspicions. You can watch him all evening and not see anything wrong because there's nothing to see. Then, when he gets ready to make his big haul, you're off guard and he takes you without your suspecting a thing.

"Your manner has a lot to do with how you get by. I never went past high school but most of the people I played against would have bet I was a college graduate. I'd done a lot of traveling and reading, and I'd hobnobbed with important people enough to know how they act—and how they want their associates to act.

"Another thing, I never went into a big game that I didn't lose a few big hands. I did it intentionally, investing for the big win. If the players are any good at all, it doesn't stand to reason that one player is going to win every big pot. You're tempted to do it, but you scare the marks out of the game if you succumb.

"Twice during my career, I even lost the Big Killing because I saw that conditions weren't right and that I'd stand a good chance of getting caught if I went ahead and built things up to a huge pot. I just sat back, took a fairly good-sized loss and waited for the right time.

"There's a certain type of loud-mouth loser who's sure he's been cheated whenever he loses a dollar. Most of the time, this idiot couldn't beat you if you let him run through the deck and pick out his hand. With a player of that kind in a game, I never went for the big killing. I always waited for another evening when he wasn't around.

"If I liked a mark, I never took him for as much as I did if I found him obnoxious. No matter how poor a player he was, I usually let him off easier than he deserved. When a player got under my skin, though, I was absolutely merciless.

"A cheap politician in New York City once irritated me so much that after all his money was gone, I took his watch, his diamond ring, and even the suit of clothes he was wearing. I actually made him call and have another suit sent over, so that he could leave the suit he'd worn into the game.

"On the other hand, a nice, middle-aged business man who loved to play poker, win or lose, once begged me to take a $10,000 mortgage on his business, in order to stay in the game—and I refused to do it.

"It wasn't that I had suddenly become a philanthropist or that I was soft-hearted. No true gambler can afford to be lenient while he's gambling. More than once, I've seen a player permitted to stay in a game on credit, develop a streak of luck and clean the players who were so lenient with him.

"I refused to take the mortgage on the mark's business for several reasons. One, the story would have spread all over town that I'd not only taken all the man's cash but had put him in a spot where he could lose his livelihood to me. Since I intended to operate in the community for awhile, it would have been terrible advertising for me and would have scared marks away from games in which I was involved.

"Two, in addition to my liking the man, he was popular with everyone in the community, and taking a mortgage on his business establishment would have made me decidedly unpopular. People would have resented it and would have tried to make life uncomfortable for me.

"Three, since this happened in a state where gambling was and still is illegal, there would have been a question about the validity of the mortgage if the heavy loser had later decided to go into court. Trying to make a gambling debt stand up in a state where gambling is against the law is usually a waste of time and money."

Asked if he had been acquainted with many crooked gamblers, Valance laughed. "Lots of 'em," he replied, "but the only ones who ever admitted it were hustlers who were working with me on a deal. A crooked gambler would have to be either out of his mind or completely cornered to admit being a cheat. I saw some of the greatest operate and saw the methods they used, but not one of them ever admitted a thing to me, even though they knew I was onto their tricks. Mudcat Mooney, Verzani and a few others talked freely to me because I was working with them. They knew I could never put the finger on them without incriminating myself, too.

"I think it was Yellow Kid Weil, one of the greatest confidence men of all time, who once said that a crooked gambler never admits his crookedness unless he's senile, and since he's senile, such an admission doesn't count.

"In the first quarter of this century, big-time gamblers were glamorous figures. Since their occupation, itself, was illegal almost everywhere in the country, doing something illegal in the pursuit of their occupation didn't bother them. A good many professional gamblers assumed that the other professional gamblers they knew were just as crooked as they were, themselves.

"It always amuses me to read about the glamorous gamblers of the Old West. I worked all through that part of the country, and nearly every saloon and pool hall had gambling games, no matter how small the town. I don't think I ran across a single dealer in a single establishment who was strictly on the up and up. Every dealer was a card sharp, capable of making a deck of cards do whatever he wanted it to do. The counter dice games were controlled by electro-magnets. The wheels of fortune were gaffed so that the operator could stop them on any number of his choice. Every dice game ran in six-ace flats whenever the occasion warranted. Even the inevitable punchboard was rigged.

"Actually, it was bad, stupid business for the proprietors of the western gambling halls to employ such tactics. They'd have made twice as much money if they'd operated straight. As long as you give the sucker a fighting chance, he'll come back with more money. If he loses constantly, he soon grows tired of the routine and quits, unless he's a compulsive gambler and an utter fool. At the time I quit, poker was the big game. The blanket roll had become well enough known so that shooting dice on the bedspread or a thick rug was difficult to make popular. In most games where any money was involved, the players had to bank the dice against a board when they threw them. Loaded dice could beat the game, but I always remembered Mudcat's advice and stayed away from such things.

"As I started to say, poker had become my major source of income—and in the last ten years of my career as a gambler, I'd guess that I only cheated in one round out of a 100. Maybe I wouldn't even have had to cheat then, but that hundredth game was the Big Kill, usually for thousands of dollars, and I didn't want to leave anything to chance.

"Looking back, I think the average card hustler could have played straight and above-board and taken the marks for almost as much as he did with trickery.

"I've gone to Las Vegas a few times in recent years, and the games there are honest above reproach. I'll bet that the casinos make twice as much money, operating as they do, as they'd make if they hustled the customers.

"I played some Blackjack in Las Vegas and won more than enough to pay for my trips. Sure, I won, but the house was going great. The way most of the marks played made me sick to my stomach. Nobody needed to cheat them. They were cheating themselves far more than any crooked dealer would dare to do—cheating themselves with their dumb play.

"I went into a nice poker club in Gardena, California, a few years ago, and I itched to play. It was all I could do to stay out of the game, but I'd sworn after that one-year jail sentence that I'd never play poker for money again. I know how to win by fair means or foul, you see, and I know I'd be tempted to try some of my old techniques if the cards ran against me."

If he had it to do over again, would he be a crooked gambler?

His answer was quick and decisive, if complicated. "Not today. I should say not! A crooked gambler can't make the grade today. There's not much of a place for him to operate, and what there is wouldn't appeal to me at all. No crooked gambler today can operate for long without attracting the notice of the police—and when he does, he's in trouble. The chances are, he'll spend more time behind bars than out.

"But remember that I was a poor kid from a poor family, living in an area where there wasn't much opportunity for the likes of me. I had no profession or trade. If I hadn't hooked up with Mudcat Mooney, I'd have probably spent my life in that grain elevator, grubbing out a bare living.

"Gambling got me out into the world. It got me a pretty fair education. It gave me an exciting life. Probably the most important thing it did was give me the stake for real estate investments that made me far more money than I ever got in crooked card games. I've lived high, I've known interesting people, I've traveled around the world and I've been in complete retirement since 1940, without a worry.

"I did things that were wrong and dishonest—things I wouldn't dream of doing now—but times were different and attitudes were different.

"This sounds terrible, I know, and it runs contrary to all the copy book maxims, but I think it was the luckiest day of my life when Mudcat Mooney took me under his wing."

It took considerable persuasion to get Kid Valance to talk, much as he wanted to reminisce. He did it, finally, only with the stipulation that his identity would be so thoroughly disguised that nobody who knows him today would identify him. Names have been altered. Is Denver actually where he lives? Maybe! maybe not. Is 89 his correct age? Somewhere in that neighborhood. Do his assets total exactly $50,000? No. That amount is on the low side, but 31 years of living well and traveling widely without taking the slightest interest in making more money have substantially depleted his fortune. Who will inherit his remaining funds when he dies? His plans are so specific that revealing them would be a give-away, but whatever money is left will go to a worthy cause. Does he have any living relatives? No. He's the last of his line, and was disowned by his father about 60 years ago.

Has he repented his sins? We doubt it—but he has been scrupulously honest since 1930. He has made and continues to make generous contributions to the church of his choice. He put one old friend who was down on his luck back on his feet with an outright gift of $10,000.

Has there been any romance in his life? Yes, but the subject is a painful one for him to discuss. "Gambling and marriage," he said ruefully, "aren't compatible, if you're talking about the kind of gambling I did, barnstorming all over, never settling down. To be honest, I knew I wasn't anywhere near good enough for the one woman I really loved. She wanted to marry me, but I knew that it wouldn't be fair to her and that she'd wind up hating me. I couldn't have any permanent involvement, so I had a series of quick romances during my years on the road. They were a poor substitute for marriage and they cost me a lot of money, but they were the best I could do."

Is he lonely?

"Of course," he said, "but what man my age isn't? The parade has passed me by, and all the friends who meant much to me are dead. I'd be lonely now even if I hadn't been a crooked gambler. That has nothing to do with it. When I was a gambler, I had the ability to make friends quickly at any level of society, and I've had no difficulty making friends in the octogenarian club. I can't expect young people to spend any time with me. They live in a different world and there'd have to be something wrong with them for them to be interested in a doddering old man."

What, today, gives him the greatest pleasure?

"Reading," he said. "I read everything—novels, non-fiction of all kinds, a few good magazines, and the newspapers. God bless the magazine and newspaper editors and publishers. Without them, I'd be more dead than alive. With them, I think I know what's going on in the world and why. They keep my interest in current events alive."

Does he miss the old life?

"Sometimes," he admitted. "It was exciting—but I have a suspicion that its grown more glamorous than it really was, the farther I get away from it. There was nothing glamorous about those eight months in jail, I can tell you. And my years of travel after 1940 were wonderful times, seeing the world. The ten years in real estate were exciting, too. I thought at the time I was still gambling, but I realize now that anybody with money during the Depression couldn't help but make more. You miss anything that's fun and exciting, after it's over. Now that you've got me thinking about it, I guess I miss the crooked gambling years less than the years that followed."

Does he miss not having had a family?

"Sure," he said, "but I'd have been a rotten father. I think one thing that kept me from marrying was that—well, a man wants his children to be proud of him—and my children wouldn't have had anything to be proud of."

Does he have any plans for the future?

"I'll probably have to go into one of these old people's setups before long. There'll come a time when I can no longer take care of myself. But the old people's homes today are a lot nicer than they used to be." He grinned broadly. "I understand that a lot of wealthy old birds in those places just love to play poker. Maybe when the time comes that I have to join them, I can start a new career." ♠

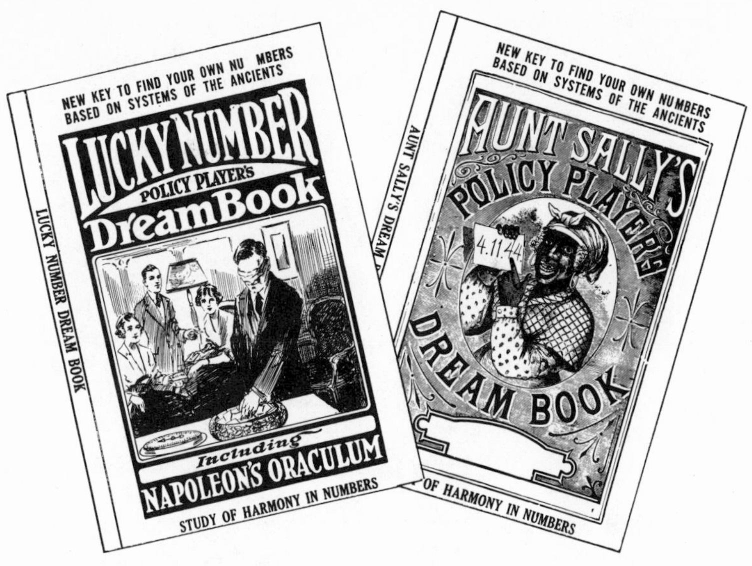

Luck and superstition

Anyone who didn't flunk arithmetic can be taught to figure mathematical probabilities. True odds may be determined by analysis of existing facts. Past performance can be weighed against present competition.

If you can't figure your chances of filling an inside straight in a poker game, you can find the information, along with carefully compiled statistics showing your chances of improving any poker hand that's dealt you.

The psychology of good gambling can be acquired. A good system of money management can be worked out and followed.

You can learn how to ferret out "edges," bets in which you have an advantage. You can recognize the odds in almost any betting situation that arises, if you'll take the trouble to do it.

And then, armed with an abundance of sound, factual information, you can start betting.

So what happens? Yon lose, that's what happens—while some lucky fugitive from the loony bin bets blindly and wildly—and wins heavily.

"Lucky" is the key word, and Lady Luck is the most fickle jade that ever breathed sweet promises into a gambler's ear.

Professional gamblers don't depend on luck because they've learned from long and sad experience that nobody can count on it. They don't depend on it, but they recognize its existence and hope it will be with them. With superb skill and superior knowledge, they'll tell you, plus a little luck, you can win big money. With the same superb skill and superior knowledge, minus the luck, you can—well, you can lose your shirt.

There are times in every gambler's life when the law of mathematical probability seems to have been repealed. There are times when what happens is completely unpredictable because it's so completely different from what *should* happen.

A 40 to 1 candidate for the glue works, a broken-down horse that couldn't catch a stalled bus, suddenly gets the inspiration to win one race before it goes out to pasture, and breezes away from the other horses, winning by four lengths.

A candidate for the Triple Crown, a horse that nobody in his right mind would bet against, decides one afternoon that it just doesn't feel like running—and nothing can change its mind.

Or you get the correct odds when eight is your point—and promptly crap out. Even worse, you roll out two, three and 12 in succession, followed by a four, which you fail to make.

One of the soundest Blackjack players in the world, an expert who beats the house at the game consistently, tells of sitting next to a middle-aged matron one evening at the blackjack table. Following every accepted betting procedure, he lost $58. "So help me," he says, "that woman had a nine up and a Queen down and took a hit, because the dealer's exposed card was a Jack. And do you know what the dealer hit her with? A deuce! She played the worst Blackjack

I've ever seen in my life—and left the table with a $300 profit. Everything she did was wrong—but not wrong for her that night. When she doubled down on a pair of tens and got hit with two Aces, I decided that I knew absolutely nothing about the game.

"And my luck was just as bad as hers was good. With a seven and four dealt, I got hit with a deuce, followed by a King.

"What can you do when the cards run like that? Run up the white flag. Surrender! Get out of the game and find a quiet bar where you can spend the rest of the night brooding, and cursing your luck."

Some gamblers maintain that they can always tell when they're going to be lucky. How? They get a "feeling." They can't describe it, but it's there and they always recognize it.

One pro snorts in derision when he hears a statement like that, which is frequently. Pure bunk, he says. "Those guys *always* have that feeling, and they remember the times when they're right. If they lose, they forget as quickly as possible. For once, they were wrong, so forget it! Most good gamblers are eternal optimists. If they didn't have a feeling they were going to win, they wouldn't get into the game.

"I've kept a record, just for fun, of the times I felt particularly lucky during the last five years. The record shows that I *was* particularly lucky on roughly 47 percent of those occasions. And, just like everybody else, I later bragged, 'I knew when I went into that game that I was going to be a big winner. I felt it in my bones.' It makes a good story when you tell about your omniscience. The only thing wrong with it is that your foresight is wrong just as often as it's right.

"As far as lucky feelings are concerned, I remember one night when I made five straight passes in a floating crap game in New York. I suddenly had a premonition that the streak was over, and I dragged all but $5. So I rolled out an 11. I knew for *sure* that the streak was over at that point, so I shot $5 again. A six-ace! To make a painful story as short as possible, I made nine straight passes altogether, and had only five bucks up on each of the last four, because I knew for sure every time that I was going to crap out. I could feel it."

A sports celebrity was taking a horrible beating in a crap game one night. Nothing he did worked out. A friend said, philosophically, "Well, ol' buddy, I guess you just don't live right."

The professional athlete turned on his friend in a towering rage. "Don't live right?" he exploded. "I don't drink or smoke. I'm one of the few guys on the team who's absolutely faithful to his wife. I contribute more than I should to every charity. I give ten hours a week to working with juvenile delinquents. I'm a patsy for anybody's hard luck story. I go to church whenever the schedule will permit it. I try to follow the Golden Rule in everything I do.

"So I don't live right! Our miserable, blankety-blank manager is a confirmed lecher. The night he goes to bed sober is a rarity. And when he gets boozed up, he cuffs his wife around. He's a confirmed liar, and he has larceny in his soul. He'd cheat his own grandmother if he thought he could get away with it. He's selfish, he's egotistical and he's mean. And last night, he won $6,000 in a crap game! Don't you talk to me about living right!"

Most casual gamblers think of themselves as lucky. Perhaps that's why they're gamblers. Why are they lucky? They don't know. It's just a state of affairs that exists.

Some professional gamblers who make a living from gambling, on the other hand, insist that they're unlucky. It's only their superior ability, they'll tell you, that keeps them ahead of the game. "With what I know about poker, I'd be a millionaire if I could just have average luck," one of them confides.

"Hope for luck, always," one of these pros advises, "but never count on it. If I counted on luck, I wouldn't bet minimums when I'm losing. I'd think that the next bet would be lucky. The Martingale player counts on luck to break his losing streak, and he's living proof that you *can't* count on it. I've never seen one yet who did well."

"Luck is a fact," a man who has done consistently well in Las Vegas observes. "It's always there, but you never know when it's going to favor you. You can't deny its existence when you see it working. Why does one guy win $12,500 at Keno? The only possible answer is that he got hit by Lady Luck. You certainly can't attribute his windfall to skill, because there's no skill in the world that can make you a winner at that game. Why does one man out of a million win a big lottery? There's no answer except luck. Look at some of the ignoramuses who go to the track, pick a horse by closing their eyes and jabbing their forefinger at the program—and win on a 15 to 1 shot. You can't come up with any explanation except luck for that sort of thing.

"Luck is all around you, all the time—and not just in the area of gambling. I've never known a successful man who wouldn't admit, when pressed, that luck had something to do with his rise in the world. An honest movie star will tell you that there are hundreds of good, competent performers in the business who've never gotten anywhere. 'Sheer talent will get you bit parts,' one of them once told me. 'Talent and a lucky break will make you a star. You need the combination—and if you'll look at some of the actors and actresses who've made it big, you'll probably reach the conclusion that luck is more important than ability'."

Since luck exists, and every gambler admits that it does, how can a betting man take advantage of it? Come up with a sure-fire answer to that question and the world is yours.

One serious student of the gambling scene is convinced that luck runs in cycles or streaks. "For every bad run of luck," he insists, "you'll have a good one. The catch is that you don't know when either will start or end."

He takes an unorthodox approach to the problem. "Everybody has always insisted that if you flip a coin and it comes up heads nine times in a row, the odds against it coming up heads on the tenth flip are still even—that the nine preceding flips have nothing to do with the odds on the tenth toss, that no matter what has happened previously, it's a one to one bet that a coin will come up heads on a single flip.

"I recognize the logic of that. But let's think about it. Flip a coin 1,000 times and it'll come up heads 500 times, or mighty close to it. However, during that 1,000 flips of the coin there will be frequent periods when heads will fail to show and other periods when you'll flip nothing but heads. Mathematical probability is going to give you roughly 500 heads in 1,000 flips, so if you get ten tails in a row, there's going to be a heavy preponderance of heads somewhere along the line.

"Regardless of mathematics and the theory of probability, if I'm in a crap game and the shooter makes ten consecutive passes, I'm going to bet against him on his eleventh throw. And if he wins, I'll bet against him again on the twelfth. Maybe it's true that the mathematical odds on every throw of the dice remain the same, regardless of what's gone before—but how often do you see a crapshooter make 13 or 14 straight passes?

"There are cycles of luck," he insists, "and they eventually even out. If I win six consecutive hands at Blackjack, I may or may not win the seventh—but somewhere along the line, I'm going to have six losing hands."

This man has kept records of play on Blackjack, craps and Roulette, and the house percentage on all three games works out inexorably, within a fraction of a percentage point—but there are times shown by his records when there are lengthy streaks of steady house wins along with other streaks of house losses.

His records show that the streaks exist. But no matter how long he studies his figures, he hasn't been able to arrive at any pattern in them. He can see that the streaks are there, but he hasn't anything even resembling an explanation of why they occur when they do or why they last for a certain period.

"Nevertheless," he insists, "if I'm scoring red and black on a Roulette game and red has come up 500 times in 900 spins of the wheel, I'm going to put my money on black on the next 100 spins. What's more, I'll bet you that I come out ahead of the game."

He believes it, whether it's true or not.

The great preponderance of gamblers don't spend much time trying to analyze luck cycles. Instead, they woo Lady Luck.

And how they woo her! They form the most superstitious group of human beings to be found anywhere outside the remotest jungles.

If you don't think so, go into a hotel room where a friendly game is in progress and toss your hat onto the bed! Or try to get one of the players to take the third light from a match.

One Chicago crapshooter acquired a reputation because of his violence whenever anyone tossed a two-dollar bill into the game. He became hysterical. If the owner of the two-dollar bill insisted on his rights, this player would pick the bill up and tear it to bits, handing its owner two singles in its place. As far as he was concerned, a two-dollar bill in a crap game was an unbeatable jinx and getting rid of it at a personal cost of two dollars was a bargain.

The late W. "Biggie" Levin, a highly successful producer and television show packager, once managed a high-priced act consisting of a group of sports stars who weren't averse to picking up a couple of thousand dollars apiece a week during their off-season.

One member of the group took a ribbing one cold winter night when he came to the theater wearing red flannel underwear. After the show, he got into a crap game and won $400, a distinct reversal from his usual losing procedure.

Back at the hotel in the wee small hours of the morning, another member of the group said to him, "I'll bet it was that red flannel underwear that changed your luck." The winner of the $400 looked thoughtful.

The next night, he returned to the game and won about $300. "Still wearing the red flannels?" a member of the group asked. "Yep," he nodded, unsmiling.

When Biggie met with the group about five weeks later to discuss contractual arrangements on an augmented tour, he walked into the hotel room, stopped short, sniffed, and gasped. "What's that awful smell?" he demanded. "Is there a dead rat in the room?"

Nobody answered. He went to the window, opened it wide, and stayed near it throughout the conference. When he left, one member of the act followed him down to the lobby.

"Something's gotta be done," the fellow said earnestly. "I gotta stand next to him onstage, and he sweats, and I get so nauseated I'm afraid I'm gonna throw up."

"What are you talking about?" Biggie demanded, and got the story. The lucky crapshooter's luck had continued and he was convinced that his change of fortune was directly attributable to his red flannel underwear.

"He's reached the point," Biggie was told, "where he won't even take it off at night. He *sleeps* in it. He's worn that same blankety-blank suit of drawers for five weeks, and you can smell him comin' a mile away."

"Is he still winning?" Biggie asked.

"He ain't even been in a crap game for the last ten days," the complainant answered. "But we can't get him to change. He says the red flannels are his good luck in everything, not just shooting craps, and he's afraid that taking 'em off will make him unlucky."

Biggie went to the music rehearsal at the theater the next morning, and noticed that everyone backstage gave the wearer of the red flannels a wide berth.

The act came onstage, and the orchestra leader stopped the entrance music abruptly. "Where's the janitor?" he shouted.

The janitor shuffled down the aisle from the back of the theater.

"A skunk's gotten into this theater," the orchestra leader yelled. "You better find it and get it out before the matinee, or everybody will want their money back."

The janitor nodded and began a systematic search, looking under every row of seats.

Biggie decided it was time for desperate measures. As soon as the act's rehearsal was finished, he buttonholed "Lucky."

"I want to talk to you privately," he said. He looked around and motioned to a shower stall. "This ought to be private enough." He stepped toward the shower stall door and motioned "Lucky" in ahead of him. Then, quickly, he blocked the doorway and turned on the faucet for the shower head, full blast.

"Lucky" screamed, and fought to get out, but Biggie blocked the doorway so determinedly and efficiently that he got drenched, too.

"It was worth it, though," he said. "I was soaked to the skin, but so was he. We both had to take off all our clothes and send to the hotel for dry ones. He was so sore at me that I was afraid I'd lose the act. I finally got him into a friendly crap game that night and deliberately let him win $50 from me. That convinced him his luck was holding. I offered him ten bucks for his necktie, and he wanted to know why. 'I had a tie just like it once,' I told him, 'and I couldn't lose at anything when I was wearing it. Craps, cards, the horses—anything.' His eyes lit up and he refused to sell the tie. According to the other fellows in the act, he wore it every day for the balance of the tour."

A Las Vegas pit boss tells about a crapshooter with an objectionable superstition. He insisted upon rubbing the dice vigorously against his crotch before every roll. After several complaints from female crapshooters who found his fetish distasteful, the casino manager told the pit boss to forbid the gesture.

"What's the matter?" the man demanded. "I ain't hurtin' anybody."

"Some of the customers find it objectionable," the pit boss explained.

"What's objectionable about it?" the shooter asked. "I ain't exposin' myself."

"I won't argue about it," the pit boss replied. "You can't do it, and that's that. It's orders from up front."

The crapshooter hurled the dice angrily at the pit boss. "If you're gonna take my luck away from me," he declared, "I won't play." He stalked out of the casino and never returned.

The same pit boss has a story about a crapshooter who always downed a shot of bourbon after his third consecutive pass, and tossed off another shot after each subsequent one. It was a routine the player had followed for years, and he was convinced that the shots of bourbon brought him luck.

On this particular evening, he made his third point, tossed off a shot of bourbon, and rolled out the dice again. "Ee-o-leven!" Another shot of bourbon and another roll of the dice. Six-ace! Another shot of bourbon. He rolled out a five-three, picked up the dice and tossed them against the board. Six-deuce. Another drink and another roll—a five. Again, he made the point, and downed a fifth shot of bourbon. A seven turned up on his next roll. That called for another shot of bourbon. He rolled again, a nine, and eventually made it.

He lurched forward to pick up the dice, clawed at them and muttered thickly, "Pass the dice." As he slumped gently to the floor, he said, "Jus' too lucky," and passed out.

A certain comedian who was married to a red-head was a consistent winner at the crap tables in Las Vegas. He always insisted upon his wife standing with him at the table and always rubbed his clenched fist against her head before releasing the dice.

One evening she joined him at the crap table promptly at the appointed time and he looked at her in astonishment. "What's happened to your hair?" he shouted.

"I got a bleach job this afternoon," she said, smiling. "How do you like it?"

He pointed a quivering finger at her. "I'll give you exactly one hour to get the red back into it," he shouted. "And if it isn't there, we're getting a divorce! What're you trying to do, ruin my luck?"

A western gambler known as "Big Hat" Quirk always wore a broad-brimmed Stetson whenever he wagered any money. One evening, he sat down at the Baccarat table in one of the plusher casinos in Las Vegas and was quietly and politely asked to remove his hat. "This hat," he declared loudly and indignantly, "is my luck. I'd sooner remove my right arm at the shoulder socket."

After considerable argument, he made a counterproposal. He would remove his hat if, when he got ready to leave, he would be permitted to put it back on and make one final bet with the house limit removed. The casino manager nodded approval to the dealer, and "Big Hat" bared his head.

He limited himself to $20 bets, and his luck was miserable. After he'd lost about $200, he announced that he was ready to leave, reached into his pocket and pulled out an enormous roll of bills, from which he peeled five of $1,000 denomination. He put on his hat firmly and with considerable relief. "Five thousand against the bank," he announced, and tossed out the money.

He won, and announced solemnly, "Nobody'll ever get me to take this hat off again."

One gambler in Las Vegas blew a deep breath against the dice before every roll.

"Do you think that brings you luck?" the man standing next to him at the crap table asked.

"I know it does," the shooter replied with conviction. "Las Vegas has a very dry climate, right?"

"Right," his neighbor nodded.

"So the dice are usually very dry. I have a very damp breath, and I always exhale against a six and an ace. My breath forms a condensation on one six and one ace. That not only gives the six and ace a little extra weight but makes them adhere to the table when they roll across it. The opposite sides come up —and the opposite sides of a six and ace are an ace and a six."

"Does it really work?" his neighboring player asked.

"Well, not all the time," the shooter admitted. "The load of condensation isn't quite heavy enough. But I've been on a hot liquid diet all day, and tonight oughta be the time I break the bank."

"Apparently," the man in whom he confided said later, "the hot liquids he'd been drinking had been too light, because the only six-aces he threw while I was at the table came when he had a point to make."

Harlem is the international headquarters for the Dream superstition, but plenty of gamblers who have never been to Harlem believe in lucky dreams.

Joe Frisco used to tell about the night he had a dream in which a seedy little tout sidled up to him and whispered, "Bet Phantaseus Mallaire tomorrow, on the nose. It's a boat race." In the dream, he brushed the tout aside and continued toward the clubhouse. An old crone barred his way and said in a quavery voice, "I'm a clairvoyant, and I see you winning much money on a horse named Phantaseus Mallaire." During the course of the dream, five different people told him to bet Phantaseus Mallaire.

When he got up the next morning, he called one of his favorite bookies and said, "I d-d-on't know the n-n-number or the t-t-track, but I want to put f-f-fifty bucks on F-f-f-." He simply couldn't say 'Phantaseus Mallaire.'

But he was determined. He bought a *Racing Form,* intent on finding the horse's number. He combed through the day's entries at every track in the country, to no avail. There was simply no horse named Phantaseus Mallaire listed.

He printed an approximation of the horse's name and took the slip to a bookie, who finally told him that there simply was no horse with such a name running, anywhere.

Shortly before noon, he found a fellow horse player and gave him the story.

"Was the tout wearing a black-and-white checked cap?" the friend asked, and Joe nodded. "A baggy pair of black pants?" Joe nodded again. "And did the old fortune teller have a shawl tied around her head?"

"Th-that's right," Joe said.

His friend shook his head. "I'm surprised you'd fall for it, Joe," he said. "I've had the same dream five or six times. Don't you see—the tout and the old dame are working together. They want you to give 'em your money to bet for you on the horse. And there *isn't* any horse named Phantaseus Mallaire. But by the time you wake up and check it out in the *Daily Racing Form,* they've got your money and there's nothing you can do about it."

Good luck charms are legion. A company that manufactures and sells rabbits' feet, cured and affixed to gold mountings, has a backlog of orders it can't fill until it finds an additional source of rabbit's feet.

"They always want the left hind foot," the man who runs the firm reveals. "They'll pay extra for it. Nothing else will do. It has to be the left hind foot."

"But how do they know they're actually getting a left hind foot?" he was asked.

"We guarantee it," he replied. "Of course, we don't explain that all four feet are left hind feet, depending on whether the rabbit is on its back or right-side up and whether you're looking at it from the front or the rear."

An advertising executive with an out-of-work relative once started a mail order business for the unemployed kinsman, and got out a cheap catalogue featuring lucky charms, amulets, dream books, hexes and kindred items. The business was a smashing success.

"We expected to get our orders from a very low class clientele," he revealed, "and were dumbfounded when business came in from affluent, well educated people. It surprised me so much that I checked on some of the orders and found that a great many otherwise intelligent people are firmly convinced that some silly charm is lucky for them. Buckeyes are very big with successful businessmen who had a buckeye when they were kids and thought it brought them luck. You'd be surprised how many Southerners carry a little black-eyed pea in their pockets, sometimes in a gold or silver mounting. A copper bracelet sells big, largely to men whose grandmothers made them wear one when they were children. It was supposed to ward off disease and bring luck—and they seem to think it delivered results.

"Numerology is big in the luck department. I'll bet you that at least three men out of five have what they think is their lucky number, and you'd be surprised how many will pay good money for bill clips, rings, tie tacks and similar items carrying the number they feel brings them luck. If you think people aren't superstitious about numbers, look at all the tall buildings that don't have a thirteenth floor."

An enthusiastic gambler who will bet on almost

anything at almost any time refuses point-blank to bet one thin dime on anything on the 16th of the month. His young son was struck by a car and killed on the 16th, 12 years ago, and the date has been off-limits for him ever since.

Professional numerologists can show you long lists of gamblers who have slightly altered their names so that the letters will conform numerologically with their lucky numbers. Some of them swear that adding an "e" or eliminating an "s" from their name has improved their luck.

One confirmed numerologist who makes frequent visits to Las Vegas always goes into the casino for the first time at 5:55 in the afternoon and makes a $5 bet at the blackjack table. If he arrives during the evening, he won't start betting until 5:55 the next afternoon. His lucky number is five.

He swears that the only time he ever suffered a substantial loss, he discovered the next day that his watch had been five minutes slow. If the fifth seat from the left at the blackjack table is already occupied, he won't play.

Is one person actually luckier than another?

"Of course!" a psychiatrist says. "No question about it. Luck starts with the foetus. One woman is undernourished and violates all the rules of pre-natal care, while another gives her unborn child every aid to health. One child is born with a congenital disease while another is robust. The babies don't have one thing to say about which position they're in.

"One child is lucky enough to be born into a loving family, while another gets little attention. One is born into a well-to-do home and another to poverty-stricken parents. One is born free and another into virtual bondage. You don't choose your parents, and yet they are the greatest influence for good or bad, riches or poverty, sickness or health, happiness or misery, in your entire life. If you want to call the circumstances of your birth Divine Providence, go ahead—but I think that's rather stuffy. I can't imagine any truly divine source giving all the advantages to one innocent babe and none to another. As far as I'm concerned, the parents anyone happens to get are pure luck. To say that one person is no luckier than another is absolute idiocy.

"You see winners and losers all around you, every day. You see people who are always lucky in everything, and others who just can't win. You see people whose luck undergoes a sharp reversal for better or worse, not because of anything they do but in spite of anything they do. Call it providence, fate or whatever you will, but it gets down to luck.

"I have a movie star patient, worth millions, who has almost no talent aside from a personality that projects. Actors who could replace him and do a better job are all around him. Off the screen, everything he touches turns to gold. He almost kicks success in the teeth with his actions and practices, and yet he continues to thrive. His one contribution to success consisted of being in the right place at the right time—which was pure luck.

"Sure, the ideal combination is one of intelligent effort and luck—but without the luck, intelligent effort won't do the job. It will enable you to get by, but it won't make you a ball of fire."

Is there, in his opinion, any way to improve luck?

"Yes," he answers, suprisingly. "Think lucky. Convince yourself that your luck is tops, whether it is or not. Believe that you have horseshoes and four-leaf clovers in every pocket.

"I'm convinced that luck begets luck. Most people who are down on their luck quit trying. And the person who thinks he's lucky will do all the necessary things to reach a desired goal. He'll spend time and exert effort on what may look like a wild longshot because he has confidence in his luck, where the chap who thinks he's unlucky believes it's useless to do his homework.

"The people who think they have better than average luck are usually right. They do have, because they've encouraged it. Positive thinking is just as important a contribution to luck as it is to anything else.

"I have one patient who's a rabid gambler. He thinks his luck is invincible, which it isn't; I'd say it's only slightly above average. He's told me story after story to prove his phenomenal luck, and the stories are always about a certain time when he hit the jackpot. 'But haven't you suffered losses almost as great as your wins?' I asked him. 'Oh, a few,' he answered, squirming slightly, 'but you can't win 'em all.' The spectacular wins are imbedded in his memory and the equally spectacular losses have been quickly erased.

"He's a good gambler, because he never panics in the face of adversity. He has a sound method of handling his gambling money, and no string of losses makes him swerve from it and begin a splurge of desperation betting. He's supremely confident that he's lucky and that his tested technique will eventually win. He bets heavily when he's winning and lightly when he's losing, which is the opposite of what many 'unlucky' gamblers do. His system is as sound as any gambling system can be, and his faith in his luck makes him stick with it.

"Another patient, a casual gambler, is supremely lucky—truly. He'll walk up to a slot machine, put in a single quarter—and walk away with several dollars' profit or even the jackpot. He makes an occasional 'hunch' bet on a horse—never with any handicapping or analysis—and wins much more often than he loses. He's won the Kentucky Derby pool in his office for three straight years. His luck in charity raffles makes mathematical probabilities look silly.

"He takes his luck for granted. He's never excited when he wins; he expected it to happen. He's more astonished when he loses; with his luck, losses shouldn't happen.

"What accounts for his exceptional luck? I don't know. What accounts for one bright boy being born to Southern sharecroppers and another, no brighter, to the multimillionaire president of a large corporation? What causes one child to have loving parents and another to be cursed with irresponsible ones?"

Is this psychiatrist superstitious?

He takes awhile to answer. "I know I shouldn't be," he answers sheepishly, "but I'm afraid I am. For years, I loved to play poker, maybe because I played a fairly good game and won. My father had been a champion marble shooter in his youth and had collected the most amazing collection of marbles I've ever seen, playing 'for keeps.'

"When I started to play marbles, he gave me his 'lucky shooter,' an aggie he's always used, and convinced me that it was invincible. He told me to carry it in my trousers pocket and to rub it whenever I needed luck.

"I always rubbed that aggie in a poker game. I rubbed it at least once during the course of every hand I played. I did it automatically, almost without being aware of what I was doing. It became an instinctive or subconscious gesture.

"And then, somehow, I lost that aggie, that lucky shooter. I thought maybe it had gone to the dry cleaning establishment in a pair of pants, and I went to the cleaning establishment, where I rummaged through box after box of unclaimed items. No aggie. I had my wife search the house for it, after I'd done the same thing without finding it. I offered my son and daughter a $5 reward if either of them would find it.

"The aggie never turned up. And I began playing the most miserable game of poker you ever saw. It seemed to me that I could hold four Aces and lose. Nothing worked. If I had a full house, Jacks on eights, somebody else in the game would have Queens on nines.

"Now, I knew the game better than most players do. I'd made a study of it. But playing with the same people in the same game I'd enjoyed for years, I played one entire evening without winning a single pot. I went back the following week, determined to wipe the lucky aggie from my mind—and I lost $90. It became an obsession with me to overcome the loss of that lucky aggie—and I dropped money consistently, week after week, without a single streak of luck.

"I finally quit the game, convinced in my own mind that I'd never win again until I found my lucky aggie. I haven't played a hand of poker since."

He smiled. "Now, as a psychiatrist, I can give you a simple explanation of why I began to lose at poker after years of winning. I can show you how loss of the lucky piece warped my judgement, and how a series of perfectly normal losses made me panic and abandon my usual sound game. My explanations are sound enough, but as a poker player who lost his lucky aggie, they don't mean a damned thing to me.

"Eleven years ago, a black cat ran across the road in front of us as my wife and I were starting on a vacation trip. About five miles past that point, we had a rather serious car accident. After that, my wife absolutely refused to continue further in the car if a black cat ran across our path.

"Last summer, we were starting out for a weekend at a nearby lake, and a black cat bounded across the road. My wife ordered me to turn around.

"I wanted that weekend. I'd been looking forward to it. So I stopped the car and reasoned with her. To think that a black cat crossing the road could possibly have any direct effect on us was childish, wasn't it? The car wreck 11 years previously had been caused by the collapse of the highway at a faulty culvert, and that gap in the pavement would have been there whether a black cat crossed our path or not. I made her admit the logic of everything I said, and she finally agreed—reluctantly—to continue the trip.

"We had driven about 30 miles past the black cat when the right front tire blew out and swerved the car into a ditch.

"Now, I know that what happened 30 miles and half an hour after our encounter with the black cat had nothing to do with what happened previously. The tire was faulty and was going to blow out whether we passed a black cat or a rhinocerous. Sure, I know that. But I also know that from now on, no black cat is going to cross my path. If I see a black cat in front of me, I'll turn around.

"There was a time when I used to deliberately walk under a ladder, to show my defiance of superstition. And one day I asked myself, 'Has anything good ever happened to you *because* you walked under a ladder?' I couldn't think of a thing. 'If it's not doing you any good, bringing you any luck,' I then asked myself,

---

ARE YOU PSYCHIC?

Well-known psychics are, by their own admission, poor gamblers.

"Whenever I try to predict something for my own personal gain," one of them says, "I invariably fail. I know I have psychic powers, but they simply don't work when it comes to gambling. In almost any kind of gambling situation, bet against me and you'll have a winner."

Edgar Kayce, who performed completely unexplainable feats in the area of extra-sensory perception, was not a wealthy man. On the occasions when he attempted to utilize his abilities to get some money, he invariably met with disappointment.

One psychic reveals, "My advice to business men clients on gambles in the stock market has been good—but the instant I try to go into the market, myself, I'm in trouble."

'why tempt Fate?' And I haven't walked under a ladder since.

"A great deal of modern superstition has its basis in that kind of muddy reasoning. You know that spilling some table salt couldn't possibly bring you bad luck and that tossing some of it over your left shoulder couldn't possibly counteract bad luck. If you toss some of the salt over your shoulder and don't have bad luck, it proves nothing. You wouldn't have had any bad luck, anyway. Spilling salt doesn't cause bad luck, to begin with. Does it? How did that superstition start? Could it possibly have any basis in fact? On the other hand, you *have* spilled some salt, and what have you got to lose if you throw some of it over your left shoulder? You end up by throwing it. Why take unnecessary chances?

"Yes," the psychiatrist concluded, "I hate to admit it, but I guess I'm superstitious. Most people are, whether they admit it or not."

A good poker player, James Mahoney, has strong convictions about one superstition. "You know the story about Aces and Eights, the Dead Man's Hand, the hand Wild Bill Hickok was holding when he was shot in the back? The hand is supposed to be bad luck. Now, actually, a pair of Aces and a pair of eights isn't a bad hand. It'll win more pots than it'll lose. Yeah? I've held Aces and Eights on six different occasions, and every one of the six has been an absolute disaster. The first time I held 'em, I bet 'em—and was beaten by three fours. And I didn't win another pot throughout the rest of the game. I bet 'em again, the second time I held them—and was soundly beaten by a full house. The third time, I refused to bet 'em and tossed in my hand. The pot was taken by a pair of Jacks. I refused to play the hand the fourth and fifth times I held it. And while I didn't lose any money on a hand I didn't play, I had such phenomenally bad luck for the rest of the evening that you wouldn't believe it. The biggest over-all losses I've ever suffered at poker have been on the occasions when I held Aces and Eights. The last time I held the hand, I got up from the table, tossed in my cards and walked out of the game."

Another poker player has a peculiar obsession about the nine of Diamonds, a card reputed by a member of the famous Greek Syndicate to be the luckiest of all cards.

"Maybe for him, but not for me," this poker player says. "I have never, not even once, won a hand of poker on a hand that held the nine of Diamonds. It's pure poison. Deal me the nine of Diamonds and I refuse to play the hand."

"What," he was asked, "would you do if you were dealt four Aces and the nine of Diamonds?"

He considered. "It wouldn't ever happen," he answered. "No hand that's a sure winner will *ever* contain the nine of Diamonds. There'll always be another hand in play that's better than any hand that includes the nine of Diamonds."

Another player says solemnly that he always bets on a pair of one-eyed Jacks, never on a pair that have both eyes showing. "The one-eyed Jacks are lucky," he explains. "They're the lowest pair I'll bet."

Doesn't he ever lose on a pair of one-eyed Jacks?

"Sometimes," he admits, and adds, "but even when I lose on them, playing them is lucky. If I get 'em and play 'em, I always wind up the evening a winner."

One expert Bridge player who always shows a yearly profit on his play will do almost anything to get himself and his partner seated in the North and South positions. He's firmly convinced that he invariably does better sitting North and South than East and West. "It has something to do with the magnetic currents," he explains vaguely.

An opponent who knew about his idiosyncrasy pulled a large magnet from his pocket and put it on the table in front of him one evening, and the expert flew into a violent rage. "You're not allowed to do that," he roared. A quick thumbing through the rule book showed nothing that prohibited a player's having a magnet in his possession.

The expert, unnerved, lost two 700 rubbers and stalked away from the table, convinced that his opponent had been unfairly tampering with "the magnetic currents."

Many a bridge couple surreptitiously visit their host's bathroom before the game just so they can sit with the bath tub direction.

One Las Vegas gambler doesn't miss a bet when it comes to superstitions. He carries a rabbit's foot in his left pants pocket and rubs it frequently. A piece of string is tied in three knots around his left wrist. He has a lucky coin in his right pants pocket which he puts out on the table at crucial times. He makes a peculiar hex sign at the dealer, croupier or stick man before each round of play starts. He frequently mutters an incantation which sounds something like "Ostagazoozlum." From time to time, he gets up, walks three times around his chair, always to the left, and resumes his seat.

One night when he had dropped $500, he got up to leave and the player next to him said, "This oughta prove to you that all your mumbo-jumbo is pure nonsense. It didn't do a thing for you! You lost five hundred bucks."

"Yeah?" the superstitious one answered coldly. "How much do you think I'd have lost if I hadn't taken all these precautions?" ♠

Bibliography

Editors of GAMBLER'S DIGEST have poured through hundreds of books on gambling and related subjects —rare manuscripts, pamphlets, letters, advertising brochures, magazines, newspapers, photographic files and even recorded tapes, in an effort to assemble the most complete treatise on gambling in all its forms ever assembled.

Most professional gamblers aren't writers. Most of them don't want to be quoted, even anonymously. No crooked gambler will ever admit that he's a "hustler," even to his closest friends. He becomes a source of possible information only after he has retired and needs money.

A high percentage of the gambling that's done throughout the world is illegal—and what few records of illegal gambling exist are highly secret. Even when those who control illegal gambling are willing to talk "off the record," their information is varied and, in some cases, highly suspect.

Numerous fictions about gambling have been built by word of mouth, and running them down has been difficult. A fiction, repeated often enough, is accepted as a fact until proven otherwise.

Every gambler, the editors of GAMBLER'S DIGEST quickly learned, is strongly opinionated, as are some of the writers who have tackled the subject. And there is little uniformity in the spread of their convictions. What one man regards as a "best bet," for example, is classified by another as a sure way to lose money. Controversy exists in nearly every area, and some of it will never be resolved.

Most authors of books on gambling have been understandably reticent about "best bets," perhaps feeling a liability in the event that their best bets turn out to be losers for some reader. If any bet were a certain winner, it would cease to be a bet, and one of the fascinations of gambling is that probability doesn't follow a set, predictable pattern.

Some of the best information dug up in our research cannot be credited in our bibliography, because it comes from sources who refuse to be named, who not only have no desire for kudos but who will go to almost any length to preserve their anonymity. Consequently, the source of considerable material in GAMBLER'S DIGEST must be its editors.

Many of our source books have been highly specialized, dealing at great length with one small part of the gambling panorama.

Books devoted exclusively to Contract Bridge, for example, are numerous, ranging from books for beginners to books dealing with the intricacies of advanced play by experts. Some substantial bridge books deal with only one phase of the game, the author's particular system of bids and responses.

It would take the average reader months to assimilate all the information on chess to be found in the many volumes that cover every phase of the game.

Poker, too, could have a lengthy bibliography all its own.

While some areas of gambling have been covered in the minutest detail, others are almost completely lacking in information. Where can you learn the fine points of Jai-Alai—or cockfighting? What book can make you a championship billiard or pool player?

Rules of games have been easy to acquire, thanks to the late Edmond Hoyle, who wrote a short treatise on Whist which was published in 1742 and went through 16 editions during his lifetime. All editions of *Hoyle's Games* during his lifetime carried a frontispiece warning against piracy, with the information that nine pirates had been prosecuted by Hoyle and his publisher, Thomas Osborne, and that no copy was genuine without the two men's signatures. Hoyle died in London on Aug. 29th, 1769, at the age of 97, and he is still the basic authority for rules of table games.

In addition to the current *Hoyle's Games,* we have referred to the 1790 London edition, published by Charles Jones, Esq., and the first American edition, published in 1845 by Henry F. Anners of Philadelphia.

Other excellent rule books for cards and allied games which must be included in our bibliography include the U.S. Playing Card Co. *Official Rules of Card Games,* Morehead's *Official Rules of Card Games,* published by Crest, and the Albert Whitman & Co. book, edited by Paul H. Seymour, *Let's Look in Hoyle.*

More detailed explanations of play are to be found in *A Handbook of Card Games,* by George F. Hervey, published by Paul Hamlyn, London. An excellent book for card gamblers is John R. Crawford's *How to Be a Consistent Winner in the Most Popular Card Games,* published by Doubleday and also available in a Dolphin Book edition. Crawford, a recognized authority, discusses winning strategy in Bridge, Canasta, Poker, Gin Rummy, Pinochle, Hearts, Blackjack, Cribbage, Pitch, Samba and Oklahoma.

Who Dealt This Mess? is an amusing book of card

game cartoons by H. T. Webster, in conjunction with Philo Calhoun, published by Doubleday.

Clem Stein, Jr.'s *Bridge and Gin Gambitry,* published by Home Library Press, is both amusing and practical, applying the theories of Stephen Potter's *The Theory and Practice of Gamesmanship* to card games. The Potter book is now available in a paperback Bantam Book edition.

Oswald Jacoby on Poker is a well-written book by a skillful card player and actuarial expert who knows his way around. While it covers far more than poker and bridge, the paperback *Oswald Jacoby on Gambling,* from Hart Publishing Co., is one of the best small investments a gambler can make, since it covers Roulette, Blackjack, Craps, Chuck-a-Luck, horse racing, baseball, basketball, and football as well. Jacoby, an international authority on gambling games, includes in this book some tables and percentages that any gambler would do well to study. His books on bridge are, of course, among the best, as are Goren's *Easy Steps to Winning Bridge,* and *Point Count Bidding Made Easy,* published by Doubleday.

When Edward O. Thorp's book on how to win at Blackjack, *Beat the Dealer,* first appeared, it caused a sensation in gambling circles. His "counting" system for Blackjack worked—for the person who could and would take the time and trouble to master it. It worked so well, in fact, that casinos immediately began figuring ways to combat it.

More recently, Lawrence Revere's *Playing Blackjack as a Business,* published by Paul Mann Publishing Co. of Las Vegas, has attempted to simplify "counting" strategies in Blackjack, starting with basics and taking the reader as far as he cares to go into the intricacies of IBM-computed Blackjack play. If the reader learns nothing except the basic strategy, a chart of which is included in GAMBLER'S DIGEST, with Mr. Revere's permission, he will be infinitely superior to most of the players at any Blackjack table. Revere says a gambler can learn his simple Five-Count Strategy in four hours, to greatly increase his advantage. More advanced Revere strategies take longer to learn.

Twenty-one, the Art of Blackjack is a simplification of "counting" systems, published by Gaming Systems Co., who also publish an anonymous system book, *Dice.*

With many excellent books on chess, we selected for our bibliography, Fred Reinfeld's *Beginner's Guide to Winning Chess,* published by Follett, Reinfeld's *The Complete Chess Player,* available in a Crest paperback edition, and E. S. Lowe's *Chess in 30 Minutes,* published by E. S. Lowe Co.

The competent Jacoby and Crawford are coauthors of a beautiful and almost unbelievably comprehensive book on Backgammon, *The Backgammon Book,* published by Viking, that has to be rated the definitive book in its field. Our other Backgammon source book was *Backgammon Standards,* by Walling and Hiss, published by Simon and Schuster.

The official amateur and professional rule books have guided us in the preparation of sports material, as has the advice of Bob Martin, Mr. Odds-Maker.

In the field of casino gambling games, we highly recommend six Gambler's Book Club paperbacks by Walter I. Nolan: *The Facts of Baccarat, The Facts of Blackjack, The Facts of Craps, The Facts of Keno, The Facts of Roulette,* and *The Facts of Slots.* All are quoted in GAMBLER'S DIGEST.

Winning at Casino Gaming, published by Rouge et Noir and written by its staff, deals with all aspects of casino gambling throughout the world, even getting into the subject of extra-sensory perception as an aid to casino gamblers.

Dice, How to Win the Las Vegas Way, by Ben Holiday, published by the Coast Publishing Company of Las Vegas, is one of a series of entertaining and informative books covering Blackjack, Roulette, Bingo and Keno, and Slots and Pinball. Other books in the series, which bears the endorsement of Nick the Greek, cover poker, horse racing and bridge.

How to Win at Cards, Dice, Races, Roulette, by Mike Goodman, is published by Holloway House, and lays deserved stress on the statement that no gambler can expect to win consistently unless he takes the trouble to learn the fine points of the game in which he's involved.

The Weekend Gambler's Handbook, by Major A. Riddle, as told to Joe Hyams, originally published by Random House and now available in a Signet paperback edition, is an entertaining book on casino gaming with a chapter of good advice on "good games to stay away from." Riddle's years as President of The Dunes in Las Vegas give him a perspective that the casual gambler hasn't acquired.

Allan N. Wilson's *Casino Gambler's Guide,* published by Harper and Row, contains detailed factual information on casino gaming that is not known to the general public.

The big, lavishly illustrated, beautifully produced *Complete Illustrated Guide to Gambling,* by Alan Wykes, published by Doubleday, shows painstaking and scholarly research on the author's part, with background information on all types of gambling, dating back almost to the creation of man. Along with much information, the book is packed with interesting anecdotes about gamblers and gambling.

Esquire's Book of Gambling, published by Harper and Row, is a compendium of gambling information and stories that have appeared in *Esquire* magazine as far back as 1935, blended into an entertaining book.

John Scarne, the author of *Scarne's Complete Guide to Gambling,* published by Simon and Schuster, is an authority on dishonest gambling, and his big, comprehensive book gives information on cheating and how to detect it that is not found in most general books on gambling.

The Clyde B. Davis book, *Something for Nothing,* published by Lipincott; *You Can't Win,* by Ernest E. Blanche, published by Public Affairs Press, and *Heads I Win, Tails You Lose,* by Charlotte Olmsted, published by MacMillan, also deal with the perils and pitfalls of gaming.

Harland B. Adams' *The Guide to Legal Gambling,* published by Citadel Press, makes a strong argument for legalization as a way to safeguard the casual gambler from unfair odds and dishonesty.

A special acknowledgement must be made to John Luckman of Gambler's Book Club, who is a consultant to the University of Nevada library in its task of assembling a comprehensive library on the subject of gambling. Mr. Luckman has given access to his lengthy list, including the Gambler's Book Club Gambling Classic Reprints.

One of these Classic Reprints, *Gamblers Don't Gamble,* by Mickey MacDougall, first of the modern-day gambling detectives and authorities on cheating, is worthy of special mention. MacDougall opened a whole new field of detection that called for inside knowledge of sleight-of-hand. A few who followed him have been highly successful.

The basic book for card mechanics—those who cheat at cards by manipulation of the pasteboards—is S. W. Erdnase's *Expert at the Card Table,* a book that has been reprinted many times and contains far more basic sleights than most crooked gamblers are capable of executing. Erdnase's real name was Andrews, a self-admitted crooked gambler, he was accused of having murdered two people. He shot himself and the young lady who was with him when he was cornered by police in San Francisco in 1905. The illustrator of the Erdnase first edition, a perfectly respectable artist, was still living at the time this book was being compiled.

While Erdnase has long been the bible of card manipulators, it would be extremely difficult reading for the average person, since it was written for people who already knew something about card manipulation.

More modern and explained in greater detail are the publications on card manipulation by Ed Marlo, certainly one of the greatest card manipulators who ever lived. Never a full-time public performer, his semi-private exhibitions invariably have both card magicians and professional gamblers hanging on the ropes, glassy-eyed.

Among his many books are some that deal solely with one particular phase of card handling. *Action Palm* explains in detail how to palm off cards while the deck is in action. *Tabled Palm* shows all the variations and possibilities of palming cards while the deck is on the table.

The Faro Shuffle explains in detail how to do a perfect shuffle—which, repeated a certain number of times, returns the deck to its original order. Mr. Marlo and his students do this perfect shuffle, which requires splitting the deck at the 26th card and interlacing the two halves in perfect order, with ease and consistency.

Seconds, Centers and Bottoms not only explains how to deal the second card from the top or cards from the bottom without detection, but shows how to deal cards from the center of the deck. Marlo's original methods for switching a card or cards are explained in *Card Switches.*

Three Marlo books which were never displayed sold for $50 each. They were *Riffle Shuffle Systems, Patented False Shuffle* and *Control System. Riffle Shuffle Systems* contained a section, "If I Were a Card Cheat," which showed in detail how to indetectably run up desired hands in the process of riffle shuffling a deck of cards. The three books have just been combined by Marlo into one new book which brings together all the latest innovations in card control systems.

The Cardician, another Marlo work, published by Magic, Inc., contains enough challenging material to keep any would-be card mechanic busy for several years.

Lessons in Dishonesty, by L. L. Ireland, another Magic, Inc., book, is particularly good on second deals, bottom deals and false card counts.

Jean Hugard's *Close-Up Card Magic* and John N. Hilliard's *Card Magic,* both published by Carl Jones, are definitive books on card magic, both containing a number of sleights that might be used by crooked gamblers. Hugard and Glenn Gravatt's *Encyclopedia of Card Tricks,* published by Max Holden, was intended solely for magicians, but card mechanics found in it considerable material they could use.

Dai Vernon, one of the world's most polished manipulators, is the author of *Early Vernon* and *Ultimate Secrets of Card Magic,* both published by Magic, Inc., and both informative for the person who thinks he may have been bilked in a card game.

In the field of dice, Marlo's *Shoot the Works* and Frank Garcia's *Marked Cards and Loaded Dice,* the former dealing with techniques and the latter with *modus operandi,* are definitive books. The Garcia book is published by Bramhall House.

One of the first comprehensive exposes of crooked gambling of all kinds was *The Open Book,* published by J. H. Johnson of Kansas City, Mo., who seems also to have been the author.

Any serious student of crooked gambling should have the book list of Gambler's Book Club and the 144-page book catalogue of Magic, Inc. Most of the books in the latter are for professional and amateur magicians, but a part of the crooked gambler's operations stem from the field of sleight-of-hand magic.

The editors feel that anyone who plays cards, particularly with strangers, should not only be aware that cheating exists but should know how to detect card manipulators.

In horse racing, Tom Ainslie is generally accepted as the outstanding authority. Among his books on which John and Ann Hussey have drawn for information are his *Complete Guide to Thoroughbred Racing, Horse Sense, Science in Betting,* and *Scientific Handicapping. The Daily Racing Form* is the fountainhead of timely information. Joe Ullman's *What's the Odds?,* a Gamblers Book Club reprint, gives an authentic picture of a bookie. Another useful book is GBC's *Dutching the Horses.*

The field of lotteries and Bingo has received remarkably thorough coverage. John Samuel Ezell's *Fortune's Merry Wheel,* published by the Harvard University Press, tells a fascinating story in entertaining style and is a comprehensive study of lotteries. *Gambling in America,* by Herbert L. Marx, Jr., published by H. W. Wilson Company, covers not only lotteries but other gambling activities. Henry Chafetz' *Play the Devil,* published by Bonanza Books, adds its own slant to the picture. *Epic of New York City* by Edward Robb Ellis, published by Coward-McCann, Inc., is particularly pertinent in view of the new lottery and current trend toward legal gambling in New York. Much of our coverage on lotteries, Bingo, pools and parlay cards has necessarily depended on information from the daily press and current news magazines.

Cardano, the Gambling Scholar, by Oystein Ore, originally published by the Princeton University Press and now available in paperback from Dover Publications, chronicles Cardano's stormy and exciting life, which ended in 1576. It also contains a translation of his *Book on Games of Chance,* the first serious study of the theory of probability. While Cardano applied the theory to games of chance, it has become an important factor in both science and business. Professor Ore makes the story of Cardano's efforts to formulate a science of gambling highly entertaining.

I. A. Todhunter's *History of the Mathematical Theory of Probability from the Time of Pascal to That of Laplace,* published by Macmillan in 1865 and reprinted in 1949 by Chelsea Publishing Co. has further information on the evolvement of the laws of probability and chance.

The Handbook of Percentages, by Charles E. Shampaign, originally published in 1930 by the Joe Treybal Sporting Goods Company of St. Louis and recently reprinted by Gambler's Book Club, bears the lengthy sub-title, "Containing Rules for the Playing of the Games with Descriptions, Technicalities, Probabilities, Percentages, Instructions, Examples, Etc. American Method of Playing with Numberous Tables and Tabulations to Which Is (sic) Appended an Elaborate Treatise on the Doctrine of Chance." This is said to have been the first work published in the United States on mathematical odds, with information to gambling house operators on how to figure percentages correctly. John Luckman of GBC says that the book was published exclusively for "inside" gamblers, people deriving income from gambling, and was sold only by firms which furnished equipment to gambling houses.

John Cohen's *Chance, Skill and Luck: The Psychology of Guessing and Gambling,* a Penguin publication is a more recent study of "psychological probability" (1960).

Odds, by J. Brussel, published by Falcon Press, depends heavily on the frequency and chance tables of the Oliver Odson book, *You Can't Lose.*

Gambling, edited by Robert D. Herman, is published by Harper & Row, and is a series of articles and papers on gambling as a social problem, with sections on Forms of Gambling, The Gambling Enterprise, Gambling as a Pathology, and Gambling, Crime and Public Safety.

The *Psychology of Gambling,* by Edmund Bergler, M.D., published by Hill and Wang, is an excellent source of information on the clinical study of gamblers.

The *Annals of the American Academy of Political and Social Sciences* for May, 1950, contains excellent material on the social aspects of gambling, including an article by Virgil Peterson, former FBI man and director of the Chicago Crime Commission on "Obstacles to Enforcement of Gambling Laws." An article on "The Professional Gambler," by Albert H. Morehead, the games expert, classifies various types of professional gambler, and "The Psychodynamics of Gambling," by Dr. Robert M. Lindner, a practicing psychoanalyst, contains interesting case studies of gamblers of several types.

Alcohol, Drugs and Gambling in Industry, a brochure published by the Bureau of Business Practice, devotes only four of its 48 pages to gambling, which would seem to indicate that there are far more serious problems in industry than gambling.

The history of gambling is a world history and must properly be so covered. The *Encyclopedia Brittanica,* the *World Book Encyclopedia,* published by Field Enterprises, and the *Encyclopedia Americana* served as starting points.

Perhaps one of the most helpful books in compiling gambling's history is, surprisingly, the *Dictionary of the Bible,* edited by James Hastings and published by T. and T. Clark, and Charles Scribner's Sons.

Customs of Mankind, by Lillian Eichler, published by Garden City Publishing Co., has been a valuable source of much unique and interesting information, as have the Wykes *Guide to Gambling* and Ezell *Fortune's Merry Wheel* previously mentioned.

China, Egypt, Greece and India are the original sources of much gambling, and the editors of GAMBLER'S DIGEST have considered it necessary to dig deeply into the gambling history of those countries.

The Four Hundred Million, A Short History of the Chinese, by Mary A. Nourse, published by the

Blakistan Co., proved an excellent source book, as did Kenneth Scott Latourette's *The Chinese, Their History and Culture,* published by MacMillan.

Harper & Bros. *Short History of the Chinese People,* by L. Carrington Goodrich, is intensely interesting reading.

Jeanine Auboyer's *Daily Life in Ancient India,* another MacMillan book, is solid proof that ancient history doesn't need to be dull. In addition to its information on gambling, it gives the reader a better perspective on India.

Archaic Egypt, by Walter B. Emery, published by R. and R. Clark, Ltd., and the Clarendon Press *Legacy of Egypt* furnish ample proof that the ancient Egyptians were high-rolling gamblers.

The editors have drawn on standard works on Greek and Roman mythology, not to mention their high school textbooks, for Greco-Roman background. Among many surprising and interesting things to be found in Robert Brumbaugh's *Ancient Greek Gadgets and Machines,* published by Crowell, are illustrations and explanations of old Greek gambling devices that bear a remarkable resemblance to modern slot machines.

Sports and Pastimes of the People of England, by Joseph Strutt, published by Thos. Tegg, tells the story of gambling in still another part of the world.

George H. Devol's *Forty Years a Gambler on the Mississippi,* published in facsimile reprint by Steck-Vaughan Company, is rich in Americana, with hundreds of anecdotes that have the ring of authenticity.

Cy Rice's *Nick the Greek, King of the Gamblers,* tells the life story of a legendary figure who made gambling history. The publisher is Funk and Wagnalls.

Gambling in the Old West is covered by a variety of regional Western history books, none of them dealing solely with gambling. The reminiscences of pioneer Western "characters" are, for the most part, poorly written and inexpertly printed but authentic.

Gaming in Nevada, published by the Gaming Industries Association of Nevada, is tersely factual, as are the *Quarterly Reports* of the Nevada Gaming Commission. *Las Vegas Report,* a Las Vegas Chamber of Commerce publication is a beautifully printed brochure that brings Las Vegas gambling almost up to date.

Coverage of Gambling Around the World has been an almost impossible task, since gambling regulations, restrictions and liberalizations are changing almost constantly. For example, between the time of preparing material on gambling in Great Britain and GAMBLER'S DIGEST's going to the printers, gambling in England underwent such drastic changes that everything on the subject had to be re-written. Changes were still in progress at the time of publication, and the editors had an uncomfortable feeling that what had to be the most up-to-date material available might soon be less than current.

The editors learned, too, that official information from some countries did not always coincide with facts. Visitors to several countries whose officials had assured us that no gambling of any kind was permitted within their boundaries informed us that gambling in these countries was almost "wide open."

We quickly realized that a query to officials in this country would undoubtedly bring a response that casino-type gambling occurs in the United States only in Nevada and that slot machines are not permitted to operate in most states.

Because it is the most timely and thorough source available, we have relied for much of our information about gambling around the world on the remarkable *New Horizons World Guide—Pan Am's Travel Facts About 138 Countries,* edited by Gerald W. Whitted for Pan American Airways, with trade distribution by Simon and Schuster, Inc.

A special acknowledgement must be made in this bibliography to Jay Marshall, the magician-comedian who has appeared in top spots throughout the English-speaking world, for his vast store of anecdotes and information on gamblers and gambling, as well as on celebrities who gamble. Some of the best of the latter information, unfortunately, cannot be passed along, the libel laws being what they are.

Mr. Marshall has a remarkable library and doesn't believe that information must be within book covers to be included, if it is interesting. He writes down everything that interests or amuses him and puts it, properly classified and indexed, into his library, which he made available to GAMBLER'S DIGEST. Perhaps the bibliographic listing should be Jay Marshall's *The Book I Never Wrote,* unpublished by Magic, Inc., his publishing label.

In addition to the many sources of material mentioned, the editors of GAMBLER'S DIGEST have drawn upon their own personal experience. Friends and well-wishers have been extremely helpful.

In spite of the difficulty which acquiring authentic information on gambling entails, the editors have been astonished and pleased to find far more printed material than they thought existed on the subject.

Estimates which appear through the book are, necessarily, just that. From off-the-record conversations with people involved in illegal gambling operations, we have a strong feeling that most estimates in the past have been far too low. Our total figure of $400 billion a year may be too high. We don't think so, but cut it in half, if you will, and it still leaves gambling as the major industry.

Throughout gambling's history, efforts have always been made to minimize the amount of money involved. Legal gambling on which records exist represents only a fraction of the total. While we have no way of proving it, we have reached the conclusion that about nine-tenths of the gambling done in the United States is never made a matter of record. ♠

A glossary for gamblers

A

ABOVE (The Line)
In Contract Bridge, scores for additional tricks above the contract, for honors and penalties for sets, go above the line.

ACE
Highest card in a deck, unless specifically designated as the lowest. Counts either 1 or 11 in Blackjack.

ACEY-DEUCY
Variation of Backgammon.
A card game.
Sounds like baby-talk, but isn't.

ACROSS-THE-BOARD
To bet a combination win, place and show ticket on one horse.

ACTION
Betting or the opportunity to bet. What every gambler wants, when it's favorable.

ACTUARIES
Insurance company's odds makers.

ADDED MONEY
Money that the track adds to the purse in stakes races to attract better horses.

ADVERTISING
To make a bluff with the intention of being exposed. Common practice in Gin Rummy, where player discards the 6 of Spades if he's holding the 5, 7 and 8 of Hearts.

ALEMBERT, THE
In money management, add one betting unit after each loss, subtract one after each win.

ALLOUT
Horse has been exhausted.

ALLOWANCE RACE
One in which horses carry various weights designated in the conditions.

ALSO ELIGIBLE
Horses that are eligible to run in a race if other entrants are scratched (withdrawn).

ALSO-RAN
Horse that did not finish in the money.

AMERICAN BOWLING CONGRESS
Organized the sport of bowling in 1895.

AMERICAN TOTALIZATOR COMPANY
Manufacturer of automatic electric ticket vending machines at race tracks; also produces odds-board at mutuel tracks. Has installed and services most pari-mutuel equipment throughout the world.

ANGELS
Investors in Broadway productions.

ANIMAL FIGHTS
Bets being placed on sports events involving animals.

ANTE
Put-up money before the deal to build the pot.

ASCOT
Money management formula not known to have worked in this century.

ASSIST (Euchre)
When the dealer's partner signals his aid for partner to take three tricks.

ASTRAGALUS
Six-sided sheep ankle bone that was used by prehistoric man as dice.

AUCTION BRIDGE
A refinement of Auction Bridge produced Contract Bridge. Auction Bridge, in its turn, evolved from Whist.

AUCTION HEARTS
Variation of Hearts.

AUCTION PINOCHLE WITH A WIDOW
Modern day Pinochle using 48 cards. Three extra (widow) cards are dealt for which players bid after all cards are dealt. Nine is the lowest card used in Pinochle.

AUCTION PITCH
Card game evolving from old English game called "All Fours." First player to score seven points wins.

AUCTION PITCH WITH A JOKER
Variation of Auction Pitch.

AUTO-BRIDGE
Adult solitaire game which enables the player to play Bridge, in effect, with experts.

AUTOMATIC DOUBLES
In a tie, when throwing the dice for the first play, doubles the stakes.

B

BABY RACE
Race for two-year-old horses (babies).

BABY'S SHOES
What a crap-shooter is trying to get the money to buy, usually expressed in, "Come on, dice, baby needs a new pair of shoes!"

BACCARAT
Big-money card game popular in casinos.

EDITOR'S NOTE: The date "1811" following a definition indicates a gambling term from the *1811 Dictionary of the Vulgar Tongue,* published by Digest Books, Inc., Northfield, Ill. These terms were included here for the reader's edification and amusement.

BACCARAT BANQUE
French banking card game.
BACKGAMMON
Dice game, object being to get all pieces off the board before opponent. Basically defensive game. Increasingly popular as a gambling game in recent years because of its "doubling" feature.
BACKGAMMON BET
In golf, any player making a putt for 15 or more feet has the privilege of doubling the stakes on next hole.
BACKSTRETCH
Straight portion of track parallel to homestretch.
BAIT
A small bet designed to invite a raise, which may be reraised.
Games played in a casino that no informed gambler would dream of playing.
Practice of card sharps in allowing victim to win several small pots as a build-up for the kill.
BAMBOOS
One of three suits in Mah-Jongg having nine ranks.
BANDAGE
Tape around legs (horse racing).
BANK
Funds of the banker or dealer in a gambling game.
BANK CRAPS
Players bet against the house. Casino craps game.
BAR
Division between the two halves of the backgammon board.
BAR BET
Usually a catch or trick bet in which the victim is stuck for a round of drinks.
BAR THE BUBBLE, TO
To except against the general rule, that he who lays the odds must always be adjudged the loser: this is restricted to bets laid for liquor. (1811)
BARE-KNUCKLE FIGHTING
Boxing without gloves.
BASEBALL
Stud Poker variation in which threes, fours and nines have special functions.
BASKETBALL
Indoor court game.
BAY
Brown horse (or tan) with black mane and tail.
BEAR
One who contracts to deliver a certain quantity or sum of stock in the public funds, on a future day, and at stated price; or, in other words, sells what he has not got, like the huntsman in the fable, who sold the bear's skin before the bear was killed. As the bear sells the stock he is not possessed of, so the bull purchases what he has not money to pay for; but in case of any alteration in the price agreed on either party pays or receives the difference. Exchange Alley. (1811)
BEAR IN
Inability to run straight. To run toward the inside rail.
BEAR OUT
To run toward the outside rail instead of in a straight line.
BEGINNER
A novice gambler who doesn't know the fine points of the game. Sometimes called a "pigeon"—and sometimes surprisingly lucky.
BELOW THE LINE
In Contract Bridge, a team that makes its contracts puts its score for tricks bid below the horizontal line.
BERGEN
Variation of Dominoes.
BEST BETS IN CRAPS
The points which may be made in the greatest number of ways. True odds in the shooter's favor.
BETTING PROCEDURE
Routine of money management in placing bets, governed by wins or losses.
BETWEEN THE SHEETS
Simple card game. Every player antes.
BEZIQUE
Popular continental card game in which a special scoring board, highly complicated, perplexes the beginning player.
BIDS
Guarantees to take a certain number of tricks in card games.
BIDDING
Player states the number of tricks that he agrees to win.
BIG CASSINO
Ten of Diamonds played in Cassino.
BIG Q
Picking two horses in #1 race to finish 1-2 or 2-1. In race #2, turn in first quinella for another quinella ticket, picking horses again 1-2 or 2-1.
BIG 6 BETS
A bet on the Number Six at the casino crap table, usually with incorrect odds to bettor. Forget it.
BIG 6 & 8
Craps players may place their own bets on this part of the layout.
BIG 8 BETS
Special bet in craps, in which casino seldom offers true odds. Regarded by most gamblers as a bad bet.
BILLIARDS
Game played with cue ball and two object balls, in which player tries to make his cue ball touch both object balls with one stroke of his cue. Has balk-line and three-cushion variations for the experts.
BINGLE-BANGLE-BUNGO
First player in golf to reach the green is Bingle, player whose ball is closest to the pin is Bangle,

player sinking the longest putt is Bungo. Each wins from the other members of foursome.

BINGO

Game of chance using numbered cards and corresponding numbers picked at random. One of the most popular church gambling games, and a universal favorite with nice little old lady gamblers.

BINOCULAR

(Binocle) French word that probably prompted the name of Pinochle for a card game. In the plural, a common accessory of the horse player, used to see how badly his horse is faring in the backstretch.

BISHOP (Chess)

Bishop may move diagonally in any direction, always on squares of its own color.
Preceeded by the word Joey, a popular night-club comedian in the Las Vegas casinos.

BLACK JACK

Casino card game requiring skill and judgment. A little luck won't hurt, either.

BLACK LEGS

A gambler or sharper on the turf or in the cockpit —so called, perhaps from his appearing generally in boots; or else from game-cocks, whose legs are always black. (1811)

BLANKET FINISH

Finish that is very close. Winner cannot be determined from stands for win, place and show order.

BLANKET ROLL

Controlled throw of dice onto a rug or blanket. Blanket Bill Perzak, a dice hustler, is said to have been able to roll any number called for, from two to 12, 97 times out of 100.

BLAZE

White marking on horse's face.

BLEACHER BETTORS

Bettors usually found in a permanent bleacher location, who will bet on anything that might possibly happen in a baseball game.

BLIND

A compulsory bet made before the cards are dealt.

BLIND MAN'S BLUFF

Children's game—I'll bet you can't find me.

BLINKERS

Equipment that limits a horse's side vision. Also blinders.

BLITZ

When one side fails to score during a game of Gin Rummy. Can usually be identified by howls of anguish from player against whom it is scored.

BLITZ BET

In golf, a member of a foursome must make the longest drive, get on the green first, make the longest putt or be closest to the pin on his approach shot.

BLOODLINE

Horse's pedigree.

BLOODLINES

Sequence of direct ancestors (horse racing).

BLOT

A thing you want to do to your opponent in Backgammon and don't want him to do to you.

BLOW OUT

Short, fast workout to loosen a horse before a race.

BLUFFED

Deceived an opponent in Poker by bidding on a poor hand with the result of the opponent withdrawing his good hand. Considered a legitimate and honorable deceit.

BOAT RACE

A fixed race.

BOBBED

Cheated, tricked, disappointed. (1811)

BOBTAIL

A four-card straight or flush. Close doesn't count.

BOLITA

Illegal lottery game. See numbers.

BOLT

To run away. Horse bolts when it is nervous or does not want to race.

"BONDS" LOTTERY

British lottery, scrupulously conducted.

BONES

Dice. (1811)

BOOKIE

Receives and pays off bets. Determines odds on bets. Short for book-maker.

BOO-RAY

Gambling card game often played for much higher stakes than players anticipated.

BOOTY

To play booty; cheating play, where the player purposely avoids winning. (1811)

BOTTOM DEAL

Card dealt from bottom instead of top of the deck. Skillful card mechanic assembles certain cards at bottom of deck and deals them while giving the impression he's dealing from top.

BOULE

Form of Roulette popular in Switzerland.

BOW HERBERT ORGANIZATION

Casino poker clubs located in Gardena City, California, where Poker is designated a game of skill.

BOX CARS

A pair of sixes in craps, an undesirable "coming out" roll.

BOXING

The art of attack and defense with the fists using a pair of heavily padded mittens.

BOXMAN

One of the employees who will cheerfully take your money or chips at a casino gaming table.

BOWLING

Ball is rolled down an alley at an object or a group of objects, usually wooden pins.

BREAK
Start of the race. To break from the gate.

BREAK-DOWN
Horse unable to continue race because of injury.

BREAK THE BANK
The gambler's dream that seldom if ever materializes, in which the "house" is bankrupted. Don't count on it.

BREAKAGE (Horseracing)
Odd change left after paying off each winning bet.

BREAKING GAIT
When, in harness racing, horse runs, canters or gallops. Trotters and pacers must trot or pace only.

BREEDING
In horse racing, production of fine strains of thoroughbreds.

BREEZE
To run at own speed without pressure from rider.

BRIDGE
Social card game that quickly gets unsociable as far as your partner is concerned, when you trump his Ace.

BRIDGE BET
In golf, same as Contract Bet.

BRIDGETTE
Two-handed bridge game invented by Joel D. Gaines, endorsed by many Contract Bridge experts.

BRIDGE EXPERT
Expert in playing Bridge. What most players think they are until they play against one.

BROODMARE
Female horse used for breeding.

BRUSH
You brush your cards toward you on the table when you want the dealer to give you another card in Blackjack.

BUG
Apprentice jockey.

BUILDING A COMBINATION
Player may discard a card from his hand onto one or more on the board, therefore building a higher denomination on the board. May pick up the combination on next turn with card of that denomination in his turn.

BUILD-UP
Setting the stage to take the victim for considerable money, usually by letting him win small sums.

BULL
An Exchange Alley term for one who buys stock on speculation for time, i.e. agrees with the seller, called a Bear, to take a certain sum of stock at a future day, at a stated price. If at that day stock fetches more than the price agreed on, he receives the difference; if it falls or is cheaper, he either pays it, or becomes a lame duck, and waddles out of the Alley. See Lame Duck and Bear. (1811)

BULLFIGHTING
Spectacle where men usually excite, fight with and kill a bull in an arena for public amusement. Highly popular sports event in most Latin-American countries.

BULL RING
Small track with sharp turns, either a half-mile or five-eighths mile track.

BUNDLE
A substantial amount of money—sometimes all a player has, as in, "I bet the bundle."

BURNS (Between The Sheets)
In some games, a card is "burned" before dealing, turned face up and put on the bottom of the deck. Has no relation to the "slow burns" that build up after repeated losses.

BUST
To go broke.
A hand to which a player has drawn unsuccessfully.
In Blackjack, if you go over 21.
Contrary to use outside the field of gambling, a bust is *never* well-developed.

BUSTERS or BUST-OUTS
Dice with certain numbers missing, usually so that 2, 12 and 7 will come up more frequently than any other numbers.

CALCUTTA
Golf pool in which players are auctioned off to the highest bidder.

CALIFORNIA JACK
More complicated version of Auction Pitch.

CALL
Put enough chips in the pot to make one's total contribution exactly equal to the total contribution of the previous active player.
Stage of race at which speeds and positions are recorded.
A term in stock trading—a call is an option to buy a stock at a fixed price within a stipulated period of time.

CALL-ACE EUCHRE
Bidder says "I call on the best" and names trump. Player holding Ace of bid suit becomes his partner.

CALLED
When all players meet the bet without raising.

CALLING A COMBINATION
Player may discard onto table one of a duplicate card in his hand and call the number, reserving it for his pick up on his next turn. Cassino.

CALL-OUT (Pinochle)
First player to correctly announce that he has 1000 points, wins the game.

CALL SHOT
Variation of pool, in which player must specify what ball he will put into what pocket.

CANASTA
Favorite ladies card game, may be played with partners. From Spanish word meaning "basket."

CANCELLATION HEARTS
Variations of Hearts.
CARD
Racing program.
Also pasteboards of colorful designs used in games, referred to as decks of playing cards.
CARD-HUSTLER
A low character who bets high—because he has a sure thing. Plays cards only when he is reasonably certain of winning, by fair means or foul.
CARDS
A deck of 52 illustrated pieces of cardboard that may be dealt out in well over a million different combinations, some of which can be highly profitable and some of which may be disastrous to their holder. Sometimes referred to at the turn of the century as "The Devil's Pasteboards."
CARD SENSE
An instinct which good card players have and which poor players often think they have.
CARNIE GAMES
Originated in traveling tent shows; currently an attraction at Circus-Circus, Las Vegas.
CARNIVALS
Traveling amusement troupes, featuring rides, shows and games of chance, usually playing one-week stands.
CARRY-OVERS
Any bets that aren't won on one hole are carried over to the next in golf.
CASINO
Building or room used for gambling.
CASINO POKER
Players are playing Poker against each other, not the house. House furnishes facilities, management and supervision for a fee.
CASSINO
Italian game where face cards have no numerical value.
CASTLE
King and Rook move simultaneously in Chess, in a criss-cross.
CASUAL GAMBLERS
Those who don't make a business of gambling and don't do it compulsively—probably about 90 percent of all gamblers.
CENTRAL PROCESSING UNIT
Computer which digests information from ticket seller's machines and in split seconds relays computations to "tote" board.
CERCLES
French gambling clubs restricted to members; Baccarat and Poker main attractions.
CHALK BETTOR
Bettor who backs the favorite horse.
CHALK HORSE
Horse favored by bettors. Horse with the lowest odds.
CHANCE
Anything that isn't a certainty, in which there is some question as to the outcome.
CHARACTERS
One of three suits in Mah-Jongg having nine ranks.
What some of the people are who frequent race tracks, casinos and bookie parlors.
CHARADES
Guessing game involving no talking.
CHART
Published results of a race.
CHECKERS
Simple game of skill using a playing board and 12 men for each player. Only two players per game.
CHECKERS BET
In golf, when a player has lost a hole, he may "jump"—which means next hole is played for double the amount.
CHECKMATE
When a King is captured in Chess.
CHECKS
Waives the right to initiate the betting in a round of Poker.
CHEMIN DE FER
French non-banking card game.
CHESS
Game of strategy and skill. Games uses a board and each player has 16 men.
CHESTNUT
Brown or tan horse with brown tail and mane.
CHICAGO BRIDGE
Four-deal Bridge commonly credited to the Standard Club in Chicago.
CHICE
A group game played with five dice.
CHINESE LOTTERY, THE
Keno played during the American pioneer years. Chinese laborers brought the game to U.S. Played in China for 2000 years.
CHIP
A disc or token used in place of money; the unit of currency in betting.
CHIP COPPER
Polite description of a thief who specializes in stealing chips.
CHOPPY
Uneven stride.
CHOUETTE
Team play in Backgammon.
CHUCK-A-LUCK
Game played with three dice in a revolving cage. Odds appear to be even, at first glance, but are actually heavily in favor of the "house."
CHUTE
Portion of track that extends from the main course, allowing a straight run from the starting gate.
CINCH
Variation of Auction Pitch.

Also a common designation for a sure thing, as in "a lead-pipe cinch."

CIRCLES
One of three suits in Mah-Jongg having nine ranks.

CLAIM
To purchase a horse in a claiming race.

CLAIMING RACE
A race in which a claim to purchase any of the horses running can be entered at a stipulated price, before the race begins.

CLIP JOINT
Not a barber shop. A dive in which patrons are "taken" for a maximum amount.

CLOBBER
To defeat overwhelmingly. Hard term to define, but when you've been clobbered, you'll know it.

CLOSE TO THE CHEST
Play conservatively.

CLUBHOUSE TURN
Turn on race track nearest to the clubhouse.

CLUBS
Original suit of cards where trefoil leaves acknowledged peasantry. Latter changed to clubs.
Also, private gaming establishments open only to members.

COCKFIGHT
Contest between two gamecocks, usually outfitted with metal spurs.

COLD DECK
Seemingly pat hand dealt by card cheat, who switches deck to set a perfect hand.

COLT
Male horse four years old or younger.

COMBINATION BET
One mutuel ticket that covers a horse's win, place or show finish.

COME (Craps)
Craps players may place their own bets on this section of the layout.

COME (On The Come)
Needing to draw a proper card before having a hand that can win in Poker.

COME BETS
Craps bet placed after the first roll of the dice, betting money that the shooter will throw a 7 or 11 or repeat the number thrown before he craps out.

COME-ON
A build-up to encourage a prospective victim to bet heavily.

COMING OUT
When the craps shooter rolls the dice.

COMPUTER
An electronic device that can catalogue and deliver applicable information quickly.

CONCEALED
In Canasta, when a player melds his whole hand in one turn, he has a concealed hand and receives 100 point bonus.

CONCENTRATION
Originally a children's card game. Players try to match pairs face down on table.

CONDITION
Horse's form.

CONDITIONS
Requirements for race: age, sex, weight, purse size, etc.

CONSISTENCY
Money won by a horse.

CONSISTENCY RULE
Eliminate any horse whose consistency rating is not within 5 points of the highest rating.

CONTRACT
Tricks must be contracted for in order to be scored toward game.

CONTRACT BET
In golf, each member of the foursome predicts his score, pays $1 for each stroke over prediction, receives $1 for each stroke under.

CONTRACT BOWLING
Playing against your league average.

CONTRE-ALEMBERT
In money management, add a unit after a win, subtract a unit after a loss.

CONTRE-LABOUCHERE
Money management system.

COOL
Calm, unruffled, not "choked up" with big money at stake.

CORNER BET
In Roulette, placing a chip at the juncture of four numbers so that it actually touches part of all four.

COUNTER PLAYER
Person who counts the cards being played in a casino. Blackjack.

COUNTER (Euchre)
One side uses black cards, the other red, as counting cards for scoring. Score is kept by two cards, a 4 & 6.

CRABS
In the dice game of Hazard, the losing numbers 2, 3 and 12 were known as Crabs.

CRAPS
Gambling game played with two dice.

CRIB, THE
In Cribbage, each player places two cards face down on the table. These become the property of the dealer.

CRIBBAGE
One of the oldest card games involving a scoring board.

CRIMP
A bend put into certain cards, for purposes of identification or location. An illegal maneuver.

CROCKFORD'S
London Gambling Club, oldest in Great Britain.

CROWD
Conditions of race in which horses are bunched and have no racing room.
CUE-BALL
The ball the player strikes with his cue in pool or billiards.
CULBERTSON, ELY
Originator of bidding system in Contract Bridge.
CURSE OF SCOTLAND
The nine of Diamonds—diamonds, it is said, imply royalty, being ornaments to the imperial crown; and every ninth king of Scotland has been observed for many ages to be a tyrant and a curse to that country. Others say it is from its similarity to the arms of Argyle; the Duke of Argyle having been very instrumental in bringing about the union, which, by some Scotch patriots, has been considered as detrimental to their country. (1811)
CUSHION
Reserve bankroll.
In billiards, the felt-covered ridge bordering inside of rails on pocket billiard tables.

DAILY DOUBLE
Dee Dee. Usually first two races of the day. Bettor must pick the winner in each race, and one ticket covers both horses.
DAILY RACING FORM
The "Variety" of racing, published by Triangle Publications, Inc., in Highstown, New Jersey.
DAM
Horse's mother.
DANDOLOS, NICHOLAS
Legendary "Nick, the Greek."
DASH
Sprint race of six furlongs or less.
DEAD HEAT
Finish in which two or more horses reach the wire simultaneously.
DEALER
One who distributes cards in a card game.
DEALER'S CHOICE
Game in which the dealer may designate the form of Poker to be played and what cards are wild.
DECK
A pack of playing cards.
DECLARATION
In High-Low Poker, a statement made before the showdown that one is trying for high, low, or both.
DECLARE
To scratch (withdraw) horse from race.
DECLARER
In cards, player who undertakes to fill his, or his team's, contract.
DESTROY
To kill a horse, usually as result of irreparable injury.
DEUCES
Playing card bearing the index number two.
DEVIL'S BOOKS
Cards. (1811)
DIAMONDS
Original suit of cards representing merchants.
DICE
Perfect cubes, with sides numbered from one through six, upon the turn of which men have risked fortunes. A pair of dice will always alight in one of 36 combinations.
DISCARD PILE
Cards previously in play, then discarded.
DISQUALIFY
To disallow a horse's finish because of some infringement of rules during running of race.
DISTANCE ELIMINATION RULE
Eliminate any horse that has not run today's distance at today's track.
DISTRIBUTION
In Bridge, the number of cards in each of the four suits that fall to each of four hands.
DIVISION
Situation resulting when there are too many entries for one race, and two races are run.
"DIX"
Lowest trump card in Pinochle.
DOCTORS
Loaded dice, that will run but two or three changes. They put the doctors upon him; they cheated him with loaded dice. (1811)
DOER
Horse who is good eater, indicating good form.
DOMINOES
Board game consisting of small flat blocks bare on one side, and having dots similar to dice on the other. Probably derived from early Oriental games.
DOMINO HEARTS
Variation of Hearts.
DON'T-PASS BETTOR
One who places bets on Bank-Crap layout that tosser won't win.
DON'T PASS LINE
Line on which players may place their own bets in craps.
Betting even odds that the shooter loses.
DOUBLE (Contract Bridge)
100 points for first trick if not vulnerable, 200 points if vulnerable, above the line. 200 points for subsequent tricks set, not vulnerable, and 300 points if vulnerable.
DOUBLE DOWN
In Blackjack, player has option to double the size of his bet, turning both of his cards face up and drawing only one additional card, face down.
DOUBLE PINOCHLE
Two Queens of Spades and two Jacks of Diamonds.

DOUBLETONS
In Bridge, a holding of any two cards in a suit.

DOUBLETS
Two thrown dice with the same number of spots on upper face.

DOUBLE UP
Betting twice as much as was previously bet and lost.

DRAG
Take chips out of the pot as change.

DRAGGING (Baccarat)
After winning, reducing amount of subsequent bet.

DRAGONS (Red, Green & White)
Tiles used in Mah-Jongg.

DRAW
Pull cards from the pack spread face down, to determine seats, first deal, etc.
Receive cards from the stock to replace discards.

DRAW (Pool)
Stroking the cue ball with the cue below center.

DRAW AWAY
To run ahead of other horses in race. To draw clear. Of a horse who wins "going away."

DRAW POKER
Variation of Poker in which a player may discard and receive replacement cards.

DRAWING LOTS
In Biblical times, the casting of lots was a decision factor for all manner of crises, policies and judicial procedure.

DREAM BOOKS
Best sellers claiming to translate dreams into numbers for bets on policy.

DRIVE
To run at full capacity under pressure. Usually the exertion in the homestretch.

DROP
Withdraw from the current deal.

DUMMY
The exposed hand in Bridge being played by the declarer in addition to his own hand.
In sport, the amateur who plays for money with a stranger.

DUTCH (Horse Racing)
Betting two or more horses in the same race to finish the same.

E

EARLY FOOT
Horse that specializes in fast speed from starting gate and in early portion of race.

EASE UP
To gradually reduce a horse's speed.

EDGE
Eldest hand; player nearest the dealer. Ante by dealer only. Used as "an edge," an advantage or extra percentage.

EIGHTER FROM DECATUR
The eight-point in dice.

EIGHT LENGTH RULE
Eliminate a horse that wasn't able to finish within eight lengths of the winner of his last race.

EIGHTS
Card game where eights are wild.

ENGLISH
In pool, a spin applied to the cue-ball.

ENTIRE
Horse that has not been castrated.

ENTRY
Two or more horses owned or trained by the same person, entered in race as one and covered by the same mutuel ticket.

E.O. (Even-Odd)
English game involving roulette wheel but with even-odd designations instead of numbers.

ESPADS
Original suit of cards (swords) from Spain symbolizing nobility and military.

EUCHRE
Euchre is a trick-taking game, probably forerunner of Whist.

EVEN MONEY
A wager in which neither side gets odds.

EXACTA
Betting situation in which bettor must pick the horses who finish first and second in one race. One mutuel ticket covers both choices.

EXECUTIVE PACKAGES
Also called gambling junkets, in which plane loads of prospective players are brought to casinos at little cost to players, with the expectation they will wager heavily at tables.

EXTEND
To pressure a horse to run at full capacity.

F

FACE CARDS
King, Queen and Jack.

FADE
Situation in which horse tires and reduces speed.
Covering a wager, as "I'll fade you."

FADER
A dice player who bets against the shooter—who "fades" him.

FAIR SHAKE
An honest count. A game in which the player has no undue advantage taken of him.

FALTER
To stop running. To tire and reduce speed.

FAN-TAN
Oriental guessing game.

FARO
Banking game in which players bet on cards drawn from a dealing box.

FARRIER
Blacksmith.
FAST CLOSE
A burst of speed in the homestretch. Fast finish.
FAST TRACK
Hard, dry track that allows greater speeds than a deep, soft track.
FEVER
The five-point in dice.
FEY, CHARLES
Invented the slot machine and put it into operation in 1895.
FIELD
Bets from craps players can be placed in the field.
FIELD BET
A bet placed on horses entered and racing beyond the 12 post positions, running "in the field."
FILLY
Female horse, four years old or younger.
FIVE-CARD STUD POKER
Variation of Poker.
FIVE-OF-A-KIND
Four of a kind plus a wild card. Poker.
FIVE SPOT WIN
Five dollar bet for first place winner.
FIVE-TEN
At Caliente Race Track in Tijuana, pick the winners in six consecutive races, five through ten . . . and qualify for sucker bettor of the day!
5 Y 6
Six horse parley in Venezuela, with heavy payoff on large ticket sale.
FIXED FIGHT
Winner of the fight is decided before the fight starts.
FIXED LIMIT
Betting limit that is not affected by the size of the pot.
FLAT
Normal racing strip, as opposed to turf (grass) or jump course.
Also, a form of loaded dice.
FLAT JOINT
A crooked carnival gambling game.
FLOATING CRAP GAME
A game with an impermanent location, "floating" from place to place, under cover, to avoid police raids.
FLOORMAN
A supervisor of casino gaming tables.
FLUSH
A poker hand with all five cards of the same suit but not in sequence.
FOLD
Refuse to put more money into the game. Withdraw from competition.
FOLLOW (Pool)
Stroking the cue ball above center.
FOOTBALL POOLS
A form of betting on football games, usually with odds against the bettor.
FORCING BID
An opening bid of two that demands the responder keep the bidding open to game.
FORM
A horse's physical condition.
FOUR FLOWERS
Tile used in Mah-Jongg.
FOUR OF A KIND
Four cards with the same face value on them. Poker.
FOUR SEASONS
Tile used in Mah-Jongg.
FOUR-WAY NUMBERS
One bet in Roulette divided into four numbers, placing individual chips on each number.
FOUR WINDS
Tile used in Mah-Jongg.
FRAMES (Bowling)
Turns, with ten turns for each player.
FRESH
Condition of horse after period of lay-off from competition.
FRIENDLY CRAPS
Dice game where players bet against each other.
FRIENDLY GAMES
Games, frequently played in private homes, in which friends occasionally finish as acquaintances.
FRONT RUNNER
Horse with fast early speed that likes the lead.
FROZEN OUT
Retired from play.
FRY
Creator of bidding system in Contract Bridge.
FULHAMS
Loaded dice are called high and lowmen, or high and low fulhams, by Ben Jonson and other writers of his time; either because they were made at Fulham, or from that place being the resort of sharpers. (1811)
FULL HOUSE
Poker hand containing three of a kind and a pair.
FURLONG
Measure of a distance. One eighth of a mile or 220 yards.
FUZZ, TO
To shuffle cards minutely: also to change the pack. (1811)

GAFF
To game by tossing up halfpence. (1811)
In modern vernacular, a device or gimmick to control outcome of a game.
GAMBLER
One who plays a game for money or other stakes.

GAMBLER'S BOOK CLUB

Publishers of most complete library of gambling books . . . Las Vegas, Nevada.

GAME

Any standard form of Poker or variant named by the dealer to be played in that deal.

GAME-AND-TABLE REVENUE

That part of winnings accruing to casino or game organizer.

GAMENIAN

Anglo-Saxon word meaning to sport or play. Origin of the word "gambling."

GAMMON

If opponent hasn't thrown off any man, the game counts double.

GARBAGE

In golf, skins and proxies worth a stipulated amount, usually 50¢.

GARDENA CLUB

Casino Poker Club in Gardena, California.

GATE

Starting gate.

GATES, JOHN "BET A MILLION"

Great gambler said to have played bridge on occasion for $1,000 a point.

GELDING

Male horse that has been castrated.

GELT

Money. (1811)

GIMPY

Sore horse.

GIN

A bonus given to a player who melds all ten of his cards before calling.

GIN RUMMY

Friendly game of cards.

GOING AWAY

Manner of winning race in which lead is increased. Indicates easy win; lack of exertion.

GOLF

A game whose object is to sink a ball into each of 9 or 18 successive holes.

GOOD GAMBLE

A good bet, an almost-sure win.

GOOSE

Device that selects the 20 numbers at random for Keno.

GO OUT

Drop from game; make contract.

GOREN

Creator of bidding system in Contract Bridge.

GRAND NATIONAL LOTTERY

Authorized by Congress in 1823 to acquire funds for beautifying Washington, D.C.

GRAND SLAM

The winning of all tricks of one hand in Bridge.

GRANDSTAND

Usually-roofed stand foı spectators at a horserace.

GRAY

Horse's color formed by black and white hairs.

GREAT MARTINGALE

Money management system whereby stakes are doubled and a dollar added after each loss.

GREENIES

In golf, a wager by a foursome on whose ball will roll closest to the pin on a par 3 shot.

GRIFTER

A cheat; confidence man.

GROUNDED

Period of suspension for jockey for infringement of rules.

H

HAND

Measure of height for a horse, approximately four inches.

Also, cards dealt to each player.

HANDICAPPING

Advantage given or disadvantage imposed. In horse racing, consideration of all entries with reference to relative chances of winning.

HANDILY

Horse's performance. Manner of racing easily without heavy urging. Using the hands to urge a horse to run.

HANDLE

Amount of money bet on a race.

Gross volume of a gambling operation.

HANDLER

In cockfighting, man who handles cocks in cock pit.

HANG

Situation in which horse can not increase his speed or effort in the homestretch.

HARNESS RACING

Sport featuring Standardbred horses pulling two-wheeled sulkies in trotting and pacing races.

HAZARD

Probable forerunner of craps, probably invented by the Arabs.

HEAD

Measure of distance the length of a horse's head.

HEADED

To lose a race by a head.

HEAD OF THE STRETCH

Beginning of the homestretch.

HEADS OR TAILS

Flat stones, pieces of wood, coins, etc., with dissimilar figures on both sides.

HEARTS

Original suit of cards symbolizing choir men.

Home gambling game. Object is to avoid taking any Hearts or the Queen of Spades.

HEAT

One trip in a race which is decided by winning two or more trials.

HEAVY TRACK
When surface of the track is in process of drying after a rain. Stage of track in drying process between "muddy" and "good."

HECKLE
Almost identical to "press," except when team is down two, the player shouts "Heckle" as an opponent is driving off the tee.

HEDGE BET
Player in golf who loses the hole and outdrives any member of the foursome on the next hole to collect the bet.

HIGH BIDDER
Player who in his judgment has the winning cards and outbets or outbids his opponents to complete the contract.

HIGH-LOW DRAW
Variation of Draw Poker in which high hand and low hand split the pot.

HIGH-LOW-JACK
Old English card game popular in the 19th century also known as "All-Fours."

HIGH-LOW SEVEN-CARD STUD
Variation of Poker in which player is entitled to use his seven cards in any way he likes, as high or low hand.

HIT
In Blackjack, to deal an additional card to a player.
To have a winning number.
To win.

HOCKEY
Game played on ice, highly competitive, fast, hazardous. Culminates in final winners in leagues battling to win the Stanley Cup Playoff.

HOLD-OUT
A mechanical device used by crooked gamblers to switch cards or dice.

HOLLYWOOD (Gin Rummy)
Variation of Gin Rummy wherein you score three games simultaneously.

HOMEBRED
Horse born in state in which it races. Illinois bred, etc.

HONORS
In most card games, the four highest cards in the deck, i.e. Aces, Kings, Queens and Jacks.

HOP THE DECK
Get the deck back into its original sequence after a cut. Usually accomplished by a sleight known as "the pass."

HORSE
Uncastrated horse five years of age or older.

HORSEMAN
An official owner or trainer of a thoroughbred race horse. An illegal maneuver.

HORSE PLAYER
One who bets on horse races.

HORSE'S CLASS
Level of his performance and amount of money the animal has won.

HORSESHOE CLUB
Casino Poker Club in Gardena, California.

HOUSE MONEY
That which belongs to operators of gambling game or casino.

HOUSE PERCENTAGE
Amount of money taken out of each pot as the fee or rental charged by the house.

HOYLE
Book of rules and instructions for card games and edited by Edmond Hoyle (1672-1769), English authority. "According to Hoyle" generically denotes honesty, according to the rules, the fair way.

HUNCHES
Bets placed on impulse rather than studied knowledge of odds.

HUSSEY, JOHN AND ANNE
Progenitors of a successful system of handicapping horse races.

HUSTLER
One who seeks advantage through the ignorance of his victims. A shark, cheat.

I

IN HAND
Situation in which horse is being restrained by rider.

INQUIRY
Situation in which there is some doubt about the result of a race. The track officials view the video of race to determine whether the claim of foul is valid.

INSIDE
Racing position nearest the rail.

INSURANCE
In Blackjack, a dealer may option 2-1 odds that his down card is not a 10 counter when his up card is an Ace. Player may not bet more than half his original bet.

INTERFERE
To block a horse's progress during race. To cause a horse to change course.

IN THE MONEY
To finish a race in first, second or third place for which there is a mutuel payoff. Horse receives purse money for a fourth-place finish, so among owners the fourth place is an in-the-money finish.

IRISH HOSPITAL SWEEPSTAKES
Lottery held in Ireland with money received going to the Irish Hospital.

IRONS
Stirrups.

ITALIAN
Bidding system in Contract Bridge.

J

JACKPOT
A deal in which everyone antes. Jacks or better to open.

JACKS UP
In Poker, pair of Jacks (or better) required to open.

JACOBY, OSWALD
Creator of bidding system in Contract Bridge. Authority on many games.

JAI-ALAI
Court game somewhat like handball using a long, curved wicker basket strapped to the wrist.

JAM
Situation in which horses are bunched with no racing room.

JAR TICKETS
Tickets with numbers on them placed in a large jar. Winning number wins money.

JOCKEY
One who rides a horse in a professional horse race.

JOCKEY CLUB, THE
Organization set up to regulate and implement rigid rules for racing.

JOKER
A playing card added to a deck as a wild card.

JOURNEYMAN
Professional, experienced jockey.

JUDGMENT
That which, when odds are even, requires educated decision of player.

JUMP-BID
Raising more than one in same suit.

JUVENILE
Two-year-old race horse.

K

KENTUCKY DERBY
The World Series, the Stanley Cup, the Rose Bowl of horse racing.

KICKER
The high extra card in a poker hand.

KING (Chess)
Object of Chess is to capture the king. King may move only one square at a time in any direction and can take a piece on any adjacent square not defended by opponent.

KING'S ROW
Farthest row away from the player in Checkers.

KITTY
In Poker, game made up of contributions from each pot.
Money put into a pot by each bowler with the eventual dividing according to rank.

KNICKERBOCKER ALLEYS
First recorded bowling match was played here in New York City in 1840.

KNICKERBOCKER WHIST CLUB
Contract Bridge was introduced here.

KNIGHT (Chess)
Knight moves one square forward, backward or sidways and then one square diagonally.

KNOCK
Rap on the table to signify check or pass.

L

LABOUCHERE
Money management system.

LAY
Horse maintains a running position until it is opportune to make a move.

LAYING ODDS
Offer a bet of a larger amount against a smaller amount.

LAYOUT
Enables the casino dealer to keep track of several wagers at the same time.

LEAD
First card played to a trick.
What a slow player is sometimes told to get out.

LEAD-PIPE CINCH
Sure winner (sometimes!).

LEAD PONY
Horse that leads the race horse to the starting gate.

LEAGUE
An organized group of men and/or women and children who meet at a scheduled time on specific days with rival teams in bowling.

LEATHER
Whip.

LEFT BOWER
In Euchre, Jack or other suit with same color as trump.

LEG
One game of a series in Bridge; a frame.

LIAR'S POKER
Variation of Poker played with serial numbers on dollar bills instead of cards.

LIBERTY BELL
The name of the first slot machine.

LINE
Pedigree.

LINE BET
In Roulette, chips on six numbers in two rows of three numbers each running across layout.
In craps, betting with the shooter.

LIQUID HAZARD
In golf, playing for $1 a hole, winner must down two shots of bourbon or scotch before teeing off for the next.

LITTLE CASSINO
Two of Spades played in Cassino.

LITTLE JOE
In dice, point 4.

LIVE (Cards)
Able or likely to be of value to another player. Usually the first card of its rank to appear.
LLOYDS OF LONDON
Insurance company in London that will bet against almost every conceivable calamity.
LOADED (Dice)
Dice that are weighted to make certain numbers come up more often.
LOBA
Rummy-type game popular in Argentina.
LONG-SHOTS
A bet in which the chances of winning are slight.
LONG SUITS
A string of four or more cards in one suit.
LOSS IN THE STRETCH RULE
Eliminate any horse that lost more than ¾ lengths in the stretch.
LOT
Object used in deciding a matter by chance.
LOTTERY
A drawing of lots in which prizes are distributed to the winners.
LOTTO
A game of chance played with cards having numbered squares corresponding with numbered balls drawn at random and won by covering five such squares in a row.
LOUISIANA LOTTERY
Last major lottery in U.S. authorized by Louisiana state legislature in 1868, a syndicate for benefit of New Orleans Charity Hospital. Last legal lottery in U.S. until 1963, when New Hampshire lottery legalized.
LOWBALL
Wierd variation of Poker where low hand wins.
LOW DEUCE
Low card in Contract Bridge.
LOW POKER
A game in which the lowest ranking hand wins the pot.
LUCK
That which, if against you, don't gamble. Bad luck is responsible for nearly all gambling losses. Wins result from skillful play, not luck.
LUG IN
To bear in, opposed to running straight.

M

MACHINES
Mutuels, slots, totalisators.
MAGIC NUMBER
Seven in craps.
MAH-JONGG
Ancient Chinese game in a form of rummy played with tiles rather than cards.
MAIDEN
Horse that has never won a race.
MAIDEN CLAIMING EVENTS
Claiming race for non-winners.
MAIDEN SPECIAL WTS.
Race for non-winners who carry uniform weights designated by the Track Handicapper.
MAKE A MOVE
To exhibit a burst of speed. To make a run.
MAKING A SWEEP
Taking every card on the table in one play.
MAN IN THE BOX
Plays alone against the other backgammon players in Chouette. Man determined by highest throw of dice.
MARATHON
Race longer than 1¼ miles.
MARBLES
Venerable gambling game with many variations, requiring some skill and coordination. Is popular with juveniles. Stakes usually are prized "shooters, Drop-eyes, or aggies."
MARCHE
When all tricks are taken by one side in Euchre. Counts 20 points.
MARE
Female horse, five years of age or older.
MARQUIS OF QUEENSBURY
Created rules for boxing in 1860.
MARRIAGE (Pinochle)
King and Queen of any suit.
MARTINGALE SYSTEM
Doubling wagers after each loss.
MATADOR
Variation of Dominoes. Player must make up a total of seven, rather than match the pieces.
MATCH GAME
Deciding game in any sports series contest.
A gambling game in which the object is to avoid removing the last match from the pile.
MATCHING COINS
Tossing coins to compare exposed faces.
MATCH RACE
Race between only two horses.
MATCH YOU
Coin-flipping bet.
MATURITY
Race for horses who are entered before their birth.
MEET
The entire race meeting of one race track.
MELD
In card games like Canasta, Pinochle and Gin Rummy, a combination of cards scoring certain number of winning points. From German, "Meldon," to announce.
MILLION DOLLAR GATE (Boxing)
Paid admissions totalling a million.
MINIMAX SYSTEM
System for money-bridge for sale at $100 a copy,

offered for sale by a player. Strictly gambitry.

MINIMUM BET
Established wager allowed by casino on a given game. Varies in each casino.

MINUS POOL
Betting situation in which so much money is bet on one horse that the odds return a pay-off of less than ten cents on the dollar. The track is responsible for making up the difference between the amount in the mutuel pool and the required pay-off.

MONEY MANAGEMENT
Any system for handling gambling money that enables the bettor to come out with a profit, in spite of losses during a given period of wagering.

MONOPOLY
Game in which players speculate mythical fortunes.

MONTE CARLO
Famous gambling casino in Monaco.

MORNING LINE
Track Handicapper's estimate of the odds of each horse at posttime. This forecast of odds is published in the track program and listed on the tote board before each race.

MOXIE
Courage, guts.

MR. ODDS-MAKER
Bob Martin of Las Vegas, gambling authority and official sports odds-maker.

MUDDER
Horse that performs well on a muddy track. A mudder is indicated in the past performance records of the *Daily Racing Form*.

MUDDY TRACK
Track's surface is very wet and slow. A muddy track is the stage between sloppy and heavy tracks.

MUGGINS
Variation of Dominoes, where the count goes by fives.

MUMCHANGE
An ancient game like Hazard, played with dice: probably so named from the silence observed in playing at it. (1811)

MUSICAL CHAIRS
Children's game—I'll bet I'm quicker than you are.

MUTUEL POOL
The total amount of money bet on all horses in a race.

N

NAMATH, JOE
New York Jets quarterback.

NATURAL CANASTA
Meld of at least seven cards without the use of wild cards.

NATURAL 8's
In craps, two 4's.

NECK
The distance of a horse's neck. To win by a neck.

NEVADA GAMING CONTROL BOARD
Information center and investigative agency which regulates Nevada gaming.

NEW HAMPSHIRE STATE LOTTERY
First legalized state lottery since 1892. N.H. only state in U.S. without sales or state income tax.

NEW YORK LOTTERY
State sponsored, approved by voter referendum, November 8, 1966.

NICK, THE GREEK
Nicholas Dandolos.

NICK, TO
To win at dice, to hit the mark just in the nick of time, or at the critical moment. (1811)

NO-BRAINERS
Pat hand in Gin Rummy.

NOLAN, WALTER
Author of *The Facts of Blackjack*.

NOSE
To win by a nose. The smallest winning margin.

NO-TRUMP
No-trump bid ranks above Spades in Contract Bridge.

NO WIN RULE
Eliminate a horse that has not won a race.

"NUMBERS" GAME
Illegal lottery based on three-digit numbers, designated as "policy wheel."

OBJECTION
A claim of foul during the running of the race. Objection is lodged by either the jockey or a steward of the race.

ODDS
The way in which a horse's probability of win is stated, as estimated by the Track Handicapper, public handicappers, and the betting public. Since all horses in a race have a total win probability of 100% (because one of them must win) every horse has an estimated probability. If one horse has a ⅓ or 33% probability of win, his odds are 2-1. Allowance made by one making a bet to one accepting a bet, designed to equalize the chances.

ODDS BETS
Bets in which odds are given or taken.

ODDS MAKING
Business that gives odds on various sports events, etc.

ODDS ON
Horse whose final odds are less than even money. Odds-on favorite.

OFF PACE
Situation in which horse runs behind the leaders of the race.

OFFICE POOL

Employees of a business put up a dollar and draw a number. Number usually based on total points, points by winning team or period when winning score was made.

OFF TRACK

Situation in which the track surface is not fast muddy, heavy, slow, etc.

OFF-TRACK BETTING CORPORATION

New York corporation established with hopes of luring away bets from illegal bookies. Profits would be turned over to New York City.

OH, HELL!

Party gambling card game. Name derived from disappointed players failing to take the number of tricks they bid.

OKLAHOMA (Gin Rummy)

Variation of Gin Rummy where the turn up card, if Spades, doubles the scoring for that hand.

OLD MAID

Simple children's card game.

ONE-ARM-BANDITS

Slot machines.

ONE-EYED JACKS

Jack with only one eye showing on face of card.

ONE MONTH RULE

Horse must have raced within 30 days of today's race.

ONE-RUN HORSE

Horse that saves all its speed and energy for one determined run.

ON THE NOSE

To bet that a horse will win, as opposed to a place or show bet.

ON THE RAIL

Running position closest to the rail.

ON THE TAKE

Law enforcement officers who have unhealthy alliances with gambling in illegal localities.

OPEN

To commence action in a card game.

OPENER

Cards of sufficient value to open the betting in a poker game.

OPTIONAL DOUBLES

Situation in Backgammon when player may either double or not, at his discretion.

ORDER IT UP (Euchre)

Bid against dealer accepting turn up card as trump.

OUTER TABLE

Right hand half of the backgammon board.

OUTRIDER

Rider of the lead pony who accompanies the race horse to the starting gate.

OVERLAY

Horse whose final odds are higher than the estimated morning-line odds.

OVERWEIGHT

Horse that carries a heavier weight than the amount assigned to him.

P

PACE

Speed of the race. Speed is recorded at each call of the race.

PACER

Horse whose right fore leg and right hind leg move in tandem; same with left side.

PADDOCK

Area where horses are saddled and paraded before they enter the track.

PAIR SPLITTING

When player is dealt two of a kind, he has the option to separate the pair and make two Blackjack hands, betting the same amount on the second hand as he had already bet on the deal.

PARI-MUTUEL

System of betting in which winners receive all the money wagered on race after the track's share has been deducted.

PARKER BROS., INC.

Holders of copyright on the game of Monopoly and many other popular home games.

PARLAY

Series of two or more bets set in advance so that original stake plus successive winnings are wagered.

PARLAY CARDS

Betting cards with numbers on them representing number of runs scored by five or six teams in baseball. Similar cards are sold for basketball and football.

PARTNERSHIP GIN

Variation of Gin Rummy where two games are going simultaneously, two players against two, with partners alternating opponents.

PART-SCORE

Trick score total less than game.

PARTY BRIDGE

Casual playing of bridge for prizes or low stakes.

PASCAL

French mathematics scholar who supposedly invented the roulette wheel in the 17th century.

PASS

Not make a bid (as in bridge). In craps, winning decision by player by throwing a 7 or 11, a natural, throwing his point the second time, a 4,5,6,8, 9 or 10.

PASSE-DIX

French dice game.

PASSERS

Crooked dice rigged to make more passes than legal dice.

PASS LINE

Line where craps players may put down their bets, betting even money that the shooter will win.

PAST PERFORMANCE
The record of a horse's recent activity. Published in the *Daily Racing Form.*

PAWN (Chess)
Pawn moves one square forward except when capturing an enemy, which permits a left or right diagonal move.

PAYOFF
Collection of a bet.
Undercover or indirect payment for a favor.

PELOTA
Also known as Jai-Lai.

PELOTA DE GUANTE
Glove-ball; popular Ecuadoran betting sport.

PERFECTA
Also Exacta. Bettor picks horses to finish first and second in one race.

PGA
Professional Golfers Association.

PIGEON
An easy mark, a soft touch, a patsy. A born loser.

PINOCHLE
Card game combining melding and trick-taking.

PIP
Any of the four large suit symbols on playing cards.

PIQUET
Old French card game from which Pinochle was derived.

PIT BOSS
Man employed by casino to oversee games, watch for errors and cheaters.

PITCHER
High bidder in the game of Auction Pitch.

PITTSBURGH PHIL
Legendary horse player who amassed millions from his betting operations.

PLACE
Second position in the finish. Second place.

PLACE BETS
Wager that a point number of your choice will come up before a 7.

PLAFOND
Continental card game.

PLATER
Horse that runs in claiming races. So called because claimers were formerly awarded silver plated trophies instead of purse money.

PLAY
Call; stay in.

PLAYER HAND
Hand farthest away from the dealing box in Baccarat.

PLAYING FOR SKINS
In golf, payment for beating all others on any hole.

PLOY
A system, strategy or tactic to confuse opponent.

POCKET
Situation during race in which horse is boxed by others and has no racing room.

POINT
A number in a gambling game on which a bet is made; 4, 5, 6, 8, 9 or 10 are point numbers in craps.

POINT SHAVING
A deliberate attempt by players in sports to hold scoring below predicted spreads between the two teams.

POKER
Card game where you try to acquire certain combinations of cards, players (can be two or more) betting on value of hand; hand with highest value wins pot, unless player is bluffed into not declaring.

POKER MACHINES
Type of slot machines with reels showing pictures of playing cards. Highly popular in New South Wales.

POLICY WHEEL
See Numbers Game.

POLLA
Horse racing pool, Peru.

POOL
Total amount bet on one race. Called pot in Poker.
Variation of billiards using 15 object balls and six pockets in the pool table.

POOL BET
Members of three or more foursomes in golf make separate $1 bets against each of the other players.
A bet of (generally) 10 or more participants—popular in offices and clubs at Derby time, bowl playoffs, World Series, etc. Each player pays a stipulated amount and "draws" his number, horse or team from a blind. Can be played by inning, quarter or race. Winner usually takes entire pot.

POOL HALL
Public hall for the playing of pool.

POST
Starting gate.

POST POSITION
Order of horses at starting gate before a race.

POT
Accumulation of all chips bet on the outcome of any one deal.

POT-LIMIT
Limitation of any bet or raise to the number of chips in the pot at the time the bet or raise was made.

PREMIUM BONDS
British lottery.

PRESS BET
In golf, when partners in foursome get behind by two strokes, they may start playing a new bet identical to original one, beginning at the next hole.

"PRESSING"
Reckless, desperate bidding, attempting to get ahead.

PROFESSIONAL BASEBALL POOL
Baseball pools run by professional gamblers.

PROGRAMMED SLOTS
Slot machines fixed for casino advantage.

PROXIES
In golf, player closest to pin on green in 2 on par 4, 3 on par 5 and 1 on par 3 . . . called greenies on par 3.

PUBLIC SELECTORS (Horse Racing)
Handicappers' choice, and therefore bettors choice to win.

PULL-UP
To slow down or stop a horse.

PUNCH BOARDS
Small board with many holes. Rolled up printed slips are punched out on payment of nominal sum to obtain a slip with lucky number on it entitling player to prize or money.

PUSH
If you tie the dealer in Blackjack, it's known as a "push" and you neither win nor lose.

PUT
A stock trading term—an option to sell stock at a fixed price within a stipulated period of time.

Q

QUADRUPLED
If a contract is redoubled in Contract Bridge, the score is quadrupled.

QUEEN (Chess)
Queen may move any number of unblocked squares in any direction, forward, backward, sideways and diagonally.

QUEEN HATASU
Queen of Egypt in 1600 B.C.

QUEER PUSHER
A player who uses counterfeit money in a gambling game.

QUINELLA
Betting similar to Daily Double except bettor picks horses in same race to run first or second, in either order.

R

RABBIT, THE
Golf game. Rabbit is "loose" when neither team has scored; rabbit is owned by team that scores a point.

RACE BIRD
Horse racing addict.

RACE HORSE KENO
Variant of Lotto with 80 numbers to a card, using names of horses. Player selects ten numbers; 20 of the 80 numbers are called.

RACING FORM
Information sheet giving pertinent data about horse races.

RACING SECRETARY
The official at race track who is responsible for planning the racing meet and establishing the conditions for each race. At many tracks, the Racing Secretary also serves as the Track Handicapper.

RAFFLES
Lotteries where one buys chances to win a prize.

RANK
Condition of horse that is fractious and refuses to be restrained during the running of the race.

RATE
To restrain or hold a horse back during a race to conserve speed and energy for the most opportune time, usually for the stretch run.

RED DOG
Sometimes called High Card Pool.

RED GRANGE
Football player No. 77 for the University of Illinois.

REDOUBLE
In Contract Bridge, bonuses for making contract and penalties for not making it which may be doubled by opponents. If bidding team elects to redouble, the "double" bonuses and penalties are doubled.

RED THREE
In Canasta, when red three is drawn, it is immediately placed face up on table. Each red three scores 100 points.

REFUSE
Situation in which a horse fails to make a good start from the gate.

RENEGE
Play an incorrect card, as trumping when you still have a card in the led suit.

REPEATER
Winning horse that won its last race. To win two or more races in succession.

RESPONDER
Partner in Bridge, who responds with adequate trump support and point count.

RESPONSES
Bids made in reply to a partner's bid.

REVERE, LAWRENCE
Author of *Playing Blackjack as a Business.*

RIDDEN OUT
Situation in which the horse makes a driving finish but has not expended all of its energy. Sometimes attributed to a horse that finished a race utilizing all of its energy.

RIDDLE, MAJOR A.
Author of *Weekend Gambler's Handbook.*

RIDGLING
Male horse that has been partially castrated.

RIFFLE
Shuffle executed by butting the two ends of the packets together and interlacing the cards while riffling them with your thumbs.

RIGHT BOWER
Jack of trump, highest card value in Euchre.

ROAN
Horse with red or gray color.

ROGUE
Horse that is usually bad-tempered and fractious.

ROMANCE BETS
Betting on love.

ROMP
Easy race in which horse is not over-extended.

ROOK (Chess)
Rook may move forward, backward and sideways but not diagonally on unblocked squares.

ROTATION POOL
Commonest form of pool, the one requiring the least skill.

ROULETTE
Gambling game where players bet on which compartment of the revolving wheel the small ball will come to rest.

ROUND
Once to, or by, each player.

ROUND DEALING
Plain, honest dealing. (1811)

ROUTE
A long race, generally one longer than seven furlongs.

ROUTER
Horse that specializes in route races.

ROUTE RACE
Any horserace longer than seven furlongs.

ROYAL CASINO
Variation of Cassino in which Jacks are 11-spots, Queens, 12 and Kings, 13.

ROYAL DRAW CASINO
Variation of Cassino in which after playing a card from his hand, player draws another from the face-down pile.

ROYAL FLUSH
Ace-high straight flush in Poker.

ROYAL MARRIAGE (Pinochle)
King and Queen of trump suit.

ROYAL SEQUENCE (Pinchole)
Ace, King, Queen, Jack and ten of trump.

RUBBER
Best out of three games in Contract Bridge.

RUNNERS
Numbers games.
Agents for policy, salesmen.

RUN OUT
For bettors, a finish other than first, second, or third. For owners, a finish other than the first four positions.

RUN, SHEEP, RUN
Children's game—"I'll bet you can't catch me."

RUN WIDE
Situation in which horse is forced to an outside position around a turn. Running wide means that the horse must cover extra ground.

S

SAFE CARD
One that the next player cannot use.

SALIVA TEST
Test administered to horses that finish in the money to determine whether illegal drugs, pain-killers, have been used.

SAMBA
Faster variation of Canasta, played with three decks instead of two.

SAVAGE
Situation in which a horse attempts to or bites another horse.

SAVE GROUND
Attempt to secure racing position on the rail so that horse has least possible distance to cover. To avoid being forced into a wide racing position.

SCALE OF WEIGHTS
Official table of weights to be carried by horse of a specific age and sex at specific distances.

SCHNEIDER
When one side fails to score during a game of Gin Rummy.

SCRATCH
To withdraw a horse from a race.

SECOND-DEAL
Dealing the second card from the top of the deck instead of the top card.

SEE
Call the bet of another player.

SEEDING
To schedule tournament players or teams so that the superior ones will not meet in earlier rounds.

SELL-OUT
Variation of Auction Pitch.

SEQUENCES
Three or more cards in the same suit and in unbroken order.

SET
Defeat of the contract (Bridge).

SET DOWN
To suspend a jockey from racing for a period of time for infringement of riding rules, usually for impeding another horse during a race.
Also, urge a horse to his maximum speed during race or workout.

SEVEN CARD STUD
Variation of poker using seven cards instead of five, and finally selecting five.

SEVEN-TWENTY-SEVEN
Uses two to ten players; object to achieve seven (low) or twenty seven (high).

SEVEN-UP
More complicated version of Auction Pitch.
In golf, bet ends when any player in foursome gets 7 "plus" points for good putting or 7 "minus" points for bad putting.

SHADING
A type of art work done on the backs of marked cards.

SHAH-MAT
Persian game, probably the origin of Chess.

SHAKE UP
Extreme pressure with whip and spurs to get a horse to extend himself.

SHASTA SAM
More complicated version of Auction Pitch.

SHED ROW
The stable area at the race track.

SHELL GAME
Ancient Chinese gambling game played with three sea shells; forerunner of carnival sucker bait.

SHILLS
Bettors "planted" by casino managers to lure visiting gamblers to the tables.

SHINER
A mirror device for reading the faces of face-down cards as they are dealt, sometimes employed by crooked gamblers.

SHOE
Dealing box in Baccarat.

SHOE BOARD
Sign that gives information about the kind of shoe each horse is wearing.

SHOO-IN
Horse that supposedly has no competition in a race. A sure bet.

SHOOTER
Craps player actually throwing the dice.

SHORE GAME
In golf, betting for $1 a hole, but no strokes are counted until the player is on the green.

SHORT
Condition when horse tires in the stretch.

SHORT PRICE
Horse whose final odds are extremely low, paying a low price.

SHOW BET
Betting on horse to take third place.

SILKS
The jockey's colors or outfit.

SINGLE-ACTION
Augmented Numbers Game which produces three winning numbers in a few hours every afternoon confining activities to one or two neighborhood blocks.

SINGLETONS
One card of a suit.

SIRE
The father of the horse.

SIX BALL WILD
Variation of Snooker, in which the player may shoot for the six ball at any time.

SIX-FURLONG SPRINTER
Horse trained to run the six-furlong race.

SIX-NUMBER BET
Placing a chip on the end of the line between two rows of three numbers.

SKILL
That which, with luck, makes winning gamblers.

SKITTISH
Condition when horse is fractious.

SKITTLES (Bowling)
Old English game, probably the forerunner of Bowling.

SLAMS
Winning all tricks by one side (Grand Slam), wining all but one trick (Small Slam).

SLOPPY TRACK
Surface of track is covered with water. This is the first stage of an off track after which the wet track becomes "muddy."

SLOT MACHINES
Machine where you insert coin, pull a handle, watch the wheels spin and wait for them to stop to see whether you won or lost.

SLOW TRACK
Stage of the off track between "heavy" and "good." Track that is soft and deep which reduces speed.

SMART MONEY
Money bet by persons who supposedly have "inside" information not available to the betting public, evidenced on tote board by sharp drop in odds on particular horse.

SMUDGE
Term used in Auction Pitch.

SNAKE EYES
In dice, two 1-spots turn up for a point of 2.

SNIP
White mark on horse's face.

SNIP, SNAP, SNORE 'EM
Simple, funny old card game played by any number with complete deck of cards, consisting mainly of matching cards with player preceding.

SNOOKER (Pool)
Variation of pool played on a special table with smaller pockets which are rounded at the edges.

SOCCER
Football game where you propel a round ball by kicking, or using any part of your body except your hands and arms.

SOCCER POOLS
Betting on soccer games.

SPADE CASINO
Variation of Cassino in which each Spade counts one point towards the game.

SPARE (Bowling)
When all ten pins are knocked down by two rolls.

SPEED RULE
Eliminate any horse whose speed rating is not within five points of the highest rating.

SPIELHALLEN
Unique West German small casinos specializing

in slot machines.

SPITE AND MALICE
Card game played with two decks, one without Jokers and the other with four Jokers.

SPIT IN THE OCEAN
Draw Poker variant, based on old French game Bouillotte.

SPLIT BET
Placing a chip on the line between any two numbers on the Roulette layout, pays 17 to 1.

SPLITS
To discard a card from a combination or set.

SPONSORS
In tennis, usually wealthy people backing the tennis player.

SPORT BETS
Bets being placed on sports events.

SPORTS LINE
Information kept on sports teams.

SPRINT
A short race, seven furlongs or less.

SPRINTERS
Horses bred for racing short distances.

SQUARE UP
Satisfy a complaint.
To square up the deck—to form the deck of cards into a neat, solid-edged packet after shuffling.

STACK
Number of chips a player takes from a banker at one time.

STADSHOTELS
Gambling casinos in Sweden.

STAKES
Type of race in which the owners put up the purse money. Often an amount of "added money" is contributed by the track.
Money or chips with which player enters the game.

STAKES RACE
Owners put up the purse money of which the winner takes the largest amount.

STAND
Refuse to draw additional cards.

STANDARDBRED
In harness racing, a purebred trotting or pacing horse.

STANDING
In Blackjack, stand on 17 through 21. Stand on 13-16 if dealer's up card is 2-6. Stand on 12 if dealer's up card is 4, 5, 6.

STAND-OFF
Two or more identical high hands which divide the pot.

STAR
White mark on horse's face.

STARTER HANDICAPS
Handicap for young horses.

STAY
Meet the bet, remain in the current pot.

STAYER
Horse bred for racing long distances.

STAYMAN
Creator of bidding system in Contract Bridge.

STAY ON
Play cool. Don't change.

STEERER
A person who receives a commission for bringing victims to a crooked gambling setup.

STEWARD
The officials at the race track who are responsible for judging all aspects of racing conduct, such as investigating claims of fouls during the running of a race.

STICK
Whip.

STICKMAN
Runs the craps game. Calls the result of each roll.

STIFF
An deliberate attempt to keep a horse from winning a race. Horse is stiffed by administration of drugs or by a poor ride.

STOCKINGS
White markings on a horse's legs.

STRAIGHT
A hand of five cards in sequence, including two or more suits.

STRAIGHTAWAY
Straight portion of the race track, as the homestretch.

STRAIGHT FLUSH
Five cards of the same suit in sequence.

STRAIGHTS
In horse racing, a bet to win.

STRAIGHT-UP BET
A bet in Roulette being placed on a single number. Pays 35 to 1.

STRATEGY
Ploy. The method used by the gambler to win gambits. Gambler's game plan.

STREAK
A run of good or bad luck.

STRETCH
Either of the straight sides on a racetrack.

STRETCH TURN
Turn into the homestretch.

STRIDE
The manner in which the horse is running.

STRIKE (Bowling)
Knocking down all ten pins on the first throw.

STRIP
Race track.
White mark on horse's face.

STRIP (Las Vegas)
Greatest concentration of high-quality gambling facilities in the world.

STRIPE
White mark on horse's face.

STRIPPERS
A deck of cards with one end tapered to be more narrow than the other. By reversing certain cards' top and bottom edges, they may be easily controlled by a card sharp.

STUD
Stallion. Male horse used for breeding.

STUDBOOK
Official thoroughbred registration.

STUD POKER
All cards dealt face up except one or more hole cards, which are revealed at a showdown. Principal form of Poker.

SUCKER BET
One which gives hustler best chance to win.

SUIT
Any of four sets of 13 cards each in a standard deck.

SURE THING
The dream of every gambler—a bet he cannot lose.

SURRENDER
In Blackjack, in some casinos there is a surrender option which gives the player the right to call off his bet by paying half of it to the dealer.

SWEEP
Taking all the cards on the table in Cassino.

SWORDS
Original suit of cards from Spain. Later changed to Spades.

SYSTEM (Bridge)
Procedures decided upon by partners (in Bridge) for bids and tactics.

SYSTEM PLAYER
Gambler who doesn't play hunches, only uses method established by himself or other authority. Usually based on mathematical formula.

SYSTEMS
Methods of handicapping and betting. A "system bettor" adheres to a formula instead of relying on chance.

T

TABLE STAKES
All the chips a player has in front of him.

TACK
Jockey's equipment.

TAKE
Track's share of the mutuel pool.

TAKE BACK
To hold up or restrain a horse, often to change position or to conserve speed.

TAKE-OUT BET
Losers in golf, may at their discretion, match the winners and pay double or nothing.

TAKE UP
A sudden slow-up to avoid trouble during race.

TAKING IN A COMBINATION
Player may take card of same denomination from the board or he may take a total of two cards to match the denomination he has in his hand. Played in Cassino.

TAKING ODDS
Accepting numerical probability ratio in betting circumstances, where the second number in the ratio is always one.

TALON
Cards laid aside or discarded.

TEAM GIN
Partnership playing of four, six, or eight handed games. One half players on each team.

TEN
Dice game in the Roman Empire.

TENNIS
Outdoor court game played with rackets and a ball.

TEN-SPOT TICKET
Ten dollar ticket in anything . . . horse racing . . . policy, etc.

THIRTY ONE
Card game for two to seven players played in hands.

THIS-TRACK RULE
Eliminate any horse who has not had one race at today's track. Race must have been run this season.

THOROUGHBRED
Bred from the best blood through a long line. Any horse eligible to registry in English or American stud-books.

THOROUGHBRED RACING
Race of thoroughbred horses.

THOROUGHBRED RACING ASSOCIATION
Founded in 1942 to institute uniformity to racing conditions.

THOROUGHBRED RACING PROTECTIVE BUREAU
Established by Thoroughbred Racing Association to investigate all accusations of illegal procedures. Serves as information bureau as well as clearing house on everyone involved in illegal racing operations.

THORP, EDWARD O.
Mathematics professor who developed system to beat Blackjack.

THREE OF A KIND
Three cards of the same rank in one hand.

THREE NUMBER BET
Placing a chip on the line at the end of a row of three numbers. Pays 11 to 1.

THREE-WAY NUMBERS
Boxing a straight number which contains same two digits, with only three different combinations of that number.

THROW
To pass a certain number of cards from right to left hand during a shuffle, keeping their order intact.